# FOUNDATIONS
## *of American*
## EDUCATION

SEVENTH EDITION

L. DEAN WEBB
Arizona State University

ARLENE METHA
Arizona State University

K. FORBIS JORDAN

**PEARSON**

Boston   Columbus   Indianapolis   New York   San Francisco   Upper Saddle River
Amsterdam   Cape Town   Dubai   London   Madrid   Milan   Munich   Paris   Montréal   Toronto
Delhi   Mexico City   São Paulo   Sydney   Hong Kong   Seoul   Singapore   Taipei   Tokyo

**Vice President and Editorial Director:** Jeffery W. Johnston
**Executive Editor:** Ann Castel Davis
**Editorial Assistant:** Penny Burleson
**Senior Development Editor:** Alicia Reilly
**Vice President, Director of Marketing:** Margaret Waples
**Marketing Manager:** Joanna Sabella
**Senior Managing Editor:** Pamela D. Bennett
**Senior Production Editor:** Sheryl Glicker Langner
**Senior Operations Supervisor:** Matthew Ottenweller
**Senior Art Director:** Diane C. Lorenzo

**Cover Image:** Stefanie Timmerman/iStockphoto
**Cover Designer:** Ali Mohrman
**Permissions Administrator:** Rebecca Savage
**Media Producer:** Autumn Benson
**Media Project Manager:** Rebecca Norsic
**Full-Service Project Management:** Element LLC
**Composition:** Element LLC
**Printer/Binder:** RR Donnelley
**Cover Printer:** RR Donnelley
**Text Font:** ITC Garamond

Every effort has been made to provide accurate and current Internet information in this book. However, the Internet and information posted on it are constantly changing, so it is inevitable that some of the Internet addresses listed in this textbook will change.

Photo Credits:

Scott Cunningham/Merrill, p. 2; © Will Hart/PhotoEdit, p. 11; Spencer Platt/Getty Images, p. 17; Comstock Images, p. 21; Monkey Business Images/Shutterstock.com, p. 28; Krista Greco/Merrill, p. 36; © Lon C. Diehl/PhotoEdit, p. 38; Patrick White/Merrill, p. 42; Russ Curtis/Courtesy of AFT, p. 44; Monkey Business Images/Getty Images, pp. 52, 396; Courtesy of L. Dean Webb, pp. 59, 349; Bettmann/CORBIS, pp. 62 (left), 83 (left), 89 (left), 119, 142, 150, 164, 171, 179; Erin Hogan/Getty Images, p. 62 (right); © Tony Freeman/PhotoEdit, pp. 65 (left), 207; Courtesy of the Library of Congress, pp. 65 (right), 156; Stockbyte/Getty Images, p. 67; Getty Images, pp. 74, 250, 257, 299, 334; Keystone/Stringer/Getty Images, p. 78 (left); AP Photo/Charles Knoblock, p. 78 (right); Brown University Special Collections Library, p. 83 (right); National Library of Medicine, p. 86; Time & Life Pictures/Getty Images, p. 89 (right); © Cindy Charles/PhotoEdit, p. 92; The Gallery Collection/Corbis, p. 100; © PRISMA ARCHIVO/Alamy, p. 111; Getty Images Inc.ñ Hulton Archive Photos, p. 117; Henry W. Brown/Bettmann/Corbis, p. 130; © Archive Images/Alamy, p. 135; © CORBIS, p. 153; John F. Kennedy Presidential Library and Museum, p. 178; REUTERS/Larry Downing, p. 190; ROGER L. WOLLENBERG/UPI/ Newscom, p. 193; Comstock Images, a division of JupiterImages Corporation, p. 198; ARTHUR TILLEY/Getty Images, p. 202; RubberBall Productions, p. 213; Laima Druskis/PH College, p. 217; Tom Watson/Merrill, pp. 224, 386, 390 (right) ; Golden Pixels/Getty Images, p. 229; © Michael Newman/PhotoEdit, pp. 233, 355, 386; UN/DPI PHOTO/S. ROTNER, p. 234; Creatas, pp. 239, 368; George Dodson/PH College, p. 254; © David Young-Wolff/Alamy, p. 261; © Spencer Grant/PhotoEdit, p. 265; SW Productions/Getty Images, p. 270; Ocean/Corbis, p. 278; © Mikael Karlsson/Alamy, p. 282; AP Photo/Marcy Nighswander, p. 289; ZUMA Press/Newscom, p. 292; © Bob Daemmrich/PhotoEdit, p. 304; Elena Rooraid/PhotoEdit, Inc., p. 308; © Jim West/Alamy, p. 316; © Tom Grill/Corbis, p. 322; © VStock/Alamy, p. 340; Courtesy of Scottsdale Unified School District, 358; © Izabela Habur/iStockphoto.com, p. 364; Tracy Barbutes/ZUMA Press/Newscom, p. 374; Anthony Magnacca/Merrill, pp. 378, 401; Valerie Schultz/Merrill, p. 390 (left); KS Studios/Merrill, p. 394; Patrick White/Merrill, p. 407. All photos of individuals in the Teacher of the Year feature were provided by the featured subjects.

**Library of Congress Cataloging-in-Publication Data**
Webb, L. Dean
  Foundations of America education / L. Dean Webb, Arlene Metha, K. Forbis Jordan -- 7th ed.
      p. cm.
  Includes bibliographical references and index.
  ISBN 978-0-13-262612-5
  1. Education--United States.   I. Metha, Arlene.   II. Jordan, K. Forbis (Kenneth Forbis)   III. Title.
  LA217.2.W43 2013
  370.973--dc23

                                   2012001875

ISBN 10: 0-13-262612-8
ISBN 13: 978-0-13-262612-5

*Dedicated to the memory of my colleague, friend, and mentor*
*K. Forbis Jordan*

# Preface

Why is the understanding of the fundamentals of American education important to today's teachers? Explore this text for answers to this fundamental question and gain an understanding of how the evolution of education affects today's teaching and learning. Become a highly qualified teacher by connecting theory and practice, by examining the philosophical and historical roots of education as well as its current structures, and by exploring the real-life challenges facing teachers and the future of education and the teaching profession.

## New to this Edition

The seventh edition brings attention to the major challenges and issues that are shaping education in the second decade of the twenty-first century. Major changes are taking place in the teaching profession, the classroom, and the board room. The increased involvement of state and federal governments in education, the movement toward national standards, the continued emphasis on student achievement data and the push to include these data in pay-for-performance compensation and value-added evaluation, the rapid growth and support for charter schools, and the minority to majority demographic shift in the student population all have major impacts on the future of education in the United States. This edition investigates each of these topics. At the same time, we emphasize the necessity of connecting theory and practice by examining the philosophical and historical roots of education, its current structure and the future of the field.

This edition represents an updating of the research and practice for all topics. All data tables have been updated. Selected dated tables and figures were eliminated and new ones added as graphic organizers. In addition, the following are new to this edition:

- Expanded coverage of the above referenced topics.
- Five new Historical Notes, five new Controversial Issues, and two new Ask Yourself features were added.
- Chapter 7 was updated and expanded through the current Obama administration.
- Expanded discussion of the racial-ethnic achievement gap and the contributing factors.
- A new section on childhood obesity was added to Chapter 10 as well as an expanded discussion of cyberbullying. The section on HIV/AIDS was deleted from the same chapter.
- The educational implications of the demographic and economic changes and challenges facing states and school districts was a discussion thread throughout the text.
- Chapters 14 (and 15) included discussion of the new Common Core State Standards. The section on the uses of technology was eliminated. Feedback from reviewers suggested it was dated by the time it was written or too large a topic to be adequately covered in the space allowed.
- Chapter 16 from the sixth edition was eliminated and the discussions of future trends integrated into preceding chapters.

## Read, Think About, and Respond to Current Educational Issues

### ABC NEWS: VIDEO INSIGHT *feature*

A total of nine ABC News videos connect chapter content to current and controversial issues in education. The videos are now available on MyEducationLab at www.myeducationlab.com.

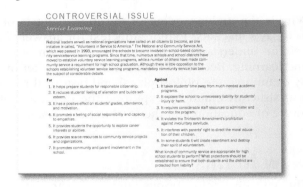

### CONTROVERSIAL ISSUES *feature*

Consider your values and beliefs as you read about and reflect on controversial school issues, complete with *for* and *against* statements for your consideration. Controversial issues features are found in Chapters 1–3, 5–8, 10, and 12–15.

## Reflect on How the Past Influences Education Today

### ASK YOURSELF *feature*

Encourages readers to think critically about and make the connection between the content being discussed and their future teaching practice. This is a great tool for readers as they develop their personal educational philosophy. This feature is found in Chapters 1–4, 9, 11, 13, and 14.

### HISTORICAL NOTE *feature*

Familiarizes readers with key individuals and hallmark educational developments in the history of education. Located in chapters 1–14, the feature encourages readers to reflect on the contribution of these historical topics or individuals.

### For Your Reflection and Analysis *margin notes*

Encourage readers to stop, think critically, and reflect on chapter content, connect it to their own thinking and beliefs, and then consider their responses. Located in every chapter, these questions help readers learn and practice reflection now and throughout their teaching careers. Readers are encouraged to answer the questions to promote reflection and group discussion.

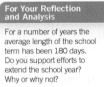

**For Your Reflection and Analysis**

For a number of years the average length of the school term has been 180 days. Do you support efforts to extend the school year? Why or why not?

### *Chapter Opening Vignettes*

Each chapter begins with a vignette featuring real education-related cases followed by a series of reflection questions that connect the vignette to the broader foundations of education.

## Prepares Teachers to Become Professionals

### *NEW!* TEACHER OF THE YEAR

Each chapter introduces one of the winners of the Council of Chief State School Officers (CCSSO) Teacher of the Year awards, asking them to respond to the question, "Why do you teach?" Video clips of these master teachers responding to this question are located on MyEducationLab.

### *Prepare for Your Licensure Examination*

Located at the end of every chapter, this case-study activity provides opportunities to assess reader knowledge in realistic case studies similar to those found in the Praxis II Principles of Learning and Teaching examination.

### *Develop Your Portfolio*

Incorporating the INTASC standards, these end-of-chapter activities serve as a guide as readers begin to develop materials to include in their professional portfolio. These activities involve readers in a range of activities such as beginning to develop a personal philosophy of education and visiting Web sites of professional organizations.

### *INTASC Correlation Matrix*

Found on the inside front and back covers, this helpful matrix connects chapter content to the INTASC standards for easy reference.

## MyEducationLab

Proven to **engage students**, provide **trusted content**, and **improve results**, Pearson MyLabs have helped over 8 million registered students reach true understanding in their courses. **MyEducationLab** engages students with real-life teaching situations through dynamic videos, case studies and student artifacts. Student progress is assessed, and a personalized study plan is created based on the student's unique results. Automatic grading and reporting keeps educators informed to quickly address gaps and improve student performance. All of the activities and exercises in MyEducationLab are built around essential learning outcomes for teachers and are mapped to professional teaching standards.

In *Preparing Teachers for a Changing World*, Linda Darling-Hammond and her colleagues point out that grounding teacher education in real classrooms—among real teachers and students and among actual examples of students' and teachers' work—is an important, and perhaps even an essential, part of training teachers for the complexities of teaching in today's classrooms.

In the MyEducationLab for this course you will find the following features and resources.

### Study Plan Specific to Your Text

MyEducationLab gives students the opportunity to test themselves on key concepts and skills, track their own progress through the course, and access personalized Study Plan activities.

The customized Study Plan—with enriching activities—is generated based on students' results of a pretest. Study Plans tag incorrect questions from the pretest to the appropriate textbook learning outcome, helping students focus on the topics they need help with. Personalized Study Plan activities may include eBook reading assignments, and review, practice and enrichment activities. After students complete the enrichment activities, they take a posttest to see the concepts they've mastered or the areas where they may need extra help.

MyEducationLab then reports the Study Plan results to the instructor. Based on these reports, the instructor can adapt course material to suit the needs of individual students or the entire class.

TEACHER OF THE YEAR

*Holly Franks Boffy Louisiana*

I'm a teacher because I believe that everybody has been given certain gifts. My gift is that of a teacher. I love my students, and I love to learn. In college, I fell in love with learning. Every day in my classroom I try to create the experiences that John Dewey wrote about 100 years ago. And I know that if I create these experiences my students will be empowered and inspired to use their gifts. My grandmother was a first-grade teacher for 30 years. My grandfather was a teacher, coach, principal, and then superintendent. When I was seven years old, he was honored by the community he served with a plaque. That plaque hangs on my grandmother's back door. It's a reminder to me that teaching is a noble profession. About a year before I was born, he wrote a message to students in the yearbook. And in that message he talked about inspiring people to continue to learn and also to serve their community. I teach because I want my students to use their gifts to make the world a better place.

### Connection to National Standards

Now it is easier than ever to see how coursework is connected to national standards. Each topic, activity and exercise on MyEducationLab lists intended learning outcomes connected to the Interstate Teacher Assessment and Support Consortium (InTASC) Model Core Teaching Standards

### Assignments and Activities

Designed to enhance your understanding of concepts covered in class, these assignable exercises show concepts in action (through videos, cases, and/or student and teacher artifacts). They help you deepen content knowledge and synthesize and apply concepts and strategies you read about in the book. (Correct answers for these assignments are available to the instructor only.)

### Building Teaching Skills and Dispositions

These unique learning units help users practice and strengthen skills that are essential to effective teaching. After presenting the steps involved in a core teaching process, you are given an opportunity to practice applying this skill via videos, student and teacher artifacts, and/or case studies of authentic classrooms. Providing multiple opportunities to practice a single teaching concept, each activity encourages a deeper understanding and application of concepts, as well as the use of critical thinking skills. After practice, students take a quiz that is reported to the instructor gradebook.

### Lesson Plan Builder

The **Lesson Plan Builder** is an effective and easy-to-use tool that you can use to create, update, and share quality lesson plans. The software also makes it easy to integrate state content standards into any lesson plan.

### IRIS Center Resources

The IRIS Center at Vanderbilt University (http://iris.peabody.vanderbilt.edu), funded by the U.S. Department of Education's Office of Special Education Programs (OSEP), develops training enhancement materials for preservice and practicing teachers. The Center works with experts from across the country to create challenge-based interactive modules, case study units, and podcasts that provide research-validated information about working with students in inclusive settings. In your MyEducationLab course we have integrated this content where appropriate.

### Teacher Talk

This feature emphasizes the power of teaching through videos of master teachers, with each speaker telling their own compelling stories of why they teach. Each of these featured teachers has been awarded the Council of Chief State School Officers Teachers of the Year award, the oldest and most prestigious award for teachers.

### Course Resources

The Course Resources section of MyEducationLab is designed to help you put together an effective lesson plan, prepare for and begin your career, navigate your first year of teaching, and understand key educational standards, policies, and laws. It includes the following:

**The Grammar Tutorial** provides content extracted in part from *The Praxis Series™ Online Tutorial for the Pre-Professional Skills Test: Writing*. Online quizzes built around specific elements of grammar help users strengthen their understanding and proper usage of the English language in writing. Definitions and examples of grammatical concepts are followed by practice exercises to provide the background information and usage examples needed to refresh understandings of grammar, and then apply that knowledge to make it more permanent.

The **Preparing a Portfolio** module provides guidelines for creating a high-quality teaching portfolio.

**Beginning Your Career** offers tips, advice, and other valuable information on:

- *Resume Writing and Interviewing:* Includes expert advice on how to write impressive resumes and prepare for job interviews.

- *Your First Year of Teaching:* Provides practical tips to set up a first classroom, manage student behavior, and more easily organize for instruction and assessment.
- *Law and Public Policies:* Details specific directives and requirements you need to understand under the No Child Left Behind Act and the Individuals with Disabilities Education Improvement Act of 2004.

**The Certification and Licensure** section is designed to help you pass your licensure exam by giving you access to state test requirements, overviews of what tests cover, and sample test items.

The Certification and Licensure section includes the following:

- **State Certification Test Requirements:** Here, you can click on a state and will then be taken to a list of state certification tests.
- You can click on the **Licensure Exams** you need to take to find:
  - Basic information about each test
  - Descriptions of what is covered on each test
  - Sample test questions with explanations of correct answers
- **National Evaluation Series**™ by Pearson: Here, students can see the tests in the NES, learn what is covered on each exam, and access sample test items with descriptions and rationales of correct answers. You can also purchase interactive online tutorials developed by Pearson Evaluation Systems and the Pearson Teacher Education and Development group.
- **ETS Online Praxis Tutorials:** Here you can purchase interactive online tutorials developed by ETS and by the Pearson Teacher Education and Development group. Tutorials are available for the Praxis I exams and for select Praxis II exams.

Visit www.myeducationlab.com for a demonstration of this exciting new online teaching resource.

## Supplemental Materials for the Instructor

The following instructor supplements can be accessed at www.pearsonhighered.com.

### Online Instructor's Manual and Test Bank

This manual provides concrete suggestions to actively involve students in learning and to promote interactive teaching using PowerPoint presentations, and ABC News videos. Each chapter contains chapter outlines, student objectives, lecture and discussion guides, extended projects and assignments, and an instructional media guide. The test bank includes multiple-choice, true/false, and essay questions.

### Online Test Bank and TestGen Software

Students learn better when they are held accountable for what they hvae learned. That is why we have developed an extensive bank of test questions per chapter in a variety of formats (multiple choice, short answer, and essay) that match the content set out in each chapter. The Test Bank is available on line at the Instructor Resource Center—www.pearsonhighered.com.

# Acknowledgments

The authors wish to recognize the many persons who have contributed to the preparation of this edition and the previous editions of this text. First, we give special recognition to the teachers and other educators who work each day to provide learning opportunities for the youth of America. Second, we wish to acknowledge the diverse scholars who have provided the past and present record of the development of elementary and secondary education and the researchers and policy analysts who are charting the future. Third, we express our appreciation to our professional colleagues for their critical comments and suggestions about ways to improve the seventh edition.

We extend our sincere appreciation to Editor Ann Davis and Project Manager Sheryl Langner. To the various reviewers of the seventh edition, we extend our sincere thanks for their constructive comments. Their efforts helped us improve the text in this seventh edition. For their participation, we extend our thanks to: Chuck Achter, Iowa State University; Brian W. Dotts, The University of Georgia; Sr. JoAnn Hohenbrink, Ohio Dominican University; Christopher J. Maglio, Truman State University; and Gerald McCain, Southern Oregon University.

# BRIEF *Contents*

# Contents

# PART II   PHILOSOPHY AND ITS IMPACT ON THE SCHOOLS

# PART III   HISTORICAL FOUNDATIONS OF EDUCATION

# PART IV    SCHOOLING IN A DIVERSE AND MULTICULTURAL SOCIETY

# PART V   LEGAL AND POLITICAL CONTROL AND FINANCIAL SUPPORT

# PART VI CURRICULUM, INSTRUCTION, AND ASSESSMENT IN EFFECTIVE SCHOOLS

# Special FEATURES

# CHAPTER
## *One*

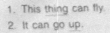

# 1

# Status of the Profession

Dr. Flynn enters the room of a patient who was recently admitted to University Hospital complaining of severe abdominal pain. Several interns follow Dr. Flynn to the patient's bedside. Dr. Flynn begins to ask the patient a series of questions. After the patient responds, Dr. Flynn turns to one of the interns and asks for a diagnosis. The intern gives a diagnosis. Dr. Flynn follows with a series of questions related to the basis for the diagnosis and possible treatment.

The ABC Corporation has just initiated a new data management plan. All middle managers have been told to report to the conference room at 8:30 A.M. on Monday. Upon arrival, the director of human resources introduces Ms. Dominguez from Data Resources, the retailer of the software supporting the new data management plan. Ms. Dominguez distributes a packet of materials and spends the remainder of the day with the managers, reviewing the materials in the packet, presenting additional information using a computer presentation platform, and showing a video related to the data management plan.

Mr. Pell stops at Amy Black's desk and answers a question. He moves to the desk of another student, observes the student writing in a workbook, points to something the student has written, and then, in a low voice, tells the student that the response is not correct and explains why. He continues around the room, stopping at almost every desk to make some remark. After about 10 minutes he goes to the front of the room and says, "Class, it appears that several people are having problems with this assignment. Let's review how to divide one fraction by another fraction." Mr. Pell walks to the blackboard and begins to speak.

Which of these individuals—Dr. Flynn, Ms. Dominguez, or Mr. Pell—is a teacher? Why? What defines the act of teaching?

*T*eaching has been considered by some to be the most noble of professions. H. G. Wells went so far as to say, "The teacher, whether mother, priest, or schoolmaster, is the real maker of history." Perhaps you are asking yourself, "What is a teacher?"; "What is this profession of teaching all about?" And, perhaps most important, "Should I become a teacher?" This chapter presents an overview of the teaching profession. After studying the chapter, you should be able to:

- Provide a demographic overview of America's teaching force.
- Evaluate your motives for becoming a teacher.
- Identify the most commonly cited satisfactions and dissatisfactions of teaching.
- Describe a typical teacher preparation program.

- Identify the most common strategies being used to recruit minorities into teaching.
- Discuss current issues related to teacher certification, including testing for certification, emergency certification, and interstate certification.
- Discuss the advantages and disadvantages of providing alternative routes for teacher certification.
- Compare projected data related to teacher supply with that projected for demand, and explore the factors contributing to teacher supply and demand.
- Identify the major elements of teacher compensation, including supplemental pay and performance-based pay.

MyEducationLab

Visit the MyEducationLab for *Foundations of American Education* to enhance your understanding of chapter concepts with a personalized Study Plan. You'll also have the opportunity to hone your teaching skills through video and case based Assignments and Activities, and Building Teaching Skills and Disposition lessons.

## The Teacher and Teaching: Definitions

Put most simply, a teacher is one who instructs another. A more formal definition from the *Encyclopedia of Education* describes teachers as "intellectual leaders who create opportunities for students to demonstrate what they know and what they know how to do" (Waid & McNergney, 2003, p. 2435). Teaching is defined in another work as "the processes of helping pupils acquire knowledge, skills, attitudes, and/or appreciations by means of a systematic method of instruction" (Shafritz, Koeppe, & Soper, 1988, p. 468). Perhaps the most provocative definition defines the teacher as an artist and teaching as an art. According to Eisner (2002), teaching can be considered an art from at least four perspectives:

> First, it is an art in that teaching can be performed with such skill and grace that, for the student as well as for the teacher, the experience can be justifiably characterized as aesthetic....
>
> Second, teaching is an art in that teachers, like painters, composers, actresses, and dancers, make judgments based largely on qualities that unfold during the course of action.... The teacher must "read" the emerging qualities and respond with qualities appropriate to the ends sought....
>
> Third, teaching is an art in that the teacher's activity is not dominated by prescriptions or routines but is influenced by qualities and contingencies that are unpredicted. The teacher must function in an innovative way in order to cope with these contingencies.... Fourth, teaching is an art in that the ends it achieves are often created in the process ... teaching is a form of human action in which many of the ends achieved are emergent—that is to say, found in the course of interaction with students rather than preconceived and efficiently attained. (pp. 154–155)

To consider teaching an art does not negate the necessity of establishing a scientific basis for the art of teaching and for developing a theoretical framework for teaching that addresses what we know and believe about intelligence, the conditions of learning, and what defines an effective teacher. The stronger the scientific basis, the greater the potential to improve teaching.

For Your Reflection and Analysis

Do you believe that teachers are "born not made"? In your experience as a student have you been exposed to teachers who were "artists" in the classroom?

## Profile of the Teaching Profession

Whatever definition is used, there is little argument that the teacher is the central element in the educational system. Research has consistently shown that the teacher is the most important school-related variable in student learning. It is of interest to review what we know about the almost 4 million teachers in America today. Table 1.1 presents some characteristics of public school teachers.

As indicated in the table, the teaching force is predominantly female and White. While only 24% of the teaching force is male, this is actually an increase from the 21% in 2000; 83% of all public school teachers were non-Hispanic White. The data also show a less experienced and younger teaching force. The average class size of secondary teachers was larger than that of elementary teachers as were the number of hours per week spent on teaching and other school related duties.

### Table 1.1 — Selected Characteristics of Public School Teachers

| Teacher Characteristics | 2001 | 2008 |
|---|---|---|
| Sex (percent) | | |
| Male | 21.0 | 24.1 |
| Female | 79.0 | 75.9 |
| Race/ethnicity (percent) | | |
| White, non-Hispanic | 84.3 | 83.1 |
| Black, non-Hispanic | 7.6 | 7.0 |
| Hispanic | 5.6 | 6.9 |
| Asian or Pacific Islander | 1.6 | 1.5 |
| American Indian or Alaskan Native | 0.8 | 0.5 |
| Average age (years) | 46.0 | 42.2 |
| Highest degree (percent) | | |
| Bachelor's | 43.1 | 47.4 |
| Master's or specialist | 56.0 | 50.9 |
| Doctorate | 0.8 | 0.9 |
| Average years teaching experience | 14.0 | 13.0 |
| Average class size | | |
| Elementary | 21.0 | 20.0 |
| Secondary | 28.0 | 23.4 |
| Average number of hours per week spent on teaching and other school related duties | | |
| Elementary teachers | 50.0 | 52.4 |
| Secondary teachers | 49.0 | 53.7 |

*Source:* Coopersmith, J. (2009). *Characteristics of Public, Private, and Bureau of Indian Education Elementary and Secondary School Teachers in the United States: Results from the 2007–08 Schools and Staffing Survey.* National Center for Education Statistics, Institute of Education Science, U.S. Department of Education, Washington, DC.

The number of teachers and other instructional personnel employed in the public school systems of the United States has grown over the years as enrollments have increased. Table 1.2 gives a historical summary of public elementary and secondary school enrollments; number of instructional staff; and number of teachers, librarians, and other nonsupervisory staff. Since 1990 the total number of teachers, librarians, and other nonsupervisory staff increased over 40%. The growth in staff reflects not only enrollment increases, but also the steady reduction in pupil–teacher ratios, the enactment of legislation requiring increased services and specialized personnel, and the increased utilization of teacher aides, librarians, guidance counselors, and other instructional support personnel.

## Why Become a Teacher?

There are many reasons why an individual might choose a career in teaching. Very few teachers would be able to identify a single reason for entering the profession. Many were positively influenced by former teachers. For others an important reason might be a practical consideration such as job security or something as forthright as the fact that their first career choices were blocked (i.e., they didn't make it into medical school or into professional sports). Others may be attracted by the long summer vacations or a schedule that allows them to spend more time with their families. A less positive reason might be that teaching is a good temporary job while waiting to prepare for or be accepted into another career.

**Table 1.2 — Historical Summary of Public Elementary and Secondary School Statistics: United States, 1869–1870 to 2007–2008**

|  | 1869–70 | 1879–80 | 1889–90 | 1899–1900 | 1909–10 | 1919–20 | 1929–30 |
|---|---|---|---|---|---|---|---|
| Total enrollment (in thousands) | 7,562 | 9,867 | 12,723 | 15,503 | 17,814 | 21,578 | 25,678 |
| Total instructional staff (in thousands) | — | — | — | — | — | 678 | 48,880 |
| Total teachers, librarians, and other nonsupervisory staff (in thousands) | 201 | 287 | 364 | 423 | 523 | 657 | 843 |
| Men | 78 | 123 | 126 | 127 | 110 | 93 | 140 |
| Women | 123 | 164 | 238 | 296 | 413 | 585 | 703 |

*Source:* Snyder, T. D. & Dillow, S. A. (2011). *Digest of education statistics, 2010.* National Center for Education Statistics, Institute of Education Sciences, U.S. Department of Education, Washington, DC.

All of the preceding reasons are indeed motives for becoming a teacher, but they are not the primary motives. Over the years, numerous researchers have asked teachers what attracted them to the profession. The three reasons given most consistently are (1) a caring for and desire to work with young people, (2) a desire to make a valuable contribution to society, and (3) an interest in a subject matter field and an excitement in sharing it with others.

The reasons one has for becoming a teacher have a significant effect on the ultimate satisfaction one finds in the job. For this reason it is important that prospective teachers question themselves about what they expect to gain from or give to teaching. The set of questions found in the following Ask Yourself feature are provided to guide you in this inquiry.

# ASK YOURSELF

## *Do I Want to Be a Teacher?*

1. What reasons do you have for wanting to teach? Are they all negative (e.g., because the schools are oppressive, or because you need a job and working as a teacher is more respectable than working as a cab driver or salesperson)? What are the positive reasons for wanting to teach? Is there any pleasure to be gained from teaching? Knowledge? Power?

2. Why do you want to spend so much time with young people? Do you feel more comfortable with children? Have you spent much time with children recently, or are you mostly fantasizing about how they would behave? Are you afraid of adults? Intimidated by adult company? Fed up with the competition and coldness of business and the university?

3. What do you want from the students? Do you want them to do well on tests? Learn particular subject matter? Like one another? Like you? How much do you need to have students like you? Are you afraid to criticize them or set limits on their behavior because they might be angry with you? Do you consider yourself one of the kids? Is there any difference in your mind between your role and that of your prospective students?

4. What do you know that you can teach or share with your students?

5. With what age youngster do you feel the greatest affinity or are you most comfortable with?

6. Do you have any gender-based motives for wanting to work with young people? Do you want to enable them to become the boy or girl you could never be? For example, to free the girls of the image of prettiness and quietness and encourage them to run and fight, mess about with science, and get lost in the abstraction of math? Or to encourage boys to write poetry, play with dolls, let their fantasies come out, and not feel abnormal if they enjoy reading, acting, or listening to music?

7. What kind of young people do you want to work with?

8. What kind of school should you teach in?

9. How comfortable would you be teaching in a multiracial or multicultural setting? Do you feel capable of working with a culturally diverse student population?

*Source: Kohl, 1976.*

| 1939–40 | 1949–50 | 1959–60 | 1969–70 | 1979–80 | 1989–90 | 1999–2000 | 2007–08 |
|---|---|---|---|---|---|---|---|
| 25,434 | 25,112 | 36,087 | 45,550 | 41,651 | 40,543 | 46,851 | 49,293 |
| 912 | 963 | 1,457 | 2,286 | 2,406 | 2,986 | 3,820 | 4,214 |
| 875 | 920 | 1,393 | 2,195 | 2,300 | 2,860 | 3,683 | 4,056 |
| 195 | 196 | 404 | 711 | 782 | — | — | — |
| 681 | 724 | 989 | 1,484 | 1,518 | — | — | — |

## Satisfactions and Dissatisfactions with Teaching

Just as each individual has personal motives for becoming a teacher, each individual will find certain aspects of the position satisfying and certain aspects dissatisfying. In fact, it is possible that a particular aspect may be both satisfying and dissatisfying. Long summer vacations are satisfiers, but the reduced salary is a dissatisfier. Working with children can be both satisfying and frustrating. Although each individual will find personal satisfactions and dissatisfactions with teaching, it is of interest to look at what practicing teachers have identified as the satisfactions or attractions of teaching, as well as the dissatisfactions or challenges of teaching. Prospective teachers in particular need to know and prepare themselves for what they will encounter when they enter the classroom.

Understanding the satisfactions and dissatisfactions of teaching is also important for those making policies that affect teachers, because teacher satisfaction has been found to be associated with teacher effectiveness which, in turn, affects student achievement (U.S. Department of Education, 1997). The good news for those considering entering the teaching profession is that teachers who have the most experience (20 years or more), rather than being the least satisfied, are the ones most likely to rank their satisfaction as "very satisfied" (Markow & Pieters, 2009).

What exactly is it that teachers find satisfying and dissatisfying about teaching? We have already mentioned what teachers most often identify as the major satisfactions of teaching: the joy of working with children and the feeling that they are making a difference in the life of a student and in the larger society. Teachers also often talk about feeling respected in today's society, being recognized for a job well done, and the fact that teaching allows them the opportunity to earn a decent salary (Markow & Cooper, 2008). Many teachers find the autonomy they exercise in their classrooms and the control they have over their own time to be attractions. For others it is the opportunity to have a lifelong association with their subject field. And for still others the security of the position and the feeling of camaraderie and cooperation they share with their colleagues are important attractions (Viadero, 2008). Teaching is one of the few professions where competition is virtually nonexistent.

Among the extrinsic factors that have been associated with teacher satisfaction and dissatisfaction are level of support from parents and administrators, availability of resources, class size, amount of time provided for planning and professional growth or collaboration with other teachers, degree of student misbehavior, and school safety (Markow & Cooper, 2008; Viadero, 2008). And, although very few teachers are motivated by salary to enter teaching, salary and benefits can influence teachers' level of satisfaction or dissatisfaction in the position, as well as their desire to remain in or leave teaching (Swanson, 2008).

Teachers are no different from other professionals in wanting to have input into the decisions that affect them and to have control over their immediate environment. Although teachers feel they are in the best position to recognize the needs of their students, they often feel they are excluded from participation in the decision-making process regarding their students. And one of the ironies of the No Child Left Behind Act of 2001, discussed in detail throughout this text, is that while it aims to promote school choice for parents and students, the curriculum and assessment systems that have been created to meet its mandates have created an environment more likely to limit than to expand teachers' choice in these areas.

A final dissatisfier, inadequate resources, the constant bane of teachers, inhibits the ability of teachers to meet the needs of individual students and prepare all students for higher levels of educational attainment or successful participation in the workforce. The nationwide recession which began at the end of the first decade of the twenty-first century has resulted in cuts in public school budgets and has exaggerated the financial challenges facing the schools.

Perhaps the ultimate indication of teacher job satisfaction or dissatisfaction is whether, given the opportunity to make the decision again, a person would become a teacher. When teachers are asked this very question, 90% of teachers said they would choose teaching again and only 8% said they would leave teaching before retirement and only 10% would leave for a better job (Alt & Henke, 2007).

## Teacher Preparation

The standards and accountability movement that has driven the reform of K–12 curriculum and assessment has also focused attention on issues related to teacher quality including teacher preparation, teacher evaluation, and teacher certification. The standards movement in teacher education has been led by the Interstate New Teacher Assessment and Support Consortium (INTASC), a group of major professional education organizations; the National Council for the Accreditation of Teacher Education (NCATE); and the National Commission on Teaching and America's Future (NCTAF). Each of these organizations has developed standards that detail what teachers should know and be able to do. The INTASC Core Teaching Standards are presented in Table 1.3 as well as on the inside front and back covers of this text. The INTASC standards have provided the content and organizational framework for many teacher education programs. Standards for experienced teachers that parallel the INTASC standards have been developed by the National Board for Professional Teaching Standards (NBPTS) and have also influenced the design of teacher preparation programs. NCATE standards are used in the accreditation of schools, colleges, and departments of education. To aid you in becoming familiar with the INTASC standards, the Organizing Your Professional Portfolio feature at the end of each chapter addresses one or more of the standards.

There are a number of ways to become a teacher. The most common is to complete a 4-year baccalaureate teacher education program that has been approved by the state or accredited by NCATE or the Teacher Education Accreditation Council. At some institutions, undergraduates majoring in fields other than education are able to accumulate enough teacher education credits to qualify for certification. An extended, or 5-year, preservice teacher education program has been implemented at a number of institutions. These programs typically emphasize field experiences, and most award a master's degree upon completion.

For the increasing number of individuals who have non-education college degrees and want to enter the profession without earning another undergraduate degree, alternative routes are available, ranging from enrolling in a compressed certification program to enrolling in a master's degree program leading to teacher certification. In the next section, we will review baccalaureate teacher education programs, the most common avenue into the profession, as well as the increasingly popular alternative certification program option.

## Table 1.3 — INTASC Core Teaching Standards

**The Learner and Learning**

**Standard #1: Learner Development.**   The teacher understands how learners grow and develop, recognizing that patterns of learning and development vary individually within and across the cognitive, linguistic, social, emotional, and physical areas, and designs and implements developmentally appropriate and challenging learning experiences.

**Standard #2: Learning Differences.**   The teacher uses understanding of individual differences and diverse cultures and communities to ensure inclusive learning environments that enable each learner to meet high standards.

**Standard #3: Learning Environments.**   The teacher works with others to create environments that support individual and collaborative learning, and that encourage positive social interaction, active engagement in learning, and self motivation.

**Content**

**Standard #4: Content Knowledge.**   The teacher understands the central concepts, tools of inquiry, and structures of the discipline(s) he or she teaches and creates learning experiences that make the discipline accessible and meaningful for learners to assure mastery of the content.

**Standard #5: Applications of Content.**   The teacher understands how to connect concepts and use differing perspectives to engage learners in critical thinking, creativity, and collaborative problem solving related to authentic local and global issues.

**Instructional Practice**

**Standard #6: Assessment.**   The teacher understands and uses multiple methods of assessment to engage learners in their own growth, to monitor learner progress, and to guide the teacher's and learner's decision making.

**Standard #7: Planning for Instruction.**   The teacher plans instruction that supports every student in meeting rigorous learning goals by drawing upon knowledge of content areas, curriculum, cross-disciplinary skills, and pedagogy, as well as knowledge of learners and the community context.

**Standard #8: Instructional Strategies.**   The teacher understands and uses a variety of instructional strategies to encourage learners to develop deep understanding of content areas and their connections, and to build skills to apply knowledge in meaningful ways.

**Professional Responsibility**

**Standard #9: Professional Learning and Ethical Practice.**   The teacher engages in ongoing professional learning and uses evidence to continually evaluate his/her practice, particularly the effects of his/her choices and actions on others (learners, families, other professionals, and the community), and adapts practice to meet the needs of each learner.

**Standard #10: Leadership and Collaboration.**   The teacher seeks appropriate leadership roles and opportunities to take responsibility for student learning, to collaborate with learners, families, colleagues, other school professionals, and community members to ensure learner growth, and to advance the profession.

*Source:* From Council of Chief State School Officers. (2011, April). *Interstate Teacher Assessment and Support Consortium (InTASC) Model Core Teaching Standards: A Resource for State Dialogue.* Washington, DC: Author. Copyright © 2011 by the Council of Chief State School Officers, Washington, DC.

## *Baccalaureate Teacher Education Programs*

From its beginnings at the Columbian School in Concord, Vermont (see the Historical Note on page 10), the formal preparation of teachers has grown to an enterprise that takes place in about 1,200 departments, schools, or colleges of education in the United States. Teacher education programs usually consist of four areas: (1) general studies, (2) content studies in a major or minor, (3) professional studies, and (4) field experiences and clinical practice. The general studies or liberal arts and science portion of the program, as well as the academic major portion, are generally similar to those required of other students at the college or university. Typically students are not admitted into the teacher education program until they have completed, or substantially completed, the general studies requirement with a grade point average (GPA) of at least 2.5. In addition, the majority of teacher education programs require the passage of a test of basic skills, often the Praxis I, prior to entering the program.

Preparation programs for elementary school teachers are somewhat different from those for secondary school teachers. In the vast majority of states, students

# HISTORICAL NOTE

## *The Columbian School: The First Formal Teacher Training Institution*

Most histories of education identify the Columbian School at Concord, Vermont, established by the Reverend Samuel Hall in 1823, as the first formal teacher training institution in the United States. Hall had gone to Concord as a supply (temporary) pastor in 1822 and in the first year observed the poor condition of the schools and came to believe that better teachers were central to any school improvement. When he accepted the pastorate in 1823 he did so with the stipulation that he be allowed to open a school to train teachers. Beginning in the unused part of a store, the school soon moved to a new brick building provided by the town.

At the Columbian School, Hall offered a review of the subjects taught in the common (elementary) school, plus advanced mathematics, chemistry, natural and moral philosophy, logic, astronomy, and the "art of teaching." In 1829 Hall published the first professional textbook on teacher education in the English language, *Lectures on Schoolkeeping*. A partial chapter outline of the book was as follows:

*Chapter III*. Requisite qualifications of teachers.

*Chapter IV*. Nature of the teacher's employment. Responsibility of the teacher. Importance of realizing and understanding it.

*Chapter V*. Gaining the confidence of the school. Means of gaining it. The instructor should be willing to spend all his time when it can be rendered beneficial to the school.

*Chapter VI*. Government of a school. Prerequisites. Manner of treating scholars. Uniformity in government. Firmness.

*Chapter VII*. Government, continued. Partiality. Regard to the future as well as the present welfare of the scholars. Mode of intercourse between teacher and scholars, and between scholars. Punishments. Rewards.

*Chapter VIII*. General management of a school. Direction of duties.

*Chapter IX*. Mode of teaching. Manner of illustrating subjects. Spelling. Reading.

*Chapter X*. Arithmetic. Geography. English Grammar. Writing. History.

*Chapter XI*. Composition. General subjects, not particularly studies. Importance of improving opportunities when deep impressions are made on the minds of the school.

*Chapter XII*. Means of exciting the attention of scholars. Such as are to be avoided. Such as are safely used.

*Chapter XIII*. To female instructors.

*Source:* Outline from *Lectures on schoolkeeping* by Samuel R. Hall is from Cubberly, E. P. (1934). *Readings in public education in the United States* (pp. 324–325). New York: Houghton Mifflin.

## For Your Reflection and Analysis

How did you determine your preference for elementary or secondary teaching?

preparing to be elementary school teachers are not required to have a major in a content area; elementary education is considered the major. It is assumed that elementary education students acquire knowledge of the subject matter through the liberal arts and science requirements. The opposite is true for secondary majors, who in most states are required to have a major in the subject field to be taught. The number of hours in the major will usually constitute two thirds of the hours taken in the upper division, with the other one third in the professional education sequence. On average, secondary education students require 10 semester hours more to complete their program than do elementary education majors.

The professional studies component of the teacher preparation program is the specialized body of knowledge and skills required by the profession. The typical professional studies component includes courses in the foundational studies in education (e.g., introduction to education, history, sociology, philosophy of education, educational psychology, child and adolescent development, comparative education, multicultural education) and the pedagogical studies, which concentrate on teaching and learning theory, general and specialized methods of instruction, and classroom management.

The fourth component of the teacher preparation program, the clinical field work, has become the focus of recent proposals and efforts to reform and strengthen teacher preparation programs. Clinical field work includes various field-based opportunities that provide candidates the opportunity to observe, assist, tutor, instruct, and/or conduct research in off-campus settings such as schools, community centers, or homeless shelters (NCATE, 2011). **Clinical field experiences** begin early in the program and are ongoing, whereas **clinical practice** "includes student teaching or internships that provide candidates with an intensive and extensive culminating activity. Candidates are immersed in the learning community and are provided opportunities to develop and demonstrate competence in the professional roles for which they are preparing" (NCATE, 2011, p. 21). Recent proposals for reforming teacher education have recommended that the clinical practice component become the centerpiece of the teacher preparation program and be extended to a much longer apprenticeship or residency.

Student teaching or internship is required for certification in almost every state. The typical length is 10 to 12 weeks. Normally, the student teacher is assigned to a cooperating teacher, who is selected based on a reputation as an "expert" teacher. A college or university professor is assigned to supervise the student teaching experience and makes periodic

Practicing teachers rate their student teaching experience as the most important part of their preparation program.

observations and visitations with the student and the cooperating teacher. During the student teaching experience, the student gradually assumes greater responsibility for instruction under the guidance of the cooperating teacher. Whereas the amount of time that the student teacher actually spends teaching may vary considerably (in part a function of the demonstrated ability of the student teacher and in part a function of the nature of the classroom), on average, student teachers will spend about 60% of their time teaching. The remaining time is spent observing, record keeping, and assisting in various classroom activities. The student teaching experience is consistently rated by practicing teachers as the most important part of their preparation program.

## Alternative Teacher Preparation Programs

As described in the Video Insight, "Teacher Shortage: Alternative Certification," in response to the shortage of qualified teachers in some teaching areas, 48 states and the District of Columbia have adopted alternative teacher preparation/certification programs to certify candidates who have subject-matter competence without completion of a formal teacher preparation program. These programs are designed

## ABC NEWS: VIDEO INSIGHT

### Teacher Shortage: Alternative Certification

This ABC News video introduces the issue of providing alternative routes to teacher certification as a strategy to meet the current and projected teacher shortage. The focus in this short video is on the benefits of attracting second-career individuals into teaching. What is left out are the concerns many educators have about these programs.

1. What do you see as the major concerns about trying to prepare individuals to enter the classroom in such an abbreviated time frame?

2. What are some alternative strategies that might be used to attract qualified individuals to the teaching profession?

3. Why have they not gained in popularity as has alternative certification?

to attract to the teaching profession qualified recent college graduates or persons with at least a bachelor's degree from other professions who have been the victims of layoffs and downsizing in the private sector or who have retired from the military (e.g., Troops to Teachers) and may want to change careers. Many such programs, including the increasingly popular Teach for America, are intended to recruit teachers for underserved rural or inner-city districts or subject areas experiencing teacher shortages.

Alternatively prepared teachers now account for as many as one third of all new teachers (Constantine, Player, Silva, Hallgren, Grider, & Deke, 2009). Several states have been particularly aggressive in developing and using alternative routes for licensing teachers: 40% of new hires in New Jersey and about one-third of new hires in Texas and California have entered the profession through alternative certification programs (National Center for Alternative Certification, 2011). The number of teachers obtaining certification through alternative routes has increased significantly in the last decade. The National Center for Alternative Certification (2011) estimates that 59,000 teachers obtained their certification through alternative routes in 2008–2009.

Alternative preparation programs may be offered through a local school district, a college or university, a private provider, the state department of education, or a partnership of any of these. There is variation among the states as to the course work and internship requirements of those seeking **alternative certification** as well as how long the internship must be and how much supervision and support are given to novice teachers. University alternative certification programs usually require students to complete all coursework and field work prior to certification. Others only require the prospective teacher to complete a six- or eight-week summer program before becoming a teacher of record in a school. The remaining coursework is completed while the teacher is serving as a full-time teacher. Still other alternative certification programs require an extended residency program where participants take courses and spend significant time in the schools working with a teacher-mentor before assuming full-time classroom responsibility (Grossman & Loeb, 2010). Teacher residency programs are most popular in urban districts and are designed to meet specific teach supply needs (e.g., math and science). Teacher residency programs have been strongly supported by the Obama administration and have received funding under the Teacher Quality Enhancement program.

The merits of alternative preparation programs are a topic of some debate and the research is mixed. Some studies have found that alternatively prepared teachers are less effective in improving student achievement and are less likely to remain in the profession than traditionally certified teachers. Other reports show no discernible difference between traditionally prepared and alternatively prepared teachers on various measures of observable teaching behaviors and student achievement, especially after the first year. One indisputable fact is that alternative preparation programs tend to attract more men and minorities than do traditional teacher education programs, which has been a major impetus for their proliferation.

## Minority Representation in the Teaching Force

In 2008 approximately 45% of public school students were classified as minority as compared to 16% of teachers. It has been predicted that by 2020, over 50% of the students in our nation's schools will be minority while less than 10% of the teachers will be minority. The underrepresentation of minority teachers "almost guarantees that most students will end their formal public school experiences without ever having had or met a teacher of color" (Stephens & Harris, 2000, p. 5).

Minority teachers are needed in the schools for a variety of reasons. Minority teachers serve as role models for all students. Minority children, many of whom come from impoverished backgrounds (see Chapter 8), derive an obvious benefit from seeing minorities in professional positions. But it is also important that all children see minorities in professional roles, rather than overly represented in nonprofessional roles. "The very presence in the classroom of teachers from racial

**For Your Reflection and Analysis**

If non-education graduates can prepare for teaching in 1 year of study, why can't education graduates also be prepared in 1 year?

and ethnic minorities reflects the growing diversity of professionals and authority figures throughout society and lets all students know what is possible" (Nichols, Bicard, Bicard, & Casey, 2008, p. 598). Minority teachers are aware of the importance of serving as a role model and, in fact, have cited this as a primary motivation for becoming a teacher (Villegas & Irvin, 2010). Minority teachers are also needed because they have the cultural framework to make instruction more culturally relevant and effective. Research suggests that this "cultural synchronicity" does provide academic benefits to minority students. Villegas and Irvine (2010) identified five specific practices of minority teachers that are associated with the favorable effects of minority teachers: "(a) having high expectations of students; (b) using culturally relevant teaching; (c) developing caring and trusting relationships with students; (d) confronting issues of racism through teaching; and (e) serving as advocates and cultural brokers" (p. 180). Given the positive impact of minority teachers on student achievement, it seems clear that increasing the supply of minority teachers should be a major strategy for decreasing the achievement gap between minority and White students described in Chapter 8.

One of the major concerns of teacher preparation programs today is that fewer minority students are entering the programs. What once was one of the few professions open to minorities must now compete with higher salaried and status professions to attract capable minority students. Various studies among Blacks, Hispanics, and Asian Americans have consistently cited teaching's lack of prestige and the associated low earning potential as major reasons minorities do not enter teaching. In an attempt to address the critical shortage of minority teachers, educators and policymakers at the local, state, and national levels have initiated a number of strategies for increasing diversity in teacher preparation programs. An overview of the most popular of these initiatives is provided in the following section.

## Strategies for Increasing Diversity

Strategies for increasing diversity in teacher education programs are of two types: strategies aimed at eliminating obstacles to participation and recruitment strategies. Strategies aimed at removing obstacles to participation include increasing scholarship, loan, and loan forgiveness programs; increasing support services and retention efforts; ensuring that testing and evaluation programs minimize the influences of race and ethnicity on entry to the profession; and, as previously noted, expanding alternative certification programs.

A number of strategies designed to increase the number of minorities in teaching go beyond traditional recruitment efforts to strategies aimed at increasing the pool of minority teacher education students. One such strategy involves identifying and encouraging interested students before their senior year in high school. This is done through Future Educator clubs, teacher cadet programs, and even magnet schools that offer a college preparatory program for students who are interested in becoming teachers (e.g., the High School for the Teaching Professions in Cincinnati and the Austin High School for the Teaching Professions in Houston). Most programs target junior high or senior high school students and are designed to engage students in learning about teaching through both classroom activities and actual teaching experiences. Such programs often provide financial aid support services, and, in some cases, transferable credits that may be taken while in high school.

An increasingly popular recruitment strategy operated as a joint venture between a college or university and local school districts is the "grow your own" program for paraprofessionals. Under the typical program, teacher aides or other professionals continue in their regular jobs, taking courses offered with flexible scheduling arrangements after school, on the weekend, and during the summer. Some districts provide time off with pay to attend classes. Tuition is often reduced or paid for by the district. And, perhaps most important, graduates are guaranteed employment in the district upon successful completion of the program and certification.

Increasing the pool of minority teacher education students is not enough if they do not stay in the profession. Minority teachers are twice as likely to leave

**For Your Reflection and Analysis**

How old were you when you first became interested in teaching? How likely would you have been to attend a magnet high school for prospective teachers if one was available?

the profession as non-minority teachers (Markow, Moessner, & Horowitz, 2006). One reason for this is that minority teachers are more likely to be placed in the inner cities, where working conditions are often the poorest and stress is the highest. Financial incentives, including housing subsidies, state income tax credits, and retention bonuses are among the strategies used by a number of districts in an attempt to retain teachers in these "hard-to-staff" schools. Also among the efforts being implemented to increase the retention of minority teachers are the mentoring programs mentioned in Chapter 2.

## Teacher Certification

Successful completion of a teacher training program does not automatically qualify an individual to teach. To become qualified for teaching, administrative, and many other positions in the public schools and many private schools, individuals must acquire a valid certificate or license from the state where they wish to practice. The **certification** or licensure requirement is intended to ensure that the holder has met established state standards and is therefore qualified for employment in the area specified on the certificate. The federal No Child Left Behind Act of 2001 stipulates that all newly hired teachers in schools receiving Title I funds must be certified in the level or subject to be taught and may not have any certification requirement waived on an emergency, temporary, or professional basis.

The certification process is administered by the state education agency. The certificate can be obtained in one of two ways: (1) The candidate can apply to the state agency, which will assess the candidate's transcripts and experiences against state requirements; or, (2) more typically, the applicant can be recommended for certification after graduation from a state-approved teacher preparation program. The certificate typically specifies at what grade and content area the holder may teach. The certificate may be good for life or, more commonly, must be renewed every 3 to 5 years. A certificate does not guarantee employment; it merely makes the holder eligible for employment.

Specific certification requirements vary from state to state, but they usually include a college degree (all states require a bachelor's degree as a minimum), a minimum number of credit hours in designated curricular areas (35 states specify course requirements in the field of education), recommendation of a college or employer, a student teaching experience, "good moral character," attainment of a minimum age, U.S. citizenship, the signing of a loyalty oath affirming support of the government, and the passing of a state-prescribed exam to assess basic skills and subject-matter mastery.

Several states have moved to a "staged" certification system. The initial certificate, often called a probationary or provisional certificate, is issued to beginning teachers who satisfy the requirements for initial certification, and it is good for a limited number of years. The standard or "professional" certificate is issued to teachers upon successful performance on an assessment performed by a school district team or by the state, using videotaped lessons, portfolios, or classroom observations. In a three-tier system, an advanced or "master" certificate is issued to teachers based on experience and demonstrated higher levels of professional performance. One way this can be obtained in most states that have the advanced certificate is to receive certification by the National Board for Professional Teaching Standards, as described later.

### *Assessment for Initial Certification and Licensure*

Public concern about the quality of the teaching force in recent years, combined with the influence of the No Child Left Behind Act, has led to an increase in state testing of prospective teachers. Not only are prospective teachers required to pass a test for admission into the teacher education program, but they also are required to pass a test for certification or licensure in 43 states. Testing for certification is seen as an accountability measure to ensure that prospective teachers have met the INTASC or other standards adopted by the state and are qualified to enter the classroom. The No Child Left Behind Act requires that all newly hired teachers in schools that receive federal funds be "highly qualified." For new elementary teachers, this means that they must pass a "rigorous" state test that covers the elementary curriculum and teaching skills. New middle and high school teachers must pass a "rigorous" state test in the academic subject matter they teach or complete an academic major in every subject they will teach.

The most commonly used tests for certification are the **Praxis Series: Professional Assessments for Beginning Teachers** developed by the Educational Testing Service. The first test in the Praxis series, Praxis I, measures reading, writing, and mathematics skills and is often taken while in college. The Praxis II exam, which is taken after completion of the teacher education program, is in two parts. The first part of the Praxis II exam measures core content knowledge in more than 70 subject areas. The second part measures knowledge of teaching and learning in four areas: Students as Learners, Instruction and Assessment, Communication Techniques, and Profession and Community. A few states also require prospective teachers to submit a portfolio demonstrating their teaching effectiveness that is evaluated by experienced teachers.

## Emergency Certification

Forty-nine states have some provision for granting **emergency (temporary) certificates** to persons who do not meet the requirements for standard certification when districts cannot employ fully qualified teachers. Emergency certificates are issued with the presumption that the recipient teacher will obtain the credentials or will be replaced by a regularly certified teacher. In most states, before the emergency certificate is granted, the district must show that an effort has been made to hire a regularly certified teacher. Although the requirements of No Child Left Behind and the growth of alternative certification programs have reduced the rate at which emergency certificates are issued, nationwide thousands of individuals enter teaching each year on emergency or temporary certificates. In many instances these teachers are concentrated in poor urban schools or rural areas.

Emergency certification does not require any professional education training prior to the assumption of teaching duties and often does not require the passage of a subject-matter test, although some states do require the passage of a basic skills test. Many professional educators question the ethics and safety of hiring untrained persons to teach: No other state-licensed profession issues "emergency" certificates to untrained persons. However, given the shortage of teachers discussed later in this chapter, it seems unlikely that the practice will be abandoned in the foreseeable future.

## Recertification

Acquiring certification once does not mean that a teacher is certified for life. Teachers are required to periodically renew their certificates to ensure they are knowledgeable about new developments in their fields. In the past, teachers could be recertified by earning a specified number of continuing education units (CEUs), which could be earned by taking approved college courses or by attending workshops, in-service training, or other acceptable activities. Increasingly, however, some states are taking measures to ensure that recertification requirements include more directed, research-proven career growth activities. For example, some states will not accept a master's degree for recertification unless it directly relates to the teacher's content knowledge or teaching skill (Education Commission of the States, 2005). About half the states accept NBPTS certification as the basis for granting recertification. Twelve states require an assessment (Praxis II, Praxis III, NES, or state-developed) for recertification (Baber, 2008).

## Reciprocity and Interstate Certification

Because each state has somewhat different certification requirements, a matter of concern related to state certification for any profession is whether the certification granted by one state will be recognized by another. The increasing mobility of teachers has encouraged state certification authorities to establish **interstate reciprocity**, which allows teachers who are certified in one state to be eligible for certification in another. It is to the advantage of each state to facilitate the employment of qualified educators and to increase the availability of educational personnel, not to establish barriers to employment. To this end, 44 states and the District of Columbia have signed the NASDTEC Interstate Agreement under the auspices of the National Association of State Directors of Teacher Education and Certifications (NASDTEC) to make it possible for an individual who has completed an approved program and holds a certificate or license issued by one state to receive an equivalent certification in another state (Iowa, Minnesota, Nebraska, New York, South Dakota, and Wisconsin are not signers). The agreement does not constitute full reciprocity in that the moving teacher may have to complete additional requirements (e.g., ESL endorsement or a course in the new state's constitution or history).

Regional interstate reciprocity agreements are also in place in a couple of areas. Eight states in the northeast (Connecticut, Maine, Massachusetts, New Hampshire, New York, Pennsylvania, Rhode Island, and Vermont) have agreed to recognize the Northeast Regional Credential, and in the Midwest nine states (Illinois, Iowa, Kansas, Michigan, Missouri, Nebraska, Oklahoma, South Dakota, and Wisconsin) have formed a regional exchange agreement under which each state's minimum certification standards are protected but the teacher applicant is given an initial 2-year license by the receiving state (National Center for Alternative Certification, 2011).

## National Certification: The NBPTS

The professionalization of teaching, as well as the prospect for some form of national certification, has been greatly enhanced by the efforts of the NBPTS, not only to develop professional standards for teaching, but also to develop certification in 25 fields. The certification fields are structured around 16 subject areas and seven levels of schooling (visit the NBPTS website at www.nbpts.org for certification fields).

Teachers with 3 years of teaching experience who hold a state teaching license can start the certification process upon payment of a fee. The process involves preparing a professional portfolio containing videotapes of classroom practice, samples of student work, and a written commentary, and going to one of the board's assessment centers for written assessment exercises focused on the candidate's content knowledge. Successful candidates are deemed **board certified**, a term used commonly in other professions. Such certification is a public acknowledgment that the teacher possesses not only the requisite knowledge but also the demonstrated ability to teach in the areas or levels of certification specified. NBPTS certification is issued for a period of 10 years and may be renewed upon satisfying a renewal requirement. As discussed in Chapter 2, a major incentive for teachers to undertake this process is that 38 states and hundreds of school districts offer financial incentives to teachers who receive board certification, and almost all states offer licensure incentives. As important as financial incentives, teachers who have been through the board certification process almost unanimously report that the experience has made them better teachers. Since its inception in 1997, more than 91,000 teachers have received national board certification (NBPTS, 2011). Overall, national board certification seems a goal beginning teachers should consider as they think about their careers.

## Teacher Supply and Demand

School districts nationwide are facing an unprecedented demand for teachers at all levels. The demand for teachers (public and private) is expected to continue, creating a demand for over 425,000 new teachers annually by 2016 and increase to

**For Your Reflection and Analysis**

How likely are you to seek national board certification when you become eligible?

440,000 by 2019 (Hussar & Bailey, 2011). The projected demand for additional teachers is a result of projected record increases in enrollment (see Figure 7.2 on page 185), as well as the record number of vacancies created by the retirement of an aging teacher population. Approximately one-third of the teaching force is 50 years of age or older and many teachers are beginning to retire: According to some estimates as many as 1.5 million teachers will retire between 2010 and 2018 (National Commission on Teaching and America's Future, 2010). The problem created by retirements is compounded by the

The increased demand for teachers in some areas has led many school districts to extensive and intensive recruiting.

growing turnover of teachers, both new and experienced, who leave the profession each year. Turnover is highest among beginning teachers and teachers serving in high-poverty, high-minority, urban, and rural schools (Ingersoll & Merrill, 2010).

The continued lowering of pupil–teacher ratios has also contributed to an increased demand for teachers. Pupil–teacher ratios in the public schools have declined from 16.0 to 1 in 2000 to 15.5 in 2007 and are projected to decline to 14.6 by the year 2019 (Hussar & Bailey, 2011). Also contributing to the demand for teachers is the growth in special education and elementary enrichment classes (Ingersoll & Merrill, 2010).

Although the demand for teachers is expected to increase, the projected supply of new teachers is not expected to be sufficient to meet the demand. The supply of newly hired teachers is a function of (1) the number of new college graduates entering teaching, (2) delayed entrants (first-year teachers who engage in other activities between graduation from college and entering teaching), (3) transfers from one state or district to another, and (4) the number of former teachers reentering teaching. In recent years, first-time teachers have come to represent a smaller percentage of newly hired public school teachers (new graduates, 18%; delayed entrants, 12%). Returning teachers make up 24% of the newly hired teachers, whereas transfers comprise about 53% of the new hires (Provasnik & Dorfman, 2005). One of the major unknowns in projecting teacher supply is the number of individuals trained as teachers who will actually enter the profession. In recent years only slightly better than half of newly prepared teachers actually entered teaching. How many of these individuals, or other prepared or interested individuals, would enter teaching if salaries and working conditions were improved and the status of the profession were enhanced is an important policy issue. However, projections by the U.S. Department of Labor, Bureau of Labor Statistics (2010) suggest that the supply of teachers will increase in response to reports of improved job prospects, better pay, greater teacher involvement in school policy and governance, and increased public interest in education. High unemployment in other professions and the proliferation of alternative certification programs should also increase the supply of teachers.

Although a shortage of teachers is expected nationwide, supply and demand will vary among states, school districts, and disciplines. In the South and West, states with the fastest growing populations will have a greater demand for teachers, while states in the Midwest and Northeast, with large numbers of teacher colleges, will have surpluses. Urban and rural districts in particular are expected to experience teacher shortages. The greatest shortages will continue to be in most areas of special education, some foreign languages (Japanese, Spanish), bilingual education, English as a second language, reading, all the sciences, computer science, and mathematics, while surpluses will exist in kindergarten, dance, social studies, health and physical education (American Association for Employment in Education, 2009). And, as always, there is a high demand for male teachers at the elementary level.

## Salary and Other Compensation

The compensation of teachers has become a major issue in efforts to strengthen the teaching profession and improve student learning. Historically, teachers' salaries have lagged behind those of other professionals with comparable training and responsibility, as well as those of many of the technical and semiskilled occupations. Although in the last decade teacher salaries increased at a higher rate than inflation, recent studies have shown that while teachers earn more than the typical worker, on the average they earn 58 cents to every dollar earned by workers in occupations with similar skill demands (Swanson, 2008). Figure 1.1 depicts the trend in average annual salaries of elementary and secondary teachers since 1991 in 1991 dollars and 2011 dollars. Although the current dollar increases appear substantial over this 20-year period, from $33,084 in 1990–1991 to $56,064 in 2010–2011, when adjusted for inflation salaries grew by only $1,334 (4.0%). And, as can be seen, during the last several years, salaries have remained almost flat or actually decreased slightly in constant dollars. This may be due to the fact that large numbers of teachers are retiring and being replaced with newer, lower paid teachers, bringing the average salary down. In 2010 salaries ranged from more than $65,000 in California, Massachusetts, New Jersey, and New York to under $45,000 in North Dakota and South Dakota (National Education Association, 2010). Salaries were highest in states in New England, the Midwest, and the Far West, and lowest in the Southeast and the Southwest.

The specific salary teachers receive depends on a number of factors, including supply and demand, union activity, the prevailing wage rate in neighboring districts, and the wealth of the district as determined by the tax base. School districts with a higher assessed value of property per pupil will typically pay higher salaries than those with lesser assessed value of property per pupil. However, many poor districts, in terms of assessed valuation, have chosen to levy higher tax rates in order to pay teachers competitive salaries. In addition, as described later, teacher shortages have led some districts to offer financial incentives to teachers who work in targeted schools or teach in target teaching assignments.

### Figure 1.1 — Average Classroom Teacher Salary, 1991–2011

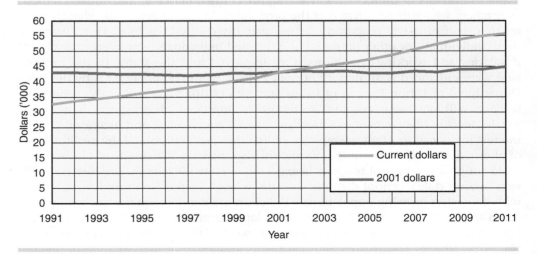

*Source:* National Education Association (2010). *Rankings and estimates: Rankings of the states 2010 and estimates of school statistics 2011.* Washington, DC: Author.

**Table 1.4 — Glenbard Township High School District 87: 2011–2012 Teacher Salary Schedule**

| Years | BA | BA+15 | MA | MA+15 | MA+30 | MA+45 |
|-------|------|-------|------|-------|-------|-------|
| 1 | $49,694 | $51,185 | $54,664 | $55,161 | $57,149 | $58,639 |
| 2 | $51,682 | $53,173 | $56,652 | $58,142 | $60,130 | $61,621 |
| 3 | $53,670 | $55,161 | $60,130 | $61,124 | $63,112 | $64,603 |
| 4 | $56,155 | $57,646 | $63,112 | $64,603 | $66,094 | $67,584 |
| 5 | $58,639 | $60,130 | $66,094 | $67,584 | $69,572 | $70,566 |
| 6 | $61,124 | $62,615 | $69,075 | $70,566 | $72,554 | $74,045 |
| 7 | | $65,100 | $72,057 | $73,548 | $75,535 | $77,026 |
| 8 | | | $75,039 | $76,529 | $78,517 | $80,008 |
| 9 | | | $78,020 | $79,511 | $81,499 | $82,990 |
| 10 | | | $81,002 | $82,493 | $84,480 | $85,971 |
| 11 | | | $83,984 | $85,474 | $87,462 | $88,953 |
| 12 | | | $86,965 | $88,456 | $90,444 | $91,935 |
| 13 | | | $89,947 | $91,438 | $93,425 | $94,916 |
| 14 | | | $92,929 | $94,419 | $96,407 | $98,395 |
| 15 | | | $96,407 | $97,898 | $99,886 | $101,874 |
| 16 | | | $98,892 | $100,383 | $102,370 | $105,352 |
| 17 | | | $98,892 | $100,383 | $104,855 | $108,831 |
| 18 | | | $98,892 | $100,383 | $104,855 | $112,309 |
| 19 | | | $98,892 | $100,383 | $104,855 | $115,788 |
| 20 | | | $101,377 | $107,837 | $112,309 | $119,267 |

*Source:* Glenbard Township High School District 87, Glen Ellyn, IL.

## Salary Schedules

More than 90% of teacher salary schedules across the nation are based on the **single salary schedule** format.[1] The single salary schedule pays equivalent salaries for equivalent preparation and experience. The trend toward the adoption of a single salary schedule for teachers began in the first quarter of the 20th century, and by midcentury it had come to dominate teacher compensation. The single salary schedule is popular with boards of education because it is easy to understand and to administer and has traditionally been defended by teacher unions as the fairest way to pay teachers (Committee for Economic Development, 2009).

There are two basic dimensions to the single salary schedule: a horizontal dimension made up of columns that correspond to levels of academic preparation (e.g., bachelor's degree, master's degree, master's degree plus 30 hours, doctorate degree), and a vertical dimension of rows of "steps" that correspond to the years of teaching experience. There is no standard number of columns or rows in a teacher's salary schedule, although there are usually more rows than columns so that the schedule tends to form a vertical matrix (see Table 1.4).

---

[1]Discussion of salary schedules is based on Educational Research Service (1987). *Methods of scheduling salaries for teachers.* Arlington, VA: Author.

## Initial Placement

The initial vertical placement of a new teacher on a specific vertical step on a scale is determined by several factors, the most common of which is teaching experience. To receive credit for any previous years of teaching, usually the teacher must have taught for 75% of the school year. Most school districts place a limit on the number of years of teaching experience credited toward initial placement on the salary schedule. Factors that affect this decision are whether the experience is in or out of the district and in or out of the state. Other factors considered in making the initial placement on the schedule are credit for related experience, credit for military service, and credit for other experience. Some districts recognize related experience such as public library experience for librarians or recreational experience for physical educators. Others grant full or partial credit for military service or for experience in the Peace Corps, Volunteers in Service to America (VISTA), or the National Teachers Corps.

## Advancement

Horizontal advancement across columns in a salary schedule is dependent on earned academic credit beyond the bachelor's degree. Vertical advancement from one step to the next within the scale is normally automatic after a stipulated period of time (usually 1 year), although longer periods may be required for advancement to the higher steps. Although teachers' groups have continued to advocate automatic advancement, in an increasing number of districts certain restrictions are being placed on vertical advancement. For example, advancement at specified points may be made contingent on (1) the attainment of additional units of academic credit or completion of in-service training programs, or (2) satisfactory performance or merit. To provide for teachers who have reached the maximum number of steps in a particular scale, some salary schedules also provide for supermaximum or long-term service increments beyond the highest step in the scale.

The single salary schedule has come under increasing criticism in recent years for its failure to recognize teacher performance, an important variable in student achievement, and because it does not provide the flexibility needed to attract teachers in hard-to-staff subjects or schools. Some individual districts have attempted to address these shortcomings by adapting the single salary schedule to include performance-based pay or labor market-based pay plans discussed in the following sections.

### *Performance-Based Pay Plans*

The growing recognition of the importance of teacher effectiveness to student performance has led to increased efforts to link teacher pay to improvements in student performance. Performance-based pay is seen as a way to both attract and retain good teachers and motivate them to greater performance and as the next logical step in the accountability movement (Yecke, quoted in Honowar & Olson, 2008). Performance-based pay initiatives have been encouraged by the federal Teacher Incentive Fund that was enacted in 2006 to support the development and implementation of performance-based pay for teachers serving in high priority schools. Under the terms of the grants, teacher pay is to be measured primarily on student achievement. Currently, about 10% of the school districts in the United States have adopted some measure of student achievement in their teacher compensation plan.

Performance-based pay plans are of two types: those that reward the individual teacher and those that reward the group performance of the school staff as a whole. Most such plans use the single salary schedule to establish the teacher's base pay and then provide performance awards to teachers who attain established levels of performance. Group-based performance awards recognize that in most organizations achievement of organizational goals is as much a result of group performance as individual performance. They are seen as a way to encourage collaboration among teachers and to promote school and school district goals. Group-based performance reward programs provide financial rewards to individual schools that meet certain prescribed standards or outcomes in such areas as student achievement, dropout rates, graduation rates, or absenteeism.

A major concern and impediment to the adoption of performance-based pay plans has been the methodological issues in measuring student learning. Using single-year measures of student achievement rather than the growth in achievement can reward teachers who teach students from higher socioeconomic backgrounds or who teach more able students, and it ignores all the many out of school variables that impact on student achievement. One proposal to address this concern is to base performance pay on the value-added method of evaluating teachers discussed in the next chapter that measures teacher performance on the gain in student test scores from one year to the next. Although a growing number of states and school districts have adopted or are considering value-added evaluation and pay, it is the subject of considerable controversy among policymakers and educators. The major arguments for and against value-added performance-based pay are presented in the Controversial Issue feature.

### Labor-Market Based Pay

As previously noted, the supply and demand for teachers varies by academic discipline and geographic area. Even within a district, preferences about where to teach create shortages in some schools. In response to these shortages, a number of states and school districts offer various incentives to attract teachers to targeted schools or target assignment areas. Twenty-five states offer incentives

**For Your Reflection and Analysis**

Should performance based rewards based on student achievement go to individual teachers or to the school as a whole?

Many teachers receive additional compensation for supplemental activities.

# CONTROVERSIAL ISSUE

## Value-Added Pay

The Obama administration has encouraged states to adopt laws that use student test data as a significant factor in the evaluation and rewarding of teachers. The proposal has gained favor with governors and lawmakers in several states, while teachers as a whole do not support basing evaluation or pay on the gain, or value added, in student test scores. The reasons often given in favor of or against value-added pay are as follows:

**For**

1. The use of gain scores allows for a more sophisticated and objective comparison of teachers and schools.
2. Basing teacher performance on growth does not penalize teachers who teach low-performing students—i.e., it accounts for differences in the starting point of students.
3. The public would be more willing to support education if they knew that teachers were accountable for student performance and paid according to performance.
4. Value-added pay would help motivate, retain, and reward good teachers.
5. Rewarding performance is consistent with the standard applied to other workers and professions.

**Against**

1. Except for self-contained classrooms, the contribution of one teacher to a student's performance is difficult to determine with any accuracy.
2. Even with the most sophisticated methodologies, it is virtually impossible to accurately control for classroom, school, and student variables beyond the control of the teacher.
3. There is little agreement about what is good teaching or how it can be evaluated using student test data.
4. Value-added pay systems encourage "teaching to the test."
5. The system is only as good as the tests teachers use; standardized tests are not available for all disciplines, and many have been plagued with issues of accuracy and validity.

Why do you oppose or favor value-added pay? Are you familiar with a school system where such pay is in operation? What effect has it had on education in that system?

to teach in targeted schools and 17 offer incentives to those who teach in target teaching assignment areas (Hightower, 2010). These take the form of student loan assistance, tax breaks, relocation assistance, or housing assistance. In addition, an increasingly popular incentive is signing or hiring bonuses.

## Compensation for Supplemental Activities

In addition to a base salary, approximately one third of the public school teaching force receives compensation during the school year for supplemental activities such as coaching, student activity sponsorship, or teaching an extra class or evening class. The amount of the supplemental pay normally depends on some consideration of the activity involved: The more student contact hours involved, students involved, and equipment and budget involved, the larger the supplement. For example, the supplement for a senior high football coach or band director may be 8% to 10% of a fixed point on the teachers' salary schedule, whereas that of the chorus director or cheerleading coach may be 4% to 5%.

## Salaries for Administrative and Support Personnel

Many teachers begin their educational careers in the classroom and then move into administrative or supervisory positions or into positions such as counselor or librarian. Most of these positions are 10- to 12-month positions and command significantly higher salaries, even on a monthly basis, than those of classroom teachers (see Table 1.5). The highest paid administrator typically is the superintendent. Superintendents in small districts earn an average of $85,000 to $100,000. Superintendents in districts with over 25,000 enrollment often earn a salary of over $175,000 per year. Principals, the administrators closest to the teacher, on the average earn 175% of the average salary of classroom teachers. However, it must be noted that most administrative and supervisory positions do require higher levels of educational preparation and experience than that required of classroom teachers.

**Table 1.5 — Mean Salaries Paid Personnel in Selected Administrative Positions, 2010–2011**

| Position | Salary |
| --- | --- |
| Superintendent | $150,000 |
| Deputy/Associate Superintendent | $128,000 |
| Assistant Superintendent | $115,000 |
| Supervisor/Director for: | |
|     Curriculum/Instruction | $95,000 |
|     Human Resources | $93,000 |
|     Finance/Business | $93,000 |
|     Technology | $85,000 |
|     Special Education | $82,000 |
|     Subject Areas | $78,000 |
| Principals: | |
|     Senior High School | $94,000 |
|     Jr. High/Middle School | $87,000 |
|     Elementary School | $81,000 |
| Assistant Principals: | |
|     Senior High School | $79,000 |
|     Jr. High/Middle school | $75,000 |
|     Elementary School | $68,000 |

**For Your Reflection and Analysis**

Do you have any interest in becoming involved in any extracurricular activities? Which ones?

## *Indirect Compensation: Employee Benefits and Services*

**Indirect compensation**, commonly referred to as fringe benefits, is an important part of any teacher's compensation package. In fact, the employee benefits provided teachers are better on the average than those provided other professionals (Allegretto, Corcoran, & Mishel, 2008) and cost school districts an average of 30% of wages. Certain benefits, such as Social Security, unemployment compensation, and workers' compensation, are required by law. Other benefits, including life insurance, health and hospitalization insurance, and long-term disability insurance, are not required by law but are voluntarily provided by the school district.

A third category of benefits includes retirement and savings plans. In most states, retirement benefits are financed jointly by teacher and public contributions. In several states, in an attempt to increase compensation without increasing state aid to education, school districts pay the employees' share of retirement as well as the employers' share. This benefit has great appeal to employees because it has a significant impact on net income without increasing gross taxable income. Consequently, in an increasing number of school districts this provision has become a popular item for negotiation. Also becoming increasingly popular are tax-sheltered annuities, which allow employees to invest part of their salaries, before the computation of taxes, in an annuity. This allows employees not only to reduce current taxes but also to supplement any state retirement plans.

One very popular category of benefits is pay for time not worked. For public school personnel this includes sick leave, personal and family leave, sabbatical leave, professional leave, religious leave, jury duty leave, military leave, and severance pay.

**Employee services** enable employees to enjoy a better lifestyle or to meet certain personal obligations at a free or reduced cost. Such services include credit unions, employee assistance programs directed at improving employee mental and emotional health, wellness programs, child care, or subsidized food services.

## Summary

There are as many definitions of *teacher* as there are reasons for becoming a teacher. It is important that those considering the profession evaluate their perceptions and expectations of teaching and their motives for considering teaching as their chosen profession.

After a period of serious criticism of the teaching profession and teacher preparation, the status of the profession appears to be improving. And a greater percentage of the teacher workforce reports being satisfied with teaching as a career. There is still a shortage of minority teachers, but more and more bright and talented individuals are entering the teaching profession, either through traditional baccalaureate programs or through the growing number of alternative certification programs. As the demand for teachers intensifies, various proposals for differential compensation, including performance-based pay and competency-based pay, are being adopted in an effort to attract qualified individuals. The next chapter discusses other efforts to make teaching more attractive by increasing professionalization and reviews other professional opportunities available to teachers.

# PROFESSIONAL DEVELOPMENT
## *Workshop*

## *Prepare for the State Licensure Examination*

Tom Metcalf, a general science teacher, and Bill Rosak, a chemistry teacher, were in discussion during their prep period in the teacher's lounge at Carlton High School. Tom had just returned from Dallas, where the annual professional meeting of Secondary Teachers of Science took place. The meeting is always held on the Friday following Thanksgiving. This year he took his wife, Sally, and they spent Thanksgiving with her parents, who live in Dallas. Tom was very excited about a new curriculum series he had learned about that provided hands-on projects his students could even do at home without any formal scientific equipment. Tom was also impressed by the fact that the curriculum included a number of projects that could be adapted for students with disabilities, because he has been having difficulty designing lessons that are appropriate for students with learning and physical disabilities in his general science class. Tom asked Bill if he would be willing to join him in requesting that the district purchase the series for use the next year.

Toward the latter part of Tom's remarks, Bill began to shake his head. "You must be crazy, Tom," he said. "There is no way I would let any kid with a physical disability come near any chemicals. Nor do I want to be responsible for some learning-disabled kids hurting themselves trying to do some take-home science experiment!" Bill went on.

Not discouraged, the very next day Tom made a request to the district textbook adoption committee that this new textbook series be approved for purchase. While waiting for the committee's response, Tom seeks the advice of his assigned mentor.

1. Under what conditions can teachers be held responsible for the injury of a student? What can teachers do to reduce their liability?

2. What approaches might Tom's mentor recommend he use to accommodate various learning styles, intelligences, or exceptionalities in his general science class? Base your response on principles of varied instruction for different kinds of learners.

3. Suggest formal and informal assessments that Tom might use to allow all students to demonstrate their accomplishments on the take-home science projects.

### Build Your Knowledge Base

1. What is your perception of what a teacher is and does? How is your perception reflected in your responses to the questions at the end of the opening vignette?

2. Was there any single event or experience that motivated you to choose teaching as a career?

3. What are the advantages and disadvantages of teaching as a career? Which are the most important to your decision to consider teaching as a career?

4. What strategies should be used to attract more top-quality students to teaching?

5. Should people be required to complete a teacher training program to become a teacher? Should there be any minimum requirements?

6. The public has increasingly expressed support for the competency testing of teachers. In your opinion, should prospective teachers be required to pass a competency test?

7. The public has also shown increasing support for competency-based pay for teachers. What are the pros and cons of competency-based pay? To what extent are financial incentives likely to improve job performance?

## Develop Your Portfolio

*The Professional Portfolio*

The professional portfolio can be used as a self-evaluation strategy, as an assessment tool to evaluate candidates for teaching positions, and to document competence for licensing/certifying agencies. The National Board for Professional Teaching Standards (NBPTS) has used the portfolio as a basis for national certification of master teachers, and a number of states require teacher portfolios prior to receiving a permanent teaching certificate.

The portfolio is an organized, goal-driven collection of evidence or artifacts. The purpose of the portfolio is to demonstrate the teacher's knowledge, skills, and abilities. The audience can be either the teacher or external reviewers. The artifacts include a wide variety of materials: lesson plans, units of study, written reports, self-reflections, essays, videotapes, photographs, and other professional documents. Reflections include written thoughts about the evidence contained in the portfolio. The portfolio serves as both a record of accomplishments and a tool for evaluating professional growth over time. You should continue to revisit/revise your portfolio throughout your education and career.

## Organizing Your Professional Portfolio

One of the first steps in developing a portfolio is to consider how you will organize the types of evidence or artifacts that you choose to include. The artifacts can be displayed in either print or electronic format. Most teachers include both formats in their portfolios.

Allow yourself ample time to develop and organize your professional portfolio into a series of appropriately labeled files. Organizing and setting up your portfolio filing system may be one of the more time-consuming portfolio tasks. However, once the system is in place you will not have to repeat this exercise again unless you decide to improve on its filing system. First you will need to prepare a series of 10 files, each labeled with one of the 10 INTASC standards presented in Table 1.3. As you read each chapter of the text, you will be directed to develop a portfolio activity that will address one or more of the INTASC standards.

Three-ring binders, labeled file folders, or forms of electronic storage (e.g., CDs or DVDs) are typically used for organizing the materials that will comprise your portfolio. Should you plan to share your portfolio with an audience other than your immediate supervisor or state licensing agency, you will need to consider the legal issues involved with sharing such information. Release forms signed by parents/guardians are necessary if you plan to share any samples of students' work or photographs or videotapes of students. An important rule of thumb is to make sure that you have blocked out any student's name. It is especially important to protect the identity of any student with special needs.

To view examples of portfolios that have been developed by other preservice teachers, as well as by beginning teachers and teachers who have received national board certification, visit www2.ncsu.edu/unity/lockers/project/portfolios/portfoliointro.html.

1. There are multiple reasons why individuals select teaching for a career. Reflect on Herbert Kohl's questions for prospective teachers presented in the Ask Yourself feature on page 6. Using these reflections as a guide, write an essay about your own reasons for choosing to pursue or continue a career in teaching. Revisit Kohl's questions and your essay throughout your training and career to determine how your early ideas have shaped your thoughts or experiences. Place your essay in the portfolio folder labeled **INTASC Standard 9, Professional Learning and Ethical Practice.**

2. Because there are a number of ways to become a teacher, it is important to maintain a detailed record of your educational program, including general studies courses, content studies in a major or minor, professional studies, and field experiences such as clinical practice, internship, or student teaching. One of the most important items to include in your portfolio is a *dynamic resumé* that will evolve throughout your education and career. As your education progresses, list important details or summaries of your education, experiences, and skills, and pursue letters of reference and recommendations. As an in-service teacher, continue to update all sections of your resumé file and include certifications, employment experience, and continuing education.

### Explore Teaching and Learning: Field Experiences

1. Arrange to shadow a teacher for a day. Keep a detailed log of the activities and tasks in the teacher's day.
   a. How much time is spent in instruction?
   b. How much time is spent in interaction with individual students or small groups of students?
   c. How much time is spent in interaction with colleagues? What were the topics?
   d. How much time is spent in interaction with the principal? What were the topics?
   e. How much time is spent on administrative duties (taking attendance, lunch count, recording grades, completing reports for the principal, etc.)?
   f. How much time is spent on student discipline?

2. Arrange an interview with an experienced teacher and a beginning teacher using questions such as the following:
   a. What are some of the most satisfying aspects of teaching?
   b. What parts of your job are most frustrating?
   c. What steps can you take to improve your working conditions?
   d. *For the experienced teacher:* What have you done to help beginning teachers?
   e. *For the beginning teacher:* What did experienced teachers do to help you in your early days of teaching?

---

## MyEducationLab

Go to Topic 1, **The Teaching Profession** in the MyEducationLab (www.myeducationlab.com) for *Foundations of American Education*, where you can:

- Find learning outcomes for the teaching profession along with the national standards that connect to these outcomes.
- Complete Assignments and Activities that can help you more deeply understand the chapter content.
- Apply and practice your understanding of the core teaching skills identified in the chapter with the Building Teaching Skills and Dispositions learning units.
- Examine challenging situations and cases presented in the IRIS Center Resources.

- Access additional video clips of CCSSO National Teachers of the Year award winners responding to the question, "Why Do I Teach?" in the Teacher Talk section.
- Check your comprehension on the content covered in the chapter with the Study Plan. Here you will be able to take a chapter quiz, receive feedback on your answers, and then access Review, Practice, and Enrichment activities to enhance your understanding of chapter content.
- Use the Online Lesson Plan Builder to practice lesson planning and integrating national and state standards into your planning.

# CHAPTER
## *Two*

# Development of the Profession

Mike, a new first-year middle school teacher and drama coach, has been contacted about joining the local teachers' organization and its state and national affiliates. He has also been contacted about joining the informal county drama coaches' association and the state association. Mike has limited funds and does not feel that he can afford membership in all three groups. Mike is also concerned about the difference between being a "joiner" or being an active contributing member in the organizations.

What principles and values should guide Mike's decision about membership? What are the relative benefits of joining the local teachers' organization or the organization for one's subject area or grade level? What responsibilities do you assume when you join a professional organization?

*T*eaching is considered by many to be "work of the most demanding sort, for teachers must make dozens of decisions daily, command a wide body of knowledge and skill, learn to react instantly, and be disposed to act wisely in difficult situations" (National Board for Professional Teaching Standards [NBPTS], 2005, p. 3). Teaching is a complex craft, calling for ongoing personal and professional reflection and commitment. This chapter focuses on teaching as a profession. The major sections of this chapter address (1) the requirements of a profession, (2) the factors working to improve the professionalization of teaching, (3) professional development for teachers, (4) evaluation of teacher performance, and (5) professional organizations for teachers. As you read and discuss this chapter and the related activities, consider the following outcome objectives and their impact on you as a potential teacher:

- Evaluate the duties of elementary and secondary school teachers in terms of the recognized criteria for a profession.
- Identify developments in the professionalization of teaching in your state.
- Develop a personal plan for professional development.
- Identify the factors that should be considered in teacher evaluations.
- Distinguish between a career ladder salary schedule for teachers and a traditional salary schedule based on education level and experience.

- Identify the programs and services provided by the major teacher organizations in your state and your school district.
- Describe the programs and services provided by the professional organization for your teaching field.

**MyEducationLab**

Visit the MyEducationLab for *Foundations of American Education* to enhance your understanding of chapter concepts with a personalized Study Plan. You'll also have the opportunity to hone your teaching skills through video and case based Assignments and Activities, and Building Teaching Skills and Disposition lessons.

## Teaching as a Profession

Is teaching a profession? Many references are made to the profession of teaching, but the actual status of teaching as a profession continues to be a matter of discussion and debate. Few would contend that teaching has attained the status of medicine or law, but some argue that teaching as an occupation compares favorably with the ministry, accounting, engineering, and similar professions. While educators and others debate whether teaching is a profession or a semi-profession, sociologists have developed what is known as the *professional model*—"a series of organizational and occupational characteristics associated with professions and professionals and, hence useful to distinguish professions and professionals from other kinds of work and workers" (Ingersoll, 2008, p. 107). These characteristics or requirements for a job to be considered a profession are discussed in the following sections.

## Requirements of a Profession

Among the most commonly considered criteria for classifying an occupation as a **profession** are those presented in Figure 2.1. The criteria discussed in this chapter include specialized knowledge and preparation, provision of essential services to society, exercise of discretion, autonomy and freedom from direct supervision, a code of professional standards, and a professional code of ethics.

### *Specialized Knowledge and Preparation*

Professions are sometimes referred to as "knowledge-based" occupations (Ingersoll, 2008). Teaching is clearly that. Teaching requires professionals who possess specialized knowledge acquired during a period of specialized study. This specialized knowledge as embodied in a typical teacher preparation program was described in Chapter 1. This specialized knowledge is also embodied in the Interstate New

### Figure 2.1 — Criteria for Classifying an Occupation as a Profession

According to the National Labor Relations Act, the occupation must:

- Be an intellectual endeavor
- Involve discretion and judgment
- Have an output that cannot be standardized
- Require advanced knowledge
- Require a prolonged period of specialized study

In addition, the American Association of Colleges of Teacher Education calls for:

- Provision of essential services to society
- Decision making in providing services
- Organization into one or more professional societies for the purpose of socialization and promotion of the profession
- Autonomy in the actual day-to-day work
- Agreed-upon performance standards
- Relative freedom from direct supervision

Teacher Assessment and Support Consortium (INTASC) principles of professional and pedagogical knowledge needed by teachers presented in Table 1.3. While there is variation among programs and members of the academic community do not all agree on the exact course of study that best produces a teacher, there is general agreement that this specialized knowledge should include:

> a broad grounding in the liberal arts and sciences; knowledge of the subjects to be taught, of the skills to be developed, and of the curricular arrangements and materials that organize and embody that content; knowledge of general and subject-specific methods for teaching and for evaluating student learning; knowledge of students and human development; skills in effectively teaching students from racially, ethnically, and socio-economically diverse backgrounds; and the skills, capacities and dispositions to employ such knowledge wisely in the interest of students. (American Federation of Teachers, 2000)

**Reflect on Diversity**
What knowledge and skills do you need to develop to be successful teaching students from racially, ethnically, and socioeconomically diverse backgrounds? How will these skills be developed?

When and how this knowledge and skills should be acquired and developed varies among the states and among teacher preparation programs. Some programs require completion of general education and academic major requirements, or even completion of the baccalaureate degree before taking professional education courses. However, most preparation programs for elementary and secondary teachers more closely resemble those described in Chapter 1. As discussed there, the content of the programs has been heavily influenced by the professional standards developed by the INTASC, the standards for colleges of education developed by the National Council for the Accreditation of Teacher Education (NCATE), and the content of the Praxis tests used in most states as a requirement for teacher certification. While most states do not dictate specific course requirements for teacher preparation programs, as described in Chapter 1 states do establish the requirements for certification that *de facto* influence program content, and 33 states rate teacher preparation institutions based on the percentage of graduates who pass the state licensing exam. A smaller number (17) hold teacher preparation programs accountable for their graduates' performance in the classroom (Hightower, 2010).

Whatever specialized knowledge and skills may be acquired as part of their formal preparation, teachers, like other professionals, recognize that this knowledge and these skills must be updated and extended on an ongoing basis. This in large part takes place through the professional development activities discussed in a following section.

## Provision of Essential Services to Society

Most Americans would acknowledge that teachers provide an essential service to society. The importance of education in a democratic society has always been recognized: "If a nation expects to be ignorant and free in a state of civilization, it expects what never was and never will be." This often-quoted statement by Thomas Jefferson reinforces the importance of education to the preservation of the nation. Teachers play a critical role in ensuring an educated populace.

This underlying belief about the role of the teacher was supported in a 2004–05 survey of new teachers, in which 85% believed that they could make a difference in the lives of their students (Markow & Martin, 2005). Other surveys of the attitudes of teachers with 1 and 2 years experience found that while this initial optimism had remained positive, it declined to about 70% (Markow & Martin, 2005).

**For Your Reflection and Analysis**

How has a teacher made a difference in your life?

## The Exercise of Discretion

Given the relative isolation of individual classrooms and the variety of decisions that a teacher must make during the typical school day, teachers routinely exercise discretion and judgment in providing services to their students. Teachers in schools with empowered site councils have even more workplace influence. However, teachers are not free agents. In most districts they cannot take vacation during the school year, work flexible schedules, work from home, or do a number of things that workers in nonschool settings often are allowed to do. Moreover, they function in an educational environment that is larger than an individual classroom, constrained by school district policies and regulations, district curriculum guides, and state and federal statutes and court decisions related to issues as far ranging as student rights to use of school property. Such district-wide concerns as scope and sequence of instruction must be considered. The individual teachers' instructional decisions need to be in harmony with those of their peers as well as the state and the district's curriculum standards and assessment policies. Responses to No Child Left Behind (NCLB) have further limited teachers' exercise of discretion in terms of deciding what should be taught and what should be assessed and how it should be assessed.

## Autonomy and Freedom from Direct Supervision

Teachers have a relatively high degree of autonomy in their actual day-to-day work, and the degree of direct supervision is rather limited. Still, teachers function in the social setting of a school with other teachers and administrators, and the culture of the school requires a degree of structure and interaction among both teachers and students. In addition, parents and taxpayers have an interest in ensuring that teachers act as responsible professionals. Some degree of supervision is necessary to provide the desired assurances.

## Code of Professional Standards

Many professions have adopted a code of professional standards that establish what is acceptable and unacceptable practice that is monitored and enforced by their members sitting as boards or commissions (e.g., a state bar association). To date, the teaching profession does not police its own members through an independent body, and this has been one of the major arguments made by those who do not consider teaching a profession. However, teachers are policed by public agencies, typically at the state level. Such bodies are referred to as professional practices boards or commissions. Their purpose is to take appropriate disciplinary action against teachers after a review or report of questionable professional conduct. While teachers' organizations have long advocated that these boards be controlled by members of the profession, as is true for similar boards in the legal and medical professions, typically their membership includes school administrators, college personnel, and members of the lay public, with teachers holding minority representation.

## Professional Codes of Ethics

Many professions also have **codes of ethics** that serve as standards for behavior of members of the profession. Codes of ethics do not have the status of law, but they indicate the aspirations of members of the profession and provide standards by which to judge members' conduct. In some instances, a professional organization monitors and enforces the code of ethics for its membership. In others, a public agency assumes the monitoring and enforcement role. Reporting of noncompliance can come from a variety of sources, including professional peers, clients, supervisors, and the public.

Each profession has its own code of ethics reflecting the activities and responsibilities of the profession. The public role of the teacher and the special relationship between the teacher and young people make the ethical considerations for teaching very different from those of other professions. As noted by the NBPTS (2011):

> Unique demands arise because a client's attendance is compulsory and, more importantly, because the clients are children. Thus, elementary, middle and high school teachers are obligated to meet a stringent ethical standard. Other ethical demands derive from the teacher's role as a model of an educated person. Teaching is a public activity; a teacher works daily in the gaze of his or her students, and the extended nature of their lives together in schools places special obligations on the teacher's behavior. Students learn early to draw and read lessons from their teacher's character. Teachers, consequently, must conduct themselves in a manner students might emulate. Their failure to practice what they preach does not long elude

students, parents, or peers. Practicing with this additional dimension in mind calls for a special alertness to the consequences of manner and behavior. Standards for professional teaching ought, therefore, to emphasize its ethical nature. (p. 1)

The National Education Association (NEA) has adopted a code of ethics for the education profession. The NEA Code of Ethics, presented in detail in Figure 2.2, contains two sections: commitment to students and commitment to the profession. The student section notes the expectations of fair, equitable, and nondiscriminatory treatment of students. The section on commitment to the profession contains standards of personal conduct in the performance of professional duties and relationships to others.

In the past, codes of conduct for teachers were adopted by local school boards. These codes often were related to personal as well as professional conduct, regulating such things as marital status, style of clothing, and places in the community that were off limits to teachers. In those days, failure to abide by the requirements was used as justification for dismissal or other punitive action against teachers. The requirements of yesteryear are quite different from the current concept of codes of ethics that focus much more on professional conduct than on out-of-school behavior.

Consider the requirements of a profession discussed in this section and the characteristics of a profession presented in the following Ask Yourself feature in answering the question: "Is teaching a profession?" Why or why not?

> **For Your Reflection and Analysis**
>
> Do you think that teachers should have a dress code if there is one for students?

# ASK YOURSELF

## Is Teaching a Profession?

Is teaching a profession, a semi-profession, or a vocation? This debate has been on-going for over half a century. Teaching should not be considered a profession, say some, because, unlike the traditional professions of law and medicine, teachers do not practice in a free market for services where the client can fire them any time for any reason. Rather they have a "captive clientele." Those who argue teaching should be considered a profession note the attributes of a profession that teaching is said to exhibit. Yet these too are in changing: for example, at the same time that teaching may have increased standards for certification teachers may be losing autonomy to increased governmental control. Consider the following indicators of a profession and ask yourself in regard to each indicator whether teaching qualifies as a profession.

1. Professionals possess specialized skills based on a theoretical body of knowledge.

    ___ True of teachers.
    ___ Not true of teachers.

2. Professionals have extensive specialized training.

    ___ True of teachers.
    ___ Not true of teachers.

3. Professionals exercise a high degree of autonomy and discretion.

    ___ True of teachers.
    ___ Not true of teachers.

4. Professions have voluntary associations of members that regulate admissions and licensing requirements and police professional practice.

    ___ True of teaching.
    ___ Not true of teaching.

5. Professional certification or licensure is based on competency testing.

    ___ True of teaching.
    ___ Not true of teaching.

6. Professions typically require members to update their skills and knowledge through ongoing professional development.

    ___ True of teaching.
    ___ Not true of teaching.

7. A profession has a code of ethics or code of professional standards that details acceptable conduct for its members.

    ___ True of teaching.
    ___ Not true of teaching.

8. Professionals typically are afforded high social status and prestige.

    ___ True of teachers.
    ___ Not true of teachers.

**Figure 2.2 — Code of Ethics of the Education Profession**

*Preamble*

The educator, believing in the worth and dignity of each human being, recognizes the supreme importance of the pursuit of truth, devotion to excellence, and the nurture of democratic principles. Essential to these goals is the protection of freedom to learn and to teach and the guarantee of equal educational opportunity for all. The educator accepts the responsibility to adhere to the highest ethical standards.

The educator recognizes the magnitude of the responsibility inherent in the teaching process. The desire for the respect and confidence of one's colleagues, of students, of parents, and of the members of the community provides the incentive to attain and maintain the highest possible degree of ethical conduct. The *Code of Ethics of the Education Profession* indicates the aspiration of all educators and provides standards by which to judge conduct.

The remedies specified by the NEA and/or its affiliates for the violation of any provision of this *Code* shall be exclusive and no such provision shall be enforceable in any form other than one specifically designated by the NEA or its affiliates.

*Principle I: Commitment to the Student*

The educator strives to help each student realize his or her potential as a worthy and effective member of society. The educator therefore works to stimulate the spirit of inquiry, the acquisition of knowledge and understanding, and the thoughtful formulation of worthy goals.

In fulfillment of the obligation to the student, the educator—

1. Shall not unreasonably restrain the student from independent action in the pursuit of learning.
2. Shall not unreasonably deny the student access to various points of view.
3. Shall not deliberately suppress or distort subject matter relevant to the student's progress.
4. Shall make reasonable effort to protect the student from conditions harmful to learning or to health and safety.
5. Shall not intentionally expose the student to embarrassment or disparagement.
6. Shall not on the basis of race, color, creed, sex, national origin, marital status, political or religious beliefs, family, social or cultural background, or sexual orientation unfairly—
    a. Exclude any student from participation in any program
    b. Deny benefits to any student
    c. Grant any advantage to any student
7. Shall not use professional relationships with students for private advantages.
8. Shall not disclose information about students obtained in the course of professional service, unless disclosure serves a compelling purpose or is required by law.

*Principle II: Commitment to the Profession*

The education profession is vested by the public with a trust and responsibility requiring the highest ideals of professional service.

In the belief that the quality of the services of the education profession directly influences the nation and its citizens, the educator shall exert every effort to raise professional standards, to promote a climate that encourages the exercise of professional judgement, to achieve conditions which attract persons worthy of the trust to careers in education, and to assist in preventing the practice of the profession by unqualified persons.

In fulfillment of the obligation to the profession, the educator—

1. Shall not in an application for a professional position deliberately make a false statement or fail to disclose a material fact related to competency and qualifications.
2. Shall not misrepresent his/her professional qualifications.
3. Shall not assist any entry into the profession of a person known to be unqualified in respect to character, education, or other relevant attribute.
4. Shall not knowingly make a false statement concerning the qualifications of a candidate for a professional position.
5. Shall not assist a noneducator in the unauthorized practice of teaching.
6. Shall not disclose information about colleagues obtained in the course of professional service unless disclosure serves a compelling professional purpose or is required by law.
7. Shall not knowingly make false or malicious statements about a colleague.
8. Shall not accept any gratuity, gift, or favor that might impair or appear to influence professional decisions or actions.

*Source*: From National Education Association. (2002). *Code of ethics of the education profession* (pp. 1–3). Washington, DC: Author. Reprinted by permission.

# The Increased Professionalization of Teaching

Great strides in the professionalization of teaching have been made in the last decade. The factors that have contributed to the increased professionalization of teaching include these:

1. Standards for teacher education programs have been raised.
2. State licensing requirements have been increased.
3. Entry-level examinations for teachers have been mandated in most states.
4. Professional certification programs such as national board certification have been implemented.
5. Performance-based pay programs with the potential of both increasing the financial rewards of teaching and recognizing those teachers who are taking steps to increase their competencies have been implemented in some states and a growing number of school districts.
6. Teaching has come to be viewed as a career with opportunities for advancement.

Some of these were discussed in Chapter 1. Those that were not are discussed here: the widespread adoption of professional standards for teachers, the establishment of standards and certification for advanced practice, and increased opportunities for professional development and career advancement.

## Development of Professional Standards

The school reform movement and NCLB have increased the interest in and acceptance of national standards for both student and teacher performance. The National Board for Professional Teaching Standards has developed standards for experienced teachers; INTASC has developed standards for beginning teachers; NCATE has developed standards for institutions that prepare educators; states have developed teacher education program approval standards; and, as discussed in Chapter 14, content standards have been developed by a variety of content specialist organizations such as the National Council of Teachers of Mathematics and, more recently, national standards in English language arts and math by the Common Core State Standards Initiative led by the National Governors' Association and the Council of Chief State School Officers, which have thus far been formally adopted by 41 states. National standards for other areas are likely to follow. The INTASC standards presented in Table 1.3 describe the "core" knowledge, dispositions, and performances all teachers are expected to possess and demonstrate. The standards have been translated into standards for a number of subject areas and still others are being developed. These standards have been adopted or adapted for teacher licensure in a number of states.

## National Board Certification

The development of standards for experienced teachers has been the work of the NBPTS. The first group of teachers received NBPTS **national board certification** in 1995. By 2011, ninety-one thousand teachers had become board certified. National board certification is valid for 10 years. While the purpose of national board certification is to complement, not replace, state licensing of teachers, it does meet most states' definition of a highly qualified teacher under NCLB (NBPTS, 2011). To be eligible for national board certification, the teacher must hold a bachelor's degree and must have completed a minimum of 3 years of teaching. Rather than relying on satisfactory performance on a standardized test, the certification process includes both portfolio entries and constructed response exercises (NBPTS, 2011). The process assesses not only the teacher's knowledge, but also the demonstration of skills and professional judgment in the classroom. The focus is on what teachers should know and be able to do.

While the 91,000 board-certified teachers represent only a very small percentage of the national teaching force, their numbers are growing rapidly. This can be attributed in no small part to the professional and financial rewards associated with achieving board certification. In 2011, thirty-one states provided financial incentives and 49 states provided licensure incentives for teachers to secure national board certification. State incentives vary considerably. For example, Washington not only provides a $5,000 bonus for the life of the certificate, but also will provide an additional $5,000 bonus to NBCTs who agree to work in a school where 70% of the students receive free or reduced lunch; Missouri provides an annual $6,000 salary bonus for the life of the certificate. North Carolina, the state with the highest number of board-certified teachers (18,000), provides 3 days of release time to allow teachers time for portfolio and assessment center exercises and awards a 12% salary increase to those who achieve national board certification. In addition to state incentives, local school districts may provide various incentives; for example, a 5% base salary increase on the salary schedule in Grand Junction, Colorado; a $2,000 one-step advancement on the salary schedule in Claremont Unified School District (CA); or a salary increase of $5,000 per year for the life of the certificate in the Clairton (Pennsylvania) School District (NBPTS, 2011).

## Professional Development

Professional training does not end with the awarding of the degree or the professional license. Professions typically require ongoing education and training of their members. "The assumption is that achieving a professional-level mastery of complex skills and knowledge is a prolonged and continuous process and, moreover, that professionals must continually update their skills as the body of technology, skill, and knowledge advances" (Ingersoll, 2008, p. 111). Performance expectations for teachers and the requirements of NCLB have made increasing the effectiveness of every individual in the school system a major focus of school improvement initiatives. High-quality **professional development** is the primary means by which both new and experienced teachers can develop the knowledge and pedagogical skills necessary for improved teaching effectiveness. Teaching information, techniques, and methods are constantly being updated, which means that the education and training provided in the teacher education program are not enough to serve teachers throughout their careers (Davies, 2010). There are always new things to learn and new skills to master. Professional development enables the teacher to feel more confident in the classroom and be a more positive professional.

Teachers participate in professional development activities throughout their professional careers.

The federal government and most state governments have increased their support of professional development for teachers. Federal funds for staff development have been made available through NCLB. States are also encouraging and providing support for professional development by either requiring participation or providing incentive for participation. For example, 40 states have adopted formal professional development standards, and in 16 states local school districts are required to set aside time for the professional development of teachers. However, only about half the states provide state funds to support general professional development activities for all districts (Hightower, 2010).

In addition to state or district-sponsored activities, teachers have numerous avenues available for personal and professional development. Many choose to join the professional organization most closely related to their teaching field. This membership provides access to professional materials, but perhaps more important, provides contact with other teachers and access to a professional peer support network. Professional organizations as well as state departments of education and education vendors also provide professional development opportunities through attendance at conferences and focused workshops. Other options for professional growth include professional travel, reading professional literature, lesson study, learning walks, faculty study groups, professional learning communities, and action research.

*Lesson study* involves a small group of teachers working together to plan a lesson that one of them ultimately teaches while the others observe. The lesson is then revised as necessary and may be re-taught by another teacher. *Learning walks* involves a small team of teachers and administrators making numerous short visits to classrooms in the school looking for specific things, reviewing and comparing observations, and reporting to the school as a whole as well as in discussions with individual teachers. The reporting and discussing serves to focus professional development for individual teachers as well as the school as a whole. *Faculty study groups*, as the name implies, involve the entire faculty meeting in smaller groups on a regular basis to engage in an in-depth study of a school-based issue (one issue per group). Action plans are then implemented in the classrooms of the group members and results monitored.

The *professional learning community* has received increased support in the professional literature as an effective approach to professional development. In professional learning communities "teachers work together and engage in continual dialogue to examine their practice and student performance and to develop and implement more effective instructional practices" (Darling-Hammond & Richardson, 2009, p. 49). Professional learning community activities can include lesson study, peer observation, and study groups.

**Action research** has become an increasingly popular tool for teachers and administrators seeking to expand their knowledge and improve their practice. Action research is a process in which educators (1) indentify a problem in their own classroom, school, or district; (2) collect and analyze data related to the problem; and (3) develop and implement a plan for improving practice. Action research can be undertaken by an individual teacher in his or her classroom or by a group of teachers investigating a common problem.

Yet another approach to professional development is to enroll in an advanced certification or degree program in a college or university. While this option is popular because it often leads to advancement on the salary schedule, the challenge of this approach is to develop an individualized program and to select components that will improve the competencies needed by the individual as a teacher, while at the same time meeting degree requirements.

Encouraged by both state and federal mandates and support, school districts are devoting increased resources to planning and conducting relevant professional development programs for their staffs. Staff development has become increasingly important because of the growth of the knowledge base related to cognition, pedagogy, and instructional methodology as well as the ever-growing body of research emphasizing the importance of quality teaching to student achievement and the explosion in the potential of technology applications in and out of the classroom.

## Mentoring Programs

In contrast to other professions in which an entry-level employee often enters as a junior member of a team consisting of persons with a range of experience, the beginning teacher typically is assigned a classroom of students in an elementary school or a series of classes in a secondary school and is expected to assume the same responsibilities as an experienced teacher. To assist beginning teachers in their transition from student to teacher, 23 states require beginning teachers to participate in a state-funded mentoring program. Even where mentoring is not

**For Your Reflection and Analysis**

What kind of professional development should you secure for yourself? What kind should the school district provide?

Mentoring is important to the success of many beginning teachers.

required by the state, the majority of school districts operate some type of mentoring program.

The concept of **mentoring** usually involves the development of a support relationship between a beginning and an experienced teacher. An important function of the mentor is to serve as a colleague from which the novice teacher can receive basic information about the expectations and operation of the school and school district, as well as advice, guidance, and support on a range of professional issues including curriculum planning, instructional strategies, classroom management, student discipline, and working with parents and the community. The goal of beginning teacher mentor programs is to establish a professional relationship that will provide a foundation and attitude of trust through which the relationship can focus on effective instructional practices. The mentee benefits from not being in isolation and from having a role model for teaching. The mentor benefits through recognition as a successful teacher and by keeping up to date on best practices in teaching and the refinement and upgrading of professional knowledge and skills. Mentors also benefit from increased reflection, increased collaboration, an enhanced sense of professional recognition, and, in some districts, released time and a financial stipend. Research has shown not only that mentoring is important to new teacher development and student learning, but also that teachers are more likely to remain in the profession if they are involved in an effective mentoring program.

Because of the proven success of mentoring, some states and many school districts have extended their mentoring program beyond beginning teachers. For example, Florida provides a 10% salary bonus to teachers who spend the equivalent of 12 working days providing mentoring and related services to teachers who are not national board certified.

## Self-Renewal

The routine of teaching is tempered by the excitement of new students arriving each semester or school year. However, the continuing pressures of the classroom and the possibilities of teaching the same grade level or the same subject for several decades can depress even the most enthusiastic person. Traditionally, **self-renewal** has been viewed as the responsibility of the individual teacher; however, experience suggests that school districts can benefit from the development of joint self-renewal or professional renewal efforts with teachers (Cain, 2001).

School districts use a variety of approaches to address teachers' need for renewal. Among the renewal programs available in districts across the country are:

• Sabbaticals for advanced study
• Periodic change of school or teaching assignment
• Attendance at workshops or professional conferences
• Visitation programs

Another option involves providing teachers with alternative assignments in curriculum or staff development programs. The purpose of such programs is to recognize outstanding teachers by providing them with a break from the classroom while continuing to engage them in professionally challenging experiences of benefit to the school district.

Teachers who have participated in formal renewal programs bring an enhanced perspective to the classroom and the school, as well as a greater sense of professionalism. Cain (2001) noted that teachers who have participated in renewal programs tended to have a stronger philosophical center; a greater sense of personal

# CONTROVERSIAL ISSUE

## *Teacher Tenure*

*Teacher tenure* is possibly one of the most maligned and misunderstood terms in education. Originally, tenure statutes were enacted to protect teachers from political or personal abuses and to provide for a more stable teaching force. In some instances, teaching jobs were awarded as political patronage by elected school board members, superintendents, or other public officials. A school board election could result in the wholesale dismissal of teachers and principals. As teacher organizations and school districts have entered into negotiations leading to a formal agreement, tenure has become less important because those agreements typically stipulate the conditions under which a teacher may be dismissed.

**For**

1. Tenure is essential to protect the teacher from arbitrary and capricious dismissal for reasons unrelated to performance in the classroom.

2. Tenure statutes protect the rights of the individual and provide for an orderly review and due process.

3. Tenure statutes stipulate the legal procedures under which a teacher's right to employment may be reviewed and terminated.

4. Tenure statutes and regulations ensure that the teacher understands the deficiency (problem) and has an opportunity to correct it.

5. The security of tenure status may encourage some persons to enter teaching.

**Against**

1. Teachers in probationary status remain in the classroom and continue to teach.

2. Cumbersome and extensive dismissal procedures result in the retention and/or rotating assignments of incompetent teachers from one school to another or from teaching to some support role in the schools.

3. Tenured teachers often are not evaluated as frequently as probationary teachers.

4. Tenure encourages some teachers to become complacent and removes their motivation to improve.

What do you think? Should tenure be retained or repealed? Should student performance be considered in decisions about retention or dismissal of teachers? Should a person's tenure status be subject to review periodically; for example, after a 5-year cycle?

---

responsibility; a sense of collegiality; and a commitment to students, lifelong learning, and their school. They also seemed to have developed a strong appreciation for all aspects of life and the ability to see and appreciate people as individuals. In addition, they enhanced their ability to communicate, developed a sense of leadership, and demonstrated the ability to separate their egos from their work.

## Career Advancement

Traditional career opportunities in teaching probably were more accurately defined as career opportunities in education. Elementary and secondary school teaching was often viewed as a necessary entry-level experience before one became a school administrator or college professor. For the majority of teachers, career advancement ended when they attained tenure (see the Controversial Issue feature above). Today, changes in teacher salaries, teacher roles, and teacher advancement programs have improved the professional opportunities and rewards available to teachers and allowed them to advance in their chosen profession without abandoning the classroom.

## Multiple Career Paths

Providing teachers with the opportunity to advance in their careers without leaving the classroom is the goal of career ladder and teacher advancement programs. **Career ladder** programs aim to make teaching more attractive by providing teachers the incentive and opportunity to advance to more challenging and responsible levels of teaching. Career ladders are also seen as a strategy to improve the quality of teaching, improve teacher motivation, and reward high performing teachers.

Career ladders allow teachers to take on additional responsibility without leaving the classroom altogether.

The concept of career ladders assumes different duties, responsibilities, and pay at different hierarchical levels. A typical career ladder has four stages or levels. The first level is the beginning, probationary, or *apprentice teacher*. (See the Historical Note feature below for the teacher apprenticeship contract for schoolmaster in colonial America.) At the end of a 3- to 5-year apprenticeship, if the teacher is retained, promotion is made to the second level, *professional teacher*. The professional teacher receives a higher base salary with additional limited annual step increases. Depending on the program, a teacher can stay at this level for a minimum of 3 years if performance is satisfactory but can also stay at this level throughout a career.

The third level, often referred to as the *senior teacher* level, also receives a higher base salary with additional annual step increases. A teacher might stay at this level for a period of 5 years and, if performance is satisfactory, can stay at this level throughout a career. The assumption in most programs is that the majority of the district's experienced teachers will be at this level. Senior teachers may be placed on an extended contract during the summer months to work on curricular or other projects.

Attainment of the fourth level, **master teacher,** typically is more complicated and may include a formal application with a portfolio that is reviewed by school district administrators and other master teachers. The decision to seek master teacher status is voluntary. These teachers are often on a full-year contract with program development responsibilities. The first step on the pay scale of master teachers might be two times the first step on the salary schedule.

# HISTORICAL NOTE

## Apprentice Contract for Schoolmaster, 1722

Registered for Mr. George Brownell Schoolmaster ye 18th day of july 1722.

This Indenture Wittnesseth that John Campbel Son of Robert Campbell of the City of New York with the Consent of his father and mother hath put himself and by these presents doth Voluntarily put and bind himself Apprentice to George Brownell of the Same City Schoolmaster to learn the Art Trade or Mystery and with the Said George Brownell to Serve from the twenty ninth day of May one thousand seven hundred and twenty one for and during the Term of ten years and three Months to be Compleat and Ended During all which term the said Apprentice his said Master and Mistress faithfully Shall Serve their Secrets keep and Lawfull Commands gladly everywhere obey he Shall do no damage to his said Master or Mistress nor suffer it to be done by others without Letting or Giving Notice thereof to his said Master or Mistress he shall not Waste his said Master or Mistress Goods or Lend them Unlawfully to any he shall not Committ fornication nor Contract Matrimony within the Said Term at Cards Dice or any other unlawfull Game he shall not Play: he Shall not absent himself by Day or by Night from his Said Master or Mistress Service without their Leave; nor haunt Alehouses Taverns or Playhouses but in all things behave himself as a faithfull Apprentice ought to Do towards his said Master or Mistress during the Said Term. And the said George Brownell Doth hereby Covenant and Promise to teach and Instruct or Cause the said Apprentice to be taught and Instructed in the Art Trade or Calling of a Schoolmaster by the best way or means he or his wife may or can if the Said Apprentice be Capable to Learn and to find and Provide unto the Said Apprentice sufficient meat Drink Apparel Lodging and washing fitting for an Apprentice during the Said Term: and at the Expiration thereof to give unto the Said Apprentice one Suit of Cloth new Consisting of a coatvest coat and Breeches also one New hatt Six New Shirts Three pair of Stockings one pair of New Shoes Suitable for his said Apprentice. In Testimony Whereof the Parties to these Presents have hereunto Interchangeably Sett their hands and Seals the third day of August in the Eighth year of the Reign of our Sovereign Lord George King of Great Brittain &c. Anno Domini One thousand seven hundred and Twenty-One. john Campbel. Signed Sealed and Delivered in the presence of Mary Smith Cornelius Kiersted Memorandum Appeared before me John Cruger Esq. Alderman and One of his Majesties justices of the Peace for this City and County. John Campbell and Acknowledged the within Indenture to be his Voluntary Act and Deed New York the 9th Aprill 1722.

John Cruger.

*Source: Citty of N Yorke indenture, 1694–1727*, translated by Saybolt, cited by Cubberley, E. P. (1934). *Readings in public education in the United States.* New York: Houghton Mifflin, pp. 71–72.

Career ladder programs were adopted by several states in the 1980s and 1990s but primarily because of insufficient funds or non-funding, all but one have been terminated. Arizona's remains, but at this writing, elimination as a budget cutting measure has been proposed. However, career ladders are still in operation in a number of schools and school districts. In addition, the career ladder is a component of Teacher Advancement Program models which are operating in more than a dozen states.

**For Your Reflection and Analysis**

What effect might a career ladder program have on the collegial environment of the typical school?

### Teacher Advancement Programs

The Teacher Advancement Program was created by the Milkin Family Foundation as one element in a comprehensive school reform model. The multiple career paths element classifies teachers as career, mentor, and master depending on their interests, qualifications, and responsibilities. Mentor and master teachers are selected through a competitive performance-based process. They are expected to have "expert curricular knowledge, outstanding instructional skills and the ability to work effectively with other adults . . . are required to have a longer work year . . . and are held to a different performance standard than the career teachers in their school, and are compensated accordingly" (TAP, 2011, p. 1).

### Teacher–Leaders

An important ingredient of many school improvement models is the concept of teachers assuming various leadership roles and more active roles in determining the direction of a school's program. Expanded roles for teachers are also consistent with the positions of the major teacher organizations. The term **teacher–leader** has become a term commonly associated with this expanded role. Several states now offer teacher–leader endorsement as part of their licensure program.

The opportunities for teachers to assume leadership roles are many and diverse; they range from the formal roles of department chair or master teacher to an informal role as coach or mentor to other teachers or those in formal leadership roles. In addition to providing leadership at the building level, some teachers work at the district or state level in curriculum development or professional development programs, policy development or revision projects, certification, or writing grant proposals to public or private agencies to support student or faculty growth. Still others collaborate with colleges and universities in the design of teacher education programs or teaching teacher education classes. In many school districts these opportunities for assuming additional responsibilities are integrated into career ladder, differentiated staffing, or pay-for-performance systems.

## Evaluating Teacher Performance

Teacher evaluation is necessary in decisions related to retention, tenure, termination, performance rewards, and the direction of staff development. The attention focused on teacher quality, standards, and accountability by NCLB has brought renewed interest in teacher performance evaluation. Forty-nine states have adopted legislation that requires the formal evaluation of teachers. At the same time, the focus on improving student achievement has led to the adoption of teacher evaluation systems that include student performance. One recent but somewhat controversial evaluation strategy that has been adopted by a growing number of states and school districts is **value-added assessment**. (See pros and cons discussed in the Controversial Issue on page 21.) Value-added assessment purports to measure teacher effectiveness by a process that determines the difference between students' expected and actual test score growth. While most educational professionals and researchers agree that most teacher evaluation systems do not adequately discriminate between the most and least effective teachers, many are also concerned with the reliance on test data and the yearly fluctuations in value-added ratings, as well as the difficulty of using value-added methodology in areas not subject to

Observation of classroom performance by a supervisor is an important part of teacher evaluation.

standardized testing, including most electives. Nonetheless, with the indisputable evidence linking teacher effectiveness and student learning, and with the encouragement of federal funding being awarded to systems that link teacher pay to student achievement, a more widespread adoption of some student growth data in teacher evaluation seems assured.

The two types of teacher evaluation are **summative evaluation** and **formative evaluation**. Summative teacher evaluation is typically conducted annually and is designed to assess terminal behaviors or overall performance. Summative evaluation is used to make such personnel decisions as contract renewal, the awarding of tenure, performance pay, and assignment to levels on a career ladder. Formative teacher evaluation, unlike summative evaluation, is ongoing. It is intended to provide continuing feedback to the person being evaluated for the purpose of self-improvement or professional development. Where summative evaluation is externally controlled and judgmental, formative evaluation is employee directed, individualized, and geared to promote reflection and support professional growth (Black, 2000).

Teachers are evaluated using a set of criteria developed by the state or the school district. Many states have adopted or adapted the **Praxis** or INTASC standards in formulating the criteria for the evaluation of beginning teachers. An example of the evaluation criteria used by the Clark County (Nevada) School District is shown in Figure 2.3.

By far the most common method used to collect data for evaluation is the observation of teaching. The beginning teacher will normally be observed several times during the school year, usually by the principal or assistant principal. The observation is usually scheduled and may be for an entire lesson or period, or more frequent, informal observations referred to as "walk throughs" lasting 3–6 minutes may be conducted. Teacher self-evaluation, teacher portfolio assessment, peer evaluation, and student achievement data are also commonly used in combination with teacher observation. Beginning teachers typically receive a more intensive summative evaluation than experienced teachers.

## Teachers' Organizations

Teacher organizations sponsor and support a variety of activities directed at improving the working conditions of teachers, promoting the status of the teaching profession, and improving the lives of students. Teacher organizations work with and lobby local, state, and federal policymakers on important educational issues. At the local level, teacher organizations focus many of these efforts on issues of teacher governance, compensation, and terms and conditions of employment.

Beginning teachers often are confronted with the choice of which and how many professional organizations to join. They may affiliate with one of the national teachers' organizations, the National Education Association (NEA) and the American Federation of Teachers (AFT), or one of their state affiliates. They may also affiliate with organizations whose focus is on a particular subject or educational specialty. In some districts, there may be only one active teacher organization; in others, the new teacher may have the opportunity to choose among two or more organizations.

**Figure 2.3 — Clark County School District Licensed Employee Appraisal Report**

9998-500008 | **CLARK COUNTY SCHOOL DISTRICT** | CCF-8 MS (Rev. 09/09)

# LICENSED EMPLOYEE APPRAISAL REPORT

Employee's Name: _____ School/Location: _____

Social Security No.: _____ Assignment: _____ Years in CCSD: _____ Location: _____

Observation Dates: From _____ to _____ Conference Date: _____ Page 1 of _____

Report and analysis of observations, performance, and other factors which may be pertinent to performance; probationary/postprobationary status, date of last evaluation, and directions.

## LEVELS OF PERFORMANCE

| **Level 4** | Performance exceeds standards consistently at a distinguished level. | **Level 2** | Performance approaches standards and/or does not consistently meet standards.* |
|---|---|---|---|
| **Level 3** | Performance consistently meets standards and may occasionally exceed standards in some areas. | **Level 1** | Performance is below standards and is not satisfactory.* |

*Any area(s) marked Level 1 or 2 require documentation. Any area(s) marked Level 1, or 8 or more areas marked Level 2 results in an overall rating of "Not Satisfactory."

### PROFESSIONAL DOMAINS

| PLANNING AND PREPARATION | 4 | 3 | 2 | 1 |
|---|---|---|---|---|
| **PROFESSIONAL STANDARDS** | | | | |
| 1. Instructional planning was documented in written lesson plans and based on adopted curriculum documents and standards. | | | | |
| 2. Content knowledge was demonstrated in planning. | | | | |
| 3. Planning, reflected knowledge of student achievement, access/equity, students' interests and backgrounds, and other site-specific demographic data. | | | | |

| ASSESSMENT OF STUDENT ACHIEVEMENT | 4 | 3 | 2 | 1 |
|---|---|---|---|---|
| **PROFESSIONAL STANDARDS** | | | | |
| 1. Student achievement, access/equity, and other site specific demographic data were analyzed. | | | | |
| 2. Desired results for student learning/achievement were identified, measurable, and used for instructional planning to determine and monitor student progress. | | | | |
| 3. Assessment regulations and guidelines were followed. | | | | |

| LEARNING ENVIRONMENT | 4 | 3 | 2 | 1 |
|---|---|---|---|---|
| **PROFESSIONAL STANDARDS** | | | | |
| 1. An academic focus and on-task behavior were maintained. | | | | |
| 2. A classroom management/discipline plan was in place, communicated and maintained. | | | | |
| 3. Respect and courtesy were modeled by the teacher in student and parent interactions. | | | | |
| 4. The physical environment supported the teaching/learning process. | | | | |

| INSTRUCTION | 4 | 3 | 2 | 1 |
|---|---|---|---|---|
| **PROFESSIONAL STANDARDS** | | | | |
| 1. The components of an effective lesson and the basic principles of learning were used when providing instruction. | | | | |
| 2. Varied instructional strategies, approaches, and resources, aligned with instructional objectives, engaged students in learning. | | | | |

| INSTRUCTION (continued) | 4 | 3 | 2 | 1 |
|---|---|---|---|---|
| 3. Lessons had a clearly defined structure and pacing was appropriate. | | | | |
| 4. Flexible instructional groupings were utilized. | | | | |
| 5. Accommodations and/or modifications were used in alignment with instructional objectives to meet the needs of students. | | | | |
| 6. Feedback to students was provided and promoted student success and achievement. | | | | |

| PROFESSIONAL RESPONSIBILITIES | 4 | 3 | 2 | 1 |
|---|---|---|---|---|
| **PROFESSIONAL STANDARDS** | | | | |
| 1. The employee participated in the school improvement process and implemented school improvement goals. | | | | |
| 2. The employee addressed identified individual improvement goals/directions. | | | | |
| 3. The employee participated in on-going professional development to improve content knowledge and pedagogical skills. | | | | |
| 4. The employee participated in required job-related meetings and activities and performed assigned duties. | | | | |
| 5. The employee maintained student records. | | | | |
| 6. The employee provided communication to parents/guardians and students related to behavior and achievement. | | | | |
| 7. The employee worked professionally with administration, staff, parents, and community. | | | | |
| 8. The employee used multicultural resources, materials and activities to support multicultural literacy, awareness, and appreciation. | | | | |
| 9. The employee complied with all school and district policies and regulations, as well as state and federal laws applicable to teachers. | | | | |

**A narrative, which includes a PERFORMANCE SUMMARY and IMPROVEMENT GOALS/DIRECTIONS, must be included on the following page.**

I certify that I have supervised and evaluated the professional performance of the above named ☐ probationary ☐ post probationary employee, and I certify that to date this school year his/her overall performance ☐ is ☐ is not satisfactory.

_____ _____
*Signature of Employee Date

☐ A response will be made (timelines established in applicable negotiated agreement).
☐ A response was submitted on_____
Date

_____ _____
Signature of Supervising Administrator Date

_____ _____
Signature of Supervising Administrator Receiving Response Date

*A signature on this summary does not necessarily mean the licensed employee agrees with the opinions expressed, but merely indicates the employee has read the analysis, had an opportunity for discussion with his/her immediate supervisor, and understands that he/she has the privilege of discussing it with the Human Resources Division.

031 DISTRIBUTION: Original – Licensed Personnel 1st copy -- Supervising Administrator -- Work Location File 2nd copy -- Licensed Employee
CCF-8 (Rev. 09/09 MSWord)

Affiliation is often seen as an indication of the commitment to teaching as a profession and as a career and provides both the beginning and the experienced teacher the benefits that come from ongoing interaction with professional colleagues. Almost three quarters of all teachers are members of a teacher organization.

## National Organizations for Teachers

Of the two major national organizations for teachers, the NEA and the AFT, the NEA is the larger. In fact, the NEA is the largest employee union in the United States. Begun in 1857 as a professional association, the NEA has members who work at every level of education and are found in all types of school districts. In contrast, the AFT has fewer members, and its activities tend to be concentrated in urban areas. The membership of both organizations includes not only classroom teachers, but also counselors, librarians, administrators, and support personnel, as well as college and university personnel. Some persons hold memberships in both the NEA and the AFT. The NEA's membership is about 3.2 million and the AFT's about 1.5 million. The AFT's membership does not include administrators, but it does include school support staff as well as local, state, and federal government employees and health care professionals. While smaller, the AFT is affiliated with the American Federation of Labor-Congress of Industrial Organizations (AFL-CIO), which has over 12 million members.

For almost 100 years, the NEA was the umbrella organization for college and university faculty as well as elementary and secondary education teachers and administrators. Until the 1960s, leadership roles in the NEA and its state affiliates often were held by school superintendents and higher education personnel. Starting in the 1960s, elementary and secondary school classroom teachers began to assume the leadership roles. The organization's program now focuses more on services to teachers and state and local teacher organizations. The NEA advocates for improvement in teacher education programs, pushes for higher standards in teacher licensure, and assumes greater control of the professional development of teachers.

The primary goals of both the NEA and the AFT have been to enhance the professional status and working conditions of teachers and to promote a positive public perception of teachers and education. Both organizations provide a variety of professional development activities and services for their members. Publications include national research reports, journals for members (the NEA's *NEA Today* and the AFT's *American Educator*), and a variety of handbooks and related documents.

National teacher organizations work to improve the status and working conditions of teachers.

Most of these publications are oriented toward improving teacher performance and working conditions or providing source information about the status of American education. Both organizations conduct annual state and national conferences and provide workshop training activities related to professional and organizational development. Both organizations also conduct research to identify and promote promising practices.

Both the NEA and the AFT, as well as many of the other national education organizations, have affiliates at the state level. The NEA's affiliates in all states and more than 14,000 school districts serve as advocates for teacher tenure and certification, increases in teacher salaries and improved working conditions, and programs that promote child welfare. The AFT also supports many similar activities, but the general perception has been that the AFT's strength has been concentrated in the organizational units at the school district level. The AFT has 3,000 local affiliates and 43 state affiliates, with its membership concentrated in urban areas.

## Local Organizations for Teachers and Collective Negotiations

Local organizations provide many benefits, including the opportunity to interact with fellow professionals in professional and social activities. Other benefits are related to the collective representation of the teachers in discussions with the school board and administration. Both the NEA and the AFT encourage teachers to negotiate salaries and working conditions with local school boards. What actually can be negotiated by the teacher union is often determined by state law or court decisions. The most commonly negotiated items include salary and benefits, reductions in force, leaves, tenure, performance evaluations, seniority, class size, hours of work, and grievance procedures. In most of the states, teachers are actively involved in formal and informal negotiations with school boards and the results of these negotiations affect the direction school districts take in almost all areas of operation. In some states, the negotiations are voluntary; in others, school boards are required by state law to enter into a contract with the local teachers' organizations about salaries and working conditions. The result has been an increase in the control and input that teachers have over issues related to their salaries and conditions of employment.

## Specialized Organizations for Teachers

In addition to the inclusive organizations for all teachers, professional organizations have been formed for each discipline and role in the school. Through research reports, publications, conferences, and workshops, these organizations play an important role in keeping members up to date on developments in their areas, as well as in providing professional development for members. Typically they are less politically active than the two national teachers' organizations.

Some specialized organizations such as the Council for Exceptional Children (CEC) include as their members parents and interested citizens as well as professional educators. Others, such as the National Conference of Teachers of English (NCTE), the National Council of Teachers of Mathematics (NCTM), the National Council for the Social Studies (NCSS), and the National Science Teachers Association (NSTA), draw their members from teachers at all levels of education. Subject-matter organizations typically do not become involved in direct discussions with school officials about working conditions of teachers; however, they may adopt statements of principles or standards about total teaching load, textbook selection procedures, and selection and use of instructional materials. The subject-matter groups are involved in the development of the content standards for their subject areas. In this way, the specialized organizations do assume an advocacy role for changes in state or federal legislation related to their teaching area. Table 2.1 lists some of the major specialized organizations with which teachers typically affiliate.

**For Your Reflection and Analysis**

As a new teacher, what kinds of assistance do you expect from the local teachers' organization?

**Table 2.1 — Major Specialized Professional Organizations for Teachers**

American Alliance for Health, Physical Education, Recreation and Dance—www.aahperd.org
American Association for Gifted Children—www.aagc.org
American Council for the Teaching of Foreign Languages—www.actfl.org
American Montessori Society—www.amshq.org
Association for Career and Technical Education—www.acteonline.org
Council for Exceptional Children—www.cec.sped.org
International Reading Association—www.reading.org
International Society for Technology in Education—www.iste.org
Modern Language Association—www.mla.org
Music Teachers National Association—www.mtna.org
National Art Education Association—www.naea.org
National Association for Bilingual Education—www.nabe.org
National Association for Multicultural Education—www.nameorg.org
National Association for Music Education—www.menc.org
National Association for the Education of Young Children—www.naeyc.org
National Council for the Social Studies—www.ncss.org
National Council of Teachers of English—www.ncte.org
National Council of Teachers of Mathematics—www.nctm.org
National Science Teachers Association—www.nsta.org

Examples of other organizations oriented to specific support roles in the schools include the American Library Association (ALA) and the American Association for Counseling and Development (AACD). A broader based organization is the Association for Supervision and Curriculum Development (ASCD), which includes teachers, administrators, and college professors. Specialized organizations for school district central office personnel and building principals include the American Association of School Administrators (AASA), the National Association of Secondary School Principals (NASSP), and the National Association of Elementary School Principals (NAESP). With some exceptions, these groups tend to be stronger at the state and national levels. Both the NASSP and the AASA have recently initiated assessment programs to improve the professional knowledge and skills of administrators.

## Teachers' Organizations and Public Policy Issues

In an effort to respond to public policy issues with a stronger political voice and collaborate on specific campaigns, in 2000 the AFT and NEA formed the NEAFT partnership. The NEAFT is governed by a joint council with members from both organizations. The council has the authority to make decisions and to advance goals that are in conformity with the policies and directives of each organization's governing body. This arrangement enables the two organizations to be more effective in representing their membership and presenting a united front on public policy issues of mutual agreement. The NEA and the AFT have found common ground in the last decade in their opposition to NCLB, specifically the heavy reliance on test scores to evaluate and categorize students, teachers, and schools as well as in opposition to vouchers, arguing they increase segregation by race and socioeconomic status. They also stand together in support of efforts to improve early childhood education; lower racial, ethnic, and socioeconomic achievement; and secure equitable evaluation and compensation of teachers.

Both the NEA and the AFT independently and together seek to advance the welfare of members and the condition of education by actively lobbying state and federal legislators and policymakers as well as education officials at the federal, state, and local levels. Both the NEA and the AFT as well as other national education associations have lobbyists in Washington who seek to advance their positions. Representatives of these associations (e.g., the Council for Exceptional Children or the National Bilingual Association) often testify before Congress and state legislatures on matters related to the passage and implementation of education legislation. It is also not uncommon for the major organizations to file *amicus* (friend of the court) briefs when education cases are being considered by the U.S. Supreme Court or even state supreme courts. And, teachers' unions do have a strong political voice because of their very size and wealth and the fact that teachers tend to vote in large numbers.

## Summary

One outcome of the school accountability movement has been an increased expectation of teachers. Advances have also been made in procedures for evaluating teachers, and school districts are providing increased opportunities for professional development. The effect of accountability on teacher quality and quantity is not known. Enforcement of higher standards may cause teachers to leave the profession or may attract more as the reputation of the profession is enhanced. The old view of teaching as a stepping-stone to careers in administration and higher education is being replaced by the perception of teaching as a career in itself. As job rewards and leadership opportunities have increased, other changes in working conditions have made the teaching profession more attractive.

In Chapter 3 you will have the opportunity to reflect on the major philosophies and the influence of these philosophies on current educational process and the teaching profession.

# TEACHER OF THE YEAR

*Jackie Johnson*
*Alaska*

I never wanted to be a teacher. I wanted to work in a zoo. While working at the zoo I began to teach classes to all ages. I loved that magical moment when I saw people truly understood something for the first time. From this, I knew I had to be a teacher. In my own classroom I love those magical moments when kids really, finally understand something for the first time. I love leading them to their own path of discovery, and I love watching them become inquisitive about their world. Recently one of my students discovered bugs for the very first time, and she has gotten so into them that she can't wait to become an entomologist when she grows up. I teach because it's the one job in the world that allows me to play, create, and explore every day, right along with my students.

# PROFESSIONAL DEVELOPMENT
## *Workshop*

## *Prepare for the State Licensure Examination*

Jason Schein has been a psychology teacher at Albert Einstein High School for 7 years. He is an alumnus of Albert Einstein High School and also completed his student teaching at the school. Known for his unique and innovative teaching methods, Mr. Schein was recently named the Teacher of the Year by his school district. For the past 5 years he has volunteered to accept a student teacher from the local university, which has had the reputation of preparing excellent teachers.

This semester Mr. Stephen Weissman, a senior who is completing his degree in education, was assigned to do his student teaching at Albert Einstein High School under the supervision of Mr. Schein. Following 2 weeks of observation and participation in Mr. Schein's advanced placement psychology class, tomorrow Stephen is scheduled to introduce an 8-week unit, "Psychological Disorders." Last Friday Stephen met with Mr. Schein and discussed his overall unit goal as well as each of his weekly lesson plans. He assured Mr. Schein that he had incorporated the American Psychological Association's (APA's) National Standards for High School Curricula in designing the unit.

Later this afternoon, during his regularly scheduled meeting with Mr. Schein, Stephen will ask him to review the handout that he plans to distribute tomorrow. The handout briefly describes the goals for the unit and provides a brief summary of each of the following weekly lessons: Weeks 1–2: Characteristics and Origins of Abnormal Behavior; Weeks 3–4: Research Methods Used in Exploring Abnormal Behavior; Weeks 5–6: Major Categories of Abnormal Behavior; and Weeks 7–8: Impact of Mental Disorders.

Tomorrow Stephen also plans to share with the class the unit homework assignments as well as the criteria that will be used for grading. While Stephen has not finalized his decision about assignments, he is considering asking each student to choose a psychological disorder, identify the symptoms of the disorder as classified in the APA's *Diagnostic and Statistical Manual*, and develop an appropriate treatment plan from each of the following orientations: (1) behavioral, (2) cognitive, (3) psychoanalytic, (4) humanistic, (5) feminist, and (6) biomedical. In addition to this written assignment, Stephen is also considering using the objective and essay examination that accompanies the textbook at the end of the unit.

### *Mr. Schein's Observation Notes of Mr. Weissman*

*First Day.* Stephen Weissman briefly shared information about himself and why he chose to teach the unit on "Psychological Disorders." While it was obvious that Stephen was very enthusiastic about the topic, it was also evident that several of the students in class were not paying close attention. However, when Stephen began to talk about the assignments and grading, most of the disinterested students began to pay more attention. For a moment the entire room was silent. Then, the silence changed to loud murmurs as several students voiced their opinion: "No way. This isn't college."

Stephen continued with a PowerPoint presentation on mental illness that provided an overview of the unit. The presentation lasted until the end of the class. His presentation was sensitive, humorous, and thoughtful. He included excellent visuals including graphics, cartoons, video, and photographs. Throughout the presentation Stephen incorporated segments of music that seemed to be popular with the students as evidenced by their body movements and desk tapping sounds. The presentation ended with three questions: (1) What exactly is "a psychological disorder"? (2) Who determines what is "normal" and "abnormal" behavior? and

(3) How have judgments about abnormality changed throughout history? Most students were attentive to the PowerPoint presentation.

(A scheduled faculty meeting that afternoon followed by a doctor's appointment for Mr. Schein precluded a meeting at the end of Stephen's first day of teaching.)

*Second Day.* Stephen again used a PowerPoint presentation that lasted the entire period to present the lesson. About halfway through the presentation several students at the back of the class (James, Ashley, and Helen) began to whisper and pass notes and Robbie appeared to be falling asleep. By the end of the class, desks were being shuffled and several students were not even pretending to pay attention to Stephen's presentation.

*Mr. Schein's Notes from Meeting with Stephen Weissman*

I complimented Stephen on his excellent PowerPoint presentation and his command of the subject matter but noted that he should have included some opportunities for student engagement during the lesson. I also mentioned that there were numerous new concepts presented and suggested that they may need to be reinforced throughout the unit. I also told Stephen that I thought the three questions he posed to his students at the end of his PowerPoint presentation were excellent and asked him how he plans to address these basic questions in future lesson plans.

Lastly we talked about classroom management and discussed alternatives for dealing with disruptive students.

1. Recommend *two* different strategies that Stephen might use to engage his students to become active participants throughout the unit. Explain your rationale for recommending the two strategies and why you are convinced that those strategies will be effective.

2. Describe an overall assessment plan that Stephen might use in evaluating his students' progress. Because his students are accelerated and gifted, should his criteria for grading differ from the criteria for grading used with a regular heterogeneous class? Give reasons why or why not.

3. What classroom management techniques might Mr. Schein suggest to Stephen to address disruptive behavior in the classroom?

## Build Your Knowledge Base

1. Which professional organization(s) do you plan to join as a new teacher, and for what reasons?

2. In what ways does teaching differ from professions such as law, medicine, and accounting?

3. To what extent will you have the knowledge and skills expected of a teacher?

4. What are the provisions for collective bargaining for teachers in your state?

5. What responsibility does the beginning teacher have for continued professional development? What are the professional development requirements for teachers in school districts with which you are familiar?

6. What steps can you take to make your teacher evaluation a positive experience that will help you improve your performance?

7. What steps are taken to monitor the extent to which teachers comply with codes of ethics in your local school districts?

8. What reasons might there be for not joining a professional organization?

## Develop Your Portfolio

1. As a pre-service or prospective teacher, begin recording examples of professional development activities in which you have participated during the past year. For example, you might have attended a lecture presented by a noted educational authority on a topic relevant to your discipline. You may choose to attend a professional organization meeting. Write a 2- to 3-page essay that includes a brief description of the activity, along with a detailed list of the concepts, ideas, or questions you considered because of the

experience. How has the experience influenced your thinking? Place your essay in your portfolio under **INTASC Standard 9, Professional Learning and Ethical Practice**.

2. Odden (2000) proposed that the schools follow the example of private-sector, high-performance organizations and incorporate into their structure incentives for teachers or schools in which student performance has improved. On the other hand, Holt (2001) has raised questions about the merits of discarding the traditional salary schedule in favor of performance pay. Prepare a brief position paper of 1 to 2 pages listing the pros and cons of both Odden's and Holt's proposals. Place your position paper in your portfolio under **INTASC Standard 9, Professional Learning and Ethical Practice**.

### Explore Teaching and Learning: Field Experiences

1. Arrange an interview with the principal and an experienced teacher in the same school concerning the teacher evaluation process that is being used in the school. Possible questions include the following:
   a. What is the purpose of the teacher evaluation process?
   b. What role does the person being evaluated have in determining the content of the evaluation process?
   c. What are the components of the evaluation process, that is, portfolio of classroom materials and lesson plans, pre-observation conference, observation, post-observation conference? Ask the teacher if you may examine the portfolio.
   d. To what degree are other teachers involved in the evaluation?
   e. What specific positive actions can be attributed to the evaluation process?

2. In a school near you, interview teachers and administrators to identify the dominant teachers' organization. Arrange an interview with the organization's leader(s). Develop an interview protocol of five questions. Possible questions include the following:
   a. What is your organization doing to improve working conditions for teachers?
   b. What benefits would I receive by becoming a member of your organization?
   c. What is your organization's position on the employment of teachers who do not qualify for a regular teacher's license or certificate?
   d. What is your organization's position on the courses and experience that should be required for teacher certification?

## MyEducationLab

Go to Topic 11, **Professional Development**, in the MyEducationLab (www.myeducationlab.com) for *Foundations of American Education*, where you can:

- Find learning outcomes for professional development along with the national standards that connect to these outcomes.
- Complete Assignments and Activities that can help you more deeply understand the chapter content.
- Apply and practice your understanding of the core teaching skills identified in the chapter with the Building Teaching Skills and Dispositions learning units.
- Examine challenging situations and cases presented in the IRIS Center Resources.

- Access additional video clips of CCSSO National Teachers of the Year award winners responding to the question, "Why Do I Teach?" in the Teacher Talk section.
- Check your comprehension on the content covered in the chapter with the Study Plan. Here you will be able to take a chapter quiz, receive feedback on your answers, and then access Review, Practice, and Enrichment activities to enhance your understanding of chapter content.
- Use the Online Lesson Plan Builder to practice lesson planning and integrating national and state standards into your planning.

# The Major Philosophies

It is late Friday afternoon and classes have been dismissed at John F. Kennedy High School. A few students remain in the chemistry laboratory cleaning equipment and in the visual arts and industrial arts classrooms putting finishing touches on semester projects that are due Monday. The sound of a lonely basketball dribbling in the gymnasium echoes down the corridor. The school seems rather eerie in its stark quietude—a far cry from the loud sounds and activities of an hour before.

The faculty lounge also is empty except for a group of four teachers engaged in a heated discussion. Ms. Jenkins, who has taught an introductory biology course for 7 years, appears agitated over the school district's new policy concerning electives. She makes a passionate argument to the rest of her colleagues at the table, alleging that it is a mistake to allow students a choice in determining their own program of study. Her major thesis is that adolescents are not capable of making such choices and, if left to their own whims, they will opt for the easiest, least demanding courses and will avoid the mathematics, life science, and physical science courses that most colleges and universities require. Mr. Rhodes, a soft-spoken and gentle individual who has taught courses in anthropology, sociology, and psychology for 3 years, attempts to argue an opposing viewpoint. He directs his comments to the entire group, but his attention is focused primarily on Ms. Jenkins. His counterargument is that adolescents, and even very young children, are capable of decision making. In fact, according to Mr. Rhodes, most individuals, if left on their own, will choose what is good for them and are capable of making high-quality educational decisions at a very early age.

Do you agree with Ms. Jenkins or Mr. Rhodes? What additional arguments might you give to support your position?

The opposing viewpoints expressed by these teachers regarding decision making and choice are examples of basic philosophic issues. Their different points of view concerning choice reflect both their personal philosophies as well as their philosophies of education.

For many, philosophy connotes a certain type of abstract or theoretical thinking that seems far removed from the day-to-day life of the elementary or secondary classroom teacher. However, every teacher and every classroom reflects a set of assumptions about the world. Those principles or assumptions comprise one's personal philosophy as well as one's educational philosophy. In this chapter, we will outline some of the basic philosophic questions and review the major traditional philosophies (idealism, realism, and neo-Thomism) and contemporary (pragmatism and existentialism) philosophies. Last, we will describe the analytic approach to the study of philosophy, along with its application to educational practice.

As you study the philosophies outlined in this chapter, you may begin to question your personal philosophy. To help you better understand the philosophies and where your personal philosophy fits within that framework, consider the following objectives:

- Describe the three branches of philosophy.
- Compare the metaphysics of idealism, realism, neo-Thomism, pragmatism, and existentialism.
- Compare the epistemology of idealism, realism, neo-Thomism, pragmatism, and existentialism.
- Compare the axiology of idealism, realism, neo-Thomism, pragmatism, and existentialism.
- Identify the philosophies that take an optimistic view of human nature and those that take a pessimistic view.
- Explain philosophic analysis in education.
- Discuss your philosophy of life and how it has changed over time.
- Explain the relationship between personal philosophy and philosophy of education.
- Identify the common principles of Eastern philosophies.

## MyEducationLab

Visit the MyEducationLab for *Foundations of American Education* to enhance your understanding of chapter concepts with a personalized Study Plan. You'll also have the opportunity to hone your teaching skills through video and case based Assignments and Activities, and Building Teaching Skills and Disposition lessons.

## What Is Philosophy?

One formal definition of philosophy as a discipline of inquiry states that philosophy is "the study of the fundamental nature of knowledge, reality, and existence" (*New Oxford American Dictionary*, 2005, p. 1278). Perhaps the simplest, yet comprehensive, definition is that philosophy is the "love of wisdom and the search for it."

The formal study of philosophy enables us as human beings to better understand who we are, why we are here, and where we are going. Whereas our personal philosophy of life enables us to recognize the meaning of our personal existence, our **philosophy of education** enables us to recognize certain educational principles that define our views about the learner, the teacher, and the school. To teach without a firm understanding of one's personal philosophy and philosophy of education would be analogous to painting a portrait without the rudimentary knowledge and skills of basic design, perspective, or human anatomy. Although you may not have thought about your personal philosophy in a formal sense, you certainly have personal beliefs that have shaped your life. After you have studied and discussed this chapter, you should be able to better articulate your personal philosophy of life.

## Branches of Philosophy

Although there is much debate and little agreement about which of the schools of philosophy is most accurate, relevant, or even complete, there is general agreement concerning the basic components or branches of philosophy: metaphysics, epistemology, and axiology. These branches are concerned with the answers to the following three basic questions that are important in describing any philosophy:

- What is the nature of reality?
- What is the nature of knowledge?
- What is the nature of values?

The framework these questions provide enables us to use a descriptive approach to study the major schools of philosophy. These branches and questions are discussed in the following section and summarized in Figure 3.1.

**Figure 3.1 — Summary of Branches of Philosophy**

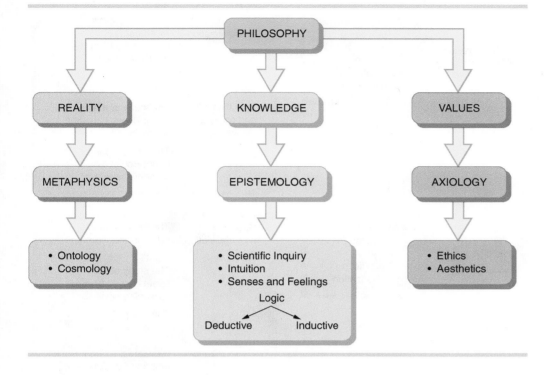

## Metaphysics: What Is the Nature of Reality?

Of the three basic questions, *What is the nature of reality?* is perhaps the most difficult to answer because the elements of reality are vague, abstract, and not easily identifiable. Despite its abstraction and vagueness, most philosophers would agree that the study of the nature of reality (meaning of existence) is one of the key concepts in understanding any philosophy.

The branch of philosophy that is concerned with the nature of reality and existence is known as **metaphysics**. Metaphysics is concerned with the question of the nature of the person or the self. It addresses such questions as whether human nature is basically good, evil, spiritual, mental, or physical.

Metaphysics can be subdivided into the areas of ontology and cosmology. **Ontology** raises fundamental questions about what we mean by the nature of existence and what it means for anything "to be." **Cosmology** raises questions about the origin and organization of the universe, or cosmos.

## Epistemology: What Is the Nature of Knowledge?

The branch of philosophy that is concerned with the investigation of the nature of knowledge is known as **epistemology**. To explore the nature of knowledge is to raise questions about the limits of knowledge, the sources of knowledge, the validity of knowledge, the cognitive processes, and how we know. There are several "ways of knowing," including experimental research, intuition, personal experience, sense perception, authority from an expert, and logic. **Logic** is a key dimension in the traditional philosophies. Logic is primarily concerned with making inferences, reasoning, or arguing in a rational manner, and logic includes the subdivisions of deduction and induction. **Deductive logic** is reasoning from a general statement or principle to a specific point or example. **Inductive logic**, on the other hand, is reasoning from a specific fact or facts to a generalization. Figure 3.2 further describes these two types of logic.

**For Your Reflection and Analysis**

Should schools concern themselves with questions regarding the origin of the universe? Why or why not?

**Figure 3.2 — Types of Logic**

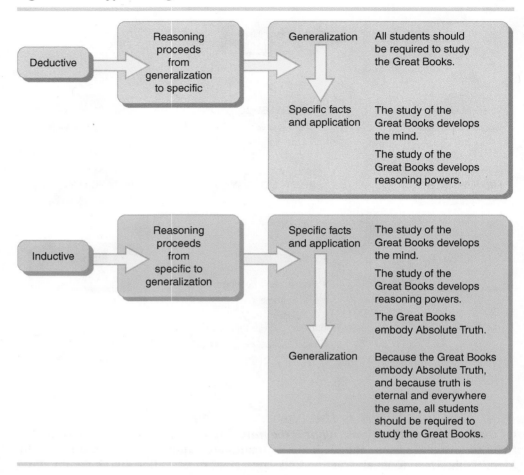

**Reflect on Diversity**
Give examples of diversity in the expression of the aesthetic experience between cultural and racial groups in the schools.

## Axiology: What Is the Nature of Values?

Whereas epistemology explores the question of knowledge, **axiology**—the study of the nature of values—seeks to determine what is of value. To evaluate, to make a judgment, to value literally means applying a set of norms or standards to human conduct or beauty. Axiology is divided into two spheres: ethics and aesthetics. **Ethics** is concerned with the study of human conduct and examines moral values—right, wrong, good, or bad. **Aesthetics** is concerned with values in beauty, nature, and the "aesthetic experience." The creative production of beauty is usually associated with music, art, literature, dance, theater, and the so-called fine arts.

One of the ongoing debates in education centers on the question of whether moral education, character education, ethics, or values education should be a responsibility of the school. The accompanying Controversial Issue feature poses arguments for and against the place of moral education, character education, ethics, or values education in the classroom; the Ask Yourself feature on page 58 lists a number of questions that are asked by the three branches of philosophy. The questions provide a framework for you to examine and perhaps articulate your own philosophy of life. Your answers to these questions also reflect some of the basic assumptions you hold about the purpose of schooling, what should be taught and how, the nature of the learner, and the role of the teacher. Your philosophy of life and philosophy of education are interdependent and provide a basis for your view of life, as well as your view of teaching.

# CONTROVERSIAL ISSUE

*Should Moral Education, Character Education, or Values Education Be a Responsibility of the School?*

Although axiology, or the study of values, is a major component or branch of all philosophies, the question of whether moral education, character education, or values education should be taught in the school is a controversial issue today. This is despite the fact that through most of American history, the didactic teaching of moral values, including religious values, has been considered to be a basic feature of the school. The No Child Left Behind Act's support for the teaching of character education has brought the topic more squarely into public debate.

Today, some parents and educators suggest that ethical questions and moral dilemmas do indeed have a place in the educational enterprise. Others have expressed strong opinions against the school's role in moral or values education. The arguments, pro and con, concerning moral education, character education, or values education are as follows:

**For**

1. The teaching of values is not a new phenomenon and follows the earlier works of Plato, Aristotle, Dewey, and Piaget, who linked values to cognitive development, which has a place in the classroom.

2. A character education curriculum is a powerful tool for teaching basic American values.

3. The discussion of moral dilemmas integrates critical thinking and ethics, developing moral reasoning skills.

4. The school is the best place for assisting learners to understand their own attitudes, preferences, and values. The role of the school is to help students sort through value confusion so they can live by their values.

5. Students should excel in their core academic subjects. They should also excel in the basic virtues or morals.

**Against**

1. The teaching of values is not the purview of the school, but that of the family and church, mosque, or synagogue.

2. Too many teachers lecture their students about the importance of certain "appropriate" values without demonstrating those values by their own actions or behaviors.

3. No individual is "valueless"; thus, all teachers, by the nature of their position, have the potential of imposing their values on their students.

4. The function of the school is to educate, not proselytize or indoctrinate; therefore, moral education, character education, and values education do not belong in the classroom.

What is your view of moral education, character education, or values education?

# Traditional Western Philosophies and Their Educational Implications

The so-called traditional philosophies include the oldest Western philosophies of idealism, realism, and theistic realism (neo-Thomism). These philosophies all include the belief in certain pre-established metaphysical truths.

## Idealism

**Idealism** is considered the oldest philosophy of Western culture, dating back to ancient Greece and Plato. For the idealist, the world of the mind, ideas, and reason is primary.

### Metaphysics

Idealism stresses mind over matter. For the idealist, nothing exists or is real except for an idea in the mind of the person or the mind of God, the Universal Mind. The universe can be explained as a creative and spiritual reality. One of the basic tenets of idealism is that mind is prior. When we seek what is ultimate in the world, if we push back behind the veil of immediate sense experience, we will find that what is ultimate in the universe is in the nature of mind or spirit, just as it is mind that is ultimate in the world of personal experience (Wingo, 1974).

If the mind is prior, in the sense that it is ultimate, then material things either do not exist (i.e., are not real), or, if they do exist, their existence depends in some

# ASK YOURSELF

## *What Is My Philosophy of Life?*

| Philosophic Questions | Branches of Philosophy |
|---|---|
| 1. Are human beings basically good, or is the essential nature of the human being evil? | What is the nature of reality? (Metaphysics—ontology) |
| 2. What causes certain events in the universe to happen? | What is the nature of reality? (Metaphysics—cosmology) |
| 3. What is your relationship to the universe? | What is the nature of reality? (Metaphysics—cosmology) |
| 4. What is your relationship to a higher being (God)? | What is the nature of reality? (Metaphysics—ontology) |
| 5. To what extent is your life basically free? | What is the nature of reality? (Metaphysics—ontology) |
| 6. How is reality determined? | What is the nature of reality? (Metaphysics—ontology) |
| 7. What is your basic purpose in life? | What is the nature of reality? (Metaphysics—ontology) |
| 8. How is knowledge determined? | What is the nature of knowledge? (Epistemology) |
| 9. What is truth? | What is the nature of knowledge? (Epistemology) |
| 10. What are the limits of knowledge? | What is the nature of knowledge? (Epistemology) |
| 11. What is the relationship between cognition and knowledge? | What is the nature of knowledge? (Epistemology) |
| 12. Are certain moral or ethical values universal? | What is the nature of values? (Axiology—ethics) |
| 13. How is beauty determined? | What is the nature of values? (Axiology—aesthetics) |
| 14. What constitutes aesthetic value? | What is the nature of values? (Axiology—aesthetics) |
| 15. Who determines what is right, just, or good? | What is the nature of values? (Axiology—ethics) |

fashion on the mind. For example, an idealist would contend that there is no such thing as a chair; there is only the idea of a chair.

The idealist's concept of reality considers the self as one in mind, soul, and spirit. Such a nature is capable of emulating the Absolute or Supreme Mind.

### Epistemology

Because idealism accepts a primarily mental explanation for its metaphysics or reality, it is not surprising that idealists also accept the premise that all knowledge includes a mental grasp of ideas and concepts. And, because the mind is the primary reality, it is important to master the science of logic because logic provides the framework for unifying our thoughts. Although traditional idealists consider reason, logic, or revelation to be the primary ways of "knowing," modern idealists also accept intuition as a way of knowing.

Some idealists believe that the search for truth, rather than truth itself, is the ultimate challenge. But, they also believe that most of us resort to the lowest level

**For Your Reflection and Analysis**

If you were an idealist, what eternal ideas would you recommend be taught in the schools?

(mere opinions about truth) and never reach "Ultimate Truth." Nonetheless, although we may never grasp Ultimate Truth, we do have the potential to aspire to wisdom, to improve the quality of our ideas, and to move closer to Ultimate Truth.

## Axiology

For the idealists, values are rooted in existence and are part of reality. Idealists contend that values are absolute and eternal; there are universal standards of moral behavior that have been applied throughout history and apply equally to all people everywhere. What is good and beautiful does not depend on where or when you live. Goodness, truth, and beauty are found in the absolute goodness, truth, and beauty found in nature (Gutek, 2004). Figure 3.3 provides an overview of idealism and its educational implications.

Although we may never grasp Ultimate Truth, we have the potential to aspire to wisdom.

## Leading Proponents

The Greek philosopher Plato (428–347 B.C.), a disciple of Socrates, is considered the father of idealism, a philosophy he taught to students from all over Greece (see the Historical Note, "Plato's Academy" on page 60). Plato believed that individuals should be attentive to the search for truth, which is perfect and eternal and cannot be found in matter because it is uncertain and subject to change. In his famous "Allegory of the Cave," found in *The Republic* (1958/360 B.C.), Plato implied that each of us lives in a cave of shadows, doubts, and distortions about reality. However, through education and enlightenment, the real world of pure ideas can be substituted for those distorted shadows and doubts.

Judaism and Christianity were both influenced by the philosophy of idealism. Judeo-Christian teaching suggests that ultimate reality could be found in God through the soul. Augustine (354–430), a prominent theologian of the fourth and fifth centuries, applied a number of Plato's assumptions to Christian thought, providing the rationale for the religious idealism that influenced Western thought for centuries (Ozmon, 2012).

Idealist thought influenced the writings of a number of major philosophers, including René Descartes, Immanuel Kant, and Georg Wilhelm Friedrich Hegel. The French philosopher Descartes (1596–1650), in his famous dictum *"Cogito, ergo sum"* (I think, therefore I am), declared that as humans we may doubt everything, but we

**Figure 3.3 — Idealism at a Glance**

| The Nature of Reality (Metaphysics) | The Nature of Knowledge (Epistemology) | The Nature of Values (Axiology) | The Nature of the Learner | Purpose of Schooling | Curriculum and Instruction |
|---|---|---|---|---|---|
| The mind and eternal ideas that represent perfect order | A rational, orderly body of truth | Absolute, eternal, and universal; a reflection of the ideal—God | A mind, soul, and spirit capable of emulating the Absolute Mind | Education should stress eternal ideas of the past and promote spiritual and intellectual development | The liberal arts and Great Books taught by lecture, discussion, and Socratic dialogue |

# HISTORICAL NOTE

## *Plato's Academy*

Contrary to the popular use of the word *academy* or the depiction in Raphael's fresco *The School of Athens*, shown at the beginning of Chapter 5, Plato's academy was not a formal institution of learning. Rather, the academy (*akademeia*) was the name of a beautiful public park named after the hero Akademos and located about a mile from the center of Athens. The area had been planted with olive trees and adorned with statues and temples, and it was the site of festivals and athletic contests.

About 387 B.C. Plato began writing and meeting his followers there. Eventually they took over the site and established a school for the study of philosophy and mathematics. Plato taught there for the next 40 years. Students came from all over Greece to study with Plato, but he accepted only those "intoxicated to learn what was in their souls"

(Planeaux, 1999, p. 2). Aristotle came to study at the *akademeia* and stayed 20 years. Once at the *akademeia*, a student listened as Plato walked about the gardens reading from his *Dialogues* (philosophical discussions or debates) and lecturing, "and they all enjoyed moderate but pleasant banquets. . . . The meals were conducted according to an elaborate set of rules, but Platon (sic) did not hold these feasts simply to celebrate to dawn. He held his banquets so that he [and his companions] might manifestly honor the gods and enjoy each other's company and chiefly to refresh themselves with learned discussion" (Planeaux, 1999, p. 2).

When Plato died in 427 B.C., he was buried on the grounds of the *akademeia*. Headed by a series of individuals elected for life, the *akademeia* continued unto Roman times.

**Reflect on Diversity**
To what extent have other religions such as Islam been influenced by the philosophy of idealism?

### For Your Reflection and Analysis

Can you think of examples of categorical imperatives that might be espoused by idealists and that would be relevant to education today?

cannot doubt our own existence. Descartes not only accepted the place of the finite mind and ideas as advanced by Plato, but he also determined that all ideas, save one, depend on other ideas. The only idea that does not depend on any idea other than itself is the idea of a Perfect Being or God. The process used by Descartes, later known as the **Cartesian method**, involved the derivation of axioms on which theories could be based by the purposeful and progressive elimination of all interpretations of experience except those that are absolutely certain. This method came to influence a number of fields of inquiry, including the sciences (Ozmon, 2012).

Immanuel Kant (1724–1804) also incorporated the major tenets of idealism into his thinking. Kant believed there were certain universal moral laws, known as **categorical imperatives**, which guide our actions or behaviors. One of Kant's categorical imperatives was "treat each person as an end and never as a mere means." This moral maxim became one of the primary principles in moral training or character development in education (Ozmon, 2012).

The German philosopher Hegel (1770–1831) approached reality as a "contest of opposites" such as life and death, love and hate, individual and society. According to Hegel, each idea (thesis) had its own opposite (antithesis). The confrontation between the thesis (e.g., man is an end in himself) and its antithesis (e.g., man cannot be merely an end to himself—he must also live for others) produces a resolution or synthesis (e.g., man fulfills his true end by serving others). This synthesis becomes a new thesis, which when crossed with a new antithesis, forms a new synthesis, and so on (Morris & Pai, 1976).

## Realism

**Realism**, like idealism, is one of the oldest philosophies of Western culture, dating back to ancient Greece and the time of Aristotle. Classical or Aristotelian realism is the antithesis of idealism. For the realist, the universe exists whether or not the human mind perceives it. Matter is primary and is considered an independent reality. The world of things is superior to the world of ideas.

### Metaphysics

Realism stresses the world of nature or physical things and our experiences and perceptions of those things. For the realist, reality is composed of both matter (body) and form (mind). Matter can be shaped or organized into being only through the mind. Moreover, the interaction of matter and form is governed not by God but by scientific, natural laws. Unlike the idealists, who believe *reality* is in the mind and internal, realists believe reality is external and can be verified.

### Epistemology

The major ways of knowing for realists are perception, rational thinking, and sensing. **Sense realism** is a school of realism that asserts that knowledge comes through the senses, which gather data and transmit them to the mind to be sorted, classified, and categorized. From these data we make generalizations. Some realists, such as Aristotle, believed that perception (knowledge through the senses) was not sufficient to understand reality. Aristotle argued that the use of deductive logic is more effective than perception in understanding the physical world. The process of deduction entails the establishment of a first or major premise, followed by a second or minor premise, and the drawing of a conclusion (*syllogism*) from them. For other realists, knowledge is established by the **scientific method**, which includes the systematic reporting and analysis of what is observed and the testing of hypotheses formulated from the observations.

### Axiology

Realists believe that values are derived from nature. Natural law and moral law are the major determinants of what is good; that which is good is dependent on leading a virtuous life, one in keeping with these natural or moral laws.

Although realism does not adhere to any hard and fast set of rules, realists believe that deviating from moral truth will cause injury both to persons and to society. To protect the common good, certain codes of conduct or social laws have been written and must be followed (Power, 1982).

For the realist, aesthetics is the reflection of nature. What is valued is that which reflects the orderliness and rationality of nature. Figure 3.4 provides an overview of realism and its educational implications.

### Leading Proponents

Aristotle (384–322 B.C.), a pupil of Plato, is considered the father of realism. Aristotle disagreed with Plato's premise that only ideas are real. For Aristotle, reality, knowledge, and value exist independent of the mind and their existence is not predicated by our ideas. Aristotle believed that knowledge can be acquired through the senses and that to obtain knowledge one had to first understand the physical world (Dunn, 2005).

> **For Your Reflection and Analysis**
>
> Consider yourself a realist. To what extent might you use the scientific method as a basis of inquiry in a beginning music class? In a class of preschoolers?

### Figure 3.4 — Realism at a Glance

| The Nature of Reality (Metaphysics) | The Nature of Knowledge (Epistemology) | The Nature of Values (Axiology) | The Nature of the Learner | Purpose of Schooling | Curriculum and Instruction |
|---|---|---|---|---|---|
| Physical things or nature and our experience or perception of those things | The discovery of logical, orderly truth of the external world via sensing and the scientific method | Natural law or moral law governing what is good | An orderly, sensing, and rational being capable of understanding the world of things | Develop reason, teach natural law, and help students master the principles of scientific inquiry | Liberal arts and sciences taught through lecture, discussion, and scientific method |

Today's students follow the precepts of Aristotle by formulating, testing, and discovering knowledge through the scientific method.

Two other advocates of realism were Francis Bacon (1561–1626) and John Locke (1632–1704). Bacon, a philosopher and politician, advanced a rigorous form of inductive reasoning that included empirical observation, analysis of observed data, inference leading to hypotheses, and verification of hypotheses through observation and experimentation (Dunn, 2005). Locke followed a similar path; his advocacy of realism stemmed from his study of knowledge. Locke was a proponent of the theory of the *tabula rasa* first proposed by the Islamic scholar Avicenna (980–1037). The theory of tabula rasa proposes that there are no such things as innate ideas. When we enter the world, our mind is like a blank sheet of paper, a *tabula rasa*. Knowledge is acquired not by the mind, but by the use of our five senses and reflection (Ozmon, 2012).

Other major philosophers who contributed to realism were the Czech educator and theologian John (Jan) Amos Comenius (1592–1670), and Jean-Jacques Rousseau (1712–1778), a French philosopher known for his political and educational theories (both discussed in Chapter 5). Another realist and follower of Rousseau was Johann Heinrich Pestalozzi (1746–1827), a Swiss educator known for his child-centered philosophy discussed in Chapter 6. Pestalozzi and Rousseau had a profound influence on the progressive educators of the early 20th century.

## Neo-Thomism

The third of the traditional philosophies is **neo-Thomism**. Neo-Thomism, or its antecedent, Thomism, dates to the time of Thomas Aquinas (1225–1274). Neo-Thomism, also referred to as **theistic realism**, incorporates both theism (belief in God) and realism (belief in objective reality guided by rational law) (Gutek, 2004). For the neo-Thomist, God exists and can be known through faith and reason.

### Metaphysics

Neo-Thomists believe that God gives meaning and purpose to the universe. God is the Pure Being that represents the coming together of essence and existence. Things exist independently of ideas. However, both physical objects and human beings, including minds and ideas, are created by God. Thus, although both

**Figure 3.5 — Neo-Thomism at a Glance**

| The Nature of Reality (Metaphysics) | The Nature of Knowledge (Epistemology) | The Nature of Values (Axiology) | The Nature of the Learner | Purpose of Schooling | Curriculum and Instruction |
|---|---|---|---|---|---|
| Physical objects and human beings, including our minds and ideas, are a creation of God | Faith and reason enable us to know God | Goodness follows reason. Beauty follows knowledge. Ignorance is the source of evil | A rational being with a soul modeled after God, perfection | Cultivate the intellect and develop spirituality through a relationship with God | Basic skills, liberal arts, and theology taught through drill and practice, demonstration, and recitation |

physical objects and God are real, God is pre-eminent. Neo-Thomists conceive of the essential nature of human beings as rational beings possessing souls, modeled after God, the Perfect Being.

### Epistemology

Although some philosophers believe that one can come to know God only through faith or intuition, neo-Thomists believe that it is through both our faith and our capacity to reason that we come to know God. They also believe there is a hierarchy of knowing. At the lowest level is scientific or synthetic knowing. At the second level is analytic or intuitive knowing. At the highest level is mystical or revelatory knowing (Morris & Pai, 1976). Thomas Aquinas clarified that truth or knowledge could not deviate from, or be inconsistent with, revelation (Jacobsen, 2003).

### Axiology

For the neo-Thomist, ethically speaking, goodness follows reason. That is, values are unchanging moral laws established by God that can be discerned by reason. As a corollary, ignorance is the source of evil. If people do not know what is right, they cannot be expected to do what is right. If, on the other hand, people do know what is right, they can be held morally responsible for what they do. In terms of aesthetics, the reason, or intellect, is also the perceiver of beauty: that which is valued as beautiful is also found pleasing to the intellect (Morris & Pai, 1976). Figure 3.5 provides an overview of neo-Thomism and its educational implications.

### Leading Proponents

Thomas Aquinas, the 13th-century theologian from whom neo-Thomism takes its name, is credited with interfacing the secular ideas of Aristotle and the Christian teachings of Augustine. Aquinas, like Aristotle, viewed reality via reason and sensation. Aquinas believed God created matter out of nothing and gave meaning and purpose to the universe. In his most noted work, *Summa Theologica*, he used the rational approach suggested by Aristotle to answer various questions regarding existence and Christianity. Aquinas found no conflict between finding truth via faith and reason and finding truth via rational observation and study. Many of the supporting arguments of Christian beliefs rely on Aquinas' works, and Roman Catholicism considers Thomism its leading philosophy (Ozmon, 2012).

# Contemporary Philosophies and Their Educational Implications

The modern or contemporary philosophies have their beginnings in the early 20th century and include pragmatism, existentialism, and analytic philosophy. These philosophies share the belief that there are no pre-established truths. At best there is a relative truth.

## *Pragmatism*

**Pragmatism**, also known as **experimentalism**, focuses on experience or the things that work. Primarily viewed as a philosophy of the 20th century developed by Americans such as Charles Pierce and John Dewey (see Chapter 7), pragmatism has its roots in European and ancient Greek tradition.

### Metaphysics

Unlike traditional philosophers, who view reality as a given, pragmatists regard reality as an event, a process, a verb (Morris & Pai, 1976). As such, it is subject to constant change and lacks absolutes. Meaning is derived from experience, which is simply an interaction with one's environment (Garrison, 1994).

### Epistemology

According to pragmatism's theory of knowledge, truth is not absolute but is determined by function or consequences. In fact, pragmatists shun the use of the word *truth* and at best speak of a "tentative truth" that will serve the purpose until experience evolves a new truth. Knowledge is arrived at by scientific inquiry, testing, questioning, and retesting—and is never conclusive.

### Axiology

Whereas traditional philosophers concentrate on metaphysics and epistemology, pragmatists focus primarily on axiology or values. As with truths, values to the pragmatist are only tentative. They are constructed from experience and are subject to testing, questioning, and retesting. For the pragmatist, whatever works, or leads to desirable consequences, is ethically or morally good. The focus on consequences is not to imply that the pragmatist is concerned only with what works for the self. In fact, the pragmatist is concerned with social consequences. "What works" is what works for the larger community. For Dewey, democracy was the key component of pragmatism. He was convinced that democracy could not exist without community. Democracy is more than government; it includes a free community capable of influencing the political, social, and economic institutions that affect its citizenry (Brosio, 2000).

Regarding aesthetic values, for pragmatists what is beautiful is not determined by some objective ideal but by what we experience when we see, feel, and touch. Accordingly, art is a creative expression and shared experience between the artist and the public. Figure 3.6 presents an overview of pragmatism and its educational implications.

### Leading Proponents

In the 19th century, the two individuals who had the greatest impact on pragmatist philosophy were Auguste Comte (1798–1857) and Charles Darwin (1809–1882). Comte influenced pragmatism by suggesting that science could solve social problems. For pragmatists, problem solving is a key ingredient in scientific inquiry. Darwin's theory of natural selection implied that reality was open ended, not fixed, and subject to change. Pragmatists applied Darwin's ideas to education, which they inferred was also open-ended and subject to biological and social development (Ozmon, 2012).

Pragmatism is primarily associated with the Americans Charles Peirce (1839–1914), William James (1842–1910), and John Dewey (1859–1952). Peirce, a mathematician and logician, believed that true knowledge depends on verification of ideas through experience. Ideas are merely hypotheses until tested by experience. Peirce regarded

**For Your Reflection and Analysis**

An 80-year-old woman who is dying of cancer has requested assistance from her son, husband, physician, and the Hemlock Society to aid her in the design of her suicide. How might a pragmatist deal with this ethical dilemma?

**Figure 3.6 — Pragmatism at a Glance**

| The Nature of Reality (Metaphysics) | The Nature of Knowledge (Epistemology) | The Nature of Values (Axiology) | The Nature of the Learner | Purpose of Schooling | Curriculum and Instruction |
|---|---|---|---|---|---|
| Experience and interaction with environment | Tentative truth determined by the scientific method or function | Ethical conduct and moral codes are determined by what works; aesthetics are determined by experimental consequences | An evolving and active being capable of interacting with the environment | Education should stress function or experience; model a democratic society | An integrated curriculum taught through problem solving, group projects, and discussion |

learning, believing, and knowing as intimate parts of doing and feeling and lamented that educators often ignored this important relationship (Garrison & Neiman, 2003).

William James, a psychologist and philosopher, incorporated his view of pragmatism into both psychology and philosophy. James emphasized the centrality of experience. According to James, there are no absolutes, no universals, only an ever-changing universe. He suggested that experience should take precedence over abstractions and universals because experience is open ended, pluralistic, and in process (Ozmon, 2012).

James's contemporary, John Dewey, had the greatest influence on American pragmatism. As discussed in more detail in Chapter 4, for Dewey (1916), experience was also central. Dewey's major contribution to pragmatism was "to complete the alignment of pragmatism with science and elevate science as the primary mode of knowledge in the modern world" (Winn & Grinell, 2008, p. 161). Dewey's scientism is extended to the work of Richard Rorty (1931–2007). In the rapidly changing

The teaching of Dewey is evident in classrooms where children actively participate in projects and social activities.

world following World War II, Rorty contended that reality derived from inquiry and that changing times can produce changing realities.

## Existentialism

**Existentialism** appeared as a revolt against the mathematical, scientific, and objective philosophies that preceded it. Existentialism voices disfavor with any effort directed toward social control or subjugation. Existentialism focuses on personal and subjective existence. For the existentialist, the world of existence, choice, and responsibility is primary.

### Metaphysics

Unlike the realists and neo-Thomists, who believe that essence precedes existence, the existentialist believes that existence precedes essence. For the existentialist there is neither meaning nor purpose to the physical universe. We are born into the universe by chance. Moreover, according to existentialism, because there is no world order or natural scheme of things into which we are born, we owe nothing to nature but our existence (Kneller, 1971). Because we live in a world without purpose, we must create our own meaning (Gutek, 1988).

In addition to existence, the concept of choice is central to the metaphysics of existentialism. To decide who and what we are is to decide what reality is. Is it God? Reason? Nature? Science? By our choices we determine reality. According to existentialists, we cannot escape from the responsibility to choose, including the choice of how we view our past.

### Epistemology

Similar to their position concerning reality, existentialists believe that the way we come to know truth is by choice. The individual self must ultimately decide what is true and how we know. Whether we choose logic, intuition, the scientific method, or revelation is irrelevant; what matters is that we must eventually choose. The freedom to choose carries with it a tremendous burden of responsibility that we cannot escape. Because there are no absolutes, no authorities, and no single or correct way to the truth, the only authority is the authority of the self.

### Axiology

For the existentialist, choice is imperative, not only for determining reality and knowledge but also for determining value. Every act and every word is a choice and hence an act of value creation. And here is the dilemma, say the existentialists: because there are no norms, standards, or assurances that we have chosen correctly or rightly, choice is at times frustrating and exasperating. It is often much easier to be able to look to a standard or benchmark to determine what is right, just, or of value than to take responsibility for the choices we have made. Yet, the existentialists suggest, this is a very small price we pay for our free will. Figure 3.7 presents an overview of existentialism and its educational implications.

### Leading Proponents

The leading proponent, indeed the "father of existentialism," was the Danish philosopher–theologian Soren Kierkegaard (1813–1855). Kierkegaard renounced scientific objectivity for subjectivity and personal choice. He believed in the reality of God and was concerned with individual existence.

Another expositor of existentialism was Martin Buber (1878–1965), a Jewish philosopher–theologian. He incorporated the principle described as an "I-Thou" relationship whereby each individual recognizes the other's personal meaning and reality. Buber suggested that both the divine and human are related, and that through personal relationships with others, one can enhance one's spiritual life and relationship with God (Ozmon, 2012).

## Figure 3.7 — Existentialism at a Glance

| The Nature of Reality (Metaphysics) | The Nature of Knowledge (Epistemology) | The Nature of Values (Axiology) | The Nature of the Learner | Purpose of Schooling | Curriculum and Instruction |
|---|---|---|---|---|---|
| Existence precedes essence; the individual determines personal reality by choice | The individual is responsible for personal knowledge | Values consist of personal choices | A free individual capable of authentic and responsible choices | Education should stress individual responsibility and choice | Humanities, values education taught through self-discovery, decision making, and the Socratic method |

Also contributing to existential thought were Edmund Husserl (1859–1938) and Martin Heidegger (1889–1976). Husserl focused his attention on philosophy as an empirical study of meaning through what he termed "intuitive conscious experience." According to Husserl, to get to this level of consciousness, one must strip away the assumptions and presuppositions of the culture and get back to the immediate original consciousness. He referred to this method as **phenomenology**. Heidegger expanded and revised phenomenology to create another philosophical method known as **hermeneutics**, or the interpretation of lived experience (Ozmon, 2012). Phenomenology had a major influence on the critical theory and postmodern movements that followed.

Undoubtedly, the most widely known existentialist was Jean-Paul Sartre (1905–1980). Sartre claimed that free choice implies total responsibility for one's own existence. There are no antecedent principles or purposes that shape our destiny. Responsibility for our existence extends to situations of the gravest consequence, including the choice to commit suicide. Sartre's major philosophic work, *Being and Nothingness* (1956), is considered one of the major philosophic treatises of the 20th century. According to Sartre, because there is no God to give existence meaning, humanity exists without any meaning until we construct our own.

Existentialism had a major impact on educators such as John Holt (1981), Charles Silberman (1970), and Jonathan Kozol (1972, 1991), who were supporters of the open schools, free schools, and alternative schools that flourished during the mid-1960s. One of the best-known educational existentialists was A. S. Neill (1883–1973), who founded Summerhill School outside London shortly after World War I. Summerhill offered an educational experience built on the principle of learning by discovery in an atmosphere of unrestricted freedom (Neill, 1960).

One of the current spokespersons for the existential philosophy of education and one of the leading educational philosophers of the last half of the twentieth century is Maxine Greene (b. 1917). Greene has consistently reiterated the existential challenge to examine ourselves, what some existentialists call *wide awakeness*; according to Greene (2008), "without the ability to think about yourself, to reflect on your own life, there's really no awareness, no consciousness" (p. 1). The role of education is to nurture "a specific kind of reflectiveness and expressiveness, a reaching out for meanings, a learning to learn" (Greene, 2001, p. 7).

The search for meaning, purpose in life, and individual existence continues to challenge contemporary youth.

## Analytic Philosophy

As we study the major philosophies and their corollary educational theories, it becomes evident that these descriptive schools of thought, or "isms" as they are often called, are very broad in their aims, are quite eclectic, and at times appear to lack clarity. Critics of the descriptive approach to philosophy point out that the philosophies of idealism, realism, neo-Thomism, and the like have major limitations in that they try to prescribe certain things and make normative judgments. Moreover, they render educational statements that are jargon-ridden and unverifiable. For these reasons, a number of philosophers began to move away from traditional thinking about philosophy and theory as disciplines and focused their attention on analytic philosophy or clarification of the language, concepts, and methods that philosophers use (Ozmon, 2012; Partelli, 1987). The resulting so-called analytic movement was less concerned with the underlying assumptions about reality, truth, and values addressed by descriptive philosophy than with the clarification, definition, and meaning of language. That is, analytic philosophers are not interested in which values are true, which behaviors are good, or which art is most beautiful. Rather, they are concerned with questions such as "Can these values or behaviors be tested empirically, and do the terms used have clear meaning to the reader?" as well as how people discuss and describe these values or behaviors.

Analysis in philosophy began in the post–World War I era when a group of European natural scientists and social scientists formed what became known as the Vienna Circle. These scholars were particularly concerned about the alienation between philosophy and science that existed at that time. One of the major outcomes of the work of the Vienna Circle was the clarification of the joint roles of both science and philosophy. For example, it was determined that if the testing of hypotheses through experimentation and observation were to be the purview or charge of science, then the proper role of philosophy should be the analysis of the logical syntax of scientific language (Magee, 1971).

The concept of **logical positivism**, or **logical empiricism**, grew out of the thinking of the Vienna Circle. One of the most important logical positivists was Ludwig Wittgenstein (1889–1951). Wittgenstein (1953) argued that the role of the sciences should be to discover true propositions and facts, whereas the role of philosophy should be to resolve confusion and clarify ideas. The assumptions that were made by the logical positivists became so rigid and restrictive that their popularity began to wane. Today, very few individuals identify themselves as logical positivists.

By the 1950s, logical positivism shifted to linguistic analysis, or the analytic philosophy movement. **Analytic philosophy** assumes that language statements have immediate meaning because of their inner logic, or that they have the possibility of being made meaningful by being stated in empirical terms that can be verified and tested. According to analytic philosophers, if language has no method of verification, it has no meaning. Many of the words or statements we use are emotional or subjective and have meaning specific to the person who used them (Gutek, 2004). For example, the terms *adaptation, inclusion, adjustment, professionalism, reform, growth,* and *tolerance* imply multiple meanings and would be defined in different ways by different disciplines. Similarly, in philosophy, statements such as "Existence precedes essence" or "Self-actualization is the highest goal for mankind" are not verifiable and hence have limited meaning.

An early spokesperson for the analytic philosophy movement was Israel Scheffler (b. 1923). In his first major work, *The Language of Education* (1960), Scheffler focused attention on how **philosophic analysis** can help teachers formulate their beliefs, arguments, and assumptions about topics that are particularly important to the teaching and learning process. Scheffler and other analytic philosophers concerned with education believed that each prospective teacher should learn the art or science of philosophic analysis. One of the first steps in learning this process is to raise questions about the assumptions we make, the values we hold, the theories we propose, the procedures we use, and the methods we trust.

**Reflect on Diversity**
How can teachers ensure that their language carries the intended meaning to students of different cultural and experiential backgrounds?

**For Your Reflection and Analysis**

Do you consider yourself to have an analytical temperament? Explain.

Since the 1970s, analytic philosophy has focused its attention on political philosophy, ethics, and philosophy of the human sciences. The impetus for this shift was to better understand the connections between concepts and ethical values. An example of some of the analytic work that has focused on complex ethical and political problems is an examination of "Who should have the right to determine the form and content of children's education? Should it be the state? Parents?" (White & White, 2001). The analytic approach to philosophy is the dominant trend in philosophy today (Shouler, 2008).

## The Major Eastern Philosophies

While the focus of this chapter has been on the major Western philosophies, to ignore the non-Western or Eastern philosophies would ignore their influence on Western philosophical thought. Unlike most Western philosophies, most Eastern philosophies are integrated with religion. Common principles of Eastern philosophies are the interconnectedness of all beings and parts of the cosmos; the importance of inner balance, peace and tranquility; living a virtuous life; and mysticism. Eastern philosophies stress meditation and searching inside oneself to discover the Absolute Truth which exists in the universe, what is valuable, and most importantly, to understand and control oneself. "He who conquers others is strong; he who conquers himself is mighty" (Lao Tzu). Another concept found in many of the Eastern philosophies is the concept of life as a journey of self-improvement. The major Eastern philosophies of Hinduism, Buddhism, Confucianism and Taoism are discussed in the following sections.

### Hinduism

Hinduism is both a religion (the oldest and third largest) and a philosophy. Hinduism represents a wide range of traditions and beliefs that have evolved over 3,000 years. Hinduism sees the entire universe as one divinity, the eternal, perfect, supreme reality that transcends all forms and that every person is divine. Hindus also believe in reincarnation, that the soul is transmitted to another body after death, and in karma—that what we experience in this life is the result of our actions in past lives (incarnations) and that our future incarnations will depend on how we live in our present life.

The four goals of life for a Hindu are (1) to observe moral law and spiritual discipline (*dharma*); (2) to obtain economic prosperity (*artha*); (3) to gratify the senses (*kama*); and (4) freedom from *samsara*, the cycle of reincarnations (*moksha*). Of these, *dharma* is the most important. To observe *dharma* 20 ethical guidelines are prescribed, 10 *yamas* or restraints (e.g., patience, honesty, sexual purity), and 10 *miyamas* or observances (modesty, charity, worship). "The purpose of *dharma* is not only to attain a union of the soul with the supreme reality, it also suggests a code of conduct that is intended to secure both worldly joys and supreme happiness" (Das, 2011, p. 1). Hinduism is the major religion of India, followed by 80% of its population.

### Buddhism

Buddhism as a philosophy is concerned with living a moral life. Meditation is the avenue to spiritual development and insight. Buddhism is based on the teachings of Siddhartha Gotama (566–486 B.C.). The teachings of Buddha are summarized in the Four Noble Truths: (1) to exist is to suffer (suffer disappointment, pain, fear, depression, etc.); (2) suffering is the result of craving or desiring things that have no permanence (e.g., passion, wealth, prestige) and whose loss is inevitable; (3) suffering can be ended by giving up these cravings and desires; (4) eliminating these desires and finding release from suffering is to reach *nirvana*. Nirvana can be achieved by following the Eightfold path or principles: (1) having a right view (seeing things as they really are); (2) a right intention (a commitment to ethical conduct); (3) right speech; (4) right action; (5) right livelihood (earning a righteous living);

(6) right effort; (7) right mindfulness (paying attention to one's own actions); and (8) right concentration, focusing through meditation. Buddhists, like Hindus, believe in karma and a cycle of reincarnations that only ends when one reaches nirvana. And, like most Eastern philosophies, Buddhism stresses harmony with the universe and pacifism. Although it began in India, most Buddhists today are found in China, Tibet, Korea, Japan, and other countries in Southeast Asia.

## Confucianism

A major philosophy of China is Confucianism, based on the teachings of Confucius (551–478 B.C.). As opposed to the other Eastern philosophies which place emphasis on connecting with the spiritual world, Confucianism is concerned with existence in this world and the issues inherent in relationships. There are five basic relationships in Confucianism: (1) ruler to subject, (2) father to son, (3) husband to wife, (4) elder brother to younger brother, and (5) friend to friend. Of these, the most important is father to son. Confucius developed a set of principles to guide social and ethical conduct in these relationships. One of the central tenets of Confucian philosophy is the principle of reciprocity, a negative formulation of the Christian Golden Role which says, "Do not do unto others what you would not have them do unto you."

Confucius taught that every individual should strive for continual self-improvement and to practice the Five Constant Virtues in their relationships with others: (1) benevolence, (2) propriety, (3) loyalty, (4) intellect, and (5) trust. These virtues, if practiced, would bring about a society based on the principles of wisdom and justice (Ozmon, 2012). While once the official philosophy of the Chinese emperors, the Communist takeover of China brought with it a suppression of Confucianism. Today its followers are found mainly in China, Japan, Korea, and Vietnam.

## Taoism

A third and complementary Chinese philosophy is Taoism. Most Chinese practice Taoism in conjunction with Confucianism. The Tao (the Way) is the ultimate, infinite, unchanging, and perfect force of nature that governs the cosmos. The Tao is often compared to a river—always fluid, moving along naturally, quietly, and cutting a path. One of the major principles of Taoism is *wu we*, the art of non-action, of yielding to the Tao. Yielding to Tao means one should not attempt to control life events but should let them flow along their natural path; i.e., "let nature take its course." In keeping with this philosophy, Taoists do not try to force their will or ideas on others; Taoists are non-aggressive and non-competitive.

Taoism is concerned with living a good and moral life in harmony with oneself and nature. Taoist teachings regarding proper and ethical conduct emphasize the practice of the Three Jewels of Taoism: compassion, moderation, and humility. Taoists believe that all things have an opposite, a *yin* and a *yang*. The *yin* is commonly described as black, feminine, passive, moon, while the *yang* is described as white, masculine, active, sun. When the *yin* and the *yang* are balanced in oneself or the university, there is harmony. Taoism emphasizes the importance of maintaining harmony as well as health and vitality through practices such as *tai chi*, meditative breathing, and acupuncture, all of which have gained popularity in the West. Ultimately, a happy and virtuous life results from being in harmony with Tao. Taoism is widely practiced in China but is also practiced in many other Asian countries and, indeed, wherever populations of Chinese are found.

## Summary

The study of philosophy enables us to better understand our philosophy of life. One of the most effective methods of developing a philosophy of life is to respond to three basic questions: What is the nature of reality? What is the nature of knowledge? What is the nature of values? These three questions and their accompanying responses comprise the branches of philosophy.

The philosophies of idealism, realism, and neo-Thomism are considered the classical or traditional philosophies, whereas pragmatism and existentialism represent the contemporary or modern philosophies. The traditional philosophies are more concerned with the past, truths, and absolutes, whereas the contemporary philosophies are more concerned with the present or future and do not subscribe to the idea of "absolute truths."

Although the study of descriptive philosophy provides a mechanism for translating basic philosophic tenets into educational practice, it is quite restrictive. Most philosophies are too broad in scope and lack precise meaning and clarity. Today, many philosophers and educators believe that a more effective way to study philosophy is by philosophic analysis, which is concerned with clarifying the language we use to describe our educational concepts and assumptions.

The origins of some of the major Eastern philosophies predate those of western philosophy. As compared to most Western philosophies, most Eastern philosophies are integrated with religion and are more concerned with the search for inner peace and harmony with the universe. The major Eastern philosophies are Hinduism, the major religion of India, and Buddhism, Confucianism, and Taoism, all practiced in China, Japan, Korea, and other nations of southeast Asia.

In the next chapter, we will examine how the traditional philosophic views have led to a number of theories of education. We will also explore the impact of these theories on educational programs and practices.

# PROFESSIONAL DEVELOPMENT *Workshop*

## *Prepare for the State Licensure Examination*

It was a typical Monday morning in late April. The 7:00 A.M. traffic had already slowed down to a snail's pace. The driver, José Santora, had been teaching American history at the same junior high school since he graduated from college 6 years earlier. For the past 3 years he had carpooled with three other teachers from the same school: Bruce Parlius, who taught social studies; Shana Cohen, a science teacher; and Cal Crane, an English teacher.

On this particular morning, Shana seemed very quiet and withdrawn. Cal asked Shana if there was something wrong. He had noticed she was not her usual animated self. There was a long silence. Finally, she answered by relaying the following incident. Over the weekend she had been shopping at the supermarket near the school when she ran into the principal, Phil Aronsky. Phil told her that late Friday afternoon he received a telephone call from the mother of one of her students. Phil explained that the mother was quite upset after learning from her son that Shana had spent the entire class period talking about the importance of evidence-based research in the sciences, especially medicine. Phil told Shana that the mother was irate because her son had come away from her class feeling that any alternative to science, relative to health and well-being, was not acceptable.

José was the first to speak. His words were carefully directed at Shana. "You know, I have been teaching history for the past six years. The first day of every class I always tell my students that there is no 'single' or 'right' interpretation of history. Each historian interprets the events from his or her own reality or experience. One of my goals is to teach tolerance and acceptance of different viewpoints. This lesson stretches beyond history. It impacts life in general."

Cal immediately added, "I never told you guys about the incident that happened to me two years ago. Shortly after I introduced a new unit on American literature, one of my seventh-grade students told his parents that I was a 'racist.' The student came to this conclusion based on my assigned reading of *The Adventures of Huckleberry Finn* by Mark Twain, which he inferred had deprecated his values, his family values, and the values of our country. I was called in by our former principal to explain my decision making relative to the assigned reading. What happened was that I had to meet with the parents of the seventh grader and explain why I felt it important for the students to read Twain's work."

Shana, who had been attentive to her colleagues' comments, said, "This whole experience has really soured me about teaching. I decided to become a teacher when I was in first grade. I loved school, I loved my teachers. And, I love teaching now. I was motivated to help others grow to love learning like I did. After this experience, I am beginning to have some doubts about my professional goals. If I have to justify every professional decision I make regarding the curriculum and what I choose to teach, then it is not worth it! I'd rather pursue some other profession and not have to put up with having to explain myself every time I make a professional decision."

Bruce, who was sitting in the back seat next to Shana, had been listening quietly to all the comments. He now spoke out: "Shana, I have not had the experiences that you, José, and Cal have had relative to the issue of professionalism and the right to choose the curriculum and assignments. So, on that level, I really cannot make any comment. But, I can tell you this. What is going on here is a difference in philosophy. It doesn't really have anything to do with professionalism. What is going on here is a variety of views about how we come to know what is 'right' and what is 'good,' for us and our students. In short, there is no 'right' answer because we are all right in making the choices we make even though those choices may contradict your choice or my choice. What is most important is that we are able to articulate to the student, parent, administration, and the public why we believe it is important that we teach what we teach. The bottom line is that we must be able to have a strong rationale for the decisions we make, knowing that oftentimes our decisions may be in direct conflict with another person's values or decisions. Shana, when you go into that meeting this afternoon and face both Phil and the mother of your student, you need to relax and just be your usual calm and articulate self. Tell the parent that you respect her values and her desire for the best education for her son. But, also communicate that as a teacher your role is to prepare her son to be able to tolerate and accept different viewpoints based on different philosophies, even though those viewpoints may contradict theirs. If we as teachers can get that lesson across, then we will have made one of the most important contributions to teaching and learning."

1. Which philosophies do you think are exemplified by Shana's classroom presentation on the importance of evidence-based research in science? Least exemplified? Give reasons why.

2. Do you agree or disagree with Bruce's conclusion that what is really at stake here is a difference in philosophies? Which philosophy would you attribute to Shana? To José? To Cal? To Bruce?

3. What advice would you give Shana in preparation for her meeting with her principal and the mother of her student?

4. How has your philosophy of life influenced your priorities and values?

## Build Your Knowledge Base

1. Consider the vignette at the beginning of this chapter. Which philosophy would you ascribe to Ms. Jenkins? To Mr. Rhodes? Explain.

2. Which of the philosophies discussed in this chapter is most like your own? In what ways? Which is the most unlike your own? In what ways?

3. List all the ways of knowing. Does what is to be known (i.e., the subject matter) dictate the approach to knowing? Explain.

4. Construct an argument using deductive logic (deductive reasoning) to explain the following statement: "Teaching does not imply education and education does not imply learning."

5. The metaphor "learning is essentially growing" depicts which philosophy? Name three other metaphors that depict three other major philosophies.

6. Give examples of words or phrases in your discipline that could be considered jargon or have subjective multiple meanings.

## Develop Your Portfolio

1. As a professional educator, one of the most important questions that you will be asked throughout your career is "What is your philosophy of education?" To help you begin to think about your philosophy of education, it is important to first consider some of the basic underlying philosophical questions about life such as those included in the Ask Yourself feature "What Is My Philosophy of Life?" Prepare a 2- to 3-page reflection paper titled "My Philosophy of Life." In your paper respond to the following questions: (a) Are human beings basically good or evil? (b) How is knowledge determined? (c) Are there certain moral or ethical values that are universal? Place the reflection paper in your portfolio under **INTASC Standard 4, Content Knowledge**.

2. Group Activity: Divide into groups of five. Each member of the group will research and prepare a response to the question "What kinds of educational activities best help students develop their thinking and reasoning skills?" from the point of view of one of the following philosophers: Plato, Aristotle, Thomas Aquinas, John Dewey, and Soren Kierkegaard. As a group discuss the various points of view. Record the discussion on audio or videotape. Following the discussion, each participant should prepare a reflection paper that summarizes the dialogue and includes his or her reactions and thoughts to the original question. Include which position or school of thought you tend to agree with the most, which you agree with the least, and what experiences or feelings influenced your position. Title your paper "Philosophy of Education" and place it in your portfolio under **INTASC Standard 4, Content Knowledge**.

## Explore Teaching and Learning: Field Experiences

1. Contact the principal of a nearby school and request a copy of the school's written mission, goals, and curriculum. See if you can identify the primary philosophic principles that undergird the school's approach to teaching and learning.

2. Interview three teachers at different grade levels on the topic of values education. Ask the following questions: What values guide you in your daily relationship with students? In your teaching, how do you model the values that you expect of your students? What values do you want students to practice in the classroom, on the playground, or in school activities?

## MyEducationLab

Go to Topic 7, **The History and Philosophy of Education**, in the MyEducationLab (www.myeducationlab.com) for *Foundations of American Education*, where you can:

- Find learning outcomes for the history and philosophy of education along with the national standards that connect to these outcomes.
- Complete Assignments and Activities that can help you more deeply understand the chapter content.
- Apply and practice your understanding of the core teaching skills identified in the chapter with the Building Teaching Skills and Dispositions learning units.
- Examine challenging situations and cases presented in the IRIS Center Resources.

- Access additional video clips of CCSSO National Teachers of the Year award winners responding to the question, "Why Do I Teach?" in the Teacher Talk section.
- Check your comprehension on the content covered in the chapter with the Study Plan. Here you will be able to take a chapter quiz, receive feedback on your answers, and then access Review, Practice, and Enrichment activities to enhance your understanding of chapter content.
- Use the Online Lesson Plan Builder to practice lesson planning and integrating national and state standards into your planning.

# The Impact of Educational Theories on Educational Practice

During a typical micro-teaching session in a methods class, three prospective teachers had just finished presenting 20-minute lessons in their subject field using the instructional technique of their choice. What surprised the instructor was that no two students had used the same technique.

Jim, a physical education major, had chosen demonstration as the major technique for his session on chipping in golf. Beth, an art major, had used the group project as the technique for her lesson on basic design; and Sam, a history major, had used lecture as the principal technique to teach about the Spanish–American War. During the class critique, all three students expressed how well prepared they felt they had been and how appropriate each of their instructional

techniques had proven to be. The class concurred with their self-assessments. Then, in a surprise move, Beth turned to Sam and added, "You know, even though I felt that your lesson on the Spanish–American War was excellent and your mini-lecture held my attention, I would not feel comfortable giving a lecture to an art class."

"What do you mean?" asked Sam, flabbergasted at her comment.

"Just what I said, Sam," Beth replied. "Maybe it's the subject matter of art or maybe it's just me. It just doesn't fit with basic design!"

Do you agree with Beth? What is the relationship between the preferred method or instructional technique used by teachers and their philosophy of education?

Like Beth, many students enrolled in pre-professional teacher education programs do not recognize the relationship between the study of philosophy and educational practice. One explanation for this is that much of the subject matter of teacher education is taught in a fragmented fashion, with little or no connection to theory and practice. As a result, the student or novice teacher is unable to discern how educational concepts such as the purpose of schooling, nature of the learner, curriculum, instructional methods, classroom management, assessment, and the role of the teacher are associated with both educational philosophy and one's philosophy of life. For, as Hogan and Smith (2003) point out, "no teacher, beginner or experienced, is wholly innocent of theory, of having an underlying philosophy" (p. 177).

In this chapter, you will be introduced to several major educational theories or *applied philosophies* and their impact on educational practice. Based on these theories and their application to practice, you will be encouraged to formulate your own philosophy of education. Information regarding the impact of the major educational theories on the purpose of schooling, nature of the learner, curriculum, instructional methods, classroom management, assessment, and the role of the teacher will be presented.

To help you study these important concepts, consider the following outcome objectives:

- Define an educational theory and explain its relationship to philosophy as a discipline.
- Identify the various underlying protests that led to the establishment of the theories of perennialism, progressivism, behaviorism, essentialism, social reconstructionism, and postmodernism.
- Compare the purpose of schooling from a perennialist, progressivist, behaviorist, essentialist, social reconstructionist, and a postmodernist perspective.
- Describe the nature of the learner from a perennialist, progressivist, behaviorist, essentialist, social reconstructionist, and a postmodernist perspective.
- Compare the curricula of perennialism, progressivism, behaviorism, essentialism, social reconstructionism, and postmodernism.
- Compare the instructional methods that characterize perennialism, progressivism, behaviorism, essentialism, social reconstructionism, and postmodernism.
- Compare the preferred classroom management methods of perennialism, progressivism, behaviorism, essentialism, social reconstructionism, and postmodernism.
- Compare the assessment strategies of perennialism, progressivism, behaviorism, essentialism, social reconstructionism, and postmodernism.
- Describe the role of the teacher from a perennialist, progressivist, behaviorist, essentialist, social reconstructionist, and a postmodernist perspective.
- Formulate your educational theory (philosophy of education).

Having examined the assumptions that underlie the major philosophies, it is now appropriate to examine how these basic assumptions translate to educational theories and practice. The major traditional and contemporary philosophies that were discussed in Chapter 3 each have a corollary educational theory. It is the combination of philosophy and theory that will enable you to frame your own philosophy of education.

## MyEducationLab

Visit the MyEducationLab for *Foundations of American Education* to enhance your understanding of chapter concepts with a personalized Study Plan. You'll also have the opportunity to hone your teaching skills through video and case based Assignments and Activities, and Building Teaching Skills and Disposition lessons.

## Theories of Education

The term *theory* can be defined in two ways. First, a theory is a hypothesis or set of hypotheses that has been verified by observation or experiment. Second, a theory is a general synonym for systematic thinking or a set of coherent thoughts. Thus, a **theory of education** is a composite of systematic thinking or generalizations about schooling (Kneller, 1971). A well-thought-out theory of education is important, for it helps to explain our orientation to teaching and allows us to defend our position with respect to how learning takes place. In short, a theory of education enables teachers to explain what they are doing, and why. It provides academic accountability. As you become acquainted with each of the theories of education, you may conclude that most teachers incorporate several theories in their practice.

The major theories of education examined in this chapter are perennialism, progressivism, behaviorism, essentialism, social reconstructionism, and postmodernism. Each theory was developed as a protest against the prevailing social and educational climate of the time. For example, perennialism came about as a protest against secularization and the excessive focus on science and technology, at the expense of reason, that dominated society and its educational institutions at the time.

As you review each educational theory, keep in mind the similarities and differences among the theories and the reason or rationale behind the protest that led to its development.

# Perennialism

Eternal or perennial truths, permanence, order, certainty, rationality, and logic constitute the ideal for **perennialism**. The philosophies of idealism, realism, and neo-Thomism are embedded in the perennialist theory of education. The educational focus of perennialism is on the need to return to the past, namely, to universal truths and such absolutes as reason and faith. The views of Plato, Aristotle, and Thomas Aquinas are reflected in this educational theory. Although perennialism has been historically associated with the teachings of neo-Thomism, it has also received widespread support from lay educators.

## Purpose of Schooling

Perennialists consider the purpose of schooling is to teach the eternal truths, cultivate the rational intellect, and develop the spiritual nature of the individual. For the ecclesiastical perennialists, the highest goal of education is union with God. They also believe that education is preparation for life and that—although formal education may end—learning is a lifelong process.

## Nature of the Learner

Perennialists believe that all students are rational beings who exemplify value and worth. Ecclesiastical perennialists also believe that students have been endowed with both an intellect and a soul.

## Curriculum

For the ecclesiastical perennialist, Christian doctrine is an important aspect of the curriculum. The holy scriptures, the catechism, and the teaching of Christian dogma play a significant role. The cultivation of the intellect while stressing faith and reason through a relationship with God best describes the curriculum of the ecclesiastical perennialist.

Both ecclesiastical and lay (secular) perennialists emphasize a strong liberal arts curriculum that includes such cognitive subjects as philosophy; mathematics (especially algebra and geometry); history; geography; political science; sociology; theology, languages, and literature (in particular the **Great Books**); physical and life sciences; and the fine arts and humanities. Mastery of these subjects is considered necessary for the cultivation of the intellect. In addition, perennialists contend that character training and moral development have an appropriate place in the design of the curriculum.

More contemporary perennialists such as Mortimer Adler (1902–2001) have advocated a curriculum which is more general, with less emphasis on specific subject matter. Rather, they view the curriculum as the context for developing intellectual skills and emphasize the importance of teaching principles, which are unchanging, as opposed to details of fact which are ever-changing. These perennialists maintain that education involves confronting the problems and questions that have challenged people over the centuries.

## Instructional Methods

Adler (1984) suggested three specific methods of instruction: (1) didactic instruction, (2) coaching, and (3) the Socratic method described in Chapter 5. Each method is carefully chosen to develop the student's intellect.

Prior to studying the great works of literature, philosophy, history, mathematics, and science, students would be taught methods of critical thinking and questioning

> **For Your Reflection and Analysis**
>
> If you were a perennalist, what 10 books would you choose as the Great Books? At what grade level(s) should they be introduced to students?

Both Robert Hutchins (left) and Mortimer Adler (right) advocated the Great Books and the enduring lessons of the past.

strategies to prepare them to engage in "dialogue" with the classical writers. For the ecclesiastical perennialists, any type of teaching method that brings the learner into direct contact with the Supreme Being would be encouraged.

## Classroom Management

Perennialists are concerned with training not only the intellect, but also the will. They believe that the teacher has the obligation to discipline the student in order to train the will. They would consider the most appropriate classroom environment for training the will to be one that reinforces time on task, precision, and order. In addition to orderliness and structure, for the ecclesiastical perennialist the learning environment would also reflect an appreciation for prayer and contemplation.

## Assessment

The objective examination would be the favored evaluation tool of the perennialist teacher. Because the study of the classical tradition of the Great Books promotes an exchange of ideas and insights, the essay examination would also be used.

## The Perennialist Teacher

Perennialists view the teacher who is well educated in the liberal arts to be the authority figure and the "intellectual coach" who engages students in the Socratic dialogue, directs discussions, and corrects errors in reasoning. The perennialist teacher must be a model of intellectual and rational powers. He or she must be capable of logical analysis, be comfortable with the scientific method, be well versed in the classics, possess a good memory, and be capable of the highest forms of mental reasoning.

## Leading Educational Proponents

Jacques Maritain (1882–1973), a French Catholic philosopher who served as ambassador to the Holy See, was perhaps the best spokesperson for the ecclesiastic perennialist position. According to Maritain (1941), intelligence alone is not sufficient to fully comprehend the universe. Having a relationship to a Spiritual Being is necessary for understanding the cosmos or universe. Robert M. Hutchins (1899–1977), former chancellor of the University of Chicago, was a noted spokesperson for the lay perennialist perspective. Both Maritain (1943) and Hutchins (1936) argued that the ideal education is one that is designed to develop the mind, and this can be best done by a curriculum that concentrates on the Great Books of Western civilization.

As discussed in Chapter 7, the 1980s saw a resurgence of perennialism. In his *Paideia Proposal: An Educational Manifesto* (1982), Mortimer Adler advocated a curriculum that would be appropriate for all students. Adler, like Hutchins, opposed differential curricula (e.g., vocational, technical, academic) and contended that all students in a democratic society should have access to the same high-quality education that includes language, literature, mathematics, natural sciences, fine arts, history, geography, and social studies. Also like Hutchins, Adler favored the Great Books tradition and maintained that by studying the great works of the past, one can learn enduring lessons about life.

Allan Bloom, another prominent perennialist of the 1980s, was concerned with what he perceived as the intellectual crisis of liberal education, particularly in the university. In his book *The Closing of the American Mind* (1987), Bloom refers to "cultural illiteracy" as the crisis of our civilization. Like Hutchins and Adler, Bloom advocates teaching and learning about the Great Books because they provide knowledge and information that have lasting significance.

Today the perennialist curriculum can be found in low-income multicultural public schools as well as elite academies. The curriculum of St. John's College and Ursinus College in Pennsylvania, which emphasize the importance of studying the Great Books of the Western tradition, are excellent examples of perennialist curriculums built around the major works of philosophy and literature. On a lesser scale, the Core Curriculum at Columbia University and the Common Core at the University of Chicago have required courses in the Great Books. Figure 4.1 presents an overview of perennialism.

**Reflect on Diversity**

How appropriate is a curriculum that concentrates on the Great Books of Western civilization for a school with a majority Asian population?

**For Your Reflection and Analysis**

As a response to Allan Bloom's perceived "crisis in our civilization," what suggestion would you make for revamping the general studies curriculum at the university level?

Figure 4.1 — Perennialism at a Glance

| Purpose of Schooling | Nature of Learner | Curriculum | Instructional Methods | Classroom Management | Assessment | The Perennialist Teacher | Leading Proponents |
|---|---|---|---|---|---|---|---|
| Teach eternal truth<br>Cultivate intellect<br>Develop spiritual nature<br>Prepare for life | Rational being with soul<br>Exemplify value and worth | Christian doctrine<br>Liberal arts<br>Philosophy<br>Mathematics<br>History<br>Geography<br>Political science<br>Sociology<br>Theology<br>Foreign language<br>Science<br>Fine arts and humanities<br>Great Books<br>Character training<br>Moral development | Didactic instruction<br>Coaching<br>Socratic method<br>Critical thinking<br>Questioning strategies<br>Discussion<br>Lecture | Training the will<br>Time on task<br>Precision<br>Order<br>Structure<br>Regularity<br>Prayer<br>Contemplation | Objective exam<br>Essay exam | Educated in liberal arts<br>Authority figure<br>Disseminator of "truth"<br>"Director of mental calisthenics"<br>"Intellectual coach"<br>Rational<br>Logical<br>Well versed in classics<br>Scholar | Jacques Maritain<br>Robert Hutchins<br>Mortimer Adler<br>Allan Bloom |

# Progressivism

**Progressivism** focuses on real-world problem-solving activities in a democratic and cooperative learning environment. This view of education is grounded in the scientific method of inductive reasoning. As an educational theory, it encourages the learner to seek out processes that work and to do those things that best achieve desirable ends. Progressivism came about as a protest against the emphasis on universal truth and the past at the expense of experience and social relevance. The philosophy of pragmatism is embedded in the progressivist theory of education.

## *Purpose of Schooling*

Progressivists believe that the school should model life, particularly a democratic society. Dewey envisioned such a democratic community to be pluralistic in nature and include moral, economic, educational, and political goals. To prepare students to best operate in this democracy and in the larger democratic society, the school should encourage cooperation, not competition, and develop problem-solving and decision-making skills.

## *Nature of the Learner*

Progressivism embraces the notion that the child is an experiencing organism who is capable of "learning by doing." Progressivists perceive students to be evolving and active beings capable of interacting with their environment, setting objectives for their own learning, and working together to solve common problems. They are also capable of establishing rules for governing their classrooms, and testing and evaluating ideas for the improvement of learning (Noddings, 1997).

## *Curriculum*

The progressivist curriculum can best be described as experience centered, relevant, and reflective. Such a curriculum would not consist of a given set of predetermined facts or truths to be mastered, but rather a series of experiences to be gained. For Dewey (1963) "anything, which can be called a study, whether arithmetic, history, geography, or one of the natural sciences, must be derived from materials which at the onset fall within the scope of ordinary life-experiences" (p. 73). However, while he maintained that experience was the basis of education, Dewey (1938) cautioned that not all experiences are equal:

> The belief that all genuine education comes about through experience does not mean that all experiences are genuinely or equally educative. Experience and education cannot be directly equated to each other. For some experiences are mis-educative. Any experience is mis-education that has the effect of arresting or distorting the growth of further experience. (p. 25)

The curriculum of progressivism would integrate several subjects but would not reflect universal truths, a particular body of knowledge, or a set of prescribed core courses. Rather, it would be responsive to the interests, needs, and experiences of the student. Lerner (1962) described such a curriculum as child centered, peer centered, growth centered, action centered, process and change centered, and equality centered. It is also community centered. It would feature an **open classroom** environment in which students would spend considerable time in direct contact with the community or cultural surroundings beyond the confines of the classroom or school. Students would experience the arts by frequenting museums and theaters. They would experience social studies by interacting with individuals from diverse social groups and social conditions. They would experience science by exploring their immediate physical world. All students would be involved in a "social" mode of learning (Westheimer & Kahne, 1993).

The progressivist is not interested in the study of the past but is governed by the present. Unlike the perennialist and the essentialist, who advocate the importance of the cultural and historic roots of the past, the progressivist advocates that which is meaningful and relevant to the student today.

## Instructional Methods

For the progressivist, because there is no rigid subject-matter content and no absolute standard for what constitutes knowledge, the most appropriate instructional methods include group work and the project method. The experience-centered, problem-solving curriculum lends itself to cooperative group activities in which students can learn to work together on units or projects that have relevance to their own lives. Katz and Chard (2000) recommend that as early as the first grade, project work can complement systematic instruction. The instructional strategy that would be used with the project method is the scientific method. However, unlike the perennialist and the essentialist, who view the scientific method as a means of verifying truth, the progressivist views scientific investigation as a means of verifying experience.

Because the progressivist curriculum is an emerging rather than static curriculum, any teaching method that fosters individual and group initiative, spontaneity of expression, and creative new ideas would be used. Classroom activities in critical thinking, problem solving, decision making, and cooperative learning are examples of some of the methods that would be incorporated in the curriculum. Any form of learning that takes away from students' autonomy, such as rote learning, is discouraged (Gingell, 2008).

## Classroom Management

Progressivism views learning as educating "the whole child," including the physical, emotional, and social aspects of the individual. As a result of this holistic view of education, the environment is considered fundamental to the child's nature. The type of classroom management that would appeal to a progressivist would be an environment that stimulates or invites participation, involvement, and the democratic process. The atmosphere of the classroom would be active, experience directed, and self-directed (Dewey, 1956).

The progressivist teacher would foster a classroom environment that practices democracy and emphasizes citizenship. Students and parents would be encouraged to form their own councils and organizations within the school to address educational issues and to advance social change. Teachers would advocate parental involvement, site-based management, and democratic decision making with regard to the administration of the school.

## Assessment

Because progressivism supports the group process, cooperative learning, and democratic participation, its approach to evaluation differs from the more traditional approaches. For example, the progressivist would engage in formative evaluation, which is process oriented and concerned with ongoing feedback about the activity under way, rather than the measurement of outcomes. Monitoring what the students are doing, appraising what skills they still need to develop, and resolving unexpected problems as they occur would be typical examples of the type of evaluation used by the progressivist.

## The Progressivist Teacher

The metaphor of the "teacher as facilitator" or "director of learning" might best describe the progressivist teacher. Such a teacher is not considered to be the authority on, or disseminator of, knowledge or truth, like the perennialist or essentialist teacher. Rather, the teacher serves more as a guide who facilitates learning by assisting students to sample direct experience. Although the teacher is always interested in the individual development of each student, the role of the progressivist teacher is focused beyond the individual. Progressivism by its very nature is socially oriented; thus, the teacher would be a collaborative partner in making group decisions, keeping in mind their ultimate consequences for the students. The teacher's role is to help the students acquire the values of the democratic system.

**For Your Reflection and Analysis**

What type of process-oriented evaluation would you be most comfortable using in your teaching?

# HISTORICAL NOTE

## *John Dewey*

John Dewey, perhaps America's most well known philosopher, was born in Burlington, Vermont, in 1859. After graduating second in his University of Vermont class at the age of 19, he taught school for three years while continuing to read and study philosophy. In 1882 he began graduate study of philosophy at the newly founded John Hopkins University, studying under such recognized philosophers as Charles Sanders Pierce, G. Stanley Hall, and George S. Morris. After graduation in 1884 he accepted a position at the University of Michigan. University faculty were required to perform inspections at schools throughout the state, and it was while performing these visits that he developed an interest in education.

In 1894 he was recruited by the University of Chicago to head the department of philosophy and what became the department of pedagogy. It was here that he founded his famous laboratory school where his theories of education were applied. The relationship between education and democracy and school and society were central to Dewey's vision of the school. The school was a mirror of democracy and learning came through experience. "Learning by doing" was the motto over the door of the school. Conflict with the president over the administration of the school led to his resignation in 1904 and a move to Columbia University where he stayed for the remainder of his academic career.

Dewey was not only a philosopher but also a political and social activist. He was involved in a variety of causes including women's suffrage and the unionization of teachers. He helped found the American Civil Liberties Union and the American Association of University Professors and was involved in the beginnings of what was to become the National Association for the Advancement of Colored People. Dewey was one of the leaders of the Progressive Movement that brought social and political reform in the late 1800s and early 1900s. He provided the intellectual foundation and rationale for the generation of progressive educators.

## *Leading Educational Proponents*

As discussed in Chapter 7, while progressivism traces its roots to Pestalozzi and Rousseau, the term *progressive education* is associated with a movement that gained momentum in the first decades of the 20th century at a time when many liberal thinkers alleged that American schools were failing to prepare all students to be effective participants in the social, economic, and political life of a democratic society. As discussed, Francis W. Parker (1837–1902), superintendent of schools in Quincy, Massachusetts, and later head of the Cook County Normal School in Chicago, is considered the father of progressive education. However, as is also discussed, John Dewey (1859–1952), perhaps more than any other American educator, is credited with having advanced progressivism (see Historical Note on the life and contributions of Dewey.) Dewey's approach to progressivism differed from that of earlier progressive educators in that, rather than focusing on the individual learner, Dewey emphasized the importance of the teacher–student interaction and the social function of the school as a model of democracy. Dewey's work at the laboratory school at the University of Chicago as well as his position at Teachers College, Columbia University, provided the clinical testing ground for his educational theory for almost a half a century.

Ella Flagg Young (1845–1918), a colleague of Dewey's at the University of Chicago and superintendent of the Chicago Public Schools, also served as an important spokesperson for progressivism by emphasizing the central role of experimentation and democracy in the classroom and the school. William H. Kilpatrick (1871–1965) further advanced progressive education by introducing the experience-centered curriculum, including the project method.

Progressivism fell into disfavor after World War II, but as Ravitch (2000) has noted, it has never disappeared. Vestiges of progressivism could be found in **non-graded schools**, alternative schools, the whole-child movement, and **humanistic education**. In the last decades of the 20th century, progressive education was given renewed attention. The most visible examples can be found in the stated Common Principles of the Coalition of Essential Schools which include:

• Schools should focus on helping students to learn to use their minds well.

• Program design should emphasize depth over breadth and should be shaped by the intellectual and creative competencies that students need.

A century apart, both Ella Flagg Young and Theodore Sizer advanced the principles of education.

- School goals should apply to all students.
- Teaching and learning should be personalized as much as possible.
- The governing metaphor of the school should be "student as worker, teacher as coach."
- Multiple assessment and student demonstration of mastery through exhibition.
- The school should demonstrate and model nondiscrimination and democratic practice (Coalition of Essential Schools, 2011)

As these goals demonstrate, more than 50 years after his death, John Dewey is still very much alive in American schools.

Figure 4.2 presents an overview of progressivism.

## Behaviorism

**Behaviorism** is an educational or learning theory that is predicated on the belief that human behavior can be explained in terms of responses to external stimuli. The basic principle of behaviorism is that education can best be achieved by modifying or changing student behaviors in a socially acceptable manner through the arrangement of the conditions for learning. For the behaviorist, the predictability and control of human behavior are paramount concepts. The control is obtained not by manipulating the individual but by manipulating the environment.

The basic principles or philosophical foundations of behaviorism are as follows:

1. Most behaviors are learned.
2. Most behaviors are stimulus specific.
3. Most behaviors can be taught, changed, or modified.
4. Behavior change goals should be specific and clearly defined.
5. Behavior change programs should be individualized.
6. Behavior change programs should focus on the here and now.
7. Behavior change programs should focus on the child's environment (Zirpoli, 2005, p. 13).

Figure 4.2 — Progressivism at a Glance

| Purpose of Schooling | Nature of Learner | Curriculum | Instructional Methods | Classroom Management | Assessment | The Progressivist Teacher | Leading Proponents |
|---|---|---|---|---|---|---|---|
| Model a democratic and pluralistic society  Encourage cooperation  Develop problem-solving and decision-making skills  Educate physical, emotional, and social needs | Experiencing organism  Capable of learning by doing  Evolving and active being  Capable of interacting with environment  Capable of setting objectives for learning  Capable of cooperative problem solving  Capable of establishing classroom rules  Capable of testing and evaluating ideas | Experience centered  Relevant  Reflective  Integrated  Problem solving  Responsive to student's interests and needs  Child centered  Growth centered  Action centered  Process centered  Equality centered  Community centered | Group activities  Project method  Critical thinking  Problem solving  Decision making  Cooperative learning | Democratic and participatory  Self-directed | Formative evaluation  Ongoing feedback  Monitoring student progress  Appraising skills | Teacher as facilitator  Director of learning  Guide  Collaborative partner | Francis W. Parker  John Dewey  Ella Flagg Young  William H. Kilpatrick |

There are two major types of behaviorism: (1) **classical conditioning**, or stimulus substitution behaviorism; and (2) **operant conditioning**, or response reinforcement behaviorism. Classical conditioning, based on the work of Russian physiologist Ivan Pavlov (1849–1936) and American experimental psychologist John B. Watson (1878–1958), demonstrates that a natural stimulus that produces a certain type of response can be replaced by a conditioned stimulus. For example, Pavlov found that in laboratory experiments involving dogs, a natural stimulus such as food will produce a natural response such as salivation. However, when Pavlov paired the natural stimulus (food) with a conditioned stimulus (bell), he found that eventually the conditioned stimulus (bell) produced a conditioned response (salivation). Watson eventually used Pavlov's classical conditioning model to explain all human learning.

The operant conditioning model can best be described by the work of psychologists E. L. Thorndike (1874–1949) and B. F. Skinner (1904–1990). Both Thorndike and Skinner suggested that any response to any stimulus can be conditioned by immediate reinforcement or reward. Skinner later determined that an action or response does not have to be rewarded each time it occurs. In fact, Skinner found that random reward, or intermittent reinforcement, was a more effective method for learning than continuous reward. Skinner concluded that behavior could be shaped by the appropriate use of rewards.

As a theory of education, behaviorism came into being as a protest against the importance placed on mental processes that could not be observed (e.g., thinking, motivation). Today, behaviorism continues to be a viable theory not only in the classroom but in clinical settings as well. For example, cognitive–behavioral therapy has emerged as an effective therapeutic intervention in psychology for identifying and modifying faulty thinking, attitudes, and problem behaviors.

## Purpose of Schooling

Behaviorists' view of the purpose of schooling is to increase appropriate behaviors, decrease inappropriate behaviors, and teach new behaviors by incorporating a variety of behavioral techniques (Zirpoli, 2005). The school sets the stage for modifying and reinforcing behaviors.

## Nature of the Learner

Behaviorists believe that "most behaviors are learned, are stimulus-specific, and can be taught and modified. They also believe that students have the capacity and disposition to change" (Zirpoli, 2005, p. 34).

## Curriculum

Unlike the curricula of perennialism, which prescribes a particular subject matter, or essentialism, which emphasizes a core of fundamental knowledge, the behaviorist curriculum is not interested in content per se, but is interested in environmental variables such as teaching materials, instructional methods, and teacher–classroom behaviors, because they directly influence the learner's behavior (Wittrock, 1987). The behaviorist curriculum includes cognitive problem-solving activities in which students learn about their belief systems, recognize their power to influence their environment, and employ critical thinking skills.

## Instructional Methods

Behaviorist theory is primarily concerned with the process of providing contingencies of reinforcement as the basis for any instructional strategy or method. According to the behaviorists, if there are appropriate opportunities for the learner to respond, and appropriate reinforcers that are readily available, then learning will occur. Behaviorists employ a variety of instructional methods to promote generalization and maintenance of learned behaviors. Computer-assisted instruction, or any type of interactive method that provides immediate feedback and reinforcement, would be favored by behaviorists. Other instructional methods employed by behaviorists include strategies such as problem solving, anger control, self-instruction, and self-reinforcement training. These strategies have been effectively used to modify both cognition and behavior (Zirpoli, 2005).

**For Your Reflection and Analysis**

What types of problem solving activities would you use to help students learn about their belief systems?

## Classroom Management

For the behaviorist, classroom management is an integral part of the process of learning. Emmer (1987) described two general principles that guide the behaviorist teacher in classroom management:

1. Identify expected student behavior. This implies that teachers must have a clear idea of which behaviors are appropriate and which are not appropriate in advance of instruction.
2. Translate expectations into procedures and routines. Part of the process of translating expectations into procedures is to formulate some general rules governing conduct. (pp. 438–439)

Other components of good management include careful monitoring or observation of classroom events; prompt and appropriate handling of inappropriate behavior; using reward systems, penalties, and other consequences; establishing accountability for completion of assignments; and maintaining lesson or activity flow (Emmer, 1987). Behaviorism is widely used in special education and mainstream classroom environments.

## Assessment

Measurement and evaluation are central to the behaviorist teacher. Specified **behavioral objectives** (e.g., the behaviors or knowledge that students are expected to demonstrate or learn) serve not only as guides to learning for the student but also as standards for evaluating the teaching–learning process. For the behaviorist

B. F. Skinner advocated reinforcement as a method of shaping behavior.

teacher, only the aspects of behavior that are observable, and preferably measurable, are of interest to the teacher. Advocates of behavioral objectives claim that if teachers know exactly what they want students to learn and how they want them to learn, the use of behavioral objectives can be an efficient method for gauging how much learning has occurred. Measurement and evaluation also provide a method for obtaining accountability from teachers because they are pivotal to the learning process. Two other types of evaluation commonly used by behaviorist teachers are performance contracting and teaching students to record their own progress.

### The Behaviorist Teacher

Because education as behavioral engineering entails a variety of technical and observational skills, the behaviorist teacher must be skilled in a variety of these techniques. Moreover, because behavioral engineering depends on psychological principles, the teacher must be knowledgeable about psychology, in particular educational psychology, which emphasizes learning. Because behaviorism focuses on empirical verification, the teacher must also be well versed in the scientific method.

The behaviorist teacher is very concerned about the consequences of classroom behavior. Therefore, the teacher must be able to recognize which reinforcers are most appropriate. In addition, the behaviorist teacher must be skilled in using a variety of schedules of reinforcement that are effective and efficient in shaping and maintaining desired responses.

To establish the behaviors that will be most beneficial to the learner, behaviorist teachers are most concerned with the student achieving specific objectives or competencies. For this reason the teacher must be capable of planning and using behavioral objectives, designing and using various types of instruction, reinforcement strategies, and intervention strategies. Two of the most appropriate metaphors for describing the behaviorist teacher are "the controller of behavior" and "the arranger of contingencies."

### Leading Educational Proponents

As noted, classical conditioning had its beginnings with Pavlov and Watson, both of whom maintained that classical conditioning was the key mechanism underlying all human learning. Also as previously discussed, the behaviorists Thorndike and Skinner are known for the concept of operant conditioning, which suggests that reinforcement of responses (operant behavior) underlies all types of learning. Another noted behaviorist, psychologist David Premack, determined that organisms often freely choose to engage in certain behaviors rather than other behaviors. Consequently, providing access to the preferred activities can serve as reinforcement for engaging in non-preferred activities. To apply the **Premack principle** in the classroom with individual students or the entire class, the teacher first must determine and record the relative frequency and desirability of actions. To be effective the less preferred behavior (e.g., completing an assignment) must come before the more preferred behavior (e.g., playing computer games). Figure 4.3 provides an overview of behaviorism.

## Essentialism

As described in Chapter 7, **essentialism** began in the 1930s as a protest against the perceived decline of intellectual rigor and moral standards in the schools. Essentialists then and now often base their criticisms of American education on

**Figure 4.3 — Behaviorism at a Glance**

| Purpose of Schooling | Nature of Learner | Curriculum | Instructional Methods | Classroom Management | Assessment | The Behaviorist Teacher | Leading Proponents |
|---|---|---|---|---|---|---|---|
| Increase or reinforce appropriate behavior Modify or change in-appropriate behavior Increase or reinforce new behavior | Capable of and disposed to modifying or changing behavior Capable of learning new behavior | Individualized Cognitive problem solving | Classical conditioning Operant conditioning Computer-assisted instruction Problem solving self-instruction Self-reinforce-ment training | Identifying expected behavior Translating expectations into procedures Formulating rules of conduct Monitoring Observing Responding promptly to inappropriate behavior Using rewards Using penalties Establishing accountability | Behavioral objectives Performance contracting Student self-evaluation | Skilled in variety of technical and observational skills Trained in educational psychology Skilled in scientific method Plans and uses behavioral objectives Designs and uses various types of instruction, schedules of reinforcement, and intervention strategies | Ivan Pavlov John W. Watson E. L. Thorndike B. F. Skinner David Premack |

comparisons with other countries such as Japan and Germany. They have argued that the curriculum in American schools was watered down and full of frills, and that in an attempt to provide equality, educational standards had been lowered and the more able students were badly served. Moreover, they contended that the schools had not only lost sight of their major purpose, to train the intellect, but they also were failing in their responsibility to transmit the culture and traditions that are the basis of the American tradition (Wingo, 1974). The philosophies of idealism and realism are embedded in the essentialist theory of education.

**For Your Reflection and Analysis**

What subjects might be considered a "frill" by an essentialist?

## Purpose of Schooling

For the essentialist the primary purposes of schooling are to train the intellect and teach students the culture and traditions of the past. It should also provide students with the knowledge and skills necessary to successfully participate in a democratic and technological society.

## Nature of the Learner

Essentialists believe that students have the capacity to become culturally literate and to develop disciplined minds. To do so, rigorous academic and moral training are required to overcome their natural tendencies.

## Curriculum

The essentialist philosophy supports the belief that there is a critical core or body of knowledge that all students should possess. The curriculum of the essentialist school would provide instruction in these "essentials," which would include those "skills and subjects that have contributed to human survival, productivity, and civility" (Gutek, 2004, p. 281). At the primary level this would include reading, writing, and mathematics. At the upper elementary grades, history, geography, natural science, and foreign languages would be added. At the secondary level, the curriculum would place a major emphasis on a common core that includes four years of English, three years of mathematics, three years of science, three years of social studies, and a half year of computer science. For the college-bound student, foreign languages would be required. Overall, essentialists maintain that the educational program should not permit any "frivolous subjects," but rather should adhere to sound academic standards and return to the "basics."

Like the perennialists, who advocate intellectual discipline as well as moral discipline, the essentialists maintain that moral development and character training deserve an important place in the curriculum. William Bennett (1993), former U.S. secretary of education, strongly endorsed essentialism because it advocates moral literacy. Bennett proposed the use of stories, poems, essays, and other works to help children achieve moral literacy and acquire the traits of character that society most admires.

## Instructional Methods

The methods of instruction to support such a curriculum include the more traditional instructional strategies such as lecture, recitation, discussion, and the Socratic dialogue. Written and oral communications also occupy prominent places in the instructional milieu of the essentialist school. Like perennialists, essentialists view books as an appropriate medium for instruction. Essentialists have also found various educational technologies supportive of their educational theory.

In general, essentialists prefer instructional materials that are paced and sequenced in such a way that students know what they are expected to master. Detailed syllabi, lesson plans, learning by objectives, competency-based instruction, and computer-assisted instruction are other examples of teaching strategies that would be acceptable to the modern-day essentialist.

## Classroom Management

For the essentialist, students attend school to learn how to participate in society, not to manage the course of their own instruction. They prepare for life by being exposed to fundamental knowledge and values, as well as by exercising discipline. Thus, the essentialist teacher would take great pains in designing and controlling a classroom environment that creates an aura of certainty, an emphasis on regularity and uniformity, and a reverence for what is morally right. The essentialist classroom would emphasize discipline and character training with clear expectations for behavior and respect for others.

## Assessment

Of all the theories of education, essentialism is perhaps most comfortable with assessment, evaluation, and testing. In fact, the entire essentialist curriculum reflects the influence of the testing movement. The increased use of IQ tests, standardized achievement tests, diagnostic tests, and performance-based competency tests, as well as the "high-stakes testing" mandated by the No Child Left Behind Act (2001), are examples of the influence of the testing and measurement movements supported by essentialists. Competency, accountability, mastery learning, and performance-based instruction have gained increasing acceptance by many educators as a result of essentialists' influence on educational practice.

## The Essentialist Teacher

The essentialist teacher, like the perennialist teacher, is an educator who has faith in the accumulated wisdom of the past. Rather than having majored in educational pedagogy, the essentialist teacher would probably have majored in a subject-matter discipline in the liberal arts, sciences, or the humanities. The essentialist educator is viewed as either a link to the "literary intellectual inheritance" (idealism) or a "demonstrator of the world model" (realism). An essentialist teacher would be well versed in the liberal arts and sciences, a respected member of the intellectual community, technically skilled in all forms of communication, and equipped with superior pedagogical skills to ensure competent instruction. One of the most important roles of the teacher is to set the character of the environment in which learning takes place (Butler, 1966).

## *Leading Educational Proponents*

Essentialism's greatest popularity emerged in the twentieth century. As noted in Chapter 7, in the 1930s and 1940s William C. Bagley and Arthur E. Bestor led the essentialist criticism of the progressivism of Dewey and his followers. They formed the Essentialist Committee for the Advancement of American Education. In the 1950s, Admiral Hyman G. Rickover (1900–1986) became the spokesperson for the essentialists. According to Rickover (1963), the quality of American education declined considerably as a result of "watered-down" courses and "fads and frills." He called for a return to the basics, with particular emphasis on mathematics and science.

A major revival of essentialism occurred with the **back-to-basics movement**, which gained support in the 1970s and was echoed in the education reform reports of the 1980s. *A Nation at Risk* (National Commission on Excellence in Education, 1983), the premier example of these reports, recommended a core of "new basics": English, mathematics, science, social studies, computer sciences, and, for the college-bound student, a foreign language.

One of the individuals most identified with the contemporary essentialist movement is E. D. Hirsch Jr. Hirsch's 1987 best-selling *Cultural Literacy: What Every American Needs to Know* became a manifesto for the back-to-basics movement. In *Cultural Literacy* Hirsch identified 5,000 names, dates, facts, and concepts from the fields of art, religion, science, and culture that he maintained an individual must know to be considered educated. **Cultural literacy**, he claimed, had become the "common currency for social and economic exchange in our democracy" and is therefore "the only available ticket to citizenship" and "the only sure avenue of opportunity for disadvantaged children" (p. xiii). *Cultural Literacy* was such a success in the popular press that Hirsch followed it with a dictionary of cultural literacy and books about what children should know at various grade levels. Hirsch also developed the Core Knowledge curriculum, which offered the same academic credit to students in more than 1,000 Core Knowledge schools nationwide.

In a similar vein was Diane Ravitch and Chester Finn's *What Do Our 17-Year-Olds Know?* (1987). After analyzing the results of the history and literature sections of the National Assessment of Educational Progress (NAEP), Ravitch and Finn concluded that the students had failed in both subjects. They then advanced the

Two prominent 20th-century spokespersons for Essentialism include Admiral Hyman Rickover and Diane Ravitch.

essentialist position that there is a body of knowledge that is so important it should be possessed by all Americans.

Another very visible essentialist is William Bennett, secretary of education during much of President Ronald Reagan's second term. From his position Bennett designed the curriculum for the model essentialist high school, *James Madison High School* (1987), and the model elementary school, *James Madison Elementary School* (1988). According to Bennett's design, all students except those in vocational programs would have the same curriculum of high academic standards.

The success of the essentialist position is evidenced by the steps taken in a number of states to mandate curricula, strengthen graduation requirements, and increase student assessment. Essentialism is the dominant philosophy in our schools today. Figure 4.4 presents an overview of essentialism.

## Social Reconstructionism

Throughout history there have been individuals who have aspired to improve, change, or reform society, including its educational institutions. Social reconstructionists differ from these revolutionaries in that they believe not only that society is in need of change or reconstruction, but also that education must take the lead in the reconstruction of society. **Social reconstructionism** began in the 1920s and 1930s with a group of progressive educators known as the "Frontier Thinkers." These educational reformers looked to the schools for leadership in creating a "new" and "more equitable" society than that which led up to the Depression. They advocated changes beyond what Dewey envisioned in

### Figure 4.4 — Essentialism at a Glance

| Purpose of Schooling | Nature of Learner | Curriculum | Instructional Methods | Classroom Management | Assessment | The Essentialist Teacher | Leading Proponents |
|---|---|---|---|---|---|---|---|
| Train intellect Teach past culture and tradition Teach knowledge and skills | Capable of becoming culturally literate Capable of a disciplined mind | Critical body of knowledge Reading Writing Mathematics Upper elementary History Geography Natural science Foreign language Secondary common core English Mathematics Science Social studies Computer science Foreign language Back to basics Moral development Character training | Lecture Recitation Discussion Socratic dialogue Written communication Oral communication Books Computer-assisted instruction Paced and sequenced materials Detailed syllabi Lesson plans Learning by objectives Competency-based instruction | Discipline Clear behavior expectations Respect for others | IQ tests Standardized achievement tests Performance-based tests Competency-based tests "High-stakes tests" Mastery learning | Well versed in liberal arts, sciences, or humanities Intellectual Skilled communicator Superior pedagogical skills | William C. Bagley Arthur E. Bestor Hyman G. Rickover E. D. Hirsch Jr. William J. Bennett Chester Finn Diane Ravitch |

his theory of progressivism; his emphasis was on the democratic social experience, theirs was on social reform. Social reconstructionists charge progressive education with failing to deal with any of the crises of the time (war, prosperity, depression) and failing to elaborate any theory of social welfare (Counts, 1932). Social reconstructionism can be traced to the philosophies of both pragmatism and existentialism.

## Purpose of Schooling

Social reconstructionists consider the purpose of schooling to be to critically examine all cultural and educational institutions and recommend change and reform as needed. In addition, the school's purpose is to teach students and the public not to settle for "what is," but rather to dream about "what might be." Most important, the purpose of schooling is to prepare students to become change agents.

## Nature of the Learner

Social reconstructionists believe that students are the critical element in bringing about social change. They contend that students are capable of initiating and adapting to change, especially if they are influenced by appropriate adult role models.

## Curriculum

Because the majority of social reconstructionists believe in the importance of democracy and the proposition that the school is the fundamental institution in modern society, the curriculum of the social reconstructionist school would reflect democratic ideals and emphasize civic education. It would also emphasize **critical theory** and the development of **critical literacy** or critical thinking skills. The curriculum would provide an opportunity for students to gain firsthand experiences in studying real social problems and controversial issues. Such a curriculum denounces any form of the politics of exclusion. Instead, it challenges all unequal power relationships and focuses on power as applied to class, gender, sexuality, race, and nationalism (Blake & Masschalein, 2003). Rather than concentrate on separate subjects, students would consider societal problems such as the place of biomedical ethics in improving the quality of life, the need to conserve our natural resources, and the issues of foreign policy and nationalism. In addition to the formal or official curriculum, attention would be given to the **hidden curriculum** (see discussion in Chapter 14), which represents the unintended norms, values, and beliefs implicitly communicated by the organization and operation of the schools.

## Instructional Methods

The instructional methods of the social reconstructionist would include cooperative learning, problem solving, and critical thinking. The focus would be on active learning and on activities outside the school such as tutoring younger students, public cleanup projects, or promoting consumer legislation. Activities such as these contextualize skills learned at school in a way that helps students appreciate their usefulness (Kincheloe, Slattery, & Steinberg, 2000). Instead of merely reading and studying about the problems of society, students would spend time in the community becoming acquainted with and immersed in society's problems and their possible solutions. They would analyze, research, and link the underlying issues to institutions and structures in the community and larger society. Finally, they would take some action or responsibility in planning for change.

## Classroom Management

The classroom environment of the social reconstructionist would be a climate of inquiry in which teachers and students question the assumptions of the status quo and examine societal issues and future trends. The social reconstructionist would strive to organize the classroom in a classless, nonsexist, and nonracist manner. There would be less emphasis on management and control and more focus on community building (Kincheloe et al., 2000). An atmosphere that promotes analysis, criticism, and action research would best describe this type of classroom environment. Conflict resolution and differences in world views would be encouraged and reinforced.

## Assessment

The type of assessment that would be favored in a social reconstructionist school would be **authentic assessment**, including formative evaluation, and would include a cooperative effort between student and teacher, student and student, teacher and administrator or supervisor, and community and teacher. Information would be shared regularly during periodic formal and informal conferences, and the student or teacher being evaluated would be an active participant in the process. Such an assessment requires participants to have the ability and willingness to think in critical terms and to expose underlying assumptions and practices. Social reconstructionists oppose standardized testing of both students and teachers and use it only if mandated by local, state, or federal authorities.

## The Social Reconstructionist Teacher

The metaphors "shaper of a new society," "transformational leader," and "change agent" aptly describe the social reconstructionist teacher. According to George S. Counts (1933), a leading figure in social reconstructionism in the 1930s, teachers "cannot evade the responsibility of participating actively in the task of reconstituting the democratic tradition and of thus working positively toward a new society" (p. 19).

Social reconstructionist teachers must also be willing to engage in ongoing renewal of their personal and professional lives. They must be willing to critique and evaluate the conditions under which they work and extend their educative role outside the domains of the classroom and school. They must have a high tolerance for ambiguity, be comfortable with constant change, and be willing to reflect on their own thinking and the cultural and psychosocial forces that have shaped it. As an educational reformer, such a teacher detests the status quo and views the school as a particular culture in evolution. Moreover, he or she views the larger society as an experiment that will always be unfinished and in flux. The social reconstructionist teacher must be willing to engage in and form alliances with community groups, neighborhood organizations, social movements, and parents to critique and question the practice of school democracy and school policy.

**For Your Reflection and Analysis**

How comfortable are you with ambiguity? Constant change?

## Leading Educational Proponents

The earliest advocates of what became the social reconstructionist movement in the United States were George S. Counts (1889–1974), Theodore Brameld (1904–1987), and Harold Rugg (1886–1960). In the wake of the Great Depression, these educators were concerned that the typical school curriculum lacked relevance to the real world and ignored the social problems surrounding the school (Kysilka & Brown, 2006). They called on the schools to take the lead in planning for the reconstruction of society and building a more ideal and more equitable social order. Counts, in his famous 1932 speech before the Progressive Education Association titled "Dare the Schools Build a New Social Order," called on the schools to focus less on the child and more on the social issues of the time, to "face squarely and courageously every social issue, come to grips with life in all its stark reality . . . develop a realistic and comprehensive theory of welfare, fashion a compelling and challenging vision of human destiny" (p. 7).

Two more contemporary spokespersons for the social reconstructionist theory of education were Ivan Illich (1926–2002) and Paulo Freire (1921–1997). Illich (1974), in his *Deschooling*

Social reconstructionists aspire to improve, change, and reform society.

**Figure 4.5 — Social Reconstructionism at a Glance**

| Purpose of Schooling | Nature of Learner | Curriculum | Instructional Methods | Classroom Management | Assessment | The Social Reconstructionist Teacher | Leading Proponents |
|---|---|---|---|---|---|---|---|
| Examine cultural and educational institutions Recommend change and reform Prepare change agents | Capable of initiating change Capable of adapting to change | Democratic ideals Critical literacy Critical thinking Political/social awareness Community problems Hidden curriculum | Problem solving Critical thinking Community projects Becoming immersed in social problems Analyzing and researching problems Planning for change | Establishing a climate of inquiry Questioning the status quo Community building Conflict resolution Encouraging criticism and differences | Authentic assessment Formative evaluation Ongoing feedback Periodic formal and informal conferences | Shaper of a new society Transformational leader Change agent Tolerance for ambiguity Comfortable with change Educational reformer Engaged in community alliances | Karl Marx George S. Counts Theodore Brameld Harold Rugg Paulo Freire Ivan Illich |

*Society,* maintained that because schools have corrupted society, one can create a better society only by abolishing schools altogether and finding new approaches to education. Illich called for a total political and educational revolution. Freire, who was born, educated, and taught in Latin America, proposed that education be drawn from the everyday life experiences of the learners. From his students, the illiterate and oppressed peasants of Brazil and Chile, Freire drew his theory of *liberation pedagogy* and reconstructionism (Gutek, 2004). In his *Pedagogy of the Oppressed* (1973), Freire maintained that students should not be manipulated or controlled but should be involved in their own learning. According to Freire, by exchanging and examining their experiences with peers and mentors, students who are socially, economically, and politically disadvantaged can plan, initiate, and take action for their own lives.

Although few current educators would consider themselves to be social reconstructionists, many have beliefs and practices that are consistent with the principles of social reconstructionism. In addition, many principles of social reconstructionism are reflected in the critical theory and postmodern movements discussed next.

Figure 4.5 presents an overview of social reconstructionism.

## Postmodernism

**Postmodernism** has been defined as a contemporary philosophy, ideology, movement, and process. It represents a combination of the philosophies of pragmatism, existentialism, social reconstructionism, and critical theory. Postmodern critical theorists are concerned with analyzing and make assumptions and generalizations about the political nature of those institutions. They raise such questions as these: Who controls the school? Who chooses the curriculum? Who hires the teachers? Who chooses the textbooks? Who writes the textbooks? In short, who has the power? From their analyses, they uncover examples of inequity between the dominant culture (male, white, middle class) and disenfranchised, disadvantaged, or marginal groups (e.g., women, racial and ethnic minorities, homosexuals, immigrants, the aged, and the poor).

Postmodernists believe that there are no eternal universal truths and values. They suggest that reality is subjective; it is not found in our ancient past, but in the eye of the beholder. Postmodernists believe that individuals construct their own meaning from personal experience and that history is itself a construction

(Newman, 1998). At the same time postmodernists believe that meaning itself is unstable and exists only within specific linguistic social contexts. Postmodernists also question "scientific realism" by refuting epistemological claims that science (in particular, the scientific method) is objective and unbiased. They claim that objective observation is not possible because the observer affects what is observed. Postmodernists suggest that the way we arrive at knowledge is not by science alone but by examining "the human past and present to see how claims of truth have originated, been constructed and expressed, and have had social, political and educational consequences" (Gutek, 2004, p. 130). They question the dominance of objectivity, universal explanations, truth, and rationality (Kincheloe et al., 2000). In their place they substitute critical inquiry and political awareness (Henderson, 2001); diversity, inclusion, and multiplicity (McLaren & Torres, 1998); and the limitations of language or the meaning of words (Biesta, 2001).

**For Your Reflection and Analysis**

Give examples of other "myths" that are perpetuated by the schools and by other institutions.

## Purpose of Schooling

Postmodernists perceive the purpose of schooling to be preparing students for critical citizenship and critical inquiry. To accomplish these tasks, the school must prepare students to recognize that schools, like other social institutions, are not value free. They have perpetuated certain myths and have reinforced a social order that is patriarchal, Eurocentric, and biased by social class and the "free market ideology" of capitalism. The school also has a responsibility to make students aware that certain groups in society have been excluded, marginalized, and exploited.

## Nature of the Learner

Postmodernists believe that students have the right to voice and question the purpose of the major institutions in society including the school. Moreover, they believe students have the capacity to understand that humans are responsible for the phenomena of wars, poverty, violence, corruption, and social, political, economic, and ecological injustices (Martusewicz, 2001).

## Curriculum

Postmodernists believe that historically the curriculum has not been unbiased. It has functioned to name and honor particular histories and experiences and has done so in such a way as to marginalize or silence the experiences of subordinate groups (Aronowitz & Giroux, 1991). In the postmodernist curriculum, any form of the politics of exclusion, including elevating Eurocentrism as a model for cultural literacy, would be unacceptable. Rather, curriculum topics such as social justice would be emphasized. The main focus of the curriculum would be one of cultural politics that would challenge all unequal power relationships (class, gender, sexuality, race, ethnicity, and nationalism). Its purpose would be to teach *literacy*, not *cultural literacy* but *critical literacy* (McLaren, 2003), which would empower students "to identify and unmask those human beliefs and practices that limit freedom, justice, and democracy" (Scott, 2006, p. 39).

Postmodernists encourage reading a wide variety of materials. For example, postmodernists might suggest the reading of the Great Books. However, they would not use the Great Books as a model for truth as do the perennialists, but as a model for questioning, critiquing, and analyzing what constitutes truth and who has the power to decide. Quintero (2007) asks, "What are the great stories? Who decides? Is there room for family stories and cultural histories that differ from stories in the standard curriculum?" (p. 202).

## Instructional Methods

Postmodernists incorporate the learning theory of **constructivism**, whereby students construct their own knowledge and meaning via hands-on, problem-solving activities. Constructivism has its roots in the philosophy of pragmatism (Dewey) and the cognitive developmental theories of Jerome Bruner (1966) and Jean Piaget (1951).

Postmodernists would also include any method that would help the student recognize and understand the notion of **hegemony**, in which the dominant culture exercises domination over subordinate classes or groups with the partial consent of the subordinate group (Wink, 2011). It would encourage students not only to question, critique, and examine the culture and its institutions, but also to recognize and pay particular attention to the contradictions and variable meanings of the language we use in our discourse and text (Derrida, 1976).

An analysis and exploration of the students' autobiographical histories, languages, and cultures would be highlighted. The previously mentioned hidden curriculum would also be examined. Lastly, the use of *text*, or "any set of symbolic objects through which we attempt to communicate something and through which we create meaning (classrooms, film, books, clothing)", would be incorporated (Martusewicz, 2001, p. 11).

## Classroom Management

The postmodernist classroom environment would be nonthreatening, supportive, and open to discussions of many controversial subjects and topics, a place where students are expected to value and treat each other with dignity and respect. Students would be encouraged to reflect on their experiences and share their personal stories and narratives. Questioning and critiquing are not interpreted as negative actions or behaviors. Rather, they are perceived as positive actions toward bringing about change. The learning environment would stimulate group problem solving, collaboration, and experimental group activities. At the same time it would encourage self-discipline and reinforce individual choice and responsibility.

## Assessment

Postmodernists would be most comfortable using various forms of authentic assessment to evaluate their students' ability to apply knowledge and skills in solving real-life problems. Some of the forms of authentic assessment that might be incorporated would be journals; personal narratives; independent and group portfolios that include photographs, videos, audiotapes, and art projects; as well as traditional writing samples. Students would also be encouraged to evaluate their own progress to determine how well they have grasped the important aspects of the learning activities (McNergney & McNergney, 2008). They would also be invited to evaluate the teacher.

## The Postmodernist Teacher

The terms *scholar-practitioner leader* (Horn, 2004), *critical thinker*, and *change agent* are metaphors that describe the postmodernist teacher. The postmodernist teacher's role is to practice and model the "doing of critical theory." These teachers practice and model questioning, critiquing, and analyzing. At the same time, they recognize the power and influence they have over their students and their students' peers, parents, and the larger community. As professionals, they constantly check how they are communicating to determine whether they are alienating or offending others, while always respecting the rights of all individuals to take issue and disagree.

## Leading Educational Proponents

While the term *postmodernism* came to be associated with a philosophical movement that originated in France in the third quarter of the twentieth century, the German philosopher Friedrich Nietzsche (1844–1900) is credited by many as being the person most responsible for laying the philosophical foundation for postmodernism. Nietzsche was among the first to reject the possibility of an objective truth and to assert that truth is subject to individual perception.

Prominent among the original French philosophers were Jean Francois Lyotard (1928–1998), Jacques Derrida (1930–2004), and Michel Foucault (1926–1984). Lyotard was primarily concerned with the role of narrative in culture and how that role has changed as we have entered the post-industrial or postmodern age. Derrida is associated with deconstructionism, which is concerned with textual criticism. Foucault

**Figure 4.6 — Postmodernism at a Glance**

| Purpose of Schooling | Nature of Learner | Curriculum | Instructional Methods | Classroom Management | Assessment | The Postmodernist Teacher | Leading Proponents |
|---|---|---|---|---|---|---|---|
| Critically examine all institutions in society Develop critical literacy Question "scientific realism" Question objectivity, truth, & rationality | Capable of becoming aware of the disequity in society Capable of understanding social, economic, political, & ecological injustices | Cultural politics that challenge all unequal power relationships Hidden curriculum | Constructivism Critique & examine autobiographical histories, languages, & cultures Examine hegemony, & hidden curriculum | Nonthreatening Supportive Open Self-discipline Individual choice Responsibility | Authentic assessment Journals Narratives Portfolios Writing Samples Student self-evaluation Teacher-evaluation | Scholar-practitioner leader Critical thinker Change agent Doing critical theory Sensitive to and aware of their influence on students Respect right of students to disagree | Michael Apple Michel Foucault Henry A. Giroux |

focused on the relationship between means and power, specifically arguing that "language is oppression" that operates to foster cultural hegemony and the exclusion of minority groups and minority perspectives.

The most noted American postmodernist was Richard Rorty (1931–2007). Rorty brought both pragmatism and analytic philosophy to the postmodernist movement. Other contemporary postmodern philosophers include Paul Feyerabend, Donna Haraway, Fredric Jameson, and Cornell West. Postmodernism is one of the most influential philosophies in education today. Figure 4.6 presents an overview of postmodernism.

## Identifying Your Philosophy of Education

Educational philosophies and educational theories do not remain static, but constantly change depending on the social, economic, and political climate at the time. Upon visiting any school, it quickly becomes evident that a variety of philosophies and theories of education can coexist in the same school, and even in the same classroom. Few teachers operate from a single philosophical or theoretical perspective. Most educators are eclectic and sample a variety of ideas, propositions, principles, or axioms that represent a smorgasbord of views.

Identifying and developing your philosophy of education may appear to be a formidable task. However, it is one of the most important tasks that you will probably be asked to perform as a prospective teacher. It is not uncommon to be asked to articulate your philosophy of education on job applications or in job interviews. School districts may require that you express your philosophical ideas and compare them to the philosophy or mission of the school district.

In Chapter 3 you were asked to respond to a series of questions that reflected your personal philosophy of life. You were also advised that the answers to those questions represented some of the assumptions you hold about teaching and learning. The time has come to combine philosophy, theory, and practice in constructing your philosophy of education. Your responses to the basic theoretical questions in the Ask Yourself feature reflect your philosophy of education. As you ask yourself these questions, recall the importance of clarity and meaning in the language you choose. Your ideas about education may change before you enter the teaching profession, and they may change one or more times during the course of your career. Nevertheless, it is vitally important that you begin to conceptualize those ideas at this stage of your professional development.

# ASK YOURSELF

## *What Is My Philosophy of Education?*

To assess your preference for an educational philosophy, answer the following questions:

1. Are students intrinsically motivated to learn?
2. Should education be the same for everyone?
3. Should certain universal truths be taught?
4. What determines morality?
5. What is the ideal curriculum?
6. What is the purpose of schooling?
7. If you were to choose one method or instructional strategy, what would it be?
8. What type of classroom environment is most conducive to learning?
9. How do you know when your students have learned?
10. What is the most important role of the teacher?
11. What is the role of the student?
12. How should prospective teachers be prepared?

## Summary

There are six major theories of education: perennialism, progressivism, behaviorism, essentialism, social reconstructionism, and postmodernism. Educational theories influence educational practice by their impact on curriculum, instructional methods, classroom management, assessment, and the role of the teacher. Each theory developed from a particular philosophy or philosophies. Most theories were formulated as a protest against the prevailing social and cultural forces at the time. The educational theories of perennialism and essentialism have much in common in that they underscore the importance of a liberal education and the wisdom of the past. Behaviorism differs from the other educational theories in that its proponents believe all behaviors are both objective and observable.

Progressivism, social reconstructionism, and postmodernism share a common theme in that each of them is more concerned with the study of the present and future than the past. Unlike the perennialist and essentialist, who emphasize the important cultural and historic roots of the past, the progressivist, social reconstructionist, and postmodernist stress that which is meaningful and relevant to the student today.

In the next chapter, you will explore the historical origins of Western education. You will also examine the beginnings of American education as it evolved in the 13 original colonies.

# TEACHER OF THE YEAR

*Jennifer Burdock Rankin Maryland*

I always thought that teachers were cool. I grew up admiring the ones that came out of their shell and went the extra mile to make sure that their students were interested, involved, and even captivated by learning. Teachers show up every day, armed with countless ways to mesmerize their students. I think it's in the hearts and souls of teachers. I relish being in a profession where I can employ my creativity and innovation to help students understand the concepts of math and language arts. I like finding exciting ways to bring information to them. I like finding ways for them to play and learn at the same time because I think learning should be fun. I teach because each day is different. Each day it's like I get on a roller coaster for an adventure that will last the whole day. I teach because every day holds a new possibility … for my students, for me, and for this world.

# PROFESSIONAL DEVELOPMENT
## *Workshop*

### *Prepare for the State Licensure Examination*

The Copper Creek School District is an urban district that in the past two decades has been transformed from a manufacturing-based to a technology-based economy. During the end of the 2012–2013 school year, the Educare Traditional K–5 Magnet School became a reality. The impetus for the school came from several members of the business community who were concerned about what they considered a lack of rigor in the schools and the fact that many graduates of the Copper Creek schools came to them unable to read, spell, or compute at a level that was demanded of them in their daily assignments.

Three focus groups and two public open hearings had been held, and numerous editorials for and against the establishment of the magnet school were printed in the *Copper Creek Examiner*. The unexpected surprise was that some of the most vocal critics of the Copper Creek schools were alumni.

Within six months after the first focus group meeting, the Copper Creek school board passed a resolution to establish Educare Traditional K–5 Magnet School. There was immediate agreement on the underlying philosophy of the school. True to its name, it would be a school that would embrace the classical tradition with an emphasis on the basic core subjects. Special features of Educare would include teacher-directed instruction in self-contained classrooms, regular homework assignments, teaching and modeling of study skills, weekly progress reports, and active participation of parents.

Several of the faculty who were selected to staff the Educare Traditional School were appointed to the curriculum committee. Representatives of the business community and parents were also asked to serve on the committee. The task of the curriculum committee is to design a model traditional curriculum with particular attention given to the basic core subjects.

1. Which basic core subjects should the curriculum committee propose that would be in keeping with the philosophy of the new school? Give a rationale or justification for your choices.

2. a. Which educational theory or theories should guide their decision making and recommendations?

   b. Which underlying philosophies are aligned with the educational theory or theories selected?

3. Describe two approaches the school district might use to improve its communication with parents and the community and to encourage their support for the new magnet school. Base your answer on some principles of communication.

### Build Your Knowledge Base

1. Reflect on the vignette at the beginning of this chapter. Which theory of education would you ascribe to Jim? To Beth? To Sam? Explain.

2. Describe the relationship between philosophy of life, educational theory, and philosophy of education.

3. Which of the theories of education presented in this chapter is most similar to your theory of education? In what ways is it different?

4. B. F. Skinner and other advocates of operant conditioning have been criticized for their emphasis on control. Are freedom and control incompatible concepts in the classroom? Explain.

5. As a social reconstructionist, list five major changes that you would propose for education and schooling in the 21st century. Should teachers and students be involved in promoting these changes? Why or why not?

6.  Choose a leading educational proponent of essentialism and, using that individual's theory, construct a letter to the editor of a newspaper suggesting how the current training of teachers should be reformed.

## Develop Your Portfolio

1.  Review each of the educational theories discussed in this chapter (perennialism to postmodernism) and reflect on which educational theorist(s) provide(s) the most effective instructional strategies (instructional methods) to encourage students to develop critical thinking skills. Prepare a reflection paper that both describes the critical thinking skills you believe are most important in your discipline or subject area and the instructional strategies (instructional methods) you might use to help your students develop their critical thinking skills. Place the reflection paper in your portfolio under **INTASC Standard 5, Application of Content**, and **Standard 8, Instructional Strategies**.

2.  Review the basic questions in the Ask Yourself feature on page 97. In preparation for constructing your philosophy of education, reflect on the question, "Are students intrinsically motivated to learn?" Prepare a reflection paper that summarizes your response. Place the reflection paper in your portfolio under **INTASC Standard 2, Learner Development**.

## Explore Teaching and Learning: Field Experiences

1.  Visit a classroom, observe a lesson, review the teacher's lesson plan, and see if you can determine which of the six educational philosophies discussed in this chapter was used in the development of the lesson.

2.  Review each of the major educational theories discussed in this chapter. Then interview the chair of the teacher education department or the associate dean for teacher education at your college or university to determine which, if any, of these educational theories is reflected in the teacher education program at your institution.

---

## MyEducationLab

Go to **Topic 7, The History and Philosophy of Education** in the MyEducationLab (www.myeducationlab.com) for *Foundations of American Education*, where you can:

- Find learning outcomes for the history and philosophy of education along with the national standards that connect to these outcomes.
- Complete Assignments and Activities that can help you more deeply understand the chapter content.
- Apply and practice your understanding of the core teaching skills identified in the chapter with the Building Teaching Skills and Dispositions learning units.
- Examine challenging situations and cases presented in the IRIS Center Resources.

- Access additional video clips of CCSSO National Teachers of the Year award winners responding to the question, "Why Do I Teach?" in the Teacher Talk section.
- Check your comprehension on the content covered in the chapter with the Study Plan. Here you will be able to take a chapter quiz, receive feedback on your answers, and then access Review, Practice, and Enrichment activities to enhance your understanding of chapter content.
- Use the Online Lesson Plan Builder to practice lesson planning and integrating national and state standards into your planning.

# 5

# American Education: European Heritage and Colonial Experience

In his Tenth Annual Report, the great American educator Horace Mann said, "I believe in the existence of a great, immutable principle of natural law . . . which proves the absolute right of every human being that comes into the world to an education; and which, of course, proves the correlative duty of every government to see that the means of that education are provided for all."

The U.S. Supreme Court, in *Brown* v. *Board of Education of Topeka* (1954), stated:

> Today education is perhaps the most important function of state and local governments. Compulsory school attendance laws and the great expenditures for education both demonstrate our recognition of the importance of

education to our democratic society. It is required in the performance of our most basic public responsibilities, even service in the armed forces. It is the very foundation of good citizenship. . . . Such an opportunity [of an education], where the state has undertaken to provide it, is a right which must be made available to all on equal terms.

However, because the Constitution makes no mention of education, the question of whether it should be considered one of the implicitly guaranteed fundamental rights has been the subject of continued debate.

In your opinion, is the right to an education one of those inalienable rights that should be guaranteed by the government? Why? What are the implications of your decision?

*W*hen the courts consider cases that involve interpretation of the Constitution or specific laws, they often review historical records and consider the context of the time to try to determine the intent of the lawmakers. Similarly, studying the history of education helps educators understand the development of educational thought and practice and evaluate present educational institutions, theories, and practices in the light of past successes and failures. To help you develop insights into the background of American education presented in this chapter, keep the following learning objectives in mind:

• Compare ancient Hindu and ancient Chinese education.
• Distinguish between the aims of education in ancient Hebrew and ancient Egyptian societies.
• Contrast Spartan and Athenian education.
• Compare the educational philosophies of Socrates, Plato, and Aristotle.
• Explain the contribution of Quintilian to the development of European educational thought and practice.

• Describe the influence of Arab scholars on Western education.
• Discuss the impact of the Reformation on the provision of education.
• Identify the contributions of Bacon, Comenius, Locke, Rousseau, Pestalozzi, Herbart, and Froebel to current educational practice.
• Describe the curriculum in colonial elementary and secondary schools and the forces that shaped it.
• Compare education in the New England, Middle Atlantic, and Southern colonies.

**MyEducationLab**

Visit the MyEducationLab for *Foundations of American Education* to enhance your understanding of chapter concepts with a personalized Study Plan. You'll also have the opportunity to hone your teaching skills through video and case based Assignments and Activities, and Building Teaching Skills and Disposition lessons.

# Education in Ancient Societies

Throughout history all societies have engaged in some form of education of their youth. In the absence of any written language this was informal, oral, and directed at the transmission of cultural values, practices, and language, as well as preparation for survival and adulthood in that particular culture and environment. With the development of written language and numeracy came the need for more formal instruction in their use. Education, as it came to be provided in non-Western and Western societies, is described in the following sections.

## *Education in Ancient Non-Western Societies*
### Education in China

While education in ancient China can be traced to about 2000 B.C., formal education appeared centuries later, primarily in the major cities, and was concerned with preparing the sons of nobility for government service. The curriculum of the schools for the nobility centered on the so-called Six Texts: rituals, music, archery, charioteering, writing, and mathematics. Schools for the common people, male and female, could also be found in the cities and smaller villages.

In later centuries the curriculum of the schools gave way to one based on the teachings of Confucius and other philosophers. Private schools began to appear for the singular purpose of preparing students for the civil service examinations. As early as the second century B.C., state-supported academies, also designed to prepare students for government service, appeared. The curriculum in these institutions was based on the Confucian Five Classics and Four Books (ethics, wisdom, spirit, and truthfulness). Confucianism considered education an ongoing process of self-improvement, the purpose of which was to "transmit a cultural heritage in order to cultivate the moral person that knows how to solve the problems of society and government" (Murphy, 2006, p. 12). Confucian education dominated the Chinese educational system into the twentieth century.

### Education in Hindu Society

Ancient Hindu education was centered on the teaching of Vedas, the Hindu sacred scriptures, but it also included the sciences, writing, and philosophy. By the sixth century B.C., the formalism and exclusiveness of the Vedas system, now confined largely to the Brahmans (Hindu upper caste), gave rise to a new religious order and movement: Buddhism. Education for the Hindu was concerned with the strengthening and purification of the body, mind, and soul, as well as creating a sense of harmony with oneself, with society, and one's environment. In time both elementary and secondary schools were established. Buddhist schools were open to students of all classes, male as well as female, although females rarely attended beyond the elementary level. Institutions of higher training attracted scholars from a number of countries and contributed much to developments in engineering, medicine, mathematics, and the physical and biological sciences. The Hindu tradition had a major influence on education throughout Central and Southeast Asia as well as China, Korea, and Japan.

## Education in Hebrew Society

The basic purpose of Hebrew education was preparing individuals to serve God. Because both Rabbinic law and the Torah obligated parents to diligently teach their children the Scriptures, and males a vocation, literacy was widespread in ancient Israel. Primary education was provided in community schools, where children learned the Scriptures, while higher education, beginning at about age 13, was provided to males at the beit midraski (House of Study). The House of Study was attached to or adjacent to the synagogue and was so valued by Hebrew society that the rabbis allowed a synagogue to be sold to build a House of Study (Mosley, 2011). The importance placed on education to the perpetuation and practice of religion by the ancient Hebrews has continued over the centuries and was reflected in the importance placed on education by the New England colonists.

**Reflect on Diversity**
How does the importance placed on education and the relationship between education and religion in Hebrew society compare with the role of education and religion in Protestant American society?

## Education in Egypt

The earliest form of education in Egypt was conducted at schools that were connected with a temple and taught writing, mathematics, and science. These Egyptian temple schools were attended almost exclusively by the children of the upper class. Their purpose was to prepare the educated bureaucracy needed to administer the vast Egyptian empire and to further the technologies needed to build the architectural monuments for which Egypt is so well known. The curriculum of the Egyptian school at the lower level emphasized writing, music, religion, astronomy, and mathematics. After six to 10 years, a limited number of students went on to advanced studies in religion, medicine, and architecture. Students were taught using an elaborate system of pictographic script known as *hieroglyphics*. Lower-level students used clay tablets, whereas students at the upper level used papyrus, a form of paper made from reeds that was invented by the Egyptians.

## *Education in Ancient Western Societies*

### Education in Greece

The Greeks are considered the first real educators in the Western world, "for they were the first western peoples to think seriously and profoundly about educating the young, the first to ask what education is, what it is for, and how children and men should be educated" (Castle, 1967, p. 11). However, although the Greeks were interested in education, they were not all in agreement as to what form it should take. For example, the content and approach to education in the two principal Greek city–states, Sparta and Athens, were quite different.

Sparta was predominantly a military state, and education reflected Spartan life. The maintenance of military strength was the most important goal of the government. The welfare of the individual came second to the welfare of the state, life was regimented by the state, and severe limits were placed on individual freedoms. Creative or strictly intellectual pursuits were discouraged. The aim of the educational system, which began at age seven for boys, was to inculcate patriotism and the ideal of the sacrifice of the individual to the state, as well as to develop and train physically fit and courageous warriors.

Whereas Sparta was renowned for its military pre-eminence, Athens was a democracy that held the individual in the highest regard. There was no compulsory education in Athens, except for two years beginning at age 18, when military training was required of all men. Athenian schools were private and restricted to those who could afford the fees.

Education in Athens prior to 479 B.C. (the defeat of Sparta), referred to as "the old education," consisted of sending boys ages 7 to 14 to several schools: the *didascaleum* or music school; the home or building of the *grammatistes* for the study of reading, writing, and arithmetic; and the *palestra* for physical education. Formal education stopped after age 14, although some youth continued their education at the gymnasia, where they received more demanding physical training, somewhat military in nature. From ages 18 to 20, a program involving military, public, and religious service was required of all young men; on completion of this service, full citizenship was granted. The aim of educating men in the Athenian state was to prepare a cultivated, well-mannered, physically fit, and agile individual ready for participation in Athenian citizenship.

**For Your Reflection and Analysis**

What aspects of the educational systems of Sparta and Athens do you find appropriate for today's students?

The traditional view of the education of girls in Athens, as in Sparta, is that they received instruction only in the home. Yet archaeological evidence suggests otherwise. Various pottery and statues depict girls going to school, as well as reading, writing, and engaging in sports. However, it is uncertain how widespread these practices were (Beck, 1964), and they may have been limited to girls from the upper class.

The "new Greek education" (after 479 B.C.) continued in much the same vein as the "old" education at the elementary level. At the secondary level, however, a new element was introduced—the Sophists, traveling teachers who charged admission to their popular lectures. In the absence of a legal profession, some Sophists developed the practice of *logography*, the writing of speeches that their clients could deliver in courts of law. Sets of speeches and handbooks on rhetoric were sold. Schools of rhetoric grew in size and number.

**Socrates (470–399 B.C.).**  In contrast to the Sophists, Socrates did not commercialize his teaching and accepted no fees. He also disagreed with the use of knowledge merely to achieve success or gain power, and he believed that knowledge was ethically and morally important to all men. According to Socrates, knowledge was a virtue that was both eternal and universal.

Socrates believed that the purpose of education was not to perfect the art of rhetoric but to develop in the individual his inherent knowledge and to perfect the ability to reason. Socrates believed that education and society were inextricably related: Society was only as good as its schools. If education was successful in producing good citizens, then society would be strong and good.

**Socratic Method.**  Socrates employed a dialectical teaching method that has come to be known as the **Socratic Method** and is similar to the inquiry method practiced today. Using this method, Socrates would first demolish false or shaky opinions or assumptions held by the student while disclaiming any knowledge himself. Then, through a questioning process based on the student's experiences and analyzing the consequences of responses, he led the student to a better understanding of the problem. Finally, he brought the student to a discovery of general ideas or concepts that could be applied to new problems.

**For Your Reflection and Analysis**

Can you recall an example from your own educational experience of the application of the Socratic Method?

> "What is courage?" he would casually ask a soldier.
> "Courage is holding your ground when things get rough."
> "But supposing strategy required that you give way?"
> "Well, in that case you wouldn't hold—that would be silly."
> "Then you agree that courage is neither holding nor giving way."
> "I guess so. I don't know."
> "Well, I don't know either. Maybe it might be just using your head. What do you say to that?"
> "Yes—that's it; using your head, that's what it is."
> "Then shall we say, at least tentatively, that courage is presence of mind—sound judgment in time of stress?"
> "Yes." (Meyer, 1972, p. 26)

**Plato.**  Socrates' most famous pupil was Plato. Plato founded the academy described in Chapter 3. Fees were not charged, but donations were accepted. As a teacher, Plato practiced a variety of methods. Sometimes he employed the Socratic Method. At other times he assigned individual exercises and problems. Sometimes he lectured, although according to Meyer (1972), he was too technical and lecturing was not his best performance. Plato's theory of education is most clearly put forward in *The Republic* (1958) and the *Laws*.

In *The Republic* Plato begins by accepting Socrates' premise that "knowledge is virtue." He then expounds on the nature of knowledge and lays out the framework for both a political and social system, including an educational system. Plato believed that the state should operate the educational system. The aim of the school was to discover and develop the abilities of the individual, to aid the individual in discovering the knowledge of truth that is within each of us, and to prepare the individual for his or her role in society. The curriculum was to include reading, especially the classics, writing, mathematics, and logic. Plato also emphasized the physical aspects of education. However, games and sports, as well as music, were important not for the purpose of entertainment but to improve the soul and achieve moral excellence.

Although Plato advocated universal education, he presumed that few possessed the capacity to reach its final stages. Those who passed the successive selection tests and reached the highest levels of wisdom and knowledge of good (i.e., the philosophers) were the best suited to rule the state; the philosopher was to be king. Thus, education is the means by which one arrives at the ultimate good. In the process, it promotes the happiness and fulfillment of the individual (because the individual is sorted into the social office to which he or she is most fitted), as well as the good of the state. Plato's belief in leadership by the most intelligent has since been espoused by countless others, including some of the founders of our nation. His belief in unchanging ideas and absolute truths has earned him the title of "the Father of Idealism."

**Aristotle.** Aristotle was Plato's most famous student. For 20 years he studied and taught at the Academy. However, as the picture at the beginning of this chapter aptly reminds us, and as discussed in Chapter 3, Plato and Aristotle differed in some important respects. In the picture Plato is shown pointing heavenward as Aristotle points earthward. And that, metaphorically, was the main difference between them: Plato was the idealist, the lover of the metaphysical, whereas Aristotle was a realist, the more scientific of the two (Winn & Jacks, 1967).

It is probably fair to say that Aristotle has had more of an impact on education than either Socrates or Plato, perhaps because he gave the most systematic attention to it. Aristotle is credited with the introduction of the scientific method of inquiry. He systematically classified all branches of existing knowledge and was the first to teach logic as a formal discipline. He believed that reality was to be found in an objective order.

Like Plato, Aristotle believed in the importance of education to the functioning of society and that education should be provided by the state; unlike Plato, he did not believe in educating girls. The aim of education, he felt, was the development of the intellect to its fullest potential through the cultivating of habits and reason. The ultimate goal was to produce a good person and good citizen.

Last, Aristotle believed that there was a common "core" of knowledge that was basic to education, which included reading, writing, music, and physical education. This belief in a core of knowledge has prevailed through the centuries and is the basis for the core course requirements in American schools and colleges today.

## Education in Rome

The Roman conquest of Greece in the second century B.C. brought thousands of Greek slaves to Rome and exposed Romans to Greece and its culture. The educational theories of the Greeks had a great impact on the Romans, and by the end of the first century, these theories dominated Roman education. The formal Roman school system that evolved (and that influenced education throughout Europe for centuries) was composed of the elementary school, known as the *ludus*, and the secondary school or **grammar school.** At the ludus children ages 7 to 12 years were taught reading, writing, and accounting. Girls could attend the ludus, but usually that was as far as their education extended. Grammar schools were attended by upper-class boys ages 12 to 16 years who learned grammar (either Greek or Latin) and literature. From ages 16 to 20, boys attended the school of rhetoric, where they were instructed in grammar, rhetoric, dialectic, music, arithmetic, geometry, and astronomy. Universities were founded during the early years of the Roman Empire. Philosophy, law, mathematics, medicine, architecture, and rhetoric were the principal subjects taught.

### Quintilian (A.D. 35–95)

The most noteworthy Roman educator was Quintilian, tutor to the emperor's grandsons. His influence on Roman schooling has had a subsequent impact on education through the centuries. Quintilian was so respected that he was made a senator and was the first known state-supported teacher (Wilkins, 1914). His *Institutio Oratoria* (*Education of the Orator*) is considered to be "the most thorough, systematic and scientific treatment of education to be found in classical literature, whether Greek or Roman" (Monroe, 1939, p. 450).

Quintilian believed that the goal of education should be to cultivate the intellect and moral nature. Accordingly, in addition to instruction in grammar and rhetoric, Quintilian recommended a broad literary education that included music, astronomy, geometry, philosophy and gymnastics. Such an education was to take place in the schools, preferably the public schools, not home schooling with private tutors as had been the practice in Rome. Similar to arguments of those who oppose homeschooling today (See the Controversial Issue discussion of homeschooling below), Quintilian maintained that public (i.e., group) education provided the opportunity for emulation, friendships, and learning from the successes and failures of others.

Progressive for his time, Quintilian disapproved of corporal punishment:

> because it is a disgrace . . . (and) because if a boy's disposition be so abject as not to be amended by reproof, he will be hardened . . . (by) stripes. Besides, after you have coerced a boy with stripes, how will you treat him when he becomes a young man, to whom such terror cannot be held out? (Monroe, 1939, pp. 466–467)

In many other respects Quintilian's views seem remarkably modern. Recognizing that "study depends on the good will of the student, a quality that cannot be secured by compulsion," Quintilian supported holidays because "relaxation

# CONTROVERSIAL ISSUE

## *Homeschooling*

While the homeschooling movement continues to grow at an estimated 8% to 10% per year, the major educational organizations as well as the National Parent Teacher Association oppose homeschooling. Among the pros and cons most often cited are the following:

**For**

1. Homeschooling allows the tailoring of the curriculum to each individual student's interest and learning styles.
2. Parents are free to incorporate religious and spiritual beliefs into the homeschool curriculum.
3. Homeschooling sponsors closer family relationships.
4. Students are freed from peer pressure and competition and therefore develop greater self-esteem and confidence.
5. Greater flexibility in learning times is provided; learning need no longer revolve around a school calendar.
6. Education takes place in a safe and drug-free environment.

**Against**

1. A heavy time commitment is required of parents.
2. Homeschoolers have limited opportunities to interact with diverse populations.
3. Students have limited opportunities to compete in team sports.
4. Parents are with their children all day, every day.
5. Expenditures for education are increased.
6. Homeschools are not required to meet the "quality" teacher requirements under the No Child Left Behind Act.

If the homeschooling movement continues to grow, what possible impacts might it have on local school districts? What standards should the state require home schools to meet?

brings greater energy to study, and also games because it is the nature of young things to play" (Castle, 1967, p. 138). He believed in the importance of early training to child development. Of the proper methods of early instruction Quintilian said: "Let his instruction be an amusement to him; let him be questioned and praised; and let him never feel pleased that he does not know a thing . . . let his powers be called forth by rewards such as that age prizes" (cited in Monroe, 1939, p. 455). He also maintained that children should not be introduced to specific subject matter until they are mature enough to master it. Last, Quintilian emphasized the importance of recognizing individual differences when prescribing the curriculum. He charges the teacher to "ascertain first of all, when a boy is entrusted to him, his ability and disposition . . . when a tutor has observed these indications, let him consider how the mind of his pupil is to be managed" (cited in Monroe, 1939, p. 465).

The Roman system of education eventually spread throughout Western Europe. The schools of medieval Europe retained the standard curriculum of the Roman schools: grammar, rhetoric, logic, mathematics, geometry, music, and astronomy. Figure 5.1 provides an overview of education in Sparta, Athens, and Rome.

**For Your Reflection and Analysis**

Should Quintilian's works be required for teacher education students today? Why or why not?

## Education in the Middle Ages

The period between the end of the Roman Empire (A.D. 476) and the 14th century is known as the Middle Ages. The Germanic tribes that conquered the Romans appropriated not only their land but also much of their culture and their Catholic

**Figure 5.1 — Education in Ancient Societies**

| EDUCATION IN SPARTA | CONTRIBUTION TO WESTERN EDUCATION |
|---|---|
| • Goal of education: to promote patriotism and train warriors<br>• Welfare of individual is secondary to the welfare of the state<br>• Curriculum emphasized exercise and games, military training, dance, and music | • Recognition of importance of physical and moral training |

| EDUCATION IN ATHENS | |
|---|---|
| • Goal of education: to prepare the well-rounded individual for participation in citizenship<br>• Emphasis on the development of reason<br>• Curriculum: reading, writing, mathematics, logic, physical education, music, and drama<br>• Schools: *didascaleum* (music school); *grammatistes* (reading, writing, and arithmetic) | • Concept of liberal education<br>• The Socratic method as a teaching method<br>• Importance of reason/the scientific method |

| EDUCATION IN ROME | |
|---|---|
| • Goal of education: to develop the intellectual and moral citizen<br>• Emphasis on education for citizenship<br>• Curriculum: reading, writing, arithmetic, grammar, literature, music, rhetoric, astronomy, geometry, and philosophy<br>• Schools: *ludus* (elementary); grammar school (secondary); schools of rhetoric (from ages 16–20); universities | • Roman curriculum and organization adopted throughout Europe<br>• Recognition of individual differences<br>• Recognition of importance of play and relaxation |

religion. The Roman Catholic Church became the dominant force in society and in education. By the end of the 6th century, public education had all but disappeared, and what remained took place under the auspices of the church. At the secondary level, monastic schools originally established to train the clergy now educated boys in the established disciplines of the Roman schools. Theology was studied by those preparing for the priesthood. One important function of the monastic schools was preserving and copying manuscripts. Had it not been for the monastic schools, many of the ancient manuscripts that survive today would have been lost.

## Thomas Aquinas (1225–1274)

The most important scholar and philosopher of the Middle Ages was the Dominican monk St. Thomas Aquinas. As discussed in Chapter 3, his philosophy, called scholasticism or neo-Thomism, is the foundation of Roman Catholic education. Aquinas was able to reconcile religion with the rationalism of Aristotle. He believed that human beings possess both a spiritual nature (the soul) and a physical nature (the body). He also maintained that man is a rational being and that through the deductive process of rational analysis man can arrive at truth. When reason fails, man must rely on faith. Thus, reason supports what man knows by faith: reason and faith are complementary sources of truth. In accordance with this philosophy, the schools were to teach both the principles of the faith and rational philosophy. The curriculum was to contain both theology and the liberal arts.

## The Medieval Universities

During the later Middle Ages, as the Crusades opened Europe to other parts of the world and many of the Greek masterpieces that had disappeared from Europe but had been preserved by Arab scholars were rediscovered, an intellectual revival occurred that manifested itself not only in scholasticism but in the establishment of several of the world's great universities. The University of Salerno, established in 1050, specialized in medicine; the University of Bologna (1088), in law; the University of Paris (1150), in theology; and Oxford University (1167), in liberal arts and theology. By the end of the Middle Ages, almost 100 universities had been established. Some, such as the University of Paris, grew out of a cathedral school, in this case Notre Dame. Others evolved from associations called *universitas*, which were chartered corporations of teachers and students, organized for their protection against interference from secular or religious authorities.

**For Your Reflection and Analysis**

If the student guild or union were in effect today, what changes might it recommend for undergraduate education?

Initially, most universities did not have buildings of their own but occupied rented space. The curriculum at the undergraduate level followed the seven liberal arts. Classes started soon after sunrise. The mode of instruction was lecture in Latin, with the teacher usually reading from a text he had written. Student guilds or unions, commonplace at the time, ventured to tell the professors how fast to speak. At Bologna the students wanted to get full value for their fees and required the professors to speak very fast. By contrast, the Parisian students insisted on a leisurely pace, and when the authorities ordered some acceleration, the students not only "howled and clamored" but also threatened to go on strike (Meyer, 1972). More exciting than the lectures were the disputations at which students presented and debated opposing intellectual positions. The disputations also served to prepare students for the much dreaded day when they would defend their theses. The Historical Note on the next page provides a glimpse of the life of the university student in medieval times. Note the differences and similarities with present-day student life.

Of all the institutions that have survived from medieval times to the present, with the exception of the Catholic Church, the university bears the closest resemblance to its ancient ancestors. As it was then, it is still an organization of students and professors dedicated to the pursuit of knowledge. It still grants the medieval degrees: the bachelor's, the master's, and the doctor's. In most universities students are still required to study a given curriculum, and if they seek the doctorate, they are required to write a thesis or dissertation and to defend it publicly. The gowns worn at academic ceremonies today are patterned after those worn by our medieval ancestors. Deans, rectors, and chancellors still exist, although their duties have changed (Meyer, 1972).

## Influence of Arab Scholars

Without the Arabs much of the classical Greek knowledge would have been lost to the world. Arab scholars vigorously sought out and translated the ancient Greek manuscripts. Many of the original Greek manuscripts disappeared and it was the Arabic translations that were later translated into Latin and other languages. However, Arab scholars "were not simply transmitters of Greek concepts; they were creators in their own right" (Covington, 2007, p. 3). For example, the Arab mathematician Muhammad ibn Musa al-Khwarizmii invented algebra, and the physicist Alhasan ibn al-Haitham not only correctly deduced the path of light rays, establishing the principle of linear perspective, but also introduced the experimental method, "insisting that theories had to be verified in practice, a key element to modern science that was missing from the less empirical Greek tradition" (Covington, 2007, p. 6). Also of note are the Arab contributions to the advancement of medicine and medical education. Not only did the Arabs establish hospitals throughout their far-flung empire, but also, as early as the beginning of the 10th century, Arab physicians were required to pass an examination and possess a license (Totah, 1926). The most famous and influential Arab philosopher–scientist of the late 10th and early 11th centuries, Avicenna (mentioned in Chapter 3), wrote more than 100 treatises on Aristotelian philosophy and medicine. His five-volume *The Canon of Medicine* is said to be the most famous single work in the history of medicine ("Avicenna," 1997).

Numerous other advances in mathematics and science made by Arab scholars were adopted by Western educators and European culture. One of the most enduring examples is the adoption of the Arabic numbering system to replace the cumbersome Roman numbering system, which used Latin letters. The spread of Arab science was greatly facilitated by the construction of paper mills, the first outside China. Paper replaced parchment and papyrus, making the production of manuscripts cheaper and easier to disseminate (Covington, 2007). Last, it should be noted that the institutions of higher education established by the Arabs throughout Spain, in Egypt, and in the Middle East provided the model for those that were established in Europe during the Middle Ages (Ulich, 1971).

**For Your Reflection and Analysis**

How does the depiction of Arabs described in this section compare with that found in the popular press today?

# HISTORICAL NOTE

## Life of the Medieval University Student

Although academic life was rigorous, students had many privileges. They were exempt from military service and from paying taxes. A student who shaved his head and assumed a few other burdens became one of the clerical class and was allowed some of the benefits associated with it. For example, if he broke what would be considered civil law, he was tried under church law, not civil law. However, in keeping with his clerical status the student was required to be celibate. If he did stray, he could continue with his studies but lost his privileges and would be denied a degree.

Medieval students were not without vices. Taverns often surrounded the universities and featured women and gambling. More seriously, students at Oxford were said to roam the streets at night, assaulting all who passed. In Rome the students went from tavern to tavern committing assault and robbery. At Leipzig they were fined for throwing stones at professors, and at Paris they were excommunicated for shooting dice on the altars of Notre Dame.

Although these acts were the exception rather than the rule, such actions, as well as the attitude of the students, who held townspeople in low regard, were sufficient to lead to open hostilities between "town" and "gown." Some separation still exists between town and gown in many university communities, perhaps a legacy from our medieval ancestors.

*Source:* Based on accounts in A. E. Meyer (1972). *An educational history of the Western world.* New York: McGraw-Hill.

# Education During the Renaissance

The Renaissance, which began in the 14th century and reached its high point in the 16th century, was so called because it represented a renaissance or rebirth of interest in the cultures of ancient Greece and Rome. It was a period of great change: the decline of the feudal system; the rise of nation–states and nationalism; the growth of cities; a revival of commerce; the introduction of gunpowder, new forms of art, literature, and architecture; and the exploration of new worlds. The dominant philosophy of the Renaissance was **humanism.** Humanism viewed human nature as its subject. It stressed the dignity of the individual, free will, and the value of the human spirit and all nature. Rejecting scholasticism and the model of the scholar–cleric as the educated man, the humanists considered the educated man to be the secular man of learning described in the classics. They also looked to the classics, primarily the works of Quintilian, for commentary on education. Quintilian's *Institutio Oratoria* (*Institutes of Oratory*) had been found and taken to Italy by Byzantine scholars when Constantinople (Istanbul) fell to the Muslims in 1453.

The foremost humanist of the Renaissance and the one with the greatest impact on educational thought was Desiderius Erasmus (1466–1536) of the Netherlands. Erasmus studied at the University of Paris and Oxford University and was a professor at Cambridge in England. Like other humanists, Erasmus believed in the importance of teaching Latin and Greek. His *Colloquies* used dialogues to not only teach Latin style but also to instruct in religion and morals, and were among the most important textbooks of his time. The use of text to teach both language and Christian doctrine and morals provided a model for the *New England Primer*, which was to become the most important textbook in colonial America.

In the *Education of Young Children*, Erasmus argued for early childhood education. In *Upon the Method of Right Instruction*, he proposed the systematic training of teachers, who he believed must be both broadly educated and experts in their subjects, be of gentle disposition, and have unimpeachable morals. His views on pedagogy are found in his treatise *Of the First Liberal Education of Children*, in which he asserted that the needs and interests of the student take precedence in the selection of materials and methods, not those of the church or the medieval guilds. In this treaty he, as had Quintilian 15 centuries earlier, deplored the use of corporal punishment and promoted the value of play and games.

Erasmus's philosophy expresses a belief in the potential of the individual to improve himself (Erasmus does not address the education of females), as well as the importance of education to the development of the intellect and morality. In his emphasis on individuality and inherent human rights, Erasmus was ahead of his time and pointed the way to the Enlightenment.

The first products of the Renaissance in education can be seen in the famous Italian court schools connected to the courts of reigning families, perhaps the best known being the ones operated by Vittorino da Feltre at Mantua from 1423 to 1446 and by Guarino da Verona at Ferrara from 1429 to 1459. Like many modern preparatory boarding schools, they housed boys from ages 8 or 10 to age 20. They emphasized what Woodward (1906) called the "doctrine of courtesy"—the manners, grace, and dignity of the antique culture. At the court schools a humanist curriculum included the so-called **seven liberal arts** (grammar, logic, rhetoric, arithmetic, geometry, astronomy, and music), as well as reading, writing, and speaking in Latin, study of the Greek classics, and, for the first time, the study of history. Following the teachings of Quintilian, games and play were also emphasized, individual differences were recognized, and punishment was discouraged. The goal was to produce well-rounded, liberally educated courtiers—the ideal personality of the Renaissance—for positions as statesmen, diplomats, or scholars.

The classical humanist curriculum, if not the humanist student-centeredness, is reflected in the Latin grammar school, the dominant form of secondary education in colonial New England. Moreover, the humanist belief that the human condition could be improved by education is reflected in the educational writings of many

**For Your Reflection and Analysis**

Which, if any, of the seven liberal arts should be required subjects today? Why?

of the Founding Fathers. And, although the Protestant reformers discussed later in this chapter are generally not considered humanists, they also shared the humanist belief in the importance of education, the importance and responsibility of the individual in determining his destiny, and the role of the school in teaching moral principles.

## Education During the Reformation

The period of history known as the Reformation formally began in 1517 when an Augustinian monk and professor of religion named Martin Luther nailed his *Ninety-Five Theses* questioning the authority (and abuses) of the Roman Catholic Church to the door of the court church in Wittenburg, Germany. In the years that followed, a religious revolution swept the European continent, resulting in a century of war and the reformation of the Roman Catholic Church. Those who protested the authority of the Church came to be known as Protestants. The invention of the printing press enabled their doctrine and the Bible translated in the vernacular to be spread rapidly. Where the Renaissance produced educational thought and practice that prestaged secondary education in America, the Reformation did the same for elementary education.

**For Your Reflection and Analysis**

Speculate on the impact of the invention of the printing press on education.

### Martin Luther (1483–1546)

One of the major practices rejected by Martin Luther and other leaders of the Reformation was that the Scriptures were read and interpreted almost exclusively by priests because most other people were illiterate. Luther not only objected to the power and authority this provided the church, but also he believed that every individual was responsible for his or her salvation, a salvation that came through faith, not works, and that could best be obtained by prayer and reading and studying the Scriptures. To do this, however, it was necessary that every child be provided a free and compulsory elementary education. Luther believed that education should be supported by the state and that the state should have the authority and responsibility to control the curriculum, the textbooks, and the instruction. In his 1524 *Letters to the Mayors and Aldermen of All Cities of Germany in Behalf of Christian Schools*, Luther stressed the spiritual, economic, and political benefits of education.

The curriculum he recommended was to include classical languages, grammar, mathematics, science, history, physical education, music, and didactics (moral instruction). Theology was also to be taught and the study of Protestant doctrines accomplished through the catechism (a question-and-answer drill).

Although formal schooling was important to the establishment of a "priesthood of believers," Luther thought it should occupy only part of the day. At least one or two hours a day should be spent at home in vocational training, preparing for an occupation through an apprenticeship. Secondary schools, designed primarily as preparatory schools for the clergy, taught Hebrew as well as the classical languages, rhetoric, dialectic, history, mathematics, science, music, and gymnastics. A university education, whose purpose was seen as providing training for higher service in

The nailing of Martin Luther's thesis on the door of the church at Wittenburg marked the beginning of the Reformation.

the government or the Church, was available only to those young men who demonstrated exceptional intellectual abilities.

### John Calvin (1509–1564)

One of the major theologians of the Protestant Reformation, and perhaps the one most important to American history, was John Calvin. Raised as a French Catholic, Calvin, like Luther, came to reject the authority of the Catholic Church and accepted the doctrine of salvation by faith through prayer and the study of the Scriptures. Calvin's views on education were very similar to those of Luther. He too stressed the necessity of a universal, compulsory, state-supported education that would not only enable all individuals to read the Bible themselves and thereby attain salvation, but also would profit the state through the contributions of an orderly and productive citizenry. The school was also seen as a place for religious indoctrination through catechistic instruction. Calvin also supported a two-track educational system consisting of common schools for the masses and secondary schools teaching the classical, humanist curriculum for the preparation of the leaders of church and state.

Calvin's influence was widespread, both in the Europe of his day and later in the colonies of the New World. His advocacy of a universal primary education provided by the vernacular schools (described below) was adopted by Protestant theologians and educators throughout Europe and was brought to the New World by the Puritans (English Calvinists who sought to purify or reform the Church of England) who settled in New England, as well as members of the Dutch Reformed Church who settled in New York, and Presbyterian Scotch Calvinists who settled in the Middle and Southern colonies. The efforts of each of these groups reflect the Calvinist emphasis on the importance of education to the religious, social, and economic welfare of the individual and the state. The legal mandates adopted by Calvinist communities in Europe (e.g., holding parents responsible for the education of their children) became the models for similar laws in the New England colonies. And the Calvinist proposal for state-supported education had great appeal to the growing middle classes in Europe and the American colonies.

### Vernacular Schools

**For Your Reflection and Analysis**

What are the disadvantages of teaching in the vernacular?

The initial product of the belief that it was necessary for each person to be able to read the Scriptures was the establishment of **vernacular schools**—primary or elementary schools that offered instruction in the mother tongue or "vernacular." Instruction in the native tongue also reflected and served to reinforce the spirit of nationalism that had begun to emerge during the Renaissance. The vernacular schools provided a basic curriculum of reading, writing, mathematics, and religion.

Vernacular schools were established throughout Germany by Philip Melanchthon and Johann Bugenhagen following Luther's teachings. Elementary schools that followed the teachings of Calvin also began to appear in other Protestant strongholds, especially those in the Netherlands, Scotland, and Switzerland. And it was the vernacular school that served as the model for the elementary schools that were established in colonial America.

## Later European Educational Thought

The Reformation opened the door not only to the questioning of superstition and religious dogma, but also to investigation of the laws of nature. The Reformation gave way to the Age of Enlightenment or Reason, so called because of the great reliance placed on reason and scientific inquiry. Philosophers and scholars believed that observation and scientific inquiry were the avenues to the discovery of the "natural laws" that dictated the orderly operation of the universe.

## Francis Bacon (1561–1626)

The English philosopher Francis Bacon (mentioned in Chapter 3) was central to this movement. He was also important to education because of the emphasis he placed on scientific inquiry, rather than on accepting previously derived hypotheses. He emphasized the need for education to develop what today is termed *critical thinking skills*. The Utopia described in Bacon's *The New Atlantis* envisioned a research university not inconsistent with modern ideas.

## Jan Amos Comenius (1592–1670)

Bacon had a major influence on Jan Amos Comenius, a Moravian bishop. Like Bacon he was a proponent of sense realism, which is the belief that learning must come via the senses through observational experience. Accordingly, education must allow children to observe for themselves and experience by doing. The notion of sensory learning was later expanded by Locke, Rousseau, and Pestalozzi.

Comenius also shared Bacon's belief in the scientific method and in an ordered universe that could be discovered through reason and experience. Comenius attempted to identify the developmental stages of children and is said to be the first educator to propose a theory of child growth and development. He proposed a set of teaching methods that incorporated both the deductive method and whatever instructional method was most appropriate for the specific developmental stage of the child.

Comenius proposed that teaching be straightforward and simple and proceed from concrete examples to abstract ideas, that it deal with things before symbols, and that it have practical application. He affirmed Quintilian's beliefs with regard to individual differences, motivation, and corporal punishment. Finally, he believed in a general learning, ***paideia,*** which should be possessed by all educated persons.

Comenius was perhaps the first educator to propose universal public education. He had a profound effect on Western education through his influence on the thinking of such educational leaders as Johann Pestalozzi, Horace Mann, John Dewey, and Mortimer Adler (1984) who dedicated his *The Paideia Program: An Educational Syllabus* to Comenius.

## John Locke (1632–1704)

Although the English philosopher John Locke is best known for his political theories, which served as the basis for the American and French constitutions, he also had a profound influence on education. As discussed in Chapter 3, Locke taught the ***tabula rasa*** concept of the human mind, which says that we come into the world with our minds a blank slate. We then learn through sensation. Locke recommended a curriculum that included, beyond the "three Rs," history, geography, ethics, philosophy, science, and conversational foreign languages, especially French. Mathematics was also emphasized, not to make the scholar a mathematician but to make him a reasonable man.

The curriculum Locke recommended anticipated that of the academy described in the next section. And, as is evidenced in the writings of the Founding Fathers on whom he had such an influence, Locke believed the goal of education was to create the moral, practical individual who could participate effectively in the governing process.

Locke's political philosophy, in keeping with his respect for the lessons of science, proposed that there were inherent laws of nature and therefore man had certain natural rights. These natural rights came from God or nature, not from rulers or governments. Among these rights, according to Locke, were those espoused later in the Declaration of Independence: life, liberty, and the pursuit of happiness.

## Jean-Jacques Rousseau (1712–1778)

A century later, another philosopher who is best remembered for his political theories but who also had a profound effect on educational theory, Jean-Jacques Rousseau, advanced the natural law argument. Rousseau is associated with an educational movement called **naturalism**. Its emphasis on freedom and the individual has had a significant influence on educational theory and practice. Rousseau's book *Social Contract* had a major influence on the thinking of those involved in both the French and American revolutions.

Rousseau expounded a theory and philosophy of education that influenced many educators, including John Dewey and other progressives. Rousseau has also been called the "father of modern child psychology" (Mayer, 1973). Like Comenius, Rousseau believed in stages of children's growth and development and in the educational necessity of adapting instruction to the various stages. His major thoughts on education are contained in his novel *Emile*, which puts forth the ideal education for a youth named Emile. The education of Emile was to be child centered, concerned with developing his natural abilities. He was to learn by his senses through direct experience and was not to be punished. Emile's education was to progress as he was ready and as his interests motivated him and was to be concerned with his physical growth and health. Finally, Emile was to be taught a trade in order to prepare him for an occupation in life.

### Johann Pestalozzi (1746–1827)

Johann Heinrich Pestalozzi, a Swiss educator, put Rousseau's ideas into practice. Pestalozzi has had a profound impact on education throughout much of the Western world. The Prussian government sent teachers to be instructed by him, and educators came from all over the world, including the United States, to observe and study his methods. Horace Mann and Henry Barnard came under his influence. Edward A. Sheldon, superintendent of schools in Oswego, New York, established a teacher training school at Oswego in 1861 that followed Pestalozzi's methods.

Pestalozzi's philosophy of education incorporated the child-centered, sensory experience principles of Rousseau. Like Rousseau, he believed in the natural goodness of human nature and the corrupting influence of society. He also supported Rousseau's idea of individual differences and "readiness" to learn. His belief in the development of the total child to the child's maximum potential was given its greatest recognition during the second half of the 20th century in the movement for the education of disadvantaged students.

Perhaps more than Rousseau, Pestalozzi recognized the importance of human emotions in the learning process. It was important, he believed, that the child be given feelings of self-respect and emotional security. It also was important that the teacher treat students with love. In fact, it can be said that the ideal of love governs Pestalozzi's educational philosophy. Pestalozzi was especially fond of poor children and recognized the need to provide them with a school environment that addressed their physical and emotional needs.

Like Comenius, Pestalozzi believed that instruction must begin with the concrete and proceed to the abstract. Materials should be presented slowly, in developmental order from simple to complex, from known to unknown. The **object lesson** provides concrete illustrations of a principle or concept that are within the child's experience.

### Johann Herbart (1776–1841)

One of the Prussian educators who studied under Pestalozzi was Johann Friedrich Herbart. His pedagogical theory included three key concepts: interest, apperception, and correlation. Instruction can be successful only if it arouses interest. Interests are derived from both nature and society; thus, the curriculum should include both the natural and social sciences. All new material presented to the child is interpreted in terms of past experiences by the process of apperception, the association of new ideas with ideas already present. Additionally, ideas can be reinforced and organized in the mind by the proper correlation of subjects in the curriculum.

Herbart maintained that any suitable material could be learned if presented systematically. The five steps in the Herbartian teaching methodology are as follows:

1. *Preparation*—preparing the student to receive the new material by arousing interest or recalling past material or experiences;

2. *Presentation*—presenting the new material;

3. *Association*—helping students see the relationship between old and new ideas;

4. *Generalization*—formulating general ideas or principles; and

5. *Application*—applying the ideas or principles to new situations.

Herbart's ideas had a significant influence on American education. Before the end of the century, teachers across the country were organizing lessons around the five steps in the Herbartian methodology. Although the Herbartian movement was short lived, the Herbartian ideas and pedagogy had a profound influence on teaching methods and the curriculum, particularly at the elementary level, long after the movement itself faded (Kliebard, 1995). As late as the 1950s the Herbartian steps could be found in teacher education tests (Connell, 1980). But, perhaps most important, 200 years later his theories of learning have been incorporated into constructivism and validated by what emerging brain research has revealed about how we learn (see discussion in Chapter 14).

### Friedrich Froebel (1782–1852)

Friedrich Froebel, also a student of Pestalozzi, was a leader in the 19th century's movement to break with subject-centered instruction and focus on the needs and capabilities of the child. Froebel is known for the establishment of the first kindergarten (1837) and for providing the theoretical basis for early childhood education. Although Froebel accepted many of Pestalozzi's ideas associated with child centeredness, Froebel was more concerned with activity than Pestalozzi, but less concerned with observation. According to Froebel, the primary aim of the school should be self-development through self-expression, which would take place through games, singing, or any number of creative and spontaneous activities that were to be part of an **activity curriculum**. Froebel was also concerned with the development of creativity in children. He viewed the classroom as a miniature society in which children learned social cooperation.

Froebel developed highly stylized educational materials that were mass produced and used throughout the world. They were designed to aid self-expression and bring out the "divine effluence" (the fundamental unity of all nature with God) within each child. Materials referred to as *gifts* and *occupations* were used. The gifts were objects that did not change their form (e.g., wooden spheres, cubes), symbols of the fundamentals of nature. The occupations were materials used in creative construction or design whose shape changed in use (e.g., clay, paper). Used together they were said to ensure the progressive self-development of the child.

One of Froebel's pupils, Margaretha Schurz, opened the first kindergarten in the United States in Watertown, Wisconsin. John Dewey adopted many of Froebel's principles and used them in his famous laboratory school at the University of Chicago. Today, the kindergarten is recognized for its importance in the educational process and as a socializing force. It is the cornerstone of the American educational system.

Table 5.1 gives an overview of the educational theorists we have discussed and their influence on Western education.

**For Your Reflection and Analysis**

Recall your own experience in the primary grades. To what extent was your education similar to Froebel's activity curriculum?

## Education in the "New" Old World Before Jamestown

The English, the predominant settlers of the American colonies, had the greatest influence on the educational system that emerged in the colonies, but the French and Spanish also played a role. The French empire in the New World spread from

**Table 5.1 — Western European Educational Thought (1200–1850)**

| Theorist | Educational Theories | Influence on Western Education |
|---|---|---|
| Aquinas (1225–1274) | Human beings possess both a spiritual and a physical nature. Man is a rational being. Faith and reason are complementary sources of truth. | Provided basis for Roman Catholic education. |
| Erasmus (1466–1536) | The liberally educated man is one educated in the seven liberal arts, steeped in the classics and in rhetoric. Systematic training of teachers is needed. Follower of Quintilian. | Advanced the need for the systematic training of teachers and a humanistic pedagogy. Promoted the importance of politeness in education. |
| Luther (1483–1546) | Education is necessary for religious instruction, the preparation of religious leaders, and the economic well-being of the state. Education should include vocational training. | Provided support for concept of free and compulsory elementary education. Promoted concept of universal literacy. |
| Calvin (1509–1564) | Education serves both the religious and political establishments: elementary schools for the masses, where they could learn to read the Bible and thereby attain salvation; secondary schools to prepare the leaders of church and state. | Concept of two-track system and emphasis on literacy influenced education in New England and ultimately the entire nation. |
| Bacon (1561–1626) | Education should advance scientific inquiry. Understanding of an ordered universe comes through reason. | Provided major rationale for the development of critical thinking skills. Proposed the concept of a research university. |
| Comenius (1592–1670) | Learning must come through the senses. Education must allow the child to reason by doing. There is a general body of knowledge (*paideia*) that should be possessed by all. | Provided theory of child growth and development. Concept of *paideia* profoundly influenced numerous Western educational leaders. |
| Locke (1632–1704) | Children enter the world with the mind like a blank slate (*tabula rasa*). The goal of education is to promote the development of reason and morality. | Provided support for the concept of the reasonable man and the ability and necessity for the reasonable man to participate in the governing process. |
| Rousseau (1712–1778) | Major proponent of naturalism, which emphasized individual freedom. The child is inherently good. Children's growth and development goes through stages, which necessitates adaptation of instruction. Education should be concerned with the development of the child's natural abilities. | Naturalism provided the basis for modern educational theory and practice. Father of modern child psychology. |
| Pestalozzi (1746–1827) | Education should be child centered and based on sensory experience. The individual differences of each child must be considered in assessing readiness to learn. Children should be educated to reach their maximum potential. Ideal of love emphasized the importance of emotion in the learning process. Instruction should begin with the concrete and proceed to the abstract. | Concept of maximum development of each child provided support for education of the disadvantaged. Pestalozzian methods were exported throughout Europe and to the United States. One of the earliest theories of instruction formally taught to teachers. |
| Herbart (1776–1841) | The aim of education should be the development of moral character. Any material can be learned if presented systematically: preparation, presentation, association, generalization, and application. Instruction must arouse interest to be successful. Education is a science. | Elevated the study of educational psychology. Demonstrated the significance of methodology in instruction. Advanced the concept that education is a science and can be studied scientifically. |
| Froebel (1782–1852) | The aim of education should be to ensure self-development through self-expression. Self-expression takes place through an activity curriculum. The school should promote creativity and bring out "divine effluence" within each child. | Established first kindergarten. Provided theoretical basis for early childhood education. |

Pictograph on Arizona Canyon wall shows Spanish soldiers and priest exploring the Southwest.

Canada to Louisiana. French priests, particularly the Jesuits, followed explorers and fur traders into the wilderness to convert and educate the Native Americans. The Catholic influence on education, which can still be seen in cities as far apart as Quebec and New Orleans, can be traced to the Jesuits, a teaching order that had been influential in establishing a number of secondary schools and universities in Europe, as well as to orders of teaching sisters.

The Spanish empire in the New World was no less vast, encompassing at various times the entire Southwest, Florida, and California. Spanish Catholic priests, especially the Franciscans, followed the explorers and established a vast network of missions throughout the Southwest where they sought to convert and educate the Native Americans. On the heels of the priests came Spanish settlers migrating north from Mexico. By 1800 almost 25,000 Spanish-speaking people were living in the Southwest. What little formal education most children of these settlers received took place at one of the missions. These missions also often taught Native Americans not only the Spanish language but also agricultural and vocational skills. Children of more affluent settlers were schooled at home by tutors or were sent to schools in Mexico or Spain.

## Native American Education

When the Spanish, French, and later English came to what was to be called the "New World," the land already had as many as 11 million inhabitants representing 300 tribes and 200 languages (see Figure 5.2). The education of these millions of native peoples did not originate with the mission schools. In fact, prior to the arrival of Europeans in the New World, each native group had a comprehensive formal and informal system for educating and training their children and youth in what Tuscarura has described as the "three basic courses" of native education: (1) economic or survival skills, (2) knowledge of cultural heritage, and (3) spiritual awareness (Szasz, 1999). Embedded in this "curriculum" were the core values of native educational practice: (1) the spirit of belonging, (2) the spirit of mastery, (3) the spirit of independence, and (4) the spirit of generosity (Brendtro, Brokenleg, & Van Bockern, 2002). The free and spontaneous nature of Native American education, which relied on oral tradition, not the written word, was very different from the more formalized approach of the Europeans. As a result, the European colonists perceived it as unreliable and as a lesser form of education than the traditional school model they employed (Hale, 2002).

**Reflect on Diversity**
To what extent are the core values of native educational practice evidenced in non-Native American education today?

**Figure 5.2 — Native American Culture Groups**

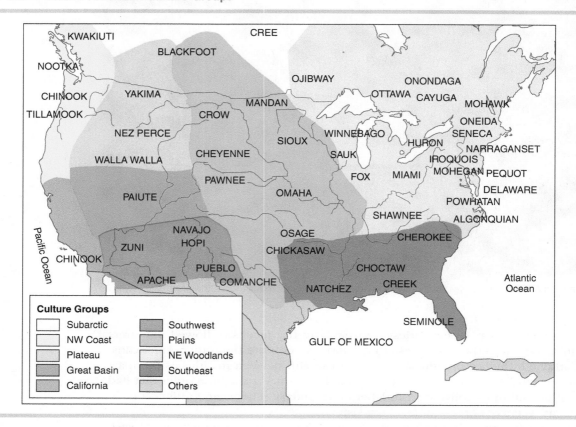

*Source:* R. Stefoff (2001). *The Colonies*, Tarrytown, NY: Benchmark Press, p. 21. Copyright © Marshall Cavendish Corporation. Reprinted from *The Colonies* with permission of Marshall Cavendish Benchmark.

# Education in Colonial America

The first English settlement in North America was at Jamestown (Virginia) in 1607. In 1620, the Pilgrims, a group of Separatist Puritans (Protestants who wanted not only to purify but also to separate from the Church of England), settled at Plymouth (Massachusetts). Ten years later a group of nonseparatist Puritans founded the Massachusetts Bay Colony. This colony became a focal point of migration, and other New England colonies (Rhode Island, New Haven [Connecticut], New Hampshire, Maine) developed from this base (Cohen, 1974). Many of the colonists who came to the New World were filled with a sense of religious commitment, largely Protestant, which shaped their views on life and education. However, the settlers in other regions did not all share their economic and political traditions, religion, society, or education. These variations are explored in the following sections.

## Education in the New England Colonies

According to Cubberley (1934), the Puritans who settled New England "contributed most that was of value for our future educational development" (p. 14). The New England colonists, who were generally well educated themselves, sustained a vigorous emphasis on education even in the hostile new environment. In fact, by 1700 the New England colonies could boast of literacy rates that were often superior to those in England (Cohen, 1974).

Initially, the Puritans attempted to follow English practice regarding the establishment and support of schools by relying on private benefactors and limiting the role of the state. However, the general absence of wealthy Puritan migrants soon led to the abandonment of this practice and, because of fears that parents were neglecting the education of their children, to a more direct role for the state (Cohen, 1974).

## First Education Laws

The Massachusetts Law of 1642 ordered the selectmen of each town to ascertain whether parents and masters (of apprentices) were, in fact, providing for the education of their children. The selectmen were also to determine what the child was being taught. The child of any parent or master failing to meet his obligation could be apprenticed to a new master, who would be required to fulfill the law. Although the law neither specified schools nor required attendance, it is said to have established the principle of compulsory education. Five years later, the Education Law of 1647 ordered every township of 50 households to provide a teacher to teach reading and writing, and all townships of 100 or more households to establish a grammar school. Although there was no uniform compliance or administration of these laws, they show how important education was to the Puritans and demonstrate their belief in the necessity of a literate citizenry for the functioning of political society. The laws also served as models for other colonies and are considered the first education laws in America.

**For Your Reflection and Analysis**

Give examples of existing education laws or policies that are directed at maintaining or strengthening the social order. How effective are they?

## Religious Influence

In New England, as in the other colonies, the institutions of secular government, including education, were closely aligned with the dominant religious group. The Puritans brought with them many of the educational views of the Reformation, namely, that education was necessary for religious instruction and salvation as well as for economic self-reliance and the exercise of citizenship by an educated laity. As the Massachusetts Law of 1642 explained, there was a need to ensure the ability of children "to read and understand the principles of religion and the capital laws of this country." This purpose is also evidenced by the first words of the Massachusetts Education Law of 1647, also called the "old Deluder Satan Law": "It being one chief project of that old deluder, Satan, to keep men from knowledge of the Scriptures." The founding of Harvard College in 1636 was also based on religious motives: to ensure that there would be an educated ministry for the colony. The colonists were fearful that there would be no replacements for the ministers who first came with them, and they dreaded "to leave an illiterate Ministry to the churches, when our present Ministers should lie in the Dust" (Cubberley, 1934, p. 13).

**For Your Reflection and Analysis**

How do the basic purposes of education in Colonial America compare with those of today?

## Elementary Schooling

The New England colonists not only shared Calvin's view of the aim of education but they also adopted the two-track system advocated by Calvin and other scholars of the Reformation. Town schools and dame schools were established to educate the children of the common folk in elementary reading, writing, and mathematics. The **dame schools** were held in the kitchen or living room of a neighborhood woman, often a widow, usually a person with minimal education herself, who received a modest fee for her efforts. Girls were allowed to attend the dame schools, and some did attend the town schools, but most received only a minimal education. In Puritan New England the view was that a little reading, spelling, and needlework was all the education that was needed or appropriate for females.

The dame school provided the only education many colonial children received.

Girls needed to be able to read so that they could study the Bible, but writing, arithmetic, grammar, and geography were considered unnecessary.

So-called writing or reading schools were concerned with the teaching of these disciplines and operated on a fee basis. **Charity** or **pauper schools** were operated by various denominations or wealthy benefactors for the children of the poor who could not afford to attend other schools.

Education was also made available as a result of the apprenticeship system, whereby a child was apprenticed to a master to learn a trade. In addition, the master was required by the terms of the indenture to ensure that the apprentice received a basic education. For some children this was the avenue by which they learned what little reading and writing they knew.

Instruction in the schools was primarily religious and authoritarian. Students learned their basic lessons from the **hornbook**, so called because the material was written on a sheet of parchment, placed on a wooden board, and covered with a thin sheath of cow's horn for protection. The board was shaped like a paddle and had a handle with a hole in it so it could be strung around the child's neck.

### The New England Primer

The *New England Primer* was used with slightly older children. The primer is an excellent example of the interrelationship between education and religion. Although editions of the primer varied somewhat in the 150 years of its publication, which began in 1690, it usually featured an alphabet and spelling guide, followed by one of the things that made the primer famous—24 little pictures with alphabetical rhymes as illustrated in Figure 5.3.

The primer also included the Lord's Prayer, the Apostles' Creed, the Ten Commandments, a listing of the books of the Bible, and a list of numbers from 1 to 100, using both Arabic and Roman numerals. Another prominent feature of the primer was a poem, the exhortation of John Rogers to his children, from John Foxe's *Book of Martyrs*, with a picture of the martyr burning at the stake as his wife and children look on. The primer ended with a shortened version of the Puritan catechism (Ford, 1962).

### Secondary Grammar Schools

Secondary grammar schools existed for the further education of the male children of the well-to-do. They also served as preparatory schools for the university where the leaders of the church and political affairs were to be trained and which required proficiency in Latin and Greek for admission. The Boston Latin School, established in 1635, became the model for similar schools throughout New England.

Education at the grammar school was quite different from that at the dame or town school. The emphasis was on Latin, with some Greek and occasionally Hebrew. Other disciplines included those necessary for the education of the Renaissance concept of the educated man. The course of study in the grammar school was fairly intensive and lasted for 6 to 7 years, although students "tended to withdraw and return, depending on familial need and circumstances; and since school was conducted on a year-round basis and instruction organized around particular texts, it was fairly simple for a student to resume study after a period of absence" (Cremin, 1970, p. 186).

### University Education

Education in the university in the early colonial period was also based on the classically oriented curriculum of English universities. As Cohen (1974) described it:

> The undergraduate courses revolved around the traditional Trivium and Quadrivium but without musical studies, the Three Philosophies (Metaphysics, Ethics, Natural Science), and Greek, Hebrew, and a chronological study of ancient history. As in English universities logic and rhetoric were the basic subjects in the curriculum. . . . Compositions, orations, and disputations were given the same careful scrutiny as at English universities. (p. 66)

**Figure 5.3 — An Alphabet Including Religious and Secular Jingles**

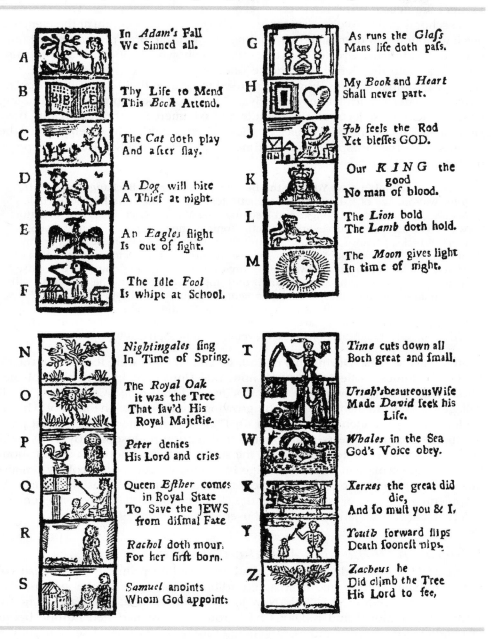

*Source:* From *The New England Primer*, by P.L. Ford (Ed.), 1962. New York: Teachers College Press. Copyright 1962 by Teachers College Press. Reprinted by permission.

## Education in New England During the Later Colonial Period

**Social and Economic Changes.** The Age of the Enlightenment or Age of Reason that swept the Western world in the 17th century had found its way to the shores of the American colonies by the 18th century. As in Europe, it brought greater concern for independent rationality, a repudiation of supernatural explanations of phenomena, and a greater questioning of traditional dogma. At the same time that the Enlightenment was sweeping the colonies, the population of the colonies increased rapidly and their economy outgrew their localized base of farming and fishing. Trade and commerce increased, and a new mercantile gentry emerged (Cohen, 1974). The mercantile activities of the new middle class called for a freer environment and increased religious toleration.

**Birth of the Academy.** It was inevitable that the educational system would change to meet the needs of the intellectual, economic, and social order. The writing and dame schools began to give way to town schools. The curriculum at the elementary level, although still dominated by reading and writing, now placed greater importance on arithmetic. Greater concern was also shown for practical and vocational training at both the elementary and secondary levels.

Many grammar schools, however, refused to change their classical curricula. As a result, numerous academies and private venture schools sprang up in the larger towns, teaching subjects useful in trade and commerce. If the prestigious Boston Latin School would not teach mathematics, others would. Advertisements for these schools filled the newspapers of the time. One such 1723 advertisement appearing in New York City read:

> There is a school in New York, in the Broad Street, near the Exchange, where Mr. John Walton, late of Yale College, Teacheth Reading, Writing, Arethmatick, whole Numbers and Fractions, Vulgar and Decimal, The Mariners Art, Plain and Mercators Way; Also Geometry, Surveying, the Latin Tongue, the Greek and Hebrew Grammers, Ethicks, Rhetorick, Logick, Natural Philosophy and Metaphysicks, all or any of them for a Reasonable Price. The School from the first of October till the first of March will be tended in the Evening. If any Gentlemen in the Country are disposed to send their Sons to the said School, if they apply themselves to the Master he will immediately procure suitable Entertainment for them, very Cheap. Also if any Young Gentlemen of the City will please to come in the Evening and make some Tryal of the Liberal Arts, they may have the opportunity of Learning the same things which are commonly Taught in Colledges. (Seybolt, cited in Rippa, 1997, pp. 61–62)

**Growth of Colleges.** During this period, several colleges were founded in the New England colonies: Collegiate School, now Yale University, in 1701; the College of Rhode Island, now Brown University, in 1764; and Dartmouth College in 1769. The colleges of this era also reflected the growing secularism of the society. This was evidenced in a broadened curriculum. In 1722 Harvard established its first professorship in secular subjects: mathematics and natural philosophy. By 1760 the scientific subjects accounted for 20% of the student's time. Another manifestation of the growing secularism was the change in graduates' careers. Theology remained the most popular career, but an increasing number of graduates were turning to law, medicine, trade, or commerce as the New England colleges became centers of independence, stimulation, and social usefulness (Cohen, 1974).

## Education in the Mid-Atlantic Colonies

Whereas the New England colonies had been settled primarily by English colonists who shared the same language, traditions, and religion, the settlers of the mid-Atlantic colonies (New York, New Jersey, Pennsylvania, Delaware) came from a variety of national and religious backgrounds. Most had fled Europe because of religious persecution and were generally more distrusting of secular authority than the New England colonists. Whereas the schools in the mid-Atlantic colonies were as religious in character as those in New England, their diverse religious backgrounds made it impossible for the government in any colony to agree on the establishment of any one system of state-supported schools. Thus, it fell to each denomination to establish its own schools. The consequence of this pattern was the absence of any basis for the establishment of a system of public schools or for state support or regulation of the schools. As a result, many young people, especially those in rural areas, had no access to education beyond what might be provided in the home.

### New York

The colony of New Netherlands was established in 1621 by the Dutch. Initially, New Netherlands was similar to the New England colonies. Schools were supported by the Dutch West India Company and were operated by the Dutch Reformed Church.

After the colony was seized by the British and became the royal colony of New York (1674), state responsibility and support were withdrawn and, except for a few towns that maintained their own schools, formal schooling became a private concern. Education at the elementary level was by private tutors for the upper class, private venture schools for the middle class, and denominational schools for the lower class.

Most notable of the denominational schools were those operated by a missionary society of the Church of England, the Society for the Propagation of the Gospel in Foreign Parts (SPG). The apprenticeship system also was very strong in New York and provided the means by which some children gained an education. However, because few towns established their own schools and the provision of education was principally left to the will or ability of parents to send their children to private or denominational schools, illiteracy rates were high (Cohen, 1974).

Education at the secondary level was even more exclusively private or parochial. The private venture secondary schools were few in number and questionable in quality.

Higher education was absent for any but the few who could afford to leave the colony. It was not until 1754 that the first institution of higher education, Kings College, now Columbia University, opened in the colony.

## New Jersey

New Jersey was originally part of New York. As in New York, education in New Jersey was primarily private and denominational. The religious diversification was great and each of the sects—Dutch Reformed, Puritan, Quaker, German Lutheran, Baptist, Scotch-Irish Presbyterian—established its own schools. The SPG also operated schools for the poor. A few towns, mainly those in the eastern region settled by the Puritans, established town schools. Secondary education was limited. Because of the primarily rural, agrarian economy, the private venture secondary schools found in the other mid-Atlantic colonies were lacking. However, the proximity to New York and Philadelphia did provide access to their secondary institutions for those who could afford it (Cohen, 1974).

It is in the realm of higher education that the colony of New Jersey most distinguished itself. Prior to the Revolution more colleges were founded there than in any other colony: the College of New Jersey, now Princeton University (1746), and Queens College, now Rutgers University (1766).

## Pennsylvania

The Pennsylvania colony was founded in 1681 by a Quaker, William Penn. The Quakers, or Society of Friends, were very tolerant of other religions; consequently, a number of different religious groups or sects settled in Pennsylvania. William Penn advocated free public education, and the Pennsylvania Assembly enacted a law in 1683 providing that all children be instructed in reading and writing and be taught "some useful trade or skill." Yet the colony did not develop a system of free public education, primarily because of the great diversity among the settlers. A few community-supported schools were established, but as in the other mid-Atlantic colonies, formal education was primarily a private or denominational affair.

However, the major difference between Pennsylvania and the other mid-Atlantic colonies was that the various denominations did, in fact, establish a fairly widespread system of schools in Pennsylvania. The SPG founded a number of charity schools, including a school for black children in Philadelphia. The Moravians also established a number of elementary schools, including the first nursery school in the colonies, and a boarding school for girls, and they were active in efforts to Christianize and educate the Native Americans. They devised a script for several Native American languages and translated the Bible and other religious materials into these languages. In their pedagogical practices they were influenced by the educational philosophy of Comenius, who was a Moravian bishop.

The Quakers were the most significant denomination in terms of educational endeavors. Their belief that all people were created equal under God led not only to the education of both sexes and to the free admission of the poor, but also to the education of Blacks and Native Americans. A school for Black children was established in Philadelphia as early as 1700. Because the Quakers do not have a ministry, they were not as interested in the establishment of secondary schools leading to that vocation. In their secondary schools they emphasized practical knowledge rather than the classical curriculum studied at most secondary schools at that time.

Schools were also established at the secondary level by other denominations. A number of private secondary schools were opened during the later colonial period, many offering such practical subjects as navigation, gauging, accounting, geometry, trigonometry, surveying, French, and Spanish. Among them was Benjamin Franklin's Philadelphia Academy, opened in 1751.

### Benjamin Franklin (1706–1790)

Franklin was strongly influenced by the writings of John Locke and was a proponent of practical education to prepare the skilled craftsmen, businessmen, and farmers needed by the colonies. In his 1749 *Proposals Relating to the Education of Youth in Pennsylvania,* he outlined the plan for a school in which English, rather than Latin, was to be the medium of instruction. This break with tradition was important, for in effect it proposed that vernacular English could be the language of the educated person. Franklin also proposed that students be taught "those Things that are likely to be most useful and most ornamental. Regard being had to the several Professions which they are intended" (p. 1).

From this statement of principle, Franklin went on to detail what should be the specific subject matter of the academy:

> All should be taught "to write a fair hand" and "something of drawing"; arithmetic, accounts, geometry, and astronomy; English grammar out of Tillotson, Addison, Pope, Sidney, Trenchard, and Gordon; the writing of essays and letters; rhetoric, history, geography, and ethics; natural history and gardening; and the history of commerce and principles of mechanics. Instruction should include visits to neighboring farms, opportunities for natural observations, experiments with scientific apparatus, and physical exercise. And the whole should be suffused with a quest for benignity of mind, which Franklin saw as the foundation of good breeding and a spirit of service, which he regarded as "the great aim and end of all learning." (Cremin, 1970, p. 376)

**For Your Reflection and Analysis**

To what extent do you agree with Franklin on what should be the "great aim and end of all learning"?

As time passed, Franklin's academy gave less emphasis to the practical studies and came to more closely resemble the Latin grammar school. Before he died Franklin declared the academy a failure as measured against his initial intent (Cremin, 1970).

Franklin was also instrumental in the founding in 1753 of the College of Philadelphia, now the University of Pennsylvania. Unlike its sister institutions, the College of Philadelphia was nonsectarian in origin (although it later came under Anglican control). The curriculum of the college was perhaps more progressive than those at other institutions. Students were allowed a voice in the election of courses, and the curriculum emphasized not only the classics but also mathematics, philosophy, and the natural and social sciences. A medical school was established in connection with the college.

### Delaware

Delaware, founded in 1638 as a Swedish colony, New Sweden, fell under Dutch control in 1655, then under the rule of the English with their conquest of New Netherlands. Education in Delaware was greatly influenced by Pennsylvania. Pennsylvania's general abandonment of the responsibility for the provision of education to private or denominational groups after 1683 was followed in Delaware. Although a number of elementary schools were established in the colony, the level of literacy remained low. During the colonial period, formal secondary education was available on a very limited basis and no institution of higher education was established in Delaware (Cohen, 1974).

## Education in the Southern Colonies
### Influence of Social and Economic Systems

The southern colonies (Maryland, Virginia, the Carolinas, and Georgia) differed significantly from the New England and mid-Atlantic colonies. The Southern colonies were royal colonies administered by governors who were directly accountable to the king. Unlike the New England Puritans, who sought to reform the Church of England, the colonists in the southern colonies accepted the Church of England as the established church. (The exception was Maryland, which was founded by Lord Baltimore as a refuge for English Catholics.) (And the Church of England asserted that it was the responsibility of parents to educate their children, not the government. Consequently, local governments were not required to establish or support schools. Whereas religious dissatisfaction was the principal motivation for the settling of New England, the reasons for settlement of the southern colonies were primarily economic.

Rather than small farms and commerce, the economy of the southern colonies was based on the plantation and slave system. The plantation system created distinct classes dominated by the aristocratic plantation owners. The relatively small population of the southern colonies was widely dispersed. This factor limited the growth of any public or universal system of education.

### Elementary and Secondary Education

As a result of the social and economic structure of the southern colonies, educational opportunities were largely determined by social class. The children of the plantation owners and the wealthy commercial classes in the Tidewater cities received their education from private tutors or at private Latin grammar schools before being sent to a university. In the early colonial period, it was common for the children of the plantation aristocracy to be sent to England to receive their secondary or, more often, their university education. However, as the number of colonial colleges grew, this practice declined.

For the majority in the less affluent classes, the only education available was at the elementary level, informally through the apprenticeship system, or formally at endowed (free) schools, charity schools, denominational schools, or private venture schools. Virginia was the most active of the southern colonies in attempting to ensure the education of apprenticed children, especially orphaned children. Often this education took place in so-called workhouse schools.

The endowed or free schools were few in number and actually were not free except to a small number of poor boys. The charity schools were primarily those operated by the SPG. The influence of the SPG in the southern colonies was significant and represented "the nearest approach to a public school organization found in the South before the Revolution" (Cohen, 1974, p. 129). Schools operated by other denominations were also established in the southern colonies. In some rural areas where other schooling was not available, several small planters or farmers might build a schoolhouse on an abandoned tobacco field. These "old field schools" generally charged a fee and offered only the most basic education.

At the secondary level, except for the private venture schools and a few public grammar schools in the larger towns or cities, few schools existed. And even the number of private venture schools was limited. As a result of the public neglect of education, overall the educational level of the southern colonies was below that of most of the northern colonies, especially those in New England.

## Higher Education: The College of William and Mary

The only institution of higher education established in the South prior to the Revolutionary War was the College of William and Mary, established in 1693 to train ministers for the Church of England and take Christianity to Native Americans. Like Harvard, the only older institution of higher education in the colonies, it also originally offered the traditional curriculum. However, by the first quarter of the 18th century it began to broaden its curriculum. It was the first college to offer an elective system and, perhaps foreshadowing Virginian supremacy in the public affairs of the country, William and Mary emphasized law and politics earlier than any other college in the country.

Figure 5.4 presents an overview of education in colonial America.

**Figure 5.4 — Education in Colonial America**

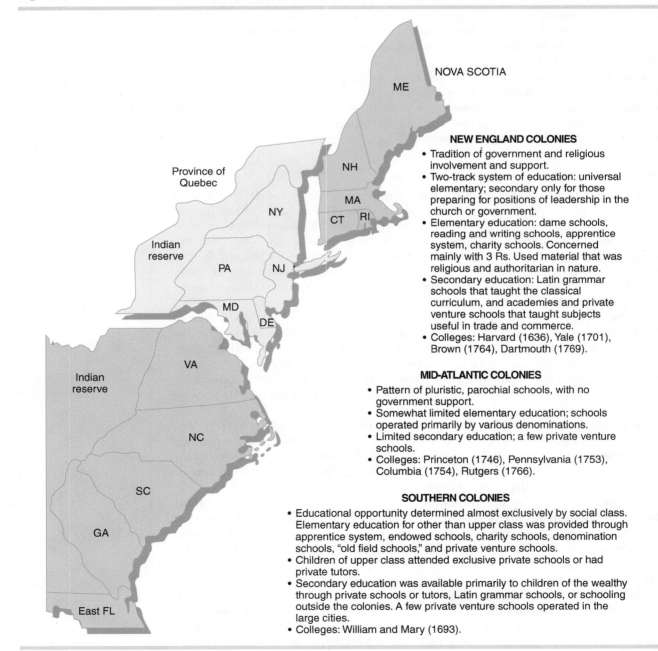

**NEW ENGLAND COLONIES**

- Tradition of government and religious involvement and support.
- Two-track system of education: universal elementary; secondary only for those preparing for positions of leadership in the church or government.
- Elementary education: dame schools, reading and writing schools, apprentice system, charity schools. Concerned mainly with 3 Rs. Used material that was religious and authoritarian in nature.
- Secondary education: Latin grammar schools that taught the classical curriculum, and academies and private venture schools that taught subjects useful in trade and commerce.
- Colleges: Harvard (1636), Yale (1701), Brown (1764), Dartmouth (1769).

**MID-ATLANTIC COLONIES**

- Pattern of pluristic, parochial schools, with no government support.
- Somewhat limited elementary education; schools operated primarily by various denominations.
- Limited secondary education; a few private venture schools.
- Colleges: Princeton (1746), Pennsylvania (1753), Columbia (1754), Rutgers (1766).

**SOUTHERN COLONIES**

- Educational opportunity determined almost exclusively by social class. Elementary education for other than upper class was provided through apprentice system, endowed schools, charity schools, denomination schools, "old field schools," and private venture schools.
- Children of upper class attended exclusive private schools or had private tutors.
- Secondary education was available primarily to children of the wealthy through private schools or tutors, Latin grammar schools, or schooling outside the colonies. A few private venture schools operated in the large cities.
- Colleges: William and Mary (1693).

## Summary

The schools of the United States can trace their ancestry to those of ancient Greece and Rome. Educational idealism is based on the philosophy of Plato. The scientific method popularized in the 20th century is rooted in the philosophy of realism espoused by Aristotle. And a number of the more progressive educational positions of this century were advanced by the Roman educator Quintilian: opposition to corporal punishment, advancement of the concept of readiness learning, and support for the recognition of individual differences in learners. The concept of universal public education that we enjoy today was a product of the Reformation. It was brought to New England by the Puritans, who held the view that education was necessary for religious instruction and salvation as well as for good citizenship. However, the earliest American educational systems were not free, were limited at the secondary levels and, in ways that would be prohibited today, were dominated by the religious establishment. In the next chapter we will continue to trace the evolution of the American educational system from the Revolution to the 20th century.

## TEACHER OF THE YEAR

*Sally Broughton Montana*

I teach because it is my passion to preserve and protect this great representative democracy in which we live. I want my young students to become empowered, engaged, and participating citizens. What an awesome responsibility. When I see my young students testify before a board and tell politicians and policy makers how to make their community better, I know that I am helping them to become engaged, participating citizens in our democracy. When I see their contributions to the community my heart swells with pride: a warning system for our local radio station, a new playground, a safe walking path to school, a helmet law to protect the children. I want my students to know that the sky is the limit. I want them to have the skills, the responsibility, and the knowledge necessary to pursue whatever they want. I love teaching and cannot imagine doing anything else. Each day is a joy as I work with children and watch them learn, grow, spread their wings ... and fly.

# PROFESSIONAL DEVELOPMENT
## *Workshop*

## *Prepare for the State Licensure Examination*

Mr. George Theosolis is a fifth-grade teacher at the Eleanor Roosevelt Elementary School, where he has been teaching for the past decade. Although George enjoys being in a self-contained classroom and teaching a variety of subjects, his real love is history. Because of George's commitment and creativity, numerous students throughout the school have been actively engaged in several major history projects, including the construction of a huge diorama to be unveiled in late May that will showcase America's colonial history.

George has developed a reputation for being the in-house historian. His finest moments have occurred when he dresses up as one of history's most noteworthy figures. He has gone so far as to study the speech and idiosyncratic mannerisms of many American spokespersons, including several American presidents. Today, George Theosolis is Ben Franklin and in a few minutes is scheduled to enter his fifth-grade class dressed as Franklin to introduce a new unit entitled *America's Break with Tradition*. George is not sure how much his students already know about Franklin, and his objective is for his students to become acquainted with Franklin's important contributions to America's past, present, and future.

Besides his love of history, George Theosolis has become the school's guru on *constructivist* teaching. Last summer he took a professional development class at the university entitled "Jean Piaget: Constructivism & Creativity." Since that experience, George has been convinced that Piaget's theories about learning styles are keys to motivating children to learn. According to Piaget, students are not passive bystanders in relationship to their environment, nor to their educational experiences. Rather, when they become involved in their education by either relating to it or experiencing it, they gain personal meaning.

This afternoon George will be introducing several group projects that will enable students to interact with other students while solving individual and societal problems. By the end of the week, George's objective is that each student will be committed to a group project or will become involved in a single issue that he or she will pursue, which will culminate in the May celebration. George also intends that each student complete an individual writing project related to some topic addressed by the unit.

1. Give examples of various writing projects that George Theosolis might assign his fifth-grade students. Describe the benefits of those assignments and the criteria he would use for grading the writing projects.

2. What form of preassessment should George use to determine what students know about Benjamin Franklin before beginning the unit? Defend your choice.

3. What are the essential elements of constructivist teaching? Which of these have been incorporated into George Theosolis's instruction?

### Build Your Knowledge Base
1. How would Aristotle and Plato answer the question posed at the beginning of this chapter: Should the right to an education be guaranteed by the government?
2. What impact did the Reformation have on the education of common people?
3. What ideas of Pestalozzi and Froebel are in practice in the schools of your community?
4. Describe the status of higher education in colonial America.
5. Contrast education in the New England, mid-Atlantic, and southern colonies. Do any legacies of these differences remain today?
6. What was the contribution of the apprenticeship system to education in the colonies?

## Develop Your Portfolio

1. Rousseau believed in stages of children's growth and development, and in the educational necessity of adapting instruction to the various stages. Faced with the reality that, in any given class, you will probably encounter students who are at various stages of growth and development, prepare an artifact that demonstrates how you will be sensitive to adapting your instruction to your students' needs. Place your artifact in your portfolio under **INTASC Standard 1, Learner Development**.

2. Johann Friedrich Herbart, who studied under Pestalozzi, believed that the aim of education should be the development of moral character. Review the Controversial Issues feature in Chapter 3, page 57, "Should Moral Education, Character Education, Ethics, or Values Education Be a Responsibility of the School?" Reflect on the pros and cons of this issue and develop a position paper that summarizes your views on this subject. Place your paper in your portfolio under **INTASC Standard 4, Content Knowledge**.

## Explore Teaching and Learning: Field Experiences

1. Check out a book on the history of education in the colonial period, explore Internet resources, and prepare a three- to five-page summary of the history of the American kindergarten movement. How does today's program compare with the program in which you were a student? What are the differences and similarities?

2. Using public library materials, newspaper reports, interviews with local citizens, and governmental records, summarize the evolution of public and private precollegiate and collegiate education in your community. What factors influenced decisions about the location and mission of educational institutions in your region?

## MyEducationLab

Go to **Topic 7, The History and Philosophy of Education** in the MyEducationLab (www.myeducation-lab.com) for *Foundations of American Education*, where you can:

- Find learning outcomes for the history and philosophy of education along with the national standards that connect to these outcomes.
- Complete Assignments and Activities that can help you more deeply understand the chapter content.
- Apply and practice your understanding of the core teaching skills identified in the chapter with the Building Teaching Skills and Dispositions learning units.
- Examine challenging situations and cases presented in the IRIS Center Resources.

- Access additional video clips of CCSSO National Teachers of the Year award winners responding to the question, "Why Do I Teach?" in the Teacher Talk section.
- Check your comprehension on the content covered in the chapter with the Study Plan. Here you will be able to take a chapter quiz, receive feedback on your answers, and then access Review, Practice, and Enrichment activities to enhance your understanding of chapter content.
- Use the Online Lesson Plan Builder to practice lesson planning and integrating national and state standards into your planning.

# 6

# American Education: From Revolution to the Twentieth Century

**The Boston Examiner**   Thursday, July 13, 1867
***"New U.S. Commissioner of Education Deplores Training of Teachers"***
In an address last evening to the National Education Association meeting in New York, Mr. Henry Barnard, the newly appointed United States Commissioner of Education, commented on the inadequate training possessed by the vast majority of teachers who teach our young. According to Commissioner Barnard: "Too many of those we have entrusted to guide and guard our nation's youth have little knowledge beyond that which they are attempting to impart. Indeed, we might well question whether their knowledge is superior to that of many of their fellow tradesmen. Not only is the depth and breadth of their knowledge of the curriculum matter a subject of concern, but where knowledge is possessed, there exists most often an absence of any training in pedagogy." The commissioner went on to say that "teachers will not be elevated to that place in society and receive that compensation they so richly deserve until they are required to undertake a special course of study and training to qualify them for their office."

Do these comments sound familiar? Which of the concerns expressed by Barnard remain concerns today? Which are no longer concerns?

At the time Henry Barnard made these remarks, the nation was fewer than 100 years old but had already more than tripled in size and increased tenfold in population. Before the century was over, the population would double again. The educational system grew with the nation, sometimes responding to, and sometimes leading, social and economic changes.

As you study the history of American education from the birth of the nation to the beginning of the 20th century, think about the following objectives:

• Describe the impact of Thomas Jefferson and Noah Webster on American education in the early 19th century.

• Identify the contributions that monitorial schools, Sunday schools, infant schools, and free school societies made to the expansion of educational opportunities in the early national period.

• Compare the curriculum and purposes of the academy with those of the grammar school and the high school.

• Discuss the development of common schools in the United States and the roles that Horace Mann, Henry Barnard, Emma Willard, and Catharine Beecher played in that development.

- Outline the development of secondary education in the United States.
- Discuss the factors leading to the growth of higher education in 19th-century America.
- Compare the educational opportunities provided to Native Americans, Hispanic Americans, and Black Americans in the 19th century.
- Trace the development of teacher education in the United States.

**MyEducationLab**

Visit the MyEducationLab for *Foundations of American Education* to enhance your understanding of chapter concepts with a personalized Study Plan. You'll also have the opportunity to hone your teaching skills through video and case based Assignments and Activities, and Building Teaching Skills and Disposition lessons.

# Education in the Early National Period

On July 4, 1776, the 13 colonies declared their independence from England. Education was one of the casualties of the war that followed. Illiteracy increased as rural schools closed their doors, and even the larger town Latin grammar schools were impacted. Almost all schools suffered from a shortage of funds and teachers (Pulliam & Van Patten, 2007). Institutions of higher education lost professors and students to fighting on both sides of the conflict. Many schools were taken over by the war effort, and others became casualties of the war.

After the Revolutionary War, the leaders of the new nation set about the business of devising a government that would encompass the ideas for which they had fought. The first attempt at self-governance under the Articles of Confederation provided little authority to the central government and established no executive or judicial branches. When this government proved inadequate, delegates from each state met in the summer of 1787 and drafted the Constitution, which after ratification in 1789 launched the new republic. Perhaps because of the former colonists' suspicion of a strong central government, or perhaps because of the association of education with theology, neither the Articles of Confederation nor the Constitution mentioned education.

## Northwest Land Ordinances

Despite the fact that neither the Articles of Confederation nor the U.S. Constitution mentioned education, there can be no doubt that the nation's founders recognized the importance of education to a country in which the quality of representation depended on its citizens' ability to make informed choices at the ballot box. To ensure that the settlers in the Northwest Territory did not neglect education, Congress passed perhaps the most important piece of legislation under the Articles of Confederation, the Land Ordinance of 1785. This ordinance, which prescribed the terms of admitting new states into the union from the Northwest Territory, required that the 16th section of land in each township in the Territory be set aside for the support of education. The land could be sold or leased, but the proceeds were to go to fund education. The 16th section, which was the section closest to the geographical center of the township (see Figure 6.1), was a strategic choice for the possible location of a school. Two years later, Article Three of the Northwest Ordinance, which incorporated the Northwest Territory, proclaimed: "Religion, morality, and knowledge being necessary to good government and the happiness of mankind, schools and the means of education shall be forever encouraged."

## Nationalism and Education

The spirit of nationalism that dominated the new republic shaped the views of the Founding Fathers regarding what type of education was needed for the new nation. Whereas the primary purpose of colonial education had been sectarian, emphasis was now placed on citizenship and the nation–state. Education was seen as the best way to both prepare citizens to participate in a republican form of government and maintain order.

The Founding Fathers were aware that changing their form of government was only the beginning of the revolution. As Benjamin Rush, a proponent of universal education, remarked: "We have changed our form of government, but it remains to

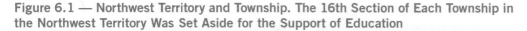

**Figure 6.1 — Northwest Territory and Township. The 16th Section of Each Township in the Northwest Territory Was Set Aside for the Support of Education**

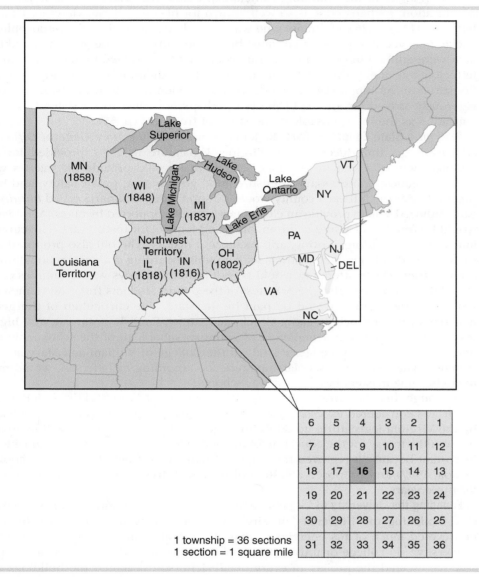

1 township = 36 sections
1 section = 1 square mile

*Source:* L. Dean Webb. *The History of American Education: A Great American Experiment.* 1st ed. (2005). Electronically reproduced by permission of Pearson Education, Inc. Upper Saddle River, NJ.

affect a revolution of our principles, opinions, and manners, so as to accommodate them to the forms of government we have adopted" (Cremin, 1982, p. 1). Rush and his compatriots worked tirelessly at devising endless versions of political and educational arrangements.

Although they differed on many details, there were at least four beliefs common to their discussions: (1) that the laws of education must be relative to the form of government, hence a republic needs an educational system that motivates citizens to choose public over private interest; (2) that what was needed was a truly American education purged of all vestiges of older, monarchical forms and dedicated to the creation of a cohesive and independent citizenry; (3) that education should be genuinely practical, aimed at the improvement of the human condition, with the new sciences at its heart; and (4) that American education should be exemplary and a means through which America could teach the world the glories of liberty and learning (Cremin, 1982).

## Thomas Jefferson

Although many of the Founding Fathers expressed their views on the importance of education, perhaps none is so well known for his educational views as Thomas Jefferson (1743–1826). Jefferson, who was strongly influenced by the philosophy of Locke, believed that government must be by the consent of the governed and that men were entitled to certain rights that could not be abridged by the government. Jefferson was one of the chief proponents of the addition of a Bill of Rights to the Constitution. As Rippa (1997) noted, "Few statesmen in American history have so vigorously strived for an ideal (liberty); perhaps none has so consistently viewed education as the indispensable cornerstone of freedom" (p. 55).

**Plan for a State Education System.** Jefferson's *Bill for the More General Diffusion of Knowledge*, introduced in the Virginia legislature in 1779, provided for the establishment of a system of public schools that would provide the masses with the basic education necessary to ensure good government, public safety, and happiness. Under the bill each county would be subdivided into parts called *hundreds*; each hundred was to provide an elementary school, supported by taxes. Attendance would be free for all White children, male and female, for three years. The curriculum would be reading, writing, arithmetic, and history. The bill also proposed that the state be divided into 20 districts with a public boarding grammar school built in each district. Those attending would be not only those boys whose families could afford the tuition, but also the brightest of the poorer students from the elementary schools, whose tuition would be paid by the state. The curriculum of the grammar school was to include Latin, Greek, geography, English, grammar, and higher mathematics. Finally, on completion of grammar school, 10 of the scholarship students would receive three years' study at the College of William and Mary at state expense. The remaining scholarship students, according to Jefferson, would most likely become masters in the grammar schools.

Although this plan, viewed in today's light, appears strikingly elitist, in Jefferson's day it was considered excessively liberal and philanthropic. In fact, it was defeated by the Virginia legislature, no doubt in large part because of the unwillingness of the wealthy to pay for the education of the poor. Nonetheless, the plan is considered important because it removed the stigma of pauperism from elementary schooling (Rippa, 1997) and proposed a system of universal, free, public education—if only for three years.

**Founding the University of Virginia.** Jefferson's interest in education also extended to establishing the University of Virginia. After leaving the presidency in 1809, he devoted much of his energies to that effort. Sometimes called "Mr. Jefferson's University," no college or university ever bore so completely the mark of one person. He created the project in every detail: Jefferson designed the buildings and landscape (even bought the bricks and picked out the trees to be used as lumber), chose the library books, designed the curriculum, and selected the students and faculty. The university opened in 1825, a year before Jefferson's death on July 4, 1826, exactly 50 years after the adoption of the immortal document he wrote—the Declaration of Independence (Rippa, 1997).

## Benjamin Rush

Benjamin Rush (1745–1813), a medical doctor and professor, was a graduate of both the University of Edinburgh (Scotland) and Princeton. At the outbreak of the Revolutionary War, he was a professor at the College of Philadelphia. Rush was deeply interested in education as well as a broad range of social issues: he was strongly opposed to the death penalty and encouraged penal reform and the establishment of institutions for the mentally ill. Together with Benjamin Franklin, he organized the first abolition society in Philadelphia, the Society for the Relief of Free Negroes Unlawfully Held in Bondage.

Rush wanted to establish a system of schools in Pennsylvania and eventually the entire nation that would provide public support for a system of free schools.

**For Your Reflection and Analysis**

How different are the wealthy of today from the wealthy of Jefferson's time in terms of their willingness to pay additional taxes to support the public schools?

According to the plan he laid out in *A Plan for the Establishment of Public Schools and the Diffusion of Knowledge in Pennsylvania*, a plan similar to Jefferson's for Virginia, Rush proposed that in every town of 100 or more families a free school be established where children would be taught to read and write English and German as well as arithmetic. An academy was to be established in each county "for the purpose of instructing youth in the learned languages (Latin and Greek), and thereby preparing them to enter college." The higher education provisions of the plan included four colleges where males would be instructed in mathematics and the "higher branches of science" as well as one university located in the state capital where "law, physic, divinity, the law of nature and nations economy, etc. be taught . . . by public lectures in the winter season, after the manner of the European universities." Rush's educational plan was intended to tie together the whole educational system: The university would supply the masters for the academies and free schools, while the free schools, in turn, would supply the students for the academies.

Rush was an advocate of the education of women and founded one of the first female academies in the United States, the Young Ladies Academy of Philadelphia. However, he was not an egalitarian. To a large extent, Rush's support of women's education was based on his view of their particular duties in a republic. In his *Thoughts upon Female Education* (1787), Rush espouses the idea of "republican motherhood," the idea that a woman's primary duty was to bring up her sons to be virtuous citizens and that to do this they must themselves be educated.

The Founding Fathers recognized the importance of education to the preservation of the new republic.

Rush was also an advocate for the education of Blacks. Rush saw the education of Blacks to be a moral and economic imperative: "let the young negroes be educated in the principles of virtues and religion . . . let them be taught to read and write—and afterward instructed in some business whereby they may be able to maintain themselves" (Binderman, 1976, p. 21).

## Noah Webster

It was a teacher, Noah Webster (1758–1843), who had the greatest influence on education in the new republic. Whereas the nation's founders had sought political independence from England, Webster sought cultural independence. Webster believed that the primary purpose of education should be the inculcation of patriotism, and that what was needed was a truly American education rid of European influence (Madsen, 1974). These goals could best be accomplished, he believed, by creating a distinctive national language and curriculum. To this end, Webster prepared a number of spelling, grammar, and reading books to replace the English texts then in use; an American version of the Bible; and what became the world-famous *American Dictionary of the English Language*.

Of his textbooks, the most important was the *Elementary Spelling Book*, published in 1783, often referred to as the "blue-back speller" because of the color of the binding. By 1875, 75 million copies of the speller had been sold (Spring, 2008), many of which were used again and again. The book included both a federal catechism with political and patriotic content and a moral catechism whose content

**For Your Reflection and Analysis**

What textbook or book from your elementary or secondary education had the greatest influence on you? Why?

was related to respect for honest work and property rights, the value of money, the virtues of industry and thrift, the danger of drink, and contentment with one's economic status (Rippa, 1997; Spring, 2011). According to the noted historian Henry S. Commager, "No other secular book had ever spread so wide, penetrated so deep, lasted so long" (cited in Rippa, 1997, p. 60).

Webster supported the concept of free schools in which all American children could learn the necessary patriotic and moral precepts. As a member of the Massachusetts legislature, he worked for the establishment of a state system of education and is credited by some as initiating the common school movement, which culminated in Horace Mann's work in the 1830s (Spring, 2008). He also supported the education of women, because they would be the mothers of future citizens and the teachers of youth. However, he envisioned a rather limited and "female" education for them and counseled parents against sending their daughters to "demoralizing" boarding schools. A staunch patriot whose proposals sometimes bordered on the fanatic (e.g., the proposal that the first word a child learned should be "Washington"), Webster has been called the "Schoolmaster of the Republic."

## Educational Innovations

Although Webster and others promoted the establishment of a uniquely American education, some of the major innovations in American education in the first quarter of the 19th century were of European origin. Among these were the monitorial school, the Sunday school, and the infant school. The period also witnessed the efforts of the free school societies and, more important, the rise of the academies. Each of these made a contribution, but the primary pattern of schooling that developed in the first half of the 19th century emerged from the common school movement, which is discussed in the next section. However, a review of these alternatives illustrates how the country, in the absence of established state systems, was searching for a suitable educational pattern for the new and developing nation (Gutek, 1991).

### Monitorial Schools

**Monitorial schools** originated in England and were brought to America by a Quaker named Joseph Lancaster. In the Lancasterian monitorial system, one paid teacher instructed hundreds of pupils through the use of student teachers or monitors, who were chosen for their academic abilities. Monitorial education was concerned with teaching only the basics of reading, writing, and arithmetic. The first monitorial school in the United States was opened in New York City in 1806, and the system spread rapidly throughout the states. One such school in Pennsylvania was designed to accommodate 450 students:

> The teacher sits at the head of the room on a raised platform. Beneath and in front of the teacher are three rows of monitors' desks placed directly in front of the pupils' desks. The pupils' desks are divided into three sections . . . and each section is in line with one of the rows of monitors' desks . . . a group of pupils would march to the front of the room and stand around the monitors' desks, where they would receive instruction from the monitors. When they finished, they would march to the rear part of their particular section and recite or receive further instruction from another monitor. While this group was marching to the rear, another group would be marching up to the front to take their places around the monitors. When finished, the pupils would march to the rear, and the group in the rear would move forward to the second part of their section to receive instruction from yet another monitor. Because each of the three sections had a group in front, one in the rear, and one in the middle working on different things, a total of nine different recitations could be carried on at one time. (Spring, 2011, p. 65)

**For Your Reflection and Analysis**

What virtues do the schools attempt to instill today?

The monitorial system was attractive not only because it provided an inexpensive system for educating poor children, but also because submission to the system was supposed to instill the virtues of orderliness, obedience, and industriousness. As already noted, the system gained wide appeal. However, in time the system declined. It appeared to be suited only for large cities with large numbers of students rather than small towns and rural areas. It was also criticized because it afforded only the most basic education. However, instead of being an educational dead end, as depicted by many educational historians, Lancasterian monitorialism may have been the model for the factory-like urban schools that emerged in the United States in the late 19th century (Gutek, 1991).

## Free School Societies: Charity Schools

The Lancasterian system was considered ideal for the schools operated by the various free school societies. These societies operated charity schools for the children of the poor in urban areas. In some instances, as in New York City, they received public support. Overall they were not a major factor in the history of education; nonetheless, for a period they did provide the only education some children received. For example, by 1820 the Free School Society of New York City (renamed the Public School Society in 1826 and placed under the city department of education in 1853) was teaching more than 2,000 children (Cremin, 1982).

## Sunday Schools

Another educational plan introduced to America was the **Sunday school**, begun by Robert Raikes in 1780 in England. The first Sunday school in America opened in 1786 in Virginia. Its purpose was to offer the rudiments of reading and writing to children who worked during the week, primarily in the factories of the larger cities, and to provide them with an alternative to roaming the streets on Sunday. Although the Bible was commonly its textbook, originally the Sunday school was not seen as an adjunct of the church and was not intended to promote conversion. By 1830, however, the initial practical purpose had been superseded by religious interests and these schools had become primarily religious institutions operated by Sunday school societies with an evangelical mission. They grew in number, reaching out to the frontier and becoming available to children from homes of all sorts. In new communities they often paved the way for the common school (Cremin, 1982).

**Reflect on Diversity**
To what extent does poverty affect the quality of education a child receives today?

## Infant Schools

The **infant school** was originated in England by Robert Owen, who also established one of the first infant schools in the United States at his would-be Utopia, a collective at New Harmony, Indiana. Established primarily in the eastern cities, these schools were taught by women and were designed for children ages 4 to 7 who, because they would go to work in a factory at a very early age, probably would not receive any other schooling. The primary schools designed along this model did not survive long. However, in a few cities the primary schools had been designed as preparatory to entry into the elementary school and often became part of the town school system. In the 1850s, the followers of Froebel revived the idea behind this form of infant school in the form of the kindergarten.

## The Growth of the Academy

More significant in foreshadowing the coming changes in patterns of formal schooling was the growth of the academy. Although the current concept of academy evokes the image of an exclusive private institution with a college-preparatory curriculum, or perhaps military training, in the late 18th and 19th centuries the term was more broadly applied. As we have seen, Franklin's academy and similar institutions were interested in providing an alternative to the traditional curriculum of the Latin grammar schools by providing a "practical" education.

The variations among academies were great. Some were indeed prestigious and exclusive, whereas others were nothing more than log cabins. Stimulated by the founding of the United States Military Academy at West Point in 1802 and the Naval Academy at Annapolis in 1848, many academies were established as military schools. Admission to some was open to all comers, whereas others catered to special clients. Some were boarding schools, and some were day schools. Some were teacher owned, others were organized by groups of parents or individuals, and yet others were run by denominations or various societies. In several states public support was given to the academies.

The curriculum of the academy usually depended, at least in part, on the students who were enrolled, but most offered an education beyond the three Rs. In the larger academies, Latin and Greek were offered along with English grammar, geography, arithmetic, and other studies deemed "practical" or in demand. By the end of the early national period, some of the larger academies were also offering courses designed to provide preparation for teaching in the common schools (Cremin, 1982; Madsen, 1974).

### Academies for Women

A number of the academies were established for women and are important for the role they played in providing females the opportunity for an education beyond the elementary school. Some of these academies bore the name *seminaries* and were important in the training of female teachers, teaching being about the only profession open to women at the time. In 1821 the Troy Female Seminary in New York was opened by Emma Willard, a lifelong activist for women's rights. Opposed to the finishing school curriculum of the female boarding schools, Willard proposed a curriculum that was "solid and useful."

**Reflect on Diversity**
Are single-sex classes or schools necessary to ensure equal educational opportunities for girls and boys? Why or why not?

Mount Holyoke Female Seminary in Massachusetts, founded in 1837 by Mary Lyon, provided a demanding curriculum that included philosophy, mathematics, and science. To be admitted to Mount Holyoke, as at many of the leading seminaries, students had to demonstrate mastery of not only the basics, but also Latin. Mount Holyoke, like Troy, was oriented to the training of teachers. Its success is indicated by the fact that more than 70% of the alumnae from the first 40 years taught at one time. Catharine Beecher, the sister of Harriet Beecher Stowe, founded both the Hartford (Connecticut) Female Seminary (1828) and the Western Institute for Women (1832) in Cincinnati and was instrumental in the founding of female seminaries in Iowa, Illinois, and Wisconsin.

Following the path forged by the female seminaries in New England, seminaries sprang up in other regions of the country, being especially popular in the South. By the mid-19th century there were more than 6,000 academies in the United States enrolling 263,000 students. The academy is considered by most educational historians as the forerunner of the American high school. Its broad range of curricular offerings responded to the demands of the growing middle class and demonstrated that there was an important place in the educational system for a secondary educational institution for non-college-bound as well as college-bound youth. The broadened curriculum, combined with the more liberal entrance requirements, allowed the entrance of people of various religious and social backgrounds and was a major step in the democratization of American secondary education (Rippa, 1997). Figure 6.2 gives an overview of the 19th-century educational institutions discussed in this chapter.

## The Common School Movement

The period from 1830 to 1865 has been designated the age of the **common school** movement in American educational history. During this period, the American educational system as we know it today began to take form. Instead of sporadic state legislation and abdication of responsibility, state systems of education were established. State control as well as direct taxation for the support of the common schools—publicly supported schools attended in common by all children—became accepted practices. The common school movement was the product of a variety of economic, social, and political factors.

**Figure 6.2 — 19th-Century Educational Innovations and Their 20th-Century Descendants**

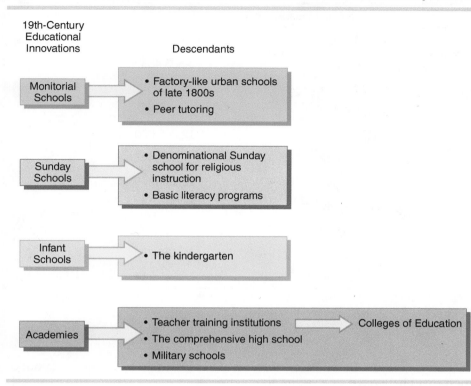

## Moving Forces
### Changing Demographics: A Larger and More Urban Population

Between 1830 and 1860, 1,220,178 square miles of territory were added to the United States. During the same period, the population exploded from 13 million to 32 million (see Table 6.1). Of this growth, 4 million came from immigration. Not only was there an increase in immigration, but the national origins of the immigrants also were different. Before this era the majority of immigrants had come from Northern Europe and shared much of the cultural and religious backgrounds as the inhabitants of their new homeland. Beginning in the 1830s and 1840s, larger numbers came from Ireland, Germany, and Southern Europe and were often Roman Catholic and often spoke a language other than English. Most settled in the larger cities of the Northeast and Midwest, providing the much-needed labor for the growing industrial complex but at the same time contributing to the problems facing growing urban areas.

At the same time that the United States was growing rapidly, it was becoming increasingly urban. Not only did the new immigrants tend to settle in the cities, but also more and more people moved from the farm to the city. Improved methods of agriculture made farming less labor intensive at the same time that employment opportunities were created by the growing number of factories. In 1820 there were only 12 cities in the 23 states with a population of more than 10,000; by 1860 the number had increased to 101 in the 33 states, and 8 had a population of more than 100,000 (Binder, 1974).

The growth in the cities was a result of the growth in industrialization. For example, in 1807 only 15 cotton mills were in operation in the United States; by 1831 there were 801 mills employing 70,000 workers (Rippa, 1997). These changing economic and social patterns gave rise to an increasing urban population, which included concentrations of children who needed schooling, a more industrialized

Table 6.1 — Area and Population of the United States, 1790–1890

| Year | Land Area (square miles) | Population |
|------|--------------------------|-----------|
| 1790 | 864,746 | 3,929,214 |
| 1800 | 864,746 | 5,308,483 |
| 1810 | 1,681,824 | 7,239,881 |
| 1820 | 1,749,462 | 9,638,453 |
| 1830 | 1,749,462 | 12,865,020 |
| 1840 | 1,749,462 | 17,069,453 |
| 1850 | 2,940,042 | 23,191,876 |
| 1860 | 2,969,640 | 31,443,321 |
| 1870 | 2,969,640 | 39,818,449 |
| 1880 | 2,969,640 | 50,155,783 |
| 1890 | 2,969,640 | 62,947,714 |

*Source:* U.S. Bureau of the Census. (1975). *Historical statistics of the United States, colonial times to 1970* (p. 8). Washington, DC: U.S. Government Printing Office.

economy that required a trained workforce, and in certain areas a Roman Catholic population that challenged Protestant domination.

### Demands of the Working Class

In this context the common schools were seen by the working class, who could not afford to educate their children at private expense, as avenues for upward social and economic mobility. Critical of pauper or charity schools, the newly emerging workingmen's organizations were open in their support of tax-supported common schools. The common schools were seen as providing the education necessary for protection against the tyranny of the upper class and for equal participation in a democracy. The leaders of business and industry also supported common schools. They saw them as a means of ensuring a supply of literate and trained workers.

### Social Control

The dominant English-speaking, upper-class Protestants saw a different merit in the common schools. This group viewed the common schools as agencies of social control over the lower socioeconomic classes. According to Gutek (1991), social control in this context meant

> imposing by institutionalized education the language, beliefs, and values of the dominant group on outsiders, especially on the non-English speaking immigrants. Common schools were expected to create such conformity in American life by imposing the language and ideological outlook of the dominant group. For example, by using English as the medium of instruction, the common schools were expected to create an English-speaking citizenry; by cultivating a general value orientation based on Protestant Christianity, the schools were expected to create a general American ethic. (pp. 87–88)

Most social groups also saw the common schools as a means of controlling crime and social unrest. Knowledge was seen as "the great remedy for intemperance: for in proportion as we elevate men in the scale of existence . . . so do we reclaim them from all temptation of degrading vice and ruinous crimes" (Binder, 1974, p. 32).

## The Frontier Movement

Interest in the establishment of common schools was not limited to the industrialized regions of the East. As the frontier moved ever westward, the one-room schoolhouse, often the only public building in a community, became the symbol of civilization and the center of efforts to keep literacy, citizenship, and civilization alive in the wilderness (Gutek, 1991).

The spirit of the frontier movement itself also contributed to the common school movement. The frontier movement was fueled by individuals who placed more value on the worth of the individual than on his or her social class. The frontier was also a place where a practical education was more important than the ability to read or write Latin. In effect, the philosophy of the common school was consistent with and supportive of the values of the frontier.

## Extended Suffrage

On the political front, the age of the common school coincided with the age of the common man. In the early years of the republic, the right to vote in many states was limited to those who owned property. Gradually this began to change and many states, especially those on the frontier, extended suffrage to all white males. The result of the extension of suffrage was not only increases in the number of common men holding public office, but also increases in the pressure for direct taxation to support common schools.

## Education Journals and Organizations

Two of the most important mechanisms for spreading the ideology of the common school were educational periodicals and educational organizations. Between 1825 and 1850 more than 60 educational journals came into existence (Spring, 2011). Among the most important were the *Massachusetts Common School Journal* and the prestigious *American Journal of Education*. Although many of these journals did not survive, collectively they served both to popularize education and to keep teachers informed of educational innovations and ideas from home and abroad.

Of the educational organizations, the most noteworthy were the American Institute of Instruction; the Western Literary Institute and College of Professional Teachers; and, on a more national scale, the American Lyceum. The latter was founded in 1826 by a Connecticut farmer, Josiah Holbrook, as an organization devoted to advancing the education of children and adults. By 1839 there were 4,000 to 5,000 local **lyceums** in the United States actively presenting programs, demonstrations, mutual instruction, and informative lectures by notable speakers. Many of these speakers, Horace Mann among them, were in favor of school reforms and in support of the common school. Cremin (1982) credits educational organizations with spearheading the common school movement, "articulating its ideals, publicizing its goals, and instructing one another in its political techniques; indeed, in the absence of a national ministry of education, it was their articulating, publicizing, and mutual instruction in politics that accounted for the spread of public education across the country" (p. 176).

## Protestant Religious Accommodation

Religious intolerance had been part of American life since the earliest colonial days. Roger Williams and Anne Hutchinson, the founders of Rhode Island, had been banished from the Massachusetts Bay Colony because of their disagreement with Puritan practices. Historically, public support for the schools had been rejected if the result would be support being given to another's religion. Common school reformers addressed the problem by proposing that the schools practice nondenominational Protestantism. Thus, as will be discussed later in this chapter, although Catholicism would be excluded, the schools would be Protestant nonsectarian. They would promote republican virtues and Christian morality, but free of the doctrine and

**For Your Reflection and Analysis**

Do you subscribe to any professional education journals? How valuable have they been to your professional development?

without the interpretation of any particular Protestant denomination (Kaestle, 1983). Although this accommodation was criticized in those parts of the country where sectarian bias was strong, support for the common schools could not have been obtained without it.

## *Leading Proponents of the Common School*
### Horace Mann

If any one person were to be given the title "Father of American Education," that person would be Horace Mann (1796–1859). Elected to the Massachusetts legislature in 1827, Mann, a brilliant orator, soon became the spokesperson for the common school movement. He led a campaign to organize the schools in Massachusetts into a state system and to establish a state board of education.

Upon the creation of the state board of education in 1837, Mann gave up his political career and a chance at the governorship to become the board's first secretary and the chief state school officer. He served in this position for 12 years and used it as a platform for proclaiming the ideology of the common school movement, as well as other educational ideals. In addition to his numerous lectures, editorships, and other writings, each year Mann wrote a report to the legislature reciting current educational practice and conditions and making recommendations for improvement. These reports, distributed in other states and abroad, were significant in influencing educational legislation and practice throughout the country.

In his own state, Mann campaigned vigorously to increase public support for education and public awareness of the problems facing education in the form of dilapidated, unsanitary facilities and substandard materials, as well as the shortcomings of the local school committees. Mann was also critical of the status of the teaching profession and the training of teachers. As a result of his efforts, state appropriations to education were doubled, 50 new secondary schools were built, textbooks and equipment were improved, and teachers' salaries in Massachusetts were raised more than 50%. Mann also fought for the professional training of teachers and established three **normal schools** (teacher training institutions), the first such schools in America. The first of these normal schools was established in 1839 at Lexington, Massachusetts.

In his Tenth Annual Report (1846), Mann asserted that education was the right of every child and that it was the state's responsibility to ensure that every child was provided an education. Although Mann himself did not promote compulsory attendance but rather regular attendance, this report was instrumental in the adoption by the Massachusetts legislature of the nation's first compulsory attendance law in 1852.

Like several prominent educators of his time, Mann had visited the Prussian schools and observed the Pestalozzian methods. His Seventh Report (1843) gave a positive account of his observations. He was particularly impressed with the love and rapport shared by the teachers and students involved in these schools. He also shared Pestalozzi's and Catharine Beecher's belief that women were better teachers than men for the common schools.

Mann's view of the role of the common school in promoting social harmony and ensuring the republic would be guided by an intelligent, moral citizenry was neither original nor unique. However, at a time when the common school movement was spreading across the nation, when it came to defining its basic principles and articles of faith, he was unquestionably its chief spokesperson (Binder, 1974).

District schools enrolled male and female children of all ages.

## Henry Barnard

Another major leader of the common school movement was Henry Barnard (1811–1900). Like Mann, he served in the state legislature (for Connecticut), worked to establish a state board of education, and then became the board's first secretary (1838–1842). He then served in a similar capacity in Rhode Island (1845–1849) and later became the first U.S. commissioner of education.

Much of Barnard's influence on educational theory and practice came through his numerous lectures and writings and, more important, through his editorship of the *American Journal of Education*. Barnard is also credited with initiating the teachers' institute movement discussed later in this chapter. Barnard's greatest successes lay in his democratic philosophy ("schools good enough for the best and cheap enough for the poorest") and as a disseminator of information about better schools. He is sometimes called the "Father of American School Administration" (Pulliam & Van Patten, 2007).

## Catharine Beecher

Catharine Beecher (1800–1878), the founder of the Hartford Female Seminary and the Western Institute for Women, was a strong supporter of the common school and saw her task as focusing attention on the need for a corps of female teachers to staff the common schools. She set forth a plan for a nationwide system of teacher training seminaries. Although the plan was not adopted, her efforts on behalf of the common school were a force in its acceptance, and her work on behalf of women pointed to a new American consensus concerning female roles (Cremin, 1982).

## *Growth of State and Local Support and Supervision*
### Increased State Support

The idea of having universal common schools was one thing, but paying for them through direct taxation of the general public was another. Until the 1820s or 1830s, the only really free education was that provided by the charity schools, or in certain other schools if the parents were willing to declare themselves paupers. Often local or county taxes levied on specific activities, for example, liquor licenses or marriage fees, provided partial support for the schools, but the remainder of the expenses were charged to the parents in the form of a **rate bill**. The rate bill was, in effect, a tuition fee based on the number of children in the family attending school. Even though the fee might be small, poor parents often could not afford it, so their children either did not attend school or took turns attending.

One of the major goals of the common school movement was to secure greater state support for the common schools. Beginning in the first quarter of the 19th century, several states began to provide aid for public schools. Funds came from the permanent school fund (derived largely from the sale of public lands), direct taxation, or appropriations from the general fund. Conditions were usually placed on the receipt of funds; local support had to equal or exceed state support, for example, and the schools had to be kept open a minimum length of time.

By 1865 systems of common schools had been established throughout the northern, midwestern, and western states, and more than 50% of the nation's children were enrolled in public schools. The lowest enrollments were in the South, where the common school movement had made little progress. As enrollments grew, the pressure to make these schools completely tax supported increased. In 1827 Massachusetts became the first state to abolish the rate bill. Pennsylvania's Free School Act of 1834 was a model for eliminating the pauper school concept. Other states soon followed these examples and by constitutional or legislative enactment adopted the concept of public support for public schools open to all children. But

**For Your Reflection and Analysis**

How does the current practice of some districts charging fees for participation in extracurricular activities affect the participation of children from low-income families?

it was not until 1871 that the last state (New Jersey) abolished the rate bill, making the schools truly free.

## Creation of State Boards and State Superintendents of Education

As is usually the case, increased support is accompanied by increased efforts to control. The effort to establish some control or supervision was marked by the creation of an office of state superintendent, or commissioner of education, and a state board of education. In 1812 New York became the first state to appoint a state superintendent, Gideon Hawley. His tenure in office was filled with such controversy that in 1821 he was removed from office and the position was abolished and not recreated until 1854. Nonetheless, by the outbreak of the Civil War, 28 of the 34 states had established state boards of education and chief state school officers. By and large, these officers and boards were vested with more supervisory power than real control. Initially their major responsibilities involved the distribution of the permanent school funds and the organization of a state system of common schools.

## Creation of Local School Districts and Superintendents

The creation of a state system of common schools paralleled the establishment of school districts and the establishment of local and county superintendents. The New England states instituted the district system in the early years of the 19th century, and it spread westward during the next three decades. Initially the districts were administered by a school committee, then by the district or county superintendent, whose primary duty was to supervise instruction. The development of the position of county superintendent of schools helped bring about some degree of standardization and uniformity in areas that had numerous small, rural school districts (Gutek, 1991).

The evolution of the office of city school superintendent quickly followed that of the district and county office. The first city superintendent was appointed in Buffalo in 1837, and others soon followed in Louisville, St. Louis, Providence, Springfield (IL), Cleveland, Rochester, and New Orleans. The early superintendents functioned mostly as assistants or representatives of the school board. Most boards continued to operate as both an executive and legislative body. Many school board members were businessmen and were reluctant to delegate any of their executive functions to the superintendent. They considered themselves more competent to conduct the financial affairs of the district than the superintendent (American Association of School Administrators, 1952). It was not until the second half of the 19th century that superintendent and school board relationships began to change and the superintendent began to assume the powers and duties associated with a chief executive officer.

## *Organization and Curriculum*

The common schools varied in terms of size, organization, and curriculum, depending on their location. In rural areas the one- or two-room school was dominant; progress was not marked by movement from one grade to another but by completing one text and beginning another. In larger cities and towns, grading had been introduced. On the frontier the curriculum was often limited to the three Rs; in larger cities it tended to be broader. In the second quarter of the 19th century, a greater variety of textbooks appeared for use in the common schools. For example, the extremely popular *McGuffey Readers* continued to teach "the lessons of morality and patriotism, but the stern, direct preachments of earlier schoolbooks were replaced or supplemented by stories and essays designed to appeal to youthful interest" (Cremin, 1982, p. 96). Rote learning, drill, and practice did not disappear from the classroom, but a more Pestalozzian approach that placed value on the sensitivities and individuality of the child was making some inroads.

**For Your Reflection and Analysis**

What would be the advantages and disadvantages of attending a one- or two-room rural school over a large, urban school?

# Secondary School Movement

Public **secondary schools** offering education beyond the elementary school did not become a firmly established part of the American educational scene until the last quarter of the 19th century. However, the beginnings of the movement occurred well before the Civil War. Perhaps not unexpectedly, the lead was taken by those states that had been first to establish systems of common schools. Boston inaugurated the high school movement in 1821 with the opening of the English Classical School, renamed the Boston English High School in 1824. The school was open to boys only and was intended to be an alternative to the Latin grammar school and to provide a "practical education." Such an education, as we have seen, could otherwise be obtained only at a private academy.

The success of the English High School for boys led education reformers to push for a high school for girls. The school was opened in 1828 and, although very successful—in fact, because it was so successful—was closed after only three years. The girls who enrolled in the school tended to stay, and being "neither trade- nor profession-minded, and unlike the boys, rarely obtained employment or other opportunities before they graduated from school. Thus, . . . [it] was but a waste of taxpayers' money" (Herbst, 1996, p. 44). (See the Controversial Issue feature on page 146 for the arguments for and against single-sex schools and classes.)

In 1831, the first American **comprehensive** (and coeducational) **high school**, offering both English and classical courses of study, was opened in Lowell, Massachusetts. In 1838 Philadelphia opened a coeducational high school with three tracks: a four-year classical curriculum, a four-year modern language curriculum, and a two-year English curriculum.

## Slow Beginnings

In the years before the Civil War, the high school movement expanded slowly. By 1860 there were only 300 high schools in the nation, compared with more than 6,000 academies; of the former, more than 100 were located in Massachusetts, the only state to require communities of 50 families or more to provide secondary-level education.

The initial slow growth of the high school movement can be partially explained by the fact that, unlike the common school, the high school was not being overwhelmingly demanded by the masses. It appeared to be more a reformer's response to urbanization and industrialization. Middle- or upper-class reformers, adopting the philosophy and rhetoric of the common school advocates, viewed their efforts as democratizing secondary education, providing a means of maintaining social values, and promoting economic progress. Prior to the Civil War, most high schools were located in urban areas, where there were a sufficient number of students and tax support.

## The Movement Grows as Industry and the Economy Grow

In the years after the Civil War, however, a number of factors came together to create a greater demand for secondary education. These factors were similar to those that fueled the common school movement: population growth due in large part to increased immigration and a rapid growth in industry and technological change, which intensified the demand for skilled workers. At the same time, a high school education was increasingly seen as necessary to the full realization of one's social and economic goals. This was as true for artisans and small entrepreneurs in the cities and for businessmen and professionals in rural communities (Herbst, 1996). Last, economic growth created a larger tax base that could be used to support an expanded educational system.

The convergence of these factors created a demand for secondary education that brought a dramatic increase in the number of public high schools, from about 500 in 1870 to 6,000 in 1900. During the 1880s the number of high schools increased

# CONTROVERSIAL ISSUE

## *Single-Sex Schools and Classes*

While Title IX has helped correct some of the blatant discrimination and inequity that have existed in educational institutions, its efforts to bring about gender equity have not been totally successful. The proposal for single-sex schools has been suggested as a possible remedy to ensure that both males and females obtain equal educational opportunities. The reasons stated by opponents on each side include the following:

**For**

1. Girls who attended private, single-sex schools have higher levels of academic achievement in reading, mathematics, and science compared to those who attended coeducational private or public schools.

2. Girls in single-sex schools are more likely to explore nontraditional subjects such as computer science, advanced physics, and advanced mathematics. They are also more inclined to participate on athletic teams and play in a variety of sports.

3. Boys in single-sex schools are more likely to study subjects such as English, foreign languages, art, music, and drama.

4. Both boys and girls tend to have a more positive attitude toward learning when they attend single-sex schools.

5. In their respective single-sex schools, girls are more confident, and boys display fewer discipline problems. Single-sex schools have great potential for high-risk students from low-income and underprivileged backgrounds (Riordan, 1990).

**Against**

1. Single-sex schools fail to prepare the student for "real-life" experiences where males and females are in direct competition with one another for grades, honors, and admission to competitive and prestigious academic programs and institutions.

2. Allowing single-sex institutions runs the risk of dismantling the public school system and replacing it with the private school model.

3. Currently the majority of single-sex schools are private, which may make them more vulnerable to a return to the past, where sexual stereotypes and traditional gender roles prevailed.

4. There is no need for a single-sex school because the federal government has published new guidelines that support single-sex classes under certain conditions.

5. Educational gender inequity continues to exist in spite of the numerous educational, social, and legal efforts that have been initiated to bring about needed change. There is no guarantee that establishing a single-sex school will resolve or eliminate the multiple inequities that exist relative to gender and schooling.

Have you ever attended a single-sex class or school or known someone who has? If so, how effective was the experience for you or for them? What is your position on single-sex schools?

tenfold and surpassed the number of academies (see Figure 6.3). By the end of the century, free public high schools had pushed out the majority of fee-paying academies. Although still only a small percentage of the eligible population attended high school, in 1900 more than half a million students were enrolled and 62,000 graduated.

## *Tax Support and Compulsory Attendance Laws Further Secondary Education and Literacy*

The public secondary school movement was given further impetus by the decision of the Michigan Supreme Court in the famous *Kalamazoo* case (*Stuart et al. v. School District No. 1 of the Village of Kalamazoo, 1874*). By its ruling that the legislature could tax for the support of both elementary and secondary schools, the court provided the precedent for public support of secondary education. And in the decade between school years 1879–1880 and 1889–1890, total expenditures for the public schools increased 81%, from $78 million to $141 million (Snyder & Dillow, 2011). By the end of the century, the publicly supported high school had replaced the academy in most communities and had become an established part of the common school system in every state.

**Figure 6.3 — The Development of Secondary Schools in the United States, 1630–1930**

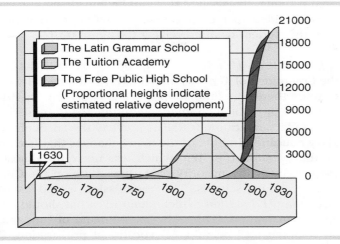

*Source:* From The History of Education (p. 699) by E. P. Cubberly, 1948. Cambridge, MA: Riverside Press. Copyright Riverside Press. Reprinted by permission.

The *Kalamazoo* decision having quashed the argument that public funds could not be used for secondary education, compulsory attendance laws soon followed. The passage of child labor laws was also instrumental in driving the adoption of compulsory attendance laws. By 1918, all states had enacted laws requiring full-time attendance until the child reached a certain age or completed a certain grade. By 1900 children attended school an average of 99 days per year, twice as many as they had a century earlier (Snyder & Dillow, 2011).

One result of this increase in school attendance was a decline in the illiteracy rate from 20% of all persons over 10 years of age in 1870 to 7.7% in 1910 (Graham, 1974). However, illiteracy rates varied by segment of the population. As a result of the pre–Civil War prohibition on teaching Blacks in most southern states and inadequate education after the war, Blacks had the highest illiteracy rate: 30.4% in 1910. The illiteracy rate was also high among the older population, which had not been the beneficiary of universal, compulsory education. Whites who were the children of a foreign-born parent had the lowest illiteracy rate, 1.1%. Literacy rates also varied by region. The South, which not only had the highest population of Blacks but also had been the slowest in developing systems of common schools, had the highest illiteracy rate (Graham, 1974).

## The Committee of Ten

As previously noted, in its origins the high school had been viewed as a provider of a more practical education. The need to assimilate the children of the new immigrants, and the more technical demands of industry, placed additional pressures on the schools to include a curriculum that could be immediately useful and that included vocational training (Graham, 1974). However, some educators did not share this esteem for the "practical curriculum." In 1892, in an effort to standardize the curriculum, the National Education Association established the Committee of Ten. The committee was chaired by Charles Eliot, the president of Harvard University, and was largely composed of representatives of higher education. The committee recommended an early introduction to the basic subjects and uniform subject matter and instruction for both college-bound and terminal students, with few electives. In addition, although four curricula were recommended (classical, Latin-scientific, modern language, and English), the entire curriculum was dominated by college-preparatory courses. Using the psychology of mental discipline as a theoretical rationale, the committee claimed that the recommended subjects would be used profitably by both college-bound and terminal students because they trained the powers of observation, memory, expression, and reasoning (Gutek, 1991). Vocational training, they believed, should come after high school. The committee also recommended that each course meet four or five times weekly for 1 year, for which the student would receive a **Carnegie unit**.

## The Seven Cardinal Principles of Secondary Education

The view of the Committee of Ten was immediately challenged by many educators, and within 25 years there was little support for its position. In 1918 the National Education Association appointed another committee, the Commission on the Reorganization of Secondary Education (CRSE), to review the curriculum and organization of secondary education in light of the many changes that had swept American society. Unlike the Committee of Ten, which was made up almost exclusively of university representatives, the majority of the members on the CRSE represented elementary and secondary schools. The commission issued its seven *Cardinal Principles of Secondary Education*, which identified what should be the objectives of the high school curriculum: (1) health, (2) command of fundamental academic skills, (3) worthy home membership, (4) vocational preparation, (5) citizenship, (6) worthwhile use of leisure time, and (7) ethical character. Compared with the recommendations of the Committee of Ten, only one of these seven principles, command of fundamental processes, was concerned with college preparation; and unlike the Committee of Ten report, which focused on goals outside the curriculum, the curriculum was seen as the instrument through which students would achieve the goals.

The cardinal principles received wide agreement and represented significant revision of the curriculum philosophy of the high school. After a decade of debate over whether secondary education in the United States should follow the European model of dual systems (academic and vocational/industrial) or a unitary, "democratic" system, the *Cardinal Principles* provided the blueprint for the American comprehensive high school and its distinguishing feature—academic and vocational studies under the same roof (Wraga, 2000).

By the mid-1920s four basic patterns of curricular organization were in evidence in the comprehensive high school: (1) the college preparatory program, which included courses in English language and literature, foreign languages, mathematics, the natural and physical sciences, and history and social sciences; (2) the commercial or business program, which offered courses in bookkeeping, shorthand, and typing; (3) the industrial, vocational, home economics, and agricultural programs; and (4) a modified academic program for students who planned to terminate their formal education on high school completion. The typical high school program was four years and was attended by students ages 14 to 18. Exceptions were the six-year combined junior–senior high schools (Gutek, 1991).

## The Junior High School

The two-year and three-year **junior high schools** that began to appear in some urban districts, offering grades six and seven or grades six through eight, were an outgrowth of the Committee of Ten's recommendation that academic work begin earlier and that elementary schooling be reduced from eight to six years. Their growth was also encouraged by the work of G. Stanley Hall, who wrote the first book on adolescent development and emphasized the developmental differences between childhood and preadolescence that would justify a reorganization of the eight–four system (eight years of elementary school and four years of high school). The concept appealed to a group of reformers who were concerned about attrition and preparing students for the world of work. They felt the junior high school would prevent dropping out and would provide students the opportunity to explore their vocational interests or even receive vocational training before high school.

The first junior high school was established in Columbus, Ohio, and another followed the next year in Berkeley, California. Other cities followed suit, but it was not until after World War II, with the rapid growth in enrollments and school

**For Your Reflection and Analysis**

Of the seven cardinal principals, which ones have the most relevance today?

**For Your Reflection and Analysis**

Did you attend a junior high? If so, what educational experiences do you recall that reinforce the positive value of the junior high school over other organizational plans?

construction, that school reorganization driven by overcrowding and space availability brought an end to the dominance of the eight–four pattern and cemented this rung of the U.S. educational system ladder.

# Developments in Higher Education

As discussed in the preceding chapter, nine colleges were founded during the colonial period. In the period following the Revolutionary War, the same nationalistic, democratic spirit that gave rise to the common school also produced an increase in public institutions of higher education. The increase was also spurred by people moving westward who wanted colleges close at hand as well as some denominations choosing to establish their own colleges rather than have their members educated at colleges operated by other denominations. Thus, of the colleges founded before 1860, fewer than 10% were state institutions.

By and large, the colleges were very small. For example, it was not until after the Civil War that Harvard had a graduating class of 100. During the late colonial and early national periods, the curriculum of the colleges became more "liberal," but it retained its heavy classical overlay and its emphasis on religion.

The first state institutions of higher education were established in the South: the University of Georgia in 1785, the University of North Carolina in 1789, the University of Tennessee in 1794, and the University of South Carolina in 1801. In the second quarter of the 19th century, the same nationalistic, democratic spirit that gave rise to the common school also produced an increase in public institutions of higher education. These appeared primarily in the Midwest: Indiana University in 1820, the University of Michigan in 1837, and the University of Wisconsin in 1848.

In both public and private institutions, lecture and recitation remained the most common modes of instruction, and discipline remained strict. Also, although the curriculum of public institutions gave more emphasis to the sciences and modern languages than the curriculum in the denominational institutions, over growing objection, the classical curriculum remained dominant in both public and private institutions of higher education in the early national period. The classical curriculum was supported by the *Yale Report* of 1828, a report by Yale scholars that argued that the classical curriculum helped develop mental discipline and proper character and provided the best preparation for professional study.

## *The Dartmouth College Case*

In 1816 the New Hampshire legislature, dominated by the liberal Jeffersonian Republicans and concerned by what appeared to be the anti-liberal sentiments of the board of trustees, enacted legislation to convert Dartmouth College from a private to a state institution. In the *Dartmouth College* case (1819), the U.S. Supreme Court upheld the original contract from the king of England that had given private status to the college. The case was important not only in affirming the constitutional principle that the state could not impair contracts, but also in providing a strong foundation for the system of private colleges secure from government control that we have today.

## *The Morrill Acts and the Establishment of Land-Grant Institutions*

By the mid-19th century, there was growing recognition among farmers and laborers of the importance of an education to improving their social and economic status. Because these groups found the majority of existing colleges unresponsive and irrelevant to their needs, they urged the establishment of a new institution, the industrial college. In response, the first Morrill Act was passed by Congress and signed by President Lincoln in 1862. The act granted 30,000 acres of land to each state for each senator and representative it had in Congress based on the 1860 census. The act specified that the income from the land was to be used to support at least one college that would "teach such branches of learning as are related to agriculture and mechanical arts, . . . in order to promote the liberal and practical education of the industrial classes in the several pursuits and professions of life."

The Second Morrill Act of 1890 provided for direct annual grants of $15,000 (increasing annually to $25,000) to each state for the support of land-grant colleges. The bill also provided that no grant would be given to any state that denied admission to its land-grant colleges because of race without providing "separate but equal" institutions.

As a result of the Morrill Acts, 65 new land-grant colleges were established. Among the first of the new institutions of higher education were the universities of Maine (1865), Illinois and West Virginia (1867), California (1868), Purdue and Nebraska (1869), Ohio State (1870), and Arkansas and Texas A&M (1871). Seventeen states, mostly in the South, also established separate land-grant colleges for Blacks under the provisions of the Second Morrill Act. Together, the Morrill Acts provided the incentive for both a shift to a new type of curriculum and for greatly expanded state systems of higher education.

## Higher Education for Women

Significant developments were also being made in the higher education of women during this period. As discussed earlier, a number of women's seminaries or colleges had been opened prior to the Civil War. A few coeducational colleges also existed before the Civil War (e.g., Oberlin, 1833; Antioch, 1853; and the State University of Iowa, 1858). However, only 3,000 women in the entire nation were attending colleges or universities that offered A.B. degrees (Newcomer, 1959). It was not until the Civil War that women's higher education really began to flourish. Several women's colleges (e.g., Vassar, 1861; Wellesley, 1875; Smith, 1875; Radcliffe, 1879; and Bryn Mawr, 1880) were established and offered programs comparable to those found in the colleges for men. In addition, perhaps in part because of the impact of the Civil War casualties on enrollments and finances, an increasing number of formerly all-male institutions began admitting women, albeit selectively. By 1880 almost one-half of the colleges and universities admitted women (Pulliam & Van Patten, 2007). However, although a wide curriculum was open to women, severe restrictions were placed on their access to facilities, libraries, and lectures. In the end, teaching remained the most accessible and socially acceptable career option for women.

## The Emergence of the Modern University

Some historians have called the period between the end of the Civil War and the beginning of the 20th century the "Age of the University." During this period more than 200 colleges were established in the United States. Not only did the number of institutions of higher education grow, but so also did their role. Many of the new institutions, as well as many of the older institutions, bore the name *university.* In contrast to the small, single-purpose, largely undergraduate colleges, the emerging universities were large and multipurpose with graduate departments and they emphasized research, influenced by the German universities where many of their faculty had studied. By the end of the 19th century, the American university had come to look much as we

After the Civil War, women increasingly sought higher education.

know it today, with an undergraduate college of liberal arts and sciences, a graduate college, and various professional colleges.

## Founding of Junior Colleges

The initiative for the establishment of **junior colleges** came in the late 19th century from a number of university presidents. Some viewed the first two years of higher education as more appropriate to secondary education. They wanted to free their faculty from what they considered secondary education responsibilities so that they could devote themselves more to research and graduate education. Others, such as President William Rainey Harper, who had put a two–two plan (two years under class, two years upper class) in place at the University of Chicago, felt the arrangement would meet the needs of those who could not afford to attend four years, as well as those who were not interested in research or were not academically qualified for it.

In 1901 the first free-standing public junior college, Joliet (Illinois) Junior College, was established. Although initially established to offer courses that would transfer to four-year institutions, it soon began to offer terminal and vocational programs as well (Gutek, 1991). In 1907 California passed a law permitting school boards to offer high school graduates courses similar to those required during the first two years of college (Rippa, 1997). By the early 1920s, the concept of the junior college was well established. During the late 1920s, encouraged by the Smith-Hughes Act, which provided federal aid to vocational education, junior colleges developed more extensive vocational and technical education programs. In subsequent decades they not only expanded rapidly, but as their goal was expanded to include serving the broad-based needs of the community, they became transformed into today's community colleges (Gutek, 1991).

**For Your Reflection and Analysis**

Did you attend a community or junior college? Would you support the movement toward having all lower division education take place at a community college?

# Education of Minorities

The progress of education in the United States has not been uniform across all regions, socioeconomic classes, or races. To many, the schoolhouse door was closed and the promise of equal educational opportunity an unrealized dream. Native Americans, Hispanic Americans, Asian Americans, and Black Americans in particular have had to struggle to realize the promise of an equal education.

## Education of Native Americans

The formal education of Native Americans was initiated by missionaries who equated education with Christianity and the virtues of civilized life. The Society for the Propagation of the Gospel and the Moravians were among the more active of the missionary groups. Just as education for the White colonists was primarily for the purpose of training for the ministry, so too was it hoped that education would equip Native Americans to become missionaries to their people. However, the efforts of missionary or philanthropic groups were limited, and the town and grammar schools enrolled few Native Americans. Efforts to provide any higher education were even more limited. In 1653 a college was founded at Harvard to instruct Native American students in the same classical education received by Whites. Dartmouth College was originally established for the education of Native Americans, but it was soon dominated by the children of the White colonists.

The initial response of Native Americans to the formal, traditional education offered by the colonists was distrust and rejection. Benjamin Franklin quoted one Native American leader as saying:

> Several of our young people were formerly brought up at the colleges of the
> Northern Provinces; they were instructed in all your Sciences; but, when they came
> back to us, they were bad Runners, ignorant of every means of living in the Woods,
> unable to bear either Cold or Hunger, knew neither how to build a Cabin, take a
> Deer, or kill an Enemy, spoke our Language imperfectly, were therefore neither fit
> for Hunters, Warriors, nor Counsellors; they were totally good for nothing. (cited in
> Kidwell & Swift, 1976, p. 335)

## Treaties and Mission Schools

During the first century of the new republic, much of the education of the Native Americans came about as a result of federal legislation or negotiated treaties. According to the terms of the treaties, 389 of which were signed with various tribes between 1778 and 1871, in return for relinquishing their land, Native Americans were given money payments, guarantees of the integrity of the land they retained, and promises of educational services (Kidwell & Swift, 1976). The predominant means by which the federal government met its obligation to provide educational services was through support of mission schools operated on the reservations by religious groups. The objective of the education was to assimilate Native Americans into American society. Most of the schools followed a program of studies known as the 50/50 curriculum: half of the time was spent in the traditional common school academic subjects, as well as the religion of the sponsoring denomination; and the other half of the time in vocational and agricultural training for boys and domestic arts for girls. Native language and culture were excluded from the curriculum (Hale, 2002).

The mission school experience was not a positive one for most American Indians or for the missionaries. The missionaries failed to recognize that American Indians were intensely religious and were invested in preserving their religion and culture at all cost (DeJong, 1993). The federal government provided a little money but no standards. The net result of 100 years of effort and hundreds of thousands of dollars was "a small number of poorly attended mission schools, a suspicious and disillusioned Indian population, and a few hundred alumni who for the most part were considered outcasts by whites and Indians alike" (DeJong, 1993, p. 59). In 1917 this arrangement, which in effect constituted government support of sectarian education, ended (Butts, 1978).

## Boarding Schools

After the Civil War the **assimilation** approach became popular. As discussed in Chapter 8, this approach advocated the immersion of Native Americans into the predominant White culture and was established on the belief that the most lasting and efficient way to advance this assimilation was to remove Native American children from their tribal setting and subject them, in a strict disciplinary setting, to an infusion of American values, language, and customs.

The first major boarding school was established in 1879 at Carlisle, Pennsylvania, by General Richard Pratt. At the boarding school, students were given new names and forbidden to speak in their native tongue. Vocational and industrial training were emphasized at this and other off-reservation boarding schools. By the turn of the century, 25 off-reservation boarding schools had been established (Szasz, 1999). However, they were subject to much criticism. The physical and living conditions were often inadequate, and the discipline was strict and harsh. Disease and death were common. The dropout rate was high. Students often returned to the reservation rather than enter White society, and upon return to the reservation they found that they were unable to apply the training they had received or that it was irrelevant.

Class at Carlisle Indian boarding school, circa 1900.

## Reservation Day Schools and Public Schools

In the last quarter of the 19th century, in part as a response to the criticisms of the boarding schools, government schooling expanded rapidly in the form of Bureau of Indian Affairs (BIA)–operated day schools on the reservation. The reservation day schools offered several advantages over the off-reservation boarding school; not only were they less expensive, but they also were more acceptable to parents. Consequently, day schools increased in number after the turn of the 20th century.

Although Native Americans in the eastern United States who were not under the jurisdiction of the federal government had already been attending off-reservation public schools, a newer phenomenon was the public school located on the reservation. These schools initially had been built to accommodate the White people who rented land on the reservation. The on-reservation public schools tended to encourage not only assimilation but also learning. As one Indian agent wrote, "Indian children progress much faster when thrown in contact with white children than they do when they are all kept together with whites excluded" (Szasz, 1999, p. 11).

## The Meriam Report

In 1924 Congress granted U.S. citizenship to all Native Americans. At the same time, the appalling living conditions and reprehensible treatment of Native Americans were brought to public view by a number of reformers determined to improve their plight. In response the BIA commissioned the Brookings Institution to conduct an independent study of Native American life in the United States. The Meriam Report, issued in 1928, documented the intolerable conditions of Native American life and noted that much of their poverty was caused by their loss of land. It also criticized the BIA educational program, exposing the inadequate industrial training, overcrowded dormitories, inadequate diet, and physical punishment in the boarding schools. The report discouraged the practice of boarding schools and encouraged the construction of day schools that could also serve as community centers. It accused the reservation system of creating isolation and concluded that the best way to improve the living standards of Native Americans was to educate them so they could be assimilated into White society (Kidwell & Swift, 1976).

The Meriam Report marked the beginning of a change in BIA policy. After 1928, BIA appropriations for education increased dramatically, efforts were made to deal with conditions in government schools, and curriculum reform was initiated. Soon a major share of the BIA's budget was allocated to education, with the goal of assimilating Native Americans into mainstream society.

## *Education of Hispanic Americans*

The story of the involvement of the United States in the education of Hispanics is largely to be told in relation to the Spanish-speaking peoples of the southwestern United States and begins with the acquisition of this territory from Mexico in 1848 at the end of the Mexican-American War. For the Mexicans who chose to remain in the territory after the U.S. takeover, or for those who fled across the border in the years that followed, life became marked by discrimination, prejudice, and segregation. The education provided Hispanic students, like that provided Native American students, was designed to promote, if not force, assimilation and deculturalization. Instruction in the segregated schools was in English and the use of Spanish was forbidden, even on the playground.

During the Depression years, many rural Mexican Americans moved to the cities, bringing their problems to a wider consciousness. Often they settled in poverty-ridden barrios. Until World War II the segregation of Hispanics was permitted in California and other states. Then, in 1944 Gonzalo Mendez moved his family to a farm he was to run for its Japanese owners, who were in an internment camp. When the Westminster school district refused to enroll his children, he joined other parents in suing Westminster and three other school districts. In 1946 a U.S. district court rejected the school district's argument that the segregation was based not on race but on the need to provide special instruction to Hispanic children (a defense that had been successfully used by the Del Rio School District in Texas in 1930).

**For Your Reflection and Analysis**

How successful have been efforts to assimilate Native Americans into mainstream society?

**Reflect on Diversity**
Should assimilation continue to be a goal of the education of Native Americans? Why or why not?

In fact, the court said, the only special instruction these students needed was to learn English and this was actually impeded when they are segregated (*Mendez v. Westminster School District*, 1947). Accordingly, the court determined that segregation was illegal because it had no basis in state law or educational need. Although some, including the NAACP and its attorney, Thurgood Marshall, who had filed an *amicus curiae* brief in the case, were disappointed that the court did not overturn "separate but equal," the decision did have a broad impact. Encouraged by the decision, the segregation of Mexican Americans was challenged in the courts in other states and within two years ***de jure* segregation** had been overturned in Texas and Arizona. However, despite these and other court victories, the desegregation of Hispanic children was far from being achieved and equality of opportunity still an unrealized dream.

## Education of Asian Americans

Asian immigration to the United States in any significant numbers did not occur until the mid-1850s, when Chinese workers were recruited as cheap labor to work in the mines and railroads of the West. Throughout the 19th century and well into the 20th century, Asian Americans experienced much of the discrimination in the schools and the larger society as did other minorities. For example, from 1871 to 1885, by their deliberate exclusion from the state school law, Chinese children were excluded from the public schools in California. When the decision of the state supreme court in *Tape v. Hurley* (1885) (see Historical Note on page 237) forced a change in the law, most school boards responded by providing segregated, so-called Oriental schools. Typically, these facilities were inferior to the facilities attended by White students. Sometimes Asian Americans were allowed to attend White schools but were segregated in different rooms or on a different floor. In the classroom the special language needs of students were largely ignored as school systems attempted to force mastery of the English language and were reluctant to employ Asian American teachers or staff. The result was that many Asian American children experienced serious difficulties (Weinberg, 1997).

Following World War I the rigid policy of segregation began to break down as parents became more persistent and Chinese students were regularly admitted to public high schools. However, elementary schools remained highly segregated, in large part because of housing patterns and attendance zones. Even in the years after World War II when many middle-class Chinese moved out of segregated neighborhoods and into integrated neighborhoods, schools in the many ethnic neighborhoods (Chinatowns) remained basically segregated. Instruction in these schools was typically in English only, leading to the *Lau* case discussed in Chapter 7.

## Education of Black Americans

Although Blacks came to America before the Puritans—20 arrived at the Jamestown colony in 1619, not as slaves but as indentured servants—their educational history was anything but similar. The vast majority of Blacks living in the United States during the first 300 years of its history lived in the South and, until after the Civil War, as slaves. On the eve of the Civil War, there were about four million Black slaves and 500,000 free Blacks out of a total U.S. population of 31 million.

### Education of Slaves and Free Blacks Prior to the Civil War

For the vast majority of enslaved Blacks, education was virtually nonexistent. A few slave owners educated their slaves, and missionary or philanthropic groups such as the SPG provided limited and sporadic schooling. However, by the third decade of the 19th century, the rise of militant abolitionism and the fear of slave revolts if the slaves "got too high an opinion of themselves" had led to the enactment of the so-called Black Codes, which, among other things, prohibited the education of slaves.

The education of free Blacks was also very limited. In the decades preceding the Civil War, as common school systems were developed in the North, Blacks more often than not found themselves in segregated schools. An important legal support for this segregation (and also the legal basis for segregation for the remainder of the century) was provided by the Massachusetts Supreme Court decision in *Roberts v. City of Boston* (1850), which said that separate-but-equal schools did not violate the rights of Black children.

Despite the difficulties, some free Blacks did obtain an education. In some communities the children of freed slaves attended public schools or the private schools established by various religious, philanthropic, or abolitionist societies. The outbreak of the Civil War in 1861 found about 4,000 Blacks in schools in the slave states and 23,000 in the free states (West, 1972). A few Blacks even obtained a higher education. A small number went abroad to England or Scotland, a few attended the limited number of American colleges that admitted Blacks (notably Oberlin in Ohio and Berea in Kentucky), and others attended one of the three Black colleges established before 1860: Cheyney State College (1839) and Lincoln University (1854) in Pennsylvania, and Wilberforce University (1856) in Ohio.

Many of the free Blacks who gained a higher education prior to 1860 did so under the auspices of the American Colonization Society, which was established in 1817 to send free Blacks to the Colony of Liberia in Africa, founded by the society in 1822. The education of the free Blacks was undertaken to provide the doctors, lawyers, teachers, clergy, and civil servants needed by the colony. Although not all those educated by the society went to the colony, or if they went did not remain, enough did so as to provide the colony and the Republic of Liberia, established in 1847, with its leadership elite (Pifer, 1973).

## Education During Reconstruction

During the post–Civil War period known as Reconstruction (1865–1877) hundreds of teachers supported by various northern churches, missionary societies, and charitable **educational foundations** moved to the South to educate newly liberated Blacks. The first of these educational foundations, established in 1867, was the Peabody Fund for the Advancement of Negro Education in the South. It later merged with the Slater Fund to support industrial education and teacher preparation. Among the others, the largest was the General Education Board set up by John D. Rockefeller in 1902 (Pifer, 1973; West, 1972).

Another major force affecting the education of Blacks in the South during Reconstruction was the Freedmen's Bureau. The bureau was responsible for the establishment of some 3,000 schools, and by 1869 some 114,000 students attended these schools. (The Historical Note on page 156 gives an account of one teacher in a freedmen's school.) These schools followed the New England common school model in terms of their curriculum (reading, writing, grammar, geography, arithmetic, and music) and moral outlook (the importance of certain values and the responsibility of citizenship), but added a new dimension—industrial training. In the view of northern educators, industrial training would prepare Blacks for the occupations they were considered most suited to perform in the South (Gutek, 1991).

## The Higher Education Debate: Booker T. Washington and W. E. B. DuBois

One of the first and most important institutions of higher education for Blacks in the immediate post–Civil War period was the Hampton Normal and Agricultural Institute, founded in 1868 by General Samuel Chapman Armstrong, a representative of the Freedmen's Bureau. The Hampton Institute was founded for the education of Blacks, but beginning in 1878 it also admitted Native Americans. Industrial education was the basic mission of the Hampton Institute. Booker T. Washington (1856–1915) was one of the hundreds of young Blacks who flocked to the few normal schools or colleges that admitted Blacks. At Hampton, Washington developed

**For Your Reflection and Analysis**

Why was assimilation a goal of Native American education but not of African American education?

# HISTORICAL NOTE

## Zeal for Learning Among Freedmen, 1868

Dear Brethren and Sisters;

Since I last wrote I have commenced my school and have now been teaching just four weeks. Everything was finally arranged so that on Monday Nov. 30th I opened school with twenty-five scholars. Since then the number has been steadily increasing and now it numbers forty-two with a prospect of large additions after their great holiday Christmas week is past.

From all the accounts of Freedmen's schools which I had heard and read previous to coming here I expected to find them anxious to learn but after all, I confess I was unprepared for the amount of zeal manifested by most of them for an education. I can say as one did of old, "The half had not been told me." I am surprised each day by some new proof of their anxiety to learn. Nearly all ages, colors, conditions and capacities are represented in my school. Ages ranging from five to sixty-five; Colors from jet-black with tight curling hair to pale brunette with waving brown hair.

Some, a few of them could read quite readily in a second reader and many more knew the alphabet and were trying patiently to spell out short easy words, while by far the greater number could not distinguish a letter. I have had as many as nineteen in my alphabet class at one time but it is now reduced to four.

One old woman over sixty, after spending three weeks on the alphabet and finally conquering it, said she wanted to learn to spell Jesus first before spelling easy words for said she, "Pears like I can learn the rest easier if I get that blessed name learned first." So now she looks through the Bible for that name and has learned to distinguish it at sight from other words. The older members of the school are as quiet and orderly as I could desire but the children are not so very different from other children. They love mischief and play and the prevailing vice among them is deceit. But education has all the charm of novelty to them and they learn with astonishing rapidity. They come to school as well provided with books as children usually do.

Your Sister in Christ,
Pamelia A. Hand

*Source: The Black American and Education* (pp. 73–74) by Earle H. West. Copyright © 1972 by Merrill Publishing Company. Reprinted by permission.

Booker T. Washington and students at the Tuskegee Institute.

the educational ideas that led to his establishment of the Tuskegee Institute in 1881. Washington emphasized the dignity of labor and, rather than an academic education, advocated a practical education that would provide Blacks the marketable skills that would allow them to be self-sufficient.

Others, such as W. E. B. DuBois (1868–1963), the first Black to earn a Ph.D. from Harvard, disagreed with Washington and what they considered a position of accommodation or compromise. They argued that such a position was wrong and that it undermined the achievement of civil and political equality for Blacks to be given only one educational direction (industrial), whereas Whites had several. DuBois encouraged political activism and in 1909 joined a multiracial group of social activists in founding the National Association for the Advancement of Colored People.

Whether Washington's accommodation approach to civil rights or DuBois's militant approach hindered the movement, or whether any other approach would have made any difference, is open to conjecture. What is known is that by the time Washington began his work at Tuskegee, Reconstruction had not only begun to decline, but a backlash against Blacks also had begun. The education he advanced was perhaps the only one that would have been permitted and supported in the openly racist political and social climate that pervaded the South at the end of the 19th century.

Washington's efforts were successful: ten years after its founding, Tuskegee had a faculty of 88 and a student body of 1,200, making it one of the largest institutions of higher education in the South. It is also significant to note that Tuskegee and, even more so, the Hampton Institute were important as centers for the training of Black teachers. The traditional attention given to Tuskegee and Hampton as agricultural and industrial schools has obscured the fact they were founded and maintained primarily to train Black teachers for the South. Indeed, between 1872 and 1890, 604 of Hampton's 723 graduates became teachers (Anderson, 1978). Many of these and Tuskegee's alumni were instrumental in not only establishing and teaching in the public schools, but in establishing normal schools in rural areas throughout the South.

In addition to Hampton and Tuskegee, several other distinguished Black colleges and universities were established in the immediate post–Civil War years. These include Atlanta University, founded in 1865 by the American Baptist Mission Society; Howard University, chartered in 1868 by the Congregationalists; Fisk University, established in 1866 by the American Missionary Association; and Mehary Medical College, originally Walton College, founded in 1865 by the Methodist Episcopal Church. Somewhat later, as a result of the Second Morrill Act of 1890, Black land-grant colleges were established in each of the southern and border states—17 in all (Pifer, 1973).

## Segregated Public Schools

Yet another factor changing the face of education in the South during the Reconstruction period was legislation leading to the establishment of tax-supported public or common school systems. Many freedmen recently elected to state legislatures were a force in this movement. Many of these Black legislators as well as some White legislators advocated integration in the newly established schools. In fact, many of the state statutes or constitutional provisions established the schools without making reference to either integration or segregation. However, none of the southern states actually instituted an integrated system, and the segregation that began as custom became law in all the southern states. Yet the efforts of the various groups and agencies did result in a dramatic reversal of the educational status of Black Americans from a literacy rate estimated at 5% or 10% at the outbreak of the Civil War to one of 70% by 1910.

From the end of Reconstruction through the turn of the century, a system of racial segregation was established in the South that remained in effect until the desegregation movement of the 1950s and 1960s. The practice of segregation was sanctioned by the 1896 U.S. Supreme Court decision in *Plessy v. Ferguson*, which said that separate railroad cars did not violate the Constitution. But the "separate but equal" doctrine, while always producing separate, rarely produced equal. Nonetheless, after the 1870s the federal government effectively withdrew from the promotion of the civil and educational rights of Blacks.

During this same period, ever-increasing numbers of White children from immigrant and lower socioeconomic families were entering the enlarged public school system; between 1880 and 1895 White enrollment in the public schools increased 106% compared to 59% for Black enrollment (Fraizer, cited in Hare & Swift, 1976). The "rise of the poor whites" placed increased financial demands on public revenues and often resulted in funds being diverted from Black schools to improve other schools (Gutek, 1991). To this was added the disenfranchisement of Blacks by many southern states and the delegation of authority to local school boards to divide state education funds as they saw fit. From the court approval of segregation, the loss of political power, and the decreased financial support emerged the "separate but inferior" system that dominated so much of the South until well after the mid-20th century.

**For Your Reflection and Analysis**

Do you consider Booker T. Washington a realist or an accommodationist? Explain.

**Reflect on Diversity**
To what extent do the poor and minorities continue to compete for limited educational resources?

# Teacher Education

The formal training of teachers in the United States did not begin until the 19th century. In colonial America, teachers at the elementary level were often young men who taught for only a short time before studying for the ministry or law. Given the strong relationship between church and education, more often than not they were chosen more for their religious orthodoxy than their educational qualifications. In fact, they were often viewed as assistant pastors and in addition to their teaching they were expected to perform various duties related to the functioning of the church. In many small communities, the minister himself was the schoolmaster.

Unfortunately, too often the "career teachers" were individuals who had been unsuccessful at other occupations or those whose personal character and civil conduct left something to be desired. It was also not uncommon in colonial America to find teachers who were indentured servants—persons who had sold their services for a period of years in exchange for passage to the New World. Perhaps the closest thing to any teacher preparation was that received by those individuals who entered teaching after serving as apprentices to schoolmasters. (See the Historical Note on page 40.) In fact, some historians refer to the apprenticeship training received by Quaker teachers as the first teacher education in America (Pulliam & Van Patten, 2007).

A distinction was made between teachers at the elementary level and those at the secondary level, not in the teacher training they received but in the higher status the secondary teachers held in society and the higher education they possessed. Teachers in the Latin grammar schools and academies typically were graduates of secondary schools and, not uncommonly, had received some college education, whereas those at the elementary level very often had little more than an elementary education themselves.

As noted in Chapter 1, most histories of education consider the Columbian School at Concord, Vermont, to be the first formal teacher training institution. However, a good argument can be made that the first such institution was actually the previously mentioned Troy Female Seminary opened by Emma Willard in 1821. Willard established the seminary to train female teachers in both the subject areas and pedagogy. She also wrote a textbook on pedagogy, as did Catharine Beecher, the head of Mount Holyoke. Each graduate of the Troy Female Seminary received a signed certificate confirming her qualifications to teach. Long before the first state-supported normal schools in Massachusetts were opened by Horace Mann, the Troy Seminary had prepared 200 teachers for the common schools (Rippa, 1997). In fact, this and other academies were responsible not only for expanding educational opportunities for women but also for preparing a large number of individuals for the teaching profession, and thus they were strongly supported by Horace Mann.

## Establishment of Normal Schools

The greatest force, however, in increasing the professional training of teachers was the establishment of normal schools. As we have seen, Horace Mann, Henry Barnard, Catharine Beecher, and others who worked for the establishment of common school systems recognized that the success of such systems was dependent on the preparation of a sufficient quantity of adequately trained teachers. This, in turn, demanded the establishment of institutions for the specific training of teachers, that is, normal schools. These educational leaders also believed that the teaching force for the common schools should be female, not only because women supposedly made better teachers at the elementary level but also because they were less expensive to hire. For example, in 1849 Iowa male teachers were paid almost twice as much as female teachers: $14.53 per month vs. $7.64 per month (Cordier, 1988). While they decreased, gender differences in teacher salaries remained in most school districts well into the twentieth century.

The growing enrollments in the common schools also created a growing demand for teachers. The response in one state after another was the establishment of normal schools. The New York State Normal School at Albany, the next established (1844) after those in Massachusetts, was headed by David P. Page. His book, *Theory and Practice of Teaching or the Motives and Methods of Good School Keeping,* published in 1847, became the standard text in teacher education. In addition to state-supported schools, to meet the ever-increasing demand for teachers in urban areas, a number of larger cities operated normal schools. These normal schools typically had higher entrance requirements than the state or private schools (generally the completion of two or three years of high school) and also provided the opportunity for much more observation and practice experience. In most instances they were authorized to issue teaching certificates (Angus & Mirel, 2001). By 1865 more than 50 normal schools were in operation, and by 1900 a reported 350 normal schools were operating in 45 states.

Admission to most normal schools required only an elementary education and was free to residents of the state. The course of study lasted one or two years and included a review of material to be taught in the elementary school, instruction in methods of teaching, "mental philosophy" (i.e., educational psychology), and classroom management. Overriding the curriculum was a concern for the development of moral character. A prominent feature of the normal school was the model school, the forerunner of the laboratory school, where students could practice teaching.

## Teacher Institutes

Despite the spread of normal schools, as late as 1900 only a bare majority of teachers had attended normal schools. Before this time, the most important institution in the training of teachers was the **teacher institute**. A common practice of school districts was to hire individuals with no formal training, with the condition that their continued employment depended on attendance at a teacher institute. The typical institute met once or twice a year and lasted from several days to four weeks, usually in the summer. In less populous areas the institutes were often conducted by the county superintendent of schools. Some were offered in connection with institutions of higher education. The primary purpose of many institutes was to provide a brief course in the theory and practice of teaching, with great emphasis placed on elevating the moral character of the teacher (Spring, 2011). At some institutes, teachers were inspired by noted educators, instructed in new techniques, and informed of the most modern material (Binder, 1974).

## Normal School Curriculum and Standards Strengthened

Toward the end of the 19th century, the character of the normal school began to change. The growing population had not only created an increased demand for elementary or common school teachers, but the secondary school movement also created a concomitant demand for secondary school teachers. To meet this demand, normal schools began to broaden their curriculum to include the training of secondary school teachers. At the same time, they began to require high school completion for admission. The passage of teacher certification statutes that specified the amount and type of training required of teachers contributed to the expansion of the normal school program from two to three years, and eventually, during the 1920s, to four years. By this time normal schools were beginning to call themselves state teachers' colleges. In time, with the broadening of the curriculum to embrace many of the liberal arts, the "teacher" designation was dropped and most became simply "state colleges." Some of these former normal schools have become the largest and most respected universities in the United States.

> **For Your Reflection and Analysis**
>
> Are you attending or have you attended an institution that began as a normal school? What influence has this history had on the institutional climate?

## *Universities Enter Teacher Training*

During the late 19th century, the universities became increasingly involved in teacher education. Teacher training at the college or university level had been offered at a limited number of institutions as early as the 1830s, but it was not until toward the end of the 19th century that universities entered the field of teacher preparation to any measurable extent. Their involvement stemmed in part from the increased demand for secondary school teachers. The universities had always been institutions for the education of those who taught in the grammar schools, academies, and high schools. However, they prepared these students not as teachers per se, but as individuals who had advanced knowledge of certain subject matter. The increased demand for secondary school teachers, the late entrance of the normal schools into the training of secondary school teachers, and the growing recognition that the professionalization of teaching demanded study of its theory and practice led to the increased involvement of universities in teacher education. The University of Iowa established the first chair of education in 1873; other midwestern universities followed, and in 1892 the New York College for the Training of Teachers (Teachers College) became a part of Columbia University. After the turn of the century, teacher training departments became commonplace in most universities.

## Summary

The Founding Fathers recognized the importance of education to the development of the new nation. As the nation marched through the 19th century and became an industrial giant, the demand for skilled workers and the demand of the working class, who saw education as a path to success, combined to expand the offering of publicly supported education through the secondary school. The growth of higher education can also be attributed to these forces. Indeed, today it is the recognition of education's importance to our national prominence and its vital role in ensuring our continued economic prosperity that has served as the motivation for much of the current activity to reform our nation's schools.

Unfortunately, although the educational opportunities afforded much of the population were greatly expanded in the 19th century, the history of the education of minorities was basically one of neglect and segregation. It would not be until the third quarter of the 20th century that any marked progress would be made in improving the education of Native Americans, Asian Americans, Hispanic Americans, and Black Americans. In the next chapter, many of these efforts will be detailed, as well as those designed to improve the professional training of teachers.

# PROFESSIONAL DEVELOPMENT *Workshop*

## *Prepare for the State Licensure Examination*

Terry Wosinski, a second-year social studies teacher at Daniel Webster Junior High School, has become increasingly concerned about the conduct of one student in his third-period history class who is having a negative effect on the entire class. Terry is worried that he is on the verge of either losing his cool or losing control of the class. At issue is the inappropriate and aggressive behavior of a large 13-year-old boy named Forrest. Forrest consistently gets out of his seat and on his way to pick up a dropped pen, sharpen a pencil, or put something in the trash will poke someone on the arm, thump them on the head, or in some other way make physical contact—not enough to really harm, but enough to disrupt and annoy. When he is seated he talks to or at students around him. Forrest rarely completes an assignment, but when he does his work, it is well above average.

Terry has tried to get to know Forrest better to see if there is anything happening outside the school that would be contributing to his behavior, but Forrest has been reluctant to share anything about his home or family situation. Terry repeatedly and sternly tells Forrest to stay in his seat and to not do whatever inappropriate thing he is doing. He has also made Forrest stay after school for detention on numerous occasions but after a day or two at best Forrest resumes his misbehaviors. Terry is reluctant to go to Neil Jones, the assistant principal, for advice or intervention because he does not want to be seen as not being able to manage his class.

1. Describe behavioral theories of classroom management that might be used to manage Forrest's behavior.
2. Explain the importance of clear expectations and consistency in administering consequences to classroom management.
3. Give examples of several desist behaviors that Terry might use to deal with Forrest's physical and verbal misbehaviors.

### Build Your Knowledge Base

1. In what ways do Henry Barnard's concerns in the opening of the chapter echo the concerns regarding teacher education expressed in the media today?
2. In what ways were Thomas Jefferson's plans for an educational system elitist? Egalitarian?
3. What was the significance of each of the following to expanding educational opportunities in the United States?
   a. Monitorial schools
   b. Sunday schools
   c. Infant schools
   d. Free school societies
4. Describe the contributions of Horace Mann and Henry Barnard to the common school movement.
5. What influence did Prussian educators have on American education in the early 19th century?
6. Describe the impact of the Second Morrill Act on the provision of education for minorities in the United States.
7. What impact has the historical neglect of the education of minorities had on their education and on the educational system today?

8. What was the contribution of Emma Willard to women's education? To teacher education?

9. Compare the role of the university with that of the normal school in the education of teachers.

## Develop Your Portfolio

1. We gain much insight about contemporary education through our reading of the history of education. Read an article from the professional education literature for the period from 1850 to 1890, and an article on the same or a similar topic in a recent journal (2010 or later). Prepare an artifact that compares and contrasts the educational concepts, methodologies, and general ideas presented in both journals. Place your artifact in your portfolio under **INTASC Standard 1, Learner Development**.

2. In 1918 the National Education Association appointed the Commission on the Reorganization of Secondary Education, The commission issued seven cardinal principles of secondary education, which identified what should be the objectives of high school curriculum: (1) health, (2) command of fundamental academic skills, (3) worthy home membership, (4) vocational preparation, (5) citizenship, (6) worthwhile use of leisure time, and (7) ethical character. Re-examine the educational theory of social reconstructionism, particularly the contributions of critical theory as presented in Chapter 4. Prepare a table that lists each cardinal principle in the left column and summarizes how a critical theorist might react to it in the right column. Place your artifact in your portfolio under **INTASC Standard 4, Instructional Content Knowledge**.

## Explore Teaching and Learning: Field Experiences

1. Arrange interviews with key local citizens and review historical information so that you can write a three- to five-page history of the organization and development of the school district from which you graduated, a local district, or one in which you might teach.

2. Identify two to three colleges and universities in your community. Contact the institutions for information, and then trace their development from their original sponsor, mission, and source of funds to their current status. Indicate the kinds of changes that have taken place.

## MyEducationLab

Go to **Topic 7 The History and Philosophy of Education** in the MyEducationLab (www.myeducationlab.com) for *Foundations of American Education*, where you can:

- Find learning outcomes for the history and philosophy of education along with the national standards that connect to these outcomes.
- Complete Assignments and Activities that can help you more deeply understand the chapter content.
- Apply and practice your understanding of the core teaching skills identified in the chapter with the Building Teaching Skills and Dispositions learning units.
- Examine challenging situations and cases presented in the IRIS Center Resources.

- Access additional video clips of CCSSO National Teachers of the Year award winners responding to the question, "Why Do I Teach?" in the Teacher Talk section.
- Check your comprehension on the content covered in the chapter with the Study Plan. Here you will be able to take a chapter quiz, receive feedback on your answers, and then access Review, Practice, and Enrichment activities to enhance your understanding of chapter content.
- Use the Online Lesson Plan Builder to practice lesson planning and integrating national and state standards into your planning.

# 7

# Modern American Education: From The Progressive Movement to the Present

In the 1930s, faculty and students at Oglethorpe University created a "time room" where artifacts from the history of civilization were preserved in their original form, on film and paper. Film footage presented a verbal and visual condensed version of significant events in the history of the world.

Suppose you and your classmates were requested to create a time room on the history of American education. What artifacts would you include in your room? If you made a video chronicle of education, what would it include?

As you may have discovered in answering the preceding questions, capturing the most noteworthy happenings from a period of time, whether in a capsule, a room, or a chapter, is a challenge. The challenge becomes greater the more rapidly changing the times and the more diverse the areas to be included.

In this chapter, discussion of the history of American education begun in Chapters 5 and 6 is brought to the present. Although from a historical perspective this period encompasses a relatively short amount of time, it has witnessed the most rapid expansion of education in our nation's history and some of the most marked changes. So much has taken place that this text cannot focus in detail on every contributing personality or intervening variable. Consider the following objectives as you study this chapter:

- Identify the major economic, political, and social forces affecting education in the 20th century.
- Describe the progressive education movement in the United States.
- Compare the impact of the Great Depression, World War II, and the Cold War on education.
- Evaluate the progress of the Civil Rights movement and the War on Poverty.
- Outline the developments in education during the 1970s, 1980s, and 1990s.
- Trace the fluctuation of federal support for education in the 20th century.
- Detail the major provisions of the No Child Left Behind Act and their impact on the schools.
- Describe how the influence of the federal government increased under the Obama administration.

**MyEducationLab**

Visit the MyEducationLab for *Foundations of American Education* to enhance your understanding of chapter concepts with a personalized Study Plan. You'll also have the opportunity to hone your teaching skills through video and case based Assignments and Activities, and Building Teaching Skills and Disposition lessons.

**For Your Reflection and Analysis**

What are some of today's most pressing problems facing "new immigrants" to the United States?

# The Twentieth Century Unfolds

## *The People and the Nation Grow*

The 20th century brought marked changes in American social, economic, political, and educational life. Population growth continued at a staggering rate: from 50 million in 1880, to 76 million in 1900, to 106 million in 1920. Although birthrates declined, improvements in medicine and sanitation led to lower infant mortality and a lower overall death rate. As in the last decades of the previous century, a significant portion of the population growth was the result of immigration. In the first 2 decades of the 20th century, the average number of immigrants arriving in this country doubled from the previous 2 decades, from an average of 450,000 immigrants per year to an average of almost 900,000 per year. Continuing with the trend that had begun in the last century, the majority of these "new" immigrants were from southern and eastern Europe—Italy, Poland, Russia, Austria–Hungary—and were primarily Catholic or Jewish. Concerns that the new immigrants were of an undesirable "racial stock" and tended to be illiterate, criminal, and "ill-fitted to the demands of a Teutonic civilization" led to demands in the popular media that immigration be restricted (Ravitch, 2000, p. 65).

At the same time that the population was experiencing rapid growth, it was becoming increasingly urban. According to the 1920 census, for the first time in our nation's history, the number of those living in towns of 2,500 or more (54.2 million) exceeded those living in rural areas (51.6 million). Much of the growth of the cities came from the new immigrants. The immigrants tended to congregate in crowded segregated neighborhoods in tenement houses. Living conditions in the slums and tenements in many of the major American cities equaled or exceeded the squalor, poverty, and unsanitary conditions of the European slums the immigrants had left behind.

America experienced growth not only at home but also on the international scene. In the last years of the 19th century and the beginning of the 20th century, the United States acquired Guam, the Philippines, Puerto Rico, Hawaii, the Virgin Islands, and the Panama Canal Zone. The nation also engaged in a war with Spain; landed troops in Mexico, Nicaragua, and Haiti; helped put down a revolt in China; and in 1917 entered the fight to "make the world safe for democracy."

## *Economic Growth*

The economic growth of the United States during this period was even more profound than the population growth. Whereas the population increased less than fourfold in the post–Civil War to pre–World War I period, production increased tenfold. This was a period of rapid growth for the railroads and other transportation and communication industries. The expansion of the railroads brought an end to the frontier and linked all parts of the nation, as did an ever-expanding network of telephone lines. At the same time, the trans-Atlantic cable and transworld shipping linked America with other nations. The expansion in the transportation industry opened up new markets for the growing agricultural and manufacturing industries. By 1920 the United States had become the largest manufacturing nation in the world.

Paradoxically, this period of stellar economic growth is also regarded as a dark chapter in American history because of the abuses in industry (Gray & Peterson, 1974). The business leaders who helped bring about the growth and contributed to the abuses have been referred to as "robber barons," and the business and political corruption of the era touched every aspect of American life. The plight of workers (including children) in factories, the unsafe and unsanitary working conditions, the horrors of industrial accidents, and descriptions of life in the poverty-ridden slums filled the tabloids and stirred political and social reforms.

## Politics and Reform

Antitrust legislation was enacted in an attempt to control monopolies and their unfair business practices. The progressive movement that emerged at the turn of the century was responsible for a flood of labor legislation addressed at regulating the labor of women and children, wages and hours, and health and safety conditions. Workers also sought to improve their plight through labor unions. Increased union activity met with harsh resistance and persecution; violence and loss of life were not uncommon. Yet by 1920 one-fifth of all nonagricultural workers in the nation were organized, a considerable achievement in light of employer hostility (Kirkland, 1969).

In the political arena, the progressive movement gained momentum in the years after 1900. Decrying the excesses of big business, the progressives challenged the cherished ideal of limited government and urged the government to protect consumers against unfair monopolistic practices, workers (particularly women and children) against exploitation, and the less fortunate against any form of social injustice. Reform became the "order of the day" on the local, state, and national levels as progressives sought to wrest control of government from the business community and use it to bring about social change.

## Changes in Education

Significant changes in the educational arena accompanied those in the social, economic, and political arenas. The urbanization of the population and the popularity of the automobile made possible the building of larger schools and contributed to the consolidation of rural school districts. The number of school districts in the United States gradually decreased from more than 130,000 at the turn of the 20th century to approximately 15,500 in 2000. State control of education increased in a number of areas: certification of teachers, requirements for teacher education programs, curricular requirements for the schools, standards for school facilities, and provisions for financial support.

At the same time, the size of the school population increased more rapidly than the overall population. In the 3 decades between 1890 and 1920 the school-age population increased 49% and school enrollments 70%. A significant portion of the increase in school enrollment, especially in the larger cities, came from the new immigrants or the children of new immigrants.

The growth in the student population was accompanied by an 80% growth in the number of teachers and other nonsupervisory personnel. During the same period, the average length of the school term increased by 27 days. More teachers and longer terms translated into significant increases in expenditures (see Table 7.1).

> **For Your Reflection and Analysis**
>
> For a number of years the average length of the school term has been 180 days. Do you support efforts to extend the school year? Why or why not?

# Progressivism in Education

## The Beginnings of Progressive Education

The progressive reform movement, which had such a widespread impact on political, social, and economic life, also found expression in education. In the pre–World War I period, paralleling the call of the social and political reformers, education reformers called for curricular and administrative reforms. They also called for making the schools, particularly those in the cities, more sanitary, more open to air and sunlight, and more conducive to creative activity. They asked for lowered pupil–teacher ratios and added the provision of basic health care and food services to the responsibilities of the school. Progressivism also sought to improve the operational efficiency of school districts and rid them of political corruption.

Pedagogical progressivism traces its intellectual roots to Rousseau and its beginnings in America to Francis W. Parker (1837–1902), superintendent of schools in Quincy, Massachusetts, and later head of the Cook County Normal School in Chicago. Parker studied in Europe and became familiar with the work of Pestalozzi and Froebel. He shared their belief that learning should emanate from the interests

**Table 7.1 — Historical Summary of U.S. Public Elementary and Secondary School Statistics, 1870–1930 (all dollars unadjusted)**

| | 1870 | 1880 | 1890 | 1900 | 1910 | 1920 | 1930 |
|---|---|---|---|---|---|---|---|
| **Enrollments** | | | | | | | |
| Total school age (5–17 yrs.) population (thous.) | 12,055 | 15,066 | 18,543 | 21,573 | 24,009 | 27,556 | 31,417 |
| Total enrollment in elementary and secondary schools (thous.) | 6,872 | 9,867 | 12,723 | 15,503 | 17,814 | 21,578 | 25,678 |
| Percent of population aged 5–17 enrolled in public schools (in private schools) | 57.0 (NA) | 65.5 (NA) | 68.6 (9.5) | 71.9 (6.4) | 74.2 (5.2) | 78.3 (4.9) | 81.7 (7.8) |
| **Attendance** | | | | | | | |
| Average daily attendance (thous.) | 4,077 | 6,144 | 8,154 | 10,633 | 12,827 | 16,150 | 21,265 |
| Average length of school terms (in days) | 132.2 | 130.3 | 134.7 | 144.3 | 157.5 | 161.9 | 172.7 |
| Average number of days attended per pupil enrolled | 78.4 | 81.1 | 86.3 | 99.0 | 113.0 | 121.2 | 143.0 |
| **Instructional staff** | | | | | | | |
| Total classroom teachers/nonsupervisory staff (thous.) | 201 | 287 | 364 | 423 | 523 | 657 | 843 |
| Men | 78 | 123 | 126 | 127 | 110 | 93 | 140 |
| Women | 123 | 164 | 238 | 296 | 413 | 565 | 703 |
| Average annual salary of instructional staff | $189 | $195 | $252 | $325 | $485 | $871 | $1,420 |
| **Finance** | | | | | | | |
| Total revenue receipts (thous.) | (NA) | (NA) | $143,195 | $219,766 | $433,064 | $970,120 | $2,088,557 |
| Percent of revenue receipts from: | | | | | | | |
| Federal government | (NA) | (NA) | (NA) | (NA) | (NA) | .3 | .4 |
| State government | | | 18.2 | 17.3 | 15.0 | 16.5 | 16.9 |
| Local government | | | 67.8 | 67.7 | 72.1 | 83.5 | 82.7 |
| Total expenditures per pupil in ADA | $16 | $13 | $17 | $20 | $33 | $64 | $108 |

Source: Snyder, T. D. & Dillow, S. A. (2011). *Digest of Education Statistics 2010* (NCES 2011–015). National Center for Education Statistics, Institute of Education Sciences, U.S. Department of Education. Washington, DC.

and needs of the child and that the most appropriate curriculum was an activity-based one that encouraged children to express themselves freely and creatively.

The practice school of the Cook County Normal School was organized as a model democratic community. Art was an integral part of the curriculum, as were nature studies, field trips, and social activities. Rather than deal with multiple, discrete subject matter, the curriculum attempted to integrate subjects in a way that made it more meaningful to the learner. In all things Parker's aim was to make the child the center of the educational process.

## John Dewey

Among the parents of children at Parker's school in Chicago was John Dewey, professor of philosophy and pedagogy at the University of Chicago. Dewey was impressed with the philosophy and methods of the school and in 1896 established his own laboratory school at the University of Chicago. Through his many writings and articulation of his philosophy, Dewey provided the intellectual foundation for progressive education. In fact, Dewey was said to be "the real spokesman for intellectual America in the Progressive Era" (Bonner, 1963, p. 44).

Dewey's progressivist educational theories are discussed in Chapter 4. He rejected the old, rigid, **subject-centered curriculum** in favor of the **child-centered curriculum** in which learning came through experience, not rote memorization. The problem-solving method was the preferred approach, and motivation was at the center of the learning process. The goal of education was to promote individual growth and to prepare the child for full participation in a democratic society.

Dewey maintained that the child should be viewed as a total organism and that education is most effective when it considers not only the intellectual but also the social, emotional, and physical needs of the child. He thought that education was a lifelong process and that the school should be an integral part of community life, a concept that gave support to the development of the community school. Dewey wrote some 500 articles and 40 books. His influence was felt not only in philosophy and education, but also in law, political theory, and social reform. He left an imprint on American education that was unparalleled in the 20th century. His classic *Democracy and Education* (1916) provided perhaps the strongest statement of his educational theories and provided the rationale for a generation of educators who were part of what was to be known as the progressive education movement.

## Ella Flagg Young

Ella Flagg Young was an important figure in the progressive education movement, both in her own right and through her influence on Dewey. Dewey acknowledged that he was constantly getting ideas from Young: "More times than I could say I didn't see the meaning or force of some favorite conception of my own until Mrs. Young had given it back to me . . . it was from her that I learned that freedom and respect for freedom mean regard for the inquiring and reflective processes of individuals" (McManis, 1916, p. 121). Like Dewey, Young proposed that teaching methods give fullest expression to the individual interests of the child, that education recognize the total experiences the child brings to the school, and that the "curriculum must provide the child with experience that builds on his or her natural interests and tendencies" (Webb & McCarthy, 1998, p. 231).

From her positions as principal of the Chicago Normal School, superintendent of Chicago schools, and president of the National Education Association, as well as through her numerous presentations and publications, Young played a visible and important role in education in the years leading up to World War I. She strove to bring greater democracy to education by providing teachers with a greater voice and by encouraging the extension of the principles of democracy to the classroom.

## Progressive Education Association

The formation of the Progressive Education Association (PEA) in 1919 gave progressivism a vigorous organizational voice (Cremin, 1962). The association adopted

**For Your Reflection and Analysis**

To what extent did your elementary school experience reflect the progressive child-centered philosophy?

**For Your Reflection and Analysis**

What activity in your educational experience was the best example of creative self-expression? Was it intended as such by the teacher, or did it take place by accident?

seven guiding principles: (1) the child's freedom to develop naturally, (2) interest provides the motivation for all work, (3) the teacher as guide in the learning process, (4) the scientific study of pupil development, (5) greater attention to everything that affects the child's physical development, (6) cooperation between the school and home in meeting the natural interests and activities of the child, and (7) the progressive school should be a leader in educational movements (*Progressive Education,* 1924, pp. 1–2).

The PEA published the journal *Progressive Education* from 1924 to 1955. In its early years, *Progressive Education* devoted considerable space to the concept of "creative self-expression." According to Harold Rugg, professor at Teachers College, Columbia University, and a leading spokesperson for the PEA, creative self-expression was the essence of the progressive education movement (Cremin, 1962).

Another well-known spokesperson for progressive education, William H. Kilpatrick, was also on the faculty at Teachers College. Kilpatrick translated Dewey's philosophy into a practical methodology, the **project method**. The project method was an attempt to make education as "lifelike" as possible. At the heart of the educative process was to be "wholehearted purposeful activity," activity consistent with the child's own goals. Kilpatrick shared Dewey's belief in the importance of problem solving, but he went beyond Dewey in his child-centered emphasis and in his rejection of any organized subject matter (Cremin, 1962).

During the 1930s (1932–1940), the PEA conducted a study of almost 3,000 students from progressive and nonprogressive high schools regarding the schools' effectiveness in preparing graduates for college. The results of the study, *The Eight-Year Study,* showed that students from progressive high schools not only achieved higher than students from traditional high schools but also were better adjusted socially.

## Influence of the Progressive Movement on Higher Education

The influence of the progressive education movement was also felt in higher education. The great model of progressive higher education was the University of Wisconsin. The Wisconsin model was based on the idea that "the obligation of the university was to undertake leadership in the application of science to the improvement of the life of the citizenry in every domain" (Cremin, 1988, p. 246). This was accomplished through faculty research and service, the training of experts, and extended education.

College and university enrollments rose steadily during the pre–World War I years and then surged after the war, partly as a result of those who had come to higher education as part of the Student's Army Training Corps and then stayed after the war ended. Enrollments rose from almost 600,000 in 1919–1920 to 1.1 million in 1929–1930.

Most of these students were seeking a professional or technical education, primarily in education, business, and engineering, and enrolled not in the universities but in the growing number of junior colleges and the teacher education institutions. The number of junior colleges increased from 52 in 1920, to 277 in 1930, to 456 in 1940 (U.S. Census Bureau, 1975); the number of colleges for teachers grew from 45 in 1920 to four times that number by 1940 (Pulliam & Van Patten, 2007). The normal schools across the country were as typical of the progressive service orientation in higher education as the state universities: "they presumed to prepare scientifically trained experts; they extended their learning to all comers; and they prided themselves on their sensitivity to popular need" (Cremin, 1988, p. 248).

## The Child Study Movement

During the first two decades of the 20th century, as the progressive movement was gaining momentum, two related movements were taking place that would have far-reaching consequences: the child study and measurement movements. The child study movement began with the pioneering work of G. Stanley Hall. Hall established a center for applied psychology at Johns Hopkins University in 1884, the year Dewey graduated from the same institution. Later, as president of Clark University, he brought together the first group of scholars interested in the scientific study of the child through the observation of children at various stages of development.

Hall and his colleagues recognized that emotional growth and personality development were just as important as cognitive development in understanding the child. They saw the child as an evolving organism and believed that once educators understood how the child developed, they would be better able to foster that development (Perkinson, 1977). These early efforts were important in laying the foundation for educational psychology and developmental psychology and for the recognition and inclusion of this discipline in teacher education. Child study, the stage theory of learning propounded by theorists such as Jean Piaget, the specialties of child, adolescent and developmental psychology, and the study of exceptional children can all trace their beginnings to Hall.

## The Measurement Movement

Another cornerstone of educational psychology was laid by Lewis M. Terman, Edward L. Thorndike, and other psychologists involved in the development of the measurement movement. Although intelligence and aptitude tests had been in use for some time, the real breakthrough came when French psychologists Alfred Binet and Theodore Simon developed an instrument based on an intelligence scale that allowed comparison of individual intelligence to a norm. Of the many adaptations of the Binet-Simon scale the most important for education was the so-called Stanford revision by Lewis Terman of Stanford University. It was also Terman who developed the **intelligence quotient (IQ),** a number indicating the level of an individual's mental development. Meanwhile, Thorndike and his students at Columbia developed scales for measuring achievement in arithmetic, spelling, reading, language, and other areas (Cremin, 1962).

World War I was a major factor in the growth of the measurement movement. The military needed a massive mobilization of manpower. It also needed a way to determine which men were suited for service and for what type of service. Out of this need, a number of group intelligence tests were developed and ultimately were administered to hundreds of thousands of recruits. One unexpected result of this massive testing was the discovery of a large number of young men with educational (as well as physical) deficiencies: approximately one-quarter of all recruits were judged illiterate. Deficiencies were particularly high among rural youth.

Within a decade of the end of the war, the measurement movement had become a permanent part of American education. According to Heffernan (1968), the "apparent objectivity of the test results had a fascination for school administrators and teachers. Certainty seemed somehow to attach to these mathematically expressed comparisons of pupil achievement" (p. 229). Throughout the country students were classified, assigned, and compared on the basis of tests results. Often the tests were wisely used to diagnose learning

The testing of World War I recruits was a major step in the development of intelligence tests.

difficulties and assess individual differences. Unfortunately, they were also used to make comparisons without consideration of differences in school populations, to make judgments about the quality of teaching, and, most distressing, to make subjective judgments about students' potential (Heffernan, 1968). Regrettably, these misuses of tests continue today.

## Education During the Great Depression

The crash of the stock market in October 1929 ushered in the greatest depression our nation has ever experienced. The period was marked by the failure of banks and businesses, the closing of factories, mass unemployment, bread lines, soup kitchens, and tent cities. Unemployment was particularly high among minorities and young people. As many as 6 million young people were out of school and unemployed from 1933 to 1935. Many had no occupational training or experience. In a labor market overrun with experienced workers, they had few opportunities for employment (National Policies Commission, 1941).

The Great Depression also had a serious impact on the operation of schools. In many states, especially in the hard-pressed South and Southwest, schools were closed or the school year shortened. By the first quarter of 1934 an estimated 20,000 schools nationwide, including 85% of the public schools in Alabama, had closed, affecting more than 1 million pupils. Ten states were estimated to have schools with school terms of less than three months and 22 with terms of less than six months (National Education Association [NEA], 1933). As the Depression deepened, students were increasingly asked to bring their own supplies or, in extreme cases, to pay tuition. In school districts throughout America, the local school boards were unable to pay their teachers and issued them promissory notes agreeing to pay them when revenues were collected. And in almost every school district the number of teachers was reduced, class size increased, and the number of courses in the high school curriculum cut (Gutek, 1991).

Until the Great Depression, the relationship of the federal government to education was clear: Education was viewed as a function of the states and local school districts. These entities were responsible for operating educational programs. Beginning in 1933, with the creation of the Civilian Conservation Corps (CCC) and later the National Youth Administration (NYA), this established relationship changed markedly. The CCC and the NYA were two of the federal emergency agencies created under President Franklin D. Roosevelt's New Deal to provide "work relief" for the unemployed. The CCC provided temporary work for more than 2 million people 18 to 25 years of age on various conservation projects. The NYA administered two programs: (1) a work relief and employment program for needy, out-of-school youth ages 16 to 25 and (2) a program that provided part-time employment to needy high school and college students to help them continue their education. At its peak in 1939–40, approximately 750,000 students in 1,750 colleges and 28,000 secondary schools participated in NYA programs.

When it became clear to officials of both the CCC and the NYA that many participants lacked not only vocational skills but also basic skills in reading, writing, and arithmetic, they moved to meet these needs by means of educational activities operated and controlled by the agencies themselves. Although both of these measures were terminated as the war economy stimulated employment, the fact that the federal government actually operated and controlled educational activities that could have been offered by state or local educational systems marked a departure from the past that was of concern to many educators, including the NEA (National Policies Commission, 1941).

Other New Deal programs provided relief to the financially depressed schools. The Public Works Administration (PWA) provided assistance for the building of numerous public buildings, including almost 13,000 schools. The Works Projects Administration (WPA, originally the Works Progress Administration) provided

**For Your Reflection and Analysis**

What were probably the greatest challenges faced by teachers during the Great Depression?

employment for 100,000 teachers in adult education, art education, and the 1,500 WPA-operated preschools. The WPA adult education program served as many as 4 million adults primarily in their own communities. Perhaps its most important program was the adult literacy program. Between 1933 and 1938, 1.5 million adults, about one-third of them Black, were taught to read. In addition, under a program that became the forerunner of the National School Lunch Program, the Department of Agriculture distributed surplus foods to the schools.

## Indian New Deal

Several New Deal measures were directed at improving the plight of Native Americans and became known as the Indian New Deal. The Indian New Deal was an attempt to remedy the conditions described by the Meriam Report (see Chapter 6). Among the actions taken was the cessation of the sale of allotted Indian land, the organization of tribal councils as legal bodies, the investment of the Bureau of Indian Affairs (BIA) with the right to contract with states for educational services, and the ending of the boarding school system (although because of distance constraints, several off-reservation boarding schools still exist). The Johnson-O'Malley Act of 1934 provided supplemental funds to public schools to provide for the special costs associated with transportation, school lunches, or activities such as graduation.

Native American education was also the beneficiary of other programs of Roosevelt's New Deal—WPA, PWA, and CCC—because they provided job training, income, and improvements on the reservations, including construction of schools and roads and conservation of land, water, and timber. The total result of the New Deal was "the most dynamic program of Indian education in the history of the Indian Service" with a "curriculum more suited to the needs of the child; . . . community day schools and a decreased emphasis on boarding schools; and a better qualified faculty and staff" (Szasz, 1999, p. 48).

## *George S. Counts and Social Reconstructionism*

The experience of the Depression had a significant impact on many progressive educators who came to believe that the schools had a responsibility to redress social injustices. At the 1932 convention of the PEA, in an address entitled "Dare Progressive Education Be Progressive?" George S. Counts challenged the child-centered doctrine and urged educators to "reconstruct their collective social, economic, political, and educational experience to solve the immediate problems of the Great Depression and in so doing create a more just, equitable, and truly 'New Social Order'" (Gutek, 2006, p. 6). In effect, Counts asked the schools to take the lead in planning for an intelligent reconstruction of society. Although the social reconstructionism movement never gained much of a foothold in American education, it served to associate progressive education in the minds of many people with "an economic radicalism that smacked of socialism and communism" and ultimately contributed to its growing unpopularity in the postwar years (Spring, 1976, p. 8).

Counts was joined in his deep concern about the socioeconomic conditions in America and his belief that educators should do something to address these conditions by liberal progressive educators such as William H. Kilpatrick and Harold Rugg. In 1935, these individuals joined with other social reformers to form the John Dewey Society for the Study of Education and Culture and began publishing a journal, *The Social Frontier,* which became the focus of educational extremism during the 1930s. The position of Counts, Rugg, and other social reconstructionists was sharply criticized by many conservative progressives and was responsible for a deepening schism within the PEA. While many of the social reconstructionists moved on to other interests (e.g., challenging communism), the social reconstructionist movement forever connected education to social protest (Watkins, 2006).

## William C. Bagley and the Essentialists

Although progressive education and innovations such as the community school and the project method were popular, protests against the child-centered ideal and its lack of emphasis on fundamentals gained momentum under another professor of education at Teachers College, William Bagley, and other educators associated with the educational theory of essentialism discussed in Chapter 4. Like Arthur Bestor in the 1950s and the reform reports in the 1980s, Bagley looked at American education and judged it weak, lacking in rigor, full of "frills," and inadequate in preparing youth for productive participation in society. The essentialists were also critical of the social reconstructionists and argued that instead of attempting to reconstruct society, educators would serve society better by preparing citizens who possessed the knowledge of the fundamental skills and subjects that provide a basis for understanding, and for the collective thought and judgment essential to the operation of our democratic institutions (Bagley, 1938).

### For Your Reflection and Analysis

Would Bagley be supportive of the seven cardinal principles of education? Why or why not?

## The Influence of the Second World War

As the war with Nazi Germany spread in Europe and American factories were increasingly called on to supply the Allied war effort, the American economy began to recover from the Depression. Once this country entered the war, every institution, including the schools, was dominated by the war effort (see Figure 7.1). According to a statement made by the NEA shortly after the Japanese attack on Pearl Harbor,

> When the schools closed on Friday, December 5, they had many purposes, and they followed many roads to achieve those purposes. When the schools opened on Monday, December 8, they had but one dominant purpose—complete, intelligent, and enthusiastic cooperation in the war effort. (Education Policies Commission, 1942, p. 3)

### Impact on Schools

The war had a heavy impact on the schools. Not only did large numbers of teachers leave the classroom for the battlefield, but enrollment also dropped significantly as youth chose not to return to school or to go to work. By the end of the war more than one-third of the teachers employed in 1940–1941 had left teaching (Kandel, 1948). High school enrollments declined from 6.7 million in 1941 to 5.5 million in

**Figure 7.1 — A War Policy for American Schools: A Statement of the Educational Policies Commission of the National Education Association**

The responsibilities of organized education for the successful outcome of the war involve at least the following activities:

- Training workers for war industries and services.
- Producing goods and services needed for the war.
- Conserving materials by prudent consumption and salvage.
- Helping to raise funds to finance the war.
- Increasing effective manpower by correcting educational deficiencies.
- Promoting health and physical efficiency.
- Protecting school children and property against attack.
- Protecting the ideals of democracy against war hazards.
- Teaching the issues, aims, and progress of war and the peace.
- Sustaining the morale of children and adults.
- Maintaining intelligent loyalty to American democracy.

*Source:* Educational Policies Commission. (1942). *A war policy for American schools.* Washington, DC: National Education Association. Reprinted by permission.

1944 (Knight, 1952). In addition, financial support, which was already low because of the Depression, was further reduced as funds were diverted from education to the war effort. Some assistance was provided by the Lanham Act of 1941 to school districts overburdened by an influx of children from families employed in defense industries or on military bases. The so-called impact aid continues today under the provisions of Public Laws 815 and 874.

Colleges and universities were also affected by the war. Enrollments declined sharply; the enrollment of civilian students was cut almost in half between 1940 and 1944. There was also a severe reduction in instructional staff and revenues. Institutional income in 1944 and 1945 was 67% of what it had been in 1940 (Knight, 1952). Income would have been reduced even more dramatically had it not been for the specialized training and large research projects commissioned by the federal government. These vast research enterprises transformed many universities into what Clark Kerr (1963) termed "federal grant universities."

Colleges and universities also played a vital role in preparing men for military service, for war industries, and for essential civilian activities. By the end of 1943, 380,000 men were involved in specialized training in 489 colleges and universities, many as part of the Army Specialized Training Program or the Navy College Training Program (Knight, 1952).

## The Postwar Years

Toward the end of the war, in an effort to assist veterans whose schooling had been interrupted by military service, the Servicemen's Readjustment Act of 1944 was passed. The G.I. Bill of Rights, as it became known, provided benefits to 7.8 million veterans of World War II to help them further their education. The benefits were subsequently extended to veterans of the Korean, Cold, and Vietnam wars; eventually almost 15 million veterans were involved. The G.I. Bill also initiated a great postwar popularization of higher education. More men and women representing a greater age range and varied social, economic, cultural, and racial groups attended colleges and universities than ever before (Cremin, 1988) (see Table 7.2).

> **For Your Reflection and Analysis**
>
> Which of the educational institutions (elementary-secondary or higher education) felt the most negative impact of World War II? Explain.

> **For Your Reflection and Analysis**
>
> What is your position in the debate about the appropriateness of ROTC on college and university campuses?

**Table 7.2 — Degree-Granting Institutions of Higher Education, Faculty, and Enrollments, 1919–1920 to 2008–2009**

| Year | Total Institutions | Total Faculty | Total Enrollment |
| --- | --- | --- | --- |
| 1919–1920 | 1,041 | 48,615 | 597,880 |
| 1929–1930 | 1,409 | 82,386 | 1,110,737 |
| 1939–1940 | 1,708 | 146,929 | 1,494,203 |
| 1949–1950 | 1,851 | 245,722 | 2,659,021 |
| 1959–1960 | 2,008 | 380,554 | 3,639,847 |
| 1969–1970 | 2,525 | 450,000 | 8,004,660 |
| 1979–1980 | 3,152 | 675,000 | 11,569,899 |
| 1989–1990 | 3,535 | 824,220 | 13,538,560 |
| 1999–2000 | 4,084 | 1,027,830 | 14,791,224 |
| 2008–2009 | 4,409 | 1,371,390 | 19,102,814 |

Source: Snyder, T. D. & Dillow, S. A. (2011). *Digest of Education Statistics 2010* (NCES 2011–015). National Center for Education Statistics, Institute of Education Sciences, U.S. Department of Education. Washington, DC.

While returning servicemen filled college and university classrooms, within a decade the postwar "baby boom" hit the public schools. Between 1946 and 1956, kindergarten and elementary school enrollments increased 37%, from 17.7 million to 24.3 million.

## The Critics and the Decline of Progressive Education

One of the foremost critics of progressive education in the postwar years was Arthur Bestor. In his most famous critical study, *Educational Wastelands,* Bestor deplored the anti-intellectual quality of American schools, which he argued had been caused by progressive education. Bestor advocated a rigorous curriculum of well-defined subject-matter disciplines and the development of the intellect as the primary goal of education. Bestor later became one of the founders of the Council on Basic Education, an organization dedicated to the promotion of a basic academic curriculum. Two other leading critics of the contemporary educational scene were Robert Hutchins and Admiral Hyman Rickover, the father of the atomic submarine. Both Hutchins and Rickover advocated a return to the classical liberal arts curriculum. Rickover also favored the multitrack, ability grouping of most European schools to the American comprehensive high school and focused his attention on the academically talented, who he believed were central to maintaining America's competitive edge with the Soviets.

Progressive education was also hurt by its identification with an educational program known as **life adjustment education**. Focusing on the youth who do not attend college, life adjustment education stressed functional objectives, such as vocation and health, and rejected traditional academic studies. Critics of progressive education found in life adjustment education a perfect target: "it continued an abundance of slogans, jargon, and various anti-intellectualism; it carried the utilitarianism and group conformism of latter-day progressivism to its ultimate trivialization" (Ravitch, 1983, p. 70).

However, in the end it was not its critics that killed progressive education. It died because it was no longer relevant to the time. The great debate about American education continued until 1957 when the Soviet Union launched *Sputnik,* the first space satellite. Then, in a nation suddenly concerned with intelligence and the need for increased science and mathematics skills, progressive education seemed out of step. By the time it disappeared in the mid-1950s, progressive education had strayed far from the "humane, pragmatic, open-minded" approach proposed by Dewey (Ravitch, 1983).

## The Montessori Movement

Concerns about academic standards also contributed to a revival of an approach to early childhood education developed by an Italian physician and educator, Maria Montessori. Although Montessori's approach had been introduced in this country before World War I, it was not until the 1950s that a second and more widespread interest led to the establishment of hundreds of Montessori schools. Its resurgence in the 1950s was fueled in part by parents searching for more academically oriented early childhood programs than those found in most public schools. Its movement gained further attention in the 1960s as many Head Start programs adopted the Montessori approach (Gutek, 2011).

Although they were different in many ways, Montessori shared with Froebel a belief that "children possessed an interior spiritual force that stimulated their self-activity" (Gutek, 2011, p. 334). In keeping with this belief, the Montessori method emphasizes sensory training and the use of didactic materials, learning episodes, and physical exercises in a structured environment. The role of the Montessori teacher is to be aware of the child's readiness to learn, to make sure the child has the materials to learn, and to guide the child through experiences. (See additional discussion of Maria Montessori in the Historical Note.)

# HISTORICAL NOTE

## *Maria Montessori*

Maria Montessori was the first woman in Italy to receive a medical degree. Her early career involved working with children with intellectual disabilities at the University of Rome psychiatric clinic and pedagogical school that prepared teachers of children with intellectual and emotional disabilities. The methods she developed were extended to children without disabilities at her first class at Bambino (Children's House), opened in 1907 in a Rome slum area. This gave her an opportunity to test and perfect ideas, methods, and materials. The schools proved so successful that other Montessori schools were established in Rome and other cities.

The Montessori Method, as it came to be called, emphasized sensory training using a set of materials and physical activities developed by Montessori. Interest and motivation are at the heart of the method. Materials are intended to arouse the student's interest, and interest provides the motivation for learning. Instruction is highly individualized and is designed to develop self-discipline and self-confidence.

Through numerous lectures and extensive writings, Dr. Montessori disseminated her ideas, and educators from throughout the world came to Italy to observe her program and be trained in her approach. By 1915, almost 100 Montessori schools were in operation in the United States. In 1929 the International Montessori Association was formed. Montessori fled fascist Italy for Spain in 1934 and worked in several places in Europe and Asia before her death in 1952. Although the Montessori Method has been considered controversial by some educators, today thousands of Montessori schools operate in virtually every country in the world.

# From *Sputnik* to the New Federalism

Few times in history has a single event had such an impact on education as the launching of *Sputnik* in October 1957. The event seemed to confirm the growing fear that the United States was losing the Cold War technological and military races with the Soviet Union because of a shortage of trained teachers, engineers, and students.

## *Curriculum Reforms*

Reacting to public pressure, in 1958 the federal government passed the National Defense Education Act (NDEA). By directing significant federal funding to specific curricular areas, particularly mathematics, science, and modern foreign languages, the federal government for the first time attempted to influence the curriculum in general elementary and secondary education. The NDEA sponsored the efforts of academic specialists to revise the curriculum according to the latest theories and methods. Soon the "new math," "new chemistry," "new grammar," and other "new" revisions were being developed and introduced in the schools. Summer institutes were held to train teachers in the use of the new materials and methods. The NDEA also provided funding for science, mathematics, and foreign language laboratories; media and other instructional material; and improvement of guidance, counseling, and testing programs, especially those efforts directed at identification and encouragement of more capable students. Student loans and graduate fellowships were also funded under the NDEA.

The curriculum reforms initiated by the NDEA of 1958 and an expanded version of that act in 1964 were further stimulated by James Conant's widely publicized study of secondary education, *The American High School Today* (1959), which recommended increased rigor and an academic core of English, mathematics, science, and the social sciences. Underlying these curricular reforms was the learning theory of Jerome Bruner, which stressed the teaching of the structure of the disciplines (i.e., the major concepts and methods of inquiry of the discipline) and the stage concept of child development formulated by Jean Piaget (1970). According to Bruner (1966), some form of the structure of a discipline could be taught to students at each stage of their cognitive development. These theories provided the rationale for the **spiral curriculum** sequencing pattern, whereby subject matter

Presidents Kennedy and Johnson declared a war on poverty, using education as a major weapon in the fight.

**Reflect on Diversity**
What are the weaknesses of the cultural deprivation theory as an explanation for the underachievement of minority students?

is presented over a number of grades with increasing complexity and abstraction. His theories of the way children construct knowledge provided the theoretical framework for the constructivist theory discussed in Chapter 4.

The NDEA set the stage for the federal government's increased involvement in education. In the decade that followed, the federal government waged another war in which it became, for perhaps the first time in our nation's history, a major force in the educational arena. This war was the War on Poverty.

## Education and the War on Poverty

In the early 1960s, large numbers of Americans became aware that at least one-quarter of the population had been bypassed by the postwar prosperity and lived in dire poverty. The results were rising crime rates, a decline in qualified manpower for military service, and a number of other social and economic problems. Books, reports, and high-impact media coverage such as Edward R. Murrow's documentary on migrant farm workers, "Harvest of Shame," brought a flood of interest in the elimination of poverty. As a result, the Democratic administrations of John F. Kennedy in 1963 and Lyndon B. Johnson in 1964 declared a War on Poverty. In an effort to win this "war," federal legislation was passed to subsidize low-income housing, improve health care, expand welfare services, provide job retraining, undertake regional planning in depressed areas such as Appalachia, and improve inner-city schools.

Education was viewed as a major factor in the elimination of poverty. Poor children as well as those of certain minority groups, it was noted, consistently failed to achieve. In the optimistic view of many politicians, social scientists, and educators, the "cultural deprivation" (i.e., lack of middle-class attitudes and incomes) of the poor was attributable to a lack of education, and if the poor were provided the skills and education for employment, they could achieve middle-class economic and social status and break the "cycle of poverty."

### Federal Education Legislation

On the education front, the War on Poverty was waged by a number of initiatives. The Vocational Education Act of 1963 more than quadrupled federal funds for vocational education. The purpose of the act was to enhance occupational training opportunities for persons of all ages by providing financial assistance to vocational and technical programs in high schools and nonbaccalaureate postsecondary institutions. The Manpower Development and Training Act, enacted the same year, was directed at providing retraining for unemployed adults.

The Economic Opportunity Act (EOA) of 1964 established the Job Corps to train youth between 16 and 21 years of age in basic literacy skills and for employment, and it also established a type of domestic Peace Corps, Volunteers in Service to America (VISTA). Perhaps the most popular and controversial component of the EOA was Project Head Start, a program aimed at disadvantaged children 3 to 5 years of age who would not normally attend preschool or kindergarten. President Johnson predicted that Head Start would "strike at the basic cause of poverty" by addressing it at its beginning—the disadvantaged preschool child. As the name suggests, the intent of the program was to give disadvantaged children a head start in the educational race so that once in school they might be on equal terms with children from nondisadvantaged homes. Although the Head Start Program has perhaps not lived up to all of President Johnson's expectations, it has proved to be the most successful of the compensatory education programs.

The centerpiece of the education legislation enacted as part of the War on Poverty was the Elementary and Secondary Education Act of 1965 (ESEA). The most far-reaching piece of federal education legislation to date, the ESEA provided more than

$1 billion in federal funds to education. The ESEA included five major sections or titles. The largest, receiving about 80% of the funds, was Title I, which provided assistance to local school districts for the education of children from low-income families. The compensatory education programs funded through Title I were intended to maintain the educational progress begun in Head Start. Other sections of the ESEA provided funds for library resources, textbooks, and instructional materials; supplemental education centers; educational research and training; and strengthening state departments of education. The act was expanded in 1966 and 1967 to include programs for Native American children, children of migrant workers, students with disabilities (Title VI), and children with limited English-speaking ability (Title VII).

In the same year that the ESEA was enacted, Congress passed the Higher Education Act, which provided direct assistance to institutes of higher education for facility construction and library and instructional improvement, as well as loans and scholarships to students. The year 1965 also saw the establishment of the National Foundation of the Arts and the Humanities to promote and encourage production, dissemination, and scholarship in the arts and humanities.

Between 1963 and 1969, Congress passed more than two dozen major pieces of legislation affecting education. These laws dramatically increased federal involvement in education and provided vast sums of money for elementary and secondary schools, vocational schools, colleges, and universities. In 1963–64, federal funds for elementary and secondary schools totaled almost $900 million. By 1968–69 this amount had skyrocketed to $3 billion, and the federal government's share of the financing of education had risen from 4.4% to 8.8%. Perhaps equally as important as the increased funding was the shift in emphasis from identification of gifted students, which had marked the 1950s, to a concern for disadvantaged students.

## The Civil Rights Movement

### The Brown Decision

Not only were the schools given a major role in the War on Poverty but they also became a stage for much of the drama of the civil rights movement. In the landmark *Brown v. Board of Education of Topeka* (1954) decision, the U.S. Supreme Court ruled that segregated educational facilities have no place in public education and generate a feeling of inferiority that affects the child's motivation to learn. However, instead of being the climax of the struggle for racial equality in education, *Brown* marked the beginning of the Civil Rights revolution. Although the Civil Rights movement began with Blacks, perhaps because the basic vision of what was wrong was most visible in the history of Blacks in America, the general principles of the movement were later applied to advancing the rights of women, racial and ethnic groups, the aged, and the disabled (Sowell, 1984).

The *Brown* decision met with massive nationwide resistance in the form of legal maneuvers and violence, resulting in countless confrontations between federal authorities who sought to enforce the law and local police or citizens who sought to obstruct it. The most dramatic physical confrontation in the struggle to

One of the most dramatic moments in school desegregation was the integration of Little Rock Central High School.

integrate the public schools took place in Little Rock, Arkansas, when President Eisenhower sent federal troops to ensure that, over the objections of the governor, Orval Faubus, nine Black students were safely enrolled in Central High School. A more violent confrontation involving the integration of higher education resulted in the loss of two lives when federal marshals were required to enroll James Meredith at the University of Mississippi, again over the objections of the state's governor, Ross Barnett.

In the early years of school desegregation, attention was focused on the *de jure* segregated districts in the southern states. Initially, districts attempted to accomplish desegregation by adopting freedom of choice plans. In most instances, these plans had little impact on the level of segregation, and a decade after *Brown,* little progress toward integration had been made.

At the same time that school desegregation was making limited progress, the civil rights movement was gaining momentum on other fronts. Freedom rides, sit-ins, boycotts, and other forms of nonviolent protest appealed to the national conscience and focused national attention on a movement that would not be denied. President John F. Kennedy pressed for the passage of a federal civil rights statute that would end segregation in public facilities, attack discrimination in employment, and require nondiscriminatory practices in programs and institutions receiving federal funds. Five days after President Kennedy was assassinated, his successor, Lyndon B. Johnson, appeared before Congress and sought its passage, declaring it the most fitting honor of his memory. The Civil Rights Act of 1964, when passed, became one of the most significant pieces of social legislation in the United States in the 20th century.

## The Civil Rights Act and Desegregation

The Civil Rights Act of 1964 further involved the federal government in the activities of the schools. Title VI of the act prohibits discrimination against students on the basis of race, color, or national origin in all institutions receiving federal funds. Title VII forbids discrimination in employment based on race, religion, national origin, or sex. The act authorized the withholding of federal funds from any institution or agency violating the law. It also authorized the U.S. attorney general to take legal action to achieve school desegregation and provided federal financial assistance to school districts attempting to desegregate.

The passage of the Civil Rights Act of 1964 and the education acts of 1965 combined with the growing intolerance of the Supreme Court to the resistance to the *Brown* decision led to the creation of a "carrot-and-stick" mechanism that dramatically increased the pace of school desegregation. The carrot was the increased federal expenditures for education, which increased from $2.0 billion in 1965–66, to $3.2 billion in 1970, to $4.9 billion in 1974. The Civil Rights Act of 1964 and a series of Supreme Court decisions between 1968 and 1972 that favored more aggressive measures to integrate in the South (e.g., *Swann v. Charlotte-Mecklenburg Board of Education* [1971], which allowed forced busing) and attacked **de facto segregation** in the North were the stick. The Supreme Court ruled that *de facto* segregation created by local zoning ordinances, housing restrictions, attendance zones, *gerrymandering,* or other deliberate official actions designed to segregate African Americans were just as illegal as *de jure* segregation (*Keyes v. School District No. 1 of Denver, Colorado,* 1973).

## Further Advances in Civil Rights in Education

The civil rights movement in education also made advances in several other areas. Previously, instruction in most schools was given only in English. In the 1960s, however, attention was turned to the growing Hispanic population of the large cities and in the Southwest. In 1968 the Bilingual Education Act was passed, giving federal funds to school districts to provide bilingual education to low-income students with limited English proficiency. Additional support for bilingual education was provided by the U.S. Supreme Court ruling in *Lau v. Nichols* (1974), which said that schools must provide special language programs for non-English-speaking children. In response, Congress passed the Bilingual Education Act of 1974, which provided for bilingual education for all children with limited English ability, as a means of promoting their participation in the regular classroom as soon as possible.

While litigation and legislation were expanding the educational opportunities afforded Black and language-minority students, Native Americans were attempting to gain greater control and assume greater responsibility for the education of their youth as well as to restore native language and culture to the curriculum. Self-determination came closer to reality with the passage of the Indian Education Act of 1972, which established the Office of Indian Education, and the Indian Self-Determination and Educational Assistance Act of 1975, which expanded the rights of Native Americans with regard to the education of their youth and sought to ensure increased educational opportunity for those youth.

On other fronts, Title IX of the 1972 Education Amendments, which prohibited sexual discrimination against employees and students in educational programs receiving federal funds, was a major victory in the extension of the civil rights movement to women. Another victory in the movement to extend civil rights to women came in the same session of Congress when Title VII of the Civil Rights Act of 1964, which prohibited discrimination in employment, was extended to cover academic institutions. With the legal support of Title IX and Title VII, women brought political pressure on local school districts and colleges and universities in an attempt to end sex discrimination in admissions, access to courses, extracurricular activities, instructional materials, counseling and counseling materials, employment, and policies and regulations governing the treatment of students and employees.

> ### For Your Reflection and Analysis
>
> In what ways have males benefited from the extension of civil rights to females?

In 1975, the landmark Education for All Handicapped Children Act (EHA) established the right of all children with disabilities to a free and appropriate education. The EHA, often referred to as the Bill of Rights for Handicapped Children, not only guaranteed the educational rights of children with disabilities, but it also defined and expanded the rights of all children. Each of these topics is covered in greater detail in later chapters.

## Social Unrest

The late 1960s and early 1970s also saw a series of urban riots and the sometimes passive, sometimes violent student rights and anti–Vietnam War movements. College campuses were the scenes of sit-ins, marches, and even the bombing and burning of campus buildings. Both the student rights and antiwar movements tended to have a negative impact on the civil rights movement through a subliminal process of guilt by association. Many members of academia as well as the larger society became disenchanted with the civil rights movement, "not because they disagreed with or were unsympathetic to its legitimate claim, but because the Student Rights movement, which they strongly opposed, got its impetus, simulation, and example from the Civil Rights Movement" (Tollett, 1983, p. 57). A campaign against demonstrations and riots and for the restoration of law and order helped put Richard Nixon in the White House in 1969 and re-elect him in 1972.

During the 1980s the civil rights movement was slowed considerably by the actions of both the courts and the Reagan administration. The budget of the Office of Civil Rights was cut, investigations were "cursory," and enforcement and compliance were loosened. The Department of Justice not only seemed uninterested in enforcing civil rights plans, it attempted to block efforts to broaden the scope of civil rights and to strengthen affirmative action and opposed even the continuation of existing desegregation plans. Magnet schools, which attempted to attract White students to predominantly minority schools, were one of the favored strategies of the Reagan administration in out-of-court settlements of desegregation cases.

## The 1970s: Retreat and Retrenchment

During the Nixon administration (1969–1974), support for many of the initiatives begun during the Kennedy and Johnson administrations was reduced. The Nixon administration represented a conservative reaction to student demonstrations and the demands of the civil rights movement. The conservative reaction included a retreat from the programs of the War on Poverty, a demand for an end of bilingual and multicultural education and involuntary bussing, a push for greater accountability, and increased emphasis on testing. On the other hand, the 1970s witnessed increased attention to the needs of people with disabilities. The Vocational Rehabilitation Act of 1973 sought to increase the physical access of persons with disabilities to educational institutions, vocational training, and employment. During the Ford administration (1974–1977), the Education for All Handicapped Children Act of 1975 (now the Individuals with Disabilities Education Act), which is discussed in Chapter 9, was enacted.

The Carter administration (1977–1981) was unable to secure the passage of any major education legislation, but it was able to oversee an increase in the federal education budget, from 8.8% of the total elementary and secondary revenues in 1977 to 9.8% in 1980 (see Table 7.3). And, under Carter's administration the Department of Education was established. Carter kept his campaign promise to the NEA and overcame congressional opposition, and in 1979 the Office of Education was elevated to department status, making its secretary a member of the president's cabinet. Carter appointed Shirley Hufstadler, a federal appeals court judge, as the first secretary of education.

The decade of the 1970s was a time of financial uncertainty for the schools. Not only were schools faced with spiraling operating costs but teachers hurt by inflation also were becoming more strident in their salary demands. At the same time, revenues for the schools were actually declining. The decline in revenues was a result of two forces: (1) the "revolt" of taxpayers against rising taxes, especially property taxes, which are the major source of tax revenues for the schools; and (2) a decline in enrollments, which brought with it a reduction in state revenues, because most states, to a large extent, base their aid to local school districts on enrollment. In 1971, for the first time since World War II, the total number of elementary and secondary students enrolled in the public schools declined.

Revenues and enrollments were not the only things in education declining during the 1970s; test scores and public confidence in the schools were also declining. The decline in Scholastic Aptitude Test (SAT) scores witnessed in the 1960s continued into the 1970s: SAT scores fell almost 60 points from 1970 to 1980. Concern about the lower academic achievement of students led many parents and politicians to call for a "back-to-basics" curriculum and to seek greater accountability from the schools. Parents in poor schools began to look to the courts to remedy the inequalities that were reflected in inferior schools and reduced educational opportunity. In 1973 the California Supreme Court handed down a decision in *Serrano v. Priest* that has since been followed by the courts in almost two dozen states. In *Serrano*, the court held that the quality of a child's education could not depend on the wealth of the district (See Chapter 13 Historical Note on page 361). The concern for student achievement, the push for a back-to-basics curriculum, and the demand for greater accountability that began in the 1970s have continued unabated to the present.

## The 1980s: Renewed Conservatism and Reform

The election of Ronald Reagan to the presidency in 1980 brought a resurgence of conservatism in both politics and education. Reagan's New Federalism called for reduced taxes and reduced federal spending for social programs, including education, and encouraged a greater role for state and local governments, as well as a greater involvement of the business community in supporting schools and setting goals and standards. The National Education Consolidation and Improvement Act of 1981 sought to consolidate the massive array of federal aid programs into several large block programs. However, Reagan's proposal for the entire block was less

**Table 7.3 — Public Elementary and Secondary School Revenues, by Source, 1940–2008 (in thousands of dollars)**

| School Year Ending | Federal | | State | | Local | | Total |
|---|---|---|---|---|---|---|---|
| | Amount | Percent of Total | Amount | Percent of Total | Amount | Percent of Total | |
| 1940 | 39,810 | 1.8 | 684,354 | 30.3 | 1,536,363 | 68.0 | 2,260,527 |
| 1950 | 155,848 | 2.9 | 2,165,689 | 39.8 | 3,115,507 | 57.3 | 5,437,044 |
| 1960 | 651,639 | 4.4 | 5,768,047 | 39.1 | 8,326,932 | 56.5 | 14,746,618 |
| 1964 | 896,956 | 4.4 | 8,078,014 | 39.3 | 11,569,213 | 56.3 | 20,544,182 |
| 1968 | 2,806,469 | 8.8 | 12,275,536 | 38.5 | 16,821,063 | 52.7 | 31,903,064 |
| 1972 | 4,467,969 | 8.9 | 19,133,256 | 38.3 | 26,402,420 | 52.8 | 50,003,645 |
| 1976 | 6,318,345 | 8.9 | 31,776,101 | 44.6 | 33,111,627 | 48.5 | 71,206,073 |
| 1980 | 9,503,537 | 9.8 | 45,348,814 | 46.8 | 42,028,813 | 43.4 | 96,881,165 |
| 1982 | 8,186,466 | 7.4 | 52,436,435 | 49.7 | 49,568,346 | 45.0 | 110,191,257 |
| 1984 | 8,567,547 | 6.8 | 60,232,981 | 47.8 | 57,245,892 | 45.4 | 126,055,419 |
| 1986 | 9,975,622 | 6.7 | 73,619,575 | 49.4 | 65,532,582 | 43.9 | 149,127,779 |
| 1988 | 10,716,687 | 6.3 | 84,004,415 | 49.5 | 74,840,873 | 44.1 | 169,561,974 |
| 1990 | 12,700,784 | 6.1 | 98,238,633 | 47.1 | 97,608,157 | 46.8 | 208,547,573 |
| 1992 | 15,493,330 | 6.6 | 108,783,449 | 46.4 | 110,304,605 | 47.0 | 234,581,384 |
| 1994 | 18,341,483 | 7.1 | 117,474,209 | 45.2 | 124,343,776 | 47.8 | 260,159,468 |
| 1996 | 19,104,019 | 6.6 | 136,670,754 | 47.5 | 131,928,071 | 45.9 | 287,702,844 |
| 1998 | 22,201,965 | 6.8 | 157,645,372 | 48.4 | 146,128,674 | 44.8 | 325,976,011 |
| 2000 | 27,097,866 | 7.3 | 184,613,352 | 49.5 | 161,232,584 | 43.2 | 372,943,802 |
| 2002 | 33,144,633 | 7.9 | 206,541,793 | 49.2 | 179,815,551 | 42.9 | 419,501,976 |
| 2004 | 41,923,435 | 9.1 | 217,384,191 | 47.1 | 202,718,474 | 43.9 | 462,026,099 |
| 2006 | 47,553,778 | 9.1 | 242,151,076 | 46.5 | 230,916,934 | 44.4 | 520,621,788 |
| 2008 | 47,707,260 | 8.2 | 282,662,805 | 48.3 | 254,358,830 | 43.5 | 584,728,896 |

Source: Snyder, T. D. & Dillow, S. A. (2011). *Digest of Education Statistics 2010* (NCES 2011–015). National Center for Education Statistics, Institute of Education Sciences, U.S. Department of Education. Washington, DC.

than what formerly had been spent for the ESEA alone. In fact, in every budget request made while he was in office, President Reagan proposed reductions in federal spending for education, and from fiscal years 1980 to 1989, federal funds for elementary and secondary education declined by 17%, and for higher education by 27% (Snyder & Dillow, 2011). Reagan's conservative education agenda included not only a reduced federal role but also the elimination of the Department of Education, high standards, greater accountability, increased parental support, a return to the basics, and a return of prayer to the classroom.

Much of the conservative agenda regarding federal aid to education stemmed from the fact that many conservatives blamed the schools for the social unrest of the 1960s and early 1970s and for many of the social problems that were seen as undermining the very moral fabric of the country. The conservative response to the presumed educational excesses of the 1960s and 1970s led to a continuation of the public debate about the condition of education. Whereas *Sputnik* and technological competition with the Russians had focused attention on the educational system in the 1950s, it was the declining ability of the United States to compete in world markets that brought the educational system into the forefront of public debate in the 1980s. In response to the growing belief that the decline in the quality of the educational system, as measured in part by student achievement test scores and comparisons with students from other industrialized nations, was a major factor in the nation's declining economic and intellectual competitiveness, President Reagan appointed the National Commission on Excellence in Education. Its report, *A Nation at Risk: The Imperative for Educational Reform* (1983), in strong and stirring language described a "rising tide of mediocrity" that was eroding the educational foundations of society and declared that it would have been seen as "an act of war" if any unfriendly power had imposed our educational system on us.

*A Nation at Risk* has been described by some as a "bombshell" on the American educational scene, by others a "call to action," and by still others as a "conservative call to arms" (Horń, 2002). However it is described, there is no question that *A Nation at Risk* was a landmark report in the history of educational reform in the United States. *A Nation at Risk* and the series of reports that followed collectively are responsible for what has been referred to as the "Educational Reform Movement of the 1980s." This reform movement has been characterized as having two waves. The first wave responded to the recommendations of *A Nation at Risk* and similar reports and acted on the assumption that what was wrong with schools could be fixed by top-down state actions directed at improving achievement and accountability. States enacted higher graduation requirements, standardized curriculum mandates, increased the testing of both teachers and students, and raised certification requirements for teachers. School districts throughout the nation increased their emphasis on computer literacy, homework, and basic skills; established minimum standards for participation in athletics; and lengthened the school day and the school year.

**For Your Reflection and Analysis**

Which of the initiatives from the first wave of reform are still emphasized today?

The second wave of reform, beginning in 1986, focused not on the state level, on state mandates and centralization of authority, but on the local level and on the structure and processes of the schools themselves. A major theme of the second wave was the redistribution of power among the critical stakeholders of the schools. The belief was that the most effective reforms were those that emanated from those closest to the students, namely, educators and parents. The recommendations from the second wave of reform, coming from such noted educators as John Goodlad, Theodore Sizer, and Ernest Boyer, called for change from the bottom up, not from the top down, and dealt with such issues as decentralization, site-based management, teacher empowerment, parental involvement, and school choice. The second wave of reform was associated with a number of prescriptions: year-round schools, longer school days and school years, recast modes of governance, alternative funding patterns, all-out commitments to technology, and various combinations of these and other proposals (Kaplan, 1990). This wave of reform also sought to balance the concern over the impact of education on the economy and the push for excellence of the first wave with a concern for equity and the disadvantaged students who might become further disadvantaged by the "new standards of excellence." Other state and local responses to the second wave of reform continued into the 1990s and are discussed in the chapters that follow.

## The 1990s: National Goals, National Standards, and Choice

By the end of the 1980s the adoption of myriad reform initiatives had not produced any significant change in educational outputs. As a result, the quality of education and the perceived need to "fix it" remained major topics of public debate. Responding to the ongoing criticism of both education and his administration's failure to offer any remedies, in the fall of 1989 President George H. W. Bush co-convened, with the National Governors Association, an "education summit" at Charlottesville, Virginia, chaired by Arkansas Governor Bill Clinton. As an outcome of the meeting, in early 1990 the National Governors Association and the Bush administration approved six national education goals to be accomplished by 2000. However, President Bush was unable to gain congressional support for his plan for implementing the goals, largely because of the controversy surrounding a key feature of the plan: **vouchers** to promote school choice.

The 1992 election saw education assume a place of prominence on the political agenda not previously held. A major factor in the victory of Bill Clinton was his promise to be a more effective "Education President." The Clinton administration's plan to implement the national goals was called Goals 2000: Educate America Act. Goals 2000 adopted the six goals articulated by the National Governors Association and added two goals related to parent participation and teacher education and professional development (see Figure 7.2). The act not only formalized the national education goals but also formalized the development of national standards and new assessment systems and established a "new federal partnership to reform the nation's educational system" (U.S. Department of Education, 1994).

The adoption of Goals 2000 also marked a turning point in the aim of state and federal education policy: "Emphasis shifted from educational inputs to educational outcomes and from procedural accountability to educational accountability. Equity was reconceptualized as ensuring all students access to high-quality educational programs rather than providing supplemental and often compensatory services" (Goertz, 2001, p. 62). The reauthorization of the ESEA, included under the Goals 2000 umbrella as the Improving America's Schools Act, encouraged comprehensive reform at the state and local levels to meet the national goals. A major provision of the act required states (with the input of local school districts) to develop school

## Figure 7.2 — The National Education Goals

1. *School Readiness.* By the year 2000, all children in America will start school ready to learn.

2. *High School Completion.* By the year 2000, the high school graduation rate will increase to at least 90 percent.

3. *Student Achievement and Citizenship.* By the year 2000, all students will leave grades 4, 8, and 12 having demonstrated competency over challenging subject matter including English, mathematics, science, foreign languages, civics and government, economics, arts, history, and geography, and every school in the United States will ensure that all students learn to use their minds well, so they may be prepared for responsible citizenship, future learning, and productive employment in our Nation's modern economy.

4. *Teacher Education and Professional Development.* By the year 2000, the Nation's teaching force will have access to programs for the continued improvement of their professional skills and the opportunity to acquire the knowledge and skills needed to instruct and prepare all American students for the next century.

5. *Mathematics and Science.* By the year 2000, United States students will be first in the world in mathematics and science achievement.

6. *Adult Literacy and Lifelong Learning.* By the year 2000, every adult American will be literate and will possess the knowledge and skills necessary to compete in a global economy and exercise the rights and responsibilities of citizenship.

7. *Safe, Disciplined, and Alcohol- and Drug-Free Schools.* By the year 2000, every school in the United States will be free of drugs, violence, and the unauthorized presence of firearms and alcohol, and will offer a disciplined environment conducive to learning.

8. *Parental Participation.* By the year 2000, every school will promote partnerships that will increase parental involvement and participation in promoting the social, emotional, and academic growth in children.

*Source:* H. R. 1804 Goals 2000 Educate America Act, Sec. 101. (1994).

improvement plans that establish challenging content and performance standards, implement assessments to measure student progress in meeting these standards, and adopt measures to hold schools accountable for the achievement of the standards. Unlike previous federal programs that bypassed state education policies, these initiatives were designed to be integrated with state and local reform initiatives (Goertz, 2001).

Throughout the remainder of the 1990s, the calls for school reform continued and standards and accountability became the key words in promoting school reform. However, states and local school districts faced a number of challenges in their efforts to establish challenging academic standards and accompanying assessment systems. In state after state, standards became the battleground for ongoing "curriculum wars" as educators and policy makers faced off over such issues as whole language versus phonics or whose history to teach (Campbell, 2010). However, despite the challenges, and in no small part due to the work of the various national subject-matter teachers organizations in establishing content standards in each of the major academic disciplines (see Chapter 14), by 2000 academic standards were in place in 48 states and schools were expected to align their curriculum with these standards.

The push for standards was accompanied by the enactment in almost every state of so-called **high-stakes testing** that would determine who would be promoted and who would graduate from high school. However, as the testing was initiated, several states experienced serious problems associated with test construction and, more important, with the high numbers of students who were being failed by the tests. In most states the students who performed the poorest on the exams were low-income and minority students, especially those with limited English speaking ability and children from low-income, mostly urban districts—the victims described in Kozol's *Savage Inequalities* (1991). Lost in the focus on standards and improving performance was the question of whether the standards movement would lead to school improvement for many marginalized students (Campbell, 2010).

The fall of 1996 saw not only the re-election of President Bill Clinton but also record enrollments in the public schools. The impact of the "baby boom echo"—the children of the 76 million baby boomers born between the end of World War II and 1964—was strengthened by continued immigration, pushing public and private school enrollments beyond the record 1971 baby boom enrollments of 51.3 million. Enrollments in the fall of 1996 reached 51.5 million, grew to 53.4 million by the turn of the century, and were projected to increase to 58.5 million by 2019 (see Figure 7.3), with the greatest increases occurring in the South and West. The growing enrollments combined with growing teacher retirements to worsen the teacher shortages already impacting many districts.

## School Choice

The Republican takeover of Congress and many state legislatures in the 1994 elections put Goals 2000 in conflict with a renewed conservative agenda, "Contract with America," which had as a key feature support for choice and privatization in education. And, although some indicators, such as SAT scores, improved throughout the 1980s and 1990s in the wake of the reform movements, large numbers of parents continued to be dissatisfied with school systems that valued diversity over diction and affirmative action over arithmetic and were demanding the right to send their children to the school of their choice funded at public expense. Support for school choice came from parents across the socioeconomic and ideological spectrum. Low-income and minority parents saw choice as a way to extend educational opportunities to students who historically had not had the resources to choose between public and private schools, or even among public schools. Other parents saw choice as providing the opportunity to protect their children from the violence in the schools or to provide them with a more academically challenging or enriched experience. Religious conservatives saw choice as a way to support schools that

**Figure 7.3 — Actual and Projected Numbers for Enrollment in Elementary and Secondary Schools, by Grade Level: Fall 1994 Through Fall 2019**

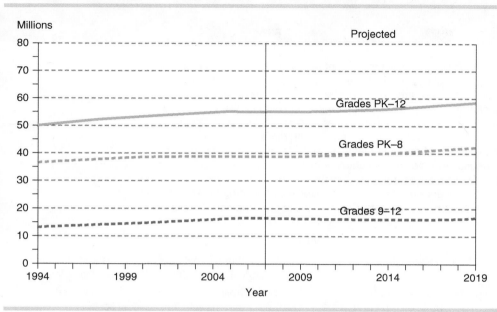

*Source:* Hussar, W. U., & Bailey, T. M. (2011). *Projections of Education Statistics to 2019.* National Center for Education Statistics, Institute of Education Sciences, U.S. Department of Education, Washington, DC.

promoted a particular religious ideology. However, while almost all parents and politicians supported the concept that parents should be given greater choice in the school their child attended, how this was to be achieved was very much in debate. The most often seriously considered approaches were school vouchers, charter schools and privatization.

The use of vouchers, including their use at private schools, was upheld by the U.S. Supreme Court in 2002 (*Zelman v. Simmons-Harris,* 2002). Following the *Zelman* decision, voucher supporters anticipated their widespread adoption elsewhere. However, this has not occurred. A major reason seems to be that the growing array of alternative school choice options (see Figure 7.4), in particular charter schools, contributed to a decreased interest in pursuing the contentious voucher alternative (Metcalf & Legan, 2002).

**Figure 7.4 — The Choice Continuum**

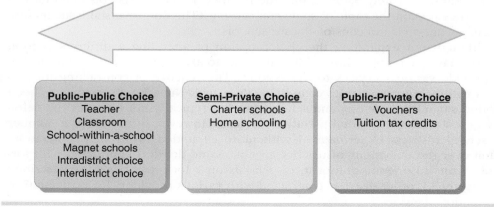

# CONTROVERSIAL ISSUE

## *Charter Schools*

One of the most obvious outcomes of the school reform movement has been the emergence of charter schools. These schools are public schools in which state and school district controls typically have been relaxed. Parents and teachers have a greater voice in school decisions. After a somewhat modest beginning, the number of charter schools is increasing rapidly. Impetus for the state legislation authorizing charter schools has come from a variety of sources: parents seeking a particular curricular emphasis in the schools, teachers wanting relief from state and district requirements so that they can address the educational needs of at-risk students, parents desiring a specific type of school environment, and entrepreneurial firms seeking an entrée into the education market.

Opinions about charter schools are divided; some people view these schools as the panacea for all of the wrongs in education, whereas others view them as being divisive and leading to separatism based on personal values and philosophies of parents. Consider these pros and cons for the charter school option:

**For**

1. Provides parents and students with a choice in the public school system.
2. Permits each school to determine its philosophy and curricular emphasis, with a coherent academic mission and high standards.
3. Increases the heterogeneity of students in schools by attracting private school students into the charter schools.
4. Have an image of being smaller and safer than the typical public school.
5. Gives teachers greater freedom and the challenge of starting and designing a program for a new school.
6. Have been given operational and programmatic freedom in return for results-based accountability.

**Against**

1. Can ignore the national education goals and state goals and content standards in developing their programs.
2. May be controlled by for-profit firms that impose standardized programs with limited local school choice.
3. Fail to provide teachers with the same salaries and fringe benefits they would receive in the public schools.
4. Have encountered fiscal accountability and management problems in the use of public funds.
5. Do not have the perceived independence because they are still a part of the public education system and thus are subject to changes in local and state requirements.

To what extent have charter schools been effective or not effective in your state? Give reasons why or why not. Would you consider teaching in a charter school? Give reasons why or why not.

---

**For Your Reflection and Analysis**

What would influence your decision to work in a charter school if you were asked to do so?

Another proposal for increasing parental choice, one that gained increased favor in the 1990s, was **charter schools**. As discussed in Chapter 13, charter schools are publicly supported schools established upon the issuance of a charter from the state, local school board, or other designated entity. In 1997 President Clinton lent support to the movement by pledging $100 million to help create 3,000 more charter schools by 2000. In fact, by 2003 approximately 2,500 charter schools were in operation in 37 states and the District of Columbia, and by 2011 the number had risen to approximately 5,400. While the number of charter schools continues to grow, they remain the topic of some controversy. (The Controversial Issue feature discusses the pros and cons of charter schools.)

Although not expanding the choice option of attending a different school, another favorite among choice advocates was to allow private contractors to bid to provide various services to the schools. The practice of contracting for services with private companies or individuals outside the school systems has been around since the New England schools but has typically not been for the delivery of instructional or administrative services. However, in the 1990s a number of school districts experimented with more expanded forms of privatization, often over the objections of teacher groups. Some districts contracted with for-profit firms to operate one or more schools on a for-profit basis. As described in Chapter 13, other districts contracted with various providers for leadership or instructional services.

## The End of a Presidency, the End of a Century

During President Clinton's second term, debate at the federal level continued over whether there should be a federal Department of Education, voluntary national testing, and private school choice. Faced with a larger Republican majority in Congress and weakened by personal scandals and threats of impeachment, Clinton held off significant reductions in federal spending for education, but he was unable to advance any of his major education proposals.

The final year of the 20th century brought a tragedy that captured the nation's attention like no other event on school grounds since the days of forced integration. That event was the massacre at Columbine High School, which resulted in the deaths of 14 students and one teacher. This event came to symbolize what was increasingly being acknowledged as a crisis in education: violence in the schools (see Chapter 10). Fighting in the schools was matched by fighting in the courts, in legislatures, and in school board meetings as the battles over the curriculum, the role of religion in the schools, standards and testing, and the provision of choice continued into the new century.

# A New Century Begins

The new century began where the last one left off—with the public as well as the educational establishment divided over the issues of state and national standards, accountability, school choice, and the place of religion in the schools. Despite the fact that the 1990s had witnessed rising test scores and an unparalleled economic prosperity that had been said to be at risk as a result of the quality of the schools, the cries for educational reform continued.

## No Child Left Behind

The reform offered by the first president of the new century, George W. Bush, was embodied in his education plan, the No Child Left Behind (NCLB) Act of 2001. No Child Left Behind has been said to be the most sweeping education reform legislation since the ESEA of 1965. No Child Left Behind required that by the 2005–06 school year all states must have developed standards for what every child should know and learn in math and reading and that 95% of all students in grades 3–8 be tested annually, and at least once in grades 10 to 12, to determine their progress in meeting the standards. NCLB set a target of 100% of tested children meeting a state-established "proficient" level on state standards by 2014. Schools, school districts, and the states are required to document the progress of the school population as a whole as well as its subgroups (racial, ethnic, gender, and non-English proficient) in making **adequate yearly progress (AYP)** toward meeting the established proficiency standards and at least one other non-test criterion (e.g., graduation rate). If even one of the subgroups fails to make AYP, the entire school is considered to be underperforming and subject to sanctions. Accountability is required of schools in the form of annual report cards to let parents know if the school is making AYP.

If any subgroup does not make AYP on the same indicator for two consecutive years, the school is placed on a list of schools in "need of improvement," is required to file a plan for improvement, and is provided technical assistance by the school district to help it improve. At the same time, parents must be notified that the school had failed to make AYP and offered the option of transferring their children to another school that is making AYP. If the school does not make AYP the next year, parents may request and the school must provide approved supplemental services, such as after-school tutoring or summer school. If a school in need of improvement fails in the fourth year it enters "corrective action status" and is subject to various actions including the replacement of staff, implementation of new curriculum, or restructuring. If the school does not make AYP after five years, it enters restructuring status and subject to closure, conversion to a charter school,

**Reflect on Diversity**
Only 15% of eligible students, most of whom come from low-income and minority families, participate in the tutoring available under NCLB. Speculate on why so few students take advantage of this support?

The No Child Left Behind Act of 2001 has driven the direction of education in the first decade of the 21st century.

or takeover by the state. The apparent theory behind NCLB was that teachers and schools would try harder and test scores would go up if scores were made public (Ravitch, 2011) and sanctions were threatened or imposed.

States have faced many challenges in meeting the mandates of NCLB. Some of these are described in the video, "No Child Left Behind," which is featured in the Video Insight box. One of the major challenges has been generating the increased revenue necessary to develop and administer tests and maintain data management and reporting systems necessary to meet the testing requirements of NCLB. Federal funding has provided less than half of the costs required to meet the NCLB mandates. In state departments of education and local school districts that are already facing budget shortfalls, "unfunded mandates" became perhaps the most common objection to NCLB.

Perhaps the most contentious issue in the implementation of NCLB has been the determination of what is to be considered proficient on state assessments. Because of the variation in the rigor of state tests, as well as in the setting of state proficiency levels, states have differed dramatically in the way they viewed school performance and in the percentage of students categorized as proficient. Because of these variations, the number of schools identified as needing improvement varied significantly from state to state. Overall, urban districts serving high proportions of minority and poor students, as well as rural districts, reported the highest percentage of schools in need of improvement.

## ABC NEWS: VIDEO INSIGHT

### No Child Left Behind

As discussed in this chapter, the NCLB Act has been the subject of considerable debate. This ABC News video narrated by journalist Dan Harris discusses some of the major issues raised by a 2005 bipartisan panel representing all 50 state legislatures. The video features a sixth-grader in Texas who stays home on the day of the required state standardized test with the consent of his father, who is concerned that in the era of NCLB children "go to school to prepare for the test, not for life."

As you think about the video and the issues surrounding NCLB raised in this chapter, respond to the following questions:

1. What was meant by the senator from New York when he said NCLB is a one-size-fits-all law?

2. According to the report by the bipartisan panel, NCLB is "flawed in fundamental ways." What are some of the major flaws? What would be required to fix the flaws?

Go to MyEducationLab and select the topic *Standards and Accountability*, then *Activities and Applications* to view the video *No Child Left Behind*.

Student achievement on many state tests has reportedly gone up since the implementation of NCLB. However, this may be a result of the quality of the tests or the fact that many states lowered the standard for what would be considered proficient. Support for this position is provided by studies that have shown that the gap between students' scores on the National Assessment of Educational Progress, the so-called Nation's Report Card, and passing on state tests exceeds 20% in all but five states. In Texas, for example, the state reported in 2007 that 85% of its 4th graders were proficient in reading while the NAEP found that only 29% were. Also of concern to many educators is that numerous studies have shown that in many states higher scores on state assessments have not produced transferrable learning and skills that have been reflected in improvement on other assessments, such as the NAEP or SAT (Darling-Hammond, 2007a) or indicators such as college readiness.

The highly qualified teacher requirement of NCLB has brought another set of implementation issues. NCLB requires that all teachers of core academic subjects be "highly qualified." A highly qualified teacher under NCLB is one who has a minimum of a bachelor's degree, full state certification and licensure, and demonstrated competency as defined by the state in each core academic subject he or she teaches. New teachers can demonstrate competency by passing a "rigorous" state test. Veteran teachers may demonstrate content knowledge by any of these means or by meeting the requirements of a "high, objective, uniform state standard of evaluation" (HOUSSE). However, as with the "proficient" issue, NCLB did not specify what constitutes "rigorous testing" or HOUSSE but left this up to the states. Given this leeway, what has emerged is the perpetuation of a system of widely differing requirements and practices. Some states have said that having a state license is all that is necessary to be considered highly qualified, whereas others have established elaborate evaluation systems. However, while a number of states have lowered standards for entry into teaching and some have even proposed removing certification as a requirement for teaching, most states report that almost all of their teachers are highly qualified and that the number of teachers with emergency or temporary certificates, as well as the number of teachers teaching out of field, has decreased dramatically. The districts that have the greatest difficulty attracting and retaining teachers who meet the highly qualified requirements continue to be rural schools and the high-poverty schools in urban areas.

In many respects the NCLB Act represents a culmination of the reforms of the 1980s and 1990s in its calls for high standards, greater accountability, and increased choice in schooling. However it is more extreme, comprehensive, and some would say radical: "Particularly because there was no reason to believe that annual tests—coupled with fear and humiliation—would produce the miraculous goal of 100 percent proficiency: a goal not achieved by any nation on earth" (Ravitch, 2011, p. 49). And, in fact, by the time George Bush left office it was reported that as many as 75% of schools in some states were failing to make AYP with hundreds subject to the most severe sanctions, including the removal of staff and state takeover. At the same time the severe economic recession that had gripped the nation had also left schools with little prospect of finding the funds to turn these schools around. Schools around the country facing a declining tax base were struggling to even keep schools open and staff paid. Class sizes grew, facilities and equipment upgrades were postponed, programs and services were cut or eliminated, administrative costs reduced, hiring freezes imposed, and staff let go.

## The Obama Administration: Increased Federal Involvement

One of the most significant results of NCLB has been that the federal government came to play a much more active role in education than ever before. The U.S. Department of Education not only must approve state testing programs as well as accountability plans, but also enforces the provisions of NCLB related to supplemental services, choice, and highly qualified teachers. The involvement of the federal and state governments in the educational enterprise was increased further by President Barack Obama's school reform program called Race to the Top. In 2009, the first year of the Obama administration, the continuing economic crisis led Congress to approve an almost $800 billion economic stimulus plan with almost $100 billion earmarked for education. While most of these funds were targeted to help local school districts prevent massive teacher layoffs, $4.35 billion was allocated to the Race to the Top (RTT) program.

The Race to the Top program was the largest competitive grant program ever administered by the U.S. Department of Education. Awards were based on the extent to which states demonstrated a commitment to reform in four areas:

- Adopting standards and assessments that are valid and reliable for all students and that prepare students to succeed in college and the workplace and to compete in the global economy;
- Building data systems that measure student growth and success, and inform teachers and principals about how they can improve instruction;
- Recruiting, developing, rewarding, and retaining effective teachers and principals, especially where they are needed most; and
- Providing the support and interventions necessary to turn around the lowest-achieving schools.

The selection criteria receiving the greatest weight and attention reflected the education priorities of the Obama administration: (1) improving teacher and principal effectiveness by including student test gains in performance evaluations, rewards, and other personnel decisions; (2) adopting common standards, specifically the standards developed by the Common Core Standards Initiative discussed in Chapter 14; and (3) ensuring successful conditions for high-performing charter schools and other innovative schools with a focus on the quality of a state's charter school law. A quality charter school law was defined as one that has no cap on the number of charter schools, that provides equitable funding for charter schools as other public schools, and regulates how charter authorizers approve, monitor, reauthorize, and close charter schools.

To become competitive in the selection process, or perhaps to use RTT as "political cover" to bolster their own arguments for reform, states enacted the policy changes that federal leaders had hoped would occur (Manna, 2010). According to the New Teacher Project (2010) RTT resulted in more education reform than in the previous two decades combined. The state changes included policies:

> to overhaul teacher evaluation, including some that give student achievement data substantial weight in those judgments. Teacher policies governing entry into the profession through traditional or alternative routes also received attention. These changes were intended to create more options for aspiring teachers . . . Policies to facilitate the development of public charter schools . . . In some states, state changes altered the rules governing how charters are opened or can operate while increasing . . . the number of charters that can exist. Other changes created additional options for states wishing to intervene in schools that perform poorly for several consecutive years, including changes that made it easier for states themselves to either take over schools or dictate particular changes in school management. (Manna, 2010, p. 115)

Since their adoption many states have found the continued economic crisis to be an obstacle to implementing the proposed initiatives. In fact, a number of school districts have backed out of RTT saying they would have to spend more money than they would receive. Criticism directed at RTT by politicians, educators, scholars, and policy makers at all levels has also dampened enthusiasm for RTT. The NEA's concern over the use of student achievement gains in teacher evaluations led to a vote of "no confidence" at its 2010 convention. In addition, seven leading civil rights groups, including the NAACP and the National Urban League, issued a public statement disagreeing with the administration that its "emphases on expanding charter schools, closing low-performing schools, and using competitive rather than formula funding are detrimental to low-income and minority children" (McNeill, 2010, p. 1). Other critics express concern that the reforms that are being pushed, many a continuation of NCLB strategies, are not supported by research or results—that an over-reliance on test scores as a measure of quality or effectiveness has only resulted in a narrowing of the curriculum and more teaching to the test, and that charter school students do not outperform their counterparts in the public schools even though charter schools tend to enroll fewer English language learners or students with disabilities (Ravitch, 2010). Still others are concerned with the increased federal involvement and what they perceive as the nationalization of education policy and a move toward a nation curriculum represented by the requirement of adoption of common core standards.

The Obama administration continued the emphasis on teacher quality and standardized testing.

Despite the concerns over RTT, the education priorities of the Obama administration seem to have changed little as it approached the long overdue reauthorization of NCLB (originally scheduled for 2007). Obama's blueprint for reauthorization of NCLB sent to Congress in 2010 continues to stress the importance of highly effective teachers and proposes that states also develop criteria for highly effective principals that would also include student achievement gains. It also continues to emphasize standards and assessments and the collection of data. However it did propose several important changes in NCLB in the way student progress is measured, that the goal that all students be proficient on a state assessment by 2014 be replaced with a new measure of proficiency—whether students are "college and career ready" when they graduate from high school, and that the school improvement process give greater flexibility to states and districts in identifying "persistently lowest-achieving schools" and the types of interventions that are used with these schools.

When Congress had failed to make any significant progress on a comprehensive bill to reauthorize NCLB by the fall of 2011, and with parents, educators, and state policymakers urging that NCLB be overhauled, the Obama administration announced a plan to grant flexibility and waivers to states in meeting NCLB proficiency standards and school labeling if they agree to adopt certain education reform principles. Citing estimates that unless the NCLB standards are changed over 80% of the public schools would be labeled as failing in 2011, the administration offered states the opportunity to apply for flexibility: (1) regarding the NCLB requirement of 100% proficiency by 2014, (2) regarding how schools are identified as failing and in tailoring interventions (rather than the "one-size-fits-all" approach of NCLB), and (3) in the use of federal education funds by allowing districts to transfer funds between funding streams while still protecting funding for the most needy students. In exchange for this flexibility states must agree to develop "rigorous and comprehensive" plans that address the "three critical areas that are designed to improve educational outcomes for all students, close achievement gaps (between racial and ethnic groups), increase equity, and improve the quality of instruction"

(U.S. Department of Education, 2011, p. 1). According to the Department of Education these three critical areas are:

- **Transitioning to College- and Career-Ready Standards and Assessments:** To request ESEA flexibility, a State must have already adopted college- and career-ready standards in reading/language arts and mathematics designed to raise the achievement of all students, including English Learners and students with disabilities. The State will then help its schools and districts transition to implementing those standards and will commit to administering statewide tests aligned with college- and career-readiness.

- **Developing Systems of Differentiated Recognition, Accountability, and Support:** Under ESEA flexibility, a State will establish a differentiated recognition, accountability, and support system that gives credit for progress towards college- and career-readiness. The system each State develops will recognize and reward the highest-achieving schools that serve low-income students and those that show the greatest student progress as Reward Schools.

  For a State's lowest-performing schools — *Priority schools,* generally, those in the bottom 5 percent — a district will implement rigorous interventions to turn the schools around. In an additional 10 percent of the State's schools — *Focus Schools*, identified due to low graduation rates, large achievement gaps, or low student subgroup performance — the district will target strategies designed to focus on students with the greatest needs.

- **Evaluating and Supporting Teacher and Principal Effectiveness:** Each State that receives the ESEA flexibility will set basic guidelines for teacher and principal evaluation and support systems. The State and its districts will develop these systems with input from teachers and principals and will assess their performance based on multiple valid measures, including student progress over time and multiple measures of professional practice, and will use these systems to provide clear feedback to teachers on how to improve instruction.

As of this writing it is unknown how many states will apply for waivers or for which waivers they will apply. Perhaps spurred by the action by the Obama administration to address some of the greatest concerns regarding NCLB, Congress has agreed on a date to take up the reauthorization of the NCLB version of the Elementary and Secondary School Act but there are no details on the actual legislation. The new version of the law may reform NCLB in ways that make the need for the waivers moot, or it may reform NCLB in ways that will negate the waivers. Being the "law of the land," it will provide direction for the nation's schools for, presumably, the next decade.

## Summary

Much of the history of education in the twentieth century can be seen in terms of a swing from one view of education to another. The progressive education movement, which began at the turn of the century and continued to gain popularity through the 1930s, gave way in the post–World War II years to a more conservative view of the purpose of education, which was a response to a perceived decline in the nation's technological supremacy. In the 1960s, the tide turned again in favor of a more liberal and child-centered approach, and schools became a vital weapon in the War on Poverty. The schools were also placed center stage in the civil rights struggles of the 1960s and 1970s.

The late 1970s and 1980s once again saw renewed interest in the basics and a national cry for reform of the entire educational system. Beginning in the 1990s, education assumed an unprecedented place on the political agenda and played a major role in the election of Bill Clinton, the "Education President," in 1992. The Republican

---

## TEACHER OF THE YEAR

*Amber Damm*
*Minnesota*

Jonathan Kozol in *Ordinary Resurrections* writes, "Good teachers . . . are specialists at opening small packages. They give the string a tug, but do it carefully. They don't yet know what's in the box. They don't know if it's breakable." Mohammed's transition to Middle School was bumpy at best. At 6' 2" he towered over his peers, but reading at a second grade level he also towered in learned helplessness. His struggle began long before he came to my classroom. He and his family were refugees from the war in Somalia. When he came to my class he pretended that he was learning for a long time. Strife and laughter and tears and arguments ensued for probably a good six months, until he decided to fill the cracks in his education and literacy with diligence and effort and hope. That year Mohammed gained three years in reading. It was a powerful experience to watch, as his defensiveness and angst was filled with real learning. I am smarter, I am more creative, I am more empathetic because of the struggles, and the laughter, and the joys, and the strengths of my students that have bumped into my life forever.

takeover of Congress in 1994 led to renewed efforts at the federal and state levels to advance a conservative education agenda that included support for increased choice, vouchers, privatization, and school prayer. These efforts continued into the new century. The standards and accountability movements that began in the 1990s gained momentum in the new century with the passage of the No Child Left Behind Act. The NCLB created new and expanded roles for the state and federal governments as well as challenges and opportunities for school districts. The expanded federal involvement begun under NCLB, as well as its emphasis on testing, teacher quality, and the promotion of charter schools, was further expanded under the Obama administration and the Race to the Top program. The impact of these changes on the organization and operation of the schools and their curriculum and instruction are explored in the chapters which follow.

# PROFESSIONAL DEVELOPMENT *Workshop*

## *Prepare for the State Licensure Examination*

Ms. Knight is a third-year science teacher at John Dewey High School. Her class contains students at all ability levels as well as three limited English language learners. Ms. Knight is attempting to design science projects that are based on student interests and that build on experiences and materials common to the daily lives of the students. She believes this would be consistent with the constructivist perspective she has been taught at State College. As her first major student assignment, she has asked students to collect a minimum of six different materials and design a project using these materials, to make a class presentation of the project, and to submit a written paper describing the project and the science supporting it. Ms. Knight reserved the computer lab for two classes to give students the opportunity to do research on the Internet.

On the scheduled day student presentations varied considerably, with some students making PowerPoint presentations, others poster displays, and still others reading a short and poorly written paper. Several students had nothing ready to present or a paper to turn in. Three students said they forgot it was due that day; three others said they did not understand the assignment. As each student made their presentation Ms. Knight tried to make some positive and encouraging comments. Her efforts were undermined by Jeff Smith and Larry Hughes, two of the students who did not have a presentation ready. They made jokes and comments throughout the presentations and laughed at students when they misspoke or when their demonstrations did not go as planned.

Ms. Knight is discouraged with the results of this first assignment. She wonders if instead of trying to be creative she should have just prepared a lecture or PowerPoint presentation.

1. What accommodation should Ms. Knight have made for the varying ability levels of the students?

2. What criteria should Ms. Knight use to assess the class presentations? The writing projects? Justify your choices.

3. a. What strategies can Ms. Knight use to try to ensure that students understand and complete assignments?

   b. How should Ms. Knight deal with the disruptive behavior of Jeff and Larry?

### Build Your Knowledge Base

1. What criteria did you use in deciding what artifacts to include in your "time room" or video on the history of education?

2. Compare the high school curricula of 1930, 1960, 1990, and 2012.

3. Describe the impact of the two world wars on American higher education.

4. To what extent did the schools either change society or adapt to changes in society in the 20th century?

5. Trace the changing involvement of the federal government in education in the 20th century. What has been the impact of declining federal financial support?

6. What is your response to Joel Spring's (2005) assertion that the end of the common school is at hand?

7. What have been the most significant positive and negative changes in education during your lifetime? What changes/reforms do you think need to be made?

### Develop Your Portfolio

1. Gather information on the current use of academic content standards in your discipline or subject field. If you are not familiar with the content standards in your subject area, contact your state department of education or specialized organizations such as the Council for Exceptional Children, the National Conference of Teachers of English, or the National Council for Teachers of Mathematics. Next, interview a teacher in your discipline regarding his or her views on the use of academic standards. How successful has this teacher been in aligning the curriculum with the standards? What steps has he or she taken to address the problem of those students who have performed the poorest on the high-stakes testing? Summarize the teacher's responses and incorporate your views regarding standards, testing, and accountability. Place your reflection paper in your portfolio under **INTASC Standard 6, Assessment.**

2. Using photos, illustrations, news clippings, or other materials, create an artifact that displays what you perceive to be the most important noteworthy happening that took place during the period of modern American education from the progressive movement to the present. Describe the event and how the noteworthy happening has impacted education today. Place your artifact in your portfolio under **INTASC Standard 4, Content Knowledge**.

### Explore Teaching and Learning: Field Experiences

1. Using the following online source (**http://www.unlv.edu/projects/ohpsp/index.html**), compare and contrast the recorded views of principals across three decades: the 1970s, the 1980s, and the 1990s. For guidance, you might focus on questions such as the following:
   a. What were the primary issues or concerns expressed by the principals? How did the concerns differ? How were they similar?
   b. Across the 3 decades, were there differences in the ways that principals discussed issues related to student learning?

2. Divide the 20th century into five periods (1900–1919, 1920–1939, 1940–1959, 1960–1979, and 1980–1999). Identify and trace shifts/changes in the dominant economic, social, political, and educational issues through these periods.

## MyEducationLab

Go to **Topic 7 The History and Philosophy of Education** in the MyEducationLab (www.myeducation-lab.com) for *Foundations of American Education*, where you can:

- Find learning outcomes for the history and philosophy of education along with the national standards that connect to these outcomes.
- Complete Assignments and Activities that can help you more deeply understand the chapter content.
- Apply and practice your understanding of the core teaching skills identified in the chapter with the Building Teaching Skills and Dispositions learning units.
- Examine challenging situations and cases presented in the IRIS Center Resources.

- Access additional video clips of CCSSO National Teachers of the Year award winners responding to the question, "Why Do I Teach?" in the Teacher Talk section.
- Check your comprehension on the content covered in the chapter with the Study Plan. Here you will be able to take a chapter quiz, receive feedback on your answers, and then access Review, Practice, and Enrichment activities to enhance your understanding of chapter content.
- Use the Online Lesson Plan Builder to practice lesson planning and integrating national and state standards into your planning.

children learn the beliefs, values, and expectations of the larger society. As Goodlad (2004) observed, while teachers "are not democracy's anointed stewards . . . (they do) have potentially powerful roles to play in ensuring that our public educational institutions provide the apprenticeship that responsible citizenship requires" (p. 2).

## The Family

Although the organization of the family varies from culture to culture and from one period of history to the next, there are certain basic functions that all families serve. One of those is the socialization function. Children are born into families, and, for a significant period in their life (in particular their early years), the family is the only world that the children know. Thus, the family is the first and most important socializing agent for the young. It is the family that first introduces the child to the world at large, and it is the family that transmits a particular culture's values to the young. Parents pass on their perceptions, values, beliefs, attitudes, experiences, and understandings to their children. The family is the point of origin for gender role socialization as well as ethnocentricism and prejudice (Sociology Central, 2011). These primary impressions are long lasting and very difficult to modify or change. They also have significant impact on children's later educational development and success in school. Parent–child interactions, the use of language in the home, attitudes, rituals, and child-rearing practices are a few of the many influences that are associated with a child's social behavior as well as educational achievement or attainment.

Although the family has traditionally been the major instrument of socialization for the young, in the last quarter century increasing responsibility for socialization has been transferred to the school or other institutions. The major reason schools and other institutions have taken on a greater role as socializing agents is the changing structure of the family. During the past three decades, the family configuration has changed dramatically. Fewer than 25% of U.S. households are made up of a married man and woman and children (U.S. Bureau of the Census, 2011). Blended families with children from former marriages living together and extended families where two or more generations live together are increasingly common. A growing number of children, especially minority children, live with grandparents. In many families both parents work outside the home, often in more than one job. When they do spend time together, it is often spent watching television. Little family interaction occurs and less time is given to teaching children acceptable values and behaviors. As a result, the school has taken on the function of teaching certain subjects that were once considered the purview of the family. For example, sex educa-

**Figure 8.1 — Socializing Agents That Transmit Culture**

## THE INDIVIDUAL

Family

School

Church

Community

Neighborhood

Peer Group

Electronic Media

Sports

The Arts

Print Media

Workplace

Technology

*Source:* Information from Human Diversity in Education: An Integrative Approach (p. 66) by K. Cushner, A. McClelland, & P. Safford. (1996). New York: McGraw-Hill.

**For Your Reflection and Analysis**

What were the childrearing practices in your home during your formative years? How were gender roles perceived?

Extended families play a major role in the socialization of children in many cultures.

**For Your Reflection and Analysis**

Has your family configuration changed during the past two decades?

**For Your Reflection and Analysis**

Describe the peer groups in your early life that served as an agent of socialization for you.

tion and values education, domains that were traditionally considered the responsibility of the family and church, have been transferred to the school.

## The Peer Group

The peer group, which consists of friends who are of approximately the same age and social status, is one of the most important institutions for shaping the child's social behaviors. In fact, "peer relationships play a unique role in a child's development—one that cannot be entirely duplicated by parents or other socializing agents" (Ladd, 2007, p. 155). Each peer group has its own set of rules, its own social organization, its own customs, and, in some cases, its own rituals and language. Children develop friendship patterns at a very early age. In the earliest years these interactions are supervised by parents and tend to parallel and reinforce the socialization learned in the family (Sociology Central, 2011). By the age of 11, peer groups are fairly well established. Although the peer group relationship may be transitory, its influence can be profound. And, unlike the family influence, which tends to lessen with time, the peer group influence becomes stronger throughout childhood and adolescence.

In adolescence, many youth begin to question their family values and attitudes and become more influenced by the values and attitudes of their peers. Peer group socialization becomes linked to puberty and the role of sexuality and sexual relations (Sociology Central, 2011). The peer group also reflects and reinforces what constitutes appropriate gender roles and social behavior in the culture (Curry, Jiobu, & Schwirian, 2008). From their interactions in the peer group, children learn about themselves and their behavior, peer relationships, and the situations and contexts in which social relationships are conducted (Ladd, 2007).

## Religion

From the very beginning of the United States as a nation, religion has been a major force in American society. Religion influenced Roger Williams and Ann Hutchinson to leave the Massachusetts Colony and found the colony of Rhode Island and the followers of Joseph Smith to cross the unsettled West to establish a settlement near a great salt lake in what was to become Utah. More currently, 65% of Americans indicated that religion is an important part of their daily lives (Newport, 2009), as have 60% of high school seniors (Wallace, Forman, Celdwell, & Willis, 2003). Religious institutions serve as primary agents for the transmission of values and function as agents of social control by reward and punishment (Gollnick & Chinn, 2009).

Religion, with its accompanying beliefs and values, serves as an important socializing agent. Religion provides a moral code or plan for living; provides social and emotional support when needed; and chronicles and ritualizes such important events as birth, marriage, and death. And, to many, it provides answers regarding proper conduct, the meaning of life, and the afterlife (Curry et al., 2008). Religion influences our attitudes regarding tobacco and alcohol use, the role of the family, sexuality, sex roles, discipline, child rearing, and our political identities.

## The Mass Media

**Mass media** refers to television and videos, electronic media (video and computer games), the Internet, popular music, movies, music videos, radio, newspapers, and magazines. The socialization effects of both television and the electronic media stand out because they have become almost as strong as those of the home, school, and neighborhood in their influence on children's development and behavior. Indeed, young people spend more time with media than any other activity including formal schooling. Twenty-five percent of high school students play video or computer games or use the computer three or more times per day, and 30% watch three or more hours of TV per day (CDC, 2010). A large increase in media use and media exposure occurs when children enter the 11- to 14-year-old age group: from under 8 hours per day for the 8- to 10-year-olds to just under 12 hours for the 11- to 14-year-olds (Rideout, Fochr, & Roberts, 2010).

While spending time with media is not in and of itself bad, there is concern about the effect of exposure to media on antisocial behavior and health. Research on the effects of media violence on children documents that young people "learn their attitudes about violence at a very young age and, once learned, those attitudes are difficult to modify. Conservative estimates are that media violence may be associated with 10% of real-life violence" (Strasburger, 2009, p. 2265). Research has also shown that the more children play violent games, the more likely they are to have a hostile personality and to be physically aggressive (Gentile & Gentile, 2005). Related research has found a strong relationship between viewing television at an early age and subsequent bullying (Zimmerman, Glew, Christakis, & Katon, 2005). Still other research has linked media exposure to childhood obesity, eating disorders, early onset of sexual intercourse, and tobacco and alcohol use (Strasburger, 2009).

Considerable variation exists among young people depending on their race, ethnicity, gender, and the amount of time spent with media. For example, among 8- to 18-year-olds, boys spend 42 minutes more per day playing video games than girls. And both Blacks and Hispanics spend more time watching TV and listening to music than their White peers: Black and Hispanic youth spend an average of 13 hours a day exposed to media, compared to about 8.5 for White youth (Rideout, et. al, 2010). Variations also exist in terms of access to media: 88% of White youth have Internet access at home compared to 78% of African American youth and 74% of Hispanic youth (Rideout, et al., 2010).

**Reflect on Diversity**
To what do you attribute the racial/ethnic differences in TV viewing and the playing of video games?

## Media and School Achievement

The relationship between media consumption and school achievement is also a matter of concern. Except for limited evidence that television viewing may increase vocabulary, most studies that have examined the relationship between television viewing and school achievement have found a negative correlation between the amount of viewing and the level of achievement, especially at the higher levels of viewing. For example, data from the National Assessment of Educational Progress show that among eighth graders, those who watch two or fewer hours of television per day had an average reading score of 266, whereas those who watch six hours or more had an average score of 238; at the 12th-grade level, the comparable scores were 292 and 256 (Snyder & Dillow, 2011). In addition, many teachers also complain that increased television viewing interferes with homework and creates in children an expectation that they must be entertained. Research has also linked increased media use to grades: 47% of students who report heavy media use (16 hours of media content per day) and 31% of moderate media users (3–16 hours of media content per day) say they get mostly Cs or below compared to 23% of light media users (fewer than 3 hours of media use per day) (Rideout et al., 2010).

Of equal concern with test scores is the effect of television viewing on attention. A 2004 study led by Christakis found that for each hour a child between 1 and 3 years of age watches television, the risk the child will have attention problems is increased by 10% (Barton, 2004).

# The Purposes and Expectations of Schooling

Just as there are a variety of theories of education that influence how we view the teaching and learning process, there are also a variety of theories or perspectives about society, its institutions, and their workings. Each perspective makes assumptions about society or a particular institution and attempts to explain their workings. When applied to the study of education, sociologists and others commonly refer to three distinct perspectives: the *functionalist perspective*, the *conflict perspective*, and the *symbolic interactionist perspective*. The functionalist perspective emphasizes the benefits of education to the social and economic order. The conflict perspective emphasizes the role of education in the perpetuation of social inequality. The symbolic interactionist perspective looks at the interactions in the schools to understand their effect on school processes and students.

## Functionalist Perspective

Functionalists believe the role of the school is to preserve and transmit a common set of values that foster social unity and maintain social order. According to the functionalist perspective, the purpose of the school is to create a common identity by teaching the economic, political, and cultural practices and norms of the dominant society (Feinberg & Soltis, 2004). These lessons are not limited to the formal curriculum, but include the hidden curriculum as discussed in Chapter 14.

The functionalists see the school as the institution where students can best acquire the necessary knowledge and skills to become responsible and productive citizens and to compete in the global economy. (The importance placed on education in terms of our nation's global standing is attested to by the attention given to, and the debate over, the achievement of American students compared with that of students in other countries.) Although there is disagreement as to what body of knowledge and which skills are the most important for students to master, philosophers, educational theorists, teachers, parents, and individuals across the economic, social, and political spectrum have underscored this purpose of schooling.

According to functionalists, education contributes to economic growth and development primarily through its effect on productivity by upgrading the skills of the labor force. They point to the research that has shown that more educated workers (1) are less likely to lose time because of unemployment and illness; (2) are more likely to innovate and be aware of, and receptive to, new ideas and knowledge; (3) produce better goods and render services with greater skill; and (4) produce more goods and services in a given period of time because of their skill, dexterity, and knowledge (Webb, McCarthy, & Thomas, 1988). Schools also prepare children to support the economic system by enhancing the development of personal attributes compatible with the industrial workplace. This purpose of schooling, aimed at training students as future workers, emphasizing the need for planning, punctuality, time on-task, cooperation, independence, and following the rules, has also been referred to as its *social efficiency* goal (Labaree, 2000).

Functionalists point out that it is not just the larger society or the employer that enjoys the benefits of schooling, but that education promotes personal growth and has a significant economic benefit for the individual. For example, the 2010 median weekly earnings of workers ages 25 and older with a bachelor's degree is $1,038 compared to $626 for those with a high school diploma, and $444 for those without a high school diploma (Bureau of Labor Statistics, 2011).

The functionalists also believe that schools play an important role in developing moral character. This was an explicit expectation of the schools throughout much of America's history. The textbooks and curriculum of the school were directed toward the development of character and moral behavior. Teachers were expected not only to exhibit high ethical and moral principles, but also to teach those principles to their students. Although the continued push for separation of church and state has greatly eliminated the religious involvement that was once the significant vehicle for much of this training, the emphasis on moral development continues to be one of the important expectations of schooling. And, as the family has relinquished more and more of its role in transmitting moral responsibility, the school has, in part, assumed this function.

## Conflict Perspective

Those who espouse the conflict perspective believe that the school is an instrument of domination used by those in power to reproduce and perpetuate socioeconomic inequities. Conflict theorists are concerned with the conflict between social classes, the workers and the "capitalists," the powerless and the powerful (Feinberg & Soltis, 2004).

Conflict theorists, similar to the Marxists, neo-Marxists, and critical theorists, believe that the schools essentially serve the wealthy and powerful at the expense of the disadvantaged. They contend that the schools serve the upper socioeconomic classes by socializing the working and lower classes to conform to the values and beliefs that are necessary to maintain the existing social order. Critical theorists argue that the classroom, with its extrinsic reward system and hierarchical relationship between teacher and student, is like a miniature factory system. Through the hidden curriculum, students are taught the goals and ideology of the capitalist system. "According to conflict theorists, the hidden curriculum works against working-class students because it instructs them not to challenge authority" (Curry et al., 2008, p. 382). Critical theorists further contend that the real purpose of schooling, which they contend is controlled by the elite, is to train the workers needed for business and industry, not to promote the movement of disadvantaged youth into the upper classes (Spring, 2008).

## Symbolic Interactionist Perspective

The symbolic interactionist perspective is both a critique and an extension of both the functionalist and the conflict perspectives. Interactionists criticize functionalists and conflict theorists for being too abstract in their depictions of what schools offer students and what teachers offer schools, as well as for failing to address what goes on in the schools on a day-to-day basis. They miss the interactional aspects of school life, what takes place between students and students and between students and teachers. "For example, the processes by which students are labeled 'gifted' or 'learning disabled' are, from an interactionist point of view, important to analyze because such processes carry with them the many implicit assumptions about learning and children" (Ballentine & Spade, 2004, p. 13).

The symbolic interactionist perspective is often combined with functionalist or conflict perspectives to provide a more complete picture of society and its institutions, including the schools. Applied by the discipline of educational sociology, interaction theory has contributed to our understanding of the effect that teacher expectations and assumptions about students based on race, ethnicity, class, and gender have on student's self-concept and achievement, as well as on the school processes and interactions that are important to decisions related to ability grouping and tracking. Combining the findings of conflict theory with the interactionist perspective, sociologists have demonstrated how school processes at the organizational level actually result in inequality and social stratifications at the classroom level. In effect, "the system of public education in reality perpetuates what it is ideologically committed to eradicating—class barriers which result in inequality in the social and economic life of citizenry" (Risk, cited in Sadovnik, 2004, p. 14).

A comparison of the three theories of the purposes of education from a sociological perspective is presented in Table 8.1.

### Table 8.1 — Comparison of the Three Theoretical Perspectives on Education

| Perspective | View of Education | Key Concepts and Processes |
|---|---|---|
| Functionalist | Sees education as essential for an orderly and efficient society | Socialization and other functions<br>Official and hidden curriculum |
| Conflict Theory | Sees educational system as perpetuating social inequality | Prestige hierarchy of schools<br>Cultural capital |
| Symbolic Interactionist | Sees education as interaction in the social setting of the school | Labeling<br>Self-fulfilling prophecy |

*Source:* Adapted from T. Curry, R. Jiobu, & K. Schwirian, © 2008, *Sociology for the Twenty-First Century* (5th ed.). Upper Saddle River, NJ: Pearson Education, p. 384.

## The Diverse Student Population

The schools reflect the society they serve. The student population is made up of children from all of the social classes, religions, races, ethnicities, languages, and exceptionalities found in the larger society. The conditions of each of these groups are reflected both in the diverse student groups and in their impact on educational achievement and attainment. Although there is practically no limit to the number of diverse groups found in the student population of our nation's schools, the most common groupings are those defined by social classes, ethnicity, race, language, exceptionality, and gender.

### Social Class

Sociologists maintain that a number of social classes exist within most societies, distinguishable by great differences in wealth, prestige, and power. The **social class** system in the United States has traditionally been represented by a hierarchy of five classes or groups: upper class, upper middle class, lower middle class, upper working class, and lower working class. One's social class, or **socioeconomic status** (SES), is determined by a number of variables, including wealth and income, education, occupation, power, and prestige. When asked to which social class they belong, the majority of Americans identify themselves as being middle class. Over the years, differences between certain classes have disappeared. For example, blue-collar workers of the working class have enjoyed greater gains in income than lower-middle-class white-collar workers, thereby eliminating some of the earlier distinctions between the two groups. At the same time, in recent years both the high-income and high-status upper class and the low-income, low-status lower class have grown, creating an ever-widening gulf between the very rich and the very poor.

Although changes are occurring among the different classes, the five-class structure still remains a viable and convenient method of differentiating one group from another. The *upper class,* which comprises only 3% of American society, includes those individuals who control great wealth, power, and influence. Members of the *upper middle class,* which includes 22% of society, do not have the family background of the upper class. They are generally leading professionals, high-level

# HISTORICAL NOTE

## The Evolving Concept of Social Class

The concept of social class and social stratification can be found as early as the time of Plato and Aristotle. Although Plato and Aristotle did not advance any particular theory to explain the causes and consequences of such stratification, they did recognize the classes that existed in their social structures. Both Plato and Aristotle discussed social class distinctions in the ideal society. Plato envisioned a utopian society that was divided into three social classes: guardians, auxiliaries, and workers. According to Plato, the guardians would be a disinterested ruling elite. Aristotle acknowledged three social classes including the very wealthy, the very poor, and the middle class. According to Aristotle, in the ideal political system, the middle class would be the dominant or ruling class.

By the 17th and 18th centuries, the concept of social class was an important subject for discussion. During this period, John Locke developed a theory of social class that identified two separate classes: property owners and laborers. In 1755, French philosopher Jean-Jacques Rousseau recognized the existence of social classes by describing what he referred to as natural inequalities and those inequities that resulted from the social order.

Perhaps more than any other political philosopher, Karl Marx demonstrated the relationship between social class and the political economy. For Marx, what distinguishes one type of society from another is the mode of production (i.e., technology and the division of labor). Marx hypothesized that each mode of production creates a particular class system whereby one class controls the process of production and the other class or classes become the producers or service providers for the dominant/ruling class. Marx was primarily concerned with modern capitalist society. He envisioned a successful working-class revolution and the birth of a classless society.

managers, or corporate executives who are well educated and financially well off. The *lower middle class,* accounting for 34% of the population, consists of middle income businesspeople; white-collar clerical workers and salespersons; skilled workers such as factory foremen; farm owners; and some building, electrical, and plumbing contractors. The *upper working class* is largely made up of blue-collar workers in skilled and semi-skilled jobs and represents 28% of the population. The *lower working class* consists of the 13% of society who are often referred to as the *underclass* and is composed of individuals with incomes at or below the poverty level who are usually poorly educated and often unemployed. The underclass includes the 2% hardcore unemployed who have lived in poverty for a lengthy period of time, such as 8 out of the last 10 years, and excludes individuals who are temporarily poor due to loss of a job or other unfortunate circumstances (Rose, 2007).

The socioeconomic distinctions among the social classes, specifically the existence of poverty, affect not only lifestyles, patterns of association, and friendships, but also patterns of school achievement and attainment. In 2010 over 15 million children in the United States were living in poverty, an increase of about 2 million from 2000. Blacks, Hispanics, and American Indians are disproportionately poor: 12% of White children live in poor families compared to 36% of Black children, 34% of American Indian children, and 33% of Hispanic children (Wight, Chau & Aratani, 2011).

The effects of poverty are seen early in the child's development. Poor mothers-to-be rarely are well nourished and often do not receive adequate prenatal care— "a recipe for lower achievement among their children" (Gardner, 2007, p. 544). Children in poverty have lower birth weight, tend to have poor vision, poor oral hygiene, more lead poisoning, more asthma, poor nutrition, less adequate pediatric care, and more exposure to secondhand smoke—all of which are likely to have a significant impact on cognitive functioning and academic achievement (Rothstein, 2004). Children in poverty often go to school with uncorrected vision problems, toothaches, and untreated chronic health problems (Berliner, 2009). Research has shown that low socioeconomic (SES) children have reduced performance compared to high socioeconomic children on measures of executive function such as working memory, cognitive flexibility, and semantic fluency (Kishiyama, Boyce, Jimenez, Perry & Knight, 2009). In addition, low SES children "often live in cognitively impoverished environments . . . have limited access to cognitively stimulating materials and experiences, and . . . receive less attention from adults than children from higher SES backgrounds" (Kishiyama, et al., 2009, p. 1113). Children in poverty are often very mobile. They may be homeless, move in with a relative, move from place to place with a parent in search of work or a place to stay. Transferring from school to school, high absenteeism, and dropping out become the norm.

Poverty's adverse effects on achievement are visible as early as the first grade, and the differences appear to increase as the child progresses through school. Low-income children are 1.4 times as likely as their higher-income peers to have a learning disability, 1.3 times more likely to be at risk for parent-reported emotional and behavioral problems, 3.1 times more likely to experience teen pregnancy, 6.8 times more likely to be victims of child abuse and neglect, and 2.2 times more likely to become a victim of violent crime (Duncan & Brooks-Gunn, 2001).

Parental income is also highly correlated with school readiness. Kindergartners from low-income homes typically start school at least one full year behind others in reading and have a vocabulary of only 5,000 words compared to 20,000 words for their middle-class peers (Evans, 2005). A number of factors are thought to be related to this lack of readiness, including the fact that

Millions of families of all races and cultures live in poverty.

**For Your Reflection and Analysis**

Identify your social class and indicate what impact your socioeconomic status has had on your educational achievement and attainment.

these children are not as likely to attend preschool and that, on average, parents below the poverty level read less to their children and tell them fewer stories than those above the poverty level (Snyder & Dillow, 2011).

## The Social Class Achievement and Attainment Gaps

Notwithstanding the popular rhetoric that schools advance economic growth, economic productivity, and **social mobility**, the goal of equal educational opportunity for all has never been fully achieved in the United States. This can be attributed in part to the fact that "poverty poses a serious challenge to children's access to quality learning opportunities and their potential to succeed in school" (KewalRamani, Gilbertson, Fox, & Provasnik, 2007, p. 16). While the attention given to the achievement disparities between students in the public schools has focused on the achievement gaps between White and Asian American students and Black and Hispanic students, the achievement and attainment gaps between rich and poor students and upper- and lower-class students are equally persistent and challenging.

A number of indicators of school success, including the sometimes controversial standardized tests (see the Controversial Issue feature on the next page), have been linked to various indicators of socioeconomic status. For example, the **National Assessment of Educational Progress (NAEP)** annually tests a national representative sample of students in public and private schools in certain subject and skill areas. The NAEP reports have consistently shown that, in general, achievement is related to parental education and student eligibility for free and reduced lunch, two indicators of socioeconomic status. According to the findings, the NAEP proficiency scores of free and reduced lunch–eligible students were consistently lower than those of non-eligible students, and proficiency scores at each age level also consistently increased as level of parental education increased. For example, in 2009 the average NAEP reading score for the fourth-grade students eligible for free and reduced lunch was 206, compared with 232 for the fourth-grade children not eligible for free and reduced lunch, while students whose parents did not finish high school had an average mathematics score of 265 compared to a score of 284 for those whose parents had some education after high school (Snyder & Dillow, 2011).

As shown in Figure 8.2, on another assessment, the Scholastic Reasoning Test (SAT), which is the test most frequently taken by college-bound seniors, the relationship between parental education and SAT scores is also evident: the lower the parental educational level, the lower the SAT scores.

Social class as measured by the educational and occupational levels of parents has also been found to be the most significant predictor of educational attainment. Regardless of race or ethnicity, students from low-income or underclass families were more likely to repeat a grade and to drop out of school than those from middle- or upper-class families. Young people from the lowest income families

**Figure 8.2 — SAT Scores of College-Bound Seniors, by Highest Level of Parental Education**

| | No High School Diploma | High School Diploma | Associate Degree | Bachelor's Degree | Graduate Degree |
|---|---|---|---|---|---|
| ☐ Critical Reading | 422 | 464 | 482 | 521 | 561 |
| ☐ Mathematics | 446 | 475 | 491 | 536 | 575 |
| ■ Writing | 419 | 453 | 469 | 512 | 554 |

*Source:* U.S. Department of Education, National Center for Education Statistics. (2008). *The digest of education statistics, 2007.* Washington, DC: U.S. Government Printing Office.

# CONTROVERSIAL ISSUE

## *Standardized Testing*

The use of standardized tests—always a controversial issue—has been even more broadly debated as a number of states and school districts have adopted so-called high-stakes tests to determine graduation from high school or grade-level retention and as the testing requirements of the No Child Left Behind Act have been enforced. Some of the most commonly given arguments for and against standardized tests follow.

**For**

1. They improve the accountability of students, teachers, and schools.

2. Student weaknesses can be identified and addressed early.

3. Schools can identify their weaknesses and focus improvement efforts on the areas of greatest need.

4. Allows for the necessary comparisons across schools, across districts, and over time that are needed for public policy purposes.

5. Helps parents know how well their children are learning.

6. Leads to improvement in teaching and student achievement.

**Against**

1. Tests are inherently biased against certain learning styles and work to the disadvantage of poor and minority students.

2. Test results are misleading: tests do not have the reliability or validity to accurately measure the proficiency of students across the ability, racial, ethnic, and socioeconomic spectrums.

3. Teachers spend too much time "teaching to the test" at the expense of other material or teaching for understanding.

4. Tests are expensive to develop and administer and take money needed for other educational programs.

5. Test results are used to make decisions that cannot be adequately informed by one measure.

6. Students and schools in poor districts, which are subject to numerous conditions beyond their control, are unfairly stigmatized and sanctioned.

What is your position? Will high-stakes testing improve education or harm it? Which students are hurt the most by such tests?

---

are twice as likely to drop out of school as those from the highest income families (Chapman, Laird, & KewalRamani, 2010). Students whose parents completed a bachelor's degree or higher were more than twice as likely to enroll in college immediately after high school graduation than students whose parents had less than a high school diploma (U.S. Department of Education, 2005).

## *Hispanic Americans*

**Ethnic groups** are subgroups of the population that are distinguished by having a common cultural heritage (e.g., language, customs, history). The 48 million Hispanics in the United States, who make up 16% of the population (see Figure 8.3), comprise the largest ethnic group in the country and the fastest growing minority group. One of every two people added to the nation's population is Hispanic (U.S. Census Bureau, 2010a). Since 2000 the Hispanic population has expanded three times faster than the population as a whole. Immigration and a high birthrate are responsible for the rapid growth in the Hispanic

**Figure 8.3 — Racial/Ethnic Composition of U.S. Population, 2010**

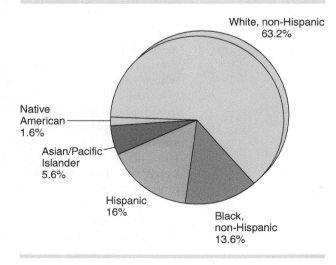

White, non-Hispanic 63.2%

Native American 1.6%

Asian/Pacific Islander 5.6%

Hispanic 16%

Black, non-Hispanic 13.6%

population. By 2050, the number of Hispanic Americans is projected to grow to 132.8 million and represent 30% of the U.S. population (U.S. Census Bureau, 2010a).

Hispanic Americans are a diverse group made up of Mexican Americans (66% of Hispanics), Puerto Ricans (9%), Cubans (3.4%), Salvadorans (3.4%), Dominicans (2.8%), and "Other," which includes persons from Spain, Central and South America, the Caribbean, and others who identify themselves as Latino or Hispanic. The median age of the U.S. Hispanic population, 27.4 years, is 9 years younger than that of the population as a whole. Over one-third of the Hispanic population is under the age of 18, compared to one-fourth of the total population. Hispanics have the highest concentration of preschoolers of any racial or ethnic group (U.S. Census Bureau, 2010a).

Hispanic Americans are geographically concentrated in three regions: the West, the South, and the Northeast. Hispanic Americans of Mexican origin are more likely to live in the West and South. Puerto Ricans are most likely to reside in the Northeast. Cubans tend to be concentrated in the South, specifically Florida, whereas people of Central American origin are found in all of these three regions of the United States.

The low educational achievement and attainment of many Hispanic American youth is no doubt associated with the previously discussed impact of socioeconomic status. In 2008, the poverty rate for Hispanic Americans was 23%, compared with 10% for non-Hispanic Whites and 11% for Asian Americans. Also, whereas Hispanic American children represent 21% of the children in the United States, they constitute 31% of all children living in poverty (U.S. Census Bureau, 2010a).

A significant explanation for the poorer academic performance of some Hispanic American children may also be their limited English-speaking ability. Over 76% of Hispanic children age 5 and older speak a language other than English at home, and of these, only about half speak English very well (U.S. Census Bureau, 2010a). Other factors that may contribute to the low achievement and low attainment of these students include the following:

- The limited education of parents, which makes it difficult for them to effectively participate in their children's education: nationally, 37% of Hispanics lack a high school degree (attainment is higher among certain Hispanic groups, e.g., Cubans with a 76% high school completion rate [U.S. Census Bureau, 2011a]);

- Hispanic children are underrepresented in preprimary education programs such as Head Start, which may explain their lack of readiness to participate in elementary school. They are also underrepresented in gifted and college preparation courses and overrepresented in remedial and vocational tracks (Walker, 2004);

- A lack of family support in terms of monitoring homework and other school-related activities (Schmid, 2001); and

- Recent immigration: 27% of children in immigrant families are poor (Wright, Chau, & Aratani, 2011).

Segregation is an important variable in explaining the achievement and attainment of Hispanic students. Hispanics are the most segregated minority student group in the United States: approximately 78% of Hispanic students attend schools where over 50% of the student body is minority: "schools that are more likely to offer their students inadequate facilities and materials, less experienced and less qualified teachers, and less successful peers" (Gandara, 2010, p. 611). Hispanics are segregated not only by ethnicity but also by poverty, and for those that are Spanish speakers, by language. Each type of segregation presents its own disadvantages. High poverty schools have higher rates of violence, absenteeism, and other at-risk behaviors. They also experience high turnover of students and faculty and offer few advanced courses (Gandara, 2010). Linguistically segregated schools not only disadvantage students because they cannot provide enough contact with English to build language development, but these schools (found mostly in urban areas) also tend to have larger classes, high student poverty rates, more unqualified teachers, and lower levels of parental involvement (Gandara, 2010).

## African Americans

The 41.8 million African Americans in the United States make up 13.6% of the total population (Figure 8.3) (U.S. Census Bureau, 2010b). The African American population is expected to reach 65.8 million, or 15% of the U.S. population, by 2050. Thirty percent of the Black population is under the age of 18, making it the second youngest racial or ethnic group (U.S. Census Bureau, 2010b).

As in the case of Hispanic Americans, explanations for the lower levels of academic achievement and attainment of African Americans (relative to Whites and Asian Americans) are linked to the lower socioeconomic status and the social milieu of African American families. For example, in 2009, the poverty rate for African Americans, 26%, was slightly less than that of Hispanic Americans (U.S. Census Bureau, 2010b). Lower average levels of parental education and lower levels of parental availability are also contributory factors. In 2010, only 33% of Black students lived with both parents compared to 75% of White students, 84% of Asian children, and 61% of Hispanic children (Child Trends, 2011). Many live in a single-mother household below the poverty level, "a consideration that puts children from any ethnic group at risk for, among other problems, poor attendance and achievement and behavior problems" (Evans, 2005, p. 586).

African American children, like Hispanic children, increasingly attend schools with high percentages of Latino and Black students, a situation which research shows could impact student achievement in mathematics and literacy as early as kindergarten and the first grade (Ready & Silander, 2009). These students disproportionately reside in tax-poor, high-poverty districts and are thus disadvantaged relative to access to resources and the type of teachers they get (Horan, 2010). They are also less likely to be enrolled in preprimary education, have higher placement

## VIDEO INSIGHT

### Acting White

In this ABC News video, the interviewer talks with Black students at East High School in Madison, Wisconsin, and rapper John Forte about the concept of "acting White." As discussed in this video, *acting White* is a derogatory term used by Black students against other Black students they perceive as being racially disloyal, in that they have "sold out" by adopting the social expectations of the White society. Using proper English, studying hard, and answering questions in class are behaviors that can be construed as acting White. Being accused of acting White can be so hurtful that many Black students will consciously underperform and hold back to avoid the charge. Sociologists and psychologists in the video suggest that this deliberate underachieving may be a contributing factor in the achievement gap between White and Black students on assessments such as the NAEP.

As you reflect on the experiences of the students in this video, answer the following questions:

1. What stereotypes of Whites held by Blacks are inherent in the term *acting White?* Is this a racial slur?

2. What stereotypes of Blacks are perpetuated by the rejection of the achievement and success orientation of students who are acting White?

3. What can you as a teacher do to help students who want to achieve academically overcome the pressure to underachieve in an effort to maintain social acceptance?

**Reflect on Diversity**
What explanations can you give for the higher expulsion rates of African American youth?

in remedial and vocational classes, are less likely to be enrolled in gifted and college preparatory classes, change schools more often, and experience higher school expulsion rates (Aud, Fox, & KewalRamani, 2010; Walker, 2004).

One particularly disturbing phenomenon that may contribute to the underperformance of some African American students is the deliberate underachievement described in the Video Insight, "Acting White."

## Asian Americans and Pacific Islanders

Asian Americans are defined as those Americans whose ancestry can be traced to such Asian countries as Cambodia, China, India, Japan, Korea, Laos, Malaysia, Pakistan, the Philippine Islands, Thailand, and Vietnam. Pacific Islanders include Polynesians, Micronesians, Melanesians, Samoans, Guamanians, Native Hawaiians, Tahitians, Northern Mariana Islanders, Palauans, and Fijians. Chinese Americans (26%), Filipino Americans (22%), and Asian Indians (18%) comprise the largest ethnic groups of Asian Americans, followed by Vietnamese, Koreans, and Japanese. Over half of the total Asian American population lives in the western part of the United States, primarily in metropolitan areas. In 2009, approximately 24% of Asian Americans were under age 18, about the same as non-Hispanic Whites (U.S. Census Bureau, 2011c).

Although their percentage of the U.S. population is relatively small (5%), the 17.3 million Asian Americans are the fastest growing racial group in the United States. Native Hawaiian and other Pacific Islanders have a population of 1.2 million. It is anticipated that by 2050, the Asian American population will more than double, to 40.6 million and will represent 9% of the U.S. population (U.S. Census Bureau, 2011c).

The Asian American student is often stereotyped as "the model student" or the "overachiever." This stereotype works to the disadvantage of such students by ignoring the varying educational experiences of Asian American students, including experiences of racism (Yoo, 2010). The model minority myth also "inherently pits Asian American students with other races and minority students creating interracial tension. . . . It creates a distorted portrait of all Asian American students as hard working, studious, persevering without complaint, while all other students of color as lazy, disruptive, and complaining" (Yoo, 2010, p. 1). Such stereotyping also masks the large variations in achievement and attainment across Asian ethnic groups as well as the experiences of Asian Americans who have been in the United States for multiple generations versus those who are recent immigrants (Ngo & Lee, 2007). For example, while some Asian groups such as Asian Indians and Japanese have been successful in receiving high school and college degrees, many other Southeast Asian American groups, including Hmong and Cambodians, have low rates of high school completion (Yoo, 2010).

**Reflect on Diversity**
How does the "model student" stereotype work to the advantage of Asian Americans?

The model minority stereotype places unfair burdens, expectations, and pressure on Asian American students to achieve and works to the disadvantage of Asian American students who encounter personal or educational problems. Not only may their problems go unnoticed, but studies have found that Asian Americans are less likely to seek help even when they have serious educational, physical, or mental health needs (Yoo, 2010). As is true for all students, higher income and educational levels of Asian American parents is highly correlated with student achievement and attainment.

Much of the research that has been done on Asian American students' achievement and attainment has concentrated on the factors contributing to their success. Cultural factors have been found to be among the most important variables. Among the cultural variables noted are high expectations of parents and teachers, valuing education, a supportive home learning environment that reinforces academic success, a high level of parental supervision, and a high value placed on self-control and education for self-improvement and family honor (Chiang, 2000; Min, 2003; Weinberg, 1997). Southeast Asian children are taught from an early age to develop a sense of moral obligation and loyalty to the family that demands unquestioning loyalty and obedience not only to parents, but also to all authority figures, including teachers and other school personnel (Morrow, 1991).

## Native Americans (American Indians and Alaska Natives)

Native Americans are a diverse population composed of American Indians and Alaska Natives (Eskimos and Aleuts). They include more than 554 tribes, each with its own culture, and 250 surviving languages. Nearly half of the nation's American Indians and Alaska Natives reside in the western states. The states with the largest percentages are Alaska (18%), Oklahoma (11%), and New Mexico (11%) (U.S. Census Bureau, 2010c).

The Native American population of 5 million currently makes up almost 1.6% of the total population and has been growing at a faster rate than the overall population. The Native American population, including those of more than one race, is expected to reach 8.6 million by 2050 (U.S. Census Bureau, 2010c). During the next two decades, the Native American population is

Although their percentage of the U.S. population is relatively small, Asian Americans are one of the fastest growing racial groups in the United States.

projected to increase at a faster rate than either the White or African American populations, but at a slower rate than the Asian American population. The Native American population is also younger than the overall population: Approximately 30% of the Native American population is under 18 years of age, with a median age of 31 years, seven years younger than the median age for the total population (U.S. Census Bureau, 2010c). The majority of Native American children and youth (approximately 90%) attend public schools. The remainder attend either Bureau of Indian Affairs (BIA)–operated schools; private, mostly religious affiliated schools; or tribal grant schools.

There are a number of explanations for the lower levels of educational achievement and attainment of Native Americans. For one thing, Native American children have the highest rate of absenteeism of any racial or ethnic group. They also have the second highest rate of suspensions or expulsions, placing them at higher risk for dropping out. Poverty is undoubtedly a major contributing factor. About 24% of the American Indian and Alaska Native population is classified as living in poverty (U.S. Census Bureau, 2010c). On reservations the poverty rate is three times the national average, and over 90,000 Native American families are under-housed or homeless ("Native American Statistics," 2010).

The limited English proficiency of many Native American parents, coupled with the English-only instruction in many schools, may also exacerbate the problems of Native American students. The average Native American student enters school with a vocabulary of 3,000 words compared to 15,000 words for the average White student (Headwater News, 2005). Native American children also tend to be disproportionately affected by health problems which impact learning and perseverance.

One explanation for the relatively low academic achievement and attainment of Native American students that has gained wide acceptance among educational researchers and theorists is the *cultural difference theory*. According to this theory, the relatively low academic achievement and attainment of Native American students results from discontinuities between the culture and language of their homes and communities and those of the mainstream society and the schools. In effect, many Native American students come from backgrounds that equip them with linguistic, interactional, and learning styles that are not typically supported or rewarded by the traditional American school, placing their cultural identity at risk in the educational environment (U.S. Commission on Civil Rights, 2003). Many Native American students also face a discontinuity between the varieties of English they speak, so-called Indian English, and that spoken by their non-Indian peers and teachers. In addition, the curriculum, teaching methods, and assessment strategies in mainstream schooling is often perceived by Native American students and their families not only as irrelevant and insensitive to their needs, but also as jeopardizing Native American views of the world, culture, and approaches to education (Barnhardt & Kawagley, 2005).

The result of all these discontinuities is a systematic and chronic miscommunication in the classroom, as well as a failure to recognize and build on the knowledge and skills that the Native American students bring with them to school (St. Charles & Costantino, 2000). As a result, Native American students experience feelings of isolation and difficulty maintaining rapport with teachers and with other students (U.S. Commission on Civil Rights, 2003).

Several additional factors identified in the literature help explain the underachievement and lower attainment of Native American students. According to a report by the U.S. Commission on Civil Rights (2003), "Native Americans students are not afforded educational opportunities equal to other American students. They routinely face deteriorating school facilities, underpaid teachers, weak curricula, discriminatory treatment, and outdated learning tools" (p. xi). Other factors mentioned in the literature include:

- The lack of well-trained teachers and administrators;
- Low student and/or parent motivation;
- Inadequate funding of the schools attended by Native Americans, many of which are small, rural schools or schools on reservations;
- Test bias, inadequate preparation for testing, and test anxiety;
- High student and staff mobility in their schools; and
- Higher rates of school violence and substance abuse (Beaulieu, 2000; Gilbert, 2000).

It is important to note that not only are there differences between Native American students and students of the dominant culture, but there also are significant differences among Native American students from different tribal groups. These differences (for example, the family's attitudes toward traditionalism, whether the student is from a multitribal home, the degree of monolingualism or bilingualism in the family, and the parents' educational background) may all impact educational outcomes as much as any of the factors previously mentioned (Callahan & McIntire, 1994).

## The Racial and Ethnic Achievement Gap

Student differences and differences in the quality of their educational experiences have combined to produce what has become perhaps the most persistent and difficult issue in education in the United States—the gap in achievement between various racial and ethnic groups. The most significant and persistent gaps are those between Black and Hispanic students and White students, between students from different socioeconomic levels, and between students and schools in different school systems. On average, Black and Hispanic students are "roughly two to three years of learning behind white students . . . regardless how it is measured, including both achievement (e.g., test scores) and attainment (e.g. graduation rate)" (McKinsey & Co., 2009, p. 1). Closing the gap is seen by both educators and policymakers as important not just for our educational system and for reducing racial and ethnic inequality, but ultimately for the economic health as a nation. Economic projections suggest that if the achievement gap between Black and Hispanic student achievement and White students had been narrowed, the Gross National Product in 2008 would have been higher by two to four percent (McKinsey & Co., 2009).

While the attainment and achievement of minorities have improved significantly, the achievement gap between White and Black students and between White and Hispanic students remains. The evidence supporting the achievement gap is typically the results of standardized tests, specifically tests such as the NAEP, the SAT, or the ACT. When scores on these tests over time are examined, the indication is that after improving for a number of years, the gap between some subgroups is again increasing. For example, as seen in Table 8.2, the average gap between the reading and math scores of 12th grade Black and Hispanic students and White students has actually increased since 1992. One positive observation is that, although the NAEP scores of Black and Hispanic students lag behind those of their White peers, their scores have increased at a faster rate than those of White students.

Not shown on Table 8.2 are the NAEP gap scores for Asian Americans and Native Americans, which for many years were not separately reported. In recent years, including 2009, the data have shown that Asian American students had the highest NAEP mathematics scores at each grade level. And Asian Americans had the highest fourth-grade reading scores and were second only to Whites in NAEP performance in reading at grades 8 and 12.

Native American children and youth tend to have lower achievement scores than White and Asian American students in reading and mathematics but higher scores than those of Hispanic American or African American students. For example, the 2009 NAEP reading scores for Native American 12th graders was 283, compared to 293 for White 12th graders, 274 for Hispanics, and 269 for Black 12th graders.

**Reflect on Diversity**
Did you take the SAT or ACT? To what extent do you feel that your scores were affected by your race, ethnicity, gender, or social class?

## Table 8.2 — Trends in NAEP Gap Scores in Reading and Mathematics

| Subject, Race/Ethnicity, and Grade | 1992 | 1994 | 1996 | 1998 | 2000 | 2002 | 2003 | 2005 | 2007 | 2009 |
|---|---|---|---|---|---|---|---|---|---|---|
| **Reading** | | | | | | | | | | |
| **White–Black gap** | | | | | | | | | | |
| Grade 4 | 32 | 38 | — | 32 | 34 | 30 | 31 | 29 | 27 | 26 |
| Grade 8 | 30 | 30 | — | 26 | — | 27 | 28 | 28 | 27 | 27 |
| Grade 12 | 24 | 28 | — | 28 | — | 25 | — | 26 | — | 27 |
| **White–Hispanic gap** | | | | | | | | | | |
| Grade 4 | 27 | 35 | — | 32 | 35 | 28 | 28 | 26 | 26 | 25 |
| Grade 8 | 26 | 24 | — | 27 | — | 26 | 27 | 25 | 25 | 24 |
| Grade 12 | 18 | 23 | — | 22 | — | 19 | — | 27 | — | 22 |
| **Male–Female gap** | | | | | | | | | | |
| Grade 4 | 8 | 11 | 6 | 6 | 10 | 7 | 7 | 6 | 6 | 6 |
| Grade 8 | 13 | 15 | 13 | 14 | — | 9 | 11 | 10 | 10 | 10 |
| Grade 12 | 10 | 14 | 16 | 16 | — | 16 | 13 | 13 | — | 12 |
| **Mathematics** | | | | | | | | | | |
| **White–Black gap** | | | | | | | | | | |
| Grade 4 | 35 | — | 34 | — | 33 | — | 27 | 26 | 26 | 26 |
| Grade 8 | 40 | — | 41 | — | 40 | — | 35 | 34 | 32 | 32 |
| Grade 12 | 26 | — | 27 | — | 31 | — | 28 | 30 | — | 30 |
| **White–Hispanic gap** | | | | | | | | | | |
| Grade 4 | 25 | — | 25 | — | 27 | — | 22 | 20 | 21 | 21 |
| Grade 8 | 28 | — | 30 | — | 31 | — | 29 | 27 | 26 | 27 |
| Grade 12 | 20 | — | 21 | — | 22 | — | 24 | 24 | — | 23 |
| **Male–Female gap** | | | | | | | | | | |
| Grade 4 | 3 | 2 | 4 | — | 3 | — | 3 | 2 | 2 | 2 |
| Grade 8 | 1 | 2 | 3 | — | 2 | — | 4 | 2 | 2 | 2 |
| Grade 12 | 4 | 4 | 5 | — | 4 | — | 3 | 2 | — | 3 |

*Source:* Snyder, T.D., and Dillow, S.A. (2011). *Digest of Education Statistics 2010* (NCES 2011-015). National Center for Education Statistics, Institute of Education Sciences, U.S. Department of Education. Washington, DC.

**Figure 8.4 — Percentage of Twelfth Graders Performing At or Above *Proficient* (2009) in Mathematics and Reading, by Race.**

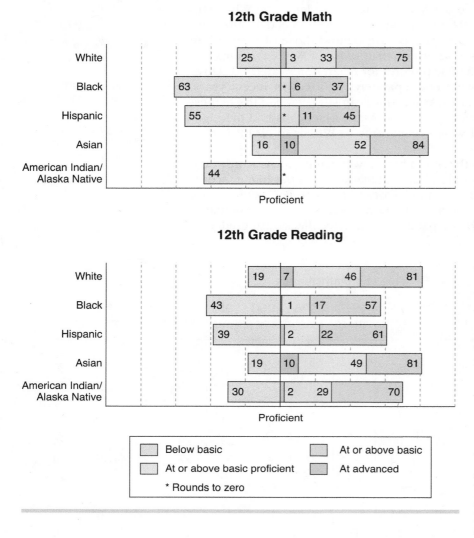

**12th Grade Math**

White · 25 · 3 · 33 · 75
Black · 63 · * · 6 · 37
Hispanic · 55 · * · 11 · 45
Asian · 16 · 10 · 52 · 84
American Indian/Alaska Native · 44 · *

Proficient

**12th Grade Reading**

White · 19 · 7 · 46 · 81
Black · 43 · 1 · 17 · 57
Hispanic · 39 · 2 · 22 · 61
Asian · 19 · 10 · 49 · 81
American Indian/Alaska Native · 30 · 2 · 29 · 70

Proficient

Below basic   At or above basic
At or above basic proficient   At advanced
* Rounds to zero

Of equal concern is the gap in achievement proficiency levels. As seen in the example in Figure 8.4, among 12th-grade students, in both reading and mathematics, Black, Hispanic and American Indian students are overrepresented among low scoring students, those below the basic proficiency level, and underrepresented at the advanced proficiency level. Similar results are true for 4th- and 8th-grade students.

## The Racial and Ethnic Attainment Gap

While the overall population and its subgroups are becoming more educated, ethnic and racial differences in educational attainment continue to exist. For example, although the proportion of the 25-year-old and older Hispanic population who have completed high school continues to increase, the gap in the dropout rate between Hispanics and other racial and ethnic groups remains significant. Most of the dropouts occur before grade 10. By the time Hispanics reach high school age, approximately 25% are two or more years over age for their grade level, a condition that places them at risk for dropping out. As seen in Figure 8.5, in 2010, 37% of Hispanic Americans 25 years of age or older had dropped out of high school, compared with 22% of Native Americans, 15% of African Americans, 11% of Asian Americans, and 8% of Whites. Hispanics as well as African Americans also tend to complete high school at an older age than Whites and Asian Americans, reflecting the fact that they are more likely than Whites or Asian Americans to fail and repeat one or more grades. In the attainment of postsecondary education, once again, the postsecondary attainment rate of Hispanic Americans has increased (from 26% in 1993 to 33% in 2010) but continues to lag behind the non-Hispanic population. As shown in Figure 8.5, 33% of Hispanic Americans 25 years old and older have attended college, compared to 60% of non-Hispanic Whites who have attended college and 69% of Asians. Hispanic college graduation rates increased from 1993 to 2010 but remained lower than those of all other racial groups. In fact, whereas 33 of every 100 White kindergarten students and 20 of every 100 African American kindergartners go on to graduate from college, only 14 of every 100 Hispanic American kindergartners later earn a bachelor's degree.

While the educational attainment rate for Hispanics is low, data indicate that Hispanic Americans, many of whom are first-generation college students, are matriculating to college at increasingly higher rates. The number of Hispanic undergraduates almost doubled between 1995 and 2009. Over the same period, the percentage of high school completers who enrolled in postsecondary

**For Your Reflection and Analysis**

To what do you attribute the proportional overrepresentation of Asian Americans in the sciences as opposed to such fields as education or social work?

**Figure 8.5 — Percentage Distribution of Adults Ages 25 and Over, by Highest Level of Education and Race/Ethnicity: 2010**

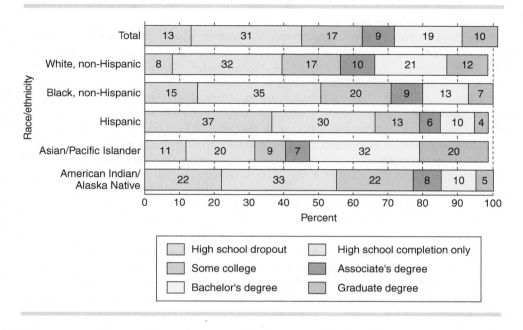

The comparative achievement of males education following completion increased from 54% to 64% (Aud, et al., 2010). It is estimated that by 2019, the number of Hispanic American undergraduates will almost equal the number of African American undergraduates (Hussar & Bailey, 2011).

Asian Americans have the highest percentage of postsecondary education completion of any racial or ethnic group—and they are completing their schooling at an ever-increasing rate. As shown in Figure 8.5, in 2010, approximately 52% of Asian Americans age 25 years and older had completed a bachelor's degree or higher, and 20% had completed an advanced degree, almost twice the percentage of Whites and almost three to four times the percentage of all other racial or ethnic groups.

## The Gender Gap in Reverse

Since the passage of Title IX in 1972, the large gaps that existed between males and females in educational achievement and attainment have seen a significant decline and in some cases have been eliminated. In fact, on the NAEP assessment of reading proficiency (see Table 8.2), females outscored males in each age group as they have since the test began. The opposite occurred in mathematics proficiency, where a very small but consistent gap in math scores between male and female students persists (see Table 8.2). In science, male students narrowly outperformed females in each age group (9-, 13-, and 17-year-olds) on the science NAEP assessment (Snyder & Dillow, 2011).

The comparative achievement of males and females on the SAT also demonstrates

Females now receive the majority of postsecondary degrees.

a clear pattern of gender difference. Males have consistently outscored females on both the reading and mathematics sections of the SAT. The gap scores on the reading test have been smaller and have narrowed over the last decade, while the larger gap in mathematics has seen only a slight decline.

At the postsecondary level, educational attainment also increased for both males and females. However, female attainment has increased at a faster pace than male attainment, with the number of females 25 and older with a bachelor's degree or more in 2006 (26.8 million) more than double the figure of 20 years earlier. For over a decade, women have earned more master's degrees than men, and since 2007 women have earned more doctorates than men, trends that are projected to continue into the next decade (Hussar & Bailey, 2011). The female advantage in postsecondary degree attainment is particularly apparent among Black and Hispanic women, who receive 66% and 61% of bachelor's degrees awarded in their respective racial groups (Knapp, Kelly-Reid, & Ginder, 2010). The success of women in postsecondary education is noteworthy in that they represent 60% or more of students with characteristics that place them at a disadvantage for completion: low income, older, married with children, or single parent (Peter & Hern, 2005). In effect, the attainment gap between males and females, or at least one that favored males, has disappeared, and the gap favoring females is projected to widen.

Although female participation in higher education has increased, females are still underrepresented in majors such as computer and information sciences, engineering, mathematics, and the natural sciences, and overrepresented in the somewhat lower-paying fields like education.

A number of theories have been suggested as to why males and females achieve differently. The most common explanations are that the differences can be largely attributed to the gender-role socialization that children receive from parents and the gender-role stereotyping and sexism they experience in school and in society. Parents are the first to teach gender roles, beginning with their simple choice of clothing, the child's living space, their toys, and so forth. Parents also interact with males and females differently. For example, research suggests that preschool girls are read to more than boys, which may contribute to later higher reading achievement for females. The gender difference in college completion rates can be explained in part by declining gender discrimination, the increased incentives for higher education, and the high secondary school dropout rate of male students.

The school experience also contributes to gender socialization, but it impacts the achievement of male and female students differently. For example, boys are more likely than girls to experience serious behavioral problems at school and engage in risky behaviors such as drug use. They are also more apt to be diagnosed with a learning disability or emotional disturbance and to be bullied, be in a physical fight, be victimized, or carry a weapon (CDC, 2010). Other factors that have been identified as contributing to the differential achievement and attainment of male and female students include the following:

1. Girls spend more time than boys talking, reading, drawing, or journal writing—all activities which give them a verbal advantage and greater phonological awareness, the key stepping stone to learning to read (Eliot, 2010).
2. Boys spend more time than girls playing catch, as well as constructing and playing high speed driving and targeting games which develop the spatial skills important in higher mathematics and science (Eliot, 2010).
3. Girls tend to be more concerned about doing well in school, are more engaged in classroom activities, and work more diligently on assignments (Ormond, 2010).
4. Textbooks and reading materials at the elementary level tend to reflect the interest and dispositions of girls. As a result, boys are bored by the books and stories they are assigned to read (Rhodes, 2010).
5. In the era of NCLB, "test oriented teachers focus energy on conventional exercises in reading, writing and other seatwork, areas in which girls tend to excel" (Von Drehle, 2007, p. 42).

**Reflect on Diversity**
Speculate on the reasons why girls are read to more than boys. Are the reasons gender-based?

6. Females are less likely to repeat a grade or drop out of school. However, girls who do repeat a grade are more likely to drop out of school than boys, and girls who drop out (often due to pregnancy) are less likely to return than boys.
7. Boys are more likely to be enrolled in gifted math and science programs, whereas girls are more often enrolled in gifted programs that focus on language arts (Sadker, 2001).
8. Boys are more likely than girls to be enrolled in higher-level high school mathematics courses (e.g., calculus) or related courses such as physics.

## Students with Exceptionalities

Students with exceptionalities include both gifted and talented students and students with mental and physical disabilities. Gifted and talented students are estimated to make up 6.7% of the student population (Snyder & Dillow, 2011). Students with mental and physical disabilities who are enrolled in federally supported programs comprise 13.2% of the student population of the public schools in the United States (Snyder & Dillow, 2011).

Education for students with disabilities has grown steadily since the 1970s, when two historic cases (*Pennsylvania Association of Retarded Citizens v. Commonwealth of Pennsylvania*, 1972, and *Mills v. Board of Education of the District of Columbia*, 1972) mandated services for special education students. In addition, two major federal laws, Section 504 of the Rehabilitation Act of 1973 and the Education for All Handicapped Children Act (EHA) of 1975, provided federal support for a wide range of programs and services for students with disabilities.

Since the passage of the EHA, renamed the Individuals with Disabilities Education Act (IDEA), the number of children served by federally supported programs increased every year until 2004. However, since 2004 the number has shown some decline. The IDEA recognizes the 13 categories of disabilities listed in Table 8.3. The growth in the number of students served under the IDEA is due not only to an

### Table 8.3 — Children 3 to 21 Years Old Served in Federally Supported Programs for the Disabled, by Type of Disability: Selected Years, 1976–1977 to 2008–2009 (numbers in thousands)

| Type of Disability | 1976–77 | 1980–81 | 1990–91 | 1995–96 | 2000–01 | 2005–06 | 2008–09 |
|---|---|---|---|---|---|---|---|
| All disabilities | 3,694 | 4,144 | 4,710 | 5,573 | 6,296 | 6,713 | 6,483 |
| Specific learning disabilities | 796 | 1,462 | 2,129 | 2,579 | 2,868 | 2,735 | 2,476 |
| Speech or language impairments | 1,302 | 1,168 | 985 | 1,022 | 1,409 | 1,468 | 1,426 |
| Intellectual disability | 961 | 830 | 535 | 570 | 600 | 593 | 556 |
| Emotional disturbance | 283 | 347 | 390 | 438 | 481 | 477 | 420 |
| Hearing impairments | 88 | 79 | 58 | 67 | 78 | 79 | 78 |
| Orthopedic impairments | 87 | 58 | 49 | 63 | 83 | 71 | 70 |
| Other health impairments | 141 | 98 | 55 | 133 | 303 | 570 | 659 |
| Visual impairments | 38 | 31 | 23 | 25 | 29 | 29 | 29 |
| Multiple disabilities | — | 68 | 96 | 93 | 133 | 141 | 130 |
| Deaf-blindness | — | 3 | 1 | 1 | 1 | 2 | 2 |
| Traumatic brain injury | — | — | — | 39 | 110 | 247 | 362 |
| Developmental delay | — | — | — | — | 178 | 339 | 354 |
| Autism | — | — | — | 28 | 94 | 223 | 336 |

*Source:* Snyder, T. D., & Dillow, S. A. (2011). *Digest of Education Statistics 2010* (NCES 2011-015). National Center for Education Statistics, Institute of Education Sciences, U.S. Department of Education. Washington, DC.

increase in the total student population, but also in large part to the growth in the number of students classified as having a specific learning disability. A child is considered to have a specific learning disability if he or she has a disorder or delayed development in one or more of the processes of thinking, speaking, reading, writing, listening, or performing arithmetic calculations. As shown in Table 8.3, the number of students with disabilities classified as specific learning disabled more than tripled and their percentage in the disabled student population rose from 22% in 1977 to 38% in 2009. The second largest category or enrollment for students with disabilities was speech or language impairment, followed by mental retardation.

American Indians/Alaska Natives and Blacks are more likely than any other racial or ethnic group to receive services under the IDEA and are represented in special education in higher percentages than in the overall student population. About 14% of American Indian/Alaska Native children and 12% of Black children received services in 2009, compared to 9% of Hispanic children, 8% of White children, and 5% of Asian/Pacific Islander children (Aud, et al., 2010).

The disproportionality of minority students in special education classrooms is a concern of policymakers and educators alike. Minority students are two to three times more likely than White students to be identified as having a developmental disability or being emotionally disturbed. These are the so-called judgmental disability categories, which involve some degree of subjectivity in the evaluation process. These minority students, many of whom come from low socioeconomic backgrounds, often never graduate from high school (Samuels, 2007).

One group of students that is **not** specifically included under the IDEA but is present in almost every classroom is students with attention deficit–hyperactivity disorder (ADHD). ADHD is recognized as a factor which may contribute to "other health impairment." ADHD is the most commonly diagnosed childhood psychiatric disorder, affecting 3% to 7% of the population. ADHD is a condition characterized by symptoms of inattention or hyperactivity–impulsivity "for at least 6 months and to a degree that is maladaptive and inconsistent with developmental level" (American Psychiatric Association, 2000, p. 80). Some students with ADHD may also have a learning or emotional disability and be receiving support under the IDEA or Section 504. Boys are three times more likely to be diagnosed with ADHD than girls; however, recent research indicates that the incidence of ADHD in girls may be higher than previously thought, but, because they exhibit lower levels of symptoms, girls may not be identified as often (Friend, 2011).

Another group of exceptional students not included under the IDEA are students who are gifted and talented. NCLB defines gifted and talented students as:

> children and youth who give evidence of high achievement in areas such as intellectual, creative, artistic or leadership capacity, or excel in specific academic fields, and who need services or activities not ordinarily provided by the schools to fully develop these capabilities. (NCLB Act, P. L. 107–110, Title IX, Part A)

No federal legislation requires states to provide services to gifted and talented students and, unfortunately, most states (29) and school districts do not offer any funding for gifted education, making the number of gifted and talented students in the United States difficult to estimate. However, the National Center for Education Statistics (Snyder & Dillow, 2011) estimates that there are approximately 3.2 million academically gifted children in the public schools, and another not estimated number of artistically or otherwise talented youth. As previously stated, Blacks, Hispanics, and Native Americans are underrepresented in programs for the gifted and talented, while Whites and Asian Americans are disproportionately represented.

## Language Diversity

For many students in the public schools, English is not their native language. Many of these **language-minority** students are immigrants and face the double challenge of attempting to adapt to a different culture and learn a new language. In 2007 over

11 million school-age students, 21% of the elementary–secondary student population, spoke a language other than English at home, and over 5% spoke English with difficulty. Among the racial/ethnic groups, higher percentages of Hispanic (69%) and Asian (64%) students spoke a language other than English at home (Aud, et al., 2010). Many of these are referred to as being limited English proficient (LEP). In 2009 there were over 5.3 million LEP students in grades PK–12, representing approximately 10.8% of the total PK–12 population (National Clearinghouse for English Language Acquisition, 2011).

In addition to the challenges associated with having limited English proficiency, LEP students often are characterized by a number of the previously discussed factors found to be associated with underachievement and underattainment. For example, LEP children often have not attended preschool and begin school less ready to learn than their non-LEP peers, they have been read to less by their parents, and they are more likely to live in households in poverty with its associated health risks.

As described in the next chapter, 80% of LEP students, approximately 4 million students, are enrolled in language instruction education programs designed to ensure that they attain English proficiency and meet the same standards for academic achievement expected of all students.

## Summary

In this chapter, the schools, the family, the peer group, religion, and the mass media were examined as agents of socialization. Of these institutions, the family has undergone the most significant changes since World War II. As a result of those changes, many of the earlier functions of the family have now been transferred to the school. At the same time, as children spend more time with media, its influence on their behavior and school achievement has increased.

There are a number of perspectives on the primary purposes and expectations of schooling; the functionalist perspective, the conflict theory perspective, and the interactionist perspective. Among these, the issue of whether the schools promote social selection or social mobility remains the most controversial.

Many people would agree that there are numerous opportunities for education, but most believe that equal educational opportunity is more a myth than a fact in the American educational system. The myth of equal educational opportunity is particularly evident when one examines differences in the educational achievement and attainment of socioeconomic groups, ethnic groups, racial groups, and males and females, as well as the challenges faced by students with disabilities and language-minority students. In the next chapter, we will look at some of the strategies that have been employed to increase equality of educational opportunity and ameliorate the effects of economic and cultural discrimination.

# TEACHER OF THE YEAR

People ask me all the time, "Why do you teach?" I always tell them "I teach because I understand the importance of being an educator and the importance an educator plays in the role of shaping a child." I came to the United States as a war refugee with absolutely nothing and I didn't speak English. I remember the teachers who shaped me, gave me confidence, loved me, cared for me, and allowed me to see the potential of who I could become. They're why I chose to be a teacher. I wanted to honor them. As a teacher now myself, I want to inspire my students to see that they can accomplish anything that they want to, despite any obstacles or any hardships that come into their lives. I want them to see that education is more than just training for a career; education is a form of self-empowerment. It's becoming an independent thinker in order to change the world for the better. If that's my legacy as a teacher, then it's the best thing I'll have been able to do with my life.

*Yung Bui-Kincer*
*Alabama*

# PROFESSIONAL DEVELOPMENT
*Workshop*

## *Prepare for the State Licensure Examination*

Kelly Fuller is a second-year, fourth-grade teacher at Martin Luther King Middle School (MLKMS), an inner-city school. MLKMS has a student body that is 15% Hispanic, many of whom are recent immigrants and non-English speakers; and 4% African Americans, many of whose families have lived in the neighborhood for decades and whose parents also probably attended MLKMS.

Kelly Fuller had just received the results of the state standardized test for her students in reading and mathematics. She was alone when she turned to the large sealed manila envelope that held the test results. Her students were still at the library working on their book report assignment, so she had time to carefully review the scores of each student.

Mrs. Fuller was disappointed to see that the majority of her students had made only a slight gain in reading and no gain in mathematics. Reading scores had increased from the 48th percentile to the 49th percentile, while mathematics scores remained at the 43rd percentile. Kelly had worked hard all year on improving student math skills and had really expected to see an improvement in math scores. She is concerned about how her students, their parents, and school and district administrators will receive the test results.

As she continued to stare at the test results, Kelly's memory flashed back to two years ago and her interview with Joe Edwards, the principal. Joe had said, "Kelly, I want you to know that one of the most difficult parts of your job here at Martin Luther King School will be to not get discouraged and disappointed. In their few short years on this earth, the kids that you will be teaching have known disappointment far beyond what you and I can even imagine. Our job is to build them up and instill in them a purpose for trying, no matter what the outcome. Students are more than just test scores to us."

Moments later, her students filed back into the class, still energized and excited about their book reports. Tommy Sanchez and Billy Middleton could hardly contain their excitement when asking Mrs. Fuller if they could do a combined book report on *The Latest Discovery of Extinct Reptiles in the Sonoran Desert*. Responding, she put aside her thoughts and disappointment regarding the state test results and refocused her attention on the 26 nine-year-olds who were settling back in their seats.

1. Differentiate between the two major types of standardized tests. Discuss the advantages and disadvantages of each approach.

2. How can Kelly best communicate the results of the state tests to students and parents to ensure that they understand the limits of the tests?

3. Statewide testing programs generally serve different purposes than teachers' classroom assessments. Explain the major purposes of a teacher's classroom assessment program.

### Build Your Knowledge Base

1. In response to the opening vignette, which describes David Marshall's paper, what are some of the possible ways he might reconceptualize the basic concept of society?

2. Describe some of the ways in which the structure of your family has changed over time. To what extent have those changes been positive? To what extent have they been negative?

3. How could you, as a teacher, mitigate the negative influence of television on children's aggressive behavior? What suggestions would you make to parents?

4. Reflect on the high school from which you graduated. To what extent did it promote upward social mobility? In what ways did it resemble a miniature factory system?

5. Discuss what is meant by the cycle of poverty. What can the schools do to break this cycle?

6. Discuss the impact of differing cultural values on school achievement and attainment. Give specific examples.

7. Discuss the common factors contributing to the underachievement of Hispanic Americans, African Americans, and Native Americans and Alaska Natives.

8. What are the levels of educational attainment of the females in your family? The males? What factors account for any differences that may exist between the two groups? To what extent are the factors evident today?

## Develop Your Portfolio

1. Review the purposes and expectations of schooling. To what extent do you tend to agree or disagree with the purposes and expectations described? Imagine that you have been asked to write an editorial for the local newspaper regarding what you believe are the purposes and expectations of schooling. Prepare your editorial from the perspective of a critical theorist. Place your editorial in your portfolio under **INTASC Standard 8, Instructional Strategies**.

2. Review the various ethnic and racial differences in school achievement that are discussed in this chapter. Begin to collect artifacts (instructional materials) that have been adapted to diverse learners, including those learners who represent a variety of ethnic, racial, and social class differences. Place your artifacts in your portfolio under **INTASC Standard 2, Learner Differences**.

## MyEducationLab

Go to **Topic 3, Schools and Society** in the MyEducationLab (www.myeducationlab.com) for *Foundations of American Education*, where you can:

- Find learning outcomes for schools and society along with the national standards that connect to these outcomes.
- Complete Assignments and Activities that can help you more deeply understand the chapter content.
- Apply and practice your understanding of the core teaching skills identified in the chapter with the Building Teaching Skills and Dispositions learning units.
- Examine challenging situations and cases presented in the IRIS Center Resources.

- Access additional video clips of CCSSO National Teachers of the Year award winners responding to the question, "Why Do I Teach?" in the Teacher Talk section.
- Check your comprehension on the content covered in the chapter with the Study Plan. Here you will be able to take a chapter quiz, receive feedback on your answers, and then access Review, Practice, and Enrichment activities to enhance your understanding of chapter content.
- Use the Online Lesson Plan Builder to practice lesson planning and integrating national and state standards into your planning.

# Responding to Diversity

At the end of the second week of school, a student, Linda Wilson, comes to the counseling office with a problem. She complains that she has been the subject of harassment by the teacher and students in the auto mechanics class. According to Linda, the boys refuse to work with her on small group projects, ignore her when she talks to them, and on various occasions have hidden her tools or put grease in her book. One day when she went to her car, she found all the air let out of her tires with a note on the windshield saying, "Do it yourself if you're such a red-hot mechanic!" She says she knows Mr. Thompson, the teacher, is aware of the students' behavior but just ignores it. According to Linda, Mr. Thompson acts as if she's stupid when she asks a question, always refers to the class as "you men," and when discussing employment opportunities makes it clear that auto mechanics is for men only. Linda says she's really interested in auto mechanics, but under the circumstances wants to drop the course.

Do you agree with Linda that she should drop the course? Why or why not? What other options would you suggest to Linda? What evidence is there of sexism, sex-role stereotyping, or sex discrimination?

As we have seen in previous chapters of this text, a variety of circumstances have combined in society and the schools to restrict the educational opportunities of many students, including students such as Linda Wilson. This chapter presents an overview of a number of programs and strategies for responding to a diverse and multicultural society while combating inequity and inequality in education. As you review these strategies, consider the following learning objectives:

- Differentiate the concepts of multiculturalism, assimilation, cultural pluralism, and multicultural education.
- Discuss the various types of bilingual education and the controversy surrounding the education of linguistic minority children.
- Describe the major compensatory education programs and their current status.
- Outline the principles inherent in the Individuals with Disabilities Education Act and their impact on American education.
- Discuss the progress of gender equity in education and the process for its attainment.

# Diversity and Culture

Multiculturalism is simply a demographic fact. Teaching only those students who share a teacher's or a community's background is neither desirable nor likely to happen. And teaching diverse groups of students only from a teacher's or community's perspective (as if all shared the same past) is unacceptable. For American teachers, *multicultural* cannot be just a lesson, a curriculum, a teaching style, or a philosophy. In the 21st century, non-White and immigrant voices and languages will be heard or ignored, honored or derided, but they will not be silenced or assimilated out of existence. (Oakes & Lipton, 2004, p. vii)

The diversity of the U.S. population in terms of race, ethnicity, socioeconomic status, gender, and exceptionalities was discussed in the preceding chapter. There are, of course, many other ways in which the population differs, including age, religion, sexual orientation, and geography. One very important difference in the population is their cultural identity. **Culture** is defined as the behavioral patterns, ideas, values, attitudes, norms, religious and moral beliefs, customs, laws, language, institutions, art, artifacts, and symbols characteristic of a given people during a given period of time.

The concept of culture can be used in a macro and micro sense. All members of a society share, to some extent, some broad ideals that define them as a member of a specific *macroculture*. For example, if introduced to someone in another country, you would probably identify yourself as "American" before you would identify your religion or political affiliation. In complex societies such as the United States, individuals will also be members of various subgroups, or *microcultures*, that are distinguished by their ethnic, racial, religious, geographic, social, economic, or lifestyle traits. Most people are members of a variety of microcultures. For example, you might be a visually impaired, Asian American male from an upper-middle-class background who is Catholic and lives in the South. The interaction of the macroculture and various microcultures can be conceived as depicted in Figure 9.1.

Culture is made up of different elements or layers that together comprise a complex system of language, symbols, customs, values, and beliefs. Teachers need to understand these elements and how they influence student learning. These elements are:

- *Language, symbols, and artifacts* (means of communication)—language, dialects preferred, proverbs, signs, sayings, jokes, stories, myths, analogies, folklore, art forms, heroes, dances, rituals, children's games, currency, holidays, history (family, national, and global).

- *Customs, practices, and interactional patterns* (means of interaction)—verbal (tone of voice, phrases used) and nonverbal (eye contact, proximity of stance, gestures) communication patterns, family behaviors, governmental and social institutions, conversational styles (formal-business, casual, ritualized), friendship patterns, community roles, and gender roles.

- *Shared values, beliefs, norms, and expectations* (values driving people, groups)—attitudes, cultural values, religious and spiritual beliefs, fears, laws, standards, norms, levels of political participation, and expectations. (Pang, 2005, pp. 39–40)

**Figure 9.1 — Macroculture and Microculture**

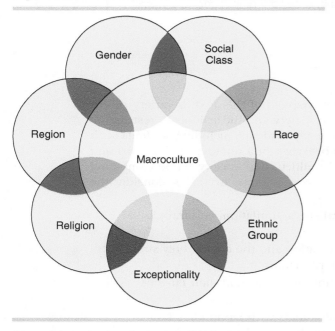

*Source:* Information from Banks, J. A. (2006). *Cultural diversity and education: Foundations, curriculum, and teaching* (5th ed.). Boston: Allyn & Bacon.

Children learn the language, customs, beliefs, norms, and expectations of their culture by the process of **enculturation**. They are taught formally and informally by their parents and other adults. Children or adults who are outside the dominant culture, or are new to the dominant culture because of their minority or immigrant status, learn the dominant culture by a process of assimilation. Throughout much of the history of the United States, the schools have attempted to force the assimilation of minorities and immigrants by encouraging English-only classrooms, the Anglicization of names, and the prohibition of the native language, even outside the school environment. Moreover, the open and hidden curriculum discussed in Chapter 14 taught and supported the values of the dominant culture over those of the minority culture.

## Cultural Influences on Teaching, Learning, and Behavior

Culture influences almost every aspect of the teaching and learning process. Cultural views on gender roles have been a major factor in the dominance of males in administrative positions in school systems as well as their underrepresentation in elementary classrooms. Culture also influences the selection of curriculum materials, what and who they portray, and how they portray the content. Culture influences the way teachers teach, how they attempt to motivate, and the very assumptions they have about students. Culture also influences how those outside the school view the teacher, or more fundamentally, the purpose of schooling. For example, Hispanic parents tend to regard the teacher as an expert and defer to them, while European Americans are more likely to be questioning and more involved in school curricular or governance issues.

Culture also has a major influence on how students think, process information, and learn—in effect, their **cognitive styles**. A number of cognitive styles have been identified and researched. Perhaps the most well known are the differences in cognitive styles found between those who are characterized as field-independent analytic thinkers and those who are characterized as field-dependent descriptive thinkers. Field-independent learners view a part of a field as discrete from the surrounding field, whereas field-dependent learners rely on the environment to place parts as embedded in an organized field. Field-independent students prefer to work on independent projects, like competition, and approach tasks on a step-by-step sequence. In contrast, students with a field-dependent style will be more likely to attend to global or holistic aspects of the curriculum and prefer group as well as multiple or cooperative activities (Cushner, McClelland, & Safford, 2009; Salend, 2011).

Research has shown that differences in learning and cognitive styles may be related to cultural factors. For example, there is some evidence that members of the dominant cultural group in the United States tend to be more field independent, whereas many members of the oppressed groups tend to be more field dependent. Research has also shown that children from cultures in which children are subject to more control and pressure to conform are more field dependent. If teachers are aware of their students' preferred learning styles and sensitive to the importance of cultural factors on learning, they will be able to design learning activities that accommodate those differences in learning styles (e.g., group versus individual learning, concrete versus abstract presentations). If teachers are unaware of or misunderstand their students' cultural learning styles, they may underestimate or overestimate the students' cognitive abilities and stereotype them (Bennett, 2011). At the same time, teachers should avoid stereotyping students and remember that within-group differences can be just as great as between-group differences. Table 9.1 provides an overview of some aspects of the preferred learning styles of African American, Hispanic, and Native American students.

## For Your Reflection and Analysis

Did you or any of your ancestors come to the United States as immigrants? What was your assimilation experience like?

## For Your Reflection and Analysis

Identify your cognitive style and how it has influenced your learning.

**Table 9.1 — Learning Styles of African American, Hispanic, and Native American Learners**

| African American Learners Tend To | Hispanic Learners Tend To | Native American Learners Tend To |
| --- | --- | --- |
| Respond to things in terms of the whole instead of isolated parts | Prefer group learning situations | Prefer visual, spatial, and perceptual information rather than verbal |
| Prefer inferential reasoning as opposed to deductive or inductive | Be sensitive to the opinions of others | Learn privately rather than in public |
| Approximate space and numbers rather than adhere to exactness or accuracy | Be extrinsically motivated | Use mental images to remember and understand words and concepts rather than word associations |
| Focus on people rather than things | Prefer concrete representations to abstract ones | Watch and then do rather than employ trial and error |
| Be more proficient in nonverbal than verbal communication | | Value conciseness of speech, slightly varied intonations, and limited vocal range |

*Source:* Irvine and York (1995) as cited in Dilworth, M. E., & Brown, C. E. (2001). Consider the difference: Teaching and learning in culturally rich schools. In V. Richardson (Ed.), *Handbook of research on teaching* (4th ed.). Washington, DC: American Educational Research Association, p. 656.

How children understand what teachers attempt to teach them is strongly influenced and possibly limited by their cultural identity (Zarrillo, 2012). Where there are significant differences between the culture of the student and the culture of the school, a *cultural dissonance* may occur. For example, many lessons that focus on skill development are presented in isolation and rely heavily on step-by-step analytical thinking. However, students with field-sensitive (i.e., field-dependent) cognitive styles may not perform well, "not necessarily because of lack of ability but rather because the instructional approach did not relate well with their strengths. If such lessons are the rule rather than the exception, over time the academic performance of the field-sensitive learner may be artificially depressed" (Friend, 2011, p. 73).

Culture is also important in how both the teacher and the learner view intelligence. There is a growing body of evidence that intelligence is defined differently between and within cultures (Sternberg, Grigorenko, & Bridglall, 2007). In particular, differences are found between cultures that emphasize the social aspects of intelligence (e.g., certain African and Latino cultures) and those that adopt the more conventional Western, cognitive concept of intelligence. Research has also found that teachers tend to reward those children who were socialized into the same view of intelligence as their own (Sternberg et al., 2007). And, given that many of the choices we make as teachers are influenced by implicit theories of intelligence, "to the extent these theories favor the behaviors, mores, and values of certain groups over others, so will our educational practice. Meanwhile, many of our children will be held back in their intellectual development" (Sternberg et al., 2007, p. 67).

Many aspects of a student's behavior and a teacher's response to it may also be influenced by culture. For example, in some cultures it would be acceptable for students to be very animated and socially engaged when working on a group project. However, many teachers would find this behavior unacceptable and would ask the group to "tone it down" or "work quietly." Some other cultural considerations related to student behavior are briefly described in Figure 9.2.

**Reflect on Diversity**
What are the limits of behavior teachers must accept because it is acceptable in the student's culture?

## Figure 9.2 — Cultural Influences on Behavior

### Interactonal Styles

- **Degree of directness.** In some cultures, it is preferable to "get right to the point" in the most unequivocable manner possible—without considering how the listener might feel about what you have to say. In other cultures, preference is given to less direct communication styles with more elaborate introductory or intervening discourse and greater deference to how the message is received by the listener.

- **Level of emotionality.** In some cultures there may be a dramatic display of emotions through voice volume, voice tone, gestures, and facial expressions, while in others this is considered inappropriate.

- **Degree of movement and vocalizations.** In some cultures, it is common for more than one person to speak at a time. In other cultures, this practice is seen as rude. Likewise, in some cultures, a higher level of physical activity and verbal exchange may be a natural accompaniment to cognitive activity (e.g., school seatwork), while in others this is not typical.

- **Displays of consideration for others.** In some cultures, consideration of others is shown by refraining from behaviors that may offend them. In other cultures, consideration is more often shown by being tolerant of the behaviors of others that one might personally find unpleasant or offensive. For example, in some cultures one may show consideration of others by not playing music loudly (because others may be disturbed by it). In other cultures, the tendency may be learn to tolerate loud music if someone else is enjoying it.

- **Attitudes toward personal space.** In some cultures, speakers customarily remain at least 2 feet apart when speaking to one another. Failure to recognize this is often interpreted as a desire to seek intimacy or as a prelude to aggression. In other cultures, closer interactions are common and physically distancing oneself may be interpreted as aloofness.

### Response to Authority Figures

- **Perceptions of authority figures.** In some cultures, students may view all adults as authority figures by virtue of their status as adults. In other cultures, position may be a primary determiner (e.g., teachers, police officers). In yet other cultures, designation as an authority figure must be earned by behavior.

- **Display of respect for authority figures.** In some cultures students show respect for authority figures by not making eye contact; in other cultures, the opposite is true. Likewise, questioning authority figures is considered disrespectful in some cultures; in other cultures this practice may be valued as an indicator of critical thinking.

- **Response to management styles.** In some cultures, having a permissive management style is viewed as a way to encourage the child's individuality and self-expression. In other cultures, such a management style would indicate weakness or lack of concern.

In considering these cultural influences on behavior, what examples can you think of that illustrate how they may be displayed in classroom behaviors? What are the implications for educators?

*Source:* From Marilyn Friend. *Special education: Contemporary Perspectives for School Professionals*, p. 73. Published by Allyn & Bacon, Boston, MA. Copyright © 2011 by Pearson Education. Reprinted by permission of the publisher.

## Culturally Responsive Teaching

In most classrooms the teacher will encounter students from various microcultures, be they racial, ethnic, religious, or socioeconomic. These students bring with them the cultural influences just discussed. Understanding and responding to the cultural context of these students is one of the most difficult challenges many teachers face. However, while it is not possible to create an environment that is culturally congruent for all students all the time, it is possible to create an affirming environment that values and respects the culture of the student and that integrates information about various cultures into the curriculum (Pang, 2005). Research has shown that perhaps the best way this can be accomplished is through culturally responsive and relevant teaching. The term **culturally responsive teaching** has been defined as:

> an approach to instruction that responds to the sociocultural context and seeks to integrate the cultural content of the learner in shaping

Schools are becoming increasingly multicultural.

an effective learning environment. Cultural content includes aspects such as experiences, knowledge, events, values, role models, perspectives, and issues that arise from the community. Cultural context refers to the behaviors, interactional patterns, historical experiences, and underlying expectations and values of students. (Pang, 2005, p. 337)

To become culturally responsive, teachers must reflect on their own cultural assumptions, values, and biases and how these influence their expectations and interactions with students. Culturally responsive teachers must be observant and alert to the classroom behaviors and verbal and nonverbal communication of students. There is no "one-size-fits-all" approach to culturally responsive teaching. Every student must be studied individually and stereotypes about a particular group discarded: Black students from rural Mississippi are as different from Black students in Watts as second-generation Cuban Americans are from new Mexican American immigrants. Nor will a piecemeal sprinkling of colorful aspects of a culture create culturally responsive teaching. Culturally responsive teaching is based on the constructivist view of learning, discussed in Chapter 4, which holds that students create their own meaning based on current and past knowledge and experience. Culturally responsive teaching occurs when teachers are sensitive to cultural differences and when culture is naturally integrated into instructional and assessment practices, classroom management, and the curriculum, not simply added on. Children need to see themselves in the curriculum and in curricular materials. When students see their cultural background and culturally derived knowledge in the curriculum, they are more likely to be engaged, see schooling as relevant, and achieve academically (Rosenberg, Westling, & McLeskey, 2008). The role of the culturally responsive teacher from the constructivist perspective is to help students build a bridge between what they already know about a topic and what they need to know (Villegas & Lucas, 2007).

## For Your Reflection and Analysis

Can you think of a teacher who could be described as culturally responsive? Defend your choice.

## Strategies for Teaching Culturally Diverse Students

A variety of strategies are available for teaching culturally diverse students. Among those the research has identified as being most effective are the following:

*Emphasizing verbal interactions.* Use activities that encourage students to respond verbally to the material in creative ways such as group discussions, role plays, storytelling, group recitations, chorus, responsive reading, and rap.

*Teaching students to use self-talk.* Encourage and teach students to learn new material by verbalizing it to themselves, such as thinking aloud.

*Facilitating divergent thinking.* Encourage students to explore and devise unique solutions to issues and problems through activities such as brainstorming group discussions, debates, and responding to open-ended questions.

*Using small-group instruction and cooperative learning.* Allow students to work in small groups, and use cooperative learning arrangements including peer tutoring and cross-age tutoring.

*Employing verve in the classroom.* Introduce *verve,* a high level of energy, exuberance, and action, into the classroom by displaying enthusiasm for teaching and learning, using choral responding, moving around the classroom, varying your voice quality, snapping your fingers, using facial expressions, and encouraging students to use their bodies to act out and demonstrate content.

*Focusing on real-world tasks.* Introduce content, language, and learning by relating them to students' home, school, and community life, as well as to their cultures and experiences.

*Promoting teacher–student interactions.* Use teaching methods based on exchanges between students and teachers. Ask frequent questions, affirm students' responses, give feedback, offer demonstrations and explanations, and rephrase, review, and summarize material. (Salend, 2011, pp. 311–312)

Creating culturally responsive teaching and effective classrooms is a process that involves virtually every aspect of educational practice. While the processes are challenging and sometimes frustrating, they are vital to the fullest development of all children of every microculture. Teachers must keep in mind that teaching is an ethical activity, and they have an ethical obligation to help every student learn (Villegas & Lucas, 2007).

# Multicultural Education

**Multicultural education** represents a broader response to diversity than culturally responsible teaching. Multicultural education is an approach to teaching and learning that is based on recognizing, accepting, and affirming a broad view of human differences and similarities. Multicultural education is for all students and all classrooms, not just minority students or classrooms for ELL students. The primary goals of multicultural education are: (1) to help students gain greater self-understanding by viewing themselves from the perspective of other cultures; (2) to provide students with cultural, ethnic, and language alternatives to the traditional Anglocentric curriculum; (3) to enable all students to learn and develop the knowledge, skills, and attitudes needed to successfully participate in and contribute to their community culture, the mainstream culture, and across other ethnic cultures; (4) to reduce discrimination against ethnic and racial groups; and (5) to help students acquire the skills they need to function effectively in an increasingly globalized and technological world (Banks, 2008).

James Banks (2008), a leading expert on multicultural education, describes multicultural education as having five dimensions:

1. The *content integration dimension,* which deals with the extent to which teachers use examples, data, and information from a variety of cultures and groups to illustrate the key concepts, principles, generalizations, and theories in the subject or discipline.
2. The *knowledge construction process dimension,* which relates to the way teachers help students understand how knowledge is created and how it is influenced by the racial, ethnic, gender, and social-class positions of individuals and groups.
3. The *prejudice reduction dimension,* which focuses on the characteristics of children's racial attitudes and how they can be modified by teaching methods and materials.
4. The *equity pedagogy dimension,* which exists when teachers use techniques and teaching methods that facilitate the academic achievement of students from diverse racial, cultural, and social-class groups.
5. The *empowering school culture and social structure dimension,* which would require the examination and restructuring of the culture and organization of the school so that students from diverse racial, ethnic, and social-class groups will experience equality and a sense of empowerment. (pp. 31–35)

## *Approaches to Multicultural Education*

To accomplish the goals inherent in these dimensions, multicultural education employs a variety of curricular, instructional, and other educational practices. Sleeter and Grant (2009) have developed a typology of the five most commonly used approaches to multicultural education. Some approaches emphasize making the curriculum more inclusive, others on improving intergroup relations. The five approaches are discussed next and illustrated in Figure 9.3.

### Teaching the Exceptional and Culturally Different Approach

The goal of the *teaching the exceptional and culturally different approach* to multicultural education is to assimilate or mainstream students of all races, classes, abilities, language dominance, and sexual orientation into the same classroom. Sleeter and Grant (2009) criticize this approach because of its identification of students as being "culturally deprived" or with "disabilities," because these terms endorse

**Figure 9.3 — Five Approaches to Multicultural Education**

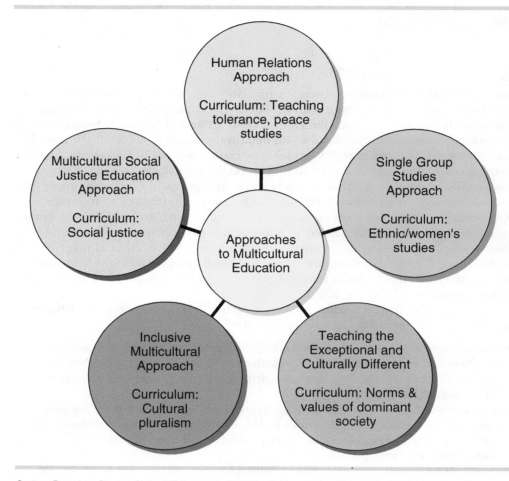

*Source:* Based on Sleeter, C. E., & Grant, C. A. (2009). *Making choices for multicultural education: Five approaches to race, class, and gender* (6th ed.). New York: John Wiley & Sons.

teacher expectations of academic deficits or behavioral problems. It is also criticized as being assimilationist and a cultural elitist approach that seeks to eliminate minority cultures.

## Human Relations Approach

The *human relations approach* to multicultural education is the approach Sleeter and Grant (2009) say is the most popular among White elementary teachers and those who work with special education students. The human relations approach attempts to help students understand the commonalities among all people and to accept their differences. Its goals are to reduce stereotyping and promote social cohesion (harmony) and tolerance. Unfortunately, if not done well, this approach can simplify aspects of culture and be simply a "tourist curricula" teaching primarily the food, clothing, and folk stories of other cultures. It is also criticized for not looking critically at issues of inequality and discrimination.

## Single-Group Studies Approach

The goal of the *single-group studies approach* to multicultural education is to promote social equality and raise the status and power of certain oppressed groups (e.g., minorities, women, immigrants, the poor, gays, and lesbians). This is done through the study of the history and culture and contemporary issues these groups face. The approach endorses the teaching of women's studies, African American studies, Chicano studies, Asian studies, and Native American studies separate from Anglo studies and, in so doing, according to critics, runs the risk of promoting cultural separatism over integration unity and exacerbating tension among groups (Sleeter & Grant, 2009).

## Multicultural Education Approach

The goal of the *multicultural education approach* to multicultural education is to reflect cultural pluralism in a democracy. The multicultural education approach to multicultural education "links race, language, culture, gender, disability, and to a lesser extend social class, working toward making the entire school celebrate human diversity and equal opportunity" (Sleeter & Grant, 2009, p. 34). The faculty mirrors the diversity of the larger population, tracking and labeling of students are eliminated, multicultural materials and curricula are integrated, and differential learning styles accommodated.

## Multicultural Social Justice Education Approach

The *multicultural social justice education approach* to multicultural education is the model Sleeter and Grant (2009) advocate. This approach extends the multicultural education approach into the realm of social action. The goal of this approach, similar to that of the social reconstructionists of the 1930s, is to prepare students to work actively to promote social justice. At the core of this model is the use of critical theory, whereby students are taught to critically analyze power relations and question classism, sexism, racism, Eurocentrism, and other social inequities as well as to develop social action skills.

Whatever approach to multicultural education you might adopt, for teaching to be truly multicultural, students must be made the center of the teaching and learning process. Individual rights and cultural differences must be respected, human rights and social justice must be promoted, the histories and life experiences of every student valued, and a belief in the potential of every child to learn reflected in all aspects of the teaching-learning process (Gollnick & Chin, 2009).

# Supporting English Language Learners

There are an estimated 5.3 million English Language Learners enrolled in U.S. schools, the fastest growing student population. About one-third of ELL students were born outside the United States. ELLs are a very heterogeneous and complex group of students with varying levels of language proficiency, educational needs, socioeconomic status, content proficiency, and immigration status (NCTE, 2008).

About 80% of these students receive language instruction from programs supported, in part, from Title III of the No Child Left Behind (NCLB) Act of 2001. What had previously been Title VII of the Elementary and Secondary Education Act (ESEA), the Bilingual Education Act was reauthorized as Title III of the NCLB. Title III brought a significant change in the program focus, from **bilingual education**, where the students are taught the content in their native language while learning English, to a focus on English acquisition (as rapidly as possible by English immersion) and achievement (in English) on

Bilingual education incorporates instruction in two languages.

Meeting the special needs of migrant children is a challenge faced by a growing number of districts.

state standardized tests. This shift reflects the divide between the two major methods of educating ELL students: bilingual education and English immersion. Bilingual education came under increasing attack in the 1990s. Concerns were voiced by a significant number of individuals, including immigrant parents. Their concerns focused on the fact that children routinely remained segregated in bilingual programs for three years or more, and in some cases more than six years. Nowhere was the opposition more heated than in California, where in 1998 voters approved Proposition 227, which mandated that ELL students be taught in a special English immersion program for no more than one year before being mainstreamed into the regular English classrooms (see the Video Insight box below). Similar initiatives followed in other states, and by 2001 opponents of bilingual education were successful in including the English Language Acquisition Act in NCLB.

The stated goal of the English Language Acquisition Act is to "help ensure that children who are limited English proficient, including immigrant children and youth, attain English proficiency, develop high levels of academic attainment in English, and meet the same challenging State academic content and student academic achievement standards as all children are expected to meet." In addition, consistent with other major NCLB programs that include provisions to ensure states comply with the intent of the act, Title III of the NCLB Act states that state and local education agencies and schools must demonstrate proficiency in state content and achievement standards in mathematics, reading or language arts, and science.

All programs supported by Title III have the same overall goals for ELL students: (1) to attain English proficiency so that they can achieve in the core academic content areas, and (2) to meet the academic achievement targets set by each state. The major program options supported by Title III are listed in Figure 9.4. The most commonly used programs are sheltered English instruction, pullout **English as a Second Language (ESL)**, structured English immersion, dual language, and transitional bilingual education. Research comparing the effectiveness of alternative programs has been controversial and inconclusive (Zehr, 2007). As a result, the educational debate between bilingual education programs and programs that focus on developing literacy in only English is likely to continue.

## VIDEO INSIGHT

### Controversy over Bilingual Education

In this ABC News video segment, you are introduced to an experiment in education that has produced its own deep, persistent controversy, namely, bilingual education.

1. In the video, English-only instruction is portrayed as being superior to bilingual education based on recent student achievement test scores. How might you explain the rapid success of English-only instruction compared to bilingual instruction? What factors other than instruction might have contributed to the improved test scores of a million California children who were taught by English-only instruction?

2. Bilingual education includes several program options involving two languages of instruction. Review the program options in Figure 9.4 and state the strengths and weaknesses of each of the options.

Figure 9.4 — Types of Language Instruction Educational Programs

**Programs that focus on developing literacy in two languages include—**

■ *Two-way Immersion* **or** *Two-way Bilingual*
- The goal is to develop strong skills and proficiency in both native language (L1) and English (L2).
- Includes students with an English background and students from one other language background.
- Instruction is in both languages, typically starting with a smaller proportion of instruction in English, and gradually moving to half of the instruction in each language.
- Students typically stay in the program throughout elementary school.

■ *Dual Language*
- When called "dual language immersion," usually the same as two-way immersion or two-way bilingual.
- When called "dual language," may refer to students from one language group developing full literacy skills in two languages—L1 and English.

■ *Early Exit Transitional*
- The goal is to develop English skills as quickly as possible, without delaying learning of academic core content.
- Instruction begins in L1, but rapidly moves to English; students typically are transitioned into mainstream classrooms with their English-speaking peers as soon as possible.

■ *Heritage Language* **or** *Indigenous Language Program*
- The goal is literacy in two languages.
- Content taught in both languages, with teachers fluent in both languages.
- Differences between the two programs: heritage language programs typically target students who are non-English speakers or who have weak literacy skills in L1; indigenous language programs support endangered minority language in which students may have weak receptive and no productive skills.
- Both programs often serve American Indian students.

■ *Late Exit Transitional, Developmental Bilingual* **or** *Maintenance Education*
- The goal is to develop some skills and proficiency in L1 and strong skills and proficiency in L2 (English).
- Instruction at lower grades is in L1, gradually transitioning to English; students typically transition into mainstream classrooms with their English-speaking peers.
- Differences among the three programs focus on the degree of literacy students develop in the native language.

**Programs that focus on developing literacy in only English include—**

■ *Specially Designed Academic Instruction in English (SDAIE), Content-based English as a Second Language (ESL), Sheltered Instruction Observational Protocol (SIOP),* **or** *Sheltered English*
- The goal is proficiency in English while learning content in an all-English setting.
- Students from various linguistic and cultural backgrounds can be in the same class.
- Instruction is adapted to students' proficiency level and supplemented by gestures and visual aids.
- May be used with other methods; e.g., early exit may use L1 for some classes and SDAIE for others.

■ *Structured English Immersion (SEI)*
- The goal is fluency in English, with only LEP students in the class.
- All instruction is in English, adjusted to the proficiency level of students so subject matter is comprehensible.
- Teachers need receptive skill in students' L1 and sheltered instructional techniques.

■ *English Language Development (ELD)* **or** *ESL Pull-out*
- The goal is fluency in English.
- Students leave their mainstream classroom to spend part of the day receiving ESL instruction, often focused on grammar, vocabulary, and communication skills, not academic content.
- There is typically no support for students' native languages.

■ *ESL Push-in*
- The goal is fluency in English.
- Students are served in a mainstream classroom, receiving instruction in English with some native language support if needed.
- The ESL teacher or an instructional aide provides clarification, translation if needed, and uses ESL strategies.

*Source:* National Clearinghouse for English Language Acquisition, Retrieved May 20, 2011. From http://ncela .gwu.edu/files/uploads/5/LIEPs0406_BR.pdf.

## Services to Immigrant Children and Youth

More than one in five children in the United States lives in a family where one or both parents are immigrants. About 75% of these children were born in the United States and are therefore United States citizens. Of the over one million legal immigrants who entered the United States in 2010, 15% were under the age of 15, 40% were from Asia, 13% from Mexico, and 10% from Africa (Monger & Yankay, 2011). The number of immigrants entering the United States has remained high for two decades (see Figure 9.5). The growth has been fueled by the increases in legal admission ceilings, the acceptance of political refugees, and the large-scale undocumented immigration that has continued to grow.

The majority of legal immigrant children, as well as the 12% of the unauthorized immigrant population that are children, are English language learners and live in low income families. These students face a number of obstacles and barriers, not the least of which are the anxiety of learning a new language, adjusting to a new culture, and understanding the Eurocentric curriculum and unique pedagogy used in the schools (Miller & Endo, 2004). Other problems noted by Salend (2011) include the following:

> In school, they may encounter racial tension and rejection from peers. . . . Immigrant youth also may fear authority figures such as the principal because they or a family member have an undocumented status. As a result, these youth may be reluctant to make friends with others, to seek help from and interactions with professionals, to attempt to gain recognition or excel in programs, or to draw attention to themselves. (pp. 107–108)

A number of factors influence how quickly immigrant youth become assimilated. Whether they are parallel or nonparallel newcomers is a major variable. Parallel newcomers, those who have had formal schooling equal to the grade level they enter in the U.S. school, may already have some experience with English and have educational experiences which make them more familiar with the routines, practices, and appropriate behavior of schools. They are assimilated more quickly than nonparallel newcomers who have had sporadic formal schooling in their home country and are one or two grade levels behind (Faltis & Coulter, 2008). Discrimination based on race or country of origin may also be a factor with immigrants from certain countries (e.g., Cuba and Vietnam) being more warmly welcomed than those from less favored nations (e.g., Haiti and Mexico) (Gollnick & Chinn, 2009).

Also important to the assimilation of newcomer students is the degree of assimilation of the parents. Immigrant children may come in conflict with parents who attempt to maintain their language and cultural practices at home. Teachers need to be sensitive to the potential conflict and help immigrant children be bicultural rather than having to choose between the culture of the home and the culture of the school (Gollnick & Chinn, 2009). The socioeconomic status of the parents, whether they are documented or undocumented, and whether they are migrant workers, moving to follow the crops, can also be important influences on the culture and educational assimilation of immigrant children. A parent who is undocumented may be less inclined to be an active and vocal participant in their child's education. And a child who is moving from one school to another will find it not only more difficult to assimilate, but also to achieve academically.

According to the research, another important factor contributing to the assimilation and success of immigrant children is the extent to which they are optimistic about their

**Figure 9.5 — Legal Permanent Residents Admitted to the United States: 1900 to 2010**

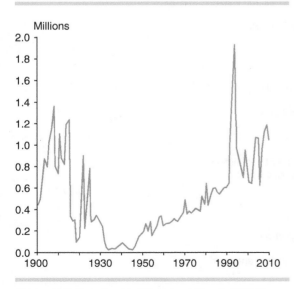

*Source:* U.S. Department of Homeland Security (2011). Retrieved May 18, 2011 from www.

future. Immigrant children who believe that the future holds better educational and economic opportunities "tend to interpret any economic, political, and social barriers they come up against in school or society as temporary, as problems they will or can overcome with the passage of time, hard work, and more education" (Faltis & Coulter, 2008, p. 59). The challenge for the teacher of these young people is to help them acquire and hold on to this vision, this optimism.

For the majority of immigrant children who do not easily become acclimated to American schooling or who have limited English proficiency, assistance is needed to help them succeed. Many immigrant children will be enrolled in one of the bilingual or ELL programs previously described. In some large cities, immigrant children may be enrolled in special newcomer schools and programs. These programs provide students, especially nonparallel students, the opportunity to acculturate in a safe environment (Faltis & Coulter, 2008). Title III of NCLB provides this assistance through a variety of programs that provide enhanced instructional opportunities for immigrant students. Among the programs are the following:

- Family literacy, parent outreach, and training programs;
- Tutorials, mentoring, and academic career counseling;
- Identification and acquisition of curricular materials, software, and technologies;
- Support for personnel, including teacher aides, to provide services for immigrant children and youth; and/or
- Basic instructional services for immigrant children and youth. (National Clearinghouse for English Language Acquisition, 2011)

# HISTORICAL NOTE

## *Tape v. Hurley:* The Chinese Struggle for Education

Except for a brief period (1859–1871) when a segregated school for Chinese children was in operation, the only education most Chinese children received in the United States in the late 1800s was by private tutors or Bible classes with the Protestant missions in Chinatown. Neither of these provisions satisfied Chinese parents. Countless letters and petitions in support of public education for Chinese children were directed to the school board and county board of supervisors, but they were ignored or denied.

In 1878, seven years after the closing of the Chinese public school, more than 1,300 merchants in San Francisco, Sacramento, and other California Chinatowns petitioned the state to provide a school—even a segregated one—for Chinese students. They noted that although they paid taxes, 3,000 Chinese were being denied an education. Their petition was denied.

In 1884, after a federal district court ruled that immigration officials could not deny reentry to a natural-born citizen of the United States who was of Chinese ancestry, the Chinese community turned to citizenship status as the key to pressing for the provision of education. The week after the decision, Joseph and Mary Tape attempted to enroll their 8-year-old daughter Mamie, a natural-born citizen of the United States, at the Spring Valley School in San Francisco near their residence. The principal, Jennie Hurley, refused admission, and the Tape family filed suit. The state superintendent of public instruction supported the board's decision,

noting that the California constitution declared Chinese to be "dangerous to the well-being of the state." On January 9, 1885, the trial court supported Mamie's request and ruled that to deny American children born in the United States the right to attend public school would be a violation of the Fourteenth Amendment. On March 3, 1885, the California Supreme Court upheld the decision.

On April 7, 1885, in a scene foretelling the desegregation of schools in the 1950s, Mamie, accompanied by her parents and attorneys and with the Supreme Court decision in hand, again attempted to enroll at the Spring Valley School. Once again Principal Hurley denied admission, arguing that Mamie needed a health certificate before she could be admitted. When threatened with legal action, she then said the classes were already overcrowded, in violation of district policy, and that Mamie would be placed on a waiting list. In the meantime, responding to the court's decision, the San Francisco School Board persuaded the legislature to pass a bill allowing districts to establish segregated schools for "Mongolians," and on April 13, 1885, the Chinese Primary School was opened at Jackson and Powell Streets. In the end the Tapes had won the battle to obtain a public education for Mamie, but desegregation was still firmly entrenched.

*Sources:* Fung, F. A. (2004, May). Lessons from the past: *Tape v. Hurley. CHSA Bulletin,* pp. 3–4; and Webb, L. D. (2006). *The history of American education: A great American experiment.* Upper Saddle River, NJ: Merrill/Prentice Hall.

The United States is the prototypical "nation of immigrants." It was founded and built by immigrants and to a large extent its future will be determined by immigrants: "Most children of immigrants will be lifelong U.S. residents and will become part of the nation's workforce. Some will serve in the U. S. military; some will be manual workers; others will become teachers or doctors. These children will play a crucial role in the viability of Social Security and Medicare . . . Even apart from the humanitarian reasons that some observers see as an adequate basis for attention to the circumstances of immigrant children, policies that help these children become successful adults are squarely in the national interest" (Greenberg, Haskins & Fremstad, 2004).

## Compensatory Education for Disadvantaged Students

**Compensatory education** offers supplemental programs or services designed to help children overcome the deficiencies associated with educational and socioeconomic disadvantages. As detailed in Chapter 8, children from low socioeconomic families are at risk for lower levels of educational achievement and attainment. Support for compensatory education has been an important part of federal educational policy and funding since the passage of the Elementary and Secondary Education Act in 1965. Title I of that act was the centerpiece of President Johnson's Great Society education program and was viewed as an important weapon in the War on Poverty.

The 2001 reauthorization of the ESEA, the No Child Left Behind Act, continued the commitment of the federal government to equal educational opportunity for disadvantaged students. Title I, Part A, of NCLB provides assistance to enable children in low-socioeconomic-level schools to meet challenging state academic content and student academic achievement performance standards. This assistance reaches 17 million students in both public and private schools. Still, Title I serves only about half the students who are eligible to receive services. Services are especially limited at the secondary level. Sixty percent of the students served under Title I are in grades one through five, 21% are in grades six through eight, and 3% are in preschool. This is the largest elementary and secondary education program, with a proposed fiscal year 2012 budget of $14.8 billion. Title I programs and services are provided both as school-wide programs to upgrade the school as a whole or as "targeted assistance programs" that may involve the "pullout" method, in which eligible students are removed from the regular classroom to receive additional instruction, usually in reading, mathematics, and language arts. Instruction lasts about 30 minutes and is delivered in smaller classes by separately hired Title I teachers.

A second major compensatory education program that also grew out of the War on Poverty is Head Start. Head Start focuses on education and early childhood development through the combination of educational programs, medical and nutritional benefits, parent involvement, and social services for preschool children ages three to five. Head Start is not operated by the schools but by community-based organizations. A related program, Early Head Start, provides educational and family support services to children younger than three years of age.

A variety of other compensatory education programs can be found in the schools, mostly operating during school hours. The following programs are the most common:

1. Programs for primary students such as Transition Head Start, which continue Head Start services into the second grade.
2. Programs for secondary education students such as Upward Bound, which are directed at dropout prevention and increasing the preparation for and participation in postsecondary education of disadvantaged youth through tutoring, instruction in basic skills, and counseling services.
3. Enrichment programs in subject areas. Almost all Title I districts offer programs in reading (e.g., Reading First). Most also offer programs in mathematics, and a lesser percentage offer programs in language arts.

4. Programs for students with disabilities. Almost three fourths of the Title I districts provide services to students with disabilities. In most districts, these students must be eligible for Title I to receive services.
5. Bilingual education and ESL. Both options of instruction are offered to LEP students. Again, normally the students must be eligible for Title I to receive services.
6. Programs for migrant students. Most such programs are found in larger school districts.
7. Psychological and social services for disadvantaged students.
8. Education for Homeless Children and Youth program. The purpose of this program is to ensure that all children and youth who experience homelessness have equal access to the same free, appropriate education, including public preschool education, that is provided to other children and youth.

In addition to federal support for compensatory education, a number of states and numerous school districts also provide resources to support compensatory education.

**For Your Reflection and Analysis**

What are the advantages and disadvantages of pulling students out of the regular class to receive compensatory instruction?

# Creating Equal Educational Opportunities for Students with Disabilities

As was noted in Chapter 8, students with mental and physical disabilities who are receiving services in federally supported programs comprise approximately 14% of the students in public schools. As also noted, in 1975 Congress passed the Education for All Handicapped Children Act (EHA) (PL 94-142). The EHA, often referred to as the Bill of Rights for Handicapped Children, and its successors have served not only to guarantee the rights of children with disabilities, but also to expand the rights of all children. In 1990 the EHA was reauthorized and renamed the Individuals with Disabilities Education Act (IDEA). The IDEA provides the framework for the delivery of services to children with disabilities; infants and toddlers with disabilities and their families receive early intervention services under Part C of IDEA, and children ages 3–21 receive services under Part B.

## *The Individuals with Disabilities Education Act*

The IDEA applies to all children with disabilities from birth to age 21. The statute defines "disabled children" as those with mental retardation, hearing impairments, speech or language impairments, visual impairments, emotional disturbance, orthopedic impairments, autism, traumatic brain injury, multiple disabilities, or specific learning disabilities.

To receive services under the IDEA, a student must not only have a disability, but the condition also must affect the student's education to an extent that requires the delivery of special education programs and related services (i.e., services necessary for the student to benefit from the special education). The major principles that are included in the IDEA are (1) the right to a free and appropriate education, (2) identification and nondiscriminatory evaluation, (3) an individualized education program, (4) least restrictive environment, and (5) procedural due process.

### Free and Appropriate Education

Perhaps the most fundamental and important principle of the IDEA is that all children ages three to 21 years with disabilities, regardless of the nature or severity of their disabilities, must have available to them a free and appropriate education

The inclusion of children with disabilities is a fundamental principle of the IDEA.

and related services designed to meet their unique needs. The IDEA does not say what programs or services must be provided to satisfy the guarantee of an appropriate education. Rather, this must be decided on a case-by-case basis through the decision-making process required for developing the student's individualized education program (IEP). The question of what should be included in the IEP has been the subject of considerable litigation. Some guidance was provided by the U.S. Supreme Court in *Board of Education v. Rowley* (1982), in which the Court stated that a free and appropriate public education did not mean "an opportunity to achieve full potential commensurate with the opportunity provided to other children," but rather "access to specialized instruction and related services which are designed to provide educational benefit to the handicapped child." Since *Rowley,* the courts have continued to support parents in their attempts to expand services to their children with disabilities, but they do tend to accept the most reasonable program rather than require the best possible program.

### Identification and Nondiscriminatory Evaluation

The first obligation imposed on the schools by the IDEA is to take affirmative steps to identify children with disabilities who may be entitled to special education. A teacher or other educator who has reason to believe a student has a disability and needs special education services may refer the student for a comprehensive evaluation to describe the child's functioning and determine whether the child has a disability. The evaluation, which assesses all areas related to the suspected disability, is to be carried out by a multidisciplinary team. Placement in any special education program is made not on the basis of a single test, but on multiple measures and procedures. Additionally, whatever evaluation mechanisms are used must be nondiscriminatory in terms of culture, race, and language, and must be designed for assessment with specific handicaps (e.g., tests for non-English speakers or tests for students with visual impairments).

If the evaluation determines that the student is not eligible for services under the IDEA, he or she may still be eligible for special education services under Section 504. On the other hand, if as a result of evaluation the team decides that the student requires special education services, an individualized education program must be prepared.

As mentioned in Chapter 8, racial and language minority children are disproportionately identified as disabled. Concerned with this problem, the most recent reauthorization of the IDEA contains provisions requiring states to have in place policies and procedures designed to prevent "the inappropriate over-identification or disproportionate representation by race and ethnicity of children with disabilities" (34 CFR 300.173) and to monitor school districts to determine whether any disproportionate representation is the result of inappropriate identification.

### Individualized Education Program

The IDEA requires that a written **individualized education program (IEP)** be prepared for each child who is to receive special education services. The IEP is designed to meet the unique needs of the child for whom it is developed and is prepared at a meeting that, under the requirements of the IDEA, must include the student's parents, teachers (special education and regular education), special education specialists or others who may contribute to the individually tailored learning plan, and, if appropriate, the student. The IEP includes a description of present levels of functional and academic performance; a statement of measurable annual goals and how the child's progress toward meeting the goals will be measured; a statement of special education and related services (e.g., transportation, physical therapy) to be provided and their duration; and a statement of any testing accommodations that the student will need to participate in state or district-wide assessments. IEPs are reviewed annually and provide the means for ensuring parent involvement in the educational decisions affecting their children, the means for accountability, the delivery of services, and a record of progress.

**Reflect on Diversity**
The IEP concept has been very successful in working with students with disabilities. How might it be used with other students?

## Least Restrictive Environment

The IDEA requires that the student receive the special education services in the **least restrictive environment (LRE)**. The least restrictive environment principle does not require all children with disabilities to be included in the regular classroom. However, the language of the IDEA establishes a clear preference for educating children with disabilities, to the maximum extent possible, in the regular classroom, where they have contact with children without disabilities: "To the maximum extent appropriate, children with disabilities . . . are educated with children who are nondisabled" (IDEA). The courts have interpreted this provision to mean that children with disabilities should not be removed from the regular educational setting unless the nature or severity of the disability is such that education in the regular classroom, even with the use of supplemental aides and services, cannot be satisfactorily achieved. In every case, a child with a disability cannot be moved from the regular classroom without a due process hearing, and schools have been required to provide supplemental services in the regular classroom before moving the child to a more restrictive environment.

The LRE principle does not require that the child be placed in a general education classroom; in fact, the IDEA does not mention inclusion. What the principle does call for is the careful consideration of all possible placement alternatives for each child with a disability before a final placement is made. In the end, it may be necessary to place the child in a segregated setting in order to provide the most appropriate education or in order to prevent the disruption of the educational process for other students. Students may also be placed in private schools at public expense if the district is not able to provide an appropriate placement. The responsibility of the school is to ensure the availability of a continuum of alternative placements such as that shown in Figure 9.6.

**Figure 9.6 — Continuum of Educational Placements for Students with Disabilities**

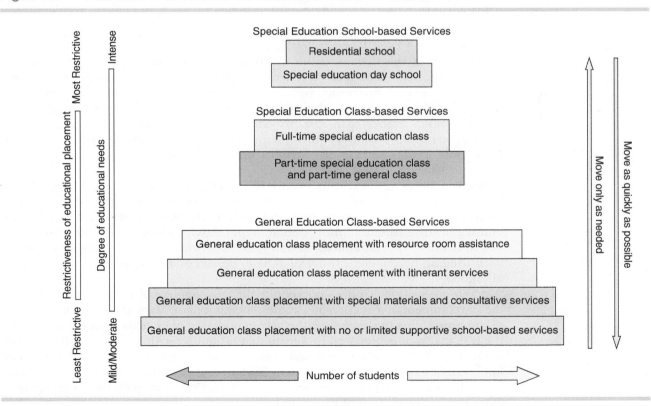

*Source:* Mercer, C. D., & Pullen, P. C. (2008). *Students with learning disabilities* (7th ed.), p. 130. Upper Saddle River, NJ: Merrill/Pearson
Copyright 2008 by Pearson Education. Reprinted by permission.

Most children with disabilities are served in the local public school under either the general education class-based services or the special education class-based services noted in Figure 9.6. Most students with mild disabilities, including those with learning disabilities, mild retardation, speech and language disabilities and serious emotional disabilities are currently served in the general education class. Instruction may be provided entirely by the general education teacher, in consultation with a special education teacher, or cooperatively with a special education teacher (Mastropieri & Scruggs, 2007).

## Procedural Due Process

The extensive procedural requirements of the IDEA are designed to ensure children with disabilities a free and appropriate education and to protect them from improper evaluation, classification, and placement. Parents have the right to obtain an individual evaluation of their child in addition to that conducted by the school district and to be involved in every stage of the evaluation, placement, and educational process. Parents must be informed of the IEP conference and encouraged to attend. In addition, the school district must inform parents in writing, or in a format understandable by them, before it initiates, changes, or refuses to initiate or change the identification, evaluation, or educational placement of the child.

When the parents and school disagree on a decision, each has the right to request a due process hearing. The request can be filed at almost any point in the process. A due process hearing is conducted by an impartial hearing officer determined in accordance with each individual state's statutory procedures for implementing the IDEA. If disagreement continues after the due process hearing, appeal may be made to the courts. While any proceedings are occurring, the child must "stay put." In other words, the child remains in the current—or last agreed-on placement—pending the outcome of the proceedings.

## Section 504 of the Rehabilitation Act

Section 504 of the Rehabilitation Act is a civil rights law that prohibits educational institutions that receive federal financial assistance from discriminating in the delivery of programs and activities, employment, and access to facilities. Section 504 is broader than the IDEA and is intended to prevent discrimination against, rather than just provide services to, students with disabilities. Section 504 seeks to remove physical and programmatic barriers to participation in schools. Under Section 504 schools must make reasonable accommodations for students with disabilities.

Section 504 is applicable to any student with a physical or mental impairment that substantially limits any major life activity, or who is regarded as having, or has a history of, such impairment. Included could be students with communicable diseases, attention deficit–hyperactivity disorder (if the student is not in need of special education and related services under IDEA), or students with lifelong health conditions such as epilepsy, diabetes, asthma, arthritis, or allergies.

Although Section 504 does not require the development of an IEP, it does require the development of a Section 504 accommodation plan. Many districts follow many of the procedures in developing the accommodation plan as they do in developing the IEP; that is, it is prepared by a team that is familiar with the student, the assessment data, and the placement and accommodation options. In addition, parents have a right to participate in any identification and placement decisions, as well as the right to a hearing by an impartial party if they disagree with the identification, education, or placement of their child.

## *The Inclusion Debate*

Just as the IDEA does not define what is meant by an appropriate education but leaves the issue to be decided case by case, it also does not define what is meant by the "least restrictive environment" but leaves this to be decided on an individual basis. The least restrictive environment issue has been central to expanded efforts to increase the number of students with disabilities who are included in regular classroom settings.

The concept of **inclusion** consists of serving students with a variety of abilities and disabilities in the regular classroom along with the appropriate support services. It is considered to be a full-time placement. Those who support inclusion argue that not only does it contribute to the academic and social progress of children with disabilities, but it also creates greater tolerance on the part of students without disabilities and better prepares them to live in an integrated society. As a result of the inclusion movement, more and more students are spending more of their time in a regular classroom than in any other school setting. The NCLB act supports inclusion and makes it clear that *all* students are general education students. Federal special education policy aims at closing the achievement gap between special education students and their peers.

The inclusion movement has generated some debate over the extent to which students are being integrated without the support necessary to make the transition successful. Many educators and parents are also concerned that inclusion is being used to save money at the expense of providing needed services to students with disabilities, and that many of the services or resources (e.g., Braillers, speech synthesizers, special computers) needed by students may either not be available in the general education classroom, or, when they are provided, may be stigmatizing when undertaken in front of nondisabled peers. Still others are concerned that many general education teachers may not have the time or training to make inclusion a success (Mastropieri & Scruggs, 2007).

To assess your support for the concept of inclusion, complete the checklist in the Ask Yourself feature below.

> **For Your Reflection and Analysis**
>
> How prepared are you to have a student with a severe disability included in your class?

# ASK YOURSELF

## *Inclusion Checklist*

The following checklist for practicing (or prospective) teachers reflects an inclusion philosophy. The more "yes" answers, the more positive the respondent is toward responsible inclusion.

1. Are you (would you be) willing to have age-appropriate students with disabilities in your class?

2. Do (would) you modify your curriculum, instructional methods, and materials to meet the diverse needs of students in your class?

3. Are you (would you be) open to suggestions and modifications in your teaching and classroom management?

4. Are you (would you be) willing to share your teaching responsibilities with other professionals?

5. Do you expect students with disabilities to be as successful in meeting their own goals as students without disabilities are in meeting theirs?

6. Do (would) you call on students with disabilities as much as you (would) call on other students in your class?

7. Do (would) you use heterogeneous grouping?

8. Do (would) you use peer tutoring?

9. Do (would) you use adaptive technology and customized software?

10. Have you attended training sessions about responsible inclusion?

*Source:* Lombardi, T. P. (1994). *Responsible inclusion of students with disabilities.* Bloomington, IN: Phi Delta Kappa Educational Foundation.

# Promoting Gender Equity

In the 1990s, the concern about gender differences in the schools focused on gender bias against girls and how the sex role stereotyping and sex discrimination found in the culture outside the school was reflected in the educational experience of girls (see, e.g., AAUW (1998), *Gender Gaps: Where Schools Still Fail Our Children*). However, by the turn of the century, researchers were increasingly acknowledging that both girls and boys are victims of gender bias in the schools. In fact, some studies suggested that boys experience the most gender bias and neglect (see, e.g., Sommers [2000], *The War Against Boys*). More recently, research has focused on the functional and structural differences between the brains of boys and girls that might explain cognitive and emotional abilities and differences. Some research suggests there are gender-based neurological differences that impact on learning, including that boys' brains tend to have more cortical areas wired for spatial/mechanical processing than girls' brains, while the frontal lobe of girls' brains, the reading/writing/word production area of the brain, generally develops earlier than that of boys' brains (King, Gurian, & Stephens, 2010). The brain research on gender differences is highly controversial and many researchers suggest that the neurological differences that have been identified reflect physical maturation more than mental development (Eliot, 2010).

Whatever the case, the fact remains that not only are there differences in the educational achievement and attainment of males and females as described in Chapter 8, but there are also differences in the educational experiences of boys and girls that affect them in every aspect of their schooling. Table 9.2 provides a partial list of some of the ways in which boys seem to be better off or advantaged in school and some of the ways in which girls seem to be better off in school.

**For Your Reflection and Analysis**

Give personal examples of differential treatment that you have experienced in elementary school, secondary school, or college.

### Table 9.2 — How Boys and Girls Are Better Off at School

**How Boys Are Better Off**

Boys outperform girls in science and mathematics.
Boys are represented in higher numbers in mathematics and science gifted programs.
Boys are more represented in computer science and engineering "high-income" careers.
Boys are overrepresented as National Merit Scholars.
Boys receive more academic help than girls.
Boys often avoid some of the inner struggles that can lead to depression and eating disorders in adolescent girls.
Teenage boys who become parents are more likely to remain and complete high school than teenage girls who become parents.
Boys are twice as likely as girls to participate in team sports.
Boys are less likely than girls to be the victims of sexual harassment and abuse.
Boys get more teacher attention of the kind that is likely to foster student achievement.

**How Girls Are Better Off**

Girls are less likely than boys to drop out of school.
Girls are less likely than boys to be diagnosed with attention deficit–hyperactivity disorder (ADHD).
Girls receive higher grades than boys.
Girls are more likely to do their homework.
Girls are less likely than boys to be diagnosed as having a learning disability.
Girls outperform boys in reading and writing.
Girls are more focused on education as a goal and are more likely to pursue college degrees.
Girls are less likely than boys to repeat a grade.
Girls are less likely than boys to have their parents contacted by the school about an academic or behavioral problem.
Girls are less likely to be the victims of violence in the school.
Girls have a lower rate of suicide.
Girls are more likely to participate in community service activities.

## Goals of Gender Equity

The goals of gender equity are the same as the goals for all forms of educational equity. As articulated by the Intercultural Development Research Association South Central Collaborative for Equity (2011) and accepted by the nine other regional equity assistance centers, these are (as adapted):

1. Goal 1: Attain comparably high academic achievement and virtually non-existent performance gaps.
2. Goal 2: Equitable access and inclusion in schools and the programs and activities within those schools.
3. Goal 3: Equitable treatment in patterns of interaction and support.
4. Goal 4: Equitable opportunity to learn: the creation of learning opportunities that present each child with the challenge to reach high standards and the requisite pedagogical, social, emotional, and psychological supports to achieve the standards that are established.
5. Goal 5: Equitable resources in regard to funding, staff, instructional materials, equipment, and learning spaces.
6. Goal 6: Accountability: the assurance that all education stakeholders accept responsibility and hold each other responsible for providing 1-5 so that every child can achieve at excellent levels in academic and other student outcomes.

Some of the strategies teachers and schools can employ in attaining these goals are discussed in the following section.

## Strategies for Achieving Gender Equity

There are numerous explanations for the gender inequality that exists in education. The three that are most often discussed in the research literature are: *gender stereotyping*, the attribution of specific abilities, behaviors, and personality characteristics and interest on the basis of gender; the *socialization* process described in the previous chapter; and *discrimination*, the denial of opportunities or rewards or other prejudicial treatment on the basis of gender. While the socialization that takes place outside the school to a large extent shapes interactions in the school, teachers need to understand the ways in which they and the culture of the school can reinforce gender inequities. Numerous strategies have been proposed to achieve gender-neutral classroom and **gender equity** in the schools. These include, but are not limited to, the following:

- Eliminate inequitable practices (e.g., encourage girls to take advanced science and mathematics courses and boys to participate in nonathletic extracurricular activities).
- Resist gender-role stereotyping (e.g., invite male and female guest speakers who are in nontraditional roles; encourage girls to pursue careers in science, math, and computing and boys to pursue careers in elementary teaching).
- Ensure that all posters, displays, and curriculum materials are free of gender bias and represent males and females of all races and in all walks of life.
- Be sensitive to gender issues (e.g., provide for the discussion of sexism, gender stratification, and the feminization of poverty).
- Correct student speech or actions that perpetuate sex discrimination or bias.
- Provide gender-neutral affirmation of skills and abilities (e.g., praise a female student for her good problem-solving ability and reinforce a male student for his sensitivity to others).
- Use instructional strategies that reinforce gender equity in the classroom and playground (e.g., ask higher-order questions of both girls and boys).

- Use a variety of instructional strategies that recognize the diverse and multiple learning styles of boys and girls.
- Ensure that testing accurately assesses the abilities of both boys and girls.
- Provide training to all instructional and support personnel in recognizing and preventing sexual harassment and in dealing with gender issues in all areas of education. (AAUW, 1998, 2001; ATPE, 2010; Eliot, 2010; Gurian & Stevens, 2004; Spade, 2004)

An increasingly popular but other somewhat controversial strategy that has been suggested to address gender equity is single-sex education. (See the Controversial Issue feature on page 146 for some of the pros and cons of single-sex classes and schools.) As described in Chapters 5 and 6, single-sex instruction was the norm for much of the first 300 years of our nation's history and has been favored by private and parochial schools. In 2006, as part of NCLB, the U.S. Department of Education issued guidelines for the creation and operation of single-sex classes and schools. The regulations require that districts ensure that enrollment in the classes or schools be voluntary and that comparable courses, programs, services, or facilities are available to both sexes. In part as a result of permission given by these regulations, but also in response to pressures to increase academic performance, single-sex schools or schools offering single-sex classes are opening at an accelerating rate—from 11 in 2002 to 524 in 2011 (NASSPE, 2011). The growth in single-sex education has been in response to public school parents who want more choice options and are pleased to have a choice that has long been available in private and parochial education. They are also attractive to parents, educators, and policymakers because of the body of evidence that suggests students in single-sex classrooms score higher on achievement tests and other measures of academic success.

The attainment of gender equity should be one of the primary goals of all educational institutions. A commitment to gender equity increases the capacity of schools to create an educational climate that encourages both girls and boys to reach their highest potential (Mobley & Holcomb, 2010). As Americans attempt to remain competitive in the 21st century's world markets, Plato's words of 2,500 years ago seem remarkably relevant: "Nothing can be more absurd than the practice . . . of men and women not following the same pursuits with all of their strength and with one mind, for thus the state . . . is reduced to a half" (*Laws*, VII, p. 805).

## Summary

Educating children with disabilities and language minority students and ensuring gender equity are strategies for achieving equality of educational opportunity. The presence of each of these strategies in the American educational system has served to expand the educational opportunities not only for the targeted populations, but also for all students. It is largely through the efforts of those asserting their rights under the constitutionally based programs that the rights of all students have been expanded. The success of our educational system and, indeed, our economic and social structure depends on the full participation of all children. This chapter focused attention on strategies for increasing the equality of educational opportunity. The next chapter turns to strategies directed at specific populations of "at-risk" youth.

# PROFESSIONAL DEVELOPMENT
## *Workshop*

## *Prepare for the State Licensure Examination*

Kevin Lewis is a third-grade teacher at Kennedy Elementary School. Kennedy is a school of 820 students in an urban school district with a predominantly minority population. Kennedy has an English language learner (ELL) population of 260 students. Spanish (68%), Vietnamese (11%), and Chinese (10%) are the most common languages spoken in the homes of the ELL students. Kevin has six ELL students in his class.

Angela Ong has been diagnosed as having a learning disability (LD) and being limited English proficient (LEP). The statement on Angela's Level of Education Performance on her IEP developed at the beginning of the year states:

> According to the Harcourt Standard English Proficiency (SELP) test, Angela's oral proficiency level is at an emergent level, meaning Angela's speech contained numerous errors in grammar, syntax, and vocabulary. Angela has been observed speaking English with her classmates but tends to avoid initiating conversation in the classroom. Angela's writing and reading skills were assessed at a preproduction level in both English and Chinese. The learning of English for Angela will be slow and should not be expected to be at the same rate for similar LEP students given Angela's identified learning disability. Angela would benefit from ELL strategies integrated into her special education instruction.

The IEP recommendation is being followed and Angela is showing improved language acquisition. However, Angela's parents are concerned that Angela is not getting as much attention in the classroom as the Spanish speakers. They have requested a reassessment of Angela's acquisition and placement. They feel that Angela would benefit more from sheltered English instruction.

The IEP team, which includes Mr. Lewis, feels that no change in the IEP is warranted. The Ongs are not satisfied and continue to insist that sheltered English would be better for Angela.

1. Is the regular classroom the best placement for Angela? Justify your response.
2. What process is required under the IDEA to resolve disagreements between the school and parents over what special education programs and services should be provided?
3. What are the advantages and disadvantages of ESL and sheltered English as instructional strategies in helping English language learners meet English proficiency standards?

### Build Your Knowledge Base

1. How has your cultural background influenced your learning and school experience?
2. Describe the multicultural education program in a school district with which you are familiar. What evidence exists that it has improved the academic performance of its participants? Is it viewed as helping or hindering progress toward racial or ethnic integration?
3. Many youth feel alienated from the school and find little identification and meaning in the educational process. As a teacher, what can you do to reach these students?
4. Discuss ways in which the Individuals with Disabilities Education Act has benefited *all* children.
5. Compare the treatment of boys and girls in the schools with their treatment in other institutions.
6. How do the missions of multicultural education, special education, and gender equity in education complement each other?

### Develop Your Portfolio

1.  Review the cultural influences on behavior described in Figure 9.2 on page 229. Write a personal reflection paper that describes the interactional styles that were practiced or reinforced in your family when you were a young child as well as the expected responses to authority that were practiced in your family when you were an adolescent. Place the reflection paper in your portfolio under **INTASC Standard 2, Learner Differences**.

2.  Research has demonstrated that differences in learning and cognitive styles may be related to cultural factors as well as socioeconomic factors. Prepare a reflection paper that describes your preferred learning and cognitive style. When did you discover your preferred learning style? How has your learning style changed over time? What cultural or socioeconomic factors might have influenced your predisposition to a particular learning style? Place your reflection paper in your portfolio under **INTASC Standard 2, Learner Differences**.

### Explore Teaching and Learning: Field Experiences

1.  Identify two schools with ethnically diverse student bodies. At each, interview the principal and two experienced teachers about the challenges of working in a school with a diverse population. Inquire about the activities/programs that a school can provide so that diversity can be viewed as an asset through which students can become more understanding of the cultural differences in the school, community, the student body, and the world at large. In what ways are your observations from the field experiences consistent or inconsistent with the content of the chapter?

2.  Locate two schools that practice inclusion of students with disabilities in the regular classroom. Interview teachers and administrators in each school to determine the merits of assigning students with disabilities to a regular classroom. Consider the impact on the workload of the teacher, experiences of the student(s) with disabilities, and experiences of the other students.

## MyEducationLab

Go to **Topic 2 Student Diversity** in the MyEducationLab (www.myeducationlab.com) for *Foundations of American Education*, where you can:

- Find learning outcomes for student diversity along with the national standards that connect to these outcomes.
- Complete Assignments and Activities that can help you more deeply understand the chapter content.
- Apply and practice your understanding of the core teaching skills identified in the chapter with the Building Teaching Skills and Dispositions learning units.
- Examine challenging situations and cases presented in the IRIS Center Resources.

- Access additional video clips of CCSSO National Teachers of the Year award winners responding to the question, "Why Do I Teach?" in the Teacher Talk section.
- Check your comprehension on the content covered in the chapter with the Study Plan. Here you will be able to take a chapter quiz, receive feedback on your answers, and then access Review, Practice, and Enrichment activities to enhance your understanding of chapter content.
- Use the Online Lesson Plan Builder to practice lesson planning and integrating national and state standards into your planning.

# Students at Risk and At-Risk Behaviors

It was twilight when Tom Wright finished packing the last box in his apartment. The movers had already taken the furniture. All that remained were a few boxes. As Tom lifted one of the boxes, an old photograph fell to the floor. He picked it up and smiled as he recognized his eighth-grade graduating class.

Twelve years had passed since that photo was taken. It seemed more like an eternity. He studied the photo for a long time. He immediately identified one of his best boyhood friends. Whatever happened to Jake Nash? He and Jake began kindergarten together and were like brothers for the entire eight years of elementary school. The last time he saw Jake was the summer after the photo was taken. Tom went on to Springview High School, but Jake moved away. It was

so sudden, Tom remembered. He and Jake had planned for high school together. But that summer Jake's life was turned upside down. Jake's mother and father divorced, and shortly afterward his younger sister, Karen, attempted suicide. In August, Jake, his mother, and his sister moved to Michigan to be near his grandparents. He and Tom promised that they would see each other often. But that never happened. They exchanged a few letters and phone calls for a year or so, then grew apart. Tom was horrified and shocked when he later learned from Jake's former neighbor that Jake had dropped out of high school in his senior year and had been indicted on drug trafficking charges on his 21st birthday.

What, if any, clues indicated that Jake was at risk for dropping out of school? For substance abuse?

*J*ake is typical of millions of youth in and out of America's schools whose life experiences and situations place them at risk for educational, emotional, and physical problems. In this chapter, at-risk children and youth are described. In addition, the methods of identifying a number of at-risk conditions and behaviors are suggested. The following objectives should guide you in your study of at-risk populations:

- Identify the predictors of being an at-risk student.
- Discuss the relationship between risk, resiliency, and protective factors.
- Identify the key elements for establishing a trusting relationship with at-risk students.
- Describe the conditions or behaviors associated with substance abuse.
- Identify the suicidal child or adolescent.
- Explain the incidence and consequence of dropping out of school.

- Suggest ways schools can promote more healthy eating habits and recommended level of physical activity.
- Name the common signs or indicators of child abuse or neglect.
- Describe the extent of the problem of violence in the schools.
- Explain why gay, lesbian, bisexual, transgender, or questioning youth are at risk for a variety of self-destructive behaviors.

**MyEducationLab**

Visit the MyEducationLab for *Foundations of American Education* to enhance your understanding of chapter concepts with a personalized Study Plan. You'll also have the opportunity to hone your teaching skills through video and case based Assignments and Activities, and Building Teaching Skills and Disposition lessons.

# At-Risk Children and Youth

**At-risk** children and adolescents are defined as those who need additional support or special services to meet academic, career/vocational, personal, or social goals. The main characteristic of this group of youngsters is that they are already experiencing or are likely to experience physical and mental health problems. In addition, they are already achieving below grade level or are likely to experience educational problems in the future.

## Identifying At-Risk Students

The key to developing and implementing effective educational programs for at-risk students is early identification. Among the most prominent behaviors or factors that identify those children and adolescents who might become at risk for a variety of self-destructive behaviors are underachievement; retention in grade; social maladjustment; discipline problems; dropping out of school; low parental support; physical problems; using and abusing drugs or alcohol; engaging in premature, unprotected sexual activity; being a victim or perpetrator of violence; and contemplating or attempting suicide. Additional risk factors include being born to, or raised by, a mentally ill parent; suffering from the loss of a significant other; having experienced prenatal trauma or poor health status at birth; experiencing chronic poverty; living in an abject environment, such as being homeless; participating in public assistance programs; and having a parent in prison (Biglan, Brennan, Foster, & Holder, 2004). Research suggests that children are usually at risk due to multiple adversities extending over a long period of time, not just a single adversity (Masten, 1997).

The research also suggests that a disproportionate number of ethnic/minority children, in particular Black, Hispanic, and Native American children; non-English-speaking children; children of single-parent families; and gay, lesbian, bisexual, and transgender (GLBT) youth are represented among the at-risk population. Certain individuals in these groups have a high incidence of at-risk behavior, including low academic achievement, dropping out of school, teen pregnancy, suicide, and being a victim of violence.

## Risk, Resiliency, and Protective Factors

Many at-risk children and youth have been able to cope with adversity and succeed despite overwhelming hardships, obstacles, and negative life events. These youngsters are *resilient* and have developed the necessary coping mechanisms and self-protective characteristics for success. According to Benard (2004), resilient children and youth share at least four attributes:

- Social competence (responsiveness, flexibility, empathy, and a sense of humor);
- Problem-solving skills (reflection, abstract thinking);
- Autonomy (a sense of one's own identity, the ability to act independently); and
- Sense of purpose or future (healthy expectations, achievement, maturity, and hopefulness).

One of the most consistent findings from the research on resiliency in children is that those who have succeeded in overcoming adversity have established a close bond with at least one competent, caring, and emotionally stable adult early in their lives (Poland, 2011b). Because schools are places where children and youth spend a significant part of their time, it is important that schools provide an environment and the conditions that help build and strengthen resiliency. Teachers and other adults

## Figure 10.1 — Keys to Working with At-Risk Children and Adolescents

1. **Establish a Meaningful Connection.** Before any at-risk child or adolescent can trust or confide in a teacher, counselor, or other adult, he or she must have a safe and meaningful connection with that adult.

2. **Be Honest and Direct.** Be honest in sharing your care and concern. However, if a child or adolescent is engaging in risky behavior, don't be afraid to challenge him or her.

3. **Seek Opportunities to Empower the Child or Adolescent.** Many children or adolescents who are at risk have internalized feelings of being "less than" and "unworthy". Compliment at-risk youngsters for the courage to talk with an adult about their problems and to seek help.

4. **Don't Be Afraid to Discuss Decision Making Relative to Sensitive Areas.** Once at-risk students have confided in you, don't be afraid to discuss their decision making relative to sensitive areas such as drug or alcohol abuse or sexual behavior.

5. **Know Your Limits.** Refer to other professionals (i.e., counselor, school psychologist, school nurse, or social worker) for their guidance and input. When you suspect a child or adolescent is at risk for self-destructive behavior such as suicide, immediately contact your school administration and the child or adolescent's parents or guardian. Follow the recommended protocol/guidelines of your school relative to appropriate intervention.

with whom the student has significant relationships can help students develop resiliency by providing encouragement and recognition, as well as by holding high expectations for student performance. Schools can also foster resilience by promoting positive peer relationships through activities that involve helping, sharing, cooperating, collaborative problem solving, and teaching peace-building skills (e.g., conflict resolution, peer-mediation, and violence prevention) (Poland, 2011b). Schools can also foster resilience by helping students build a positive outlook, helping them believe that they can succeed, "by deliberately and repeatedly providing them with situations in which they are able to master material or succeed by achieving a goal" (Poland, 2011b, p. 2). And, in today's climate, one of the most important ways schools can help build resiliency is to provide students a safe and positive learning environment.

The research suggests that the key to working with at-risk children and adolescents is to establish a trusting relationship. Figure 10.1 presents some of the keys to establishing a trusting relationship with at-risk students. The remainder of this chapter describes a number of at-risk conditions or behaviors and discusses how they might be identified. In addition, for each at-risk condition or behavior, prevention and intervention strategies are explored. The conditions or behaviors to be discussed include tobacco, drug and alcohol use and abuse; suicide; dropping out of school; teenage sexuality and pregnancy; obesity; child abuse and neglect; and violence. The conditions that place gay, lesbian, bisexual, and transgender youth at risk for a variety of self-destructive behaviors are also discussed.

## Tobacco, Drug, and Alcohol Use and Abuse

While there has been a decrease in the use of drugs and alcohol among students in the past decade, their use and abuse continue to be a major issue for the schools and the larger society. According to the *Youth Risk Behavior Surveillance—United States, 2009* (Centers for Disease Control and Prevention [CDC], 2010), the percentage of high school students from public and private schools who smoked cigarettes declined significantly from 36% in 1999 to 20% in 2009. And, in a reversal of past years, in 2009 slightly more female high school students (22.8%) smoked cigarettes than male students (22.3%). The survey also found racial and ethnic differences regarding high school students' use of cigarettes: more White students (22%) smoked cigarettes than Hispanic (18%) or Black (10%) students. In spite of the decline in smoking, in 2009 almost one in five high school students in the United States reported they were current smokers.

Although many high school students continue to use and abuse tobacco, drugs, and alcohol, significant decreases have been seen during recent years.

Smokeless tobacco (e.g., chewing tobacco, snuff, or dip), used mostly by boys, peaked in the mid-1990s before declining at all grades. According to the CDC 2009 survey, during the prior 30 days, 7% of 9th graders, 8% of 10th graders, and 10% of 12th graders reported using smokeless tobacco. Over one in six boys in 12th grade in 2009 was a smokeless tobacco user.

Both cocaine and marijuana use have also declined in the last decade. Cocaine use declined from 4% in 2001 to 3% in 2009. The highest cocaine use was reported by Hispanic youth (4%), compared to 2% for White and Black youth. More males than females used cocaine, as was also true for marijuana. And, while current marijuana use declined from 27% in 1999 to 21% in 2009, it remains the most commonly used illicit drug by youth in the United States

Not only drug use, but also alcohol use among youth has declined over the period 1999–2009, with approximately 42% of high school students reporting alcohol use in 2009, compared to 50% in 1999. Still, alcohol is used by more youth in the United States than either tobacco or illicit drugs. As with tobacco and drugs, the 2009 Youth Risk Behavior survey found racial and ethnic differences regarding high school students' use of alcohol: 44% of Hispanic and 43% of Black high school students reported current alcohol use compared to 48% of White students. Most disturbing was that 26% of high school students rode in a car or other vehicle with someone who had been drinking alcohol and 18% of high school students drove while drinking alcohol. According to the National Institute on Alcohol Abuse and Alcoholism (NIAA), half of all American children begin drinking alcohol prior to the age of 15, and those who begin to drink before 15 have four times the risk of having a lifetime of alcoholism diagnosis (Chamberlin, 2008). Current patterns of cigarette, alcohol, marijuana, and cocaine use are presented in Table 10.1.

**Table 10.1 — Percentage of High School Students Who Use Cigarettes, Alcohol, Marijuana, and Cocaine by Sex, Race/Ethnicity, and Gender—United States, 2007**

| Category | Cigarette Use Female | Male | Total | Alcohol Use Female | Male | Total | Marijuana Use Female | Male | Total | Cocaine Use Female | Male | Total |
|---|---|---|---|---|---|---|---|---|---|---|---|---|
| **Race/Ethnicity** | | | | | | | | | | | | |
| White | 22.8 | 22.3 | 22.3 | 45.9 | 43.6 | 47.7 | 17.9 | 23.0 | 20.7 | 1.7 | 3.0 | 2.4 |
| Black | 8.4 | 10.7 | 9.5 | 35.6 | 42.4 | 42.9 | 18.7 | 25.6 | 22.2 | 0.9 | 3.0 | 1.9 |
| Hispanic | 16.7 | 19.4 | 18.0 | 43.5 | 42.4 | 42.9 | 18.2 | 20.5 | 21.6 | 3.7 | 4.9 | 4.3 |
| **Grade** | | | | | | | | | | | | |
| 9 | 15.2 | 12.1 | 13.5 | 35.3 | 28.4 | 31.5 | 15.5 | 15.5 | 15.5 | 2.2 | 2.4 | 2.3 |
| 10 | 18.7 | 17.8 | 18.3 | 41.2 | 40.1 | 40.6 | 17.9 | 23.9 | 21.1 | 1.8 | 3.2 | 2.5 |
| 11 | 20.6 | 23.9 | 22.3 | 45.6 | 45.7 | 45.7 | 19.5 | 26.7 | 23.2 | 1.7 | 4.8 | 3.3 |
| 12 | 22.4 | 28.1 | 25.2 | 50.17 | 52.6 | 51.7 | 19.1 | 27.9 | 24.6 | 2.0 | 3.9 | 3.0 |
| Total | 19.1 | 19.8 | 19.5 | 42.9 | 40.8 | 41.8 | 17.9 | 23.4 | 20.8 | 2.0 | 3.5 | 2.8 |

*Source:* Centers for Disease Control and Prevention. (2010). *Youth risk behavior surveillance—United States, 2009* Surveillance Summaries (2010). *MMWR 2010, 59* (No. SS-5).

The use of other illicit drugs, including LSD and other hallucinogens, has also declined among youth, but the nonmedical use of prescription and over the counter (OTC) drugs remains high. According to the 2009 CDC survey, 20% of students had taken a prescription drug without a doctor's prescription. The most commonly used drugs were pain relievers, tranquilizers, stimulants, and depressants, including OxyContin, Percocet, Vicodin, Adderall, Ritalin and Xanax. Every day an average of 2,000 teens 12 to 17 become first time users of prescription drugs without a doctor's prescription (NIDA for Teens, 2010). OTC medications such as cough and cold medications which contain the cough suppressant dextromethorphan (DXM) are used by youth, even young youth, to get high. At high doses DXM affects memory, thoughts, and feelings.

Inhalants (glue, paints, or aerosol spray cans) are often the first drug that young adolescents use. The use of inhalants has shown a modest decrease in recent years. Their use is most common among 7th through 9th graders but can become chronic and continue into adulthood (NIDA for Teens, 2010). Another drug that showed decreased use, especially in the upper grades, was MDMA, an illegal drug called "ecstasy." For most abusers a "hit" of ecstasy will last for three to six hours, but takes only 15 minutes to enter the bloodstream and reach the brain. Ecstasy can also cause muscle tension, nausea, blurred vision, fainting, chills or sweating, increased heart rate, and increased blood pressure. In addition to effects on the body, ecstasy can affect the brain, causing confusion, depression, sleep problems, intense fear, and anxiety. For some abusers these side effects can last for days or weeks. Ecstasy can be extremely dangerous in high dosages (NIDA for Teens, 2011).

## The Effects of Drug and Alcohol Abuse

The abuse of both drugs and alcohol is related to a variety of other at-risk behaviors, including unintentional injury, school failure, risky sexual behavior (e.g., multiple sex partners or reduced condom use), unintended pregnancy, HIV-AIDS and other sexually transmitted diseases (STDs), violent and abusive behavior, and other psychological and social problems. On an individual level, drug and alcohol abuse interfere with cognitive development and academic achievement. On a societal level, neighborhoods near schools often become the target of drug dealers, many of whom are students themselves. Additionally, crimes of violence often are associated with substance abuse, particularly among teenage gang members. Research also suggests that teenage drug abuse is a contributing factor to adolescent suicide as well as to personal, social, and occupational maladjustment in later young adulthood. The prevention of drug use and abuse is not only a moral imperative but also a cost savings to society. For example, it has been suggested that for every dollar spent on drug use prevention, communities can save considerable costs for drug abuse treatment and counseling. The research also suggests that youth who do not use illicit drugs, alcohol, and tobacco prior to the age of 18 are likely to avoid chemical-dependency problems over their lifetime (National Clearinghouse for Alcohol and Drug Information, 2006).

## Identifying Alcohol and Drug Use

Parents and school personnel are better prepared to provide early intervention when they recognize the difference between normal childhood and adolescent behavior and behavior that may indicate substance use or abuse. Among the psychological and interpersonal factors that place certain children and adolescents at risk for alcohol and drug use include low self-esteem, antisocial and aggressive behavior, lack of engagement with the school, and poor school achievement. Family factors such as substance abuse by parents or siblings, coupled with environmental factors such as poverty and violence, also make certain youngsters more vulnerable than others. However, the strongest risk predictors are attitudes toward drug use and association with peers.

The differences between so-called normal behavior and behavior that reflects substance use or abuse often are a matter of degree. For example, it is normal for a child or adolescent to spend time alone. However, it is usually not normal to exhibit sudden, almost complete, withdrawal from family or peers. Overall, the best predictor of possible substance abuse is a pattern of changes, not any single behavioral change.

### Prevention and Intervention Strategies

Practically every teacher from middle school on will be confronted by students who are engaging in regular use of drugs and/or alcohol. Beginning teachers need to become familiar with the educational prevention programs offered by their district and their school (e.g., peer counseling and school-based individual and group counseling). They also need to become acquainted with the treatment programs available in the community for children, adolescents, and their families. The school counselor, social worker, school psychologist, or school nurse will be an invaluable resource for the beginning teacher who may feel unprepared to deal with this particular type of at-risk behavior.

There are literally hundreds of programs, activities, and services at the national, state, and local levels that are designed to reduce the occurrence of substance use and abuse by children and adolescents. One of the major programs at the national level is the Safe and Drug Free Schools and Communities (SDFSC) Act. SDFSC supports school-based programs that promote a sense of individual responsibility and that teach the consequences of the illegal use of drugs, how to recognize social and peer pressure to use drugs illegally, the skills for resisting illegal drug use, and the dangers of emerging drugs. A number of prevention initiatives have been directed at reducing risk factors associated with drug use, teaching resistance skills, and strengthening protective factors. The most successful of these programs attempt to address multiple risk factors. Research suggests that prevention efforts that target only one risk factor may be less effective because many youth engage in multiple risk behaviors. Regardless of the thrust of the prevention program, it is important that parental involvement be a component of the substance abuse prevention curriculum.

## Adolescent Suicide

Over 2,000 youth aged 10–19 commit suicide in the United States every year, one every four hours. Suicide ranks as the second leading cause of death among 15- to 19-year-olds. The highest rate of suicide deaths is among American Indian/Alaska Native and Hispanic adolescent males. The lowest risk group for suicides is African American females (CDC, 2010). Males are four times as likely to complete suicide as females, probably because they tend to use more lethal methods such as guns or hanging. Girls tend to attempt suicide by overdosing or cutting themselves.

For every completed suicide there are many more **suicide attempts**. In 2009, almost one in 15 high school students attempted suicide. Of these, 2% had made a suicide attempt that had to be treated by a doctor or nurse. The prevalence of having made a suicide attempt that resulted in injury, poisoning, or an overdose that required treatment by a doctor or a nurse was highest among 9th-, 10th-, and 11th-grade females. Suicide attempts were about twice as common among high school females (8.1%) than males (4.6%) (CDC, 2010). Hispanic and Black females reported higher attempted suicide rates (11.1% and 10.4%, respectively) than their White counterparts (6.5%) (CDC, 2010).

### Risk Factors for Youth Suicide

Research has shown a number of risk factors associated with youth suicide. One of the most important risk factors for suicide is substance abuse. A strong relationship has also been found between **major depression** and suicide. The clinically depressed child or youth is likely to exhibit signs of hopelessness, a change in eating and sleeping habits, withdrawal from family and friends, substance abuse, persistent boredom, loss of interest in pleasurable activities, neglect of personal appearance, and frequent complaints about physical symptoms. In early adolescence, depression is often masked by acting out or delinquent behavior. Older adolescents are more apt to resort to violence, drug or alcohol use, and sexual activity rather than face their emotional pain.

Students who have made a previous suicide attempt, have a family history of suicide, or know a friend or other significant person who has attempted or completed suicide are at high risk for suicide. The child or adolescent who experiences a significant number of stressful life events (e.g., death of a parent, separation or divorce of parents, family turmoil or conflict, lack of family support, school failure, sexual or physical assault, issues of sexual identity, or interpersonal conflict with a boyfriend or girlfriend) are also at risk. This is especially true if those stressors occur in combination with alcohol and drug use and the availability of lethal weapons, especially firearms.

Recognizing depression is key to suicide prevention.

A history of physical or sexual abuse also places youth at a higher risk of suicide. Victimization, whether as the victim or the perpetrator, specifically being threatened or bullied at school, also places youth at a higher risk of suicide behavior. Being gay, lesbian, bisexual, or transgendered may also place adolescents at increased suicide risk: over 30% of LGBTQ youth report at least one suicide attempt within the last year (Youth Suicide Prevention Program, 2010). Interpersonal problems, including poor parental relationships, lack of peer support, low self-esteem, and feelings of hopelessness and isolation have also been found to be predictive of suicidal behavior.

## Warning Signs of Youth Suicide

Research indicates that four out of five teen suicides have been preceded by clear warning signs (TeenSuicide.us, 2005). The American Academy of Child and Adolescent Psychiatry (2008) has identified the following warning signs of adolescent suicidal behaviors:

- Change in eating and sleeping habits.
- Withdrawal from friends, family, and regular activities.
- Violent actions, rebellious behavior, or running away.
- Unusual neglect of personal appearance.
- Marked personality change.
- Persistent boredom, difficulty concentrating, or a decline in the quality of schoolwork.
- Frequent complaints about physical systems, often related to emotions, such as stomachaches, headaches, fatigue, etc.
- Loss of interest in pleasurable activities.
- Not tolerating praise or rewards. (p. 1)

A young person actually planning to commit suicide may give additional warning signs including giving away personal possessions or saying things like, "I may not be around much longer to bother you"; or "Nothing really matters, I wish I could die"; or even, "I'm going to kill myself." It behooves every parent and educator to be sensitive to any one of the warning signs and recognize that it may be the youngster's last desperate plea for understanding or help. If one or more of these signs is observed, the parents and/or educator should talk to the child about his or her concerns and seek professional help if those concerns or

**Table 10.2 — Indicators of Childhood or Adolescent Suicide**

| Psychosocial | Familial | Psychiatric | Situational |
|---|---|---|---|
| 1. Poor self-esteem and feelings of inadequacy<br>2. Hypersensitivity and suggestibility<br>3. Perfectionism<br>4. Sudden change in social behavior<br>5. Academic deterioration<br>6. Underachievement and learning disabilities | 1. Disintegrating family relationships<br>2. Economic difficulties and family stresses<br>3. Child and adolescent abuse<br>4. Ambivalence concerning dependence versus independence<br>5. Running away<br>6. Family history of suicide | 1. Prior suicide attempt<br>2. Verbalization of suicide or talk of self-harm<br>3. Preoccupation with death<br>4. Repeated suicide ideation<br>5. Daredevil or self-abusive behavior<br>6. Mental illness such as delusions or hallucinations in schizophrenia<br>7. Overwhelming sense of guilt<br>8. Obsessional self-doubt<br>9. Phobic anxiety<br>10. Clinical depression<br>11. Substance abuse | 1. Stressful life events<br>2. Firearms in the home<br>3. Exposure to suicide |

*Source:* Adapted from © 1998. *Preventing Adolescent Suicide* by Capuzzi, D., & Golden, L. Reproduced by permission of Routledge/ Taylor & Francis Group, LLC.

problems persist. Table 10.2 presents some of the major indicators of childhood or adolescent suicidal behavior.

## Prevention and Intervention Strategies

The most effective way to prevent adolescent suicide is to recognize the warning signs of suicidal behavior and, when necessary, seek professional help. It is therefore critical that not only should all school personnel be trained in identifying suicidal youth, but also that students themselves be trained. The majority of suicide prevention programs for students emphasize a curriculum of decision-making, problem-solving, and general life-skills training. Many of these prevention programs also include information about how students can recognize the signs and symptoms of depression and suicidal behavior among their peers and how to access help from the school and community. Such programs are often incorporated into the health curriculum.

Some educators and parents have concerns that exposure to such programs may have a negative effect on students who are already at risk for suicide, in particular students who may have made an earlier suicide attempt. While there is no research evidence that exposure to such a curriculum has caused a suicide or suicide attempt, the research has recommended that for students who are already at risk for suicide, a prevention curriculum is not appropriate. Instead, such students need to be identified and immediately referred for treatment intervention and follow-up.

The most common suicide intervention program is the **crisis intervention team** approach. The crisis intervention team is composed of teachers, counselors, administrators, social workers, school nurses, and school psychologists who are trained to respond to a variety of crisis situations, including suicide. Their task is to work with one another to identify youngsters who appear to be depressed, overwhelmed by stress, or who display a **suicide gesture** or suicide threat. Problems are often solved at the team level; however, the crisis team may refer a student to a community mental health agency or hospital for emergency care. Other school-based intervention strategies include individual and group counseling, peer counseling, and referral to a suicide hotline for students who are in crisis when school is not in session. School personnel should not attempt to handle the suicidal student alone; they should notify parents if they suspect that a child or an adolescent is suicidal and hold the student in protective custody until the parents arrive.

The crisis intervention team also plays an important role in helping the school return to normal in the aftermath of a suicide. Grief counseling, support groups, implementation of guidelines for interacting with the media, and follow-up care are examples of strategies facilitated by the crisis intervention team.

Parents and teachers are often the last to recognize that the child or adolescent is at risk for suicide. The child's peer group will probably be the first to know that the child needs immediate help. Teachers need to be able to establish a trusting relationship with students so that they will come forward to seek the help they need to respond to a suicidal friend. Many beginning teachers feel very inadequate and uneasy about handling a suicidal student for fear that their actions may precipitate an actual suicide or suicide attempt. The truth is that talking about suicidal tendencies will not exacerbate a suicide or suicide attempt. Most youngsters at risk for suicide are relieved to be able to articulate their fears and concerns to an adult who will listen. The worst response is *no response.* Most students do not know the school nurse or school psychologist, certainly not as well as they know a teacher. They are more likely to trust a teacher and be willing to open up to the teacher.

## Dropping Out of School

A **dropout** is defined by most states and school districts as a student who leaves school for any reason before graduation or completion of a program of study without transferring to another school or institution. Approximately 25% of high school students leave school each year without a diploma. Every school day approximately 7,000 students drop out of school. Among developed countries, the United States ranks 18th in secondary school graduation rates.

As discussed in Chapter 8, there are significant differences in dropout rates among racial/ethnic groups. Fewer than half of American Indian/Alaska Native students complete high school, and only half of Black and Hispanic students graduate on time. Dropout rates also differ by family income, with those from low income families over four times higher than those from high income families (8.7% versus 2.0%) (Chapman, Laird, & KewalRamani, 2010).

Dropping out of school has serious consequences for the individual and society. Dropouts are twice as likely as high school graduates to live in poverty and are more likely to be in poor health, need health and welfare services, and to be incarcerated. Dropouts are also more likely to be unemployed than high school graduates and earn significantly less: dropouts earn approximately $630,000 less in their lifetimes than high school graduates (Chapman, et al., 2010). In addition to the cost to the individual, dropouts from the class of 2011 will cost the nation more than $200 billion in lost tax revenues and public assistance (Unlimited Justice, 2011). As summed up by former National Education Association (NEA) President Reg Weaver, society will be "paying the price, socially, economically, and politically for a generation that is more likely to be incarcerated than to be in college" (quoted by Nabozny, 2007, p. 24).

### Identifying the Potential Dropout

As with other at-risk behaviors, early identification of the potential dropout is critical. The earlier the identification, the more likely dropout prevention efforts will be successful. Fortunately it is possible for schools to identify the majority of potential dropouts by ninth grade or before with up to 85% accuracy (Neild & Balfanz, 2006).

While there is no single factor that can predict who is at risk for dropping out, research has identified a number of factors that are associated with dropping out of school. The three most often identified in the research are poor academic performance, low socioeconomic status, and behavioral problems. Many drop out because of premature transitions to adulthood such as work, pregnancy, or caring for a family member. Other factors commonly associated with dropping out include having been retained in at least one grade, being behind in academic credit, lack of basic skills, problems at home, living with a single parent, frequent moves, having a parent or older sibling who is a dropout, lack of parental involvement in the school, limited English proficiency, low self-esteem, poor relationships with peers and teachers, and school suspension. In addition, dropouts are often individuals who have undiagnosed learning or emotional disabilities and individuals who abuse drugs or alcohol. For females, pregnancy is the principal reason for dropping out of school.

## Prevention and Intervention Strategies

A number of strategies have been found to be effective in preventing students from dropping out. First, because of the importance of early identification and intervention, schools need to pay close attention to risk factors before they are compounded. Potential dropouts need to receive ongoing, comprehensive and personal attention and support from teachers, counselors, and support staff and be closely monitored for attendance and performance. Perhaps most importantly, research on dropout prevention suggests that school-based dropout prevention practices within schools are more successful when they focus on "alterable" aspects of the school environment. "In fact, many of these alterable school factors have a stronger impact on preventing students from dropping out than unalterable factors such as income levels, race, and ethnicity" (Hupfeld, 2007, p. 5). According to the research, successful dropout prevention programs have many of the same strategies:

- Building confidence by providing opportunities for success;
- Communicating the relevance of education to future endeavors;
- Helping students build internal motivations for success;
- Helping students build problem-solving skills;
- Helping students with personal issues such as health and stress management; and
- Creating caring and supportive environments with meaningful relations between teachers and students. (Hupfeld, 2007, pp. 5–6)

Some states have attempted to address the dropout problem by the adoption of punitive or disincentive policies. The most common of these are the "No pass, no drive" laws which are intended to keep teens in school by revoking their driver's licenses if they drop out of school, are chronically truant, or are not progressing toward graduation. Another proposed policy, while not punitive, is to raise the compulsory attendance age to 18.

**For Your Reflection and Analysis**

Do you support the "dropouts don't drive law" as an intervention strategy? Why or why not?

# Teen Pregnancy

Teen pregnancy has been a topic of ongoing concern for parents, educators, and policymakers. In 2009 approximately 410,000 births occurred to adolescent mothers 15–19 years of age, a birthrate of 39 per 1,000 females, the lowest ever recorded in the United States. However, significant racial/ethnic and geographic differences do exist. American Indian/Alaska Native, Black, and Hispanic teens are about two to three times more likely to become pregnant than White teens (see Figure 10.2). Birth rates are highest in the southern states and lowest in New England and the upper Midwest.

While the teen birth rate has decreased over the last two decades, the United States continues to have the highest teen pregnancy and birthrates among industrialized countries (Ventura & Hamilton, 2011), "which puts us at a terrible competitive disadvantage in the world economy" (Hoffman, 2006, p. 1).

## Consequences of Adolescent Pregnancy

Teen pregnancy has major consequences for the individual and for society. Teen childbearing perpetuates a cycle of poverty and disadvantage; "teen mothers are less likely to finish high schools, and their children are more likely to have low school achievement, drop out of high school and give birth themselves" (CDC, 2011b, p. 2). Teen mothers also often lack proper prenatal care, one of the major prerequisites for a healthy delivery. The mortality rate for teenage mothers also is

**Figure 10.2 — Birthrates from 15 to 19 years per 1,000 females, 2009**

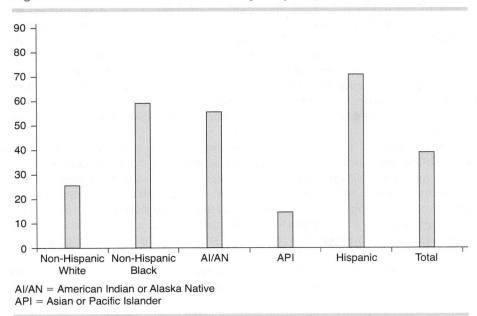

AI/AN = American Indian or Alaska Native
API = Asian or Pacific Islander

*Source:* Hamilton, B.E. Martin, J.A. & Ventura, S.J. (2010). *Teen Pregnancy and Birth Rates.* Retrieved June 19, 2008, from http://www.cdc.gov/Features/dsTeenPregnancy/

higher than for any other age group. Because teen mothers experience so many health problems before and after the birth, they place heavy demands on the social service system. In addition, teen mothers are at risk for premature delivery with accompanying low birth weight (Ventura & Hamilton, 2011). These premature infants often are at risk for a host of subsequent serious health problems. Teen mothers are also at risk for educational and psychological problems and often are overrepresented in classes for students with learning and emotional disabilities. They are also more likely to become incarcerated or be on welfare (Hoffman, 2006).

The problem of teenage pregnancy has several major economic consequences. Teen mothers are more likely to drop out of school than other teens. And, as previously noted, dropouts have a reduced earning potential and are more likely to be on welfare and out of the labor force. It has been estimated that each year teen childbearing costs taxpayers approximately $6 billion in lost tax revenues and another $3 billion in public assistance (CDC, 2011b). Moreover, there is strong evidence that the transfer of poverty from the mother to her children perpetuates a cycle of poverty for future generations.

## Prevention and Intervention Strategies

The obvious primary aim of pregnancy prevention programs is to keep teens from conceiving. This goal is addressed in most schools through a health education curriculum that focuses on abstinence as the most effective method to avoid pregnancy, sexually transmitted diseases, and the risks associated with teen pregnancy. In part because of the controversy sur-

Pregnant teens are at increased risk for dropping out of school.

rounding the teaching of sex education (see the Controversial Issue below), only about half of all schools teach methods of contraception in a required health education course (CDC, 2010). As opposed to what schools currently provide, experts suggest that the most effective programs in reducing teen pregnancy are those that use a multifaceted approach, as the problem is multidimensional, and should not only focus on sexual factors and resultant consequences, but also should include non-sexual factors such as skill training and personal development and should address the multiple sexual and non-sexual antecedents that correlate with teen pregnancy (Oringange, Meremikwu, Eko, Esu, Meremikwu, & Ehiru, 2009).

The primary goals of most intervention strategies are to provide prenatal care, parenting skills, and vocational and personal counseling to adolescent mothers in an effort to reduce the cycle of repeated pregnancies and welfare dependency. Parent resource centers, which are usually coordinated with school health clinics, have proven to be a promising intervention strategy. Such parent resource centers provide pregnant and parenting students with a wide range of health, educational, and social services, including child care. The students who are referred to such resource centers usually work with a case management team that includes a social worker, teacher, and public health nurse. This team interacts with the students' parents and closely monitors the academic progress, attendance, and health of each girl and her baby.

### For Your Reflection and Analysis

To what extent should the school bear the costs and responsibility for providing a pregnancy prevention and intervention program?

# CONTROVERSIAL ISSUE

## Sex Education in Public Schools

Despite continuing high pregnancy rates, only about half of the nation's high schools provide a comprehensive sex education program. Sex education has been a controversial issue in many school districts and has been the subject of numerous judicial challenges. The following are some of the arguments that are given for and against sex education in the public schools:

**For**

1. Early teaching of sex education can help students understand the importance of either remaining abstinent or practicing "safe sex."

2. Sex education can help dispel myths and misinformation about sex (e.g., you cannot contract sexually transmitted diseases (STD) by oral sex or you cannot get pregnant the first time you have sex).

3. Sex education can help prevent the spread of STDs and unplanned pregnancy.

4. Sex education does more than teach about sex. It teaches about sexual health, reproduction, sexuality, and provides students with a basic understanding of their bodies.

5. Many parents do not take the proper time or do not know how to talk to their children about sex.

6. Abstinence-only education has not been effective in reducing sexual activity or teen pregnancy.

**Against**

1. Teaching sex education early can arouse students' curiosity and cause some students to experiment before they are ready.

2. Sex education can go against the religious or moral beliefs of parents or students.

3. Most sex education classes are taught as a brief module in a health or physical education class and are not given enough time to teach the content effectively.

4. Teaching sex education in the school infringes on the option of parents to teach their children when and how they choose.

5. Teaching "safe sex" dilutes or sends mixed messages about the message of abstinence, the only 100% effective method of preventing STDs and pregnancy.

6. Sex education can be embarrassing or even traumatizing to some students.

What is your position on sex education in the public schools? What types of program(s) exist in a school with which you are familiar?

# HISTORICAL NOTE

## Outcasts: Three HIV-Positive Brothers Barred from School

In 1986, in Arcadia, a small town in west-central Florida, three brothers, Ricky (age 9), Robert (age 8), and Randy (age 7) Ray, were diagnosed with HIV, the virus that causes AIDS. They were among the thousands of hemophiliacs who contracted the virus through tainted blood. During this time, fear, misunderstanding, and ignorance regarding HIV/AIDS prevailed. Little was known about the transfer of HIV, and the residents of Arcadia had their own theories: medical conspiracies, mosquitoes, and using the same toilet.

When Clifford and Louise Ray learned of their sons' diagnosis, they notified the school district and attempted to enroll their sons in regular classes. The school board barred their admission. The boys were tutored at home at district expense. The Rays sued the school board. The next year the federal court in Tampa ruled that the Ray children could not be excluded from regular classes and ordered the De Soto County Schools to admit the three boys in the fall. In response, a group calling themselves Citizens Against AIDS in Schools encouraged parents to keep their children at home. The organization drew hundreds of residents to a series of rallies, where they demanded that the Ray children be quarantined. The first day of school hundreds of parents, including

the mayor, kept their children out of school. Ugly protests were followed by death threats. Finally, someone set fire to the Ray home. Quiet Ricky blamed himself for the fire, and Randy, the youngest, was desolate over the loss of his stuffed monkey. The little restuffed monkey without a tail had been with him through all of his hospital stays.

After the fire the Rays moved to Sarasota, where the Ray boys enrolled with little protest. Ricky died in 1992 at age 15. In 1998 the federal government passed the Ricky Ray Relief Fund Act, which acknowledged the government's lax screening of the blood supply and provided compensation for hemophiliacs (many of whom were children) who had contracted AIDS between 1982 and 1987. Robert died in 2000 at age 22 before his scheduled marriage. As of this writing, Randy Ray has full-blown AIDS but maintains an active life.

*Sources:* Buckley, S. (2001, September 2). Slow change of heart. *St. Petersburg Times.* Retrieved September 7, 2005, from www.sptimes.com/News/090201/news_pf/State/slow_chang_of_heart.shtml; and Voboril, M. (October 1987). The castaways: Fears about AIDS drive three boys from home. Retrieved September 7, 2005, from www.maryellenmark.com/text/magazines/life/905W-000-030.html

## Childhood Obesity

Childhood obesity has become a major health issue in the United States. Childhood obesity rates have soared over the past quarter century; today almost 25 million children are considered overweight or obese (CDC, 2010). According to some experts, "if obesity among children continues to increase, our current generation of children will become the first in American history to live shorter lives than their parents" (Clinton Foundation, 2011, p. 1).

Significant racial, ethnic, and socioeconomic differences exist in the prevalence of obesity among children. Obesity is significantly higher among Mexican-American adolescent boys (27%) than among non-Hispanic White boys (17%), and almost twice as high among non-Hispanic Black adolescent girls (29%) than among non-Hispanic White adolescent girls (15%) (Ogden & Carroll, 2010).

Obesity results from a caloric imbalance: too few calories are expended for the number of calories consumed. This imbalance is the result of the interaction of a number of genetic, behavioral, and environmental factors (see Figure 10.3). It is the *interaction* of these factors, rather than any one factor, that is thought to cause obesity. For example, while *genetic factors* may increase an individual's susceptibility to obesity, this susceptibility may need to exist along with contributing behavioral and environmental factors to have a significant impact on weight. *Behavioral factors* related to obesity include excessive energy intake through eating large portions, eating at fast food restaurants, snacking on energy dense foods and consuming sugar-sweetened drinks. Another major behavioral factor contributing to obesity is physical inactivity. The 2009 *Youth Risk Behavior* study found that almost one-fourth of students did not participate in at least 60 minutes of physical activity on any day during the seven days before the survey, and almost one-half did not attend physical education classes (CDC, 2010). The same study found that children spend a considerable amount of time in sedentary behavior,

**Figure 10.3 — Factors Contributing to Childhood Obesity**

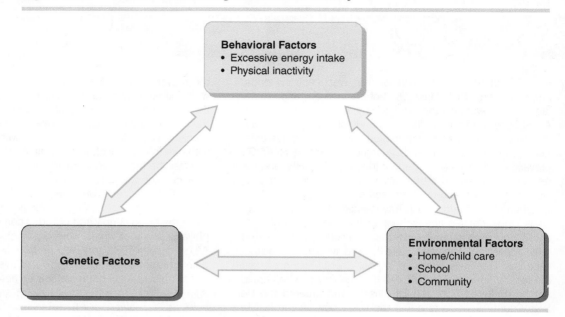

such as watching television or playing video games, another behavioral factor contributing to childhood obesity.

The various environments with which the child interacts also influence childhood obesity. In the home parents not only make major decisions about food, but also serve as role models for their children in developing healthy eating and physical activity habits. Child care providers serve a similar role. Schools not only provide the ideal environment for teaching children to adopt healthy eating and physical activity habits, but they also can have an impact through their nutrition program, their health education program, and their physical activity programs. Community environments—the presence or absence of parks, sidewalks, community recreation programs, and the availability of affordable healthy food choices—can be important influences on children's behavior related to physical activity and healthy eating. For example, one study of 200 neighborhoods found that "there were three times as many supermarkets in wealthy neighborhoods as in poor neighborhoods, leaving fast food restaurants as the most convenient meal option for many low income families" (Clinton Foundation, 2011, p. 1).

## Consequences of Childhood Obesity

Childhood obesity has major consequences for both the individual and society. Obese children and adolescents are at risk for a number of health and psychosocial problems both in their youth and as adults. Among those documented by the Centers for Disease Control and Prevention (2011) are:

- Obese youth have higher risk factors for cardiovascular disease, including high cholesterol and high blood pressure, and type 2 diabetes;
- Obese children and adolescents are at greater risk for bone and joint problems, liver disease, and asthma;
- Sleep apnea (the cessation of breathing while sleeping), while a less common complication among obese children, can lead to various cognitive difficulties (Peoples-Health.com, 2011);
- Psychosocial risks: obese children are often targets of systematic social discrimination which can cause low self-esteem, which in turn, can hinder academic and social functioning, persisting into adulthood; and

- Obese youth are more likely to become overweight or obese as adults, and therefore more at risk for adult health problems such as heart disease, type 2 diabetes, stroke, several types of cancer, and osteoarthritis.

## *Prevention and Intervention: The Role of the School*

Schools cannot solve childhood obesity on their own, but they can help students adopt and maintain healthy eating habits and recommended levels of physical activity. Based on a review of scientific research and the input of health care experts, the CDC (2008) has published 10 key strategies schools can initiate to effectively promote healthy eating and physical activity:

1. Address physical activity and nutrition through a Coordinated School Health Program.
2. Maintain an active health council and designate a school health coordinator to manage and coordinate all school health policies, programs, activities, and resources.
3. Assess the school's health policies and programs and develop a plan for improvement.
4. Strengthen the school's nutrition and physical activity policies (e.g., how often students attend physical education, which items are offered in vending machines and in the cafeteria, and which topics and skills are taught in health education).

More than one third of school age children in the United States are considered obese.

5. Implement a high quality health promotion program for school staff.
6. Implement a high quality course of study in health education.
7. Implement a high quality course of study in physical education.
8. Increase opportunities for students to engage in physical activity (e.g., walking to and from school, after school programs, and intramural sports).
9. Implement a high quality school meals program.
10. Ensure that students have appealing, healthy choices in foods and beverages offered outside the school meals program (e.g., vending machines, school store, after-school programs and activities, and fundraising campaigns).

Schools seeking to improve their physical and nutrition programs face financial challenges in ever more limited budgets as well as a resistance to expanding programs that are not directly related to improving test scores. Nonetheless, historically the schools have played a major role in promoting the physical welfare of children, and it is a role they must continue to play in combating childhood obesity.

# Child Maltreatment

Child maltreatment includes all types of abuse and neglect of a child under the age of 18 by a parent, caregiver, or other person in a custodial role. The major types of child abuse are neglect, physical, sexual, and emotional abuse, all of which can occur separately or in combination with each other. The consequences of child maltreatment can be seen in the immediate and the long term, indeed life-long. They manifest in a variety of physical, psychological, and behavioral domains, including cognitive impairments, socioemotional development, and physical and mental health. Victims of child maltreatment are more likely to abuse drugs and alcohol, experience teen pregnancy, drop out of school, be arrested as a juvenile and adult, and to meet the criteria for at least one psychological disorder (Child Help, 2010).

**Table 10.3 — Rates of Child Abuse and Neglect, Victimization (victims per 1,000) by Maltreatment Type, Gender, Race, and Ethnicity**

|  | Number of Victims | Victimization Rate |
|---|---|---|
| **Maltreatment Type** | | |
| Physical abuse | 123,599 | 1.8 |
| Neglect | 543,035 | 7.5 |
| Medical neglect | 16,837 | 0.3 |
| Sexual abuse | 66,964 | 1.0 |
| Psychological maltreatment | 52,532 | 0.8 |
| Other abuse | 66,487 | 3.7 |
| Unknown | 1,928 | 0.3 |
| **Gender** | | |
| Male | 334,262 | 8.8 |
| Female | 354,476 | 9.7 |
| **Race/Ethnicity*** | | |
| American Indian/Alaska Native | 7335 | 11.6 |
| African American | 152,159 | 16.1 |
| Asian | 6,143 | 0.9 |
| White | 300,266 | 7.8 |
| Multiple Race | 22,044 | 12.4 |
| Hispanic | 141,434 | 8.7 |

*Not all states reporting

*Source:* U.S. Department of Health and Human Services, Administration on Children, Youth and Families, Children's Bureau. (2010) *Child Maltreatment 2009.* Retrieved May 15, 2011, from www.acf.hhs.gov/programs/ch/stats_research/index.html.

In 2009, 3.3 million children, one every 10 seconds, were reported to child protective service agencies for suspected maltreatment and an estimated 772,000 claims were substantiated (USDHHS, 2010). Of these, 78% suffered neglect, 18% physical abuse, 10% sexual abuse, and 8% emotional/psychological abuse (a child may have suffered multiple forms of maltreatment). As shown in Table 10.3, approximately nine male children and 10 female children in every 1,000 were victims of child maltreatment. Approximately half of all victims were White, one quarter (24%) Black, and 22% Hispanic. The highest victimization rates were found among African Americans and American Indian/Alaska Natives.

Child fatalities constituted the most tragic consequence of child abuse. In 2009, an estimated n 1,770 children (ages 0–17), almost five every day, died from abuse and neglect. Of these, 36% was attributed to neglect alone. More than four-fifths were children younger than four years of age. Boys had a slightly higher fatality rate than girls (USDHHS, 2010).

## Child Neglect

**Child neglect** is the failure to provide for a child's basic physical, educational, or emotional needs. Abandonment, expulsion from home, refusal to allow a runaway to return home, inadequate supervision, and the refusal to provide health care in a timely manner are forms of *physical neglect.* Failure to attend to a child's special educational needs, failure to enroll a child in school, and the tolerance of chronic truancy constitute forms of *educational neglect. Emotional neglect* includes the failure to provide for the psychological well-being of the child, being inattentive to a child's needs for affection, and parental permission to use and abuse drugs or alcohol. Female parents tend to be the major perpetrators of child neglect. Because neglect often leaves no outward signs, it is often unreported.

## Physical Abuse

**Physical abuse** is the use of physical force, whether intentional or not, against a child. Examples of physical abuse include punching, beating, kicking, biting, burning, shaking, throwing, stabbing, choking, hitting, and/or otherwise harming a child. As mentioned, in 2009, approximately 18% of maltreated children were victims of physical abuse.

## Sexual Abuse

**Sexual abuse** involves engaging a child in sexual acts. Sexual abuse includes fondling a child's genitals, intercourse, incest, rape, sodomy, exhibitionism, and commercial exploitation through prostitution or the production of pornographic materials. Sexual abuse is considered to be the most underreported form of child maltreatment due to the "conspiracy of silence" that is often associated with such cases. Male parents are primarily identified as the perpetrators of sexual abuse for the highest number of victims (USDHHS, 2010).

## Emotional Abuse

**Emotional abuse** refers to behaviors (psychological/verbal abuse/mental injury) that harm a child's self worth or emotional well being. Emotional abuse almost always occurs with the forms of child maltreatment already mentioned. It includes acts or omissions by the parents or caregivers that could cause serious behavioral, cognitive, emotional, or mental disorders. Specific examples of emotional abuse include such nonphysical abusive behaviors as blaming, disparaging, or rejecting the child; habitual scapegoating, belittling, and intimidating; treating siblings unequally; deliberately enforcing isolation such as confinement to a dark closet; and continually withholding security and affection. In 2009, 8% of victims of maltreatment were emotionally or psychologically abused.

## Identifying Child Abuse and Neglect

A number of factors have been found to increase the risk for child abuse or neglect. These include a family environment where there is a great deal of stress, families that are isolated from friends, relatives or other social support systems, violence in the family, parent history of maltreatment, substance abuse in the family, and single-parent, low-income and undereducated parents. Having a physical, mental or emotional disability also places a child at high risk for maltreatment.

Some of the common signs or indicators of child physical abuse include unexplained injuries, fractures, lumps, bruises, bite marks, and burns. A pattern of accidents may also be an indicator. Children who have been subject to any form of abuse often exhibit a variety of behavior changes, including aggressive or withdrawn behavior, neglected appearance, attention-seeking behavior, anxiety, or fear. They may engage in self-destructive behaviors and exhibit low self-esteem, depression, and severe emotional problems. They may be socially isolated, have poor relationships with parents, repeatedly run away, and have a history of frequent tardiness or absence from school. The presence of one of these signs does not prove a child is being abused, but when they occur repeatedly or in combination, as they often will if the child is being abused, they warrant closer examination and possible reporting. Some of the physical and behavioral indicators of possible neglect and abuse that teachers should be aware of are listed in Table 10.4.

Parents or caregivers also exhibit behaviors that may be indicators of child abuse or neglect. For example, they may show little concern for the child, provide minimal supervision, see the child as burdensome, or rarely look at or touch the child. They may deny the existence of, or blame the child for, problems the child is having at home or at school. They may see the child as bad or worthless and ask teachers or administrators to use harsh physical discipline if the child misbehaves.

### Table 10.4 — Signs of Child Abuse and Neglect

#### Signs of Physical Abuse

Consider the possibility of physical abuse when the child:

- has unexplained burns, bites, bruises, broken bones, or black eyes;
- has fading bruises or other marks noticeable after an absence from school;
- seems frightened of the parents and protests or cries when it is time to go home;
- shrinks at the approach of adults;
- reports injury by a parent or another adult caregiver.

#### Signs of Neglect

Consider the possibility of neglect when the child:

- is frequently absent from school;
- begs or steals food or money;
- lacks needed medical or dental care, immunizations, or glasses;
- is consistently dirty and has severe body odor;
- lacks sufficient clothing for the weather;
- abuses alcohol or other drugs;
- states that there is no one at home to provide care.

#### Signs of Sexual Abuse

Consider the possibility of sexual abuse when the child:

- has difficulty walking or sitting;
- suddenly refuses to change for gym or to participate in physical activities;
- reports nightmares or bedwetting;
- experiences a sudden change in appetite;
- demonstrates bizarre, sophisticated, or unusual sexual knowledge or behavior;
- becomes pregnant or contracts a venereal disease, particularly if under age 14;
- runs away;
- reports sexual abuse by a parent or another adult caregiver.

#### Signs of Emotional Maltreatment

Consider the possibility of emotional maltreatment when the child:

- shows extremes in behavior, such as overly compliant or demanding behavior, extreme passivity, or aggression;
- is either inappropriately adult (parenting other children, for example) or inappropriately infantile (frequently rocking or head banging, for example);
- is delayed in physical or emotional development;
- has attempted suicide;
- reports a lack of attachment to the parent.

*Source:* From *Recognizing Child Abuse and Neglect: Signs and Symptoms*, by National Clearinghouse on Child Abuse and Neglect Information, 2007, Washington, DC: U.S. Government Printing Office. www.nccanch.acf.hhs.gov

There is increasing awareness that abuse of drugs or alcohol by parents and other caretakers may be related to abuse and neglect. Many states have responded by expanding the definition of child abuse or neglect to include exposing children to illegal drugs in the home environment.

As discussed in Chapter 12, state child abuse statutes require that child abuse be reported by school counselors, school psychologists, social workers, teachers, nurses, or administrators to the local child protective agency, department of welfare, or law enforcement agency. Teachers and counselors must report suspected abuse or neglect even though to do so would violate a confidence; they cannot claim privileged communication as a defense for failure to report.

Most state reporting statutes detail the procedures that are to be followed in making the report. In all jurisdictions the initial report may be made orally to a law enforcement agency, child protective services, or other designated agency. It is important that teachers be familiar with the applicable state statutes and the school district's policies on reporting child abuse and neglect. State statutes that require teachers to report suspected child abuse do not demand that reporters be certain that the child has been abused, only that there be "reasonable cause to believe" that the child is subject to abuse or neglect. Under all state statutes, school employees who report suspected child abuse or neglect are provided immunity from civil and criminal liability if the report was made in good faith.

## Prevention and Intervention Strategies

Recognizing and reporting child maltreatment are important to any intervention strategy, but schools must also be involved in preventing maltreatment. A number of school-based prevention programs have been introduced to address child maltreatment. Some are provided through specifically designed programs, others through the existing curriculum. Many school districts have incorporated the prevention program content into the health education curriculum in order to keep it outside the controversial sex education domain. The most common curriculum are (1) life skills training, (2) socialization skills, (3) problem-solving and coping skills, (4) preparation for parenthood, and (5) self-protection training (Crosson-Tower, 2003).

Because child maltreatment occurs across all socioeconomic classes and ethnic/racial groups, it is likely that most teachers will be confronted with this problem at some point during their teaching career. In fact, 16.5% of all reports of abuse or neglect are made by teachers. When abuse or neglect occurs, it is important to remember not only one's legal and professional obligation to report the abuse but also one's obligation to the student. Although these are normally delicate and emotionally charged situations, avoidance is not the appropriate response. It is always better to err on the side of the child's welfare.

For the child or adolescent victim of maltreatment, the attitude of the school personnel is critical. It is important that school personnel understand and believe that the child is not to blame and communicate this to the child. The teacher, in particular, is in a unique position to create a classroom environment that is safe, nurturing, and responsive to the needs of the vulnerable youngster. The teacher can help the abused child set healthy boundaries and know that those boundaries will be respected. Teachers need to set reasonable goals, but they also need to provide the support necessary for youngsters to feel confident and successful. Because abused children often feel powerless to control their environment, the teacher's role is to help them become more resilient and regain a personal sense of control. The first step in a child's regaining control is by having basic needs met within a safe and nurturing school environment. Because abused children tend to have low self-esteem, a caring and sensitive teacher can help them learn that they have many strengths and that they are valued and accepted members of society.

**For Your Reflection and Analysis**

What are the procedures for reporting child abuse in your state?

# School Violence

Schools are intended to be places where children and teens can feel safe. Yet the fact is that more nonfatal crimes are committed against students at school than away from school (Roberts, Zharing, & Truman, 2010). Every day thousands of children across the country are the victims of various forms of school violence, including physical attack or fighting without a weapon, theft/larceny, and vandalism. The 2009 *Youth Risk Behavior* survey reported that almost 15% of male students and 7% of female students were involved in fighting at school, and 8% of students reported being threatened or injured with a weapon on school property one or more times in the 12 months prior to the survey (CDC, 2010). Peer sexual harassment based on gender, sexual orientation, and disability is another common form of violence experienced by students: 11% of females and 4% of males reported being the victim of the most severe form of sexual harassment—rape. In recent years bullying has become one of the most serious problems facing the schools, with 20% of all students being bullied on school property (CDC, 2010). The most violent act, homicide, takes an average of 19 students each year (Roberts, et al., 2010).

Students are not the only victims of violence at school: in 2007–08, 4% of teachers reported being physically attacked by a student and 7% were threatened with injury. The percentages for both being attacked and threatened were higher in city schools than suburban, town, or rural schools. Male teachers were threatened more than female teachers (9.3% vs. 6.9%), whereas a higher percentage of female teachers were actually attacked than male teachers (3.7% vs. 4.1%) (Roberts et al., 2010).

School violence affects not only its victims, but also other students who see themselves as potential victims. Five percent of high school students reported they did not attend school because they felt unsafe at school or on their way to school. Hispanics and Blacks, both male and female, were the most likely not to attend school because they did not feel safe (CDC, 2010).

Every day thousands of school children are victims of bullying or other forms of violence.

Acts of school violence are typically not isolated events and do not come without some warning sign. A study of school shootings by the U.S. Secret Service (2001) found that over half of the school-associated homicide perpetrators gave some type of warning sign (e.g., threat or note) prior to the violent act. Seven told other students about the plan. Most attackers had been victims of bullying, and that bullying played a role in the attack. The study also found that almost all attackers had either attempted suicide or threatened suicide prior to the incident, and over 80% had experienced a major change in a significant relationship or a loss of status. Most attackers also had previously used, or had access to, guns. Other risk factors associated with violent behavior by youth include: a prior history of violence, drug, alcohol, or tobacco use, association with delinquent peers, poor family functioning, poor grades in school, and poverty in the community.

### Bullying

**Bullying** is a serious problem affecting schools, large and small, urban and rural, all across the United States. Bullying is a form of aggressive antisocial behavior that involves one or more individuals who repeatedly and intentionally harass, coerce, or intimidate another individual verbally, physically, socially, and/or psychologically, particularly when there exists an imbalance of power. Bullying differs from other aggressive behavior (e.g., jostling or rough play or teasing) that is a normal part of childhood in that the latter is benign, not malicious nor intended to harm or dominate the peer (Doll, Song, & Siemers, 2004). When aggressive peer interactions occur between children, they will typically work to resolve the conflict, especially if it involves a friend. However, if the conflict is left unresolved, or if the opportunity presents itself in an unequal power relationship, children may resort to physical or verbal aggression or social ostracism in order to prevail over or dominate classmates (Doll et al., 2004).

Almost 32% of teens report being bullied at school, with the prevalence being higher among females (33%) than among males (30%). Asian students report the lowest incidence of bullying (18%) (Roberts et al., 2010). Males are more likely to be involved in physical bullying, while females are more likely to engage in social bullying (e.g., rejection, exclusion, slander, spreading of rumors). Bullying often begins at the elementary level, peaks in middle school, and lessens in high school. Most bullying occurs when students are in school (78%), during the school day in the hallways, bathrooms, and on the playground.

Children and teens who are most at risk for being bullied tend to be those who are most vulnerable because of age, gender, physical weakness, timidity, insecurity, poor self-esteem, depression, mental capacity, or lack of protection from peers or teachers. They also tend to be those who are less popular, have fewer friends, do not get along well with others, and do not conform to gender norms (Stopbullying.gov, n.d.).

Bullying affects the overall climate of the school. And the results of bullying are felt not only by the victim, but also by the bully and by the onlookers, who may feel powerless, guilty that they did not act to stop the bullying, and afraid that they might be the next victim. Bullying can affect the self-esteem of the victims, make them depressed, drop out or avoid school, and in extreme cases like the students involved in the school shootings in Columbine or the student in the Video Insight, commit suicide.

### Cyberbullying

One form of bullying that has increased dramatically in the last several years is *cyberbullying.* Cyberbullying includes sending hateful, aggressive, or threatening emails or instant messages, spreading rumors or false information, posting embarrassing photos or personal information, and sexual harassment. Cyberbullying has increased as the number of teenagers using computers and cell phones and interacting on social networks such as Facebook and video sharing sites such as YouTube has increased. About 20% of youth aged 10–17 years report being victims of cyberbullying (Hinduja & Patchin, 2010). Cyberbullying differs from other bullying in that the bully can be anonymous and can be at some distance from the victim. It also differs from traditional bullying in that the actions of a cyberbully are viral; "that is, a large number of people (at school, in the neighborhood, in the city, in the world) can be involved in a cyber-attack on a victim or at least find out about the incident with a few keystrokes or clicks of the mouse" (Hinduja & Patchin, 2010, p. 2).

### *Prevention and Intervention Strategies*

The majority of public schools have initiated some type of formal violence prevention and/or violence reduction program. The escalation of bullying has also

**For Your Reflection and Analysis**

Have you ever been bullied? Witnessed bullying? How did you respond? What could the school have done to prevent the incident?

## VIDEO INSIGHT

### The In Crowd and Social Cruelty

This ABC News video examines both what it feels like to be part of the in crowd as well as being a victim of social cruelty, specifically bullying. The pervasiveness and seriousness of bullying is presented by real-life video taken on school campuses and by an interview with the family of a young girl who committed suicide to escape relentless bullying. Narrator John Stossell shares his high school experience of being in the "out crowd." Psychologist Michael Thompson, the author of *Best Friends, Worst Friends,* explains what it takes to be popular, why young people bully, and what some schools are doing to prevent bullying.

1. Have you ever been involved in an incident of bullying either as the bully, the victim, or an onlooker?

2. How does bullying affect the bully, the victim, and the onlooker?

3. What can you as a teacher do to combat social cruelty and bullying?

led most school districts to adopt antibullying policies and bullying prevention programs. Most of these programs attempt to reach students through a variety of in- and out-of-school activities. The most common violence prevention strategies involve the enactment and enforcement of expanded and clearly articulated discipline codes, life skills training, the establishment of peer mediation, conflict resolution, law-related education programs, and the institution of increased security measures, including security personnel and security equipment on campus. Bullying prevention programs also focus on empowering students to move off the sidelines and become a defender of the victim. They also involve staff training on how to intervene in a bullying incident and the importance of signaling by intervention that bullying is unacceptable and will not be tolerated.

Effective prevention programs also emphasize what is probably the most important action schools can take to prevent violence: recognizing the warning signs of a potentially violent youth and making appropriate referrals. These warning signs are presented in Table 10.5. It is important to note that these warning signs should be viewed as potential indicators, not as predictors of violence. Once these students are identified, they must receive coordinated services that might include the schools; social services; mental health providers; and, if necessary, law enforcement and the juvenile justice system. "A number of approaches have been developed for interventions at this stage, including anger management training, structured after-school programs, mentoring, group and family counseling, changing instructional practices, and tutoring" (National Youth Violence Prevention Resource Center, n.d., p. 1).

Another very important action schools can take, one that was a key recommendation of the Columbine Review Commission (2001), is to work to overcome the student "code of silence." Schools need to emphasize to students that warning an adult or school official about the proposed violent act could save a life. Students also need to be convinced that all threats of violence will be taken seriously and investigated (Columbine Review Commission, 2001). In an effort to encourage students to warn authority figures and make warning more comfortable, some schools have installed phone lines for anonymous tips. Youngsters need to be assured that if they report a potential violent act, their name will be kept confidential and the call will not be traced.

Because most schools will experience some episode of violence, the violence prevention program should be linked to a crisis response plan. Such a plan will typically

**Table 10.5 — Warning Signs of Potentially Violent Youth**

- Social withdrawal
- Excessive feelings of isolation and being alone
- Excessive feelings of rejection
- Being a victim of violence
- Feelings of being picked on and persecuted
- Low school interest and poor academic performance
- Expression of violence in writings and drawings
- Uncontrolled anger
- Patterns of impulsive and chronic hitting, intimidating, and bullying behaviors
- History of discipline problems
- History of violent and aggressive behavior
- Intolerance for differences and prejudicial attitudes
- Drug and alcohol use
- Affiliation with gangs
- Inappropriate access to, possession of, and use of firearms
- Serious threats of violence

*Source: Early Warning, Timely Response: A Guide to Safe Schools,* by K. Dwyer, D. Osher, & C. Warger, 1998, Washington, DC: U.S. Department of Education.

call for the establishment of a crisis response team and describe what to do both when a crisis occurs and in its aftermath. For example, members of a crisis team might be responsible for evacuating students to a safe area in the case of a violent act on campus, a bomb threat, or a natural disaster such as an earthquake; debriefing and leading a discussion or support group following the death or loss of one of the members of the school; and monitoring and supporting friends of a suicide or homicide victim.

States and the federal government have responded to the increase in school violence by enacting legislation aimed at its prevention and effective intervention. In 1994 Congress passed the Gun Free Schools Act (1994), which requires states and school districts, as a condition of receiving federal funding for elementary and secondary education, to put in place zero-tolerance policies under which students who bring guns to school are expelled for at least one year. States have not only enacted zero-tolerance statutes, but most also have mandated that a school district develop a school crisis plan and practice its implementation. Many states have also passed statutes requiring districts to adopt antibullying policies.

# Gay, Lesbian, Bisexual, Transgender, and Questioning (GLBTQ) Youth

Sexual orientation is an enduring emotional, romantic, sexual, or affectionate attraction toward another human being. Because sexual orientation develops across the life span, individuals may realize at various periods in their lives that they are heterosexual, gay, lesbian, or bisexual. An individual may identify himself or herself as homosexual or bisexual without having had any sexual experience. Others, in particular adolescents, may have had sexual experiences with someone of the same gender but not consider themselves to be gay, lesbian, or bisexual (American Psychological Association, 2005). **Transgendered** individuals are those whose birth sex is in conflict with their psychological gender identity. Questioning individuals are those who are questioning their own sexual preference. An estimated 5% to 6% of the student population, or as many as two million school-age youth, may be gay, lesbian, or bisexual (Human Rights Watch, 2005).

Too often gay, lesbian, bisexual, transgendered, and questioning (GLBTQ) students attend schools with a culture that is not only intolerant of sexual minorities, but is also complicit of intolerance and violence toward them (Savage & Horley, 2009). The *2009 National School Climate Survey*, which chronicles the experiences of GLBT youth in the United States, characterized schools nationwide as "hostile environments for a distressing number of LGBT students—almost all of whom commonly hear homophobic remarks and face verbal and physical harassment and even physical assault because of their sexual orientation or gender expression" (Kosciw, Greytalk, Diaz, & Bartkiewicz, 2010, p. 3).

The serious and persistent harassment and victimization GLBTQ students experience has serious negative consequences in terms of educational aspirations, academic achievement, and psychological well-being (Kosciw, et al., 2010). GLBTQ youth are at risk for many of the problems discussed in this chapter, substance use and abuse, dropping out of school, and sexual abuse, as well as rejection by family and peer group. Gay, lesbian, bisexual, and transgender students respond to the fear, rejection, guilt, and alienation they feel by withdrawing from friends and family, abstaining from school, failing to concentrate, developing low self-esteem, and, in the most serious cases, developing major depression or attempting suicide.

## *Improving the School Climate*

Schools have a professional and legal responsibility to ensure that all students feel safe, are supported in school, and are in an environment that is conducive to learning. The attention focused on bullying in recent years has led the majority of states and almost all schools to adopt antibullying laws or policies. Unfortunately, as a

# TEACHER OF THE YEAR

*Justin Darnell Colorado*

I teach because our under-served populations deserve more than a second-rate education. Low-income families can no longer be expected to simply work harder in the face of inequity. We talk about achievement gaps when the problem is also opportunity gaps. I owe my students the opportunity to be in a classroom that's engaging. I owe my students the opportunity to work with their peers in a positive way. I owe my students the chance to learn in an environment that is caring, comforting, and a place where they can be at their best. I owe my students "everything," because they are amazing, and they deserve an amazing future. We can take steps toward this future by stopping our use of deficit language. For instance, I prefer the term "non-dominant" to "at-risk," which to me has a negative connotation and may set students as individuals to be pitied rather than celebrated. Join me in taking a stand on their behalf.

national survey of principals found, in many cases these policies do not specifically mention sexual orientation or gender identity expression (GLEN, 2008). While it is critically important that schools adopt and enforce comprehensive bullying policies, with clearly articulated reporting guidelines and disciplinary consequences, policies are only a partial solution to improving the school climate for GLBTQ students. Among the strategies that have been recommended by experts to improve the school climate for GLBTQ students are the following:

- Provide staff development for school personnel that includes a review of psychological and social research on same-sex sexual orientation, encourages an examination of beliefs and attitudes toward such orientation, and teaches them how to help students who approach them with issues of sexual identity.

- Increase student access to appropriate and accurate information regarding sexuality and sexual identity through inclusive curriculum and community resources.

- Be aware of language. Teachers and administrators need to be aware of the language students use and take action to stop the use of stereotypical language and the use of words such as "fag" and "that's so gay," which serve to hurt and marginalize GLBTQ students (Weinberg, 2009).

- Support student clubs, such as Gay-Straight Alliance, that provide support for GLBTQ youth and address their issues in education (GLEN, 2010).

- Identify "safe spaces," such as counselors' offices or designated classrooms, where GLBTQ youth can receive support from administrators, teachers, or other school staff (CDC, 2011).

In addition to improving the school climate, counselors, teachers, and administrators should be aware of the resources in the community that can help these youth. Among the resources are telephone hotlines and such organizations as Parents and Friends of Lesbians and Gays (P-FLAG) and the Gay, Lesbian and Straight Education Network.

In its *Guide to Sexual Harassment* (discussed in Chapter 12), the Office of Civil Rights provided examples of antigay harassment that are prohibited by Title IX. These guidelines have significant implications for all schools because schools that fail to follow the guidelines in responding to this and other forms of sexual harassment risk losing federal funding.

## Summary

At-risk children and youth are a particular challenge for school personnel and mental health professionals. Because of their association with students, teachers and counselors play a vital role in identifying at-risk students. Prevention and intervention programs for a variety of at-risk behaviors have become the combined responsibility of schools, social service agencies, churches, faith communities, parent groups, and law enforcement agencies. Although for each at-risk behavior a number of prevention and intervention strategies have been devised, growing evidence supports the primacy of early identification and treatment. Creating classrooms and school environments that foster resilience and strengthen protective factors is also most important. Chapter 12 will expand the discussion of the responsibilities of teachers. We will also consider their legal rights, as well as those of their students. But first we will explore the legal basis for public education and the legal issues surrounding the church–state relationship in education in Chapter 11.

# PROFESSIONAL DEVELOPMENT
## *Workshop*

## *Prepare for the State Licensure Examination*

Mrs. Chavez, a 10th-grade math teacher at Temple High School, glanced at the clock on the wall and noted it was already 3:15 P.M. It was Friday afternoon. Just minutes before, all of her students had hurried from her classroom, bound for the parking lot or buses. As Mrs. Chavez began to organize her desk for Monday morning class, she became startled as she glanced up and saw Lucia Alvarez standing in front of her. Lucia was one of her best students and had been absent for several days, and Mrs. Chavez was pleased to see her in school. However, it was clear that Lucia had been crying. Mrs. Chavez motioned to Lucia to sit in the chair beside her desk. Lucia slowly sat down and immediately began to weep uncontrollably. In a quiet and compassionate voice, Mrs. Chavez said, "Lucia, what's wrong? Tell me and let me try to help." After a few moments, Lucia gained her composure and told Mrs. Chavez that she was four months pregnant. She began to weep again. In a barely audible voice she said, "I can't tell my parents. My father is very strict. He'll kill me! Maybe I should just save him the trouble and do it myself. I really wanted to be the first in my family to graduate from high school and go to college, and now I'll have to drop out."

Mrs. Chavez held Lucia's hand and quietly said, "Lucia, the first thing you must do is *not* focus on handling this situation alone. Because you are 15 years old and a minor, you must tell your parents and let them help you through this. If you like, either I or Mrs. Radcliff, the school counselor, would be willing to be with you when you talk to your parents."

Lucia stopped crying and seemed more in control. Mrs. Chavez asked her if the father of the baby was aware of the pregnancy. Lucia said she had not told him. Mrs. Chavez asked the age of the father. Lucia said he just celebrated his 17th birthday. Mrs. Chavez asked Lucia if she knew about the pregnancy support group that Temple High had initiated during the spring semester. Lucia said she had heard about it during the summer from one of her friends, but because it had not seemed relevant for her at the time, she did not think much about it except that it sounded like a good idea. Mrs. Chavez suggested that Lucia talk with either Mrs. Radcliff or Ms. Hernandez, the school nurse, about the support group because both of those individuals cosponsored the group, which meets weekly after school.

Lucia got up to leave, and Mrs. Chavez also got up from her chair and hugged Lucia. Mrs. Chavez's parting words were, "Lucia, let me know how either I or anyone at the school can help you." Lucia wiped away her tears and said, "Thank you. I will." After Lucia closed the door and left, Mrs. Chavez thought to herself, "Another prom baby!"

1. How should Mrs. Chavez respond to Lucia's comment about her father or her own suicide? What responsibility do teachers have to report threats of violence to self or others?

2. What family and community considerations might influence a student's decision to remain in or drop out of school?

3. If the father of the baby were 21 years of age or older, what additional responsibility would Mrs. Chavez have had relative to reporting the information?

### Build Your Knowledge Base
1. If you were confronted with a suicidal child in your classroom, what steps might you take to ensure that child's safety? What type of information and experiences do prospective teachers need to better prepare them to work effectively with children who are at risk for suicidal behavior?

2. What role do schools play in promoting educational resilience? What specific resilience-promoting strategies might you use in your classroom?
3. How can the school help in combating teen pregnancy? AIDS? STDs? How comfortable would you be in discussing safe sex with your students?
4. How does peer pressure contribute to adolescent substance abuse and youth violence? How can teachers use the power of peer influence to combat these problems?
5. How can the school and society more effectively address the problem of violence in the schools? Because the majority of youth deaths result from homicide or suicide by gunshot wounds, what can and should be done to restrict the use of firearms by minors?

## Develop Your Portfolio

1. Interview a school counselor, social worker, school psychologist, school nurse, or special education teacher regarding their experiences in working with at-risk children and youth. Prepare a reflection paper that describes your reaction to their experiences. Include a statement regarding what steps you will take to become more knowledgeable and effective in working with at-risk students. Place your reflection paper in your portfolio under **INTASC Standard 10, Leadership and Collaboration**.

2. Select one particular at-risk behavior (underachievement, retention in grade, discipline problems, dropping out of school, using and abusing drugs or alcohol, engaging in premature unprotected sexual activity, teen pregnancy, obesity, being a victim or perpetrator of violence, and contemplating or attempting suicide). Examine information and referral resources in your community that are designed to address that particular at-risk behavior. Interview a representative of one of the community agencies that provide services for that particular at-risk behavior, and inquire about the extent to which that agency interfaces and works directly with the schools. Prepare a file on "Information and Referral Resources for At-Risk Students." Include a summary of your interview in the file. Place your file in your portfolio under **INTASC Standard 10, Leadership and Collaboration.**

## Explore Teaching and Learning: Field Experiences

1. Arrange an interview with a social worker to identify the ways in which schools work with other child welfare agencies. What is the source of funds for these activities? What role does the school district have in coordinating the activities?

2. Building on the previous field experience, arrange an interview with a middle school or high school counselor to secure information about programs that have been started to address the special needs of students who are at risk of dropping out of school. How many staff members have been involved and what is the source of funds? Summarize the findings of your efforts.

## MyEducationLab

Go to **Topic 2, Student Diversity,** in the MyEducationLab (www.myeducationlab.com) for *Foundations of American Education*, where you can:

- Find learning outcomes for student diversity along with the national standards that connect to these outcomes.
- Complete Assignments and Activities that can help you more deeply understand the chapter content.
- Apply and practice your understanding of the core teaching skills identified in the chapter with the Building Teaching Skills and Dispositions learning units.
- Examine challenging situations and cases presented in the IRIS Center Resources.

- Access additional video clips of CCSSO National Teachers of the Year award winners responding to the question, "Why Do I Teach?" in the Teacher Talk section.
- Check your comprehension on the content covered in the chapter with the Study Plan. Here you will be able to take a chapter quiz, receive feedback on your answers, and then access Review, Practice, and Enrichment activities to enhance your understanding of chapter content.
- Use the Online Lesson Plan Builder to practice lesson planning and integrating national and state standards into your planning.

# Legal Framework
# for the Public Schools

Like many schools, Oceanview High School has found it difficult to find qualified teachers to fill vacancies left by "baby boomer" retirees. In particular, Oceanview has had difficulty finding teachers for its advanced placement science courses. For this reason, Mr. Kindrick, the principal, was particularly pleased when Jean Collins applied for an open science position. Mrs. Collins had recently moved to Oceanview with her family when her husband's company transferred him there. She had previously taught science at a private denominational high school.

After an interview and following the district's hiring process, Mrs. Collins began teaching at Oceanview. Toward the middle of the fall semester, Mr. Kindrick visited Mrs. Collins's class to conduct a scheduled performance evaluation. He found her to be an exceptionally gifted teacher who clearly cared about her students. On that occasion he did notice that Mrs. Collins was wearing a very large cross, five to

six inches long. A few days later he saw her at a faculty meeting and she was wearing the same cross. Within two weeks he received a call from Larry Kruz, the father of one of Mrs. Collins's students, complaining about the fact that, according to the student, Mrs. Collins wore the cross every day and that it was a distraction and seemed to get in the way as she wrote on the board and leaned over students' desks, exacerbated by the fact that she seemed to always be handling it. According to the father, he and the student, who were not Christians, were offended by Mrs. Collins's oversized cross and by what they considered her attempt to bring attention to it. They asked that Mr. Kindrick direct Mrs. Collins to stop wearing the cross.

What action should Mr. Kindrick take? What additional information might be important to his decision? What constitutional issues are involved? What, if any, action should Mr. Kindrick have taken prior to Mr. Kruz's complaint?

The U.S. Constitution protects Mrs. Collins's right to freedom of religious expression as well as students' rights not to be subjected to state actions that further the establishment of religion. It is within the rules of action or conduct provided by federal and state constitutional provisions, federal and state statutory law, regulations and decisions of administrative agencies, school board policies, and court decisions that the framework is established for the operation of the public schools. Before going into the specifics of the law as they affect teachers' and students' rights, this chapter provides a brief overview of the major sources of school law, the federal and state court systems, and their interrelationship in forming the legal basis for public education. The second half of the chapter addresses one of the most controversial issues in education today—the appropriate relationship between religion and the schools. After reading this chapter you should be able to:

- Identify federal constitutional provisions affecting education.
- Discuss the importance of state constitutional provisions affecting education.
- Compare statutory law, case (or common) law, and administrative law.
- Describe the levels of the federal court system and those of a typical state court system.
- Explain how challenges under the Establishment Clause are evaluated.
- Give the current posture of the courts with regard to prayer and Bible reading, religious expression, access to school buildings, challenges to the curriculum, and compulsory attendance.
- Distinguish between permissible and impermissible state aid to nonpublic education.

## MyEducationLab

Visit the MyEducationLab for *Foundations of American Education* to enhance your understanding of chapter concepts with a personalized Study Plan. You'll also have the opportunity to hone your teaching skills through video and case based Assignments and Activities, and Building Teaching Skills and Disposition lessons.

### For Your Reflection and Analysis

In what way does federal support of education contribute to the "common defense" of the United States?

# Federal Constitutional Provisions Affecting Education

Constitutions are the highest level of law. They are the fundamental laws of the people of a state or nation, establishing the very character and concept of their government, its organization and officers, its sovereign powers, and the limitations of its power. Constitutions are written broadly so as to endure changing times and circumstances. Although constitutions can be changed by amendment, the process is normally difficult and is seldom used. The Constitution of the United States, written more than 200 years ago, has served the needs of a fledgling nation and a world power, with only 27 amendments.

Education is not mentioned in the U.S. Constitution. It is through Article I, Section 8, the so-called General Welfare Clause, that the federal government has become involved in education. Article I, Section 8 gives Congress the power to tax and to "provide for the common defense and general welfare of the United States." Over the years, the U.S. Supreme Court has interpreted the general welfare clause as authorizing Congress to tax and to spend money for a variety of activities, including education, that were construed as being in the general welfare. However, the general welfare clause does not give Congress the authority to do anything it pleases to provide for the general welfare, only to tax for that purpose. In regard to education, this means that although Congress may levy taxes to provide support for education, it may not legislate control of education. However, in recent years the Supreme Court has ruled that the federal government can attach conditions to the use of federal funds that, if not complied with, may result in the denial or withdrawal of the funds. Exercising its authority under the general welfare clause, Congress has enacted a massive body of legislation that has provided direct federal support for a variety of instructional programs, as well as providing services and programs for identified special needs students and financial assistance to prospective teachers.

Several of the amendments to the Constitution affect schools (see Figure 11.1). Among these are the First, Fourth, Eighth, Tenth, and Fourteenth amendments. These constitutional provisions serve as the basis for education-related cases being brought to federal courts.

## First Amendment

The First Amendment addresses several basic personal freedoms. It provides that

> Congress shall make no law respecting an establishment of religion, or prohibiting the free exercise thereof; or abridging the freedom of speech or of the press; or of the right of the people peaceably to assemble, and to petition the Government for a redress of grievances.

**Figure 11.1 — Laws and Regulations Affecting the Schools**

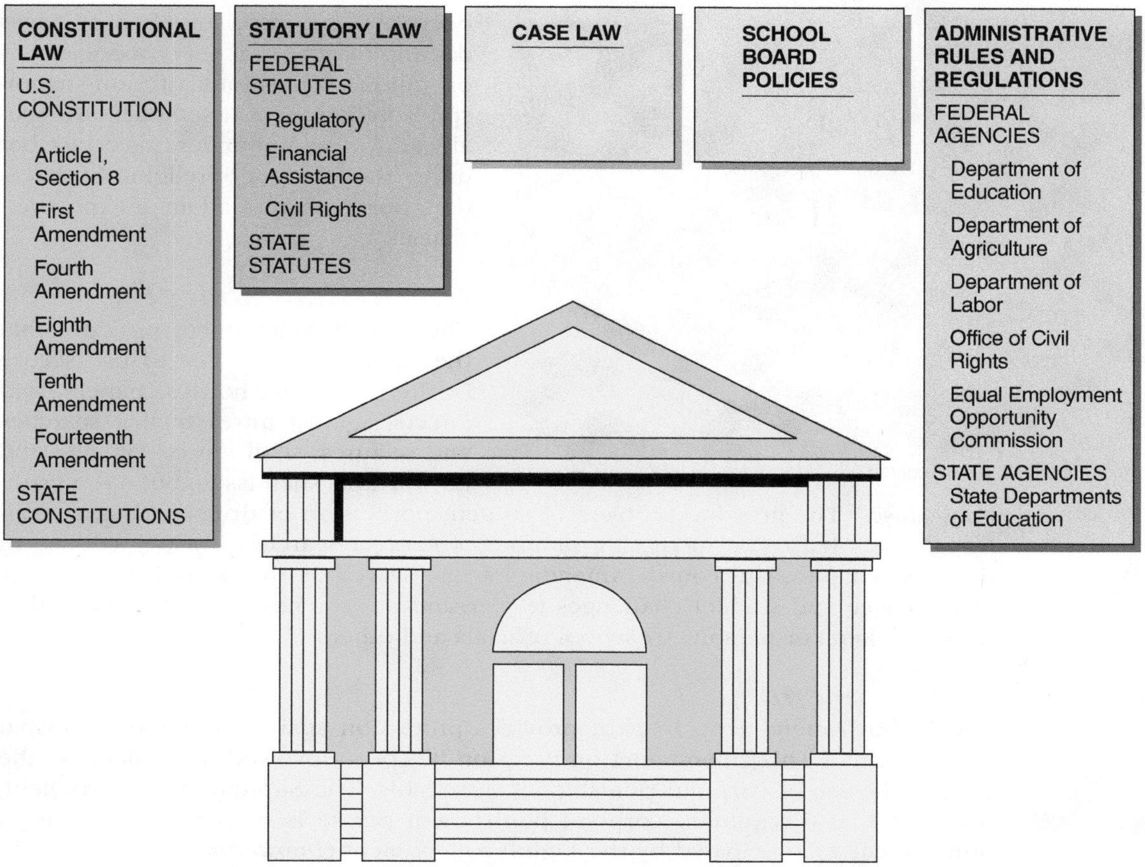
CONSTITUTIONAL LAW
U.S. CONSTITUTION
Article I, Section 8
First Amendment
Fourth Amendment
Eighth Amendment
Tenth Amendment
Fourteenth Amendment
STATE CONSTITUTIONS
STATUTORY LAW
FEDERAL STATUTES
Regulatory
Financial Assistance
Civil Rights
STATE STATUTES
CASE LAW
SCHOOL BOARD POLICIES
ADMINISTRATIVE RULES AND REGULATIONS
FEDERAL AGENCIES
Department of Education
Department of Agriculture
Department of Labor
Office of Civil Rights
Equal Employment Opportunity Commission
STATE AGENCIES
State Departments of Education

Increasingly, the first clause of the First Amendment, the establishment and free exercise of religion clause, has become the focus of litigation in education. The schools have become a battleground for some of the most volatile disputes over the appropriate governmental relationship vis-à-vis religion (Thomas, McCarthy, & Cambron-McCabe, 2009). As discussed later in this chapter, these cases have dealt with numerous issues surrounding (1) school practices objected to on the basis of promoting or inhibiting religion (e.g., released time, prayer, Bible reading), (2) curriculum content, and (3) public funds used to provide support to nonpublic schools or to students or parents of students attending nonpublic schools.

The second clause of the First Amendment, dealing with the freedom of speech and press, has also been the subject of a growing number of education cases in recent years. Both teachers and students have alleged violations of their rights to express themselves in a variety of ways. Teachers have also become more concerned with what they consider attempts to infringe on their academic freedom to select textbooks and other teaching materials and to practice certain teaching methodologies.

The third clause of the First Amendment, which deals with the rights of citizens to assemble, has been called into question in a number of education cases concerning the freedom of association. Both students and teachers have become more assertive of their rights to belong to various organizations, including those that may have goals contrary to that of the school system (see, e.g., *Melzer v. New York City Board of Education*, 2003, where the court rejected a teacher's claim that his constitutional right to freedom of association was violated when he was terminated

Students and their lockers are subject to search.

for membership in the North American Male/Boy Love Association). The question of freedom of association has also been at issue in a number of cases dealing with teachers associations or unions. Questions of non-school-sponsored student assemblies are usually addressed not under this clause but under the freedom of religion (if that is their purpose) or freedom of expression clauses.

## Fourth Amendment

The Fourth Amendment provides that the right of the people to be "secure in their persons, houses, papers, and effects, against unreasonable searches and seizures, shall not be violated and no warrants shall issue, but upon probable cause." The growing problem of student possession of drugs and other contraband has led to an increasing number of student searches. As we will see in the next chapter, the Fourth Amendment has served as the basis for a number of employee and student challenges to warrantless searches of their automobiles, desks, lockers, or persons by school officials and others.

## Eighth Amendment

The Eighth Amendment, in part, provides protection against "cruel and unusual punishments." This amendment on occasion has been involved in challenging the practice or use of corporal punishment in schools. The Supreme Court has held, however, that disciplinary corporal punishment per se is not cruel and unusual punishment as anticipated by the Eighth Amendment (*Ingraham v. Wright,* 1977). This does not mean, however, that corporal punishment may not be prohibited by state or school district regulations or that punishment can be excessive. In fact, if the punishment causes physical harm, it may be grounds for a civil action for assault and battery.

## Tenth Amendment

The Tenth Amendment states that "The powers not delegated to the United States by the Constitution, nor prohibited by it to the States, are reserved to the States respectively, or to the people." Because education is not mentioned in the Constitution, it is considered to be one of the powers reserved to the states. However, while the provision of education is considered one of the powers of the states, the supremacy clause of the Constitution (Article VI, Section 2) declares that the Constitution and the laws enacted by Congress are the supreme law of the land. Thus, the states, in exercising their authority, may not enact any laws that violate any provisions of the federal Constitution.

## Fourteenth Amendment

The Fourteenth Amendment is the constitutional provision most often involved in education-related cases because it pertains specifically to state actions, and, as previously stated, education is a state function. The Fourteenth Amendment states:

> No State shall make or enforce any law which shall abridge the privileges or immunities of citizens of the United States; nor shall any State deprive any person of life, liberty, or property, without due process of law; nor deny to any person within its jurisdiction the equal protection of the laws.

**For Your Reflection and Analysis**

How have society's views regarding corporal punishment in the schools changed since you began school?

As discussed in Chapter 12, the due process clause of the Fourteenth Amendment has been important to students in disciplinary actions and to teachers in negative personnel actions, and it has been invoked in a wide array of issues involving student and teacher rights.

## State Constitutional Provisions Affecting Education

Like the federal Constitution, state constitutions have provided the foundation for the enactment of subsequent innumerable statutes that govern the activities of the state and its citizens. However, unlike the federal Constitution, which contains no reference to education, every state constitution includes a provision for education, and all but one expressly provide for the establishment of a system of public schools. These provisions range from very general to very specific, but their overall intent is to ensure that schools and education be encouraged and that a uniform system of schools be established. For example, Article X, Section 3 (as amended, April 1972), of the Wisconsin constitution states:

> The Legislature shall provide by law for the establishment of district schools, which shall be as nearly uniform as practical; and such schools shall be free and without charge for tuition to all children between the ages of 4 and 20 years.

The constitutions of 45 states provide for the establishment of "common schools" and 35 states establish specific methods for financial support (Collins, 1969). The constitutions of 30 states expressly prohibit the use of public funds for the support of religious schools, and the constitutions of every state except Maine and North Carolina contain a provision prohibiting religious instruction in the public schools.

The wording of the state constitutional provision for education has proved to be very important to the courts in determining whether particular legislative enactments were constitutionally permissible or required. For example, an Arizona Court of Appeals ruled that the constitutional requirements that the state legislature provide for a system of "free common schools" did not require that free textbooks be provided to high school students (*Carpio v. Tucson High School District No. 1 of Pima County*, 1974). The basis for the court's decision was its interpretation that at the time the constitution was adopted the common schools consisted only of grades one through eight.

Regardless of the particular provisions related to education contained in a state's constitution, the constitution does not grant unlimited power to the state legislature in providing for the public schools. Rather, it establishes the boundaries within which the legislature may operate. The legislature may not then enact legislation exceeding these parameters or violate any provisions of the federal Constitution, which is the supreme law of the land.

## Statutory Law

**Statutory law** is the body of law consisting of the written enactments of a legislative body. These written enactments, called statutes, constitute the second highest level of law, following constitutions. Where constitutions provide broad statements of policy, statutes establish the specifics of operation. Both the Congress and state legislatures have enacted innumerable statutes affecting the provision of education. These statutes are continually reviewed and often revised or supplemented by successive legislatures. They are also subject to review by the courts to determine their intent and whether they are in violation of the federal Constitution.

### *Federal Statutes*

Despite the federal constitutional silence on education, during each session the Congress enacts or renews numerous statutes that affect the public schools. The

No Child Left Behind Act, discussed throughout this text, is one of the most recent and far-reaching federal statutes affecting education. Others, such as the Occupational Safety and Health Act (OSHA), which requires employers to furnish a safe working environment, although not directed specifically at school districts, do affect their operation. Many of the statutes enacted by Congress are related to the provision of financial assistance to the schools for a variety of special instructional programs, research, or programs for disadvantaged children. Still other federal statutes, civil rights statutes, also have had a considerable impact on educational programs and personnel. An overview of the major civil rights statutes affecting schools is provided in Table 11.1. They are discussed in more detail in relevant sections of this text.

**Table 11.1 — Summary of Major Civil Rights Statutes Affecting Education**

| Statute | Major Provision |
| --- | --- |
| Civil Rights Act of 1866, 1870 42 U.S.C. §1981 | Provides all citizens equal rights under the law regardless of race |
| Civil Rights Act of 1871 42 U.S.C. §1983 | Any person who deprives another of his/her rights may be held liable to the injured party |
| Civil Rights Act of 1871 42 U.S.C. §1985 and 1986 | Persons conspiring to deprive another of his/her rights, or any person having knowledge of any such conspiracy, are subject to any action to recover damages |
| Civil Rights Act of 1866, 1870 (as amended) 42 U.S.C. §1988 | Courts may award reasonable attorney fees to the prevailing party in any action arising out of the above acts and Title VI of the Civil Rights Act of 1964 |
| Civil Rights Act of 1964, Title VI 42 U.S.C. §2000(d) | Prohibits discrimination on the basis of race, color, or national origin |
| Equal Pay Act of 1963 29 U.S.C. §206(D) | Prohibits sex discrimination in pay |
| Civil Rights Act of 1964, Title VII 42 U.S.C. §2000(e) | Prohibits discrimination in employment on the basis of race, color, religion, gender, or national origin |
| Age Discrimination in Employment Act of 1967 29 U.S.C. §621 | Prohibits age discrimination against any individual with respect to employment unless age is a bona fide occupational qualification |
| Education Amendments of 1972, Title IX 20 U.S.C. §1681 | Prohibits sex discrimination in any education program or activity receiving federal financial assistance |
| Rehabilitation Act of 1973 (as amended) 29 U.S.C. §791 | Prohibits discrimination against any "otherwise qualified handicapped Individual" |
| Equal Educational Opportunities Act of 1974 20 U.S.C. §1703 | Prohibits any state from denying equal educational opportunities to any individual based on his/her race, color, gender, or national origin |
| Americans with Disabilities Act of 1990 42 U.S.C. §12112 | Prohibits discrimination against persons with disabilities |
| Individuals with Disabilities Education Act of 1990 20 U.S.C. §1400–1485 | Individuals with disabilities must be guaranteed a free appropriate education by programs receiving federal financial assistance |
| Civil Rights Restoration Act of 1991 42 U.S.C. §1981 et seq. | Amends the Civil Rights Act of 1964, the Age Discrimination in Employment Act of 1967, and the Americans with Disabilities Act of 1990 with regard to employment discrimination |

## State Statutes

Most of the laws affecting the public schools are enacted by state legislatures. The power of the state legislature is **plenary**, or absolute; it may enact any legislation that is not contrary to federal and state constitutions. Although much is said about local control, the courts have clearly established that education is a function of the state, not an inherent function of the local school district, and that the local district has only those powers delegated to it by the legislature. The courts have also affirmed the authority of the state to regulate such matters as certification, powers of school boards, accreditation, curriculum, the school calendar, graduation requirements, facilities construction, and the generation and spending of monies. In fact, the courts have made it clear that school districts have no inherent right to exist; they exist only at the will of the legislature and can be created, reorganized, or abolished at the will of the legislature.

State legislatures have delegated the administration of the state education system to an administrative agency, such as a state department of education, and the actual operation of the majority of the schools to the local school districts. The legislature must still pass legislation to administer the system as a whole and to provide for its financing and operation. Consequently, numerous education statutes exist in every state, and in every legislative session new statutes are enacted that affect education.

**For Your Reflection and Analysis**

What laws or statutes have recently been enacted in your state that affect certification?

## Case Law

**Case law**, also referred to as **common law**, is that body of law created by the courts. Case law is based on the doctrine of *stare decisis*, which means "let the decision stand." The doctrine requires that once a court has laid down a principle of law as applicable to a certain set of facts, it will apply it to all future cases where the facts are substantially the same, and other courts of equal or lesser rank will similarly apply the principle (Garner, 2009). However, adherence to the doctrine of *stare decisis* does not mean that all previous decisions may never be challenged or overturned. In fact, courts of appeal regularly reject the reasoning of a lower court and reverse its decision in whole or in part. It also happens, though not as commonly, that a court will reverse its own earlier decision. On other occasions constitutional or statutory changes have, in effect, overturned the previous decision.

## Administrative Rules and Regulations

Both state and federal agencies adopt rules and regulations that affect education. The regulations issued by these agencies carry the force of law and are sometimes called **administrative law**. They are subject to judicial review and will stand as law unless found to be in conflict with federal or state constitutional provisions, statutes, or court decisions.

The U.S. Department of Education is the federal agency most directly concerned with education. It issues regulations to implement federal education statutes and monitors districts for compliance. The regulations issued by the Office of Civil Rights of the Department of Education in regard to the implementation of Title IX are a prime example of the profound impact that administrative law can have on the operations of the schools.

Among the other federal agencies that have significant interaction with schools are the Department of Agriculture, which administers the National School Lunch Act; the Department of Health and Human Services, which administers Head Start; and the Department of Labor, which administers the Occupational Safety and Health Act. In addition, both the Office of Civil Rights of the Department of Education and another agency, the Equal Employment Opportunity Commission, are charged with enforcement of civil rights and nondiscrimination legislation.

The state agency that has the most direct control over and responsibility for education is the state department of education. A large body of administrative law is generated by this agency as a result of the promulgation of numerous rules and regulations relating to such areas as certification of teachers, accreditation of schools, adoption of textbooks, courses of study, minimum standards for specified areas, and distribution of state funds.

## School Board Policies

As previously stated, state constitutions and statutes delegate the actual day-to-day operation of public elementary and secondary schools to local school districts. The constitutions and statutes in these states also give to school districts the authority to enact policies and rules necessary to carry out the responsibilities delegated to them. The powers and duties of school boards are defined somewhat differently in each state. Some statutes are very general, others very vague; some outline mandatory duties, others outline discretionary duties. The board acts through its adopted policies; the policies spell out how the school district will operate. Policies impact virtually every aspect of district operations—employment of staff, administration of pupil services, curricular requirements, student discipline, school facilities, equipment, finance, and support services. School board policies guide the actions of administrators, teachers, staff, and students.

## Powers and Organization of the Courts

The courts have three basic functions: (1) settle disputes between parties, (2) interpret laws and policies, and (3) determine the constitutionality of governmental actions. In school-related matters, the courts have generally taken the position that they will not intervene in a dispute unless all internal appeals have been exhausted. For example, where school board policy provides teachers with the right of direct appeal to the board, this avenue of appeal must be exhausted before the courts will hear the appeal. The exceptions to this provision are cases involving an alleged violation of a constitutionally protected right.

The courts cannot become involved in education cases of their own initiative. A case must be brought to the court for resolution. The most common type of school case brought to the court is one that requires the court to interpret laws within its jurisdiction. Another common type of school case requires the court to determine the constitutionality of state statutes or administrative rules or regulations.

### The Federal Court System

Most education cases that come to federal courts involve alleged violations of constitutionally protected rights or interpretations of federal statutes. Sometimes a case will involve questions of both federal and state law. When this occurs, the federal court can decide on the state issue, but it must do so according to the rules governing the courts of that state.

The federal court system consists of three levels of courts of general jurisdiction: a supreme court, courts of appeals, and district courts. In addition, the federal court system includes courts of special jurisdiction, such as the Customs Court or the Tax Court. These courts normally would not be involved in education cases (see Figure 11.2).

The lowest-level federal courts are district courts. There are about 100 district courts: at least one in each state, and as many as four in the more heavily populated states, such as California, New York, and Texas. Federal district courts are given names reflective of the geographic area they serve; for example, "S. D. Ohio" indicates the Southern District of Ohio. District courts are the courts of initiation or original jurisdiction for most cases filed in the federal court system, including most education cases. They are trial courts, meaning that a jury hears the case.

**Figure 11.2 — Federal Court System**

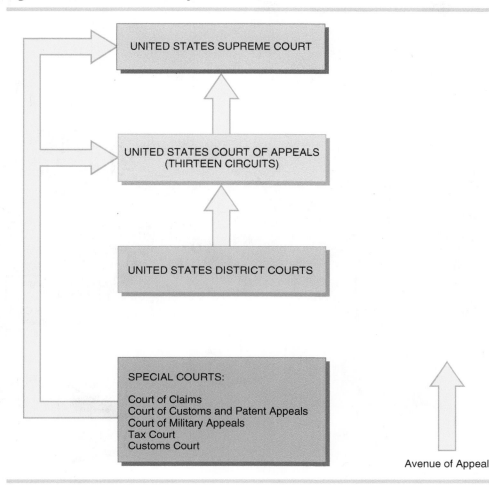

UNITED STATES SUPREME COURT

UNITED STATES COURT OF APPEALS
(THIRTEEN CIRCUITS)

UNITED STATES DISTRICT COURTS

SPECIAL COURTS:

Court of Claims
Court of Customs and Patent Appeals
Court of Military Appeals
Tax Court
Customs Court

Avenue of Appeal

The decisions of federal district courts have an automatic right of appeal to the next level of federal courts, U.S. Circuit Courts of Appeals.

There are 13 circuit courts of appeals in the federal system. Twelve of the circuit courts have jurisdiction over a specific geographic area (see Figure 11.3). The 13th, the Federal Circuit, has jurisdiction to hear appeals in specific areas of federal law (e.g., customs, copyright, international trade). A circuit court hears appeals from the decisions of district courts and certain federal administrative agencies. It hears arguments from attorneys, but it does not retry the case; there is no jury. A panel of judges, usually three, hears the case and can either affirm, reverse, or modify the decision of the lower court, or remand the case back to the lower court for modifications or retrial.

The decision of a federal circuit court is binding only on federal district courts within its geographic jurisdiction. Circuit courts have no power over state courts and do not hear appeals from them, nor does the decision of one circuit court bind other circuit courts or the district courts in other circuits. Thus, it is possible, and indeed it happens quite often, that one circuit court will rule one way, whereas another circuit court will rule in the reverse.

The highest federal appeals court, indeed the highest court in the land, is the U.S. Supreme Court (see Historical Note on Sandra Day O'Connor, the first female to serve on the Court on page 289). Decisions of the Supreme Court are absolute: there is no appeal. If Congress or citizens do not agree with a decision of the Supreme Court, the only ways they can mediate against the effect of the decision are to pass a law or to get the Court to reconsider the issue in a later case. A notable example

**Figure 11.3 — The Thirteen Federal Judicial Circuits**

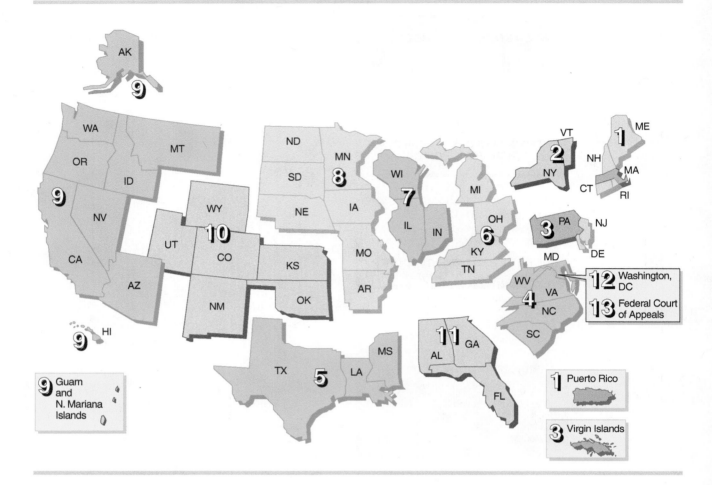

with regard to education of the Supreme Court reversing itself concerned racial segregation: in *Plessy v. Ferguson* (1896), the Court had said "separate but equal" public facilities for Blacks and Whites were constitutionally permitted, but in 1954 in *Brown v. Board of Education of Topeka,* the Court reversed this position and ruled that separate educational facilities for Blacks and Whites were inherently unequal.

The Supreme Court hears cases on appeal from lower federal courts or from the highest state courts if the state case involves questions of federal law. Although thousands of cases are appealed to the Supreme Court each year, only a small number are heard. However, in recent years the number of education cases being heard by the Supreme Court has increased.

## The State Court Systems

Because most education cases do not involve the federal Constitution or federal statutes, they are handled by state courts rather than federal courts. Although the specific structure of the court system and the names given to courts vary from state to state, in most respects state court systems resemble the federal court system in terms of having courts of limited and special jurisdiction and courts of appeal.

Most states have courts that are designated as courts of limited or special jurisdiction. The limitation may be related to the types of cases they may handle (e.g., probate courts, juvenile courts) or the amount in controversy (e.g., small claims courts, traffic courts). Generally, state court systems do not permit appeal of the decisions of courts of limited jurisdiction.

# HISTORICAL NOTE

## Sandra Day O'Connor: Breaking the Glass Ceiling on the U.S. Supreme Court

Sandra Day O'Connor, President Ronald Reagan's appointment to become the first female on the United States Supreme Court, was born in El Paso, Texas, in 1930. Her early years were spent on a cattle ranch in southern Arizona. Because of the isolation of the ranch, she attended school in El Paso with her grandmother. She received a B.A. and a law degree from Stanford University. After graduation, because of her gender, she was not able to find a job with any law firm but was offered a job as a legal secretary.

Following her husband on his Army assignment in Germany, she served as a civil lawyer for the Quartermaster's Corps before returning to Phoenix, Arizona. Once there she found it difficult to find a position with a law firm and accepted a job as an assistant attorney general instead. Turning to politics, she became active in the Republican party and served in the state senate from 1969 to 1975. In 1973 she became the first woman to serve as a majority leader of any state legislature. In 1975 she was elected to the Maricopa County Superior Court, and in 1979 she was selected by Democratic Governor Bruce Babbitt to the State Supreme Court. Two years later President Ronald Reagan kept a campaign promise to appoint a female to the Supreme Court and appointed her to the United States Supreme Court. Despite concerns about her lack of federal judicial experience and conservative concern that she might be pro-abortion, she was unanimously confirmed by the U.S. Senate.

As a member of the Court, Justice O'Connor was considered a pragmatic conservative. While most often voting with the court's conservative bloc, she approached each decision on a case-by-case basis and most often tried to find ways to win a majority vote. Among the major education cases on which Justice O'Connor was a deciding vote were *Wygant v. Jackson Board of Education* (1986), *Hazelwood School District v. Kuhlmeier* (1988), *Board of Education of Westside Community Schools v. Mergens* (1990), *Mitchell v. Helms (2000), Zelman v. Simmons-Harris* (2002), and *Grutter v. Bollinger* (2003).

Sandra Day O'Connor resigned from the Supreme Court on January 31, 2006, to spend more time with her husband who suffered from Alzheimer's disease. On August 12, 2009, she was awarded the Presidential Medal of Freedom, the nation's highest civilian honor, by President Barack Obama.

Sandra Day O'Connor

All states have courts of general jurisdiction. These courts are generally trial courts and as such hear witnesses, admit evidence, and, when appropriate, conduct jury trials. Depending on the state, courts of general jurisdiction may be referred to as district courts, county courts, circuit courts, superior courts, or supreme courts (in New York). Appeals from the decisions of courts of general jurisdiction are made to state appellate courts, often referred to as courts of appeals. Like the federal appellate courts, state appellate courts do not retry cases but sit as a panel of judges to review the record of the trial court and hear attorneys' arguments.

The final appeal in state court systems is to the state supreme court (court of appeals in New York), the final authority on questions related to the state constitution, state law, or school district policies. If the case involves federal issues, however, appeal may be taken from the state supreme court to the U.S. Supreme Court. Decisions of state supreme courts have legally binding effect only in their own state, although their analysis and rationale may influence future courts or courts in other states.

# Student and Teacher First Amendment Rights: Religion

The issue of the appropriate relationship between religion and the state has been one of the most controversial in American legal history. The experience of the nation's founders both with attempts to interfere with the free exercise of religion and with state control of education prompted a desire to erect what President Thomas Jefferson called "a wall of separation between Church and State" through the very first amendment to the Constitution, which states, "Congress shall make no law respecting an establishment of religion or prohibiting the free exercise thereof." Although the establishment and free exercise of the First Amendment make reference only to actions of the federal government (Congress), they are made applicable to the states by the Fourteenth Amendment, which prohibits state actions that violate the constitutional rights of citizens.

The free exercise of religion is not absolute. While individuals are free to believe whatever they want, they are not always free to act on those beliefs. The government may prohibit or regulate certain religious practices when it has a compelling public interest to do so. Thus, maintaining the wall of separation without being "hostile to religion" has been the challenge faced by policymakers at every level of government, as well as by public school teachers and administrators. Often they find their actions challenged in the courts, and a number of cases have reached the U.S. Supreme Court (see Table 11.2). For more than four decades, the courts used a tripartite test to evaluate claims under the Establishment Clause. The test, often called the **Lemon** test (from the case in which it was articulated, *Lemon v. Kurtzman,* 1971), asked three questions which must be answered in the negative if the policy or action is to be judged constitutional: (1) Does the policy or action have a primarily religious purpose? (2) Does the policy or action have the primary effect of advancing or inhibiting religion? (3) Does the policy or action foster an excessive entanglement between the state and religion? As will be discussed in later sections, later Supreme Courts, although not directly overturning *Lemon,* have reinterpreted it in such a way as to significantly affect its application.

The church–state issues most often contested in education can be categorized into several broad areas: prayer and Bible reading, religious expression, religious access to school buildings, curriculum content, and public support for private schools. Each of these is discussed in the following sections.

## *Prayer and Bible Reading*

The issue of school prayer has been one of ongoing—and heated—dispute. In *Engel v. Vitale* (1962) the Supreme Court ruled against the use of a prayer composed by the New York Board of Regents as part of morning exercises. The Supreme Court held that "it is no part of the business of government to impose official prayers for any group of American people" and to do so constituted a violation of the Establishment Clause. The following year, the Supreme Court rendered another significant decision affecting both school prayer and Bible reading. In *School District of Abington Township v. Schempp* (1963), the Court declared unconstitutional Pennsylvania and Maryland statutes that required daily Bible reading and, in Maryland, recitation of the Lord's Prayer. Although children could be exempted from participation in the Maryland case upon request by their parents, the Court held that such activities, held in public school buildings under the supervision of public school personnel, served to advance religion in violation of the Establishment Clause of the First Amendment. Although prohibiting Bible reading as a religious exercise, the Court in *Schempp* specifically noted that its opinion did not prevent studying the Bible as literature and studying about religion (e.g., the history of religion or comparative religion).

Not only are state-imposed prayers and Bible reading in the classroom constitutionally impermissible, so too are voluntary prayers and Bible reading, whether given by teachers or students, or even if requested by students. The courts have

**For Your Reflection and Analysis**

Do you recall being involved in any religious activities in a public school situation? Would it pass the *Lemon Test*?

found little to distinguish these from state-imposed prayers in that both are sanctioned by the school.

Although state-sponsored prayer in the classroom has been disallowed, this does not mean that students cannot engage in individual prayer, as long as it is

**Table 11.2 — Overview of Selected U.S. Supreme Court Cases Affecting Church–School Relations**

| Case | Decision |
|---|---|
| *Cochran v. Louisiana State Board of Education* (1930) | States may provide secular textbooks to children attending sectarian schools. |
| *West Virginia State Board of Education v. Barnette* (1943) | Public schools may not require the Pledge of Allegiance to the flag. |
| *Everson v. Board of Education* (1947) | States may use public funds to provide for transportation of children to and from private, sectarian schools where state constitution permits it. |
| *Illinois ex rel. McCollum v. Board of Education* (1948) | Released time program whereby religious instruction is provided during school hours on school grounds is unconstitutional. |
| *Zorach v. Clauson* (1952) | Released time program whereby students are released to go off campus to receive religious instruction and where no state support is provided is constitutional. |
| *Engel v. Vitale* (1962) | Public schools may not require the recitation of prayers. |
| *School District of Abington Township v. Schempp* (1963) | State may not promote Bible readings and prayers, even when participation is not compulsory. |
| *Epperson v. Arkansas* (1968) | State law forbidding the teaching of evolution is unconstitutional. |
| *Lemon v. Kurtzman* (1971) | State support to nonpublic schools, their personnel, and their students is unconstitutional if it (1) has a primarily religious purpose, (2) either advances or inhibits religion, or (3) creates an excessive entanglement between church and state. |
| *Mueller v. Allen* (1983) | State may provide income tax deduction for educational expenses of nonpublic school parents if also available to public school parents. |
| *Wallace v. Jaffree* (1985) | State laws authorizing classroom periods of silent meditation or prayer are unconstitutional. |
| *Edwards v. Aguillard* (1987) | Public schools may not be required to teach creationism. |
| *Board of Education of Westside Community Schools v. Mergens* (1990) | Schools must provide access to student-sponsored religious groups if access is provided to other student groups not directly related to the school's curriculum. |
| *Lee v. Weisman* (1992) | School-sponsored prayers at graduation exercises are unconstitutional. |
| *Zobrest v. Catalina Foothills School District* (1993) | School district provision of the services of a sign language interpreter to a student attending a sectarian school is constitutional. |
| *Agostini v. Felton* (1997) | State aid allocated to nonpublic schools on the basis of neutral, nonsectarian criteria is not unconstitutional. |
| *Mitchell v. Helms* (2000) | Federal Chapter 2 funds allocated to nonpublic schools for the acquisition and use of instructional materials is constitutional. |
| *Santa Fe Independent School District v. Doe* (2000) | School-sponsored, student-led, student-initiated prayer at football game is unconstitutional. |
| *Zelman v. Simmons-Harris* (2002) | Publicly financed tuition vouchers may be used at religious schools. |
| *Arizona Christian School Tuition Organization v. Winn* (2011) | Tax credits given for contributions to scholarship organizations that only give scholarships to students attending faith-based schools are not unconstitutional. |

nondisruptive and does not give the appearance of school endorsement. Sometimes there is a fine line between prayer that violates the Establishment Clause and that which does not. The Supreme Court has noted that there is a "crucial difference between the state endorsing religious speech, which the Establishment Clause forbids, and private religious speech which the Free Speech and Free Exercise clauses protect" (*Board of Education of Westside Community Schools v. Mergens,* 1990). The key is whether it appears that the prayer is school sponsored.

Under some circumstances courts have permitted schools to start the day with a "moment of silence" when the purpose of the activity was not just a cover to provide an opportunity for mandatory school prayer as a daily activity, as had been the case in the 1985 case of *Wallace v. Jaffree,* in which the Supreme Court struck down an Alabama statute that mandated a moment of silence for "meditation and voluntary prayer." However, the Court did indicate that statutes providing for periods of silence that did not demonstrate intent to encourage prayers and that demonstrated a secular purpose would probably be upheld. Accordingly, in 2001 the Supreme Court declined to review and overturn an appeal from the Fourth Circuit challenging a Virginia statute that required a daily moment of silence for students to "meditate, pray, or engage in any other silent activity" (*Brown v. Gilmore,* 2001). In refusing to block enforcement of the law, Chief Justice Rehnquist noted not only the absence of legislative intent to establish religion but also its stated secular concern about violence in the schools. Since the terrorist attacks of September 11, 2001, there has been a significant increase in the number of states and school districts that have adopted mandatory moments of silence. Although many people see these efforts as attempts to bring back government-led prayer, the legality of each is subject to determination state by state (see, e.g., *Sherman v. Koch,* 2010, Seventh Circuit upheld an Illinois moment of silence law ruling that not only did the law not mention prayer, it serves a secular purpose by settling students down at the beginning of the day).

## Prayer at School-Sponsored Activities

While it is clear that the school or teachers may not orchestrate prayer at the beginning of the day, in class, or within the curriculum, school districts continue to wrestle with the issue of if, and under what circumstances, prayers may be delivered at school-sponsored activities. Two of the most frequently litigated areas have been prayers at graduation ceremonies and at athletic events.

The issue of prayers at graduation ceremonies was addressed by the U.S. Supreme Court in 1992 in *Lee v. Weisman.* The case involved the practice of a Providence, Rhode Island, school of allowing the principal to select clergy to deliver prayers at graduation ceremonies. The clergy were instructed that the prayers were to be nonsectarian and were given a copy of "Guidelines for Civic Occasions" prepared by the National Conference of Christians and Jews. In ruling that school organized prayer, even if voluntary and nonsectarian, violated the Establishment Clause, the Court focused on the fact that the school supervised or controlled the activity by selecting the clergy to deliver the prayers and giving directions to them. In the opinion of the Court, the "psychological coercion" placed on student dissenters to attend graduation ceremonies had the effect of government coercion of students to attend religious exercises.

**For Your Reflection and Analysis**

Are you in favor of a constitutional amendment to authorize prayers and Bible reading in the schools?

The issue of prayer in the public schools continues to be the subject of legal and political debate.

In the years since *Weisman,* the courts have clarified that if a graduation prayer is not school sponsored, but truly a student's expression, it may be constitutional. This requires that the school not retain control over the content of the student speech. For example, in *Adler v. Duval County School Board* (2001), the Eleventh Circuit upheld a school's policy of letting senior classes choose a classmate to deliver an unreviewed graduation message even though the vast majority of the messages were religious in nature. The court could find nothing in the school policy that invited or encouraged a religious message.

The lower courts have applied the *Lee* coercion rationale in reviewing prayer at other school-sponsored activities. In *Santa Fe Independent School District v. Doe* (2000), the U.S. Supreme Court held that the delivery of an invocation over the public address system at a football game by an elected student council chaplain under the supervision of school faculty violated the Establishment Clause. Although noting that attendance at a football game is voluntary, the court reasoned that the social pressure or personal desire to attend does not dramatically differ from that of graduation exercises, and those in attendance may not be coerced into participating in an act of religious worship. The court also noted that the very election process itself ensured that minority view candidates would never prevail and that their views would be effectively silenced. A similar rationale was used by a Kentucky district court in disallowing a prayer at a graduation ceremony given by a student chaplain elected solely for that purpose (*Doe v. Gossage,* 2006).

**Reflect on Diversity**
Do you find anything wrong with an invocation for the safety of participants at an athletic event that did not mention any specific higher being?

## *Religious Expression*

### Religious Displays and Observances

Every year courts around the country are faced with deciding whether specific actions of school districts, teachers, or students constitute either an unconstitutional endorsement or prohibition of religion. The application of the *Lemon* test led the Supreme Court to overturn a Kentucky statute that required the posting of the Ten Commandments in every classroom in the state (*Stone v. Graham,* 1980). A similar ruling by a Michigan court found that a picture of Jesus Christ prominently displayed outside the principal's office violated the First Amendment's Establishment Clause (*Washegesic v. Bloomington Public Schools,* 1994). On the other hand, the Supreme Court declined to review an Eighth Circuit decision upholding a school board policy that allowed the use of religious symbols if used temporarily in an unobjectionable manner and as an example of the cultural and religious heritage of the particular holiday (*Florey v. Sioux Falls School District 49-5,* 1980).

The *Lemon* test has also been applied to challenges of religious observances in the public schools with the same general result: public schools may not sponsor religious practices. In practice, this means that there can be recognition of a holiday and the teacher can teach about the holiday, but any religious program must serve an educational rather than a religious purpose and cannot make any child feel excluded because of his or her religion. Holiday programs in December may include religious music and themes, but these should not dominate. Any skit should emphasize cultural, rather than religious, concepts of the holiday. Holiday displays may include religious symbols, but they should include diverse religious, cultural, and ethnic symbols and should be temporary. This does not mean that any display, program, or song that has some religious element but whose primary purpose is secular would violate the First Amendment. In fact, in *Doe v. Duncanville Independent School District* (1995), the Fifth Circuit stated that to prohibit the singing of certain songs that might be religious in origin, but were sung because of their recognized musical value, would be showing hostility to religion. (See the Video Insight, *Standing Alone,* on page 294, which deals with objections to a choral group singing Christian songs.) On the other hand, the courts have upheld school district policies that prohibit the performance of religious music at school sponsored events when there was no secular purpose for the performance (See, e.g., *Stratechuk v. Board of Education of South Orange Maplewood School District*, 2010).

Some holidays considered by many people to be secular are viewed by others as having religious connotations (e.g., Valentine's Day or Halloween). Students who object to classroom discussions or programs or activities on religious grounds may ask to be excused. Such requests are routinely granted and are provided for in school district policy.

Students as well as teachers may also request to be absent from school for religious reasons. While the courts have generally recognized the right of school districts to place limits on the number of such absences, they have also required that reasonable accommodation be made for the exercise of staff and student religious beliefs. For example, although the courts have held that it is within the discretion of school districts to limit the number of paid leaves that are provided employees for religious leave, they have also held that to allow employees to take unpaid leave is a reasonable accommodation for the employee's religious beliefs.

### Wearing of Religious Attire

Since colonial times, school officials have sought to regulate both student and teacher dress. Also, as discussed in the next chapter, the courts have given schools considerable discretion in adopting student dress codes as long as they do not burden students' First Amendment rights without adequate justification. For example, in *Cheema v. Thompson* (1995), a district refused to allow three young Khalsa Sikh children to wear ceremonial knives called kirpans to school. The kirpans are one of the five symbols of the Khalsa Sikh that are to be worn at all times. The school maintained that wearing the knives violated both school policy and state law, which prohibited the possession of weapons on school property. The case settled when the parties agreed that the knives could be worn if the blade was dulled, did not exceed two and a half inches in length, and was sewn securely into a sheath and secured in a cloth pouch.

## VIDEO INSIGHT

### Standing Alone

This ABC News video tells the story of Rachel, a young Jewish girl in heavily Mormon Salt Lake City, who objected to the overwhelmingly Christian music to be performed by the school choir. Rachel is joined in her protests by her father, who makes a strong written complaint with the choir director, who refuses to meet with him. The director's offer to add two Jewish songs to the Christmas concert failed to appease the father. Rachel and her family became the targets of harassment, especially when they filed (and won) a court order to stop the singing of two religious songs at graduation.

1. How would you have handled this situation if you were the choir director?

2. How can you as an educator respect and protect the viewpoint of one student against the majority?

3. Under what circumstances, if any, should religious music be performed in school or school-sponsored events?

While acknowledging the delicate balance that must be maintained between the rights of teachers to wear religious garb and the interest of the school in not being seen as promoting a particular religion, the courts have been almost unanimous in supporting school district prohibitions regarding the wearing of religious garb (see, e.g., *United States v. Board of Education for the School District of Philadelphia* [1990], in which the Third Circuit ruled that a district's compelling interest in maintaining religious neutrality was sufficient to prohibit a Muslim teacher from wearing her traditional Muslim dress). The courts have also tended to support school districts in restricting teacher dress that is intended to carry a specific religious message. For example, in *Downing v. West Haven Board of Education* (2001), the court found no violation of the teacher's rights when she was required to change clothes or cover a t-shirt with the slogan "Jesus 2000" on it. However, while disallowing religious dress, the courts have generally permitted teachers to wear *incidental* pieces of religious garb or religious symbols (e.g., a cross, crucifix, or Star of David).

## Pledge of Allegiance

One of the most controversial rulings ever made by the U.S. Supreme Court involved the compulsory flag salute. In *West Virginia State Board of Education v. Barnette* (1943), the Court ruled that the compulsory flag salute violated the religious freedom of Jehovah's Witnesses. Following *Barnette,* the position of the courts has been that schools may lead the Pledge of Allegiance so long as student participation is voluntary. However, because in *Barnette* the Supreme Court framed its decision as a free speech issue, not a free exercise of religion issue, challenges to the Pledge of Allegiance as a violation of freedom of religion continued. None of the challenges was successful until 2002, when the Ninth Circuit Court of Appeals held that requiring the words "under God" in the pledge violated the first prong (purpose) of the *Lemon* test and therefore violated the Establishment Clause of the First Amendment (*Newdow v. U.S. Congress*, 2002). The case was appealed to the U.S. Supreme Court, which did not address the religious issue but ruled that the noncustodial father (the mother had sole custody) who brought the challenge did not have legal standing to bring the suit. In a later case, *Newdow v. Rio Linda Union School District* (2010), also coming out of the Ninth Circuit, the court seemed to reverse itself and ruled that the Pledge of Allegiance was a patriotic, not religious exercise, whose primary effect was neither to advance nor inhibit religion and did not create an excessive entanglement with religion. And in another recent case, the Supreme Court declined to review a federal district court decision which upheld a Florida statute requiring students to recite the Pledge of Allegiance unless excused by parents but overturned the portion of the statute which said they must stand at attention (*Frazier v. Winn*, 2009). Thus while the constitutionality of the inclusion of "under God" in the pledge has not been settled by the highest court, what is settled is that students cannot be required to recite the pledge or punished for failure to do so.

## Distribution of Religious Literature

An issue of growing contention is the school's obligation to distribute or refrain from distributing religious materials to children. Absent any Supreme Court guidance, the majority of courts have applied the same equal access rationale and ruled that when school officials allow distribution of nonreligious literature, the same rules must be applied to the distribution of religious literature. For example, the Montgomery County (Maryland) Public Schools regularly distributed to families materials for children's groups such as the Boy Scouts and 4-H. However, when asked to distribute materials to promote the after-school Good News Club, a Christian evangelical group, the school refused, citing Establishment Clause concerns. The Fourth Circuit disagreed, noting that the Good News Club would be receiving no benefit other than those afforded other organizations, and ordered the district to allow the distribution of the materials (*Child Evangelism Fellowship of Maryland v. Montgomery County Public Schools,* 2004).

In cases that involve individual student attempts to distribute materials, the courts have also applied the equal access rationale but have acknowledged the authority of school officials to impose the same time, place, and manner restrictions as apply to other forms of student expression. For example, the court upheld a school in stopping a first grader from distributing candy canes with an attached religious message during a class holiday party. Parents had been instructed that the party was to be "as generic as possible" and the student was the only one to bring a nongeneric gift. The court ruled that the party was part of the curriculum and not an appropriate forum for religious advocacy (*Walz v. Egg Harbor Township Board of Education,* 2003).

## *Religious Access to School Buildings*

Partially in response to public sentiment that prayer and other devotional activities should not be banned from the school grounds, in 1984 Congress passed the Equal Access Act (EAA) (20 U.S.C., sections 4071–73). The act specified that if a federally assisted public secondary school provides a **limited open forum** to non-curriculum-related student groups to meet on school premises during the lunch hour, before or after school, or during other noninstructional time, "equal access" to that forum cannot be denied because of the "religious, political, philosophical, or other content of the speech at such meetings." Access can be denied only if the ideas that the group wishes to express are likely to lead to a material and substantial disruption of the functioning of the school.

In *Board of Education of Westside Community Schools v. Mergens* (1990), the Court clarified that a student group was curriculum related if the subject matter of the group is actually taught in a course, concerns the body of courses as a whole, or if participation in the group is required for a particular course or if academic credit is given for participation in the group. The Court also said that the direct relation to the curriculum does not mean "anything related to abstract educational goals" and that schools cannot evade the intent of the act by "strategically describing existing groups" (*Board of Education of Westside Community Schools v. Mergens,* 1990, p. 244). Subsequent courts have clarified that "access" means not simply access to the school building but also to fund-raising activities, bulletin boards, and any other resources made available to other student groups (*Prince v. Jacoby,* 2002).

Use of school facilities by community groups, for which there is no school sponsorship or supervision, although very different from use by student-initiated groups under the EAA, has also been the subject of ongoing controversy. Following *Mergens,* access to school facilities was expanded even further by the Supreme Court in *Lamb's Chapel v. Center Moriches School District* (1993), which said that school districts that allow community groups to use school facilities for civic or social purposes have created a limited open forum and cannot, therefore, bar religious groups from using the facilities on the same terms. And in *Good News Club v. Milford Central School* (2001), the Supreme Court said that to refuse access to a community group simply "because it is religious" if it is not engaged in strictly "religious activities" would constitute viewpoint discrimination in violation of the First Amendment. However, the Court did not clarify what constitutes "religious activities" as opposed to, for example, in this case teaching moral and character development from a religious perspective.

Compliance with the EAA has created a dilemma for a number of school districts: the very words in the EAA that grant access and the right to free expression to religious groups like the Good News Clubs also grant access to gay-lesbian-trangendered support groups, atheist clubs, or various controversial or unpopular groups. Schools attempting to deny access to such groups have been successful in excluding hate groups such as the Aryan Nation but not lifestyle organizations such as Gay Straight Alliance Clubs.

## *Challenges to the Curriculum*

First Amendment challenges to the curriculum generally have been brought by parents attempting to introduce religious material and curriculum or to eliminate specific courses, activities, or materials said to be advancing religion. While many people claim that the schools are hostile to religion and that all mention of religion is forbidden in the schools, in fact public school curricula may include teaching about religion or may use religious material. The Supreme Court has specifically said that the study of the Bible or teaching about religion or about different religions, when presented objectively as part of a secular program of education, is not a violation of the First Amendment (*School District of Abington Township v. Schempp,* 1963). But of course, the curriculum may neither endorse nor inculcate religion.

Teachers, like all citizens, have the right of free exercise of religion. However, in exercising their right of exercise, they cannot make their religious beliefs part of classroom instruction. Nor can they exclude from the curriculum content (e.g., the theory of evolution) that violates their individual religious beliefs. Schools have a constitutional duty under the Establishment Clause to prevent teachers from promoting religion or being hostile to it. In addition, teachers cannot require students to modify, include, or exclude religious views from their assignments. Teachers can control students' assignments for legitimate pedagogical reasons, or if it may give the appearance of endorsement of religion, but student work that includes religious expression should be assessed under ordinary academic standards including the criteria established for the assignment. For example, in *DeNoyer v. Livonia Public Schools* (1992), the Court concluded that a second grader had no right to show a videotape of her singing a proselytizing religious song. The Court upheld the teacher's rationale that the presentation wasn't in line with the assignment (developing self-esteem by giving an oral presentation), was longer than assigned, and would encourage other students to bring in long videos. And, in *Settle v. Dickson County School Board* (1995), the Court held that the teacher could give a student a zero on a research paper without violating the student's free exercise rights. The student's choice of topic was the life of Jesus Christ, but the student did not meet the teacher's requirements of using at least four sources to research a topic.

In recent years a growing number of parents have contended that certain courses, materials, and practices in the curriculum promote a nontheistic or antitheistic religion sometimes referred to as secular humanism or New Age Theology. In the cases to date, the courts have rejected the argument that the challenged courses or materials advanced any nontheistic or antitheistic creed and have reaffirmed the position taken by the Supreme Court in 1968 in *Epperson v. Arkansas.* In this case, the Court struck down an Arkansas law forbidding instruction in evolution, stating: "The state has no legitimate interest in protecting any or all religions from views distasteful to them." For example, the courts have consistently found that sex education courses present public health information that promotes legitimate educational objectives, and that the Establishment Clause prevents the state from barring such instruction merely to suit the religious beliefs of some parents (Thomas et al., 2009).

In cases in which parents or students find that a course or part of a course offends their religious beliefs, the courts generally are satisfied if the student is exempted from the challenged course or exposure to the objectionable content. However, the exemption will not be given unless the material or activity actually violates the student's religion or if the state can show a compelling interest in educating regarding a particular topic. For example, in *Ware v. Valley Stream High School District* (1989), the Court ruled that the states' compelling interest in requiring all primary and secondary students to receive instruction regarding AIDS prevention and the dangers of alcohol and drug abuse did not violate the First Amendment rights of parents who believed that such education was "evil."

The teaching of evolution is one area that has been targeted as advancing secular humanism. Following the ruling in *Epperson* that evolution is a science, not a secular religion, and that states cannot restrict student access to such information to satisfy religious preferences, attempts were made in several states to secure "balanced treatment" or "equal time" for the teaching of creationism or *intelligent design* (a theory that holds that the complexity of the universe and living things are the product of intelligent cause, not a random process). However, these statutes have also been invalidated. In *Edwards v. Aguillard* (1987), the U.S. Supreme Court ruled that creation science is a religious doctrine, and to require it be taught would violate the Establishment Clause. Similarly, the courts have declared unconstitutional a requirement that teachers read a disclaimer immediately before the teaching of evolution stating that the teaching of evolution was "not intended to influence or dissuade the Biblical version of creation" and that it is "the basic right and privilege of each student to form his or her own opinion or maintain beliefs taught by parents" (*Freiler v. Tangipahoa Parish Board of Education,* 1999). And in *Kitzmiller v. Dover Area School District* (2005), the U.S. district court ruled that "the overwhelming evidence at trial established that intelligent design is a religious view, a mere re-establishing of creationism, and not a scientific theory" (p. 43), and to teach it in the public school would be a violation of the Establishment Clause.

In addition to challenges to curricular programs, another set of challenges has focused on the use of specific curriculum materials or methods, the wearing of particular clothing in physical education classes, and coeducational dancing in physical education classes. In deciding these cases, the courts applied the same analysis used in considering religious objections to secular courses and have said that the particular method or material does not violate the Establishment Clause, but that the Free Exercise clause may give the students the right to be excused from exposure to the objectionable material or practice. Parents in a number of cases have claimed that the required use of a specific reading series violated their rights by exposing their children to beliefs that were offensive to their religious beliefs. For example, the *Impressions* reading series has been the focus of a number of challenges in recent years. The series uses the whole-language approach to teach reading, and among its readings are selections dealing with the supernatural and witchcraft. Both the Seventh and Ninth Circuit Courts have held that merely reading about these practices, or even creating poetic chants, did not constitute the practice or advancement of these practices (*Fleischfresser v. Directors of School District No. 200,* 1994; *Brown v. Woodland Joint Unified School District,* 1994). In fact, echoing what seems to be the sentiment of most courts in reviewing this type of case, the court quoted from the U.S. Supreme Court's 1948 decision in *Illinois ex. rel. McCollum v. Board of Education:* "If we are to eliminate everything that is objectionable to any [religious group] or inconsistent with any of their doctrines, we will leave public education in shreds" (p. 235).

Few areas of the curriculum have not been challenged on religious grounds. Popular targets have been AIDS and drug awareness and drug prevention curricula, global education, values clarification, and outcomes-based education. Yet another, multicultural education, is faulted for threatening traditional values and cultural heritage. This vast body of litigation has not resulted in a concrete list of what can be included and what must be excluded from the school curriculum. However, some conclusions can be drawn:

> On the one hand, schools may not tailor their programs in accordance with religious beliefs, offer religious instruction or theistic moral training, or endorse the Bible as the only true source of knowledge. On the other hand, schools may not systematically purge the curriculum of all mention of religion or ideas that are consistent with religious belief, endorse atheism, or declare that science is the only source of knowledge or that the Bible is not true. (Imber & van Geel, 2000, p. 88)

## Public Aid to Private Schools

In recognition of the financial burden placed on parents who pay property taxes to support the public schools in addition to tuition at private schools, as well as to promote school choice, legislatures have regularly attempted to provide some type of public support to these parents or to the schools their children attend. The legal issue involved in these attempts is whether the assistance violates the

**For Your Reflection and Analysis**

Many of the curriculum materials being objected to today have been used for decades (e.g., *Huckleberry Finn* and *Catcher in the Rye*). To what do you attribute the recent objections to such materials?

First Amendment prohibition against governmental actions that promote the establishment of religion.

Although most state constitutions forbid state aid to religious schools, the courts have relied on the **child benefit theory** to provide several types of assistance whose primary benefit is to the child rather than the private school itself. Using this theory, the U.S. Supreme Court in *Cochran v. Louisiana State Board of Education* (1930) upheld a Louisiana law that provided for the loan of textbooks to children attending nonpublic schools and in *Everson v. Board of Education* (1947) supported a New Jersey law reimbursing parents for the cost of bus transportation for children attending both public and nonpublic schools. However, the fact that the

The Supreme Court has recognized the right of the state to regulate private schools.

Supreme Court has said that transportation, textbooks, or the provision of other services is permissible under the federal Constitution does not mean that states are required to provide this assistance, or that such assistance may not be prohibited by state laws or constitutions. As previously stated, the constitutions of 30 states expressly forbid the use of public funds for the support of religious schools.

Following the articulation of the *Lemon* test in 1971, this test has been used to determine the constitutionality of various state aid programs. However, in recent years, the courts have abandoned a strict interpretation of the *Lemon* test and have shown a greater receptivity to various types of aid directed at providing services to students. In *Zobrest v. Catalina Foothills School District* (1993), the Court did not rely on the *Lemon* test but more on the child benefit theory, or neutrality principle, in ruling in favor of a deaf student's request that the school district provide him with a sign language interpreter in the Catholic school he attended. The Court stated:

> When the government offers a neutral service on the premises of a sectarian school as part of a general program that is in no way skewed towards religion, it follows that provision of service does not offend the Establishment Clause. (p. 2462)

Adopting this reasoning in an even more far-reaching decision in 1997, *Agostini v. Felton,* the U.S. Supreme Court modified the *Lemon* test, overturned two of its earlier decisions, and ruled that public school employees could provide Title I remedial services in the parochial school. According to the Court, although it will continue to ask if the *purpose* of the aid is to advance or inhibit religion, it has changed its stand on the criteria used to assess whether the aid has an impermissible *effect*. Rather than acting on the presumption that the mere presence of public school employees in parochial schools created an impermissible "symbolic link" between government and religion, the Court held that aid allocated on the basis of neutral, nonsectarian criteria is not invalid under the Establishment Clause.

Three years later, in *Mitchell v. Helms* (2000), the Supreme Court effectively negated the effect criterion of *Lemon*. In its decision that Title II permits the lending of computers, library books, and other instructional equipment to sectarian schools, the Supreme Court said that the effect test basically becomes one of satisfying a neutrality standard. According to the Court, if aid is offered to the "religious, irreligious, and unreligious" alike, then its allocation is neutral and thus any indoctrination that the recipient conducts cannot be attributed to governmental action. Also important to the court's rationale was that the decision as to what schools receive aid was the result of the private choice of the recipient to apply for funds, rather than the "unmediated will of the government."

According to many legal experts, after the *Agostini* and *Helms* decisions, "the new jurisprudence of the Establishment Clause, appropriated by the current Supreme Court, has now dismantled the principal constitutional barriers that prevented general taxation for the support of religious institutions" (Alexander & Alexander, 2009, pp. 201–202). At this point in history, it appears that if any wall is to separate church and state, it will come from the schools or from state institutions (see Ask Yourself, *How Tall Is the Wall?* below).

### *Vouchers*

**Vouchers** are seen as a means of providing all parents greater choice in the school their child attends. In particular, vouchers are seen as a way to extend private school options to disadvantaged students in urban areas and students attending failing public schools. Voucher bills have been introduced in more than half of the states but have met with limited voter approval. And, until the 2002 decision of the U.S. Supreme Court in *Zelman v. Simmons-Harris,* all attempts to provide vouchers for students to attend parochial schools had been overturned by the courts. The Cleveland voucher plan in the *Zelman* case was unique in that it applied only to poor students attending failing public schools. The vouchers were based on financial need and were sent directly to the parents, not the schools. The *Zelman* decision has not produced the flurry of voucher programs that supporters had anticipated. This is in part due to the fact that while vouchers are permitted under federal Constitutional provisions, most states have constitutional prohibitions against expending public funds for private schools. Most existing voucher programs are targeted to low income urban school districts.

### *Tax Credits and Deductions*

Various tax deduction and tax credit proposals have been introduced in Congress, as well as in almost every state legislature. Tax deductions for education expenses reduce a taxpayer's taxable income, while tax credits reduce the taxpayer's tax liability. Tax credits may be given to students' families or to individuals or corporations that contribute to public or nonprofit private school scholarship organizations.

Tax deductions and tax credit programs have invariably invoked challenges on Establishment Clause grounds in most states where they have been proposed. However, tax credits and tax deductions have generally been viewed favorably by both

# ASK YOURSELF

## *How Tall Is the Wall?*

Teachers have the absolute right to believe as they choose. However, the right to act on these beliefs is not absolute. The teacher's right to free exercise of religion must be balanced against the school's interest in maintaining the delicate balance between church and state, neither endorsing nor prohibiting religion. Reflect on your responses to the following questions to see how tall you think the wall of separation of church and state should be.

1. How would you respond if you were required to use a textbook that contained material endorsing practices that violated your religious beliefs?

2. How would you respond if a student asked you about your religious beliefs?

3. How far should the school go to accommodate the religious practices of students or teachers (e.g., serve kosher food or provide a place for Islamic students or teachers to fulfill their obligation to pray)?

4. If your school allowed a moment of silence, would you participate?

5. Should teachers be allowed to participate in or sponsor a student religious club?

6. Should Halloween and Easter be celebrated in public schools?

7. Should students be required to study about world religions as part of a unit on globalization?

federal and state courts. In *Mueller v. Allen* (1983), the Supreme Court upheld a Minnesota statute that permitted a state income tax deduction to parents of both public and nonpublic school students for expenses for tuition, books, and transportation. In upholding the statute, the Court distinguished this case from *Nyquist* in that the New York statute provided the **tax benefits** only to parents of nonpublic school students. Here, the Court said, a secular purpose was served in providing financial assistance to a "broad spectrum" of citizens.

The Supreme Court in 2011 also let stand an Arizona tax credit program that allows state tax credits for donations to public schools for extracurricular programs ($200 for a single taxpayer, $400 for married filing a joint return) and to private school tuition organizations ($500/$1000). The program was challenged by taxpayers who cited data showing that over half the money raised through the tax credit program went to organizations that only give scholarships to students in faith based schools and that very little of the funds actually went to low-income students. The U.S. Supreme Court rejected the taxpayers, standing to sue because they could not show they were directly affected by the tax credits, and the funding of religion came from individuals, not a legislative appropriation (*Arizona Christian School Tuition Organization v. Winn,* 2011).

## Compulsory Attendance

Each of the 50 states has legislation requiring school attendance by children of a certain age range residing within the state. The age range is normally from 7 to 16 years. Parents may satisfy this requirement by sending their children to a public or private school or by homeschooling. In addition, although attendance is compulsory, attendance in a specific district or at a particular school within the district may legally be restricted to those residing within the district or within a certain attendance zone or by voluntary or court-ordered desegregation remedies.

The residency requirement is not the same as a citizenship requirement. The U.S. Supreme Court, in *Plyler v. Doe* (1982), upheld the right of children of illegal aliens to attend school in the district of their residence. According to the Court, the state's interest in deterring illegal entry was insufficient to justify the creation and perpetuation of a subclass of illiterates within the nation's borders. On a similar note, the courts have ruled that school districts also must educate homeless youth who have no address but are living within their boundaries.

## Summary

The legal foundation of education derives from state and federal constitutional provisions, the laws of state and federal legislatures, the enactments of state and federal agencies, school board policies, and court decisions. Every state constitution includes a provision for education, and the wording of the provision has proved important in determining the obligation of the state in providing for education and the constitutionality of legislative action. Although the federal Constitution does not mention education, a number of its provisions affect education and afford protection to school personnel, pupils, and patrons.

The interaction of the institutions of religion and education has become the source of increasing legal controversy in recent years. A tension exists between the efforts of the schools to accommodate religion and yet maintain the wall of separation between church and state required by the First Amendment. Thus far, the courts generally have been consistent in their decisions that keep religious practices and proselytizing efforts out of the schools. However, the decisions of the U.S. Supreme Court in *Mergens* (1990), *Agostini* (1997), and *Helms* (2000) represent not only a potential crack in the wall of separation between church and state, but also the growing conservative thrust of the Court. In the next chapter, other constitutional rights of teachers and students are explored.

**TEACHER OF THE YEAR**

I teach because I want to shape our students into the professionals of the future. As a high school senior I said that I would never teach because I saw the challenges that my teachers faced. But some ten years after the fact, I came back to the table and said, "Never say never." I decided that teaching was a way to reach out to students and actually change their lives. I'd been a broadcast journalist and found that elements of that profession brought into the classroom helped to give students a real-world relevance. And I do believe that as a teacher I "touch the world."

*Stacey Donaldson Mississippi*

# PROFESSIONAL DEVELOPMENT
## *Workshop*

## *Prepare for the State Licensure Examination*

Mr. Reid is a sixth-grade teacher at Fairview Middle School. Fairview has been labeled "performing" on the state performance assessment. Mr. Reid's class is a heterogeneous class of 27 that includes three students with disabilities. Mr. Reid participated in the development of the IEP for each of these students. One student, Samuel, has been diagnosed as learning disabled and also suffers from ADHD. He often gets out of his seat and walks around the class, disturbing other students. Mr. Reid has moved him to the back of the class, hoping to limit his span of activity. Samuel rarely turns in any homework assignments and has trouble following directions for class assignments and activities. The work he does do is often incomplete and performed carelessly.

Mr. Reid is teaching a lesson on the Constitution and the Bill of Rights. He tells the students that it is important that they take notes because some of the information is not in the textbook. As he delivers his lecture he tries to speak slowly and clearly enough for Samuel and all students to take notes. Nonetheless, on several occasions students interrupt his lecture to ask him to clarify or repeat some comment. As he talks, he walks around the class to see how students are doing. When he gets to Samuel's desk he sees that Samuel has not written any notes. Rather, he has drawn a picture of action figures. Several other students also seem to have rather "sketchy" notes. Mr. Reid completes the lecture but senses that the lesson has not gone as he planned. After some reflection he decides to seek the advice of the designated master teacher for his grade level in designing cooperative learning activities or other instructional strategies that would involve students more.

1. Explain the least restrictive environment requirement of the IDEA and what must be included on the IEP.
2. Describe three behavioral management strategies the master teacher might suggest Mr. Reid use to manage Samuel's behavior.
3. What instructional strategies might the master teacher suggest Mr. Reid use as an alternative to lecture and note taking? Explain the advantages of each.

### Build Your Knowledge Base

1. Given the situation described in the vignette at the beginning of this chapter, how might Mr. Kindrick accommodate Mrs. Collins's desire to wear the cross and students' desires not to be exposed to this symbol of Christianity?
2. What are the provisions of your state constitution regarding education?
3. Describe the levels and types of state courts in your state.
4. What is your school (or school system) policy on silent meditation? Is there support for prayer or Bible reading? On what grounds?
5. What is meant by the *Lemon* test? How effective has it been in distinguishing permissible and impermissible aid to nonpublic school students?
6. How does the child benefit theory serve to justify educational vouchers? How does it operate in the school systems in your area? Are textbooks or bus transportation provided?
7. What First Amendment issues are currently being debated in the schools in your area?

## Develop Your Portfolio

1. Many of the curriculum materials being objected to today have been used for decades (e.g., *Huckleberry Finn* and *The Catcher in the Rye*). Interview a school librarian and a community librarian regarding their experiences in handling objections to a variety of curriculum materials. Prepare a reflection paper that describes how you would handle a situation if a parent came to you and objected to curriculum material you had selected for your class. Place your reflection paper in your portfolio under **INTASC Standard 9, Professional Learning and Ethical Practice.**

2. Review Table 11.1, Summary of Major Civil Rights Statutes Affecting Education, on page 284. Using a Web site such as http://web.lexisnexis.com/universe, select one legal case from your state that exemplifies a lawsuit pertaining to a major civil rights statute. Prepare a brief (one-page) paper that summarizes the case. Include a discussion of how the outcome of the case has impacted education in your state. Place your paper in your portfolio under **INTASC Standard 4, Content Knowledge.**

## Explore Teaching and Learning: Field Experiences

1. Contact the central office of a nearby school district and arrange to review the district's policies and procedures concerning (a) access of religious groups to school buildings, (b) distribution of religious material, and (c) absence for religious holidays. Outline the key procedures that must be followed.

2. Search the Internet for your state government's Web site or for the National Conference of State Legislatures' Web site and determine if your state's school finance system has been challenged in the courts. Review the materials to determine the constitutional arguments of the plaintiffs. Write a short synopsis of the issue(s) involved.

## MyEducationLab

Go to **Topic 4, Ethical and Legal Issues,** in the MyEducationLab (www.myeducationlab.com) for *Foundations of American Education,* where you can:

- Find learning outcomes for ethical and legal issues along with the national standards that connect to these outcomes.
- Complete Assignments and Activities that can help you more deeply understand the chapter content.
- Apply and practice your understanding of the core teaching skills identified in the chapter with the Building Teaching Skills and Dispositions learning units.
- Examine challenging situations and cases presented in the IRIS Center Resources.

- Access additional video clips of CCSSO National Teachers of the Year award winners responding to the question, "Why Do I Teach?" in the Teacher Talk section.
- Check your comprehension on the content covered in the chapter with the Study Plan. Here you will be able to take a chapter quiz, receive feedback on your answers, and then access Review, Practice, and Enrichment activities to enhance your understanding of chapter content.
- Use the Online Lesson Plan Builder to practice lesson planning and integrating national and state standards into your planning.

# Teachers, Students, and the Law

Helen Tye is a high school English teacher. Maria Collins is in Ms. Tye's third-period class. Ralph Tyler, the pitcher on the school baseball team, is also in this class. Soon after the class begins, Ralph appears to be trying to get Maria's attention, but she ignores him. He then gives a folded piece of paper to Andrew, another student, and motions for Andrew to pass it to Maria. However, Ms. Tye intercepts the note before Andrew can give it to Maria. She puts the note in her pocket and continues with the class discussion of Shakespeare's sonnets.

At home later that afternoon as she is changing clothes, Ms. Tye retrieves the forgotten note from her pocket and is shocked when she reads its contents. Ralph has described in graphic sexual terms what he would like to do to Maria. As she remembers the incident in class, Ms. Tye is afraid that Maria's attempt to ignore Ralph suggests that this is not the first time Ralph has made offensive remarks to Maria.

Is this a case of sexual harassment? What action should Ms. Tye take now? What should be done to protect both Maria's rights and Ralph's rights?

*L*ike Ms. Tye, teachers must make decisions every day that affect the rights of students, their own rights, and their professional lives. Therefore, it is imperative that teachers be knowledgeable about applicable state and federal legislation, school board policies, and court decisions. After completing this chapter, you will be able to:

- Identify the personal and professional requirements for employment of prospective teachers.
- Describe teachers' employment rights as derived from the employment contract and tenure status.
- Outline the legal requirements for dismissing a teacher.
- Provide an overview of teachers' rights, inside and outside the classroom.
- Discuss the teacher's responsibility in reporting child abuse and using copyrighted materials.
- Define the elements of negligence.
- Compare equal opportunity and affirmative action.
- Contrast the procedural requirements for suspension, expulsion, and corporal punishment.
- Trace the development of student rights in the area of search and seizure.

- Explain the restraints that may be placed on student expression and personal appearance.
- Distinguish between quid pro quo and hostile environment harassment as the concepts apply to employees and students.
- Discuss how the Family Educational Rights and Privacy Act has expanded parental and student rights.

## MyEducationLab

Visit the MyEducation-Lab for *Foundations of American Education* to enhance your understanding of chapter concepts with a personalized Study Plan. You'll also have the opportunity to hone your teaching skills through video and case based Assignments and Activities, and Building Teaching Skills and Disposition lessons.

# Teacher Rights and Responsibilities

Although school personnel are not expected to be legal experts, it is imperative that they understand their rights and obligations under the law and that these rights and obligations are translated into everyday practices in the schools. In this chapter, the basic concepts of law are presented as they relate to terms and conditions of employment; teacher dismissal; teacher rights inside and outside the classroom; tort liability; discrimination, equal opportunity, and affirmative action; and certain legal responsibilities of teachers. Although there is some variation in the application of these legal concepts from one state or locality to another, certain topics and issues are of sufficient importance and similarity to warrant consideration. Some of these topics are also discussed in other chapters of this text. Here, attention is given to the legal considerations of these topics.

## *Terms and Conditions of Employment*

As emphasized in Chapter 11, within the framework provided by state and federal constitutional and statutory protections, the state has complete power to conduct and regulate public education. Through its legislature, state board of education, state department of education, and local school boards, the state promulgates the rules and regulations for the operation of the schools. Among these rules and regulations are those establishing the terms and conditions of employment. The areas most often covered by state statutory and regulatory provisions are those dealing with certification, citizenship and residency requirements, health and physical requirements, contracts, and tenure.

### Certification

As noted in Chapter 1, to qualify for most professional teaching, administrative, and other positions in the public schools, an individual must acquire a certificate or license. The certificate does not constitute a contract or guarantee of employment; it only makes the holder eligible for employment.

All states have established certification requirements for prospective teachers. These requirements may include a college degree with minimum credit hours in specific curricular areas; evidence of specific job experience; "good moral character"; a specified age; U.S. citizenship; the signing of a loyalty oath; good health; and, as discussed in Chapter 1, a minimum score on a test of basic skills such as the Praxis examination (39 states require a test of basic skills of teacher education candidates). Where specified certification requirements exist, failure to meet the requirements can result in dismissal.

### Citizenship and Residency Requirements

The courts have upheld both citizenship and residency requirements for certification and/or as a condition of employment. With regard to the citizenship requirement, the U.S. Supreme Court has held that education is among the governmental functions that is "so bound up with the operation of the state as a governmental entity as to permit the exclusion from those functions of all persons who have not become part of the process of self-government" (*Ambach v. Norwick,* 1979, pp. 73–74).

Requirements that educators reside in the district where they are employed also have been upheld if it can be shown that there is a rational basis for the requirements. For example, a Kentucky court upheld a Kentucky law that required a superintendent to become a Kentucky resident after hiring. The superintendent was an Ohio resident hired by a Kentucky school district. The court agreed with the state that a Kentucky resident would have a better understanding of Kentucky's educational needs (*Newport Independent School District v. Commonwealth of Kentucky,* 2009). Note, however, that although residency requirements have been upheld in many jurisdictions, a number of states have statutory provisions prohibiting school districts from imposing such requirements (Thomas, Cambron-McCabe, & McCarthy, 2009).

## Health and Physical Requirements

Most states and school boards have adopted health and physical requirements for teachers. The courts have recognized that such requirements are necessary to protect the health and welfare of students and other employees. Accordingly, the courts have upheld the release or reassignment of employees in instances when their failed eyesight, hearing, or other physical or mental condition made it impossible for them to meet their contractual duties. The courts have also upheld school districts in requiring medical examinations to determine employees' fitness to perform their duties. For example, a Michigan court upheld a school board that suspended a teacher for three years and required that she undergo physical and mental examinations before returning to work. The court determined that the district had a legitimate concern, following several instances of misconduct and insubordination, that she might be experiencing a breakdown (*Sullivan v. River Valley School District,* 1998).

Although the courts have upheld school districts' imposition of health and physical requirements, they are concerned that such requirements not be arbitrarily applied, be specific to the position, and not violate state and federal laws intended to protect the rights of people with disabilities. For example, Section 504 of the Rehabilitation Act of 1973, which protects otherwise qualified individuals with handicaps from discrimination, served as the basis for a 1987 U.S. Supreme Court ruling that overturned the dismissal of an Arkansas teacher with tuberculosis (*School Board of Nassau County v. Arline,* 1987). According to the Court, discrimination based solely on fear of contamination is to be considered discrimination against people with disabilities. The Supreme Court instructed the lower court to determine if the teacher posed a "significant risk" that would preclude her from being "otherwise qualified" and if her condition could reasonably be accommodated by the district. Ultimately, the court found the teacher posed little risk and was otherwise qualified, and she was reinstated with back pay.

The significant risk standard and the provisions of Section 504 have been relied on by plaintiff teachers in cases involving AIDS. In the lead case, *Chalk v. U.S. District Court Central District of California* (1988), the U.S. District Court relied heavily on the significant risk standard articulated in *Arline* to determine when a contagious disease would prevent an individual from being "otherwise qualified." In applying the "significant risk of communicating" standard in this instance, the court found that the overwhelming consensus of medical and scientific opinion regarding the nature and transmission of AIDS did not support a conclusion that Chalk posed a significant risk of communicating the disease to children or others through casual social contact.

A major federal statute impacting on health and physical requirements for school district employees is the Americans with Disabilities Act of 1990, which prohibits employment discrimination against "qualified individuals with a disability." Such a person is defined as one who "satisfies the requisite skill, experience, education, and other job-related requirements of the (position) . . . and who, with or without reasonable accommodation, can perform the essential functions" of the position. Although the law does not require the hiring or retention of unqualified persons, it does prohibit specific actions of employers that adversely affect the employment opportunities of people with disabilities (e.g., inquiring into a disability or requiring a medical examination before an offer is made, writing job descriptions that include nonessential job functions), and it does require employers to make "reasonable accommodation" for a known mental or physical disability.

An area of current dispute in regard to health and physical requirements for school employees involves mandatory testing for alcohol or drug use. As explained later in this chapter, employees have challenged such testing as violating their rights of privacy and constituting an unreasonable search under the Fourth Amendment.

## The Employment Contract

The general principles of contract law apply to the teacher employment contract; that is, in order for the contract to be valid, it must contain the basic elements of (1) offer and acceptance, (2) legally competent parties, (3) consideration (compensation), (4) legal subject matter, and (5) agreement in the form required by law. In addition, the employment contract must meet the specific requirements of applicable state law.

To be valid, a contract must contain an offer by one party and an acceptance by another. Typically the offer of employment specifies that the acceptance must be made within a certain period of time of the offer. Until the prospective employee to whom the offer is made accepts the offer (i.e., acceptance cannot be made by a spouse or relative), the contract is not in force.

The authority to contract lies exclusively with the school board. Although the superintendent or other officials may screen candidates and recommend employment, only the school board is authorized to enter into contracts, and only when it is a legally constituted body; for instance, contracts issued when a quorum of the board is not present or at an illegally called meeting of the board (e.g., adequate notice is not given) are not valid.

To be enforceable, a contract must pertain to a legal subject matter (i.e., a contract for the commission of a crime is not enforceable). Nor can the terms of the contract violate state or federal statutes or regulations or public policy (e.g., pay less than the federal minimum wage). Last, the contract must be in the proper form required by law. In most states, this means the contract must be in writing and signed.

The employee's rights and obligations of employment are derived from the contract. The courts have held that all valid rules and regulations of the school board, as well as all applicable state statutes, are part of the contract, even if not specifically included. Accordingly, employees may be required to perform certain tasks incidental to classroom activities, regardless of whether the contract specifically mentions them. These have included such activities as field trips; playground, study hall, bus, and cafeteria duty; supervision of extracurricular activities; and club sponsorship. Teachers cannot, however, be required to drive a bus, perform janitorial duties, or perform duties unrelated to the school program (compare this with the duties required of teachers in Colonial America presented in the Historical Note on page 309). If an employee refuses to perform reasonable extracurricular duties required as a condition of employment, the courts may construe such a refusal as insubordination justifying removal.

Playground duty is among those nonclassroom duties that teachers may be required to perform.

## Tenure

**Tenure** is "the status conferred upon teachers who have served a probationary period . . . which then guarantees them continual employment until retirement, subject to the requirements of good behavior, financial necessity, and in some instances good periodic evaluations" (Sperry, Daniel, Huefner, & Gee, 1998, p. 1041). Tenure is a creation of statute designed to maintain permanent and qualified instructional personnel. Most state statutes specify the requirements and procedures for obtaining tenure, which normally include the satisfactory completion of a probationary period of three years of regular and continuous teaching service. During the probationary period, the teacher is usually issued a one-year contract that, subject to satisfactory service and district finances, is renewable at the end of each of the probationary years. If the district decides not to renew a probationary contract, in about half the states school districts are not required to give the reasons for the nonrenewal or to even provide a hearing on the decision. However, most states do require that the probationary teacher be given timely notice of intent to nonrenew (usually no later than April 1). And, in all cases, if the district attempts to break the contract of a probationary teacher during the term of the contract, the teacher must be given, at a minimum, a notice of dismissal and a hearing on the causes.

Satisfactory completion of the probationary period does not guarantee tenure. In some states, tenure is automatically awarded at the end of the probationary period

# HISTORICAL NOTE

## *Duties of a Dorchester, MA Schoolmaster, 1645*

"First. That the schoolmaster shall diligently attend his school and do his utmost endeavor for benefiting his scholars according to his best discretion.

"Second. That from the beginning of the first month until the end of the seventh, he shall every day begin to teach at seven o'clock in the morning and dismiss his school at five in the afternoon. And for the other five months, that is, from the beginning of the eighth to the end of the twelfth month he shall every day begin at eight of the clock in the morning and end at four in the afternoon.

"Thirdly. Every day in the year the usual time of dismissing at noon shall be at eleven and to begin again at one, except that

"Fourthly. Every second day in the week he shall call his scholars together between twelve and one of the clock to examine them what they have learned on the Sabbath day preceding, at which time he shall take notice of any misdemeanor or outrage that any of his scholars shall have committed on the Sabbath to the end that at some convenient time due admonition and correction may be administered.

"Fifthly. He shall equally and impartially receive and instruct such as shall be sent and committed to him for that end whether their parents be poor or rich, not refusing any who have right and interest in the school.

"Sixthly. Such as shall be committed to him he shall diligently instruct, as they shall be able to learn, both in humane learning and good literature, and likewise in point of good manners and dutiful behavior towards all,

especially their superiors as they shall have occasion to be in their presence whether by meeting them in the street or otherwise.

"Seventhly. Every sixth day in the week at two of the clock in the afternoon he shall catechize his scholars in the principles of Christian religion, either in some Catechism which the wardens shall provide and present, or in defect thereof in some other.

"Eighthly. And because all man's endeavors without the blessing of God needs be fruitless and unsuccessful, therefore it is a chief part of the schoolmaster's religious care to commend his scholars and his labors amongst them unto God by prayer morning and evening, taking care that his scholars do reverently attend during the same.

"Ninthly. And because the rod of correction is an ordinance of God necessary sometimes to be dispensed unto children, but such as may easily be abused by overmuch severity and rigor on one hand, or by overmuch indulgence and lenity on the other, it is therefore ordered and agreed that the schoolmaster for the time being shall have full power to administer correction to all or any of his scholars without respect of persons, according as the nature and quality of the offence shall require." The rule further requires that the parents "shall not hinder the master therein" but if aggrieved they can complain to the wardens "who shall hear and impartially decide between them."

*Source:* Excerpted from: *Fourth Report of the Record Commissioners, 1880.* (Boston: Rockwell and Churchill, City Printers.

unless the school board notifies teachers that they will not be rehired, whereas in other states official action of the school board is required for the awarding of tenure. In cases where the school district fails to follow applicable state laws, the courts will attempt to balance the public policy interests of employing competent and qualified teachers against the rights of the individual teacher.

The granting of tenure does not guarantee the right to teach in a particular school, grade level, or subject area. Subject to due process requirements, teachers may be reassigned to any position for which they are certified. The awarding of tenure also does not guarantee permanent employment. As discussed in the following sections, the teacher may be dismissed for disciplinary reasons (for cause) or because declining enrollments, financial exigencies, or other circumstances necessitate a reduction in force. Tenure statutes normally specify the grounds for dismissal of a tenured teacher as well as the procedures that must be followed in the dismissal. The dismissal protection afforded tenured teachers, compared with that of nontenured teachers, is perhaps the major benefit of obtaining tenure. Tenure status gives teachers the security of practicing their profession without threat of removal for arbitrary, capricious, or political motivations. In fact, the courts have said that the granting of tenure in effect awards the teacher with a **property right** to continued employment that cannot be taken away without due process of law.

## *Teacher Dismissal*

### Grounds for Dismissal

*Dismissal* is defined as the termination of employment during the term of the contract. The statutory provisions regarding teacher dismissal "for cause" vary among the states in terms of the specified grounds for dismissal as well as the legal requirements for dismissal. The behaviors that would justify dismissal apply equally to tenured and nontenured teachers. The reasons for dismissal most frequently cited in statutes are immorality, incompetency, and insubordination. Among the other commonly mentioned reasons are neglect of duty, unprofessional conduct, unfitness to teach, and the catch-all phrase, "other good and just cause." Most challenges to dismissals revolve around two primary issues: (1) whether the conduct in question fits the statutory grounds for dismissal; and (2) if so, whether the school board presented the facts necessary to sustain the charge. The burden of proof in justifying a dismissal lies with the school board and must be supported by sufficient evidence to justify the dismissal. In addition, as will be discussed in the next section, in any dismissal the school board must provide the teacher with all the due process required by state statute, school board policy, or negotiated agreement.

**Immorality.** Although **immorality** is the most frequently cited ground for dismissal in state statutes, they normally do not define the term or discuss its application to specific conduct. Consequently, these tasks have been left to the courts. A review of cases challenging dismissals related to immorality shows that they generally have been based on one or more of the following categories of conduct: (1) sexual conduct with students; (2) same-sex sexual orientation; (3) making sexually explicit remarks or talking about sexually related topics unrelated to the curriculum; (4) distribution of sexually explicit materials to classes; (5) use of obscene, profane, or abusive language; (6) public lewdness; (7) possession and use of controlled substances; (8) other criminal misconduct; and (9) dishonesty.

While the concept of immorality "is subject to ranging interpretations based on shifting social attitudes (and therefore) must be resolved on the facts and circumstances of each case" (*Ficus v. Board of School Trustees of Central School District,* 1987, p. 1140), some standards have evolved from the cases in this area that are often applied to other cases involving dismissal for immorality. The first is the exemplar standard. The majority of the public believes that teachers should be good role models for students, both in and out of the school (Imber & van Geel, 2010). The courts also recognize that there are "legitimate standards to be expected of those who teach in the public schools" (*Reitmeyer v. Unemployment Compensation Board of Review,* 1992, p. 508). Second, in most jurisdictions there must be a nexus, or connection, between the conduct of the teacher and the teacher's ability to teach, or the conduct must have an adverse effect on the school relationship or be the subject of public notoriety. For example, the Delaware Supreme Court upheld the dismissal of a teacher who had a sexual affair with a 17 year old student (a former student of his), finding that "there was a proper nexus between his alleged off-duty conduct and his fitness to teach" (p. 11) and that retaining the teacher could "reasonably undermine parents' confidence in both (the teacher) and the District" *(Lehto v. Board of Education of the Caesar Rodney School District No. 175,* 2008, p. 12). The exceptions to the principle that the behavior must affect teaching performance or become the subject of notoriety have been made most often in regard to notoriously illegal or immoral behavior.

Because the facts of no two cases are exactly the same, the connection may exist in one case involving a particular conduct but not in another. For example, the courts have held that conviction for a felony or misdemeanor, including possession of illegal drugs, does not necessarily, in and of itself, serve as grounds for dismissal. Again, the circumstances of each case are important, especially regarding the effect on the school, students, and coworkers. Thus, the courts might not uphold the dismissal of a teacher solely because the teacher once was indicted for possession of a small amount of marijuana, but they probably would support a firing based on evidence of a widely publicized conviction, combined with testimony that the teacher's criminal behavior would undermine the teacher's effectiveness in the classroom (Schimmel, Stellman, & Fischer 2011). Similarly, most courts have overturned the dismissal of homosexual and bisexual teachers based only on their private conduct, when no conviction of breaking the law had taken place (see, e.g., *Glover v. Williamsburg Local School District Board of Education,* 1998). However, dismissal has been upheld in cases where public sexual conduct was involved (see, e.g., *C. F. S. v. Mahan,* 1996).

Although cases involving alleged immoral conduct must be settled case by case, the courts have agreed on the factors to be considered in determining if the alleged conduct renders a teacher unfit to teach. These factors include (1) the age and maturity of the teacher's students, (2) the likelihood that the teacher's conduct will have an adverse effect on students or other teachers, (3) the degree of anticipated adversity, (4) the proximity of the conduct, (5) any extenuating or aggravating circumstances surrounding the conduct, (6) the likelihood that the conduct would be repeated, (7) any underlying motives, and (8) the chilling effect on the rights of teachers (*In re Thomas,* 1996).

**Incompetency.** Courts typically describe **incompetence** as lack of ability, legal qualifications, or fitness to discharge the required duties. Those conditions or behaviors that have been sustained most successfully as constituting incompetence fall into six general categories: (1) inadequate teaching, (2) lack of knowledge of the subject matter, (3) unreasonable discipline or failure to maintain classroom discipline, (4) failure to work effectively with colleagues, supervisors, or parents, (5) physical or mental incapacity, and (6) willful neglect of duty.

As with dismissals for alleged immorality, in dismissals for incompetence the courts require that there be an established relationship between the employee's conduct and the operation of the school. Additionally, the standard against which the teacher is measured must be one used for other teachers in a similar position, not some hypothetical standard of perfection, and the conduct must not be an isolated incident but a demonstrated pattern of incompetence. Most jurisdictions also require that before termination a determination is made as to whether the behavior in question is remediable, a notice of deficiency be given, and a reasonable opportunity to remediate be provided.

**Insubordination.** Regardless of whether it is specified in a statute, insubordination is an acceptable cause for dismissal in all states. **Insubordination** involves the persistent, willful, and deliberate violation of a reasonable rule or direct order from a recognized authority. The rule not only must be reasonable but it also must be clearly communicated, and it cannot be an infringement on the teacher's constitutional rights. For example, rules that limit what teachers can say or write may, in some cases, violate their First Amendment right to free speech. Normally, unless the insubordinate act is severe, a single action is not sufficient grounds for dismissal. Dismissal may also not be supported if the teacher tried, although unsuccessfully, to obey the rule or no harm resulted from the violation (Alexander & Alexander, 2009).

In cases involving insubordination, it is not necessary to establish a relationship between the insubordinate action(s) and teaching effectiveness. In a case in point, an industrial arts teacher was terminated for repeated refusal to submit lesson plans even though he had received positive performance evaluations (*Vukadinovich v. Board of School Trustees of North Newton School Corporation,* 2002). Among the actions that have been held to constitute insubordination are refusal to obey the direct and lawful orders of school administrators or school boards, unauthorized absence from duty, abuse of sick leave, refusal to follow established policies and procedures, inappropriate use of corporal punishment, refusal to meet or cooperate with superiors, encouraging students to disobey school authority, refusal to perform assigned teaching or nonteaching duties, and failure to acquire required approval for use of instructional materials.

## Constitutional Rights of Teachers

School boards in this country have historically considered it their right, indeed their responsibility, to control the personal as well as the professional conduct of teachers. School boards have sought to regulate teachers' dress, speech, religion, association, and choice of instructional content and practices. However, in the last quarter of the 20th century, teacher activism, court decisions, and enlightened legislators and school boards greatly expanded the rights of teachers.

### Procedural Due Process

In keeping with the Fourteenth Amendment, if the dismissal of a teacher involves either a property or liberty right, **procedural due process** must be provided. As previously noted, teachers who are tenured have a "property right" to continued employment. On the other hand, nontenured teachers do not have such a claim to due process unless they are dismissed during the contract year or unless the dismissal action impairs a fundamental constitutional right, creates a stigma, or damages the employee's reputation to the extent that it forecloses other employment opportunities. Nontenured teachers may also establish a **liberty interest** claim if the nonrenewal decision was made to retaliate for the teacher's exercise of a fundamental liberty.

Once it has been established that a school district action requires procedural due process, the central issue becomes what process is due. In arriving at its decision, the court will look to the procedural due process requirements in state statutes, state agency or school board regulations, or employment contracts to determine both their propriety and the extent to which they were followed.

Generally, the courts have held that an employee facing a severe loss such as termination of employment must be ensured the following procedural elements:

1. Notice of charges;
2. The opportunity for a hearing;
3. Adequate time to prepare a rebuttal to the charges;
4. The names of witnesses and access to evidence;
5. A hearing before an impartial tribunal (which can be the school board);
6. The right to representation by legal counsel;
7. The opportunity to introduce evidence and cross-examine witnesses;

8. A decision based solely on the evidence presented and the findings of the hearing;
9. A transcript or record of the hearing; and
10. The opportunity to appeal. (Thomas et al., 2009)

Notice must not merely be given; it must be timely (on or before an established date) and in sufficient specificity to enable the employee to attempt to remediate or to prepare an adequate defense. The hearing requirements will typically be specified in state statutes, school district policies, or the employment contract. A formal hearing as in a court may not be required, but the hearing must provide the employee a full and fair opportunity to rebut all charges. Table 12.1 lists some Supreme Court cases affecting teachers' rights, many of which are discussed in the sections that follow.

## Freedom of Expression

In the landmark U.S. Supreme Court decision regarding freedom of expression in the public schools, *Tinker v. Des Moines Independent Community School District* (1969), the Court ruled that neither teachers nor students shed their constitutional rights to freedom of speech or expression when they enter the schoolhouse gate. However, this does not mean that teachers or students are free to say or write anything they wish or express themselves through dress or other symbolic expression in any way they choose. Rather, in reviewing cases involving expression, the courts attempt to balance the rights of the individual against the harm caused to the schools.

In the lead case involving teachers' freedom of expression, Marvin Pickering, a high school teacher, was terminated after writing a letter to the newspaper severely criticizing the superintendent and school board for their handling of school funds. The U.S. Supreme Court (*Pickering v. Board of Education*, 1968) overturned his dismissal and ruled that teachers, as citizens, do have the right to make critical public comments on matters of public concern. The Court further held that unless the public expression undermines the effectiveness of the working relationship between the teacher and the teacher's superior or coworkers, the employee's ability to perform assigned duties, or the orderly operation of the schools, such expression may not furnish grounds for reprisal. Finding that the issue of school board spending is an issue of legitimate public concern, that Pickering's statements were not directed at people he normally worked with, nor that there was any disruption of the operation of the schools (in fact, the letter had been greeted with apathy by everyone but the board), the Supreme Court overturned Pickering's dismissal. One recent case involved disciplinary action taken against teachers who reported the alleged misconduct of an employee and then discussed the dismissal and changes in the program the employee directed with students and also encouraged parents to attend a board meeting where the proposed changes were to be discussed. The court found the teachers' speech to be protected as they spoke as citizens on a matter of public concern (*Kelly v. Huntington Union Free School District*, 2009).

If, however, the public comment is not related to matters of public concern, then it is not protected. The U.S. Supreme Court ruled in *Connick v. Myers* (1983) that free expression is not protected when a public employee "speaks not as a citizen upon matters of public concern, but instead as an employee upon matters only of personal interest" (p. 147). Thus, comments related to political advocacy, general issues of administrative management, instructional methods, or the curriculum have been found to be matters of public concern, whereas comments or complaints related to personnel actions or relations with superiors have been found to be matters of personal concern and are not protected speech.

Even if expression does involve a matter of public concern, it still is not protected if the impact of the expression undermines the effectiveness of working relationships or is disruptive to the normal operation of the schools. For example, the Fourth Circuit upheld the dismissal of a teacher who wrote and circulated a letter

**Table 12.1 — Selected U.S. Supreme Court Cases Affecting Teachers' Rights**

| Case | Decision |
| --- | --- |
| *Indiana ex rel. Anderson v. Brand* (1938) | Tenure statutes provide qualifying teachers with contractual rights that cannot be altered by the state without good cause. |
| *Keyishian v. Board of Regents* (1967) | Loyalty oaths that make mere membership in a subversive organization grounds for dismissal are unconstitutionally overbroad. |
| *Pickering v. Board of Education* (1968) | Absent proof of false statements knowingly or recklessly made, teachers may not be dismissed for exercising the freedom to speak on matters of public interest. |
| *Board of Regents v. Roth* (1972) | A nontenured teacher does not have a property right to continued employment and can be dismissed without a statement of cause or a hearing as long as the employee's reputation or future employment have not been impaired. |
| *Perry v. Sindermann* (1972) | Teachers may not be dismissed for public criticism of superiors on matters of public concern. |
| *Cleveland Board of Ed. v. Le Fleur* (1974) | School board policy requiring that all pregnant teachers take mandatory leave is unconstitutional. |
| *Hortonville Joint School District No. 1 v. Hortonville Education Association* (1976) | A school board may serve as the impartial hearing body in a due process hearing. |
| *Washington v. Davis* (1976) | To sustain a claim of discrimination, an employee must show that the employer's action was a deliberate attempt to discriminate, not just that the action resulted in a disproportionate impact. |
| *Mount Healthy City School District v. Doyle* (1977) | To prevail in a First Amendment dismissal case, school district employees must show that the conduct was protected and was a substantial and motivating factor in the decision not to renew, and the school board must prove that it would have reached the same decision in the absence of the protected conduct. |
| *United States v. South Carolina* (1978) | Use of the National Teachers Examinations both as a requirement for certification and as a factor in salary determination serves a legitimate state purpose and is not unconstitutional despite its disparate racial impact. |
| *Connick v. Myers* (1983) | The First Amendment guarantee of freedom of expression does not extend to teachers' public comments on matters of personal interest (as opposed to matters of public concern). |
| *Cleveland Board of Education v. Laudermill* (1985) | A teacher dismissed for cause is entitled to an oral or written notice of charges, a statement of the evidence against him or her, and the opportunity to present his or her side prior to termination. |
| *Garland Independent School District v. Texas State Teachers Association* (1986) | Teachers can use the interschool mail system and school mailboxes to distribute union material. |
| *Wygant v. Jackson Board of Education* (1986) | Absent evidence that the school board has engaged in discrimination or that the preferred employees have been victims of discrimination, school board policies may not give preferential treatment based on race or ethnicity in layoff decisions. |
| *School Board of Nassau County v. Arline* (1987) | People suffering from diseases are considered to have a disability, and discrimination against them based solely on fear of contamination is considered unconstitutional discrimination against people with disabilities. |

to fellow teachers objecting to a delay in receiving summer pay, complaining about budgetary management, and encouraging teachers to stage a "sick-out" during final examination week. The court ruled that any First Amendment interest inherent in the letter was outweighed by the public interest in having public education provided by teachers loyal to that service (i.e., not causing a disruption of exams by a sick-out that was both in violation of district policy and the teachers' contract and represented professionally questionable behavior), and by the employer interest "in having its employees abide by reasonable policies adopted to control sick leave and maintain morale and effective operation of the schools" (*Stroman v. Colleton County School District,* 1992, p. 159).

The exact definition of what constitutes disruptive speech was not defined by the *Pickering* court. However, a subsequent Supreme Court decision held that public employers need not prove that the speech actually caused a material disruption, only that at the time of the penalized speech the employer "reasonably believed" the speech would be disruptive (*Waters v. Churchill,* 1994). The effect of the *Waters* decision, together with *Connick,* has been to make it more difficult for public employees to prove that adverse employment actions have violated their First Amendment expression rights (Thomas et al., 2009).

**Political Activity.** Teachers have the right to engage in political activities and hold public office; however, restrictions may be placed on the exercise of this right. For example, teachers may discuss political issues and candidates in a nonpartisan manner in the classroom. However, they may not make campaign speeches in the classroom or otherwise take advantage of their position of authority over a captive audience to promote their own political views. (See, e.g., *Weigarten v. Board of Education of City School District of the City of New York* [2010], upholding school policy prohibiting the wearing of political buttons in the presence of students.) Political activity in the schools that would cause divisiveness among the faculty or otherwise be disruptive may also be restricted if the school can demonstrate that the restriction is necessary to meet the compelling public need to protect efficiency and integrity in the school.

The authority of school boards to restrict teachers' political activities outside the school setting is far less than their authority to restrict activities in the schools. The courts have upheld teachers' rights to support candidates or issues of their choice, display political buttons and stickers, and participate in demonstrations. In addition, the courts generally have upheld the right of teachers to run for and hold public office. However, the courts also have indicated that if the time and activities associated with running for or holding office interfere with the performance of teaching duties, then the teacher may be required to take a leave of absence (but only if such were required for any other time-consuming activity). In addition, the courts have found the holding of certain political offices (e.g., school board member in the employing school district) to present a conflict of interest, and therefore forbid the joint occupancy of both positions.

**For Your Reflection and Analysis**

If you felt strongly that a particular candidate would be in the best interest of your community or state, how would you work for that person's election? Would you consider running for office as an "education candidate" in order to improve education?

## Right to Associate

The courts have ruled that teachers have the right of free association and that unjustified interference with this right by school boards violates the Fourteenth Amendment. The associational rights of teachers include the right to belong to political organizations, religious or social organizations, and a union or professional association. School district actions that inhibit membership in a controversial organization can be justified only by a compelling state interest. For example, in *Melzer v. Board of Education of the City School District of New York* (2003), the court upheld the school district's decision to terminate a teacher because of his membership and active participation in the North American Man-Boy Love Association, a group that advocates sexual relations between men and boys. The court found that Melzer's membership and participation in the group was potentially disruptive to the school operations and undermined his effectiveness as a teacher because students may not feel comfortable with a teacher who advocates such views.

Although teachers have a right to form or join a union or professional association, whether they have a right to engage in collective bargaining depends on state law. About 40 states have passed laws permitting school boards to engage in collective bargaining with teacher groups. The collective bargaining laws vary

Teachers have the right to participate in demonstrations.

widely. Some states require school boards only to "meet and confer" with the teacher organization. Many specify the topics to be negotiated (typically salaries, benefits, workload, hours, grievance procedures, and other conditions of employment) and the procedures to be followed if an impasse in bargaining occurs.

Despite the recognition of the right of teachers to organize, the right to strike has not been recognized by the courts and is prohibited by 37 states, with anti-strike laws currently being considered in several others. In the 11 states where strikes are allowed by law, they usually are permitted only after the requirements for impasse resolution have been met and only after the school board has been notified of the intent to strike. When teachers strike in violation of state law or without having met the requirements of the law, the school board may seek an injunction to prohibit the strike. Violation of a court order or an injunction ordering strikers back to work may result in a contempt of court decree and fine or imprisonment. Moreover, those who engage in illegal strikes may be subject to economic sanctions, for example, withholding of salaries/wages, fines, or disciplinary actions, including dismissal (*Hortonville Joint School District No. 1 v. Hortonville Education Association,* 1979).

## Academic Freedom

**Academic freedom** is not a constitutional protection in and of itself but is "the desirable end to be achieved by the enforcement of the individual rights and freedom in the classroom as guaranteed by the Bill of Rights" (Alexander & Alexander, 2009, p. 708). Academic freedom refers to the teacher's freedom to discuss the subject-matter discipline and to determine the most appropriate instructional methodology. Academic freedom is not without limits. For example, teachers do not have the ultimate right to determine course content or select textbooks—that authority belongs to the school board. The school board may also require that teachers receive prior approval for the use of supplementary materials. Teachers also do not have the right to ignore prescribed content or to refuse to follow the designated scope and sequence of content or materials, even if the refusal is for religious reasons. Nor do teachers have the right to use profane or objectionable language in the classroom even if part of a lesson plan. For example, in *Erskine v. Board of Education* (2002), a federal district court upheld the firing of a teacher for writing the word "Negro" on the board as part of a Spanish lesson on colors.

Currently, perhaps the most contested academic freedom issue involves attempts to censor the curriculum by excluding certain offerings (e.g., evolution, sex education, and values clarification) or materials deemed to be vulgar or offensive or to promote New Age theology. The courts typically have supported school boards in the face of parental attempts to censor the curriculum or ban certain books from the school library. However, when it is the school board itself that advocates censorship, judicial support is not as easily won. The courts traditionally have recognized the authority of the school board to determine the curriculum, select texts, purchase library books, approve the use of supplementary materials, and perform a host of other curriculum-related activities. Nonetheless, in a number of instances, the courts have found that specific censorship activities violated the teacher's right to academic freedom or students' First Amendment rights to have access to information. While acknowledging that the banning of books and materials on the basis of obscenity or educational unsuitability is permissible, the courts have held that censorship motivated primarily by the preferences of school board members or to suppress particular viewpoints or controversial ideas contained in a book, or for narrow partisan political or religious purposes, is not permissible.

The controversy regarding who controls instructional and curricular matters—teachers or the school board—is likely to continue, as are parental attempts to exert greater control over the curriculum. Until definitive guidance is provided by the Supreme Court, resolution will continue case by case, attempting to balance the teacher's interest in academic freedom against the school board's interest in promoting an appropriate educational environment.

## Rights of Privacy: Employee Searches

As stated in Chapter 11, the Fourth Amendment guarantees persons the right "to be secure in their persons, houses, papers and effects against unreasonable searches and seizures." However, this right applies only to areas where the person has a reasonable expectation of privacy. Applying case law related to other public employees to education, the courts have said that school employees have reasonable expectations of privacy in regard to their lockers, personal effects, and persons. However, their expectation of privacy does not extend to those places under the control of the school, such as desks, filing cabinets, and storage areas. Where an expectation of privacy does exist, the employer may conduct a search if (1) there is reasonable suspicion that the search will produce evidence of work-related misconduct, and (2) the scope of the search is reasonably related to the objectives of the search and not excessively intrusive in light of the nature of the misconduct (*O'Conner v. Ortega,* 1987). The more personally intrusive the search, the more compelling the circumstances must be to justify the search.

The heightened concerns about substance abuse and school violence have led to an increase in searches of both students and school employees. In recent years, these searches have extended beyond searches of personal belonging to searches of persons, specifically mandatory urinalysis to screen for drugs. Historically employees have successfully challenged such tests as violating their right of privacy and the Fourth Amendment prohibition against searches without an "individualized reasonable suspicion." The only exception to the individualized suspicion standard was where an employee's history or job duties implicate student safety (e.g., driving a school bus) or where employees regularly use hazardous substances or operate potentially dangerous equipment. However, in 1999 the Supreme Court let stand a decision of the Sixth Circuit that allowed mandatory urinalysis of all applicants (including teachers and principals) for positions in the district or transfers within the district (*Knox County Education Association v. Knox County Board of Education,* 1999). The court reasoned that because educators were on the "frontline of school security," and because they occupy so-called safety-sensitive positions (i.e., positions where even a momentary lapse of attention could have serious consequences (see *Skinner v. Railroad Labor Executive Association,* 1989), the policy was justified. Also important to the court's decision was that the testing program was narrowly prescribed and not overly intrusive (it was a one-time test with advance notice), as well as the fact that educators were involved in a "heavily regulated industry," so their expectations of privacy were diminished. The pre-employment drug testing upheld in *Knox* was expanded in *Crager v. Board of Education of Knott Co.* (2004) to the random suspicionless drug testing of 25% of all employees in "safety-sensitive" positions. However, despite the support of the courts, drug testing of teachers has not become widespread.

*Teacher Rights: Freedom from Employment Discrimination and Sexual Harassment*

## Employment Discrimination

School districts and their employees are prohibited by the Fourteenth Amendment and numerous state and federal statutes from engaging in practices that intentionally discriminate against employees or students on the basis of race, gender, age, religion, national origin, or disability. Most cases alleging **employment discrimination** are brought under Title VII of the Civil Rights Act of 1964 (as amended) or one of the other civil rights statutes detailed in Table 11.1. Title VII covers recruitment, hiring, promotion, and compensation, as well as other terms and conditions of employment. Two types of employment discrimination claims are typically brought under Title VII: **disparate treatment**, which places the burden on the plaintiff to prove that he or she is a member of a group protected by Title VII, was qualified for the position, and was treated less favorably than others by some employment practice or policy; and **disparate impact**, which requires that the plaintiff show that an employment practice or policy had a more severe impact on a protected class than others. If the employer answers the challenge by showing the policy or practice is job related and consistent with a business necessity, the employee can still prevail by showing that the district could have accomplished its goal by less discriminatory means. For example, a female applicant for a high school biology teaching position was successful in a sex discrimination suit in showing that the district's requirement that applicants also have the ability to coach varsity softball had a disparate impact on women (*Civil Rights Division v. Amphitheater Unified School District,* 1983). The court rejected the district's business necessity defense because the district was unable to demonstrate that less discriminatory alternatives had been attempted.

### Sexual Harassment

Sexual harassment is considered a form of sex discrimination prohibited under Title VII. According to Title VII, sexual harassment occurs when unwelcome advances or requests for sexual favors are made a condition of being hired, receiving a raise or promotion, or any other benefit of employment (*quid pro quo* **harassment**), or where verbal or physical conduct is sufficiently severe or pervasive as to unreasonably interfere with an individual's work performance or to create an intimidating, hostile, or offensive work environment (**hostile environment harassment**).

The courts have traditionally held that under the legal principal of agency, employers can be held vicariously liable for the sexual harassment committed by employees. As a result, employers were sometimes held liable in instances in which they neither condoned nor even knew of the acts of the employee. While not abandoning this position, in two cases the Supreme Court said that in cases that involved a supervisor engaging in what heretofore would have been called *quid pro quo* harassment (the court did not like these labels), the employer will still be held strictly liable. But in cases of hostile environment harassment, the employer will not be liable if it can prove (1) it had a sexual policy in place designed to prevent and effectively address allegations of sexual harassment, and (2) the harassed employee did not follow the procedures in the policy to file a complaint or to seek help (*Burlington Industries v. Ellerth,* 1998; *Faragher v. Boca Raton,* 1998).

## Equal Opportunity and Affirmative Action

The legal principle of **equal opportunity**, whether equal employment opportunity or equal educational opportunity, is founded in antidiscrimination legislation. Equal opportunity requires that school districts and other agencies develop policies and procedures to ensure that the rights of employees and students are protected and that they are given equal treatment in employment practices, access to programs, or other educational opportunities.

**Affirmative action** goes beyond equal opportunity. The principle of affirmative action holds that ensuring nondiscrimination is not enough; what is needed are affirmative steps to admit, recruit, hire, and retain individuals who are underrepresented in the workplace or the classroom. Beginning in the 1960s and 1970s, many school districts adopted affirmative action plans that set forth their intended goals in these areas and their intended actions to achieve diversity in the workplace and classroom and to "remedy the vestiges of past discrimination."

Although achieving diversity is a desirable goal, the U.S. Supreme Court, in *Regents of the University of California v. Alan Bakke* (1978), ruled against the establishment of firm quotas that designate a predetermined number of "slots" only for minorities, resulting in so-called **reverse discrimination**, but it said that institutions could use race as one factor to be considered in admissions. Almost 20 years later, the Court seemingly retreated from that position by ruling that universities could not use racial preferences in admissions (*Hopwood v. Texas,* 1996). And, in *Wygant v. Jackson Board of Education* (1986), the U.S. Supreme Court overturned a Michigan school district's collective bargaining agreement that provided for the release of White employees with greater seniority than Black employees in order to preserve the percentage of minority teachers employed prior to the layoffs. The Court ruled that affirmative action plans must be designed to remedy location-specific past discrimination, not general societal discrimination. That is, first there must be evidence that remedial action is necessary, and second, the plan must be "narrowly tailored" to remedy the past discrimination (see also *Taxman v. Board of Education of Piscataway,* 1996, where the retention of an equally qualified Black teacher over a White teacher to preserve racial diversity was overturned by Third Circuit Court of Appeals).

Although the need for school districts to promote diversity in the ranks of their employees and student bodies has not ended, the courts have increasingly made clear that under the strict judicial review standard, any program giving consideration to race, ethnicity, or gender must have a compelling state interest and be narrowly tailored to serve that interest. These standards have been applied in recent cases involving school district voluntary race-conscious student assignment plans. The Supreme Court addressed this issue in *Parents Involved in Community Schools v. Seattle School District No. 1* (2007). The court ruled that student assignment plans adopted for the sole purpose of achieving racial diversity did not constitute a compelling state interest (e.g., to remedy the effects of *de jure* segregation) nor did the district use the most narrowly fashioned means (i.e., race neutral alternatives) to achieve their goal of promoting diversity.

**Reflect on Diversity**
What should a district do to increase the number of women in administrative positions?

## *Legal Responsibilities of Teachers*

In addition to the terms and conditions of employment previously discussed, other requirements may be made as a condition of teacher employment as long as they do not violate teacher rights or state or federal law. Some requirements, such as those related to providing reasonable care and maintaining discipline, are discussed later in this chapter. Requirements related to two topics—reporting child abuse and neglect and use of copyrighted materials—are discussed here. These topics have become increasingly important to educators in the last decade.

### Reporting Child Abuse and Neglect

Child abuse is defined in both federal and state statutes. The federal Child Abuse Prevention and Treatment Act (CAPTA), as amended by the Keeping Children and Families Safe Act of 2003, defines child abuse and neglect as:

> Any recent act or failure to act on the part of a parent or caretaker which results in death, serious physical or emotional harm, sexual abuse or exploitation. It includes an act or failure to act which represents an imminent risk of serious harm. (42 U.S.C. 5106)

Because child abuse occurs across all socioeconomic classes and ethnic/racial groups, it is likely that all teachers will be confronted with this problem at some point during their teaching careers. In fact, 16.5% of all reports of abuse and neglect in 2009 were made by educational personnel, as noted in Chapter 10 (U.S. Department of Health and Human Services, 2010a).

As discussed in Chapter 10, all states have enacted statutes requiring teachers to report actual or suspected child abuse and neglect immediately upon gaining knowledge or suspicion of the abuse or neglect. Most states detail the procedures that are to be followed in making the report. In all states the report may be made orally or in writing to either a law enforcement agency, child protection services, or other designated agency. State reporting statutes apply not only to suspected parental abuse but also to suspected abuse by school employees. Under most state supporting statutes, failure to report abuse may result in civil or criminal liability, with penalties as high as two years in jail and a fine of $4,000. A civil suit claiming negligence also may be brought against the teacher for failure to report child abuse. In addition, school districts may take disciplinary measures, including dismissal, against employees for failure to follow required reporting statutes. Because of the serious consequences of failure to report child abuse—to the child, the teacher, and possibly the district (the district could be required to pay monetary damages if liability is found)—most school boards also have adopted policies affirming the responsibility of district employees to report child abuse and detailing the procedures to be followed when abuse is suspected. Such policies are also intended to protect employees against false charges of child abuse.

As emphasized in Chapter 10, state statutes that require teachers to report suspected child abuse do not demand that they be absolutely sure that the child has been abused, only that there is "reasonable cause to believe" that the child is subject to abuse or neglect and that the report is made in "good faith." Teachers and counselors are required to report suspected abuse or neglect even if to do so would violate a confidence. Under all state statutes, school employees who report suspected child abuse or neglect are immune from civil and criminal prosecution if the report was made in good faith. In many states, good faith is presumed and the person challenging the reporter would have to prove that the reporter acted in bad faith.

## Observing Copyrights

Copyright laws are designed to protect the author or originator of an original work from unauthorized reproduction or use of the work. Because of their widespread use of print and nonprint material in the classroom, it is important that teachers be knowledgeable about and comply with federal copyright laws. Teachers can legally use copyrighted materials under three conditions: (1) they have requested and received permission from the copyright holder to use the work, (2) the work is in the public domain (i.e., it is either more than 75 years old or has been created by a governmental agency), or (3) it is considered fair use. The **fair use doctrine** allows the nonprofit reproduction and use of certain materials for classroom use without permission of the copyright owner if each copy bears the copyright notice and meets the tests of brevity, spontaneity, and cumulative effect outlined in the guidelines for classroom copying presented in Figure 12.1.

The increasing use of instructional technology has brought to light a number of issues related to use of copyrighted nonprint materials, namely television programs and videotapes. In 1981, Congress issued *Guidelines for Off-the-Air Recording of Broadcast Programming for Educational Purposes*. The guidelines provide that a nonprofit educational institution may tape broadcast television programs for classroom use if requested by an individual teacher. Programs also may be taped at home by the teacher. All copies must include the copyright notice on the program and cannot be altered in any way. During the first 10 days after taping, the material may be shown once by the individual teacher and may be repeated

## Figure 12.1 — Guidelines for Classroom Copying of Printed Material

1. A single copy may be made of any of the following for your own scholarly research or use in teaching:
   A. A chapter from a book;
   B. An article from a periodical or newspaper;
   C. A short story, short essay, or short poem;
   D. A chart, graph, diagram, drawing, cartoon or picture from a book, periodical, or newspaper.
2. Multiple copies (not to exceed in any event more than one copy per pupil in a course) may be made for classroom use or discussion, provided that each copy includes a notice of copyright and that the following tests are met:
   A. Brevity Test
      (i) Poetry: (a) a complete poem of less than 250 words and if printed on not more than two pages, or (b) from a longer poem, an excerpt of not more than 250 words.
      (ii) Prose: (a) Either a complete article, story, or essay of less than 2,500 words, or (b) an excerpt from any prose work of not more than 1,000 words or 10 percent of the work, whichever is less, but in any event a minimum of 5000 words.
      (iii) Illustration: One chart, graph, diagram, drawing, cartoon or picture per book or per periodical issue.
      (iv) "Special" works in poetry, prose, or in "poetic prose" that combine language with illustrations and are less than 2,500 words in their entirety may not be reproduced in their entirety; however, an excerpt of not more than two of the published pages of such special work and containing not more than 10 percent of the words may be reproduced.
   B. Spontaneity Test
      (i) The copying is at your instance and inspiration, and
      (ii) The inspiration and decision to use the work and the moment of its use for maximum teaching effectiveness are so close in time that it would be unreasonable to expect you would receive a timely reply to a request for permission.
   C. Cumulative Effect Test
      (i) The copying of the material is for only one course in the school in which the copies are made.
      (ii) Not more than one short poem, article, story, essay or two excerpts may be copied from the same author, nor more than three from the same collective work or periodical volume during one class term.
      (iii) There cannot be more than nine instances of multiple copying for one course during one class term.
      [These limitations do not apply to current news periodicals and newspapers and current news sections of other periodicals.]
3. Copying cannot be used to create or to replace or substitute for anthologies, compilations, or collective works.
4. There can be no copying of, or from, "consumable" works (e.g., workbooks, exercises, standardized tests and test booklets and answer sheets).
5. Copying cannot substitute for the purchase of books, publishers' reprints, or periodicals.
6. Copying cannot be directed by a higher authority.
7. You cannot copy the same item from term to term.
8. No charge can be made to the student beyond the actual cost of the photocopying.

*Source:* Excerpt from *Report of the House Committee on the Judiciary* (House Report No. 94–1476).

only once for purposes of instructional reinforcement. Additional use is limited to viewing for evaluating the program for possible purchase. After 45 days, the tape must be erased or destroyed. All other off-the-air recording (except for the purpose of time shifting for personal use) is illegal unless the program is recorded from educational television. These recordings may be shown for a period of seven days after the broadcast, but must then be erased or destroyed. The taping of television programs telecast by cable or satellite providers does not fall under these guidelines because they are not free to the public. Before taping any programs carried

Teachers are responsible for ensuring the ethical use of computers.

by cable or satellite, the particular station or network should be contacted to determine their taping guidelines.

Generally, teachers cannot duplicate audiovisual materials or convert them from one format to another (e.g., from audio tape to CD or from videotape to DVD). Use of copyrighted video purchased by the district is, of course, permitted. Other video for which public performance rights in a school setting have been obtained may also be shown if shown as part of a systematic program of instruction and not for entertainment or recreation. Teachers may also make a single copy of a recording of copyrighted music owned by the district or the teacher if the purpose is to construct oral exercises or examinations.

The copying of computer software and material on the Internet and World Wide Web has become a major area of copyright infringement. The high cost of software, combined with limited school budgets, has resulted in numerous cases of unauthorized copying of software. In 1980 the copyright law was amended to include software. According to the amendments, one archival or backup copy can be made of the master program; making multiple copies, even for educational purposes, would be a violation of the fair use principle. However, teachers and school districts can negotiate license agreements with a software company that would allow for multiple use of a particular program at a substantial savings over purchasing multiple copies. Teachers also have the responsibility to make sure students understand copyright restrictions and monitor compliance. Teachers who knowingly allow students to engage in illegal copying could be charged with contributing to copyright infringement. In the use of copyrighted audio, video, or software, as in the use of any copyrighted material, teachers are required to obey both the letter and the spirit of copyright laws and adhere to any relevant school board policies or guidelines.

Materials found on the Internet are also protected by copyright laws, including the Digital Millennium Copyright Act and the Technology, Education and Copyright Harmonization Act which defines the terms and conditions under which educational institutions can use copyrighted material in distance education and on websites. Of particular concern to school districts is illegal file sharing. Any student or school employee who uploads a copy of a copyrighted song, video, or software with the purpose of making it available to others is violating copyright, as is any person who downloads such a file. School districts have attempted to address the problem of illegal file sharing by adopting policies prohibiting the practice, blocking sites where illegal file sharing is known to take place, and disciplining offenders.

## Tort Liability of School District Employees

A **tort** is defined as a civil wrong that leads to injury to another (criminal wrongs are not torts) and for which a court will provide a remedy in the form of an action for damages. To protect both school district employees and school board members against financial loss resulting from a tort suit, many school districts purchase liability insurance. Many educators also participate in liability insurance programs through their professional organizations.

The most common category of torts in education is negligence. Basically, **negligence** can be defined as a failure to do (or not do) what a reasonable and prudent person would have done under the same or similar circumstances, resulting in injury to another. Before an educator can be found guilty of negligence, four elements must be proved:

1. The educator had a duty to provide an appropriate standard of care to another individual (student, coworker, the public).
2. The educator failed in his or her duty to provide the reasonable standard of care.
3. A causal relationship exists between the negligent action and the resultant injury (i.e., the action was the proximate cause of the injury).
4. A physical or mental injury occurred, resulting in actual loss.

**For Your Reflection and Analysis**

What impact does the potential for negligence suits have on you as a prospective or practicing teacher?

## Standard of Care and Duty

Although teachers have the responsibility of providing an appropriate standard of care for their students, the standard of care expected is not the same for all teachers and all students. Teachers of younger children are held to a higher standard of care than are teachers of more mature students. A higher standard of care also is required of teachers of students with physical or mental disabilities, as well as of physical education and vocational and industrial arts teachers because of the inherent dangers in the activities involved.

**Reasonableness Doctrine.** In determining whether the educator failed to provide the appropriate standard of care, the courts compare the teacher's actions with those of the hypothetical "reasonable and prudent" teacher—one with average intelligence and physical attributes, normal perception and memory, and possessing the same special knowledge and skills as others with the same training and experience—not some "ideal" or "super" teacher.

**Foreseeable Doctrine.** A related element is whether the hypothetical reasonable teacher could have foreseen, and thus prevented, the injury. The actions of the teacher are compared with those of the reasonable teacher to determine negligence.

## Proximate Cause

Even in situations in which the teacher has failed in a recognized duty to provide a reasonable standard of care, liability will not be assessed unless it can be shown that the teacher's action was the **proximate cause** of the injury; that is, the injury would not have occurred had it not been for the teacher's conduct. In some cases an intervening event, such as the negligent act of a third party, may relieve the teacher of liability. Because each case brings with it a set of circumstances distinct from all others, the determination of proximate cause must be made case by case.

## Educational and Professional Malpractice

Historically, most educational liability litigation has involved student injuries. However, in recent years, a new topic of negligence litigation, **educational malpractice,** emerged and became the focus of concerned discussion in both the educational and legal communities. As in medical malpractice, the term is concerned with some negligence on the part of the professional. In general, there are two kinds of educational malpractice suits: (1) *instructional malpractice* suits concerned with students who have received certificates or diplomas and have actually failed to learn (see, e.g., *Peter W. v. San Francisco Unified School District,* 1976, where a student was awarded a high school diploma even though functionally illiterate); and (2) *professional malpractice* suits involving misdiagnosis, improper advising, or improper educational placement (see, e.g., *Hoffman v. Board of Education of the City of New York,* 1979, where a kindergarten student of normal intelligence but with a severe speech impediment was placed in a class for children with intellectual disabilities based on an intelligence test that, in part, requires oral responses, and, although a psychologist recommended retesting in two years, the student was not retested for 13 years). Although there have been a number of instructional malpractice suits, none has been successful in the courts. However, the requirement that students be taught by highly qualified teachers, in accordance with state standards and to specified levels of proficiency, "may finally move the courts to abandon 30 years of stubborn dismissal of these suits" (Gray, 2010, p. 25).

As opposed to educational malpractice, students have been successful in a limited number of cases based on the theory of professional malpractice. These claims differ from educational malpractice claims in that they do not challenge academic or curriculum decisions or educational standards. Rather, they claim that specific individuals have negligently performed their professional duties. In the first successful suit of its kind in education, *Eisel v. Board of Education of Montgomery County* (1991), two school counselors were found negligent in failing to communicate to a parent a student's suicidal statements made to other students and told to them. The counselors had questioned the student about the statements, but when she denied them, they did nothing further. The court ruled that the counselors had "a duty to use reasonable means to prevent a suicide when they are on notice" of a student's suicidal intent. The student subsequently died from a murder-suicide pact.

In two cases dealing with similar facts but very dissimilar results, the courts addressed the issue of improper advising. In the first case, *Stain v. Cedar Rapids Community School District* (2001), the law related to negligent misrepresentation, which applies to accountants, attorneys, and other professionals who are in the business of supplying information to others who might forseeably rely on it, was extended to the incorrect advice given by a high school counselor. The counselor told a basketball player that a particular English course would be approved by the NCAA toward its core course requirement when, in fact, the course had not been submitted by the school for approval. After graduation, the student was notified by the NCAA that he was one third of a credit short of what was needed to participate in Division I basketball. As a result, he lost his college scholarship. In finding for the student, the court concluded that it was appropriate to extend the tort of negligent misrepresentation to the duty of a guidance counselor "to use reasonable care in providing specific information to a student when (1) the counselor has knowledge of the specific need for the information and provides the information to the student in the course of a counselor–student relationship, and (2) a student reasonably relies upon the information under circumstances in which the counselor knows or should know of the student's reliance" (*Stain v. Cedar Rapids Community School District*, 2001, p. 125). A different conclusion was reached by the Wisconsin Supreme Court in *Scott v. Savers Property and Casualty Insurance Co.* (2003) when it ruled that the district was not liable when a guidance counselor's faulty advice also resulted in a student's losing a college athletic scholarship.

## Student Rights and Responsibilities

Traditionally, it was accepted that school officials had considerable authority in controlling student conduct. Operating under the doctrine of *in loco parentis* (in place of a parent), school authorities exercised almost unlimited, and usually unchallenged, discretion in restricting the rights of students and in disciplining students. However, beginning in the 1960s students increasingly challenged the authority and actions of school officials. Subsequent court decisions broadened the scope of student rights and, at the same time, attempted to maintain a balance between the rights of students and the rights and responsibilities of school officials (see Figure 12.2 and the Controversial Issue discussion of Service Learning on p. 326). Since 1975, however, the Supreme Court has generally been less favorable towards students than it was during the early Civil Rights movement. "This shift in orientation occurred for diverse reasons, including growing concern about the level of violence and disorder in the public schools, the changed political climate following the end of the Vietnam era, and a pattern of increasingly conservative judicial appointments during the Nixon, Reagan, and Bush administrations" (Arum & Preiss, 2009, p. 69).

**Figure 12.2 — Balancing the Rights of Students and the Responsibilities of School Officials**

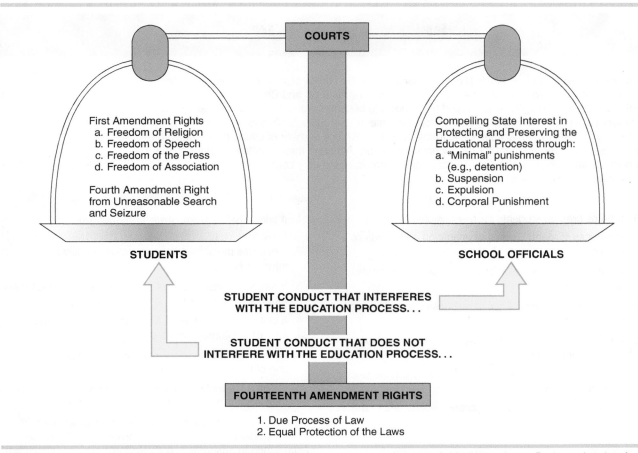

**COURTS**

First Amendment Rights
a. Freedom of Religion
b. Freedom of Speech
c. Freedom of the Press
d. Freedom of Association

Fourth Amendment Right
from Unreasonable Search
and Seizure

**STUDENTS**

Compelling State Interest in
Protecting and Preserving the
Educational Process through:
a. "Minimal" punishments
   (e.g., detention)
b. Suspension
c. Expulsion
d. Corporal Punishment

**SCHOOL OFFICIALS**

**STUDENT CONDUCT THAT INTERFERES
WITH THE EDUCATION PROCESS...**

**STUDENT CONDUCT THAT DOES NOT
INTERFERE WITH THE EDUCATION PROCESS...**

**FOURTEENTH AMENDMENT RIGHTS**

1. Due Process of Law
2. Equal Protection of the Laws

*Source:* Adapted from *The Schools, the Courts and the Public Interest* by J.C. Hogan, Copyright © 1974 by Lexington Books, an imprint of Macmillan, Inc.

## Student Discipline

Although the *in loco parentis* doctrine has been weakened in recent years, school officials do have the authority—and in fact the duty—to establish reasonable rules of student conduct designed to protect students and employees, as well as rules necessary to establish and maintain a climate conducive to learning. The authority and responsibility to establish rules of conduct carries with it the authority to discipline students for violations of these rules. The severity of the violation will determine the nature of the discipline and the due process required. Because state compulsory attendance laws give students a property right to attend school, if a disciplinary action involves exclusion from school or the removal of the student from the classroom for even a minimal period of time, some due process is required, even if in the latter instance it is only informally providing the student the opportunity to give his or her side of the story.

The concept of constitutional due process contains two components: substantive due process and procedural due process. **Substantive due process** is concerned with ensuring that government actions are reasonably related to a legitimate state purpose and are not arbitrary or capricious. The state's interest in disciplinary situations is to maintain order in the school and to protect students. Thus, to pass the substantive due process test, a school must show that its rules are reasonably related to these purposes. Even when the school's actions are related to a legitimate state interest, substantive due process can be violated when the school's actions are unreasonable or unreasonably severe. The bottom line on substantive due process is fundamental fairness.

# CONTROVERSIAL ISSUE

## *Service Learning*

National leaders as well as national organizations have called on all citizens to become, as one initiative is called, "Volunteers in Service to America." The National and Community Service Act, which was passed in 1993, encouraged the schools to become involved in school-based community service/service learning programs. Since that time, numerous schools and school districts have moved to establish voluntary service learning programs, while a number of others have made community service a requirement for high school graduation. Although there is little opposition to the schools establishing volunteer service learning programs, mandatory community service has been the subject of considerable debate.

**For**

1. It helps prepare students for responsible citizenship.
2. It reduces students' feeling of alienation and builds self-esteem.
3. It has a positive effect on students' grades, attendance, and motivation.
4. It promotes a feeling of social responsibility and capacity to empathize.
5. It provides students the opportunity to explore career interests or abilities.
6. It provides scarce resources to community service projects and organizations.
7. It promotes community and parent involvement in the school.

**Against**

1. It takes students' time away from much-needed academic programs.
2. It exposes the school to unnecessary liability for students' injury or harm.
3. It requires considerable staff resources to administer and monitor the program.
4. It violates the Thirteenth Amendment's prohibition against involuntary servitude.
5. It interferes with parents' right to direct the moral education of their children.
6. In some students it will create resentment and destroy their spirit of volunteerism.

What kinds of community service are appropriate for high school students to perform? What protections should be established to ensure that both students and the district are protected from liability?

---

## For Your Reflection and Analysis

What effect, if any, does the weakening of the doctrine of *in loco parentis* and the apparent expansion of student rights have on the willingness of educators to discipline disobedient or disruptive students?

Procedural due process is designed to ensure the processes by which students are disciplined are fair and equitable. In the lead case in student due process (*Goss v. Lopez,* 1975), the Supreme Court applied the concepts of procedural due process to disciplinary measures. The Court concluded that due process applies to school discipline because education is a property right under state law. The extent of the due process required depends on the nature of the interest being taken away; i.e., the greater the potential deprivation, the more procedural protections must be provided. Typically, if the maximum penalty that could be imposed is relatively small (e.g., a one-day detention), only a minimal amount of procedural due process is required. Even within this constitutional framework, the laws governing student discipline vary significantly from state to state.

### Suspensions and Expulsions

Short-term **suspensions** usually are defined as exclusions from school for periods of 10 days or fewer; long-term suspensions and **expulsions** are for periods in excess of 10 days. Although a teacher or administrator may initiate an expulsion proceeding, normally only the school board can expel the student. Because of the severity of expulsions, state statutes and school board regulations usually detail the grounds for expulsion, as well as the procedures that must be followed. Grounds for expulsion typically include theft or vandalism of school property, possession of weapons (may be mandated by "zero tolerance" policies featured in

# VIDEO INSIGHT

## Action, Reaction, and Zero Tolerance: How Far Is Too Far?

In this ABC News video, you are asked a variety of questions about the effect of zero tolerance in schools. You are also asked to consider zero tolerance for anything that might be construed as a threat of violence.

1. In the video segment, you are confronted with three choices relative to the students playing "cowboys and Indians." Should the officer have (1) just walked on by and ignored the situation? (2) intervened and counseled the students? or (3) considered the situation as a criminal matter? Give the pros and cons for each choice. What other possible choice(s) might you have recommended to the officer?

2. Consider the zero tolerance policies for various offenses other than firearms (alcohol, drugs, harassment, etc.). What are the most effective ways of ensuring that those policies are both understood and accepted by the students and their parents or guardians?

the Video Insight feature above), possession or use of alcohol or drugs, causing or attempting to cause injury to another, and engaging in any behavior forbidden by law. In addition, the Gun Free Schools Act of 1994 requires any school receiving federal funds to expel for one year any student who brings a firearm to school. (This can be mitigated on a case-by-case basis by the local superintendent.)

The procedures that must be followed in an expulsion usually include the right to:

1. A written notice specifying the charges, the time and place of the hearing, and the procedures to be followed at the hearing;
2. Sufficient time between the notice and the hearing to allow the student to prepare a defense;
3. A hearing before an impartial tribunal;
4. A cross-examination of witnesses and a presentation of witnesses and evidence to refute adverse evidence;
5. Representation by legal counsel or other adult;
6. A written statement of the findings/recommendations of the hearing body that demonstrate the decision was based on the evidence presented;
7. A written or taped record of the hearing, if appeal is to be made; and
8. A clear statement of the right to appeal.

In contrast to the detailed statutory guidelines pertaining to expulsions, in *Goss v. Lopez* (1975), the U.S. Supreme Court ruled that for short-term suspensions of fewer than 10 days, the student need be given only oral or written notice of the charges, an explanation of the evidence, and the opportunity to rebut the charges before an objective decision-maker. However, the Court did recognize that there might be situations that would require more detailed procedures, such as situations in which the facts are disputed and not easily resolved, as well as emergencies in which the safety of persons or property is threatened, where no due process is required prior to disciplinary action. However, even in these situations due process must be followed as soon as possible after the danger of harm has passed. Although *Goss* specified only the basics of due process that must be followed for short-term suspensions, state statutes may, and often do, require additional procedures.

**Reflect on Diversity**
What types of behaviors might be a manifestation of a disability? What disability?

Students may be disciplined for conduct off-campus that has a direct and immediate effect on school discipline or the safety and welfare of students the same as they would for on-campus conduct, and they are entitled to the same due process protections. However, students are not entitled to due process protections when suspended or expelled from extracurricular activities, because students have no property right to participate in those activities.

Special considerations are involved in the suspension or expulsion of children with disabilities. According to the 2004 revisions of the IDEA, disruptive students with disabilities can be suspended or relocated to an "interim alternative educational setting" for up to 10 days while awaiting an expulsion hearing, but they cannot be summarily suspended. Expulsion or long-term suspension is considered a change in placement and cannot take place until the IEP team has undertaken an inquiry to determine if the misconduct is a "manifestation of the disability." If it is found to be a manifestation of the disability, then change-of-placement procedures must be followed before any relocation or expulsion can take place. If it is not a manifestation of the disability, then the student is subject to the same disciplinary actions as students without disabilities.

### Corporal Punishment

As noted in Chapter 11, the U.S. Supreme Court has said that corporal punishment is not prohibited by the Eighth Amendment. However, corporal punishment that is arbitrary, capricious, or unrelated to a reasonable educational purpose may be a violation of the student's right to privacy and personal security, as well as due process rights under the Fourteenth Amendment. In addition, if the punishment is cruel or excessive, a student may have an assault and battery claim, and the administrator or teacher administering the corporal punishment may be found liable under tort law for the injuries sustained. However, punishment administered in a "privileged manner" is not a tort. Punishment is said to be privileged when it serves a reasonable educational purpose and is reasonable in its method and degree of force. The determination of reasonableness includes a consideration of the nature of the infraction; the past record of the student; the age, gender, and physical and mental condition of the student; and the force and instrument employed (Valente & Valente, 2005).

Among the other things considered by the courts in determining reasonableness and in order to be upheld, corporal punishment must:

- Be allowed by state law
- Be permitted or at least not prohibited by district policy
- Be implemented consistent with state and district requirements
- Be used as a method of correction
- Be appropriate for the offense
- Be consistent with the terms for any applicable IEP
- Not be motivated by anger or malice
- Not be cruel or excessive

More than half the states prohibit corporal punishment by state law (see Figure 12.3). In a number of others, corporal punishment is prohibited by school board policy. In the states and school districts where corporal punishment is permitted, school board policies will normally dictate the conditions under which corporal punishment can be administered. Most such policies require that the principal rather than the teacher administer the punishment and that another adult be present.

### Search and Seizure

The issues surrounding student search and seizure have increased in recent years, along with the concern about the presence of drugs and weapons in the schools. Historically, the Fourth Amendment protection against unreasonable search and

## Figure 12.3 — The State of Corporal Punishment

Corporal punishment banned by law

Corporal punishment allowed

More than half of all students are in districts with no corporal punishment

seizure has been interpreted as requiring law enforcement officials to have "probable cause" that a crime has been committed and to obtain a search warrant before conducting a search. Prior to 1985, some courts held school officials to the same standard. However, in *New Jersey v. T.L.O.* (1985), the Supreme Court ruled that school officials' interest in maintaining discipline in the schools was sufficient to justify their being held to a lesser standard than probable cause. Rather, school officials may conduct a warrantless search if it passes the two-pronged "reasonableness test": (1) there is reasonable cause or individualized suspicion that a search of that particular person will reveal evidence of a violation of the law or school rules, and (2) the scope of the search is reasonably related to the objective of the search and is not "excessively intrusive" in light of the age and gender of the child and the nature of the alleged infraction.

The court in *T.L.O.* did not say that an individualized suspicion is an absolute requirement for a reasonable search. Exceptions may exist when the privacy interests are minimal or the object of the search is very serious: imminent danger may justify an intrusive search based on reasonable suspicion. For example, in *Thompson v. Carthage School District* (1996), the Eighth Circuit Court upheld a search of all male students in grades 6 through 12 based on a report that a weapon was being concealed by a student. The court ruled that the search was minimally intrusive and justified in light of the need to uncover a dangerous weapon. On the other hand, a search of all students in an art class for a pair of allegedly stolen sneakers was not upheld by the court. The court said that deviation from the individualized suspicion requirement is justified only in special circumstances, such as protecting students from weapons or drugs (*DesRoches ex rel. DesRoches v. Caprio,* 1997).

In determining whether a particular search is reasonable, the courts have distinguished between school property (e.g., lockers) and personal property (e.g., a book bag, wallet, or purse). Searches of student personal possessions require that there be individualized suspicion that a violation of law or a school policy has occurred. On the other hand, most courts have upheld locker searches; the courts have reasoned that although a student may have exclusive use of a locker in regard to other students, because the possession is not exclusive in regard to school officials who retain control of the lockers, the student has a limited expectation of privacy. Many schools or school districts minimize the expectation of privacy by notifying students in the student handbook that lockers are subject to inspection.

A number of districts have turned to the use of drug-sniffing dogs in their efforts to combat drugs and violence. The Supreme Court has held that the use of dogs to sniff objects is not a search because it is not a violation of someone's reasonable expectation of privacy. The dogs merely sniff the air surrounding the object, that is, they explore only that which is within "plain smell" (*United States v. Place,* 1983). This holds true in schools as well, but there are limitations. Schools may use dogs to sniff lockers, possessions, and book bags. However, canine searches of students have been more limited, and because the dogs may touch the children and individually sniff them, a greater expectation of privacy is involved. Thus, most schools limit canine searches to unpopulated areas. Some schools employ private companies or local law enforcement with dogs to regularly sniff hallways and parking lots.

Strip searches, because of their intrusive nature, have been prohibited by law in a number of states (California, Iowa, New Jersey, Oregon, Washington, and Wisconsin), and in all areas are carefully scrutinized and most often disallowed by the courts. However, such searches have been allowed if they meet the *T.L.O.* reasonable suspicion standard, particularly in regard to the scope of the search. How much suspicion is needed for the search to be considered reasonable was addressed by the Supreme Court in its 2009 decision in *Safford Unified School District v. Redding,* involving a near strip search of an 8th grader based on the report of another student that she had received prescription strength ibuprofen from Redding and the report of another student that Redding and other students had brought pills to school that they were going to take at lunchtime. No pills were found. The court ruled that the "content of the suspicion failed to match the degree of intrusion" and that there was "no indication of danger to the students from the power of drugs or their quantity" (pp. 2642–2643).

While the search in *Redding* was found to be unconstitutional, the court also said that the indignity of the search did not make it unlawful if there is enough evidence to support reasonable suspicion. In a case in point, the Court upheld the partial strip search of a student suspected of being under the influence of marijuana. The student was "giggling and acting in an unruly fashion" and had dilated pupils and bloodshot eyes. A school nurse conducted a cursory medical assessment of the student as well as a search that required the student to remove his under jersey, shoes, and socks and empty his pockets. The court held that there was a reasonable basis for the search given the student's behavior and that the search was not excessively intrusive (*Bridgman v. New Trier High School District,* 1997).

Perhaps the most controversial issue in the area of student searches is drug testing of students. Thus far, the courts have invalidated blanket drug testing of the general student population on the basis of the individualized suspicion standard. However, the question of "suspicionless" random drug testing of students who wish to participate in extracurricular activities has yielded mixed conclusions. In *Vernonia School District v. Acton* (1995), the Supreme Court found a school district's policy requiring student athletes to submit to a random urinalysis not unreasonable under the Fourth Amendment. The Court not only agreed with the district's contention that the policy was justified based on its interest in

## For Your Reflection and Analysis

What would be examples of student conduct that would constitute "reasonable suspicion" for you to institute a search for drugs?

preventing injuries and deterring drug use (some of the athletes were leaders in the drug culture), but also noted that the testing procedure used was no more intrusive than the students' daily undressing in the locker room. A similar conclusion was reached by the U.S. Supreme Court in *Board of Education of Independent School District No. 92 of Pottawatomie County v. Earls* (2002), where drug testing was required of all middle and high school students who participated in "competitive" extracurricular activities. Once again the court found the required urinalysis to be only a negligible intrusion on the student's privacy, a privacy that is limited in the school environment, where the school district is responsible for maintaining a safe and orderly environment. Also important to the court's decision was the fact that the results were not turned over to law enforcement or used to discipline the students.

The *Vernonia* "special needs" argument has been used in subsequent decisions to support random searches with metal detectors. Table 12.2 lists some Supreme Court decisions affecting students' rights.

## Table 12.2 — Selected U.S. Supreme Court Cases Affecting Students' Rights

| Case | Decision |
| --- | --- |
| *Tinker v. Des Moines* (1969) | School officials cannot limit students' rights to free expression unless there is evidence of a material disruption or substantial disorder. |
| *Goss v. Lopez* (1975) | For suspensions of less than 10 days, the student must be given an oral or written notice of charges, an explanation of the evidence against him or her, and the opportunity to rebut the charges before an objective decision-maker. |
| *Wood v. Strickland* (1975) | Students may sue school board members for monetary damages under the Civil Rights Act of 1871. |
| *Ingraham v. Wright* (1977) | Corporal punishment does not constitute cruel and unusual punishment under the Eighth Amendment and does not require due process prior to administration. |
| *Board of Education, Island Trees Union Free School District v. Pico* (1982) | Censorship by the school board acting in a narrowly partisan or political manner violates the First Amendment rights of students. |
| *Bethel School District v. Fraser* (1986) | School boards have the authority to determine what speech is inappropriate and need not tolerate speech that is lewd or offensive. |
| *New Jersey v. T.L.O.* (1985) | School officials are not required to obtain a search warrant or show probable cause to search a student, only reasonable suspicion that the search will turn up evidence of a violation of law or school rules. |
| *Hazelwood School District v. Kuhlmeier* (1988) | School officials may limit school-sponsored student speech as long as their actions are related to a legitimate pedagogical concern. |
| *Honig v. Doe* (1988) | Disruptive students with disabilities may be expelled but must be kept in their current placement until an official hearing is held. |
| *Franklin v. Gwinnett* (1992) | The sexual harassment of a student may be a violation of Title IX for which monetary damages can be sought. |
| *Vernonia School District v. Acton* (1995) | Special needs can justify "suspicionless" random searching of students. |
| *Board of Education of Independent School District No. 92 v. Earls* (2002) | Drug testing of students in extracurricular activities does not violate the Fourth Amendment's prohibition against unreasonable searches; individualized suspicion is not required. |
| *Morse v. Fredrick* (2007) | Student free speech rights do not include advocating illegal drug use. |
| *Safford Unified School District v. Redding* (2009) | Student search may not be excessively intrusive in light of age and sex of student and the nature of the intrusion. |

## *Freedom of Expression*

Free speech is one of our most highly treasured and protected constitutional liberties. This is especially true within the public schools, where the Supreme Court has noted that First Amendment rights must receive scrupulous protections in schools "if we are not to strangle the free mind at its source and teach youth to discount important principles of our government as mere platitudes" (*West Virginia State Board of Education v. Barnette*, 1943). However, the Court has recognized that even the right to free speech must be balanced within the public schools to ensure student safety and learning. The First Amendment protects all forms of expression, not only verbal communication, but written and symbolic communication (e.g., dance, art, dress) as well. In 1965, several students in Des Moines, Iowa, were suspended after wearing black armbands to school to protest the Vietnam War. The wearing of armbands was prohibited by a school district policy that had been adopted to prevent possible disturbances after it was learned that students planned to wear the armbands. The suspended students filed suit, and the decision by the Supreme Court (*Tinker v. Des Moines,* 1969) has become a landmark case, not only in student expression but also in the broader area of student rights. In finding for the students, the Court said that students have the freedom to express their views by speech or other forms of expression, so long as the exercise of this freedom does not cause "material disruption," "substantial disorder," or invade the rights of others. According to the Court:

> In order for the State in the person of school officials to justify prohibition of a particular expression of opinion, it must be able to show that its action was caused by something more than a mere desire to avoid the discomfort and unpleasantness that always accompany an unpopular viewpoint . . . undifferentiated fear or apprehension of disturbance is not enough to overcome the right to freedom of expression. (pp. 508–509)

The "material and substantive disruption" standard articulated in *Tinker* has been applied to the numerous student expression cases that have followed. Subsequent rulings have clarified that although the fear of disruption must be based on fact, not intuition, school officials need not wait until a disruption has occurred to take action. If they possess sufficient evidence on which to base a "reasonable forecast" of disruption, action to restrict student expression is justified.

Freedom of expression does not include the right to use vulgar and offensive speech, even if it does not cause disruption. At a high school assembly, Matthew Fraser nominated a classmate for a student council office using what the Court described as "an elaborate, graphic, and explicit sexual metaphor." Fraser was suspended for two days. Lower courts found his suspension to be a violation of his right to free speech and that his speech was not disruptive under the *Tinker* guidelines. The Supreme Court, however, went beyond *Tinker*'s concern with the effect of the student's speech to the content of the speech, and the Court concluded that the school board has the authority to prohibit vulgar or offensive speech or conduct that is inconsistent with the educational mission of the school. In fact, the court said that schools must teach by example the "shared values of a civilized social order" (*Bethel School District No. 403 v. Fraser,* 1986).

Content was also one issue in the recent Supreme Court case of *Morse v. Frederick* (2007). The *Morse* case resulted from a student's actions at an Olympic torch rally. Students lined both sides of the street—on school grounds and across the street. Frederick and his friends displayed a banner that said "Bong Hits 4 Jesus" to attract attention and get on television. The principal saw the banner, crossed the street and told the students to take it down. All students complied except Frederick, so the principal confiscated the banner and disciplined Frederick. The Court held that because schools may take steps to safeguard those entrusted to their care from speech that can reasonably be regarded as encouraging illegal drug use, the school official did not violate the First Amendment by confiscating the pro-drug banner and suspending the student. The Court found that the student could not claim that he was not at school, because the event occurred during normal school hours, was an approved social event at which the district's student conduct rules expressly applied, the teachers and administrators walked among the students and were charged with supervising them, the student stood among other students, and the banner was plainly visible to most students. The Court also found that those who viewed the banner would interpret it as advocating or promoting illegal drug use, in violation of school policy, and that a principal may restrict student speech at a school event when that speech is reasonably viewed as promoting illegal drug use—even if the speech was not a "substantial disruption."

## Student Publications

Although students have the right to free expression and the right to publish and distribute literature published both on and off campus, school officials can enact time, place, and manner restrictions to ensure that the student expression or distribution of student publications does not interfere with the learning environment or endanger the safety of students and employees. However, the restrictions must be reasonable, must not treat speech differently based on viewpoint, and must be consistently applied to all expression. In cases in which school policies require faculty or administrative approval prior to publication, censorship is justified only if the material is libelous, obscene, or likely to cause material and substantial disruption. In addition, the procedures and standards for review must be clearly articulated.

While unpopular or controversial content, or content critical of school officials, has generally been considered insufficient justification for restricting student expression, the Supreme Court in *Hazelwood School District v. Kuhlmeier* (1988) said that school officials "do not offend the First Amendment by exercising editorial control over the style and content of student speech in school-sponsored expressive activities so long as their actions are reasonably related to legitimate pedagogical concerns." In this case a school principal deleted two articles from a school newspaper. According to the principal, he was not concerned with the content of the articles, but felt that they were not well written by journalistic standards (e.g., did not maintain the anonymity of pregnant students or give a father a chance to defend himself against condemning remarks made by a student relative to the impact of divorce on students). Believing that there was not enough time before the publication deadline to make the needed changes in the articles, he deleted the articles. The Court in *Hazelwood* made a distinction between personal expressions by students and those activities that students, parents, and the public might reasonably assume bear the "imprimatur of the school." In the latter category, the Court included not only school-sponsored publications but also "theatrical productions and other expressive activities." The effect of the *Hazelwood* decision has been to allow school officials greater discretion in determining what is inappropriate student speech and expression. When read together, the *Tinker, Bethel,* and *Hazelwood* decisions present three principles for assessing the First Amendment rights of students:

> First, vulgar or plainly offensive speech (Fraser-type speech) may be prohibited without a showing of disruption or substantial interference with the school's work. Second, school sponsored speech (*Hazelwood*-type speech) may be restricted when the limitation is reasonably related to legitimate educational concerns. Third, (personal) speech that is neither vulgar nor school-sponsored (*Tinker*-type speech) may only be prohibited if it causes a substantial and material disruption of the school's operation. (*Pyle v. South Hadley School Community,* 1994, p. 166)

These principles apply not only to print publications but also to expression on school-sponsored Web sites.

## Student Appearance

Thus far the U.S. Supreme Court has refused to accept a case that deals directly with student appearance, and the circuit courts are split as to whether dress is considered a form of expressive activity. In those jurisdictions where dress is considered protected speech, the courts will not uphold appearance regulations unless the district can show a compelling interest in having such a regulation, such as the disruptive effects of the appearance on the educational process or for health and safety reasons. For example, in *Barr v. Lafon* (2008), the Court agreed that following a racially charged altercation, the principal could prohibit students from wearing clothing bearing a Confederate flag. The court ruled that wearing the clothing could present a disruption to the school environment, and the prohibition was justified by the school's interest in maintaining an environment conducive to learning. But in *Zamecnik v. Indian Prairie School District No. 204* (2010), the court upheld students' claims that their right to free speech was violated by the school forbidding them to wear t-shirts or buttons stating "Be Happy, Not Gay." The court held that the school failed to show that it faced a threat of substantial disruption.

In jurisdictions where dress is not considered protected speech, it can be restricted for legitimate reasons. For example, schools have been successful in prohibiting dirty, scant, or revealing clothing; excessively tight skirts or pants; baggy pants; clothing displaying obscene pictures, sexually provocative slogans, or vulgar and offensive language; loose clothing in shop areas; or other dress deemed inconsistent with the mission of the school. However, student dress codes also will not be upheld if they do not provide sufficient clarity so that students know what expression is prohibited. In *Stephenson v. Davenport Community School District* (1997), a student, under threat of expulsion, underwent laser surgery to remove a tattoo of a cross from between her thumb and index finger. She later sued for damages because the procedure left a scar. The court ruled in her favor and held that the school district's policy, which prohibited "gang-related activities such as display of colors, symbols, signals, signs, etc.," was too vague to put the student on notice that the tattoo would fall within the scope of the policy.

**Gang-Related Apparel.** The response of many schools to the increase of gang-related activity on campus has been to enact dress codes that seek to restrict the wearing of clothing, jewelry, or other symbols reputed to be associated with gang membership. The response of the courts to challenges to these dress codes is to say that schools may prohibit students from wearing specific clothing or other symbols of gang membership if it can be shown that a gang problem exists and that, in fact, a relationship exists between the particular item(s) prohibited and the public policy goal of curbing gang activity on campus. However, if no gang problem exists or if a relationship between the items and gang activity cannot be established, then the school district policy will not be upheld. The dress code of one California school district prohibited the wearing of clothing identifying any college or professional sports teams. However, testimony showed that gang members were, in fact, wearing Pendleton shirts; Nike shoes; white t-shirts; and baggy Dickies, or black pants; that there was negligible gang activity at the middle school; and no gang activity at the elementary level. Absent a rational relationship between the dress code and the activity it aimed to curtail, the dress code was not upheld (*Jeglin v. San Jacinto Unified School District*, 1993). (See also *Chalifoux v. New Caney Independent School District*, 1999, school district policy too vague as to prohibit wearing of rosary beads as "gang-related apparel.")

**School Uniforms.** School uniforms are seen as one way to reduce gang activity, bullying, and school violence. They are also thought to improve discipline, academic performance, and self-esteem, and they are less expensive

Gang activity has led to increased efforts to prohibit the wearing of gang apparel.

than other clothes. As a result, a growing number of schools and school districts have adopted mandatory school uniform policies. In a number of these school districts, students have challenged the policies, alleging a violation of their First Amendment rights. To date, the courts have been unanimous in holding that uniform policies will pass constitutional scrutiny "(1) if it furthers an important a substantial state interest; (2) if the interest is unrelated to the suppression of student expression; and (3) if the incidental restrictions on First Amendment activities are no more than if necessary to facilitate that interest" (*Palmer v. Wanahachie Independent School District, 2009*, p. 520). Important to the courts in these cases is if the policy contains an "opt-out" provision whereby students, with parental permission, could request an exemption from the requirement for medical or religious reasons.

**Religious Wear.** Students have a First Amendment free exercise right to wear prescribed religious garb. For example, a policy disallowing the wearing of hats could not be used to prohibit a student wearing a yarmulke (e.g., *Menora v. Illinois High School Association*, 1982). Similarly, the suspension of a Muslim student for refusing to remove her headscarf was overturned by the court and the district was ordered to revise its dress code to provide religious exceptions (*Hearn v. Muskogee Public School District*, 2004).

## Sexual Harassment of Students

As noted in Chapter 10, as many as 80% of the students in the public schools have been victims of some form of sexual harassment. As with employees, students can be victims of *quid pro quo* harassment if the condition of some benefit is on the granting of sexual favors. More often, however, students are the victims of hostile environment harassment. In *Franklin v. Gwinnett* (1992), which involved the sexual harassment of a student by a teacher, the Supreme Court recognized that sexual harassment, if sufficiently severe, persistent, or pervasive, can create a hostile environment for the victim that limits the student's ability to benefit from, or participate in, an educational program or activity in violation of Title IX. Sexual harassment is not limited to harassment of a member of the opposite gender; the harassed and the victim can be of the same gender. Sexual harassment based on sexual orientation may also be a violation of Title IX if it is sufficiently serious to limit a gay or lesbian student's ability to participate in or benefit from the school program. Under Title IX, a student victim of sexual harassment can sue for damages. However, the Supreme Court has ruled that the school district is liable for damages only if a school official with authority to address the harassment and take corrective action had actual knowledge of the harassment and was deliberately indifferent to it (*Gebster v. Lago Vista Independent School District*, 1998).

The overwhelming majority of the student sexual harassment that occurs in the schools is student-to-student sexual harassment. The Supreme Court addressed this issue in its 1999 decision in *Davis v. Monroe*. Applying the "deliberate indifference" standard of *Gebster,* the Court ruled that schools may be liable for student-to-student sexual harassment that "is so severe, pervasive, and objectively offensive, and that so undermines and distracts from the victims' educational experience, that the victims are effectively denied equal access to an institution's resources and opportunities" (p. 1664) and to which the school responded with deliberate indifference. The court in *Davis* did recognize that not all unwelcome physical harassment nor all offensive comments are sexual harassment, and that students often engage in "insults, banter, teasing, shoving, pushing, and gender specific conduct that is upsetting to the students subjected to it" but that does not rise to the level of conduct to impose liability.

Sexual harassment of students is not limited to the classroom. The increased use of the Internet for emailing, social networking, instant messaging, and for educational purposes has had the unfortunate consequence of students experiencing sexual harassment over the Internet. Sexual harassment on the Internet

**For Your Reflection and Analysis**

As a K–12 student, were you ever sexually harassed by a peer? How did it make you feel? Did a teacher or other school officer take any action?

# TEACHER OF THE YEAR

Brian Grimm
Oklahoma

For me, education is a civil rights issue. Education is our citadel of social justice. It is, as Atticus Finch says in the novel *To Kill a Mockingbird*, "the great equalizer." It's the vehicle by which each and every one of my students can be afforded the full measure of their dream and their future. Dr. King once said, "The greatest sin of our time is not the few who have destroyed but the vast majority who sat idly by." I want a different world for my students, so I dig deep, get my hands dirty, and work hard every single day. When we work together to show our students the promise of tomorrow, we become a quiet revolution. When we realize that isolation is the enemy of excellence, but collaboration is the genesis of innovation, we become unstoppable. And when we show our students that the pulse of possibility beats strong in every single heart in every classroom across this country, we make manifest a million daily miracles. That's why I teach.

occurs when a harasser sends unwanted, abusive, threatening, or obscene messages or unwanted pornographic, lewd, or lascivious images to a victim. Unlike traditional harassment, Internet harassment can be anonymous and be perpetrated by a harasser anywhere, at any time.

To combat Internet sexual harassment, as well as cyberbulllying, most school districts and a number of states have adopted policies and laws that prohibit bullying and harassment in the public schools. In some districts harassment off campus can also be subject to disciplinary action if it has an impact on the school or its students. And the U. S. Department of Education has recognized that Internet sexual harassment, like other forms of sexual harassment, can be a violation of Title IX. Guidance in determining what sexual harassment is, and what it is not, are provided by the U.S. Department of Education in its guidelines, *Sexual Harassment Guidance: Harassment of Students by School Employees, Other Students, or Third Parties.*

## Student Records and Privacy

For every student who attends the public schools, various records are kept by school authorities. Questions about the contents of these records, and who has access to them, are addressed by a federal statute, the Family Educational Rights and Privacy Act (FERPA) of 1974. FERPA provides protection to parents and students against unauthorized access to students' educational records while guaranteeing their right to access. FERPA requires that school districts establish procedures for providing parents, guardians, and eligible students (over age 18 years) access to student records. Such procedures are to identify staff members with access to the records and to include a log of those who access the records. The act also stipulates that personally identifiable information from the records is not to be released without written permission from the parent or eligible student. However, FERPA does allow personally identifiable information to be released without permission to the following persons or under the following circumstances: (1) parents of a dependent student or educators or officials in the school district who have a legitimate educational interest, (2) officials of a school in which the student is enrolling, (3) persons who have obtained a court order, (4) persons for whom the information is necessary to protect the health or safety of the student or other individuals in case of an emergency, (5) in connection with financial aid for which the student has applied, (6) accrediting organizations in order to carry out their accrediting function, or (7) to state and federal agencies for research or statistical purposes.

Seemingly in response to the tragic shooting at Virginia Tech, proposals have been made to amend FERPA to explicitly permit higher education institutions to share certain student mental health information with parents if a mental health professional certifies in writing that sharing of the student's information with parents may protect the health and safety of the student or others. When students reach 18 years of age or enroll in a postsecondary institution, they must be allowed to see their records if they so desire.

While FERPA guarantees parents and eligible students access to records, this does not mean that records must be produced anytime or anywhere on demand. School officials can adopt rules that specify reasonable time, place, and notice requirements for reviewing. Neither does this law give parents the right to review the personal notes of teachers and administrators if these records are in their sole possession and not shared with anyone except a substitute teacher.

After reviewing the record, if the parents or the eligible student believes that information contained in the record is inaccurate, misleading, or in violation of the rights of the student, the parents or student can request that the information be amended. If school officials refuse, the parents or eligible student must be advised of the student's right to a hearing. If the hearing officer also agrees that the record should not be amended, the parents or student is entitled to place a statement of explanation or objection in the record.

## Summary

The educational process takes place in an environment in which the rights of teachers and students are constantly being balanced against the rights and responsibilities of school officials to maintain a safe and orderly environment conducive to learning. Although the rights of both teachers and students have been greatly expanded in the past quarter century, they do not include the right to say, publish, or teach whatever they feel or believe. The courts continue to uphold the rights and responsibilities of school districts to limit teacher conduct that has a negative impact on performance in the classroom, that is unrelated to the course of study, or that is materially or substantially disruptive. Teachers also have the responsibility to comply with various statutory requirements related to terms of employment, copyright, and so on, and to provide a reasonable standard of care for their students. When they do not comply with these statutory requirements or when they breach the standard of care, they can be subjected to a variety of disciplinary actions both within and outside the school system. Although every situation is unique, certain legal principles can provide direction in many situations. It is imperative that teachers not only be knowledgeable about these principles, many of which are broadly discussed in this chapter, but that they also become familiar with applicable laws and school board policy in their state and district.

In the next chapter, we will discuss a topic that sometimes is not given sufficient attention in teacher preparation programs—the governance structure of the public schools. Yet, as you will see, the way schools are organized, administered, and financed has a vital impact on the teacher and the educational program.

# PROFESSIONAL DEVELOPMENT *Workshop*

## *Prepare for the State Licensure Examination*

Mrs. Angelina Jimenez is a sixth-grade teacher at Hiawatha Elementary School. It is the first week of the school year. After giving a writing assignment, she walks around the room. The children are bent over their desks busily writing "What I Did on My Summer Vacation." Stopping at Tommy Rhodes's desk, she notices deep scratch marks on his neck. When asked how he got the marks, Tommy says his cat scratched him. After school, however, Marty Robinson, who was sitting near Tommy when Mrs. Jimenez asked the question and heard Tommy's reply, comes to her and volunteers that "Tommy has marks all over his back. I saw them during gym."

The next day Mrs. Jimenez asks Tommy about the marks and also asks him if he has any marks on his back and if she can see them. Tommy continues to say that the marks came from his cat, but he refuses to let Mrs. Jimenez see his back.

Mrs. Jimenez worries about this all weekend and tries to call Juanita Ruiz, the school principal, at home but is not able to reach her. On Monday she arrives at school 30 minutes earlier than usual, hoping to meet with Mrs. Ruiz before her first class begins. She is relieved to find Mrs. Ruiz already at her desk returning telephone calls from last Friday. Mrs. Jimenez briefly shares her concerns about Tommy and asks Mrs. Ruiz's whether she should report the scratch marks as suspected abuse. Mrs. Ruiz tells Mrs. Jimenez that she made the right decision to come in and discuss the matter. She compliments Mrs. Jimenez about taking the appropriate steps relative to this potential serious matter.

Mrs. Jimenez gets right to the point. She says, "I am truly worried about Tommy, but at the same time I must admit I am also concerned about the fallout that may follow if I do report suspected child abuse. What if I am wrong? Can I be sued? Having never been confronted with such an issue, I have no idea what comes next. Over the weekend I surfed the Internet and came across a legal case that literally brought on an anxiety attack. I learned that in one state, after a thorough review of the alleged possible abuse, which by the way was dismissed, the superintendent of a particular school district actually sent the parents a letter which included the name of the teacher who reported the alleged abuse. I have not slept since Friday just worrying about this whole matter."

Mrs. Ruiz interrupts Mrs. Jimenez by responding, "Hold on—you are putting the cart before the horse. Let's take this issue and break it down into some manageable parts. First of all, each state has passed legislation relative to protecting the confidentiality of those who report allegations of child abuse. We are fortunate to live in a state that has passed a statute that clearly protects the confidentiality of the individual(s) who make the report. Second, before you leave my office, I will arrange for you; Joan Shephard, our school nurse; and I to meet with Tommy and assess the scratch marks and see if they really do look like cat scratch marks; maybe he does have a very mean cat at home who jumped on his back. Then we will decide on whether to make a report of child abuse. But remember, when in doubt, it is always better to err on the side of protecting the student."

1. What are some of the visible signs of child abuse or neglect?
2. What are the teacher's responsibilities regarding the reporting of child abuse or neglect?
3. Enumerate some of the consequences of failing to report suspicion of child abuse.

## Build Your Knowledge Base

1. What limits can be placed on teachers expressing themselves on political issues in the classroom? Outside the classroom?
2. Describe the "reasonable teacher" guideline as it relates to tort liability.
3. What should be the role of the schools in confronting the AIDS epidemic?
4. To what extent should teachers, administrators, and school board members be held liable for the education, or lack of education, received by the students under their control?
5. What are the statutory requirements in your state regarding student expulsions? Student suspensions?
6. How does the doctrine of *in loco parentis* serve to give students expectations about the care given them in the schools? How does the doctrine serve to define the teacher's right to control and supervise students?

## Develop Your Portfolio

1. One of the important responsibilities of the teaching profession is to understand teacher rights and obligations under the law. Select one of the following issues relative to teacher rights and responsibilities: (1) conditions of employment; (2) teacher dismissal; (3) teacher rights inside and outside the classroom; (4) tort liability; and (5) discrimination, equal opportunity, and affirmative action. After researching a particular right and responsibility, prepare a reflection paper that summarizes your thinking about the legal protections and risks associated with being a teacher. Place your reflection paper in your portfolio under **INTASC Standard 9, Professional Learning and Ethical Practice**.
2. Review the U.S. Supreme Court cases affecting students' rights as shown in Table 12.2 on page 331. With the assistance of the Internet resources at the Companion Website, select one of the more controversial issues related to students' rights (e.g., freedom of expression, student appearance as symbolic speech, search and seizure). Prepare a reflection paper that summarizes your views relative to the legal decisions pertaining to certain students' rights. Place your reflection paper in your portfolio under **INTASC Standard 9, Professional Learning and Ethical Practice**.

**Explore Teaching and Learning: Field Experiences**

1. Contact the central office of a local school district to determine the due process procedures for dismissing school personnel. What specific steps are required to dismiss a teacher?

2. Contact the state department of education or view its Web site to secure information about alternative routes to licensure for teachers in the K–12 public schools. How do these requirements differ from regular certification requirements in your state? In your opinion, what are the advantages and disadvantages of a state providing alternative routes to securing a license to teach, or a student using an alternative route?

## MyEducationLab

Go to **Topic 4, Ethical and Legal Issues,** in the MyEducationLab (www.myeducationlab.com) for *Foundations of American Education,* where you can:

- Find learning outcomes for ethical and legal issues, along with the national standards that connect to these outcomes.
- Complete Assignments and Activities that can help you more deeply understand the chapter content.
- Apply and practice your understanding of the core teaching skills identified in the chapter with the Building Teaching Skills and Dispositions learning units.
- Examine challenging situations and cases presented in the IRIS Center Resources.

- Access additional video clips of CCSSO National Teachers of the Year award winners responding to the question, "Why Do I Teach?" in the Teacher Talk section.
- Check your comprehension on the content covered in the chapter with the Study Plan. Here you will be able to take a chapter quiz, receive feedback on your answers, and then access Review, Practice, and Enrichment activities to enhance your understanding of chapter content.
- Use the Online Lesson Plan Builder to practice lesson planning and integrating national and state standards into your planning.

# CHAPTER Thirteen

# Governance and Financing of Elementary and Secondary Schools

A school board election is scheduled in a few months in the school district in which David Rodriguez lives and works as a teacher; he has spent his entire life in the district. At a parent–teacher meeting at the school, a parent asks about the functions and desirable qualities of school board members in the community. As a senior teacher in the district, Mr. Rodriguez is asked to be a panelist at a public forum on school board selection. His assignment is to indicate why he decided to work in the district, what he thinks are some needs of the district, and what he thinks would be desirable qualities of school board members.

What level of education should be required of school board members? How active should teachers be in school board elections? Should the teachers association endorse specific candidates? What are some possible implications of teachers endorsing candidates for the school board? What information does Mr. Rodriguez need about the district to prepare for the meeting?

*T*he 1921 Yearbook of the National Association of Secondary School Principals stated, "We may have reached the time when the public will not grant us more money unless we can show greater efficiency in spending the dollars which have already been voted for school use." Almost a century later, this quotation may be even more relevant for the first quarter of the 21st century than the first quarter of the 20th century. Throughout your career as an educator, you will be asked to justify educational funding and to explain how schools are governed and funds are expended. Because education is one of the nation's largest industries, representing a significant large public expenditure, a high level of public interest is to be expected and justified.

In the following overview of the governance and financing structure for public elementary and secondary education in the United States, initial attention is given to the overall governance structure of public education. This is followed by a discussion of state school finance programs and revenues for the support of schools. The chapter concludes with a discussion of the present and projected status of private education in America. After reading the chapter, you should be able to:

- Describe the roles of the state and local school boards and superintendents of education.
- Discuss the impact that site-based management decision making might have on the roles and responsibilities of the classroom teacher.
- Discuss the growth of charter schools and their possible impact on public schools.

- Differentiate between the responsibilities of the state board of education and that of the chief state school officer.
- Describe the three public policy goals of school finance programs.
- Compare the major types of state school finance programs.
- Identify the major local, state, and federal revenue sources that support education.
- Discuss the role of private education in America.

# The Context of the Public Schools

The complexity of the educational enterprise in the United States is awesome: one person in five either attends or is employed in the nation's public elementary and secondary schools. Consistent with the checks and balances inherent in the American governmental system, the governance system for public elementary and secondary education also has its checks and balances. Public elementary and secondary education has been referred to as a state responsibility, a local function, and a federal concern. Among the nations of the world, the United States is unique in the emphasis placed on decentralization and, in fact, is the only nation that does not have a national or federal system of education.

As noted in Chapter 11, even though education is not referred to in the federal Constitution, an education clause can be found in each state constitution. Within the guidelines of their constitution, each state establishes the governance system for its schools, provides for the funding of the schools, and establishes various minimum standards for school operation. While no two states have exactly the same organizational structure, finance system, or educational tax support system, in many ways state provisions for education are similar. For example, the grade structure of kindergarten through grade 12 is found in all states. Statutes and regulations for teacher licenses also do not vary greatly among the states. Textbooks are published for a national market, creating a commonality in academic content among the states. National curriculum standards provide another example of the similarities, rather than the differences, in public elementary and secondary schools among the states.

# Organization for Education

Rather than a national or federal system of schools, the American education system operates through 50 separate state education agencies with instruction being provided by about 14,000 school districts in over 97,000 schools staffed by almost 3.3 million teachers.

Policies for the operation of the schools are set by governors, state legislatures, state boards of education, and local school boards. Governors and legislators not only face the public policy challenge of determining the best funding system for the schools, but also are expected to provide adequate and equitable financing for this system of schools.

Elementary and secondary education is the largest item in the budgets of many state and local governments. In the 2010–2011 school year, total expenditures for public elementary and secondary schools exceeded $530 billion. Although funds come from a combination of local, state, and federal sources, most of the money comes from state and local taxes. Federal funding is used for special programs or conditions and provided 10.5% of the expenditures for public elementary and secondary schools in 2010–2011. Figure 13.1 shows the national average of funding sources for education from each of the three levels of government.

Unlike governmental functions such as national defense and interstate commerce, which have a heavy federal orientation, the governmental structure for the public schools has evolved as a combination of state and local powers and

**Figure 13.1 — Sources of Funds for Public Elementary and Secondary Schools, 2010–2011**

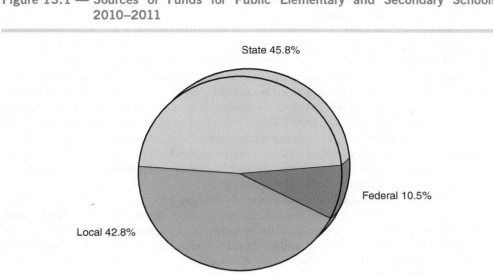

State 45.8%

Federal 10.5%

Local 42.8%

*Source:* National Education Association. (2011). *Rankings & Estimates: Rankings of the States 2010 and Estimates of School Statistics 2011.*

responsibilities. Rather than being the source of centralized educational policies and decisions, historically the federal government has had a very limited role, primarily concerned with funding for the educational needs of special populations or special programs, national research priorities, and data gathering and reporting. However, as most visibly illustrated by the mandated assessment and reporting requirements of the No Child Left Behind Act and the education agenda promoted by the Obama administration discussed in Chapter 7, the federal influence has increased significantly in the last decade.

## Education at the Local Level

Public education in the United States is a highly decentralized endeavor. State constitutions have provided for the creation of local school districts that are responsible for the actual operation of schools. The sole purpose of the school district is to operate elementary and secondary schools. Even though state and federal requirements exist, school districts and individual schools have considerable freedom in organizing their programs and the teaching/learning environment. The primary functions of school districts are as follows:

• Adopt policies and regulations for the operation of schools.

• Within the context of state guidelines, adopt the curriculum for the schools.

• Serve as links between community patrons and the schools and provide periodic reports about the students and schools.

• Provide the human and material resources needed to operate schools.

• Take the necessary steps to provide and maintain adequate facilities for instruction.

• Provide the state department of education and other agencies with required information about the schools.

### School Boards

The governing body for the operation of a school district is the **school board**, typically composed of five to seven members elected for four-year terms. The role of lay citizens in the governance of public education through a system of local school boards is a unique feature of the American educational system. In principle, school boards represent all the people; members are chosen as stewards with a public trust.

Most (95%) school board members are elected (Hess & Meeks, 2010). In most cases, there are no educational requirements for school board membership. Members come from all walks of life, though, as noted in Chapter 14, they tend to be upper middle class professionals or businessmen/women. More than 25% were former or current educators (Hess & Meeks, 2010). Typically the only prerequisite for board membership is that the board member be a resident of the school district.

The primary function of the school board is to set the **policies** under which the schools will operate. Before making decisions, the board has a responsibility to consider the beliefs, values, and traditions of the community. However, boards typically rely on the counsel and recommendations of the superintendent in making policy decisions. Board members cannot act independently; board members must function as a group, for they have power and authority only when a quorum of the board is present at a legally convened meeting.

Other functions of the school board include budget adoption, approval of expenditures, approval of the schools' organizational pattern, approval of textbooks and curriculum, employment of personnel, termination of personnel, and issuance of contracts. These legal functions are in addition to the role of the school board in engaging and informing the community. Community support is especially critical because of the role of the local property tax in financing schools in many states and the importance of maintaining a strong base of citizen support for the public schools. The typical administrative organization of a school district is illustrated in Figure 13.2.

**Figure 13.2 — Local Education Governance**

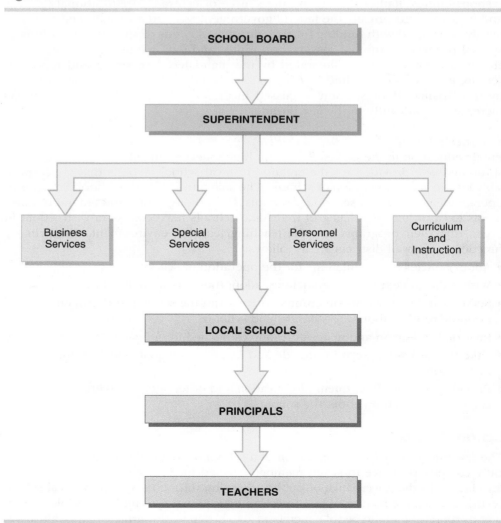

## Superintendent of Schools

One of the most important decisions the school board makes is hiring a chief administrator, usually referred to as the **superintendent of schools**. As the role and responsibilities of the superintendent have evolved, the job has become that of the chief executive officer of the school district. Typically, the educational program and related responsibilities of the superintendent include planning, staffing, coordinating, budgeting, administering, evaluating, and reporting. Basically, the superintendent's primary responsibility is to work with the school board and the school district staff to improve educational programs in the district. In many ways the school board functions like the board of directors of a corporation while the superintendent of schools, the counterpart of the chief executive officer of the corporation, is responsible for the day-to-day operation of the enterprise, the schools.

Superintendents typically begin their careers as teachers. Specialized training in educational administration beyond the master's degree is usually required for licensing or certification as a superintendent. Among a few large school districts, there has been some interest in hiring as superintendent persons who have demonstrated in fields outside of education that they possess the management and leadership skills required to be a successful superintendent of schools. Some of these school districts have looked to private-sector executives or retired military officers to assume the superintendency. Examples of this practice may be found in Minneapolis, New Orleans, Raleigh, San Diego, Seattle, and Washington, D.C.

> **For Your Reflection and Analysis**
>
> What kinds of experience and educational preparation should a superintendent of schools have?

## Building Principal

The individual with the primary responsibility for the success or failure of the educational program in each school is the **building principal.** The school principal's responsibilities are multidimensional. Not only is the principal responsible for the day-to-day administration of the school and implementation of the school district's regulations and policies, but the principal also leads the staff in establishing the vision and climate of the school. What principals understand, believe, say, and do has a profound consequence on those around them; they set the climate of the school (Sparks, 2004).

The effective principal is an advocate in the district and the community in securing the resources the staff needs in the classroom. The effective principal also serves as a buffer to protect teachers from unnecessary intrusions so that they may focus on their work with students. Skillful principals make data-driven decisions by using various sources of information to support change, establish plans, monitor progress, and document results of efforts to achieve goals. Effective principals lead staff in the development of visions of the student learning and teaching desired in their schools. The success of all students becomes the highest priority; this leads to the development of an environment that nurtures continuous improvement in teaching and creates interdependent relationships among all staff members.

Principals are responsible for the induction and professional growth of the school staff. This requires that they give attention to the development of the knowledge, skills, and attitudes of the individuals and the group that comprises the professional learning community.

Traditionally, principals have been teachers and may have served as an assistant principal before becoming a principal. Some have viewed the principalship as a career and others have considered the job to be a stepping-stone to assistant superintendent or superintendent.

> **For Your Reflection and Analysis**
>
> What kinds of experience and educational preparation should a school principal have?

## Pattern of School Districts and Enrollments in the States

Since 1950, the number of school districts in the nation has been reduced from approximately 100,000 to about 14,000. Among the states, the number of school districts varies. The number of school districts and the enrollment in each state are shown in Table 13.1. Excluding Hawaii, the number of school districts in the states ranges from as few as 17 in Nevada and 24 in Maryland to 960 in California and

### Table 13.1 — Estimated Number of Regular School Districts (2008–2009) and Fall Enrollment for Public Schools, by State, 2010–2011

|  | Districts | Rank | Fall Enrollment | Rank |
|---|---|---|---|---|
| United States | 13,809 |  | 49,086,253 |  |
| Alabama | 133 | 35 | 740,975 | 23 |
| Alaska | 53 | 43 | 132,000 | 45 |
| Arizona | 225 | 23 | 1,071,484 | 13 |
| Arkansas | 245 | 22 | 459,419 | 34 |
| California | 960 | 2 | 6,219,649 | 1 |
| Colorado | 178 | 27 | 843,958 | 20 |
| Connecticut | 166 | 30 | 566,030 | 29 |
| Delaware | 19 | 48 | 128,530 | 46 |
| Florida | 67 | 41 | 2,621,085 | 4 |
| Georgia | 180 | 26 | 1,689,648 | 8 |
| Hawaii | 1 | 50 | 179,122 | 42 |
| Idaho | 115 | 37 | 285,236 | 38 |
| Illinois | 869 | 3 | 2,106,925 | 5 |
| Indiana | 294 | 18 | 1,051,696 | 14 |
| Iowa | 362 | 13 | 491,431 | 32 |
| Kansas | 318 | 16 | 481,000 | 33 |
| Kentucky | 174 | 29 | 658,328 | 26 |
| Louisiana | 69 | 40 | 702,133 | 25 |
| Maine | 283 | 20 | 187,401 | 41 |
| Maryland | 24 | 47 | 840,628 | 21 |
| Massachusetts | 352 | 14 | 953,223 | 17 |
| Michigan | 552 | 7 | 1,662,067 | 9 |
| Minnesota | 340 | 15 | 810,123 | 22 |
| Mississippi | 152 | 32 | 496,504 | 31 |
| Missouri | 523 | 9 | 903,887 | 18 |
| Montana | 420 | 12 | 140,533 | 43 |
| Nebraska | 256 | 21 | 297,563 | 37 |
| Nevada | 17 | 49 | 456,844 | 35 |
| New Hampshire | 178 | 28 | 193,264 | 40 |
| New Jersey | 616 | 5 | 1,366,067 | 11 |
| New Mexico | 89 | 38 | 326,940 | 36 |
| New York | 696 | 4 | 2,642,524 | 3 |
| North Carolina | 116 | 36 | 1,405,706 | 10 |
| North Dakota | 187 | 25 | 92,074 | 48 |
| Ohio | 614 | 6 | 1,914,222 | 6 |
| Oklahoma | 534 | 8 | 656,655 | 27 |
| Oregon | 194 | 24 | 564,620 | 30 |
| Pennsylvania | 501 | 10 | 1,763,946 | 7 |
| Rhode Island | 32 | 46 | 138,803 | 44 |
| South Carolina | 85 | 39 | 716,524 | 24 |
| South Dakota | 161 | 31 | 123,900 | 47 |
| Tennessee | 136 | 33 | 971,537 | 16 |
| Texas | 1,032 | 1 | 4,824,778 | 2 |

|  | Districts | Rank | Fall Enrollment | Rank |
|---|---|---|---|---|
| Utah | 40 | 45 | 587,198 | 28 |
| Vermont | 292 | 19 | 85,635 | 50 |
| Virginia | 134 | 34 | 1,252,529 | 12 |
| Washington | 295 | 17 | 1,038,156 | 15 |
| West Virginia | 55 | 42 | 283,469 | 39 |
| Wisconsin | 426 | 11 | 871,929 | 19 |
| Wyoming | 48 | 44 | 88,355 | 49 |

*Sources:* Snyder, T. D., and Dillow, S. A. (2011). *Digest of Education Statistics 2010* (NCES 2011–015). National Center for Education Statistics, Institute of Education Sciences, U.S. Department of Education. Washington, DC; *Rankings of the States 2010 & Estimates of School Statistics 2011.* Used with permission of the National Education Association 2010. All rights reserved.

1,032 in Texas. As the data in Table 13.1 suggest, the number of school districts in a state is not related to either the total enrollment or the geographic size of the state.

Among the 50 states, the estimated number of enrolled pupils in 2010–11 ranged from about 6.2 million in California and 4.8 million in Texas to less than 85,000 in Wyoming and 93,000 in Vermont. The 15 states with more than 1 million pupils accounted for 64% of the almost 49 million public school pupils nationwide.

As each state organized school districts, it created different types of school districts. The most common school district organization is the unified school district, which provides educational programs for students in prekindergarten through grade 12. However, a few states (e.g., Arizona, California, Illinois, Montana, New Jersey, and Vermont) permit the operation of separate high school districts serving grades 9 through 12 and elementary districts serving students in prekindergarten through grade 8 in addition to unified (pre-K–12) districts.

## School District Budgeting

Public elementary and secondary schools are labor-intensive endeavors. Personnel costs represent the majority of expenditures in school district budgets. More than two thirds of a typical school district's current expenditures budget goes for instructional services, including teachers' salaries. Figure 13.3 shows the percentage of the budget allocated to the major budget categories in the typical school district.

School district budgets are developed by an ongoing process that involves (1) planning around district mission, objectives, programs, and projections of student enrollments, revenues, and expenditures; (2) coordinating and integrating community and staff input; (3) presentation of the proposed budget to the community and the school board and adoption by the school board; (4) effective administration of the budget; and (5) ongoing evaluation of the budget to determine if the adopted budget is functioning in a way to facilitate the accomplishment of the intended goals and objectives. In most states districts are required to submit their budget for review and approval to the state department of education.

## Site-Based Management

As the smallest management unit of the school district, the local school is the most critical unit in the educational delivery system. **Site-based management (SBM)** is the shifting of decision making over educational programs from the central administration to site-based councils composed of parents and teachers. SBM has been promoted as a way to increase teacher morale, improve the management of schools, raise student performance, and increase the involvement of school faculties, parents, and community leaders in education decision making. SBM is mandated for every school in six states (Colorado, Florida, Kentucky, North Carolina, Texas and

**Figure 13.3 — Percentage of Total Current Expenditures by Function**

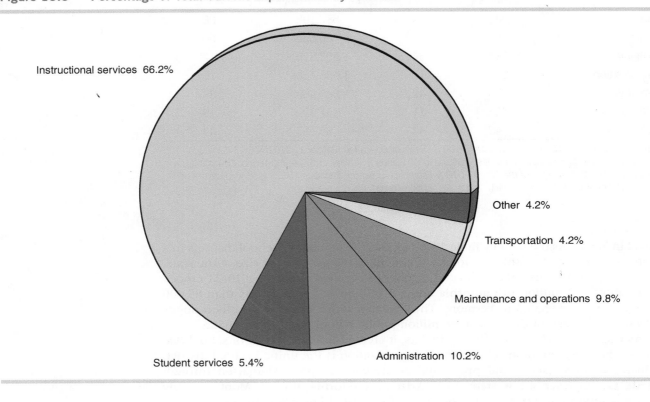

Instructional services 66.2%

Other 4.2%

Transportation 4.2%

Maintenance and operations 9.8%

Administration 10.2%

Student services 5.4%

Virginia) and several large cities (e.g., Chicago, New York City, Los Angeles) and is practiced in hundreds of other school districts throughout the nation.

An underlying assumption of SBM is that those closest to students are in the best position to make decisions that affect their welfare. Site-based management assumes that teachers should be involved in planning, discussing, and making decisions and that parents should be involved in critical aspects of school-site decision making. Research suggests that schools are more successful when teachers have a voice in decisions about their working conditions and the operation of the school.

In practice, SBM operates along a spectrum in terms of the control and authority given to the site council as well as the extent to which the council operates in a policy-making or advisory capacity. In no case, however, is complete decentralization of decision making possible because local schools, as part of a school district within a state system of education, are subject to statutes, policies, and regulations from the district and the state.

Although new assessment and accountability measures have taken away much of the site council's power over the school curriculum and student assessment, SBM is still seen as a vehicle for providing teachers the involvement in the decision-making process they want as well as providing a useful framework for responding directly to the specific needs of each school's student population (Cromwell, 2006).

## Charter Schools

A **charter school** is a nonsectarian public school that operates with greater autonomy than a traditional public school. The charter school movement began in the 1990s to provide parents and students with a choice between the traditional public school and an alternative public school that is under the control of the parents or other individual(s) holding the school's charter. Currently, legislatures in 40 states have enacted statutes providing for the operation of charter schools. The 10 states

**For Your Reflection and Analysis**

What kinds of decisions should be made at the school site, and who should make them?

that do not have charter school laws are Alabama, Kentucky, Maine, Montana, Nebraska, North Dakota, South Dakota, Vermont, Washington, and West Virginia. As of the 2010–2011 school year more than 5,400 charter schools were serving about 1.7 million students (see Figure 13.4). The number of charter schools is growing at a rapid pace: 465 new charter schools opened in 2011 alone (Center for Education Reform, 2011). More recently, Washington, D.C., and Detroit proposed to convert a number of schools into charter schools to avoid closure. The states with the largest number of charter schools are Arizona, California, Florida, Michigan, and Texas.

Charter schools grow in numbers and continue to be the most popular choice option.

The growth in the charter school movement can be attributed to several factors:

1. Students and/or their parents exercising choice by enrolling students in a charter school rather than enrolling them in the school to which they were assigned on the basis of their residence;
2. Public school staff seeking exemption from local and state rules and regulations so that they can provide innovative programs and services;
3. Community interest in special schools to provide support for programs not being provided in the regular schools; for example, performing arts, technology, or one of the sciences;

### Figure 13.4 — Number of Charter Schools, 1994–1996 to 2010–2011

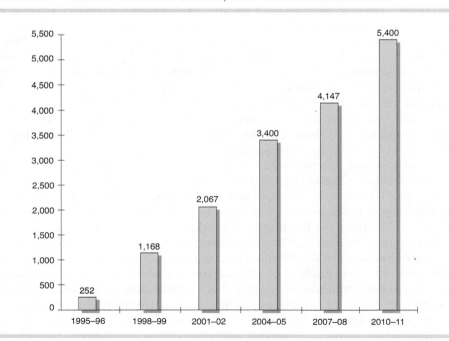

*Source:* Center for Education Reform. (2007). *Charter schools.* Retrieved February 3, 2008, from http://www.edreform.com/index.cfm?fuseAction=stateStats&pSectionID=&cSectionID=44

4. School patrons seeking relief from regulations so that the schools can explore nontraditional approaches to instruction; and

5. The conversion of financially troubled private schools to charter schools.

**Reflect on Diversity**
Speculate on why minority students are attracted to charter schools.

Rather than charter schools having a common reason for being, similar goals or programs, or sponsors with similar interests, the common characteristic of charter schools is their diversity. Sponsors include parents, teachers, community nonprofit agencies, and a diverse group of entrepreneurial interests. A new trend in the charter school movement has been faith-based charter schools without the faith: Arabic schools without Islam, Hebrew schools without Judaism, and Catholic schools without Catholicism. Because these are public schools, they must not inject religion into the school. However, for financially strapped private schools facing closure or for religious groups that would not otherwise have a separate school for their children, charters are becoming a popular option. Some charter schools are individually autonomous, and others are owned and operated by a for-profit firm or a service agency.

The procedures for approving an application to open a charter school and the strength of the charter school laws vary by state. Statutes in some states give local school boards the authority to award charters; in still others, the state board of education has the authority. In others a state charter school board, institution of higher education, municipality, or nonprofit group has the authority (Palmer, 2007). The charter to operate the school typically is granted for three to five years. Responsibility for monitoring charter schools also varies by state, but the local school board often has this responsibility if the charter school is located in its district.

The charter school movement has not advanced without controversy. Some of the controversy has focused on the characteristics of the student body of charter schools and the achievement of those students, as well as weak charter school laws that allow underperforming and fiscally irresponsible charter schools to continue to operate. According to reports by the National Alliance for Public Charter Schools (2009), more recent studies show that charter schools produce "more instances of larger achievement gains in both math and reading when compared to the traditional public schools" (p. 3). Also reported were studies that indicated high ACT scores, higher graduation rates, and greater likelihood of attending college than students from traditional public schools. Data from various research presenting a counter argument reported in the Wall Street Journal's *Smart Money* (Morgan, 2010) indicate that only 17% of charter schools produce better results than neighboring public schools, while 37% were significantly worse; that teachers in charter schools are less likely to hold state certification than teachers in traditional public schools and are paid less; and that charter schools have about twice the turnover rate of traditional public schools. Also reported were studies which suggest that charter schools typically have significantly fewer students with disabilities than neighboring public schools (Morgan, 2010).

The charter school movement has received support from administrations beginning with President Clinton. The Federal Charter Schools Program, established in 1994, has provided significant support for charter school planning and start-up. Expanded support for charter schools has been a key element of the Obama educational agenda, doubling the funding for the federal Charter School Program. Priority in funding is given to high performing charter schools and to states that have high quality charter school laws, defined as laws that do not limit the number of charter schools; provide equal funding of charter and non-charter schools; and regulate how charter school authorizers approve, hold accountable, reauthorize, and close poor performing schools. At the same time, high performing charter schools are given an expanded role in the restart provision of the School Improvement Grant program, which requires local school districts to close persistently low-achieving schools and reopen under the management of an effective charter school operation, charter management organization, or educational management organization.

It is not clear what the impact of these changes will be in terms of the number of underperforming charter schools that might be closed or the number that might open as part of the restart program. What is clear is that charter schools have gained the support of both political parties and have established a permanent place in the American educational system.

## *Education at the State Level*

The NCLB Act expanded the role of the state government in education. Under the NCLB Act, states have been required to develop and expand existing student assessment systems and provide technical assistance to schools identified as being "in need of improvement." Sanctions imposed on schools that continue to fail to make adequate yearly progress include state takeover of the operation of the schools. And, perhaps most important, because it is the state, not the local school district or the federal government, that has the legal responsibility to provide for education, it is ultimately the state's responsibility to meet the goal that all children in the state will be achieving at the proficient level by 2014.

The state-level governance structure for the education system that is responsible for meeting this goal typically includes the **state board of education** as the policy-making body, a state administrative agency referred to as the **state department of education**, and a **chief state school officer**, who serves as executive officer of the state board of education and administers the state department of education. Figure 13.5 reflects the state-level administrative organization in many states.

## State Departments of Education

As noted in Chapter 11, the legal principle of education being a state responsibility has resulted in the creation of state educational agencies that have a key role in the development of the structure and delivery system for public elementary

**Figure 13.5—State Education Governance**

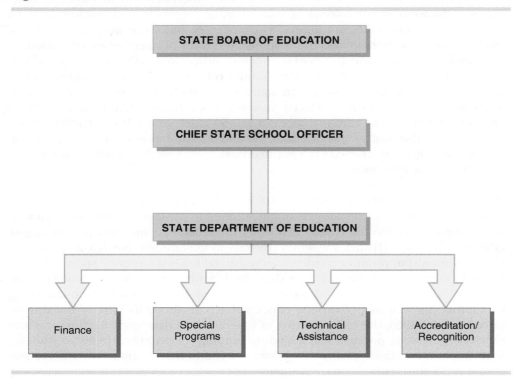

and secondary education. Each state has a state-level administrative agency whose primary functions include the following:

- Implementing the state board of education's broad policies for the operation of the state's public elementary and secondary schools;
- Monitoring schools to ensure implementation of legislative mandates;
- Disbursing state funds to operate local school districts;
- Providing the state legislature and citizens with information about the schools, including student performance and related accountability indicators;
- Providing technical assistance to the schools;
- Collecting and reporting data about the schools; and
- Being an advocate for public education.

## State Boards of Education

Most state boards of education are not responsible for the direct operation of educational institutions or schools; rather, their concern is with the overall direction of the state's schools. In two-thirds of the states, the state board of education is appointed by the governor (National Association of State Boards of Education, 2011). State boards of education have various responsibilities. These boards usually are charged with adopting regulations to ensure implementation of the constitutional and statutory mandates related to the operation of the state system of schools. Their directives and mandates become policy and are enforced within the context of the state's statutory provisions. Examples include graduation requirements for high school students and mandated curricular offerings in schools. Among the important state board functions are providing the state legislature with timely reports about the schools, proposing changes in statutes, proposing new initiatives and programs, and presenting and serving as an advocate for the budget for state support of schools.

## Chief State School Officer

Each state has either constitutional or statutory provisions for a chief state school officer. This person often is referred to as the superintendent of public instruction or education, commissioner of education, or secretary of education. In most instances, responsibilities are limited to elementary and secondary education, but in a few states the person also has responsibilities for postsecondary education.

Depending on the state, the chief state school officer may be elected or appointed. In several states where the chief state school officer is elected, the qualifications are often unstated or very broad. In states where the chief state school officer is appointed, the tendency is to select a person with professional training and experience as an educational administrator. Of the 50 chief state school officers, 24 are appointed by the state board of education and 12 are appointed by the governor. The remaining 14 are elected on a popular basis statewide (National Association of State Boards of Education, 2011).

**For Your Reflection and Analysis**

Should the chief state school officer be elected by popular vote, appointed by the state board of education, or appointed by the governor with advice and consent of the legislature?

## *The Federal Government and Public Education*

As noted in Chapter 6, education is not mentioned in the federal Constitution and is a function reserved to the states. As a result the federal government cannot dictate education policies. Historically when the federal government has felt it was in the national interest to promote particular educational goals it has done so by targeting funds in support of those goals. As described in Chapter 7, examples include the National Education Defense Act passed in response to the Soviet Union launching of Sputnik, as well as the various education acts included as part of the war on poverty. Since 1965, the major portion of federal funds have gone to programs and services for special populations, including funding for programs to serve students with disabilities, educationally disadvantaged youth, financially needy college students, and vocational education students.

The most recent emphasis of the federal government in education has been on promoting student achievement and educational excellence and preparation for global competiveness. These goals have been pursued through the enactment of such programs as the previously described No Child Left Behind Act of 2001 and the Race to the Top programs.

Since the creation of the first Department of Education in 1867, the one continuing role of the federal education agency has been data gathering and reporting. Rather than each state gathering and reporting data independently, it has been more cost effective for the function to be performed by a federal education agency, the National Center for Education Statistics. The centralization also facilitates the reporting of consistent and comparable data that can be used for a variety of purposes, including international comparisons.

**For Your Reflection and Analysis**

How much control should the federal government exercise over education?

### U.S. Department and Secretary of Education

Beginning in 1867 with the creation of the Department of Education without cabinet status, some type of federal education agency has been in existence. In 1869 the title was changed to Office of Education, in 1870 to Bureau of Education, and in 1929 back to Office of Education. The latter designation was retained until the creation of the Department of Education in 1980, when education was given cabinet status. The secretary of education is a member of the president's cabinet and is responsible for the operation of the U.S. Department of Education. The secretary has been an advocate for the president's educational initiatives. Since the position was established in 1980, the secretaries have come from a variety of backgrounds, including being a federal judge, college professor, university president, governor, chief state school officer, local school district superintendent, and domestic policy adviser.

## Financing of Education

In addition to establishing the governance structure for education, state legislatures also establish the basic structure for financing public elementary and secondary schools. The state enacts the funding system for schools and sets the taxing and spending powers of school districts, including the state's method for funding schools, the types of taxes that may be used to support education, and the tax rate that may be levied.

Methods of financing public elementary and secondary schools as well as expenditures per pupil differ in a variety of ways both within and among states. However, two basic legal principles guide the financing of the public schools in the United States. First, education is a responsibility of the state; and, second, in the design and implementation of the state school finance program, the state has an equal responsibility to each pupil within its jurisdiction. Adhering to these principles has often been difficult because the states have chosen to let the school districts, with their wide differences in enrollment, taxable wealth, and citizen aspirations, administer and deliver education.

States face major financial challenges in the coming years in providing the facilities and teachers needed for growing enrollments. Public school enrollments reached nearly 50 million in 2011 and are projected to reach almost 59 million in 2019 (Hussar & Bailey, 2011). The impact of this growth has been to (1) exacerbate the need for additional classroom space and the need to replace educationally obsolete facilities, and (2) create a demand for more teachers to cope with the enrollment increases and replace the large number of teachers and other professional staff members who are projected to retire in the next decade. Securing the funding to meet these needs presents a major financial challenge to states and school districts.

### Public Policy Goals in State School Finance

Public policy decisions about how schools should be financed are made with three goals in mind: equity, adequacy, and choice. The three school finance goals are not independent, but are interactive. One can have equity without adequacy, for equity has been interpreted merely as the equal treatment of students in different school districts in a state, while adequacy implies that the level of funding is sufficient "to provide students with the opportunity for a meaningful education that enables them to meet challenging new state standards" (Rebell, 2008, p. 432) but does not assume either equal treatment or choice. By the same token, the taxpayers of a district may exercise their choice in ways that may not result in either equity or adequacy.

### Equity

The concept of **equity** refers to the equal treatment of persons in equal circumstances. For students, this means funds used to address student needs should ensure that all students have an equal opportunity for an education. For taxpayers, this means equal tax rates on similar property regardless of the wealth of the district (the wealth of the district is expressed in terms of the assessed value of property per pupil). The problem with achieving this goal is that even if equity is achieved, it may not result in adequate or sufficient funds for schools; it may only result in equal treatment of students or taxpayers.

### Adequacy

**Adequacy** refers to the extent to which educational funding is sufficient to provide the programs and services needed by all students. Factors affecting adequacy include quality of staff, sufficient materials, and facilities. A definitive standard for adequate funding has not been established, but one can argue that the student should have access to the human and material resources required to demonstrate attainment of the applicable academic standards.

### Choice

The term **choice** has been used to refer to two goals. One goal is local control of funding decisions. Traditionally, school boards were permitted to choose the level of funding for the schools. In some cases, equity and choice have come into conflict because a district's freedom to choose the level of funding has resulted in inequitable treatment of taxpayers and students. Choice also is being used to refer to the power of parents to select the school that their child will attend: private, public, public magnet, public charter, or home school. Many states and school districts have adopted *open enrollment* policies that allow students to attend any school in the district or a surrounding district, under certain provisions.

**For Your Reflection and Analysis**

Of the three school finance policy goals, which is most important? Why?

## *State School Finance Programs*

States use several basic approaches to allocate funds to schools and in many cases may use a combination of the approaches described below. For example, a state may use an equalized foundation program to allocate the majority of funds to the school district in the form of a block grant and on top of that allocate transportation funds on a flat-grant basis of so much per route mile.

### Full State Funding

The first approach used by states to fund their schools, **full state funding**, occurs when no local tax revenues are collected for the support of schools; all funds for schools come from state-level taxes. This model is used only in Hawaii, which has one school district for administrative management of all state schools. However, several other states have such a high level of state funding that they approach full state funding. Under full state funding, students and taxpayers are treated equally, but attainment of adequacy depends solely on the funding level determined by the state. Opportunity for local district choice is limited.

### Flat Grants

The second approach, the **flat grant**, allocates funds to school districts on a per unit basis (per teacher; per classroom; per mile; or, most often, per pupil). The grants may be either uniform, a set amount per unit to all districts, or variable, with differing amounts allocated based on district financial need or program costs. No state currently uses the flat grant as the primary funding method. However, several states include a low-level flat-grant program as a part of an equalization program to ensure that high-wealth districts receive some state funds or for allocating funds to targeted programs.

## Equalized Foundation Grants

The most common school finance allocation program is the **equalized foundation grant**. Under the equalized foundation plan, the state aid is determined by multiplying the number and type of students in the district (special education, kindergarten, compensatory, English language learners, or other students may be given extra weight) by a fixed expenditure level per pupil set by the state legislature. From this is subtracted what is known as the *required local effort,* the revenue the district can collect locally through a uniform tax rate applied to the assessed value of property in the district. A poor district with low assessed property value will raise less money locally than more wealthy districts and will therefore get more state aid under an equalized program. While foundation grants are the most common method used to finance education among the states, they have often been criticized because the per pupil funding level set by the state may be at a minimum level and not be sufficient to support an adequate educational program.

## Categorical Grants

As a supplement to the basic funding approach, states often target funds for a specific educational purpose (e.g., bilingual education, education of students with disabilities, gifted education, student transportation, technology, textbooks, and instructional materials). These targeted grants often are referred to as **categorical funding**. While widely used to fund specific programs, this is not the principal method for funding schools in any state.

## State Spending Differences

As shown in Table 13.2, in 2010–2011, among the 50 states, per pupil estimated expenditures ranged from $17,750 in New York to $7,056 in Utah. The national average was $10,856 per pupil enrolled. The category of current expenditures does not include expenditures related to the building of school facilities, commonly referred to as capital outlay expenditures.

## *Sources of Revenue for Schools*

Funds for public elementary and secondary schools come from various taxes levied by local, state, and federal governments. As discussed previously, and as shown in Table 13.3 (page 357), the proportion of revenues from each source varies among and within states. The percentage of the revenues for schools from state tax sources ranged from 90.2% in Vermont and 82.9% in Hawaii to 16.8% in Illinois. The percentage of funds from local tax sources ranged from 69.7% in Illinois to 1.1% in Vermont and 4.0% in Hawaii, and the percentage from the federal government ranged from 17.3% in Alabama to 2.9% in Rhode Island.

For Your Reflection and Analysis

Which school finance formula is used to fund schools in your state?

In Title 1 schools serving low income communities the free lunch is an important part of the school day for many children.

### Table 13.2 — 2010–2011 Estimated Per Pupil Expenditures, by State

|  | PPE | Rank |  | PPE | Rank |
| --- | --- | --- | --- | --- | --- |
| U.S. Average | $10,826 |  |  |  |  |
| Alabama | 9,483 | 35 | Montana | 9,973 | 29 |
| Alaska | 11,147 | 22 | Nebraska | 10,452 | 26 |
| Arizona | 6,448 | 50 | Nevada | 8,089 | 47 |
| Arkansas | 11,999 | 14 | New Hampshire | 13,797 | 11 |
| California | 8,689 | 42 | New Jersey | 17,717 | 2 |
| Colorado | 9,588 | 33 | New Mexico | 11,346 | 21 |
| Connecticut | 14,989 | 8 | New York | 17,750 | 1 |
| Delaware | 13,960 | 10 | North Carolina | 8,303 | 45 |
| Florida | 9,124 | 40 | North Dakota | 8,880 | 41 |
| Georgia | 10,971 | 23 | Ohio | 9,512 | 34 |
| Hawaii | 11,819 | 17 | Oklahoma | 8,311 | 44 |
| Idaho | 8,101 | 46 | Oregon | 10,959 | 24 |
| Illinois | 11,896 | 16 | Pennsylvania | 13,334 | 12 |
| Indiana | 10,390 | 27 | Rhode Island | 15,803 | 5 |
| Iowa | 9,856 | 30 | South Carolina | 9,616 | 31 |
| Kansas | 9,254 | 38 | South Dakota | 9,310 | 37 |
| Kentucky | 9,612 | 32 | Tennessee | 8,393 | 43 |
| Louisiana | 10,578 | 25 | Texas | 9,128 | 39 |
| Maine | 15,032 | 7 | Utah | 7,056 | 49 |
| Maryland | 15,268 | 6 | Vermont | 17,447 | 3 |
| Massachusetts | 14,828 | 9 | Virginia | 11,753 | 19 |
| Michigan | 12,015 | 13 | Washington | 10,367 | 28 |
| Minnesota | 11,905 | 15 | West Virginia | 11,369 | 20 |
| Mississippi | 8,003 | 48 | Wisconsin | 11,791 | 18 |
| Missouri | 9,422 | 36 | Wyoming | 16,066 | 4 |

*Source:* Data from *Rankings of the States 2010 and Estimates of School Statistics 2011,* used with permission of the National Education Association © 2010. All rights reserved.

## Local Sources of Tax Revenue

The principal source of local tax revenue for schools is the *ad valorem* tax on real property, commonly referred to as the **local property tax**. This tax is levied on the value of land, residences, apartment buildings, commercial buildings, railroads, and utilities. On average, more than 90% of all local tax revenues for schools comes from the property tax. The property tax has the advantage of being a fairly stable source of revenue for school districts and one that cannot be easily avoided. It is also the tax that comes closest to being a user charge and meeting the benefits received principle of taxation, which says that those who pay the taxes are the users or beneficiaries of the services provided by the tax. However, despite its widespread use, the property tax is not considered the best source of revenue for education because it violates two major principles of taxation: equity and progressivity. The property tax is not considered equitable because it is not related to the taxpayers' ability to pay and places a disproportionate burden on people who own their own homes but have little current income, such as older people or others on fixed incomes. It is also considered a regressive tax because persons in the lower income groups pay a higher percentage of their income toward the property tax than do those in higher income groups.

**Table 13.3 — Estimated Percentage of Revenues for Public Schools from Federal, State, and Local Sources, 2010–2011**

|  | Federal | State | Local |
|---|---|---|---|
| United States | 10.5% | 45.8% | 43.7% |
| Alabama | 17.3 | 54.9 | 27.8 |
| Alaska | 12.5 | 63.5 | 24.0 |
| Arizona | 7.8 | 52.9 | 39.3 |
| Arkansas | 11.4 | 56.3 | 32.3 |
| California | 13.3 | 56.8 | 29.8 |
| Colorado | 7.1 | 44.0 | 48.9 |
| Connecticut | 7.1 | 37.2 | 55.7 |
| Delaware | 7.5 | 62.4 | 30.0 |
| Florida | 16.5 | 35.4 | 48.1 |
| Georgia | 8.9 | 42.7 | 48.4 |
| Hawaii | 13.1 | 82.9 | 4.0 |
| Idaho | 9.5 | 69.8 | 20.6 |
| Illinois | 13.6 | 16.8 | 69.7 |
| Indiana | 9.1 | 52.6 | 38.3 |
| Iowa | 10.4 | 44.8 | 44.8 |
| Kansas | 12.2 | 57.2 | 30.6 |
| Kentucky | 15.8 | 54.0 | 30.2 |
| Louisiana | 17.2 | 42.5 | 37.2 |
| Maine | 11.3 | 37.2 | 51.5 |
| Maryland | 6.0 | 45.7 | 48.3 |
| Massachusetts | 7.1 | 41.0 | 51.9 |
| Michigan | 8.8 | 56.9 | 34.2 |
| Minnesota | 9.0 | 76.9 | 14.0 |
| Mississippi | 16.0 | 53.1 | 30.9 |
| Missouri | 10.4 | 30.6 | 59.0 |
| Montana | 12.8 | 47.9 | 39.3 |
| Nebraska | 6.9 | 39.4 | 53.7 |
| Nevada | 8.0 | 34.2 | 57.8 |
| New Hampshire | 5.5 | 34.3 | 60.2 |
| New Jersey | 3.1 | 34.0 | 62.8 |
| New Mexico | 14.6 | 70.0 | 15.4 |
| New York | 8.6 | 44.9 | 46.4 |
| North Carolina | 7.3 | 51.3 | 41.4 |
| North Dakota | 10.3 | 39.7 | 50.1 |
| Ohio | 9.0 | 44.9 | 46.0 |
| Oklahoma | 13.4 | 52.5 | 34.1 |
| Oregon | 9.6 | 51.1 | 39.3 |
| Pennsylvania | 6.3 | 38.7 | 55.0 |
| Rhode Island | 2.9 | 35.5 | 61.6 |
| South Carolina | 10.3 | 45.5 | 44.2 |
| South Dakota | 19.9 | 30.2 | 49.9 |
| Tennessee | 13.7 | 47.8 | 38.5 |
| Texas | 13.4 | 41.7 | 44.9 |

*(continued)*

**Table 13.3 — *(continued)***

|  | Federal | State | Local |
|---|---|---|---|
| Utah | 12.9 | 51.4 | 35.7 |
| Vermont | 8.0 | 90.2 | 1.7 |
| Virginia | 6.0 | 42.0 | 52.0 |
| Washington | 13.4 | 58.2 | 28.5 |
| West Virginia | 13.6 | 59.4 | 27.0 |
| Wisconsin | 12.6 | 43.5 | 43.9 |
| Wyoming | 7.7 | 50.9 | 41.4 |

*Note:* Due to rounding, totals may exceed 100%.

*Source:* Data from *Rankings of the States 2010 and Estimates of School Statistics 2011,* used with permission of the National Education Association © 2010. All rights reserved.

## Local Sources for Nontax Revenues

As a result of state restrictions on local school spending, local budgetary shortages, and rising costs, many schools have curtailed or eliminated some programs and services (e.g., art, music, and extracurricular activities). In response, schools and their supporters have sought to find other sources of funding for schools, including (1) charging participation or user fees for school activities, (2) formation of nonprofit educational foundations at the school or district level, and (3) various enterprise activities.

Fees for participation in elective or extracurricular activities (e.g., driver education, athletics, and school clubs) are becoming a significant source of revenue in many school districts. However, the charging of these fees is in conflict with court cases that have sought to bring about greater equity in funding and equality of access to educational programs and services and may be in violation of state constitutional requirements for a free public education. The basic question may be whether the activity is considered a necessary part of the school program or a truly extracurricular activity being provided under the sponsorship of the school. If the activity is a basic part of the school program, then charging a participation fee may violate the state constitutional mandate of a free public education and may be considered discriminatory because a student from a low-income family may not be able to afford the fees. Families with multiple children may also question the affordability of participation. To address these concerns, many school districts provide reduced fees and/or a maximum fee per family. Despite the concerns over activity fees, given the current economic pressures faced by most school districts, they are more likely to grow in use rather than the reverse.

Another source of nontax revenues for schools is donor activities, including booster clubs and educational foundations. Some school districts have created these nonprofit foundations to secure funds for programs and services that cannot be supported from tax funds. These foundations, which are allowed to receive tax-deductible gifts from parents, interested citizens, and businesses, provide a means for districts to provide programs and services that are important components of a high-quality education for their constituents.

Enterprise activities include such things as leasing school facilities and services (e.g., leasing the roof of a building for a cell phone tower) and the sale of school access. The latter is generally through advertising on school property (e.g., buses or athletic fields) or in school publications (e.g., school yearbooks or newspapers). A growing and more controversial practice is commercialism in the schools (see the Ask Yourself feature on page 359). Commercialism can take the form of sponsored programs or activities (e.g., the XYZ Prize); sponsored educational materials; incentive programs (e.g., Box Tops for Education); Internet marketing on education-related sites; or, more commonly, advertisement on sites favored by youth. Schools have traditionally allowed, even courted, advertisements in school yearbooks or newspapers to offset the cost of the publication, as well as at athletic events to support extracurricular activities. However, most of the advertising in schools today has not been solicited by the school but has become imbedded in the education context. And it is everywhere: not just on scoreboards but on textbooks, book covers, and television and radio programs broadcast in the schools. Despite the concerns that have been raised about the negative effects of commercialism on children's health and psychological well-being, cash-strapped schools have welcomed school business "partnerships" that they hope will help avert program cuts (Molnar, Boringer, Wilkinson, Fogarty, & Geary, 2010.)

Commercialism in the form of ads is increasing in the schools.

## State Sources of Revenue

State sales and income taxes are the principal sources of the state revenues that go to the schools. All but five states have a sales tax, and all but seven have a personal income tax. Most states have both a sales tax and an income tax. Both of these taxes are more equitable than the property tax, especially if food is exempted from the sales tax base and when the income tax (the only tax related directly to the taxpayer's ability to pay) allows exemptions or credits to account for the special circumstances of the taxpayer. One tax credit that has generated controversy in recent years, not only on the Establishment grounds discussed in Chapter 11, but from the perspective of lost state revenues, is the tuition tax credit debated in the Controversial Issue on page 360.

# ASK YOURSELF

## *What Limits Should Be Placed on Commercialism in Schools?*

Advertisers and marketers of commercial products have an obvious interest in reaching children. It is estimated that in 2011 teenagers alone constituted a $209 billion annual market. Another estimate is that children aged 6–14 years spend $43 billion annually and influence their parents' decisions on many billions more (EPM Communications, 2008). The size of the youth and adolescent market has led to a dramatic increase in in-school commercialism. Many parents and many educators, concerned with children's health and childhood obesity, have called for a ban on advertising by the food market in schools. Where do you stand on this issue? To clarify your position on the issue of commercialism in the schools, ask yourself the following questions:

1. Should food and snack providers be allowed to provide in-school sampling of products?

2. Should any advertisement in schools be allowed at the elementary level?

3. Should school newspapers be allowed to accept advertisements from fast-food companies?

4. Should companies be allowed to advertise on commercial radio programs to be broadcast in school buses?

5. Should "pouring rights" that give corporations exclusive rights to sell and promote their products (e.g., Pepsi-Cola or Coca-Cola) in exchange for a percentage of the profits be allowed?

6. Given the budget financial shortages in most districts, should school districts seek to award "naming rights" to companies in exchange for sponsoring a capital project or major school event or activity?

7. Should all commercial advertising be limited to such places as scoreboards or rooftops?

# CONTROVERSIAL ISSUE

## *Tuition Tax Credits*

In 2011 the U.S. Supreme Court ruled in the Arizona case of *Arizona Christian School Tuition Organization v. Winn* that dollar-for-dollar tax credits ($500 for individuals, $1000 for couples) for donations to organizations that provide tuition support for students in private schools, including parochial schools, did not violate the First Amendment religion clause. Several other states in addition to Arizona provide tuition tax credits, and in the wake of the *Winn* decision, they have been proposed in even more. Wherever they have been considered, tuition tax credits have been the topic of heated debate. Among the arguments for and against are:

**For**

1. Tuition tax credits provide disadvantaged families with the means to exercise greater choice in the schools their children attend.

2. The tuition goes directly to the school and has no government involvement.

3. Tuition tax credits provide relief to families that are already paying taxes to support the public schools.

4. Tuition tax credits provide indirect support for private schools that play an important role in the American system of education.

**Against**

1. The major beneficiaries of tuition tax credits are families who are already sending their children to private schools.

2. Many disadvantaged or poor families do not have any tax liability and therefore do not not benefit from the tax credit.

3. Tuition tax credits reduce tax revenues at a time when most states are facing financial deficits.

4. Tuition tax credits go largely to schools that have few low income or minority students.

What is your position on tuition tax credits? How likely would you be to donate to a tuition organization if you could? Why or why not?

Another state tax issue that has grown in recent years is tax on Internet sales. The growth in Internet sales across not only state lines but also national borders has made collection of sales taxes an issue that has impacted state revenues. At the same time, many states have sought to increase sales tax revenues by extending the sales tax to services such as dry cleaning, hair care, or other personal services.

In addition to tax sources, 20 states earmark some or all of state lottery profits for public elementary and secondary schools. Although lottery funds are only a small portion of total state revenues allocated to the public schools, they are a controversial source of revenue. Not only are lotteries a regressive form of revenue generation and the involvement of government in the promotion of gambling is questionable, but also they really generate only a very small percentage of the revenues for education in any state (average of 2%). Even in those states where lottery proceeds have been earmarked for education, the budget crisis faced by states forced several states to divert lottery funds from their original educational targets or to reduce the percentage of funds allocated to education. Despite these objections, lotteries have grown in popularity over the years because they represent an acceptable means of raising revenue when tax increases would have been rejected by the taxpayers.

## Federal Sources of Revenue

The principal source of federal revenue for education is the federal income tax. A major advantage of the federal income tax is that it relies on the taxable income of the entire nation as the taxpaying base.

The states with the largest percentage of federal education revenues tend to be those in the Southeast. They are also the states with the highest percentage of children in poverty (thus the recipients of Title I funds) as well as with heavy concentrations of military bases (thus receiving federal impact aid). Other states with large amounts of federal property (e.g., national parks and forests, Indian reservations, or military bases) also receive higher proportions of federal funds.

## The Courts and School Finance

Since the early 1970s, when the first wave of school finance litigation began, state programs for financing the public schools have been challenged in more than 45 states. The contention in most of these cases has been that articulated by the California Supreme Court in the Historical Note feature below: that the state has failed to provide equal educational opportunities for students because the state system for financing education relies too heavily on the local property tax as a source of revenue for the schools, and, as a consequence, the disparities in taxable wealth among the districts create fiscal and educational inequalities. As a result of the disparities in taxable wealth, either taxpayers in different districts must be taxed at different rates to provide the same level of support, or students in these districts will have less spent on them than students in districts with greater wealth or higher tax rates. Plaintiffs contend that the result is unfair to both taxpayers and students in the low-spending districts who often receive an inadequate or inferior education.

In the landmark federal school finance case, *San Antonio v. Rodriguez* (1973), the U.S. Supreme Court rejected the argument that education is a constitutionally protected right under the U.S. Constitution requiring equal treatment in providing education. Since the *Rodriguez* decision effectively closed the door to challenges in the federal courts, challenges to existing state school finance programs have been based on the education clause in a state constitution, discussed in Chapter 11, rather than on provisions in the U.S. Constitution.

# HISTORICAL NOTE

## Serrano v. Priest: *The School Finance Reform Movement Begins*

In 1971 the education community, supporters of public education, and many policymakers were sent into a virtual euphoria by the decision of the highest court in the nation's most populous state that the quality of a child's education not be determined by the wealth of the school district in which the child resided, but by the wealth of the state as a whole. To do otherwise would be to violate the equal protection clause of the state and federal constitutions. *Serrano* was part of an era which saw the struggle against inequality and gender, race, ethnicity, and disability discrimination being both waged and played out in the schools. In *Serrano v. Priest* the struggle was concerned with the educational inequality between students in the more wealthy districts and those in the least wealthy districts. As summarized by the California Supreme Court:

> The public school system is maintained throughout the state financing plan which relies heavily on local property taxes and causes substantial disparities among individual school districts in the amount of revenue available per pupil for educational purposes. Districts with smaller tax bases, therefore, are not able to spend as much money per child for education as districts with larger tax bases. As a result of the finance scheme, substantial disparities in the equality and extent of availability of educational opportunities exist and are perpetuated among the state's school districts. The educational opportunities made available to children in the property poor districts are substantially inferior to the educational opportunities made available to children in other districts in the state. The state school finance plan thus fails to meet the requirements of the federal and state equal protection clause . . . Furthermore, as a direct result of the school plan system, they [parents in poor districts] are required to pay a higher tax rate than taxpayers in many other school districts in order to obtain for their children the same or lesser educational opportunities afforded children in those other districts.

Although the *Serrano* litigation went on for several years, and its Constitutional analysis was overruled in *San Antonio Independent School District v. Rodriguez* (1973), *Serrano* sparked a revolution in school finance that has continued for four decades. State courts in over two dozen states used the Serrano rationale in overturning their own states' school finance plan. In still other states, even if litigation was not initiated, in many instances the attention brought to bear on the inequities in school funding spurred the legislatures to reform their school finance systems.

The provision of equity was traditionally the major concern of plaintiffs in challenging state finance plans. In the 1990s, however, attention turned increasingly to whether the funding level was sufficiently adequate to provide an education that met state standards. The concern with adequacy is that even if every district were to receive equal funding per pupil, because of geographic and cost differences and variations in concentrations of high-need students, some districts would still need funds beyond the foundation base level of funding if they were to provide the same adequate education to each student. Consider, for example, the differences in the cost of the land for a school building or hiring a school social worker in New York City compared to rural New York State. Plaintiffs have prevailed in more than two thirds of these cases. In part in a response to these cases, policymakers in a number of states have initiated reform of their state finance programs in an effort to provide a sufficient level of funding to deliver an adequate education to every child in the state.

## Federal Aid for Elementary and Secondary Schools

The No Child Left Behind (NCLB) Act of 2001, the reauthorization of the Elementary and Secondary Education Act (ESEA), has become the cornerstone of the federal education agenda. NCLB marked a major expansion and change in the underlying purpose of the federal government's involvement in education. Historically, the federal government's involvement was based on the premise that an educated citizenry would contribute to the national political and economic welfare. NCLB, however, made clear that the principal reason for the federal government's involvement in public education is to raise student achievement through the promotion of academic standards and increased qualifications for instructional personnel. President Obama's blueprint for the reauthorization of ESEA (proposed at this writing) continues the emphasis on ensuring quality teachers in every classroom. It also continues the push for state standards and assessments, with the focus on those that are designed to produce graduates that are "college and career ready." As a result of the massive federal infusion of $4.35 billion as part of the American Recovery and Reinvestment Act and $10 billion under the Education Job Funds, federal aid to education rose to an all time high of 10.5% of total educational revenues in 2010 (see Table 13.3).

Support for the major federal programs such as Title I and the Individuals with Disabilities Education Act (IDEA) has been maintained for 40 years and has increased under NCLB, but other programs have been more dependent on the preferences of Congress and the executive branch. As a result, specific programs initiated by one administration may be terminated or consolidated by a subsequent administration because of different priorities. However, even though funding is limited, the federal government's involvement in education continues to be influential in providing programs for youth with special needs, and this involvement may in fact increase as student assessment programs are implemented.

Of the federally funded elementary and secondary education programs, the largest is the Title I program for the education of disadvantaged pupils. As indicated on Table 13.4, the proposed 2012 federal education budget included $14.8 billion for Title I. The Head Start program for low-income preschool children, administered by the Department of Health and Human Services, typically is not operated by public school districts but is an important component of the educational system. Proposed funding for this program in 2012 was $8.1 billion.

The second largest federally funded PK–12 education program is special education grants. The 2012 federal budget proposal included $12.9 billion for special education programs. This program has been in existence since the late 1970s, but the level of federal funding has never reached the commitment in the original legislation: 40% of the average per pupil expenditure. However, no modification has been made in program requirements or regulations because of the failure to fully fund the program.

**Table 13.4 — Federal Budget for Major Federal Education Programs (in billions), 2002–2012**

| Program | FY 2002 | FY 2004 | FY 2006 | FY 2012 Proposed |
|---|---|---|---|---|
| **K–12 Programs** | | | | |
| Title I | $10.4 | $12.3 | $14.8 | $14.8 |
| Special education grants | 7.9 | 10.5 | 11.5 | 12.9 |
| Impact aid | 1.1 | 1.2 | 1.4 | 1.1 |
| Career and technical education | 1.3 | 1.3 | 2.0 | 1.0 |
| Effective teachers and leaders state grants | 2.9 | 2.9 | 2.9 | 2.5 |
| 21st Century Community learning centers | 1.0 | 1.0 | 1.1 | 1.3 |
| English learner education | 0.7 | 0.7 | 1.1 | .8 |
| Adult and literacy education | 0.5 | 0.5 | 0.5 | .64 |
| Head Start | 6.5 | 6.8 | 7.3 | 8.1 |
| School breakfast and lunch program | 6.9 | 7.6 | 8.5 | 10.8 |

Another long-standing federal program is impact aid to school districts for the education of youth residing with parents who live or work on federal property or Indian reservations or are active-duty uniformed military personnel. Proposed funding for this program in 2012 was $1.1 billion. One program that provides significant services to low income students is not funded by the U.S. Department of Education: the School Lunch and Breakfast programs funded by the U.S. Department of Agriculture, with a 2010 budget of $10.8 billion.

# Private Education

The private school option is not new; it has provided an alternative to public education in the United States since the colonial period. In 1924, in *Pierce v. Society of Sisters,* the U.S. Supreme Court recognized the right of parents to educate their children in private schools. However, the decision also recognized the right of the state to regulate private schools, including requiring that their teachers be certified and that their curricula comply with state guidelines.

Private schools take different forms in response to parents who want broader educational opportunities for their children, who seek a more rigorous or more restrictive environment for their children, or who desire a more permissive environment than the public schools can provide. This pattern of diverse aspirations has contributed to the development of a variety of private schools that are noted more for their differences than their similarities. Such schools include church-related schools, private traditional day schools, and "free" schools in which students can pursue individual interests.

**Proprietary schools**, schools operated for profit, comprise a growing sector of the private school market. Their popularity has been attributed to parents' being attracted to the high standards that many such schools espouse, the extras (e.g., before- and after-school remediation and counseling and a wide variety of extracurricular activities), in-depth education, and smaller class size. However, proprietary schools represent only 1% of all elementary and secondary schools.

## Private School Enrollments

The number of students attending the almost 22,000 private schools in the United States totaled about 6 million students in 2009–2010, a slight decline from previous years. Some of the decline in private school enrollments has been attributed

> **For Your Reflection and Analysis**
>
> In the current era of accountability, what kinds of controls should the state exercise over private schools?

The number of students attending private schools could increase if vouchers are provided by the state or federal governments.

to the success of charter schools in providing parents an option to the local public school. Of the 6 million students attending private schools, over 78% attend church-related schools, or **parochial schools**, with about 2.2 million of these students attending Roman Catholic schools (Snyder & Dillow, 2011).

Despite the recent decline in private school enrollment in some sectors, projections suggest that the overall percentage of American students enrolled in private elementary and secondary schools will increase as overall PK–12 enrollments increase (Hussar & Bailey, 2011). If states or the federal government provide vouchers to students or if more states provide tax credits, enrollments could increase even further (see the Video Insight feature below). On the other hand, if a significant number of private, church-related schools convert to charter schools, as have a number of Catholic schools in Washington, D.C., and elsewhere, enrollments may remain stable or decline.

### Homeschooling

**Homeschooling** as a form of private schooling is another alternative to attendance in the public schools. Homeschooling is allowed in all states. The interest in homeschooling has increased dramatically in the last two decades as more and more

## VIDEO INSIGHT

### Vouchers

This ABC News video consists of interviews about vouchers to pay tuition for students in grades K–12 to attend church-related and secular nonpublic schools. Advocates for vouchers have been heartened by a decision of the U.S. Supreme Court (*Zelman v. Simmons-Harris*, 2002) that approved the voucher program for disadvantaged youth in the Cleveland Public Schools. The Court ruled that the Cleveland program did not violate the Establishment Clause of the U.S. Constitution, which calls for separation of church and state, as long as parents have a choice from a range of church-related and secular schools. With your classmates and/or other students, research and discuss the following topics:

1. Form a study group to review the wording of the Establishment Clause and the related subsequent decisions, and have the study group give a background report and lead a class discussion on the topic.

2. Have another study group review and summarize the literature about the public's attitude toward vouchers.

3. Using the information above, have a class debate on vouchers.

parents have become concerned about instruction or safety in the public schools. The number of homeschoolers increased from 850,000 in 1999 to over 1.5 million in 2007 (Snyder & Dillow, 2011). Although in most states home schools are under the supervision of the local school district, often the local district provides little or no monitoring. In some states and school districts, homeschooled children can enroll in independent study programs through a public school or participate in some form of part-time school attendance. However, where state funding is not provided for part-time students or where state athletic associations deny eligibility to part-time students, homeschoolers may be denied attendance or participation in extracurricular activities, not only including sports but also such activities as band, choir, and theater.

State statutes providing for homeschooling range from those that are very strict to those that simply treat homeschooling the same as any other form of nonpublic education. Generally, state statutes or regulations require that (1) instruction be essentially equivalent to that taught in the public schools and include the subjects required by state law, (2) the parent or other adult providing the instruction be qualified (not necessarily certified) to teach, (3) systematic reporting be made to local school authorities, and (4) a minimum number of hours of instruction per day be provided.

In about two-thirds of the states, students in homeschools must be periodically assessed for academic progress. In fact, a federal court has upheld a state statute making ineligible for homeschooling those students whose scores fall below the 40th percentile and do not improve after home remediation (*Null v. Board of Education of the County of Jackson,* 1993). The courts have also upheld the right of school officials to visit the home to observe the teaching and to examine student work. However, where states have attempted to impose requirements on homeschools that were not required of the public schools, or were unreasonable, the courts have overturned the requirements (e.g., *Clonlara, Inc. v. State Board of Education,* 1993, 180-day minimum school year requirement for homeschools but not for public schools).

## Summary

Annual expenditures for public elementary and secondary education reached $550 billion by 2010–2011. This outlay is viewed as an investment because education contributes trained workers who support the economy through their production and purchase of consumer goods and because it is believed that an educated populace is necessary for sustaining a democracy.

State governmental and organizational structures for schools differ in some ways, but the general pattern is consistent. Greater differences can be found in the patterns of school finance and the range in the proportion of funds that comes from state and local revenue sources. An ongoing challenge for all states is to provide for an acceptable balance between the conflicting goals of equity, adequacy, and choice. A second challenge is to raise the revenues for the programs in a fair and equitable manner to ensure that all students have access to an appropriate educational program and that all taxpayers are treated fairly.

The No Child Left Behind Act resulted in the federal government assuming a more active role in elementary and secondary education. The focus was on accountability, including each school's performance and annual progress on achievement tests, school report cards, and intervention for low-performing schools. This focus continued under the Obama educational agenda, with federal funding reaching an all time high percentage of revenues to education.

With this background on school organization, administration, and finance, you now have a context in which to place the discussion of the school curriculum and instructional practices in the following chapter.

**For Your Reflection and Analysis**

Should parents who home-school receive state aid?

## TEACHER OF THE YEAR

*Peggy Jackson
New Mexico*

I love to teach. I've always been a teacher. I taught my dolls. I taught elementary kids how to swim. I taught middle school kids in a teen group what to do. Today my passion is teaching high school seniors in a rural-suburban school district about the U.S. Constitution. I teach AP U.S. Government, Politics, and Economics. I believe that teaching these students is something important that I can contribute to our American democracy, because they need to be participants in society and understand what it means to be a citizen. I begin my classroom with political cartoons, then give them an inquiry-based question on a controversial issue and let them go at it and teach one another. I do a "We The People" team at my high school, and at simulated congressional hearings my students teach me. I teach my students *how* to think, not *what* to think. I'm a teacher because I believe passionately that participatory democracy is very important.

# PROFESSIONAL DEVELOPMENT
## *Workshop*

### *Prepare for the State Licensure Examination*

Rhonda Pham has been teaching mathematics for eight years at Rainer Maria Rilke Junior High School, located in the Southwest. During the past two years, Rhonda has also served as a part-time assistant principal assigned to work with beginning teachers on various issues, including classroom management.

Recently Ms. Pham was asked by the principal to meet with Jackson Dearborn, a first-year, seventh-grade English teacher who is having difficulty controlling the disruptive behavior of his students, especially in the library. According to Margaret Chatsworth, the librarian, Mr. Dearborn's students come into the library pushing and shoving and rush to the computers, causing a great deal of commotion and noise. And, despite Mr. Dearborn's presence, they spend most of their time socializing with students from other classes and use the computers to play games or send e-mail to their friends when they should be doing Internet research.

1. What are some of the major causes of disruptive behavior in classrooms?

2. Describe some of the interventions that Mr. Dearborn might use to effectively deal with the misbehavior of his students in the library.

3. Under what circumstances might coercive punishment and/or other types of penalties be used to reduce or eliminate inappropriate behavior at school?

### Build Your Knowledge Base

1. How does education being a state function affect the powers of citizens to determine programs in local schools?
2. What qualifications should a person have to be a member of a school board, principal, superintendent, chief state school officer, or U.S. secretary of education?
3. What kinds of responsibilities should teachers have in the administration of an individual school?
4. In what ways are private schools and their students different from public schools and their students?
5. How does the per pupil funding level for schools in your state compare with the levels in other states?
6. In what ways are public schools, charter schools, and private schools different, and how are they similar?
7. What educational programs should the federal government finance?

### Develop Your Portfolio

1. To better understand how schools are financed, review the following tables: Table 13.2, 2010–2011 Per Pupil Expenditures by State, on page 356; and Table 13.3, Estimated Percentage of Revenues for Public Schools from Local, State, and Federal Sources, 2010–2011, on page 357. Interview a school business manager regarding how schools are financed in your state. Use the following questions as a guide for your interview: (1) What are the major local, state, and federal revenue sources in your state? (2) How do the state taxes compare with other states? (3) How equitable is the school finance program? (4) How adequate is the funding? (5) Explain how "choice" is being used (i.e., local control of funding decisions or the power of parents to select the school their child will attend). (6) Identify the major model or funding approach (equalized foundation grants, equalized reward for tax effort, full state funding, flat grant, or other

sources of nontax revenues). (7) To what extent has your state been involved in litigation regarding the inequalities or inadequacies of school financing? After the interview, prepare a short reflection paper that summarizes your thoughts regarding the major problems of financing public elementary and secondary schools in your state. Place your reflection paper in your portfolio under **INTASC Standard 4, Content Knowledge**.

2. The proposed 2012 budget for the U.S. Department of Education recommended no funding for federal vocational education programs. Interview a principal concerning the student interest in vocational education. Include his or her remarks in a position paper summarizing the pros and cons of vocational education. Include the following information in your interview: (1) When did federal funding start for vocational education? (2) How were the federal funds used? (3) Does your state provide funds for vocational education? (4) How many students are served in the program in his/her school? (5) Are vocational education teachers certified in the same manner as public school teachers? (6) How is accountability measured? Place your position paper in your portfolio under **INTASC Standard 4, Content Knowledge**.

## Explore Teaching and Learning: Field Experiences

1. Contact the business office of a local school district and request a copy of the district's annual budget and financial report. Identify the various sources of revenue for the school district. What portions come from federal, state, and local sources? Make a pie chart that shows revenue sources similar to the one shown in this chapter. How does the pie chart for your district compare with the national one presented in the chapter?

2. Contact the business office of a local school district and request a copy of the district's annual budget and financial report. Review the document to determine the proportion of the budget allocated for teacher's salaries, utilities, classroom supplies, and salaries of central office administrators. What are their percentages of the total? Make a pie chart that shows the budget allocation for the principal functions in the budget similar to the one in this chapter. How does the pattern for your district compare with the national pattern presented in the chapter?

### MyEducationLab

Go to **Topic 5, Governance and Finance,** in the MyEducationLab (www.myeducationlab.com) for *Foundations of American Education*, where you can:

- Find learning outcomes for governance and finance, along with the national standards that connect to these outcomes.
- Complete Assignments and Activities that can help you more deeply understand the chapter content.
- Apply and practice your understanding of the core teaching skills identified in the chapter with the Building Teaching Skills and Dispositions learning units.
- Examine challenging situations and cases presented in the IRIS Center Resources.

- Access additional video clips of CCSSO National Teachers of the Year award winners responding to the question, "Why Do I Teach?" in the Teacher Talk section.
- Check your comprehension on the content covered in the chapter with the Study Plan. Here you will be able to take a chapter quiz, receive feedback on your answers, and then access Review, Practice, and Enrichment activities to enhance your understanding of chapter content.
- Use the Online Lesson Plan Builder to practice lesson planning and integrating national and state standards into your planning.

# CHAPTER
## *Fourteen*

# Curriculum and Instruction

As a new teacher, Mary Sherman has found that there is some community controversy over who should control the curriculum in the public schools. This question also is receiving considerable attention in local school board meetings and parent–teacher meetings. The community has not been able to reach consensus. Mary has read a recent Phi Delta Kappa poll that indicates teachers felt that they should have the greatest influence on what is taught in the schools. In reviewing the national content standards that have been adopted by the state for the major subject areas, Mary found that the national professional organizations had been deeply involved in the development of the standards. The state also has recently adopted a statewide assessment program designed to determine the extent to which the students have attained the standards. Mary has also seen national polls reporting that parents feel the schools' curriculum needs to be changed to meet current needs and that they should be given a greater role in determining its direction.

What steps should the local teachers' organization take to address these apparently conflicting positions? What effects will the content standards and the statewide assessment program have on Mary's role as a teacher and what she teaches in the classroom? What are the implications for the academic freedom and academic responsibility of the public school teacher?

*T*he term **curriculum** is a vague and complex notion. Curriculum theorists do not agree on any one definition. Broadly stated, curriculum is said to be all of the educational experiences of students that take place under the auspices of the school. In this chapter, the concept of curriculum is explored from its many perspectives, ranging from curriculum as content to curriculum as experiences.

This chapter also reviews various instructional practices associated with effective teaching. Rather than advocating a particular approach, the focus is on different models and strategies that teachers and schools have used for different purposes with different groups of students.

This chapter provides information to help you to:

- Review the sociopolitical and professional forces that influence curriculum policy making and design.
- Compare the subject-centered and student-centered patterns of curriculum organization.
- Describe the hidden curriculum and the null curriculum and their effects on schooling.

- Discuss the difference between educational goals and educational objectives.
- Identify the models of instruction that have been classified as belonging to the information processing family of models and the behavioral systems family of models.
- Explain the relationship between teaching and learning.

How a teacher perceives curriculum and instruction is important because it reflects and shapes how we think about and act on the education provided to students (Sowell, 2005). In this chapter various perspectives on the curriculum are examined. First, the influence of a number of sociopolitical forces on curriculum policy making and design will be reviewed. Next, the major patterns of curriculum design will be described, followed by a discussion of the null and the unintended or null curriculum. Attention is then given to the importance of instructional goals and objectives in schools. Finally, an overview of some of the more commonly employed models of instruction is provided.

**For Your Reflection and Analysis**

Who should determine the curriculum? Who should decide how to teach the content?

# Forces Influencing the Curriculum

Decisions about the curriculum are not made in a vacuum by teachers, administrators, and curriculum specialists. Such decisions occur in the context of a particular community, state, and nation at a particular time. Throughout history various professional, political, social, economic, and religious groups have attempted to influence the schools' curriculum. Their relative power and influence have varied over time, as well as their motives, methods, strengths, and successes (Marsh & Willis, 2003). The process by which they attempt to influence the curriculum is political and is directed at answering four questions: (1) Who initiates the curriculum? (2) Who determines priorities? (3) Who implements the curriculum? (4) Who is accountable for what happens?

A variety of political, commercial, and professional groups seek to determine or influence the curriculum. Political forces and professional organizations have become more active as initiators because of concerns about the importance of an educated workforce if the nation is to be competitive in a global economy. This national interest has contributed to greater uniformity in curricular content and student assessment. The professional subject-matter organizations have developed standards and goals that have been incorporated into textbooks and the instructional materials. The commercial testing companies then provide the standardized assessment instruments. This section briefly discusses the influences of the following forces on curriculum in the schools: national curriculum standards, textbooks, mandated assessments, state governments, teachers, local school boards, parent and community groups, and the federal government. The interaction of these relationships is shown in Figure 14.1.

## National Curriculum Standards

Before the mid-1980s, concerns about the curriculum were largely limited to textbook content and "what to teach when." The school reform movement and state accountability legislation changed this somewhat comfortable and isolated environment. One of the most influential developments occurred during the 1990s, when the major subject-matter professional organizations developed curriculum standards in the principal subject areas. This had a dramatic impact on elementary and secondary schools, as well as on teacher preparation programs in colleges and universities. The standards identified what students should know and be able to do, called for more rigorous content, and encouraged the development of a comprehensive curriculum that emphasized problem solving, integrated tasks, real-life problems, and higher-order thinking skills (Wiles & Bondi, 2011). Many of the states either adopted these standards in total or used them in the development of the state's curriculum standards.

Figure 14.1 — Forces and Groups Influencing Curriculum

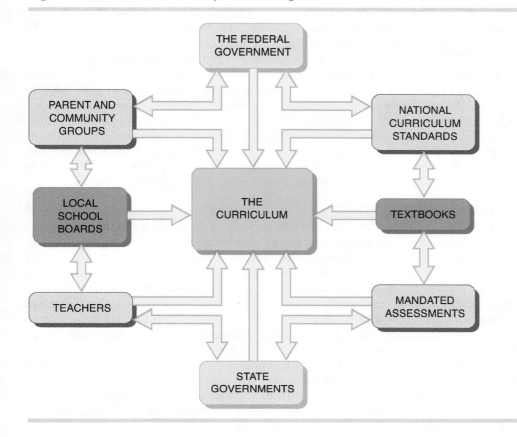

A potentially more far-reaching impact may come from the development and adoption of the Common Core State Standards. As described in Chapter 7, these standards are the work of the Common Core State Standards Initiative, a joint venture by the Council of Chief State School Officers and the National Governors Association. Released in 2010, they have currently been adopted or adapted by 41 states. The standards address two areas, English Language Arts and Mathematics, but it is anticipated that they will be expanded into additional academic disciplines. While not national standards, *per se*, the standards represent an effort to set common expectations for college and career readiness across all states that would replace the wide variations from state to state that currently exist. The standards not only include rigorous content and application of knowledge through higher order thinking skills, but are "internationally benchmarked so that all students are prepared to succeed in our global economy and society" (Core Standards, 2010, p. 1).

*Textbooks*

The influence of textbooks cannot be overstated; in the course of their educational career, students may be exposed to hundreds of textbooks and spend major portions of their time in the classroom and in doing homework using textbooks. Teachers rely heavily on textbooks and their accompanying instructor's manuals, tests, and audiovisual materials for instructional content, organization, and evaluation. Without question, textbooks and other published instructional materials influence what is taught and learned in the classroom. It is because they recognize the powerful influence of textbooks that special-interest groups have been so vocal and persistent in their attempts to influence textbook content and adoption decisions as well as the textbook industry. Textbook publishers design their books to appeal to a national market and are sensitive to major education and social trends. If a large sector of that market or a large state (e.g., Texas or California) finds material

**For Your Reflection and Analysis**

What are the pros and cons of having academic professionals set standards and goals in their subject areas?

**Reflect on Diversity**
What kinds of cultural, racial, ethnic, or gender bias have you encountered in the textbooks you have used?

objectionable, the publisher may respond in ways that not only reflect the perspective of the biggest users, but also put that perspective in the hands of students nationwide. The 21 states that choose at the state level what textbooks are to be used in all districts in the state dominate the market.

Given the potential influence of textbooks, it is not surprising that their adoption often sparks religious or political controversy over their content (see Chapter 11). While both textbook publishers and state education agencies have developed guidelines for content, it is also important that teachers be sensitive to textbook treatment of topics such as cultural diversity, gender differences, and special populations. Textbooks must also be examined to ensure they are aligned with state standards. Teachers should actively seek to participate in the textbook review or selection process. Ultimately, the influence that textbooks have on the curriculum is determined by the care taken in their selection and how useful they are in delivering information to students.

## Mandated Assessments

The increase in the last two decades in the use of national standardized tests in making major decisions affecting students and teachers has been significant. Students are admitted to postsecondary institutions, private elementary and secondary schools, and specialized programs in the public schools based on their test results. Passage of a minimum competency test for graduation is required in over half the states. Teachers, programs, and schools are considered more or less effective based on standardized test results. Under the terms of No Child Left Behind, schools considered low performing based on test results have been subject to sanctions including restructuring or state takeover. And, as discussed in Chapter 1, in a number of states and school districts, high-performing or improving schools or teachers in those schools are given financial rewards. The admission of prospective teachers and administrators into degree or certification programs, or their later certification, are determined by test results. Not ending there, in some states practicing teachers and administrators are tested for recertification.

That what is tested influences what is taught seems undeniable. Mandated assessments influence the curriculum in several ways. First, they serve an accountability function by ensuring that the standards on which the curriculum is built are indeed being taught, and their results can provide useful information for curriculum revision. At the same time, there is a danger that they can lead to a narrowing of the curriculum. Another unfortunate consequence is the practice of "teaching to the test," which has become widespread as teachers and administrators seek to ensure that they prepare students to do well on the test. If test scores are down in a particular school or certain curriculum area, district resources and instruction may be redirected to that area. Increasingly, individual students and their families invest in tutorial books, computer software, and seminars in an attempt to raise test scores. Thus, "to the extent that teaching to the test is practiced, the test becomes the curriculum, or at least, shapes the curriculum" (Tanner & Tanner, 2007, p. 156).

## State Governments

As the level of government with legal responsibility for education, the state exercises its influence over the curriculum in several ways. One important way the state influences the curriculum is through the adoption of curriculum standards in the subject areas. One example of state standards, Florida's geometry standards for grades 9–12, is found in Table 14.1. The rating of schools, students, and teachers, as well as the consequences to each based on the assessment of test results, reinforces the influence of the state on the curriculum content.

Another example of the influence of the state on the curriculum is through state statutes that mandate that students receive a passing grade in certain courses or pass a proficiency test in order to graduate from high school. In only a few states is the decision regarding the number of credits required for graduation left to the discretion of local school boards. In states where the number of Carnegie units

**For Your Reflection and Analysis**

What are the concerns about testing companies designing what knowledge should be tested? What role should they play?

**Table 14.1 — Florida Grades 9–12 Geometry Standards**

**Standard 1: Points, Lines, Angles, and Planes**   Understand geometric concepts, applications, and their representations with coordinate systems. Find lengths and midpoints of line segments, slopes, parallel and perpendicular lines, and equations of lines. Using a compass and straightedge, patty paper, a drawing program or other techniques, also construct lines and angles, explaining and justifying the processes they use.

**Standard 2: Polygons**   Identify and describe polygons (triangles, quadrilaterals, pentagons, hexagons, etc.), using terms such as regular, convex, and concave. Find measures of angles, sides, perimeters, and areas of polygons, justifying the methods used. Apply transformations to polygons. Relate geometry to algebra by using coordinate geometry to determine transformations. Use algebraic reasoning to determine congruence, similarity, and symmetry. Create and verify tessellations of the plane using polygons.

**Standard 3: Quadrilaterals**   Classify and understand relationships among quadrilaterals (rectangle, parallelogram, kite, etc.). Relate geometry to algebra by using coordinate geometry to determine regularity, congruence, and similarity. Use properties of congruent and similar quadrilaterals to solve problems involving lengths and areas, and prove theorems involving quadrilaterals.

**Standard 4: Triangles**   Identify and describe various kinds of triangles (right, acute, scalene, isosceles, etc.). Define and construct altitudes, medians, and bisectors, and triangles congruent to given triangles. Prove that triangles are congruent or similar and use properties of these triangles to solve problems involving lengths and areas. Relate geometry to algebra by using coordinate geometry to determine regularity, congruence, and similarity. Understand and apply the inequality theorems of triangles.

**Standard 5: Right Triangles**   Apply the Pythagorean Theorem to solving problems, including those involving the altitudes of right triangles and triangles with special angle relationships. Use special right triangles to solve problems using the properties of triangles.

**Standard 6: Circles**   Define and understand ideas related to circles (radius, tangent, chord, etc.). Perform constructions and prove theorems related to circles. Find measures of arcs and angles related to them, as well as measures of circumference and area. Relate geometry to algebra by finding the equation of a circle in the coordinate plane.

**Standard 7: Polyhedra and Other Solids**   Describe and make regular and nonregular polyhedra (cube, pyramid, tetrahedron, octahedron, etc.). Explore relationships among the faces, edges, and vertices of polyhedra. Describe sets of points on spheres, using terms such as great circle. Describe symmetries of solids and understand the properties of congruent and similar solids.

**Standard 8: Mathematical Reasoning and Problem Solving**   In a general sense, mathematics is problem solving. In all mathematics, use problem-solving skills: choose how to approach a problem, explain their reasoning, and check the results. At this level, apply these skills to making conjectures, using axioms and theorems, constructing logical arguments, and writing geometric proofs. Learn about inductive and deductive reasoning and how to use counterexamples to show that a general statement is false.

*Source:* Florida Department of Education. (2007). Retrieved March 12, 2011, from www.Floridastandards.org/downloads.aspx.

required for high school graduation has been mandated by the state, the number of units required ranges from 13 to 24, with the median being 21.

In addition to statutory requirements, the state influences the curriculum through the state board of education, which, in many states, is authorized to determine curriculum requirements and promulgate curriculum guidelines for all subject areas. The state department of education also influences the curriculum through the textbook adoption process, support for professional development activities, and the provision of instructional resources and curriculum guides. State curriculum guides detail the goals and objectives, competencies, and instructional activities for every subject at every grade level. (See Chapter 13 for a discussion of the roles and responsibilities of state boards and departments of education.)

## Teachers

Historically, teachers have had a significant impact on the school curriculum. Teachers were considered the primary source of knowledge in the classroom and were perceived to have the knowledge and skills to determine what was to be taught, what materials to use, and how student mastery was to be measured. They participated in the development of curriculum guides and related materials.

With the enactment of state accountability and assessment programs and the adoption of content standards, teachers now have less control over what is to be taught and when. However, they retain important influence over the curriculum because they serve as "the filters through which the mandated curriculum passes. Their understanding of it (the curriculum) and their enthusiasm, or boredom, with various aspects of it, color its nature. Hence the curriculum enacted in the classroom (may) differ from the one mandated by administrators or developed by experts" (McCutcheon, cited in Diaz, Pelletier, & Provenzo, 2006, p. 278).

School board meetings provide the venue for members of the community to make public their concerns about operation of the local schools.

## Local School Boards

The 13,800 local school boards in the United States make a host of curriculum decisions about the content and learning opportunities that are provided for students. Within the limits of state authority, local boards decide what electives will be offered, which textbooks and other instructional materials will be purchased, which curriculum guides are to be followed, what teachers will be hired, how the budget will be spent, and how to respond to innumerable other issues that directly or indirectly influence the curriculum. It is the local school board that most often feels the pressure of parents and other special-interest groups, because this body decides such matters as whether a new program will be piloted, whether such courses as sex education will be offered, or whether a program for students with hearing impairments will be offered by the district.

In recent years, there has been increased concern regarding the extent to which the school board represents all constituencies in the community. One concern is that boards are influenced too much by small but vocal groups of parents or concerned citizens. Another concern is the elitist composition of boards of education. School boards tend to be composed disproportionately of White professionals or businesspersons with college degrees and incomes above the national average (Hess & Meeks, 2010).

## Parent and Community Groups

Because of their vested interest in the local schools and their proximity to local decision makers, parents and community groups have the potential for exercising tremendous influence on the curriculum. For example, in recent years parents in some African American communities have demanded an Afrocentric curriculum that presents the Black perspective on history and current events as an alternative to the traditional Eurocentric curriculum. Such a curriculum, supporters argue, not only promotes a positive identity with their racial/ethnic group, but it also leads to improved self-esteem and academic achievement. Afrocentric public schools have been established in a number of the larger cities in the United States. In addition, in a number of areas, educators and parents have established charter schools that are Afrocentric, Chicano–centric, or Native American–centric, "emphasizing what is known, valued, and respected from their own cultural roots" (Gollnick & Chin, 2009, p. 73).

Parents also exercise their influence on the curriculum by serving on textbook adoption committees or education committees at the local, state, or national level. Parent–teacher associations, band boosters, parents of children with disabilities, parents of gifted children, and other interest groups are often active in supporting special programs or influencing legislation and supporting tax or spending referenda. Other groups bring pressure on school boards and school officials to decide whether or not to include curriculum material on sex education, substance abuse, suicide, ethnic or women's studies, and religion. Currently, various religious groups are bringing pressure on local school boards, state boards of education, political decision makers, and the textbook industry to rid the schools of all material and teaching that promote evolution and ignore religion (see Chapter 11).

## The Federal Government

Attempts by the federal government to influence the curriculum have historically focused on addressing perceived national problems or promoting programs to serve youth with special needs. Examples of these initiatives are the National Defense Education Act of 1958, discussed in Chapter 7, which was enacted in response to the launching of *Sputnik*; the Bilingual Education Act; the Individuals with Disabilities Education Act; and Title IX. However, as discussed in previous chapters, the most far reaching involvement of the federal government came with the enactment of the No Child Left Behind Act (NCLB), which gave the federal government broader involvement and places a number of requirements on schools, school districts, and states including (1) establishing standards for what students should know and be able to do in key academic subjects, (2) conducting an annual assessment of all students in reading and mathematics, (3) adopting and reporting yearly progress, and (4) adopting and reporting requirements related to preparation of teachers and paraprofessionals.

Federal involvement has been furthered by the Obama administration's Race to the Top initiative which has served as the impetus for major education reform in a number of states, involving an increase in the number of charter schools, an overhaul of teacher tenure laws, and linking teacher evaluation to student test scores. Because of the link between teacher and administrator salaries and test scores, Race to the Top has the potential of narrowing the curriculum more than NCLB, with less time available for the arts, history, foreign languages, and even physical education (Ravitch, 2010).

# Patterns of Curriculum Design

Decisions about how the curriculum should be organized involve choices about what content to study and how this content will be presented to the students. Although many structures are available and reflect alternative perspectives about the nature of the curriculum, these alternatives can be classified as being either subject centered or student centered. The subject-centered perspective is the older, more traditional, and most common structure. It views the curriculum as a program of studies or collection of courses that represents what students should know. The second perspective, the student-centered perspective, focuses on the needs and interests of the student and the process by which learning takes place.

The subject-centered and student-centered perspectives represent two ends of a continuum of curricular design. In this section, six alternative curriculum designs along this continuum are examined: subject-area design, integrated design, core curriculum design, student-centered design, and the constructivism. Various components of the curriculum organizations are compared in Table 14.2.

## The Subject-Area Curriculum Design

The **subject-area curriculum** design is the oldest and most common organization plan for the curriculum. This design views the curriculum as a group of subjects or body of subject matter. The subject matter to be included in the curriculum is that which has survived the test of time and is perceived to be of most value in the development of the intellect—said by supporters to be the primary purpose of

**For Your Reflection and Analysis**

How much input should parents and school patrons have in deciding what is to be taught?

**For Your Reflection and Analysis**

Should states be permitted to ignore national standards and goals?

**Table 14.2 — Perspectives on Curriculum Organization**

| Curriculum Design | Educational Theory | Curriculum Focus |
|---|---|---|
| Subject-area | Essentialism | A group of subjects or subject matter that represent the essential knowledge and values of society that have survived the test of time |
| Integrated | | The integration of two or more subjects, both within and across disciplines, into an integrated course |
| Core curriculum | Perennialism | A common body of curriculum content and learning experience that should be encountered by all students |
| Student-centered | Progressivism | Learning activities centered around the interests and needs of the child, designed to motivate and interest the child in the learning process |
| Constructivism | Progressivism Social Reconstructivism Postmodernism | Learning activities that encourage students to construct their own meaning based on current and past knowledge and experience |

education. The subject-area curriculum is consistent with the essentialist philosophy of education.

The subject-area design has been the dominant curriculum organization for more than a century. The subject area curriculum is supported by the essentialist and perennialist educational theories discussed in Chapter 4. As described, they propose a return to fundamentals and a curriculum of basic studies (reading, writing, and mathematics) and the elimination of "frivolous subjects."

Those who criticize the subject-area curriculum claim that it ignores the needs, interests, and experiences of individual students and discourages creativity on the part of both students and teachers. Another major criticism of this curriculum is that it is fragmented and compartmentalized. The subject-area curriculum is also faulted for failing to adequately consider both individual differences and contemporary social issues such as the growing number of English language learners. The primary teaching methods of the subject-area curriculum are lecture and discussion. Rote memorization and recitation are required of students.

The subject-area curriculum has remained the most popular and dominant curriculum design for four basic reasons. First, most teachers, especially secondary school teachers, are trained in the subject areas. Secondary school teachers usually think of themselves as American history teachers, biology teachers, English teachers, and so on. Second, organizing the school by subject matter makes it easy for parents and other adults to understand a student's education because most adults attended schools that were organized by subject matter. Third, the subject-area organization makes it easy for teachers to develop curriculum and goals: The content provides the organization and focus needed in planning. Finally, textbooks and other instructional materials are usually developed for subject-area use (Ellis, Mackey, & Glenn, 1988). Because the subject-area design has been so dominant in this country, it is possible to go into schools from Seattle to Key West and find much the same curriculum.

## The Integrated Curriculum Design

The **integrated curriculum** design emerged as a response to the multiplication of courses resulting from the subject-area design. Emphasis remains on subjects, but in place of separate courses in history, geography, economics, political science, anthropology, and sociology, for example, an integrated course in social studies might be offered. By using this latter approach, supporters claim, knowledge is integrated in a way that makes it more meaningful to the learner. The integrated design also provides greater flexibility to the teacher in choosing subject matter.

Among the more common integrated courses are language arts, which has taken the place of separate courses in reading, writing, spelling, speaking, grammar, drama, and literature; mathematics, which integrates arithmetic, geometry, and algebra; general science, which includes botany, biology, chemistry, and geology or earth science; and the previously mentioned social studies. Although the integrated design usually combines separate subjects within the same discipline, in some instances content from two or more branches of study has been integrated into a new field of study. For instance, futuristics, which integrates knowledge from mathematics, sociology, statistics, political science, economics, education, and a number of other fields, is one such new field of study.

The integrated curriculum has been widely accepted at the elementary level. Where once a number of separate subjects were taught for shorter periods of time, the typical elementary curriculum is now more likely to integrate these subjects into "subject areas" that are taught in longer blocks of time.

## The Core Curriculum Design

A core curriculum is a curriculum or course of study or set of courses representing a common set of knowledge, skills, and abilities which are deemed essential for every student. Different interpretations of the **core curriculum** concept have emerged since it was first advanced in the 1930s. For example, the response to the series of national reports critical of education in the 1980s was to recommend a core of subjects to be taken by all students. The National Commission on Excellence in Education (1983) recommended 13.5 units in "the Five New Basics," while Boyer (1983) proposed a "core of common learning" consisting of 14.5 units, and others wanted less specific but still identifiable cores. The core curriculum as defined, *de facto*, by the NCLB Act are English, reading or language arts, mathematics, science, foreign languages, civics and government, economics, art, and history and geography. More recently the previously described Common Core State Standard Initiative has promulgated a core curriculum (initially English language arts, literacy, and mathematics) which has been adapted and adopted by the majority of the states.

The common core curriculum has grown in popularity because it is said to be the best way to ensure that teachers, administrators, students, parents, textbook publishers, text developers, and educational policymakers are "on the same page." A common core curriculum also allows students to transfer to another school in the district, state, or nation and pick up where they left off. Another benefit of the common core curriculum, according to its supporters, is that it promotes equity: all students are offered the same curriculum and held to the same standards. The actual core curriculum fills only two-thirds of students' instructional time. The remainder of the time students can pursue their individual interests. The core curriculum has received support from reports such as those published by the College Board (2010) showing students who completed a common core curriculum scored 50 points higher on each of the three sections of the SAT (reading, writing, mathematics).

Despite the current support for the core curriculum concept, many educators are concerned that it is not possible to have a core curriculum for all students and still maintain high quality. Others are concerned about the impact of a universal core requirement on the schools' ability to meet the needs of different student populations, including those interested in vocational preparation. Still others are concerned about the impact of a mandated common core on the academic freedom of teachers and local control by the community.

## The Student-Centered Curriculum Design

The concept of the **student-centered curriculum** has its roots in the philosophies of Rousseau, Pestalozzi, and Froebel (see Chapter 5). In the United States, the concept was revived by the progressive education movement. There are a number of variations on the student-centered curriculum, including the experience- and activity-centered curriculum, the value-added curriculum, and the relevant curriculum. The emphasis of all student-centered curricula is on the student's freedom

**For Your Reflection and Analysis**

How is the role of the teacher different under the various curriculum types?

The student-centered curriculum includes a wide range of activities outside the classroom.

to learn, activities, and creative self-expression that engages the student in the learning process.

Whereas the traditional curriculum is organized around the teaching of discrete subject matter, in the student-centered curriculum, students come to the subject matter out of their own needs and interests. The student-centered curriculum focuses on the individual learner and the development of the whole student. The scope of this curriculum is as broad as all of human life and society, and its goal is to motivate and interest the student in the learning process. To achieve this goal, the curriculum encompasses a wide range of activities, including field geography, nature study, number concepts, games, drama, storytelling, music, art, handicrafts, physical education, community involvement projects, and other creative and expressive activities.

Student-centered designs are often criticized for being too broad and for being so inclusive they become nonfunctional. They are also criticized for being too permissive and for their lack of attention to subject-matter mastery. Modern proponents (e.g., John Holt, Herbert Kohl, and Elliot Eisner) counter that the student-centered curriculum enhances learning because it is based on the needs and interests of the learner. Student-centered curricula have operated in numerous districts and schools throughout this century, primarily at the elementary level. However, they have never been seriously considered at the secondary level.

## The Constructivism Curriculum Design

Currently, one of the most popular student-centered curricula is the constructivist curriculum design. The major theme of constructivism is that learning is an active process in which students construct new ideas or concepts based on their current and past knowledge and social and cultural experiences (Bruner, 1960). Students link their prior knowledge to the new knowledge in a continuous, active process of constructing meaning. The role of the teacher is that of a facilitator: to engage students in an active dialogue, translate information into the students' current sphere of understanding, and motivate students to think about what they are learning. The constructivist curriculum stresses real-life environments where students are encouraged to consider multiple perspectives in solving problems by using higher order thinking skills.

In the constructivist classroom, "teachers are usually less concerned with curriculum standards; instead they are committed to providing students freedom to explore and create activities, to read books of their choosing, and to learn about topics that interest them" (Diaz et al., 2006, p. 307). The constructivist curriculum is not concerned with breadth, but depth. It views the student not as a passive recipient of knowledge but as a knowledge-maker. Knowledge is an individual construct arrived at by a process of inquiry and critical thinking models of instruction described in this chapter.

**Reflect on Diversity**
How might the diverse background knowledge of students influence their construction of knowledge?

## Curriculum Contrasts

In practice, most schools do not adopt a single model but use variations of both in their curriculum organization. Historically, elementary schools have tended to be more student centered and secondary schools more subject centered. Ultimately, the choice of curriculum design reflects the prevailing philosophical orientation of the school.

# CONTROVERSIAL ISSUE

## *The Subject-Centered and Student-Centered Curricula*

The debate between the essentialists and others who support the subject-centered curriculum and the progressives and others who support a student-centered curriculum has continued unabated for almost a decade and appears likely to continue. Among the arguments the proponents of each orientation give are the following:

**Essentialists for the Subject-Centered Curriculum**

1. Introduces learners to the cultural heritage.

2. Gives teachers a sense of security by specifying what their responsibilities are for developing given skills and knowledge.

3. Reduces repetition or overlap between grade levels or different sections of the same class.

4. Increases the likelihood that learners will be exposed to knowledge and develop skills in an orderly manner.

5. Permits methodical assessment of pupil progress; assumes that knowledge is the only measurable outcome of learning experiences.

6. Facilitates cooperative group planning by educators in allocating the scope and sequence of learning experiences.

**Progressives for the Student-Centered Curriculum**

1. Releases the teacher from the pressure to follow a prescribed scope and sequence that invariably does not meet all learners' needs.

2. Has a positive influence on learners as they find that instruction is varied to meet individual needs and purposes.

3. Encourages teacher judgment in selecting the content deemed most suitable for a group of learners.

4. Increases the likelihood that content has relevance to learners.

5. Modifies instruction to accommodate developmental changes and behavioral tasks as individual differences are identified and monitored.

6. Allows much more latitude for creative planning by the individual teacher.

What other arguments can you think of for the subject-centered or student-centered curriculum?

*Source:* Shane, H. G., & Tabler, M. B. (1981). *Educating for a new millennium* (pp. 79–80). Bloomington, IN: Phi Delta Kappa. Reprinted with permission.

The major arguments in support of the subject-centered and student-centered curriculum are summarized in the Controversial Issue feature above.

Perhaps even more important than the explicit or formal curriculum is the informal or hidden curriculum. This concept, which was briefly mentioned in Chapter 8 with regard to the socialization role of the school, is discussed in the section that follows.

## The Hidden and Null Curricula

Schools teach students more than is in the explicit or formal curriculum; they are influenced by the implicit aspects in the curriculum that send them messages about what they ought to be doing and thinking. Teachers help shape the hidden curriculum in the classroom by sending signals such as smiles and frowns, gold stars and certificates, about what is considered to be important. The message may be unintended and may not be reflected in the school catalog, but a powerful message is communicated to students about what is valued and important. For this reason it is important that teachers always be aware of the hidden messages they may be communicating in their classrooms.

The hidden curriculum includes the norms and values that underlie the formal curriculum. Even though the hidden curriculum is not taught directly or included in the objectives of the formal curriculum, it impacts both students and teachers. Evidence of the hidden curriculum may be found in textbooks and other curriculum materials and in the norms and values of the school. The hidden curriculum includes the organizational structure of the classroom and the school as well as the ways in which students and teachers interact (Gollnick & Chinn, 2009).

The hidden curriculum includes the **null curriculum.** This term refers to the things students learn but are not taught. They may not be taught because they are perceived as controversial, or because other topics are seen as more relevant, or are topics with which the teacher is more knowledgeable or comfortable. The null curriculum, like all areas of the hidden curriculum, does not impact all students equally. Differences are found even within the same school or classroom in what certain students have the opportunity to learn.

In recent years, increasing attention has been focused on the hidden curriculum as more has been learned about the strength of its influence. Particular concern exists about its negative influence. For example, the lessons of the hidden curriculum tend to promote conformity and in the process may stifle creativity and independent thinking. The hidden curriculum also teaches students to avoid conflict and change. When teachers treat some students significantly different than others, bias and stereotyping of race, gender, and social class are reproduced and reinforced through the hidden curriculum (Gollnick & Chinn, 2009).

## The Curriculum Cycle

Throughout the 20th century, the curriculum in America's schools shifted between a subject-centered orientation and a student-centered orientation (see Figure 14.2). The first two decades of the century were dominated by the progressive movement and its student-centeredness. In the wake of World War I came a more conservative political posture and a renewal of interest in a more orderly academic curriculum. Out of the social upheaval of the Great Depression emerged a more liberal voice that championed concern for the individual. In the 1950s, Conant's study of secondary schools, which underscored the need for greater attention to academic studies, was reinforced by the Soviet launching of *Sputnik*. What followed was a curriculum reform movement aimed at strengthening mathematics, science, and foreign language offerings and providing greater rigor in all disciplines. The Great Society ideology of the 1960s drove the cycle in the opposite direction. The open school and alternative school movements were the most visible reflections of the increased attention being focused on students. By the early 1980s many of the curricular innovations of the previous decade had disappeared, and again a call was heard for a return to the basic academic subjects and an elimination of the frills. This mood dominated the remainder of the century.

At the turn of the 21st century, the enactment of the No Child Left Behind Act and the accompanying emphasis on standards and testing ensured that the focus remained on subject-matter mastery. This emphasis has been continued by the policies and programs of the Obama administration and is anticipated to be reflected in the reauthorization of the Elementary and Secondary Education Act.

Whatever curriculum orientation is present, it is actualized by the instructional process. That process begins with clearly defined goals and objectives for instruction and information about the roles and responsibilities of learners in

**Figure 14.2 — Cycle of Curriculum Orientation, 1900–2011**

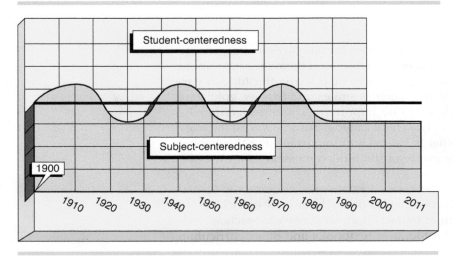

relation to specific goals and objectives. The role of educational goals and objectives in the instructional process is discussed in the following section.

# Instructional Goals and Objectives

**Educational goals** are general statements about directions toward which we want learning outcomes to lead. Educational goals are ideals one intends to reach or one's accomplishment targets. Rather than identifying specific skills, educational goals describe the attributes that should be found in an educated person. They may be goals for you as a teacher, goals for your students, or team goals (Kellough & Kellough, 2011). Examples of goal statements are as follows:

- The learner will develop basic math skills.
- The learner will develop an appreciation of poetry.
- The learner will develop an understanding of the events leading up to World War II.

Goals are achieved through the cumulative effect of a series of learnings. As defined, goals designate the desired outcome of instruction but lack the specificity to actually implement an instructional sequence (Kellough & Kellough, 2011). That is where educational objectives come into play.

## *Educational Objectives*

An **educational objective** is a clearly defined, observable, and measurable student outcome that indicates learner progress toward the achievement of a particular educational goal. Educational objectives describe learning outcomes in terms of observable student behaviors. They also describe how the behavior will be demonstrated and at what proficiency level the behavior is to be performed. The specification of objectives is necessary to ensure the alignment of the goals curriculum and is required before the design of any assessments.

Examples of behavioral objectives include:

- Using a computer spreadsheet program, enter the assigned data set in one 40-minute class.
- Differentiate between an adverb and adjective by using each in the same sentence.
- Using a ruler and a protractor, draw 45-, 90-, and 120-degree angles.

## *Taxonomies of Educational Objectives*

Educational outcomes vary in their complexity and in terms of the types of knowledge being addressed. In the development of educational objectives, a taxonomy or classification system is needed. One of the oldest and most widely used has been the hierarchy of intellectual behaviors developed by Benjamin S. Bloom in 1956 and referred to in the literature as **Bloom's Taxonomy of Educational Objectives.** A recent revision of the taxonomy by some of Bloom's students reflects the research and our increased understanding of teaching and learning in the 50 years since the original taxonomy was developed. Expanding on the one-dimensional original taxonomy, the revised taxonomy presents two dimensions: a knowledge dimension and a cognitive dimension. The knowledge dimension describes four categories of knowledge (factual, conceptual, procedural, and metacognitive) along a continuum from concrete to abstract. For example, knowing technical vocabulary (factual knowledge) is less complex than actually knowing how to do something (procedural knowledge).

The cognitive process dimension contains six ways of thinking (remember, understand, apply, analyze, evaluate, and create) along a continuum of cognitive complexity. For example, analyzing something is more complex than simply remembering it. As illustrated in Figure 14.3, the revised taxonomy can be depicted as a matrix of 24 cells representing the intersections of the two dimensions.

It is important when planning instruction to incorporate activities from the full range of levels into students' learning experiences to stimulate and develop

**Figure 14.3 — Taxonomy of Teaching, Learning, and Assessing**

| The Knowledge Dimension | **The Cognitive Process Dimension** | | | | | |
|---|---|---|---|---|---|---|
| | **1**<br>**Remember** | **2**<br>**Understand** | **3**<br>**Apply** | **4**<br>**Analyze** | **5**<br>**Evaluate** | **6**<br>**Create** |
| A. Factual Knowledge | | | | | | |
| B. Conceptual Knowledge | | | | | | |
| C. Procedural Knowledge | | | | | | |
| D. Metacognitive Knowledge | | | | | | |

*Source:* Anderson, L. W., & Krathwohl, D. R. (2001). *A taxonomy for learning,* teaching, *and assessing.* Published by Allyn & Bacon, Boston, MA. Copyright © 2001 by Pearson Education. Reprinted by permission of the publisher.

their intellectual skills. This helps students master what is popularly referred to as higher-order thinking skills. The higher-order thinking skills in the revised taxonomy of educational objectives are analyze, evaluate, and create.

Goals and objectives become the structure that schools and teachers use in making decisions about models of instruction. As described in the following section, several models may be used to achieve these educational goals and objectives.

## Models of Instruction

Historically, teachers have used different strategies, tactics, or methods of instruction depending on their personal talents, the content to be taught, and the interests and abilities of the students. As discussed in Chapter 1, teaching is often described as an art. This does not imply that teachers operate without design or planning; rather, it underscores the need for teachers to understand and be able to use a variety of strategies as they work with students of different abilities, learning styles, and intelligences. "Knowledge of a variety of instructional strategies and the flexibility to change them both within and among lessons are two of the greatest assets a teacher can have" (Borich, 2011, p. 220).

Over the years many models of instruction have been developed. Joyce, Weil, and Calhoun (2009) have categorized models of instruction into four primary families: the information processing family, the social family, the personal family, and the behavioral systems family (see Table 14.3). Rather than selecting a single model of instruction, the effective teacher is familiar with and understands how to use various models within the four families in response to different teaching/learning goals and objectives used with different students. It is not realistic for the beginning teacher to be familiar with the more than 20 models described by Joyce et al. What we have chosen for discussion in the following sections are the models in most common use in the schools today.

### The Information Processing Family of Models

Models of instruction under the information processing family represent a distinct philosophy about how people think and how teachers can affect the way in which

**Table 14.3 — Models of Instruction**

| Models | Orientation | Examples |
|---|---|---|
| Information processing family | Student-centered Constructivism | • Inquiry instruction<br>• Critical/inductive thinking instruction |
| Social family | Student-centered Progressivism | • Cooperative learning<br>• Problem-based instruction |
| Personal family | Rogerian Counseling | • Nondirective instruction |
| Behavioral systems family | Teacher-centered Behaviorism | • Direct instruction<br>• Mastery learning |

students receive, process, and use information. The models are linked to concepts and principles of information processing developed by cognitive psychologists such as Piaget and Vygotsky. Information processing models are associated with constructivist education.

The models vary in the structure of their views about information handling and in the depth of their approach from a narrow focus on memorization to specific types of inductive thinking. Two models of instruction associated with the information processing family of models—inquiry instruction and critical/inductive thinking instruction—are described in the following sections.

## Inquiry Instruction

As described in Chapter 7, **inquiry instruction** was made popular in America by John Dewey at the beginning of the 20th century. This student-centered method of instruction is also referred to as problem solving, the inductive method, creative thinking, the scientific method, or conceptual learning. The underlying presumption of inquiry instruction is that students would prefer to seek knowledge rather than having it provided to them through demonstrations and textbook readings. As the concept has developed, the ultimate form of inquiry instruction occurs when students recognize and identify the problem as well as decide the process and reach the conclusion (Hlebowitsh, 2005; Kellough & Kellough, 2011). Students use the inquiry process to develop a better understanding of current knowledge and to create new knowledge.

In inquiry instruction, the assumption is that students construct their knowledge. The teacher, the classroom, the school, and the community provide the setting and support that will encourage students through the process. Because of differences among students, knowledge is constructed through different processes and patterns of thinking. Through engagement in the learning process, the learner becomes active and assumes responsibility for acquiring and applying knowledge (Orlich, Harder, Callahan, & Gibson, 1998).

Inquiry instruction takes place when a person is faced with a problem or forced choice and he or she actively seeks out an answer to the dilemma. Students generate ideas and then identify ways to test the ideas. The five phases of the inquiry cycle are (1) identification or recognition of the problem, (2) application of thought or exploration of the problem, (3) the gathering and analysis of data, (4) identification of a tentative conclusion, and (5) testing of the conclusion (Hlebowitsh, 2005; Kellough & Kellough, 2011). The sequence of the inquiry process is illustrated in Figure 14.4.

Successful inquiry instruction depends on the effective interaction of students and teachers in a supportive learning environment. Students and teachers must be comfortable with the challenges and the freedoms associated with the student-centered

**Figure 14.4 — The Inquiry Cycle**

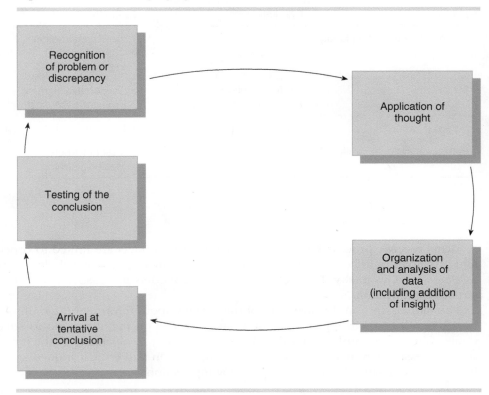

*Source:* Adapted from A *resource guide for teaching* K–12, 5th ed. by R.D. Kellough, 2011. Upper Saddle River, NJ: Prentice Hall. Reprinted by permission of Pearson Education, Inc.

**For Your Reflection and Analysis**

Which information-processing model of instruction would you feel most comfortable using?

dimensions of the inquiry process. Successful inquiry instruction in today's educational environment requires that students have easy access to research tools and educational technology and be free to use them at their own pace.

### Critical/Inductive Thinking Instruction

When the development of **critical thinking** skills is the instructional goal, the student becomes more active and responsible and the teacher becomes less dominant. The teacher initiates, organizes and provides direction for student learning, but the student is an active, rather than passive, participant. The teacher is no longer the center of activity. In both the critical thinking and the inquiry models, the teacher is a guide, facilitator, motivator, stimulator, even a cheerleader who challenges learners. In essence, the teacher empowers students. However, the teacher often assumes the role of the devil's advocate and forces students to defend and explain their positions. A self-evaluation checklist for critical thinkers is presented in the Ask Yourself feature on page 385.

Critical thinking instruction allows teachers and students to become active in identifying and seeking solutions to problems. This model is used in a wide variety of curriculum areas with students of all ages. The process of critical thinking is illustrated in Figure 14.5.

**Figure 14.5 — The Process of Critical Thinking**

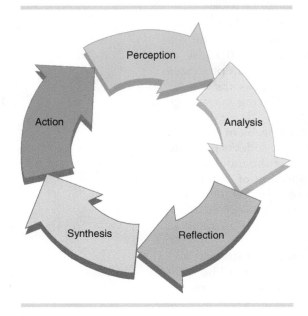

### The Social Family of Models

The social family models combine a belief about learning and a belief about society. Learning is viewed as a socially and intellectually stimulating cooperative behavior; thus,

# ASK YOURSELF

## *Are You a Critical Thinker?*

A critical thinker is one who engages in a process of identification, evaluation, analysis, and synthesis of evidence and information to guide beliefs, actions and decisions. How do you rate yourself as a critical thinker on the following criteria?

A critical thinker:

- Is open-minded and listens to and seeks alternative explanations and conclusions.

- Asks and answers questions that provide clarification.

- Is well informed.

- Uses and judges credible sources.

- Clearly states a thesis or question.

- Remains focused on the primary issue and deals in an orderly manner with the parts of a complex whole.

- Takes the total context/culture into account.

- Is sensitive to the feelings, level of knowledge, and degree of sophistication of others.

- Seeks as much precision as the subject permits.

- Takes a position only when the evidence and reasons are sufficient to do so.

Which criteria give you the most concern? What can you do to improve your critical thinking skills? How would you model critical thinking skills in the classroom? How would you help your students to become critical thinkers?

---

tasks that require social interaction will stimulate learning. A further assumption underlying these models is that a central role of education is to prepare citizens to perpetuate a democratic social order.

Social family models can be used to enhance individual teaching repertoires and also to design entire school environments. The models envision the school as a productive literate society rather than as a collection of individuals acquiring knowledge independently. Two models of instruction have been associated with the social family of models: cooperative learning and problem-based learning.

## Cooperative Learning

In **cooperative learning,** students work in small groups (usually of three to four) to complete an assignment or task. The teacher still has responsibility for setting the stage and working with students, but students work in groups rather than as individuals. Typically the groups are composed of students of varying abilities and are heterogeneous in terms of race, ethnicity, and gender. Because the group often is the unit that is evaluated, students are rewarded for helping one another rather than for competing. The likelihood of failure is reduced and the probability of success is enhanced because of the combined resources of the group.

Although there is no one model of cooperative learning, the steps or phases common to all models include:

1. The teacher goes over the goals of the lesson and motivates students to learn.
2. Information related to the lesson topic is presented, often in the form of printed materials rather than verbal presentations.
3. Students are organized into learning teams and asked to study the material.
4. Students, assisted by the teacher, work together and study.
5. Presentation of the group's work or testing on what students have learned.
6. Recognition of group and individual efforts (Arends & Kilcher, 2010).

Cooperative learning promotes both cognitive and social skills development. Research suggests that cooperative learning is associated with improved collaborative skills, higher self-esteem, and increased academic achievement (Borich, 2011). By working together, students not only develop more cooperative behavior, but they also have the opportunity to exercise leadership. At the same time, they tend to be less competitive and to be more tolerant of differences and accepting of diversity (Arends & Kilcher, 2010). Cooperative learning allows students to reap the

**Reflect on Diversity**
How can cooperative learning be used to promote diversity?

**For Your Reflection and Analysis**

Explain how the role of the teacher under cooperative learning differs from that under direct instruction.

Cooperative learning is one of the most commonly used instructional strategies at both the elementary and secondary levels.

benefits of group success while remaining individually responsible for their personal performance and achievement.

## Problem-Based Learning

**Problem-based learning (PBL)** is a student-centered curriculum model that organizes curriculum and instruction around a real world problem relevant to students. PBL has two main goals. The first is to provide students with the opportunity to identify and explore real-life problems that are relevant to the student. The second is to help students acquire an extensive, integrated knowledge base and set of research and human relations skills that can be recalled and applied to the analysis and solution of future problems. Under PBL, students are responsible for their own learning both individually and as a member of a group. They identify what they need to learn and what resources they are going to use to accomplish that learning. The teacher's role in problem-based learning is to serve as a model, coach, questioner, guide, and mentor:

> As *models* teachers think aloud with students; they model behaviors they want students to use. As *coaches*, teachers coax and prompt students; they provide feedback and encourage students to become independent and self-reliant learners. As *questioners*, they ask higher order and meta-cognitive questions that help focus student inquiry. As *guides*, teachers provide instruction about local community resources, websites, and a variety of valuable textual materials. They also teach students about effective group processes and help groups that are stuck get back on track. In some cases, teachers serve as *mentors* to a select number of students. Mentoring happens most often when students are working on projects where the teacher has particular expertise. (Arends & Kilcher, 2010, p. 327)

The PBL problems that are central to the PBL model should be complex and interdisciplinary and must be relevant to students, as well as authentic. They must be loosely structured learning situations, with just the initial presenting situation to stimulate learners to generate multiple hypotheses about the problems. Learning should be integrated from a wide range of disciplines or subjects. Ideally, PBL should not occur within a single discipline but should integrate several disciplines. Sometimes PBL problems are linked to specific curriculum standards or benchmarks. Other PBL problems may grow out of current issues in the local community or state that are of interest or relevant to students (Arends & Kilcher, 2010).

Collaboration is an essential component of PBL. Learning in PBL takes place within the context of a small group where collaboration is vital to sharing responsibility for group learning and problem solving. Collaboration involves not only sharing tasks, but also managing conflict and team building, as well as demonstrating support and respect for alternative perspectives. As with cooperative learning, teaching collaborative skills is an important role of the teacher when using PBL instruction.

## *The Personal Family of Models*

A major thesis of the personal family of models is that the better-developed, more-affirmative, self-actualizing learners have increased learning capabilities. The assumption underlying the personal family models is that academic achievement can be increased by tending to the needs of individual learners.

Personal family models can be used to moderate the entire learning environment, enhance the personal qualities and feelings of students, and provide opportunities to make students partners in the teaching/learning process. Personal family models are designed to lead the student toward greater mental and emotional health by developing self-confidence and a realistic sense of self and empathy for others (Joyce et al., 2009). In the following discussion, the focus is on one of the personal family models—nondirective instruction.

## Nondirective Instruction

**Nondirective instruction** models bring the student and teacher together in a cooperative effort in deciding what and how the student will learn. The nondirective instruction model is student centered. The role of the teacher is to guide and facilitate student learning and help students identify personal or academic problems or goals and explore how they might be resolved or attained.

The nondirective instruction model has been described by Joyce et al. (2009, pp. 337–38) as consisting of a sequence of five phases:

- *Phase One: Defining the Helping Situation*

  Teacher encourages free expression of feelings.

- *Phase Two: Exploring the Problem*

  Student is encouraged to define the problem.

  Teacher accepts and clarifies feelings.

- *Phase Three: Developing Insight*

  Student discusses problem.

  Teacher supports student.

- *Phase Four: Planning and Decision Making*

  Student plans initial decision making.

  Teacher clarifies possible decisions.

- *Phase Five: Integration*

  Student gains further insight and develops more positive actions.

  Teacher is supportive.

The nondirective model has a variety of potential applications and can be used in conjunction with other models to ensure that the teacher serves as a guide for the student. The model creates an environment in which students and teachers are partners in learning, share ideas openly, and communicate honestly with one another. The model is particularly useful when students are planning independent or cooperative learning.

## The Behavioral Systems Family of Models

Models of instruction under the behavioral systems family umbrella focus on observable skills and behaviors. These models are teacher centered, are typically highly organized, and emphasize student knowledge acquisition and skill development.

The intellectual roots of the behavioral systems model can be traced to the use of Pavlovian principles (Pavlov, 1927) to address the psychological disorders of school-age youth. The efforts were successful with some learners who had been making virtually no progress in language development or development of social skills. Progress also was made with milder forms of learning problems as well as with youth who had severe learning problems. These models of instruction have not only been quite effective with students with disabilities, but with other students as well. Two of the models of instruction classified as belonging to the behavioral systems family are *direct instruction* and *mastery learning*.

## Direct Instruction

**Direct instruction** is a teacher-centered method that is used to convey information. The most common forms of direct instruction are formal lecture, informal lecture, and teacher-led discussion. Direct instruction involves four steps:

Step One: Introduction and Review: the teacher introduces the lesson and reviews prior understanding.

Step Two: Presentation: the new skill is presented, explained, and illustrated with high-quality examples.

Step Three: Guided practice: students practice the skills under the teacher's guidance.

Step Four: Independent practice: students practice the skill on their own.

In direct instruction, the teacher controls and directs the learning process. The teacher also determines the methods of presentation, the pace of instruction, the quantity of supervised practice or reinforcement, and the form of student evaluation. Students are expected to listen, read, and answer questions as the teacher directs.

For direct instruction to be effective, the teacher must recognize that students differ in their levels of competence and that direct instruction requires more extensive and detailed daily lesson planning; for example, possibly the scripting of lectures. The teacher must also ensure that lesson objectives are clearly stated and that instruction is directed to these objectives. The structure and direction of the lecture or discussion should be obvious to the learner. Further, even with extensive preparation and a quality presentation, the teacher must realize that portions of the information contained in a lecture will have to be repeated or re-taught (Hlebowitsh, 2005).

## Mastery Learning

**Mastery learning** is based on the assumptions that all students can master a uniform set of predetermined outcomes given instruction appropriate for their learning style and appropriate reinforcements. Mastery learning is based on the behaviorist theory of education described in Chapter 6. The basic assumptions of mastery learning are as follows:

1. Students can experience success at each phase of the instructional process. The experience of success provides incentive and motivation for further learning.
2. Mastery learning of any subject is possible for every student if the learning units are small enough;
3. Most learning units are sequential and logical;
4. Most learning outcomes can be observed and measured;
5. Students learn at different rates; some students will take longer to achieve mastery than others; and
6. For high-quality learning to occur, the instruction rather than the students must be modified and adapted (Kellough & Kellough, 2011).

Mastery learning is generally taught through **group instruction** and, therefore, is primarily teacher centered.

The mastery learning instructional format assumes that the teacher presents the lesson using the most effective combination of materials and instructional strategies and then administers what is called the first diagnostic or formative test. The purpose of the test is to check learning progress and provide the students with feedback and suggestions to help them overcome any difficulties they are experiencing. After the test, students who have not mastered the material (typically set at 80%) are provided additional instruction or remedial activities. Then a second parallel test is administered to ensure that the students have achieved mastery before the class moves on to the next learning unit. Students who demonstrated mastery on the first formative test are given enrichment activities during the remedial phase of instruction. Students continue the cycle of remediation and testing until mastery is met. No student moves to the next learning unit until at least basic mastery is met.

Mastery learning enables the teacher to address the special needs of students in multicultural environments. However, critics assert that the process has been oversimplified, that mastery of the individual units does not necessarily transfer to future learning, and that students cannot be expected to learn and achieve at the mastery level indefinitely.

## Relationship Between Teaching and Learning

As discussed in Chapter 9, students vary greatly in their learning styles; that is, in the composite of cognitive, affective, and physiological behaviors that indicate how a learner perceives and processes information, solves problems, and responds to problems in the educational environment. Each student's learning style is determined by the interaction of hereditary and environmental influences. Some students learn best through seeing (visual), others learn best by hearing (auditory), while yet others learn best by touching (tactile). Some need structure and directions; others need independence and freedom. Some need total silence; others can function in a noisy environment. The accompanying Historical Note describes the work of Polingaysi Qöyawayma with Hopi students, which emphasized the importance of adapting teaching to the learning styles and experiences of the students.

**Reflect on Diversity**

For what kinds of learner differences should the teacher adjust instruction, as opposed to the student being encouraged to adjust?

## HISTORICAL NOTE

### *Polingaysi Qöyawayma*

Polingaysi Qöyawayma (1892–1990), whose English name is Elizabeth White, was an innovator in shaping American Indian education in the United States and preserving the cultural traditions of the Hopi Indians. As one of nine children in a traditional Hopi family, she was educated by missionaries and taught in schools operated by the Bureau of Indian Affairs (BIA). She was influential in Indian education because of her emphasis on the importance of basing education on the content and examples from the lives of students.

After having first been hidden by her mother to avoid attending the BIA school, in which the Hopi language could not be spoken and students were given English names, Qöyawayma became curious and followed her sister to school. When she heard about an opportunity to attend school in "the land of the oranges," she persevered until her parents reluctantly gave their permission. She rode in a wagon to Winslow, Arizona, and took the train to the Sherman Indian Institute in Riverside, California. She was there for four years without returning home. On her return, she attempted to become a missionary to the Hopis, but she found neither success nor fulfillment because of the conflict with traditional Hopi beliefs.

Polingaysi then became a teacher in the BIA schools. Very soon, she became concerned because the teaching materials, illustrations, and photographs were not within the life experiences of Indian students. To provide a more realistic educational environment, she took the students into the natural surroundings and used Hopi legends, songs, and stories. Students translated these stories into English. Polingaysi's goal was to blend the best of the Hopi culture with the best of white culture and to retain the essence of good from this blend. After initial skepticism, her supervisors began to support her teaching efforts. With the appointment of John Collier as commissioner of Indian affairs, Polingaysi found unexpected support for her teaching methods. She was chosen to demonstrate her teaching methods at a summer institute for BIA teachers. The focus was on starting the teaching/learning process by basing teachings on what students already know, rather than using a totally new set of experiences. When teachers and students met on mutual ground, students tended to come out of their shells and become active learners. In her life as a teacher, Polingaysi learned to meet criticism with serenity and to appreciate the good in both the Hopi and non-Hopi ways of life.

*Source:* Reyhner, J. (1994). Polingaysi Qöyawayma. In M. S. Seller (Ed.), *Women educators in the United States, 1820–1993* (pp. 397–402). Westport, CT: Greenwood.

Learning styles differ: Some students learn better by hearing, others by seeing.

Not only do students vary in their skills and preferences in how they receive information, but they also vary in how they mentally process the information once it has been received. Kellough and Kellough (2011) have identified four types of learners: imaginative, analytic, common sense, and dynamic. They are described as follows:

**For Your Reflection and Analysis**

Which of these learning styles is most like your own?

- The **imaginative learner** perceives information, concretely processes it reflectively, and learns well by listening and sharing with others and integrating the ideas of others with their own experiences. Imaginative learners have difficulty with traditional instruction and may be at-risk students.

- The **analytic learner** perceives information abstractly and processes it reflectively; these learners prefer sequential thinking, need details, value expert thinking, and do well in traditional classrooms.

- The **common sense learner** perceives information abstractly and processes it actively. These learners may find schooling frustrating unless they can see an immediate application; this type of learner is likely to be at risk for dropping out.

- The **dynamic learner** perceives information concretely and processes it actively. These learners prefer hands-on activities, are risk takers, and also may be at risk in traditional classrooms (pp. 207–208).

The determination of a student's learning characteristics requires a consideration of not only the student's preferred learning style, but also the student's developmental stage and learning history. Observations of visual perceptions, language pronunciation, and cognitive thinking provide indications that the student is developmentally ready to learn. Teachers need to have a sufficient understanding of developmental indicators so that they can respond to the indicators.

Learning history refers to the prior learning that a student brings to the learning opportunity. To maximize learning, teachers need to be sensitive to and knowledgeable about each student's learning characteristics (Keefe & Jenkins, 2002).

## Summary

The curriculum found in any school has been influenced by a number of sociopolitical forces, including national curriculum standards, textbooks, mandated assessments, state governments, teachers, local school boards, parent and community groups, and the federal government. The orientation of the curriculum is along a continuum from subject-centered to student-centered. The subject-centered curriculum views the curriculum as a program of studies or collection of courses that represents what students should know. The subject-area design, the integrated curriculum, and the core curriculum are examples of the subject-centered curriculum. The second perspective, the student-centered perspective, focuses on the needs and interests of the student and the process by which learning takes place. The constructivist curriculum is an example of this perspective.

A curriculum standing alone is of little value. Not until it is implemented does it take on meaning. Instruction is the process by which it is implemented. In this chapter instruction was discussed in terms of four broad categories: the information processing models, the social models, the personal models, and the behavioral systems models. Ultimately, the effectiveness of instruction will depend on the extent to which the teacher recognizes and adapts to the learning styles of students and considers student differences in the selection of alternative modes of instruction.

# TEACHER OF THE YEAR

*Jamie Yoos*
*Washington*

You're either now here, or you're nowhere.

I teach Honors Chemistry, AP Chemistry, and bicycle maintenance and that phrase, "you're either now here or you're nowhere," is a reminder both to me and to my students as we step into the classroom. I ask my students to be more than just "present" in my classroom —I ask them to be active participants, to *own* their learning and their understanding. My students recognize that learning is an active process. As their teacher I also need to be more than just present in the classroom; I must be keenly aware of my students' strengths and weaknesses so that I can challenge them or support them as needed. I truly believe in the field of education, and I believe the U.S. public education system has the potential to be the great social equalizer. All students can learn, and because of this I will continue in my field of education. I believe and have hope in our future.

# PROFESSIONAL DEVELOPMENT
## *Workshop*

### *Prepare for the State Licensure Examination*

Levi Burlington, a fourth-grade teacher, is a five-year veteran working in an elementary school with an enrollment of 380 students. The school population has 90% free or reduced lunch, and the majority of the students come from single-parent homes. The teaching faculty is almost evenly split between novice teachers (fewer than two years in the classroom) and experienced teachers nearing retirement. The school is on the watch list in terms of annual yearly progress under the No Child Left Behind Act. Some progress has been made in improving scores, but overall improvement goals have not been achieved.

Dr. Carolyn Bright is starting her second year at the school, having replaced an administrator who had been at the school since it was constructed 27 years ago. This is Dr. Bright's first administrative position; she has just completed her dissertation. Her topic was related to identification of gifted students, and her experience has been in upper-income suburban communities.

At the beginning of the school year, Dr. Bright called Levi to her office to discuss ways to "reinvent" the school with the primary focus of school improvement. To help frame the task, Dr. Bright asked Levi to review the organization of the school's instructional goals and objectives, individual teachers' methods of organizing instruction, their teaching strategies, and finally learning styles of the students.

1. How do goals and the implementation of instructional objectives influence the education of the students?
2. Why do teachers need to understand learning styles and instructional strategies?
3. What are the major provisions of the No Child Left Behind Act?

## Build Your Knowledge Base

1. As a new teacher like Mary Sherman in the opening vignette, how would you respond to a parent who is critical of the school's curriculum?
2. How would you define the terms *curriculum* and *hidden curriculum?* Should the lessons of the hidden curriculum be incorporated into the formal curriculum? If not, how can they be dealt with by the teacher? Should they be dealt with?
3. Which of the agencies or groups discussed in this chapter has had the most influence on the curriculum in your district in the last five years?
4. Which of the curriculum designs discussed in this chapter is most consistent with your philosophy of education as identified in Chapter 4?
5. Do you think you would be a better teacher if you used only one mode of instruction?
6. How can teachers best determine the learning styles of their students?

## Develop Your Portfolio

1. Many educators believe that with the enactment of state accountability and assessment programs, as well as the adoption of state and national content standards, teachers tend to have less control over curriculum and instruction. Prepare a position paper that either agrees or disagrees with this idea. Place your position paper in your portfolio under **INTASC Standard 7, Planning for Instruction**.
2. Review Table 14.2, Perspectives on Curriculum Organization, on page 376. Using "Constructivism" as the curriculum design, select three learning activities from your particular field of study that encourage students to construct their own meaning based on current

and past knowledge and experience. Place your learning activities in your portfolio under **INTASC Standard 4, Content Knowledge**.

3. Review the process of critical thinking illustrated in Figure 14.5 on page 384 and collect examples of how each step in the process can be applied to curriculum and instruction in your field of study. Place the artifacts in your portfolio under **INTASC Standard 7, Planning for Instruction**.

## Explore Teaching and Learning: Field Experiences

1. Contact the director of curriculum in a school district and arrange for an interview or a review of available documents to determine the curriculum process used in the district to develop new components of a curriculum; that is, the process for planning, design, pilot testing, implementation, and evaluation. Who has input into this process: teachers, administrators, students, parents, community leaders, outside experts?

2. Arrange for an interview with a central office administrator in a school district to determine the process used in adopting textbooks. Who has input into this process: teachers, administrators, students, parents, community leaders, consultants?

3. Contact the principal of a nearby school and make an appointment to observe a classroom lesson that uses cooperative learning strategies. Write a brief observation report that includes the objective of the lesson, a description of how children had to cooperate to complete assignments, your assessment of the percentage of time that students were on task and not "goofing off," and the roles that students with different talents played in cooperatively completing the lesson.

## MyEducationLab

Go to **Topic 10, Curriculum and Instruction,** in the MyEducationLab (www.myeducationlab.com) for *Foundations of American Education,* where you can:

- ·Find learning outcomes for curriculum and instruction, along with the national standards that connect to these outcomes.
- Complete Assignments and Activities that can help you more deeply understand the chapter content.
- Apply and practice your understanding of the core teaching skills identified in the chapter with the Building Teaching Skills and Dispositions learning units.
- Examine challenging situations and cases presented in the IRIS Center Resources.

- Access additional video clips of CCSSO National Teachers of the Year award winners responding to the question, "Why Do I Teach?" in the Teacher Talk section.
- Check your comprehension on the content covered in the chapter with the Study Plan. Here you will be able to take a chapter quiz, receive feedback on your answers, and then access Review, Practice, and Enrichment activities to enhance your understanding of chapter content.
- Use the Online Lesson Plan Builder to practice lesson planning and integrating national and state standards into your planning.

# chapter Fifteen

# Standards and Assessment

Mary Jordan is a sixth-grade teacher at Longmore Elementary School. Longmore is an inner-city school with 70% of its students on free and reduced lunch. Three quarters of its student population is minority. Longmore has been classified as a "needs improvement" school as detailed in No Child Left Behind (NCLB). The faculty has worked with a consultant over the past two years to develop and implement a school improvement plan, and state assessment scores have improved. However, Longmore still has not been able to meet adequate yearly progress (AYP). This means that Longmore will enter NCLB's "corrective action status."

A faculty meeting has been called to discuss the consequences and responses to the school's corrective action status. As the meeting begins, some teachers express concern that they might be dismissed. Others are angry and feel that they have not been given the resources they need to turn the school around. Soon discussion turns to the test itself. The question is raised as to whether the test is really an accurate measure for the students at Longmore. "The content on these national tests does not reflect the educational and life experiences of our students. We should refuse to administer that test again until they give a version appropriate for our students. It is not fair to them and it makes them feel 'less than,'" one teacher, Marvin Kehoe, declares.

As the conversation continues, the sentiment moves toward a strategy that could be considered "teaching to the test." Mary articulates what others seem to be feeling: "I know that if we focus on the test we may be taking time away from the regular curriculum, but if this is what we're being judged on, if this is what my job depends on, then I say, 'If you can't beat 'em, join 'em.'" Although Scott Johnson, the music teacher, feels some discomfort with the idea of teaching to the test, he agrees and suggests they get practice tests from private publishers and try to obtain test items from the previous year's test. Susan Moore, the reading teacher, suggests another strategy: "I think we should also try to teach test-taking skills. I know that will mean less time to teach the regular curriculum, but I feel more comfortable teaching test-taking skills than teaching to the test." The meeting ends with no resolution but with the agreement to continue the discussion next week.

1. Do you agree with Mary's suggestion to teach to the test? Is there anything wrong with teaching to the test?

2. How much time would you be willing to take from the regular curriculum to focus on the test or to teach test-taking skills?

3. Do you agree with Marvin's suggestion that Longmore boycott the test? What are the consequences of such action?

4. How can the faculty make their concerns about test bias and lack of resources known to policymakers?

As discussed in Chapter 7, standards, assessment, and accountability have become the centerpieces of the school reform agenda and the federal No Child Left Behind Act. U.S. students take an estimated 68 million tests annually to meet the requirements of NCLB (Scherer, 2005). The

Logical-mathematical intelligence is the basis for the hard sciences.

importance of standards, assessment, and accountability is evidenced by the fact that all states have adopted academic content standards and statewide assessment systems to hold schools accountable for student achievement.

This chapter begins with a discussion of standards and their role in the assessment process. Next we discuss the meaning of assessment in the context of education and its purposes. This is followed by a description of the two major types of assessment, standardized assessment and classroom assessment. We also discuss the assessment tools that are used with each type of assessment. Next we focus on the criteria for quality assessment, and the chapter concludes with a discussion of standards-based education and assessment. After reading this chapter and participating in class discussion, you should be able to do the following:

- Explain the role of standards in the assessment process.
- Define *assessment* and enumerate the major purposes of assessment.
- Explain the major differences between formal—or standardized—assessment, and informal—or classroom—assessment.
- List the various tools for classroom assessment.
- Explain the criteria for fair and accurate assessment.
- Explain the difference between traditional and standards-based assessment.

# Standards

Standards in education are benchmarks used to compare curriculum, instruction, and student learning, as discussed in Chapter 14. The three kinds of standards commonly referred to in education today are curriculum content standards, performance standards, and opportunity to learn standards. **Curriculum content standards** are defined as the appropriate content of a particular academic discipline that students at a specific grade level are expected to learn or be able to do. For example, a standard for geography might be: "Students should know the capitals of each of the 50 states in the United States." **Performance standards** are the levels of achievement expected of students at specific grade level(s) on specific assessments. For example, on the scoring rubric for the creative writing assignment presented in Figure 15.3 on page 404, the performance standard to receive a score of 4 points (Excellent) on Argument/Evidence is: "Evidence and or argument are creatively presented and strongly support the work." A less-discussed standard, **opportunity to learn standard**, specifies the resources and conditions necessary for students to achieve the performance standards. The NCLB requirement that every child be taught by a highly qualified teacher is one example of an opportunity to learn standard.

## *Curriculum Content Standards*

Curriculum content standards broadly describe what students should know or be able to do in a specific discipline. The first wide-scale effort to develop curriculum content standards was undertaken by the major national associations of teachers of specific disciplines, beginning with the first set of published standards in 1989 by the National Association of Teachers of Mathematics. Other disciplines soon followed. As described in Chapter 14, these standards not only identified what students should know and be able to do, but also called for more rigorous content and stimulated curriculum reform nationwide. These standards have been adopted in total or in part by many states. For other states the standards served as the basis for the development of state curriculum content standards. As previously discussed, more recently, the Common Core State Standards developed by the Common Core State Standards Initiative of the National Governors' Association and the Commission of Chief State School Officers have been adopted by 41 states to date. While currently only for English Language Arts and Mathematics, standards for other disciples are planned. Their widespread adoption does give substance to the concept of national curriculum standards.

State standards provide the framework for what is taught in the schools. Schools attempt to align the curriculum with these standards. The state curriculum standards also provide the framework for the statewide assessment. A sample of one state's curriculum standards, Florida's standards for grades 9–12 geometry, was presented in Table 14.1 on page 373.

The broadly stated curriculum standards are broken down into benchmarks which detail the specific knowledge and skills students should acquire at each grade level. For example, the following benchmarks for grades 6–9 are associated with the Iowa Core Science Content Standard, "Students can understand concepts and relationships in life science":

1. Students can understand structures of living things.
2. Students can understand life cycles.
3. Students can understand environmental interaction and adaptation.

## Performance Standards

Performance standards "describe the things students can perform or do once the content standards are learned" (Nitko & Brookhart, 2011, p. 9). The establishment of performance standards involves the judgment of one or more persons knowledgeable about the students or the content. This person decides when or to what extent a standard has been met. For example, there is no absolute that says a score of 78, as opposed to a score of 77 or 79, on a statewide assessment should be considered proficient. Similarly, the setting of standards of student performance on a scoring rubric, described later in this chapter, involves the subjective judgment of the teacher. However, it is an informed judgment based on professional standards for grading.

## Opportunity to Learn Standards

Opportunity to learn standards define the conditions and resources necessary for students to have an equal opportunity to learn the material on which they are to be tested. Opportunity to learn standards may include curriculum, educational experiences, instructional materials, facilities, information resources, and teachers. State standards related to class size or required classroom square footage per student are examples of opportunity to learn standards. Concerns such as those expressed by the Longmore faculty in the opening vignette about inadequate resources being made available to help students meet the AYP performance standards have led to proposals in some states to develop opportunity to learn standards that align with the content and performance standards.

Figure 15.1 illustrates the relationship between curriculum, performance, and opportunity to learn standards. The learner is the focus of each of these standards.

Standards define the knowledge and skills students need to know, the performance level they are to achieve, and the resources and conditions necessary to achieve the standards. However, standards are but hollow words unless some determination is made of the extent to which the standards have been met. This determination is made by the process of assessment, discussed in the following section.

**For Your Reflection and Analysis**

Who should decide the proficiency score on a statewide high stakes test? The state legislature? The state department of education? A panel of educators? A panel of parents?

**Reflect on Diversity**
Why might opportunity to learn standards be more likely to benefit minority students than majority students?

**Figure 15.1 — Relationship Between Curriculum Content, Performance, and Opportunity to Learn Standards**

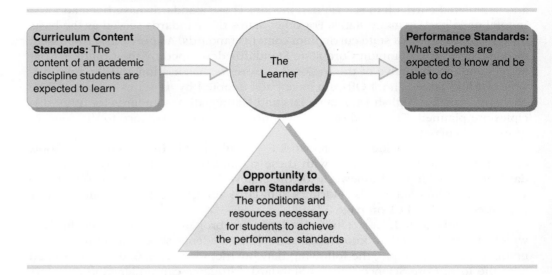

## Assessment

**Assessment** describes any process or activity used to collect information about students' knowledge, skills, aptitude, or attitudes. Assessment should be an integral part of the instructional planning process discussed in Chapter 14, not something that takes place *after* instruction ends. Historically, assessment has been used to intimidate or motivate students. As discussed in Chapter 7, under NCLB assessment is used to determine whether schools are making adequate yearly progress. In some states the statewide assessment is a high-stakes test that determines graduation from high school or promotion to the next grade level.

Statewide testing practices, particularly high-stakes testing, have been the subject of considerable controversy. Critics, including those featured in the Video Insight, "The Test," charge that, like Mary and Susan in the opening vignette thought might happen, teachers spend too much time preparing students for a test that neither reflects what is being taught nor accurately measures student learning (Nichols & Berliner, 2005). In effect, they are saying that the test is not serving the purposes of assessment described in the following section. Other arguments against state and federal mandated assessment as well as arguments in support of these tests are presented in the Controversial Issue feature on page 399.

### *Purposes of Assessment*

There are six major purposes of assessment. All either directly or indirectly involve the learner. Some serve immediate purposes (e.g., deciding the final grade in a class), while other purposes may be long range. The six most common purposes of assessment mentioned in the literature are discussed below.

### To Inform Instruction and Promote Student Learning

The primary goal of assessment should be to gather information about student understanding and skills so that decisions can be made about what and how to teach next. This purpose of assessment is referred to as formative assessment. Formative assessment provides the teacher with the information needed to decide whether to move on to the next unit or whether further review on the current material is needed. It can also provide insight into the effectiveness of the way students are trying to learn. If students are trying to learn by problem solving, for example, and assessment indicates students do not have mastery of the content, then perhaps the teacher may want to use drill and practice. Formative assessment must be used *during* an instructional

# VIDEO INSIGHT

## The Test

In this video, proponents and opponents of Florida's high-stakes testing program discuss the results of its implementation in terms of the large number of students who are required to repeat a grade or are denied graduation. Governor Jeb Bush maintains that the strict use of the test, combined with the support students receive to help them pass the test, has resulted in increased achievement. This argument is counterbalanced by numerous testimonials of parents and students about how demoralizing the test and the use of the results have become.

1. Large numbers are failing the FCAT (Florida Comprehensive Assessment Test). What does this say about the curriculum of the Florida schools?

2. One student talked about the fact that she had a GPA of 2.8 but did not pass the FCAT and was being denied graduation. To what do you attribute this situation? How do you think this occurred?

3. What, if any, testing accommodation should be made for students from disadvantaged homes or homes where English is not the primary language?

# CONTROVERSIAL ISSUE

## State and Federal Mandated Assessments

The role of the federal government in K–12 education changed with enactment of the assessment requirements in the No Child Left Behind Act. Experiences with federal guidelines, regulations, state interpretations, and local efforts to implement the NCLB Act, as well as separate, but related, state accountability programs, have resulted in achievement tests in the elementary grades and high school proficiency examinations. Reports refer to the performance of the school, not the students attending the school. Pros and cons about the legislation range from strong support to outright opposition:

**For**

1. Focus on the performance of students and schools rather than districts and states.

2. Disclosure of test performance information to the community, state agencies, and federal government.

3. Support for the federal interest in a well-trained workforce.

4. Continued interest in federal funds to provide programs and services for youth with special needs.

5. Assurances of students being accorded due process and access to programs.

**Against**

1. Insufficient funds for purchase and administration of the tests.

2. Excessive school time used for testing.

3. Possible narrowing of the curriculum as emphasis is placed on teaching for the test.

4. Questions about the capacity of any national assessment instrument to measure achievement in view of the cultural and ethnic differences of the students.

5. Federal action of this magnitude contrary to traditional governance of education in the United States.

As a prospective teacher, do you endorse the federal government becoming more active in governance of education? Should student achievement test data be used in evaluating teachers and determining their continued employment?

unit so there is time left to adjust the approaches to teaching and learning currently being employed. "Formative assessment is a loop: students and teachers focus on a learning target, evaluate current student work against the target, act to move the work closer to the target, and repeat" (Nitko & Brookhart, 2011, p. 141).

### To Diagnose Individual Student Learning Strengths and Weaknesses

**Diagnostic assessment**, also called preassessment, is used before instruction begins to assess the level of the student's knowledge and skills and to identify student interests and learning-style preferences. Diagnostic assessment can provide valuable information to inform instructional planning and to guide teachers in adapting instruction to meet individual student needs. Among the common preassessment tools are skills charts, concept maps, pretests of content knowledge, and K-W-L (Know–Want to Learn–Learn) charts.

### To Assess Student Achievement

**Summative assessment** assesses students' knowledge level or proficiency and is often made for reporting purposes, whether it be to the state or federal government or to students or parents in the form of final grades. For example, a teacher may use an end-of-unit exam or a best-works portfolio in determining the final grade for a course. However, a statewide standardized test would be used to assess student mastery of state curriculum standards.

### To Compare the Performance of Students

There are numerous reasons why students are ranked or compared. These include: selection for honors, scholarships, and college admissions or entrance to special classes or programs. Such comparisons are typically made using **norm-referenced assessments** such as the PSAT, which is used in deciding National Merit Scholars, or the Wechsler Intelligence Scale for Children, which is used in special education placement decisions. Norm-referenced assessments facilitate the comparison of students by reporting student scores in terms of percentile ranks, grade equivalent scores, or other measures that can be used for comparison purposes.

### To Assist Students in Making Decisions About Courses of Study or Career Planning

There are a variety of diagnostic assessments to help students decide what courses of study or careers they should consider. For example, career development checklists or career interest inventories can help students identify careers where the student has the greatest potential for success.

### To Evaluate Schools, Inform Program Decisions, and Evaluate Teachers

The results of an assessment can be used to measure a school's effectiveness. NCLB refers to this as determining whether the school is making AYP. As described in Chapter 7, if a school fails to make AYP for two years in a row, it is classified as "needs improvement" and must implement a school improvement plan. Then, if it does not make AYP for two consecutive years it enters "corrective action," as did Longmore in the opening vignette. If it does not make AYP at the end of a year of corrective action, the school enters restructuring status and the district is required to prepare a restructuring plan. This plan is implemented at the end of the next year if the school does not make AYP. Restructuring can include the replacement of staff, conversion to a charter school, or even closure.

School-level assessment data are also used for other purposes. For instance, it can be used to inform decisions about allocation of human and material resources or to implement school improvement programs. For example, NCLB requires that schools in corrective action must allocate at least 10% of their Title 1-A funds to staff improvement. And, as discussed in previous chapters, student assessment data are increasingly being used in the evaluation of teachers.

An array of assessment alternatives can serve the above purposes. It is important that teachers be knowledgeable about these alternatives and that they know the strengths and weakness of each alternative. It is also important that teachers be able to choose the assessment tools that are most appropriate for their own instructional goals and objectives as well as for the social, cultural, ethnic, and language background of students. Some of the more commonly used standardized and classroom assessment alternatives are discussed in the following sections.

## Standardized Assessment

The assessment alternatives available to teachers are typically classified as formal, or standardized, assessments and informal, or classroom, assessments. Standardized assessments are data-driven assessments. The results of standardized assessments are those most often reported in the media and discussed by policymakers. The two principal types of standardized assessment are the standardized achievement test and the standardized aptitude test or IQ (intelligent quotient) test. **Standardized tests** are administered, scored, and interpreted using specific guidelines and uniform standards. Standardized tests are developed by test construction experts. Directions for administration, scoring, and interpretation of standardized tests are presented in a manual that accompanies the test and are explicit. Standardized tests may be individual or group-administered and are available for most academic subjects.

The most commonly used standardized test is the multilevel battery achievement test, which contains several subtests (e.g., reading, language arts, and mathematics). Single-level achievement tests are also available for one subject. Many state-mandated achievement tests are standards-based achievement tests that have been customized by test developers to assess mastery of the state curriculum standards. Some states use one of the nationally standardized tests (e.g., the California Achievement Test, the Iowa Test of Basic Skills, the Metropolitan Achievement Test, Stanford Achievement Tests, or the Terra Nova).

The National Assessment of Educational Progress (NAEP), referred to as the "Nation's Report Card," is also a standardized test. The NAEP is administered annually to a sample of 4th-, 8th-, and 12th-grade students nationwide. The NAEP does not address any specific set of standards but is a general assessment of student knowledge in several subject areas. Not every subject and grade level is assessed every year, but they rotate. The results of the NAEP provide an indicator of how students are achieving nationwide as well as over time. Results are not reported by school or district, only by state, grade level, and selected student variables. Comparisons of NAEP results with results on statewide assessment provide an indicator of the rigor of the state assessment, a topic of concern among educators and policymakers (see discussion in Chapter 7).

Most standardized tests are **norm-referenced tests**, which compare the performance of one student to that of other students of the same age and grade (the norm group). Schools can also be compared to one another using norm-referenced tests. The tests are generally used for accountability and reporting purposes or for screening purposes to determine eligibility for special programs. "Because the format of these tests is generally multiple choice, the diagnostic

**For Your Reflection and Analysis**

What type of assessment data would be of most value to a school attempting to implement a school improvement program?

**For Your Reflection and Analysis**

Explain what is meant when test developers are referred to as the "gatekeepers of knowledge."

Standardized tests are administered, scored, and interpreted using specific guidelines and uniform standards.

**Reflect on Diversity**
How might students be disadvantaged by the selection of the norm group?

information that can be obtained is limited . . . (and) provides little information that can be used to develop specific instructional programs" (Spinelli, 2011, p. 65).

Standardized tests can also be **criterion-referenced tests**. These tests do not compare one student's scores to other students'. Criterion-referenced tests compare scores to a performance standard or criterion of mastery. Some statewide assessments are criterion-referenced tests, which assess student mastery of state-adopted curriculum standards.

**Aptitude tests** are used to determine an individual's intelligence quotient (IQ) and to predict success in a future setting. Aptitude testing is required by the IDEA for diagnosis and determination of eligibility for several classifications of special education services.

## Classroom Assessment

Classroom assessment is more directly and clearly related to standards, the curriculum, and to instruction than standardized assessment. **Classroom assessment** is used to assess student progress and inform practice. Classroom assessments are most often designed by the teacher as opposed to a commercial test developer. The teacher is also the test administrator, which may not be true for a standardized assessment. Classroom assessment also occurs more frequently than standardized assessment. In fact, a teacher engages in some form of classroom assessment daily, whether observing student progress in working on a group assignment or administering an end-of-unit exam. It is usually necessary for the teacher to use more than one of these assessment strategies to meet a particular instructional goal or to accurately assess learning. For example,

> Matching exercises . . . emphasize recall and recognition of factual information; essay questions emphasize organizing ideas and demonstrating writing skills under the pressure of time limits; and a month-long project emphasizes freely using resources, and research to more thoroughly analyze the topic. All three of these assessment techniques may be needed to ascertain the extent to which a student has achieved a given learning target. (Nitko & Brookhart, 2011, p. 5)

Some of the most commonly used classroom assessment strategies are discussed below.

### Observation Assessment

**Observation assessment** is perhaps the most common and under-rated method of classroom assessment. Teachers formally or informally observe students throughout the day. Observation assessment requires systematic collecting, recording, and scoring of observable student behavior. The most commonly used tools for these tasks are anecdotal records, checklists, and rating scales. As described by Taylor and Nolen (2008),

> An anecdotal record is a written description of student behaviors in relation to target learning objectives. . . .
> A checklist is a list of the behaviors you expect to see along with a place to check whether each specific behavior is present or absent, right or wrong. A rating scale is similar to a checklist except that, instead of indicating whether the behavior is present or absent, right or wrong, the teacher rates the behaviors on a rating scale. Rating scales can indicate how often something happens or how well something is done. (p. 107)

A sample rating scale and checklist using the same set of criteria are illustrated in Figure 15.2.

### Performance Assessment

**Performance assessment** is a method of assessment that requires students to produce, create, analyze, perform, problem solve, experiment, explain, debate, demonstrate, or otherwise perform a task to demonstrate their skills and

**Figure 15.2 — Checklist and Rating Scale for Assessing the Design of an Experiment**

————— 1. Describes the problem
————— 2. States hypotheses
————— 3. Specifies variables that must be controlled
————— 4. Clarifies independent and dependent variables
————— 5. Makes at least three measurements of dependent variables
————— 6. Organizes data in a chart or table
————— 7. Writes a description of results

Rate each item. A rating of 5 is excellent, and a rating of 1 is poor.

5 4 3 2 1   1. Describes the problem clearly
5 4 3 2 1   2. States hypotheses clearly
5 4 3 2 1   3. Controls variables effectively
5 4 3 2 1   4. Gathers data appropriately
5 4 3 2 1   5. Presents data clearly
5 4 3 2 1   6. Draws logical conclusions

*Source:* Jacobson, D. A., Eggen, P., & Kauchak, D. (2009). *Methods for teaching: Promoting student learning in K–12 classrooms* (8th ed.). Boston: Allyn & Bacon/Pearson, p. 341.

understanding. Performance assessment broadens the type of student learning that can be assessed and provides students a variety of ways to demonstrate their learning (Nitko & Brookhart, 2011). Performance assessment can be conducted using checklists, rating scales, or scoring rubrics.

A **rubric** details the desired performance criteria for the task, the levels of performance, and the grades or points assigned to each level of performance. Rubrics serve teachers and students by providing clear expectations for performance and serve as the basis for feedback and improvement. They also serve to make the assessment consistent and objective. There are two types of rubrics: holistic rubrics and analytic rubrics. Holistic rubrics are used to evaluate an entire project or activity while analytic rubric assess individual components of the project or activity. Most rubrics have between three and six levels of performance, depending on the complexity of the performance being assessed. On the sample rubric used to evaluate dance performance presented in Figure 15.3, five performance criteria are being used, with four levels of performance for each.

The term *performance assessment* is sometimes used interchangeably with the term *authentic assessment*, but the two are not the same. Performance assessment refers to what student response is being assessed, while authentic assessment refers to assessment based on tasks that are "authentic," "real life," or meaningful to the student (e.g., a personal journal). Performance assessment need not be authentic, but authentic assessments are necessarily performance assessments.

According to Nitko and Brookhart (2011), the advantages of performance assessment are:

- Performance assessment is consistent with modern learning theory, which emphasizes that students should use their previous knowledge to build new knowledge structures, be actively involved in exploration and inquiry, and construct meaning for themselves from educational experiences.

- Performance assessments may be linked more closely with teaching activities than are tests.

- Using performance assessment along with traditional objective formats broadens the types of learning targets you assess and offers students a variety of ways of expressing their learning. This increases the validity of your student evaluations. (pp. 193)

**For Your Reflection and Analysis**

Which would be the more complex performance to assess: a creative dance or a science experiment? Why?

**Figure 15.3 — Creative Writing Rubric**

Student: _____

| | **Poor**<br>**1 pt** | **Fair**<br>**2 pts** | **Good**<br>**3 pts** | **Excellent**<br>**4 pts** |
|---|---|---|---|---|
| **Argument/Evidence** | Poor<br>No argument and/ or evidence has been provided. | Fair<br>Evidence is included but does not support the work. | Good<br>Evidence and/or argument are presented and somewhat support the work. | Excellent<br>Evidence and/or argument are creatively presented and strongly support the work. |
| **Context/Use of Fact** | Poor<br>Facts are not presented. | Fair<br>Minimal amount of fact is presented and weakly used to support the work. | Good<br>Appropriate facts are used in a creative and effective way. | Excellent<br>Facts are presented in a creative manner and demonstrate a sufficient knowledge base. |
| **Role Assumption** | Poor<br>Piece does not reflect the character or situation. | Fair<br>An attempt to get into the role and situation has been made but is not consistent. | Good<br>Piece reflects the role and situation effectively with consideration for time period. | Excellent<br>Role and situation are assumed with creativity and effectiveness. |
| **Format/Organization** | Poor<br>There is no resemblance to selected format. | Fair<br>An attempt to follow rules of format is evident but not complete. | Good<br>There is little deviation from format. The piece may be over or under length. | Excellent<br>Format has been followed correctly and creatively. |
| **Persuasiveness** | Poor<br>Piece does not convey required components. | Fair<br>Piece attempts to convince audience of requirements but is not effective. | Good<br>Piece is effective in its attempt to convey believability. | Excellent<br>Piece is creative and effective in conveying believability. |

*Source:* Retrieved June 21, 2008, from http://www.rcampus.com/rubricprintpostc_cfm?Kd92w3rfl=%2Frubricprinteditc%2Ecfm%3F&

## Portfolio Assessment

**Portfolio assessment** involves the assessment of a student product, a portfolio. A portfolio is a planned collection of student work, assembled and maintained by the student or the teacher over a period of time for the purpose of documenting learning. Portfolios can be best works or student growth portfolios. *Best-work portfolios* contain samples of student work selected by the teacher with or without the input of the student that showcase the student's best work. *Growth portfolios* monitor progress and show student growth in meeting specific standards or goals across a period of time. The portfolio includes not only the final product but also earlier drafts, preliminary experiments, and so on. Students not only participate in the selection of other exhibits to include in the portfolio, but may be required to reflect on why each entry was selected and what it was intended to show. Teachers may include samples of student work, anecdotal notes, or other information the teacher believes demonstrates the student's academic or personal development. Portfolio assessment can be accomplished using checklists; rating scales; or, more commonly, rubrics.

The advantages of portfolio assessment are detailed in Table 15.1.

## Table 15.1— Advantages of Portfolio Assessment

- Provide criteria for evaluating and monitoring individual student progress
- Provide criteria for evaluating program and curriculum effectiveness
- Provide criteria for grading
- Measure students' specific strengths and weaknesses
- Diagnose students' instructional needs
- Inform classroom instructional planning and improve instructional effectiveness
- Measure growth in second-language students
- Promote reflective practice at the school and classroom levels
- Encourage student efficacy
- Support student involvement in the assessment process by allowing students to select submissions
- Promote student development in self-assessment strategies
- Motivate students to monitor and improve their performance
- Promote focus on personal growth and improvement rather than on comparisons with peers
- Provide for clear communication of learning progress to students, parents, and others
- Allow for adjustment in individual differences
- Encourage the collection of work samples
- Provide for multidimensional assessments in authentic contexts over time
- Illustrate the range of classroom learning experiences
- Allow students to demonstrate the scope of their skill mastery
- Encourage dialogue, reflection, and collaboration among teachers, parents, and students

*Source:* Spinelli, C. G. (2012). *Classroom assessment for students in special and general education* (3rd ed., p. 125). Upper Saddle River, NJ: Merrill/Pearson.

## Teacher-Made Tests and Quizzes

The most common form of classroom assessment is teacher-made tests and quizzes. Teacher-made tests and quizzes take a variety of formats, including essay, short answer, fill-in-the-blank, multiple-choice, true–false, and matching assessments. Teacher-made tests and quizzes tend to focus on whether the student has acquired specific content knowledge or cognitive skills. Constructing high-quality tests and quizzes can be difficult and time consuming, but if properly conducted, they allow the teacher to target assessment to specific standards and to what was actually taught. They also allow the teacher to direct attention to any area that the teacher feels would provide information valuable to the improvement of instruction or learning.

Whatever strategy of classroom assessment is used, it should be directly and clearly related to state and district standards and to the curriculum. A useful tool for helping teachers design classroom assessments that accurately address standards, as well as identify achievement objectives to be assessed is a table of specifications. The general format for a *table of specifications* is presented in Table 15.2. A table

## Table 15.2 — Table of Specifications for Geometry Test (Standards from Table 14.2)

| Standard | Level of Skill | | | |
| --- | --- | --- | --- | --- |
| | Knowledge | Comprehension | Application | Analysis & synthesis |
| Find measures of angles, rules, perimeter and areas of polygons | 2 items | 2 items | | 6 items |
| Identify and describe various kinds of triangles | 2 items | 2 items | 8 items | |
| Apply the Pythagorean theory to find altitude of right triangle | 2 items | | | 8 items |
| Find measure of arcs and angles related to them | 2 items | 2 items | 4 items | 4 items |

of specifications is a simple table that addresses two essential questions regarding the standard: (1) What must students learn (the standards/benchmarks) and (2) What level or type of skill is required (knowledge, comprehension, application, or analysis). By matching assessment items to the elements in the table of specifications, teachers can ensure that there is a match between what is taught and what is assessed and that the assessment measures all the important skills and abilities associated with the standard; i.e., that the assessment has content validity. It also assures that the assessment includes a variety of items that require different levels of cognition.

Standardized and classroom assessment strategies can provide the information teachers, parents, students, and policymakers need *if* they meet the criteria for quality assessment. These criteria are described in the following section.

## Criteria for Quality Assessment

Assessments are of no value unless they are fair and accurate. The increased importance placed on accountability in the current political climate has increased the importance of ensuring that assessments are fair and accurate. Fair and accurate assessment provides the information that teachers need to plan and evaluate instruction; diagnose and meet learner needs; and provide appropriate feedback to students, parents, and policymakers. Assessment that is not fair and accurate will have a negative impact on decisions about instruction and students. Three general criteria are used to determine whether an assessment tool is fair and accurate: (1) absence of bias, (2) reliability, and (3) validity. Generally, **absence of bias** means that the tool provides an accurate assessment of different subgroups and that each student being assessed has an equal opportunity to demonstrate their knowledge or skills relative to the subject of the assessment. **Reliability** is concerned with whether the tool consistently yields the same result. **Validity** addresses the issue of whether the assessment tool measures what it is intended to measure. Each of these criteria is discussed in the following sections as they relate both to standardized and to classroom assessments.

### *Absence of Bias*

The bias of an assessment instrument refers to the "qualities of an assessment instrument that offend or unfairly penalize a group of students because of the students' gender, race, ethnicity, socioeconomic status, religion, or other such group-defining characteristics" (Popham, 2011, p. 111). In effect, Marvin's concern about the state test in the opening vignette was that it was biased against Longmore's inner-city, minority students. Language and content can create bias against some student subgroups and cause them to not perform as well on an assessment. For example, a mathematics question that asks students to calculate measurements using information related to a football field might complicate the questions for females or for immigrant students who are not familiar with American football.

The issue of fairness is of particular concern in assessing English language learners and students with disabilities. Many assessment tools are in English only. When ELLs cannot understand the test items, the usefulness of the assessment is compromised (Lenski, Ehlers-Zavala, Daniel, & Sun-Irminger, 2006). The poor performance of many ELLs on these assessments places them at increased risk of being misdiagnosed with a learning disability and placed in special education programs. To provide fair and unbiased assessment of ELLs, teachers should conduct multiple forms of assessment using a variety of assessment tools (e.g., anecdotal records, checklists, rating scales, portfolios). This approach will assess the progress of students in a way that will provide direct insight into the students' literacy development and will provide the kind of information needed to plan instruction (Lenski et al., 2006).

Students with disabilities often require various accommodations when taking required assessments. For example, a student with a reading disability may require more time to complete the assessment. Students with other disabilities may need accommodations in terms of alternative modes of access or alternative modes of response. In addition to accommodation, NCLB allows alternative standards of assessments or developmentally appropriate versions of the state test for children with severe cognitive disabilities. Whatever accommodations are made should reflect those documented on the student's IEP (see the discussion of IEPs in Chapter 12).

## *Reliability*

Reliability relates to consistency. A reliable car is one that can be counted on to start and get you to where you want to go. Reliability is a concern of both test developers in the development of standardized tests and teachers in the development of classroom assessments. In the following sections, reliability is discussed in the context of both standardized and classroom assessment.

The issue of fairness is of particular concern in assessing English language learners and students with disabilities.

### Reliability Standards for Standardized Assessments

Reliability as it relates to standardized tests is "the degree to which students will earn the same score if their responses are scored by another scorer or if they take another test that is intended to measure exactly the same knowledge and skill" (Taylor & Nolen, 2008, p. 487). Quality standards for standardized tests used in education have been established by the American Education Research Association (AERA), the American Psychological Association, and the National Council on Measurement in Education and are published in the *Standards for Educational and Psychological Testing* (AERA, 1999). According to these guidelines, there are several ways to determine the reliability of a standardized test. The most common are (1) test–retest reliability, (2) alternative form reliability, (3) inter-method reliability, and (4) inter-rater reliability.

**Test–Retest Reliability.** **Test–retest reliability**, as its name implies, involves giving the same test twice to the same group, usually one to three weeks apart, and correlating scores on the first test with those on the second test. For test–retest results to be accurate it is important that no significant performance-influencing event occur in the interval between the two tests (Popham, 2011). A test is generally considered reliable if the correlation coefficient calculated for the two sets of scores is .80 or higher (1.0 is the maximum value).

**Alternative Form Reliability.** **Alternative form reliability** involves giving a group of students one test and an alternative version of the same test during the same test session. This method obviates the possibility, as with test–retest, that students might remember test items. A comparison of student scores on the two tests is then made and a correlation coefficient is calculated. As with test–retest, the closer the coefficient is to 1.0, the more reliable the test.

**Internal Consistency Reliability.** A third method used to determine reliability, **internal consistency reliability**, is not concerned with the consistency of scores but whether the items on the test function consistently (Popham, 2011). Internal consistency reliability is based on the assumption that if a test is measuring a single concept (e.g., fractions), then each of the items on the test is basically assessing the same thing. Thus a student who gets one item correct will probably respond to a similar item the same way and get it correct. Internal consistency is determined by several statistical formulae that are beyond the scope of this text but will be addressed in your course on assessment or test and measurement.

**For Your Reflection and Analysis**

What are some "performance-influencing" events that could affect student responses on the second test?

**Inter-Rater Reliability.** The last major type of reliability is **inter-rater reliability.** This form of reliability is also concerned with consistency. In this case the consistency involved is the consistency in scoring between or among two or more scorers. Inter-rater reliability is calculated by comparing the number of items raters agreed on to the total number of items on the evaluation. For example, if two observers agree on 17 of 20 items on a checklist, the rate of agreement would be 85% (17/20 × 100). The minimum acceptable rate of agreement is 80% (McLoughlin & Lewis, 2008).

The reliability of classroom assessments is also concerned with the concept of consistency. However, it is determined by a different set of strategies. These are described in the following section.

## Reliability Standards for Classroom Assessment

The four standards for determining reliability of classroom assessments are (1) generalizability, (2) sufficiency of evidence, (3) clarity of directions and expectations, and (4) quality of scoring (Taylor & Nolen, 2008). While similar to the strategies for determining reliability of standardized assessments, they differ in the ways described below.

**Generalizability.** *Generalizability* is concerned with whether the student's performance is consistent over time and on different measures of the same knowledge or skill. Generalizability in classroom assessment is similar to test–retest reliability, which is concerned with the consistency of student scores on the same test at two points in time, and alternative form reliability, which is concerned with the consistency of student scores on two versions of the same test.

**Sufficiency of Evidence.** The second reliability standard for classroom assessment is *sufficiency of evidence*. Sufficiency of evidence determines whether there is enough high-quality assessment information to make reliable decisions about students' knowledge and skills (Taylor & Nolen, 2008).

**Clarity of Directions and Expectations.** The *clarity of directions and expectations* standard is concerned that assessment directions are clear and that expectations are unambiguous so students can respond in a way that accurately reflects their knowledge and skills. For example:

> Suppose a teacher created a multiple choice test for which students are expected to select the *best* conclusion for the results of a scientific investigation. All answer choices may be viable conclusions; however, only one provides the most thorough conclusion. Students must know, from the directions, that all conclusions are possible and that they are to choose the *best* conclusion. Similarly, if students are expected to use both primary and secondary sources in a research study, the directions for the assignment should indicate this expectation. (Taylor & Nolen, 2008, p. 35)

**Quality of Scoring.** The last reliability standard for classroom assessment, *quality of scoring*, requires that the rules for scoring and the scoring process are specific and clear enough so they can be consistently applied across students and similar tasks (Taylor & Nolen, 2008). Figure 15.4 is an example of a vague scoring rubric with an assignment to describe the main character. Figure 15.5 is a scoring rubric for the same assignment; it provides more specific guidelines.

The reliability standards for classroom assessment are summarized in Table 15.3.

## *Validity*

A test is considered valid if it measures what it purports to measure. Validity and reliability are related concepts. An assessment cannot be valid if it yields inconsistent results. However, an assessment could be reliable but assess the wrong content. The validity standards for standardized assessments and classroom assessments, while similar in some respects, differ in important ways. These standards are discussed next.

**For Your Reflection and Analysis**

Give an example of an assessment that might be valid but not reliable.

**Table 15.3 — Reliability Standards for Classroom-Based Assessments**

| Reliability Standard 1: Generalizability | Is the work typical of what the student knows and is able to do in relation to the learning targets? |
| --- | --- |
| Reliability Standard 2: Sufficiency of Evidence | Is there sufficient evidence so that one can make a dependable judgment about what each student knows and is able to do in relation to the learning targets? |
| Reliability Standard 3: Clarity of Directions and Expectations | Do the assessment directions provide clear, unambiguous expectations so that students can dependably demonstrate what they know and are able to do in relation to the learning targets? |
| Reliability Standard 4: Quality of Scoring | Are the scoring rules and scoring processes systematic enough to ensure consistent evaluation over time and across diverse samples of student work that demonstrate the same learning targets? |

*Source:* Taylor, C. S., & Nolen, S. B. (2008). *Classroom assessment: Supporting teaching and learning in real classrooms.* Upper Saddle River, NJ: Merrill/Pearson, p. 28.

## Validity Standards for Standardized Assessments

The three most commonly used methods to determine validity of standardized tests are (1) content validity, (2) concurrent validity, and (3) predictive validity. Content validity as it relates to standardized assessments is actually concerned with the validity of the interpretation of results, not the test itself (Popham, 2011).

**Content Validity.** **Content validity** is the extent to which the items on a test are representative of the content area and the curriculum target being assessed. Content validity is determined by a review of the items on the test by a panel of experts or by a comparison of the items on the test to a list of content topics to determine if the test represents the content area.

**Concurrent Validity.** The second form of validity, **concurrent validity**, is determined by administering an established test and a new test at the same time, to the same group of people, then calculating a correlation coefficient for the two sets of results. The higher the correlation coefficient, the greater the relationship between the two measures. For example, if a teacher assessed reading comprehension using a reading assessment measure for which there were established validity data and at the same time used a new reading comprehension assessment for which there were no validity data, a correlation coefficient of .86 would indicate a high correlation between the two measures and that the second, newer instrument had concurrent validity.

**Figure 15.4 — Vague Scoring Rubric for Character Description**

| 4 points | The written work is a thorough and accurate description of the main character. |
| --- | --- |
| 3 points | The written work is a mostly complete or mostly accurate description of the main character. |
| 2 points | The written work is a partially complete or partially accurate description of the main character. |
| 1 point | The written work is attempted with few details or is mostly inaccurate. |
| 0 points | The written work shows no comprehension of the main character. |

*Source:* Taylor, C. S., & Nolen, S. B. (2008). *Classroom assessment: Supporting teaching and learning in real classrooms.* Upper Saddle River, NJ: Pearson/Merrill, p. 36.

**Figure 15.5 — More Specific Scoring Rubric for Character Description**

| 6 points | The written work thoroughly describes the main character, including:<br>• the main character's name,<br>• a physical description of the main character (age, sex, clothes, hair color, skin color, and what the character wears),<br>• a reasonable statement about the main character's personality (e.g., friendly) or motives (e.g., wants to get rich), and<br>• at least *two* examples of the main character's actions or dialogue that show his/her personality or motives. |
|---|---|
| 5 points | The written work addresses all four expectations but one or two required details are missing from the physical description. |
| 4 points | The written work completely addresses the first three expectations but gives only one example from the text to show personality or motives. |
| 3 points | The written work addresses all four expectations but many details are missing from the physical description OR no examples are given to show the character's personality or motives. |
| 2 points | The written work addresses the first three expectations but many details are missing from the physical description OR the work completely addresses the first two expectations. |
| 1 point | The written work addresses the first two expectations but many details are missing OR the work gives a partial physical description of the character. |
| 0 points | The written work gives only the name of the main character OR is illegible OR is off task OR shows no comprehension of the text. |

*Source:* Taylor, C. S., & Nolen, C. B. (2008). *Classroom assessment: Supporting teaching and learning in real classrooms.* Upper Saddle River, NJ: Pearson/Merrill, p. 37.

**Predictive Validity. Predictive validity** is concerned with how well the assessment predicts the student's performance on some future behavior that is represented by the test content. Predictive validity is determined by administering a test prior to the student's performance and then comparing the results to data obtained about the student's performance at a later date. For example, the predictive validity of a school readiness exam could be determined by administering the exam at the beginning of the kindergarten year and then comparing the results to teacher ratings of academic achievement at the end of the first grade (McLoughlin & Lewis, 2008).

## Validity Standards for Classroom Assessment

The validity standards for classroom assessment parallel those for standardized assessment. They are (1) representation and fidelity, (2) cognitive demands, (3) consistency of assessments, (4) alignment with instruction, (5) enhancing fairness and minimizing bias, and (6) consequences of the interpretation and use of assessment results (Taylor & Nolen, 2008).

**Representation and Fidelity.** The first validity standard, representation and fidelity, is concerned with whether the knowledge and skills students are required to demonstrate on the assessment represent the knowledge and skills embedded in the curriculum standard. For example, if a standard states that students are expected to add and subtract fractions, the teacher should ensure that the assessment represents this standard. As previously noted, teachers can obtain this assurance by preparing a table of specifications. The representation and fidelity standard parallels the content validity standard for standardized assessments.

**Cognitive Demands.** A second and related standard, cognitive demands, asks whether the assessment tool requires students to demonstrate knowledge and skills at the cognitive level specified in the performance standard. This standard is concerned with how the items on the test function and whether they require students to use targeted knowledge and skills. Meeting this standard can be determined by the table of specifications.

**Consistency Across Assessments.** Consistency of results is the concern of the third validity standard, which asks whether students respond similarly on different assessments that are intended to measure the same standards. One strategy for determining validity on this standard is similar to that used with the alternate form reliability, except in this case students are doing different versions of the same type of work rather than different versions of the same test. For example, the teacher might assess mastery of a specific concept by a quiz, a portfolio, or an oral presentation.

**Alignment with Instruction.** The fourth standard is concerned with the fundamental question of whether the assessment is aligned with the curriculum. Clearly, if there is a mismatch between what is assessed and what was taught, the assessment is not valid and the results are of no value. Again, the table of specifications is helpful in addressing the validity standard.

**Enhancing Fairness and Minimizing Bias.** This standard is basically the same as the previously discussed absence of bias standard. The concern of the fifth validity standard for classroom assessment asks whether the assessment process and tools provide students from all subgroups with an equal opportunity to demonstrate their knowledge and skills. This requires that the assessment not only be free of obvious bias in content, but also that student abilities, disabilities, and learning styles be considered in developing the assessment process. For example, students who are ELLs may require an alternative assessment if they are to demonstrate the knowledge or skills they possess.

**Consequences of the Interpretation and Use of Assessment Results.** The final validity standard addresses the issue of whether the assessment has negative consequences for students in terms of lower self-concept; decreased motivation; loss of interest in learning; or, in the case of misdiagnosis or misscoring, improper placement, failure to be promoted, or failure to graduate from high school (Taylor & Nolen, 2008).

The validity standards for classroom-based assessment are summarized in Table 15.4.

## Table 15.4 — Validity Standards for Classroom-Based Assessments

| | |
|---|---|
| **Validity Standard 1: Representation and Fidelity** | Do the knowledge and skills required by the assessments represent the breadth of knowledge and skills defined in the standards? |
| **Validity Standard 2: Cognitive Demands** | Do the assessment tools and processes require students to demonstrate the targeted knowledge and skills at a cognitive level specified in the standards? |
| **Validity Standard 3: Consistency Across Assessments** | Do different assessments of the same knowledge and skills elicit comparable work? |
| **Validity Standard 4: Alignment with Instruction** | Does assessment align with the content taught and the instructional methods used? |
| **Validity Standard 5: Enhancing Fairness and Minimizing Bias** | Do the assessment tools and processes provide an equal opportunity for individuals, regardless of group or setting, to demonstrate the targeted knowledge and skills? |
| **Validity Standard 6: Consequences of the Interpretation and Use of Assessment Results** | Are there negative consequences for students that could be prevented if assessment tools, processes, events, or decisions had been more valid? |

*Source:* Taylor, C. S., & Nolen, S. B. (2008). *Classroom assessment: Supporting teaching and learning in real classrooms.* Upper Saddle River, NJ: Merrill/Pearson, p. 28.

The development of reliable and valid assessments is central to standards-based assessment. And, standards-based assessment is a key ingredient to standards-based education. Standards-based education, the movement that has dominated education in the United States in the last decade, is discussed next, in the conclusion of this chapter.

## Standards-Based Education and Assessment

As was discussed in Chapter 7, today's standards-based reform agenda can be traced to the 1983 publication of *A Nation at Risk*. The next two decades witnessed a movement in the United States toward what can be characterized as standards-based education. Standards-based education has now become the organizing principle and driving force behind educational policies at the federal, state, and local levels (edsource, 2011). These policies are directed at:

• The establishment of challenging, concrete, and measurable academic standards and curriculum and instruction aligned with the standards and designed to address the standards.

• Assessments that monitor student progress toward meeting benchmarks and standards.

• Accountability systems that are aligned with the standards and that attach school and district rewards and sanctions to specific performance outcomes (edsource, 2011).

Standards-based education differs from traditional education in several important respects. First, focus shifts from the teacher and a curriculum decided in large part by the teacher and the school to student learning and learning experiences that allow learners to progress at their own pace toward meeting standards. Second, teachers, students, and their parents know what students are expected to learn and are able to do before instruction begins. Third, standard-based education proposes that all students can achieve the standards, albeit at different rates and different ways: no student is exempt or "left behind." Standards-based education is seen as the way to ensure that all American students graduate from high school prepared for college or a career and to succeed in a global economy.

In a standards-based model of education, assessment is embedded in the teaching-learning process, not something that is done after instruction ends. Assessment is used to diagnose student strengths and weaknesses, to evaluate instructional effectiveness, to inform practice, and to improve student learning—not simply to sort and rank students. Figure 15.6 provides a model of standards-based education and assessment as it has been presented in this text.

### Figure 15.6 — Standards-Based Education Model

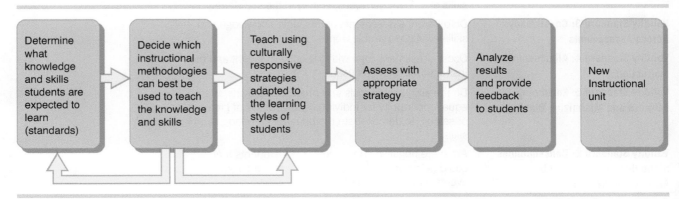

*Source:* Adapted from: Taylor, C. S., & Nolen, S. B. (2008). *Classroom assessment: Supporting teaching and learning in real classrooms*, p. 4.

# Summary

Standards are statements about expected levels of performance. There are three types of standards in education: curriculum content standards, performance standards, and opportunity to learn standards. Assessment is the process by which the attainment of standards is determined. The primary purpose of assessment is to gather information about student learning so that decisions can be made about the direction of instruction or the way students are trying to learn, with the goal of improving student learning. Assessment can be classified as either formal—or standardized—assessment or informal—or classroom—assessment. Standardized assessments are conducted using either norm-referenced tests or criterion-referenced assessments. Classroom assessments are conducted using a variety of tools, the most common being observation, performance assessment, portfolio assessment, and teacher-made tests and quizzes.

The accuracy of the results of an assessment will depend on whether it is free of bias, valid, and reliable. The validity of an assessment tool is whether it measures what it purports to measure. The reliability of an assessment tool is the extent to which it yields the same results over time and evaluators. Both standardized and classroom assessments have criteria that can be used to determine whether an assessment is valid or reliable. If an assessment tool does not satisfy these criteria, its results are of little value.

# PROFESSIONAL DEVELOPMENT *Workshop*

## *Prepare for the State Licensure Examination*

Michael Collins is a new fifth-grade teacher at John Adams Elementary School. Michael took advantage of the days before school began to review the records of the 26 students who would be in his class. He was pleased to see that most of the students were performing at or above grade level on the standardized tests in reading comprehension, science, and mathematics.

During the first two or three days of school, Michael randomly asked students questions related to the last unit they had covered in the fourth grade to determine what knowledge and skills had been mastered and what might need to be reviewed. Michael was surprised and concerned when it became clear that most of the students had mastery of little more than the most basic facts. To get a more accurate assessment of student knowledge and skills, Michael spent the first weekend of school developing a diagnostic assessment that he administered on Monday. The results were disappointing. They indicated that the class as a whole did not perform at the level that would have been expected given their scores on the state standardized assessment.

1. What were some examples of informal assessment in this scenario?

2. To what do you attribute the fact the students scored well on the standardized tests administered in the second semester of the fourth grade and their lower performance on Michael's assessments at the beginning of their fifth-grade year?

3. How can Michael use the results of the diagnostic assessment to plan for instruction? To improve student learning?

## Build Your Knowledge Base

1. To what extent, if any, can assessment be used for motivational purposes? Support your position.

2. What standardized tests have you taken in the last five years? For which of the purposes of assessment were they used?

3. Describe the concepts of reliability and validity and how they can influence test results.

4. How would you explain to a parent the discrepancy between performance on a standardized test and scores on classroom assessments?

### Develop Your Portfolio

1. Collect a sample of three or more types of classroom assessment. Review each of the assessments in terms of the reliability and validity standards for classroom assessment. Place your written review in your portfolio under **INTASC Standard 6: Assessment**.

2. Prepare a scoring rubric identifying the criteria used to assess a student research paper. Place your rubric in your portfolio under **INTASC Standard 6: Assessment**.

### Explore Teaching and Learning: Field Experience

1. Observe a teacher on the day before a major test is to be given. Then, observe this same teacher the day the test is returned to students. Did the teacher do anything to prepare students for the test? Would you classify the preparation as encouraging or intimidating? Did the teacher go over the test with students when they were returned? Interview the teacher to determine how the test results will be used.

2. Examine the contents of a student portfolio. What artifacts have been included in the portfolio? Describe the rubric, checklist, or other assessment tool the teacher is using to assess the portfolio.

3. Review a commercially prepared standardized test and the accompanying manual being used at a local school. Are the directions easy to understand? What information is provided about the validity and reliability of the test? How would you interpret the results to a parent?

---

## MyEducationLab

Go to **Topic 8, Assessment, Standards, and Accountability** in the MyEducationLab (www.myeducationlab.com) for *Foundations of American Education*, where you can:

- Find learning outcomes for assessment, standards, and accountability, along with the national standards that connect to these outcomes.
- Complete Assignments and Activities that can help you more deeply understand the chapter content.
- Apply and practice your understanding of the core teaching skills identified in the chapter with the Building Teaching Skills and Dispositions learning units.
- Examine challenging situations and cases presented in the IRIS Center Resources.

- Access additional video clips of CCSSO National Teachers of the Year award winners responding to the question, "Why Do I Teach?" in the Teacher Talk section.
- Check your comprehension on the content covered in the chapter with the Study Plan. Here you will be able to take a chapter quiz, receive feedback on your answers, and then access Review, Practice, and Enrichment activities to enhance your understanding of chapter content.
- Use the Online Lesson Plan Builder to practice lesson planning and integrating national and state standards into your planning.

# Glossary

## A

**Academic freedom.** The teacher's freedom to determine the most appropriate instructional materials and the most appropriate teaching strategies without censorship, interference, or fear of reprisal.

**Academy.** A type of private secondary school operating in the 1800s, designed to teach subjects useful in trade and commerce.

**Action research.** A process in which educators identify a problem in their own classroom, school, or district and engage in a process of data collection and analysis designed to formulate a plan of intervention or change in practice.

**Activity curriculum.** A curriculum that is determined to a large extent by student interest and that emphasizes self-expression through games, singing, or other creative and spontaneous activities.

**Adequacy.** The extent to which funding for programs and learning opportunities is sufficient.

**Administrative law.** The formal regulations and decisions of state or federal agencies.

**Aesthetics.** The branch of philosophy concerned with values in beauty, especially in the fine arts.

**Affirmative action.** Affirmative steps to recruit and hire, or recruit and retain, individuals from groups who are underrepresented in the workplace or the classroom.

**Alternative certification.** State provisions or regulations for awarding a teaching license to a person who has not followed the traditional teacher education program; exceptions typically are related to completion of a concentrated professional education sequence, teaching internships or prior experience, or credits for work experience.

**Analytic learner.** A person who perceives information in an abstract form and processes that information in a reflective manner.

**Analytic philosophy.** A philosophy that incorporates an analysis of languages and assumes that the words we use must be empirically verified and tested to be meaningful.

**Assimilation.** A response to population diversity that requires conformity to a single model, which is largely defined by traditional Western European political, social, cultural, and religious institutions.

**At risk.** A term used to describe students who are achieving below grade-level expectations or are likely to experience educational problems in the future, as well as students who are likely to experience physical and mental health problems.

**Authentic assessment.** A form of evaluation based on the cooperation between the student and teacher, student and student, teacher and administrator or supervisor, and community and teacher.

**Axiology.** The branch of philosophy concerned with the nature of values.

## B

**Back-to-basics movement.** A revival of essentialism begun in the 1970s and echoed in education reform reports of the 1980s that emphasizes the three Rs, a core curriculum, and more rigorous academic program requirements.

**Behavioral objectives.** Action-oriented statements that indicate specific behaviors or knowledge that students are expected to learn or demonstrate upon completion of an instructional sequence.

**Behaviorism.** An educational theory predicated on the belief that human behavior can be explained in terms of responses to external stimuli. The basic principle underlying behaviorism in education is that behaviors can be modified in a socially acceptable manner through the arrangement of the conditions for learning.

**Bilingual education.** Instruction to non–English-speaking students in their native language while teaching them English.

**Bloom's Taxonomy of Educational Objectives.** List and organizing scheme containing expected learnings for students.

**Board certified.** Certification awarded by the assessment board of a profession acknowledging the recipient's qualifications in specified areas.

**Building principal.** The person responsible for the administration and management of a school.

**Bullying.** A form of aggressive antisocial behavior that involves one or more individuals who repeatedly and intentionally harass another individual.

## C

**Career ladder.** A career development plan that provides differential recognition and rewards for teachers at steps of the plan, which coincide with increased experience and expertise.

**Carnegie unit.** A measure of clock time associated with a high school course used to award credit toward high school graduation.

**Cartesian method.** A process proposed by Descartes that involves the derivation of axioms on which theories can be based by the purposeful and progressive elimination of all interpretations of experience except those that are absolutely certain.

**Case (common) law.** That body of law originating from historical usages and customs.

**Categorical funding.** The practice of state funding of specific educational programs or activities (e.g., bilingual education, education of pupils with disabilities, pupil transportation, or in-service programs).

**Categorical imperatives.** Universal moral laws that guide our actions and behaviors.

**Certification.** The authorization of an individual by the state to teach in an area where the state has determined that the individual has met established state standards.

**Charity (pauper) schools.** Schools in colonial New England designed for children who could not afford to attend other fee-charging schools.

**Charter schools.** Publicly supported schools established upon the issuance of a charter from the state, local school board, or other entity and designed to provide greater autonomy to individual schools and greater choice in educational programs to parents and students.

**Chief state school officer.** The elected or appointed executive officer of the state department of education, responsible for elementary and secondary education, and sometimes for higher education; often referred to as the superintendent of public instruction or the commissioner of education.

**Child abuse.** The repeated mistreatment of a child, which can result in physical, emotional/psychological, or sexual injury or harm.

**Child benefit theory.** The legal theory that supports providing state aid to private education when the aid benefits the private school child rather than the private school itself.

**Child-centered curriculum.** Curriculum designed with the child's interest and needs at the center of the learning process; learning takes place through experience and problem solving.

**Child neglect.** Child abuse that includes an unwillingness to provide for the basic needs of the child.

**Choice.** Power or authority of (1) a local school board to select the instructional program and level of funding to be provided students in the school district, or (2) parents to select the school that their child attends.

**Classical conditioning.** A type of behaviorism that demonstrates that a natural stimulus that produces a certain type of response can be replaced by a conditioned stimulus.

**Clinical field experiences.** Opportunities provided to teacher education students to observe, assist, tutor, instruct, or conduct applied research in the classroom.

**Clinical practice.** Student teaching and internships that provide candidates with experiences that allow for full immersion in the learning community so that candidates are able to demonstrate proficiencies in the professional roles for which they are preparing.

**Code of ethics.** A set of professional standards for behavior of members of a profession.

**Cognitive styles.** The alternative processes by which learners acquire knowledge.

**Common schools.** Publicly supported schools started during the mid-1800s, attended in common by all children.

**Common sense learner.** One of four learning styles related to the perceiving and processing of information. The common sense learner perceives information abstractly and processes it actively.

**Compensatory education.** Educational programs designed to overcome the educational deficiencies associated with the socioeconomic, cultural, or minority group disadvantages of youth.

**Comprehensive high school.** A public secondary school that offers curricula in vocational education, general education, and college preparation.

**Constitution.** A written contract for the establishment of a government; the highest level of law.

**Constructivism.** (See Postmodern constructivism.)

**Cooperative learning.** Instructional system that assumes that students will study and work together in a supportive relationship rather than competitively.

**Core curriculum.** A curriculum design that emphasizes the required minimum subjects and topics within subjects that all students are expected to learn.

**Cosmology.** The branch of philosophy concerned about the nature of the universe or cosmos.

**Crisis intervention team.** Volunteer teachers, counselors, administrators, social workers, school nurses, and school psychologists who network with each other and identify the student who appears to be overwhelmed by stress or who displays suicidal gestures or suicidal threats.

**Critical literacy.** A type of curriculum that challenges all unequal power relationships and denounces any form of exclusion.

**Critical theory.** A set of principles that focuses on the political nature of education, including social control and power.

**Critical thinking.** The process of thinking and problem solving that involves the examination and validation of assumptions and evidence and the application of logic to the formulation of conclusions.

**Cultural literacy.** An assumed body of knowledge about which persons should be able to demonstrate mastery if they are to function at an optimal level in society.

**Culturally responsive teaching.** Instruction that seeks to integrate the cultural context of the learner in shaping an effective learning environment and strategies.

**Culture.** The behavioral patterns, ideas, values, religions and moral beliefs, customs, laws, language, institutions, art, and all other material things and artifacts characteristic of a given people at a given time.

**Curriculum.** All the educational experiences of students that take place in the school.

# D

**Dame school.** The elementary school in the New England colonies, usually held in a kitchen or living room and taught by women with minimal education.

*De facto* **segregation.** Segregation existing as a matter of fact, regardless of the law.

*De jure* **segregation.** Segregation sanctioned by law.

**Deductive logic.** Reasoning from a general statement or principle to a specific point or example.

**Direct instruction.** Teacher-dominated mode of instruction in which smaller learnings are integrated into meaningful wholes; basic or simpler skills (parts) are not taught in isolation from meaningful contexts (e.g., activities, problems). The teacher tells, demonstrates, restates, and helps students to state and restate rules and cognitive strategies. Knowledge is made explicit and overt, and students are taught to use this knowledge (e.g., how to figure a total cost) in their activities. With practice, this knowledge becomes covert (internalized).

**Dismissal.** The termination of employment during the term of the employment contract.

**Discrimination.** Showing bias or prejudice in the treatment of individuals because of their race, ethnicity, gender, disability, or sexual orientation.

**Disparate impact.** The situation that exists when a policy or practice has a differential impact on individuals in a protected class.

**Disparate treatment.** The less favorable treatment of an individual protected by Title VII by an employment policy or practice.

**Dropout.** A pupil who leaves school for any reason except death, before graduation or completion of a program of studies and without transferring to another school or institution.

**Dynamic learner.** One of four learning styles related to the perceiving and processing of information. The dynamic learner perceives information concretely and processes it actively.

# E

**Educational foundations.** Charitable or not-for-profit entities established to receive or distribute funds that can be used to enrich the educational opportunities for students.

**Educational goals.** Broad general statements of desired learning outcomes.

**Educational malpractice.** Failure on the part of an education professional to render a reasonable amount of care in the exercise of assigned duties with resultant injury or loss to another.

**Educational objective.** A clearly defined, observable, and measurable student behavior that indicates learner progress toward the achievement of a particular educational goal.

**Emergency (temporary) certificate.** A certificate issued to a person who does not meet the specified degree, course, or other requirements for regular certification; issued with the presumption that the recipient teacher will obtain the necessary credentials for regular certification.

**Emotional abuse.** Nonphysical abuse such as blaming, rejecting, or withholding security and affection.

**Employee services.** A benefit designed to help the employee to enjoy an improved lifestyle or meet certain obligations at a free or reduced cost (e.g., credit unions, employee assistance programs, child care).

**Enculturation.** The process of learning about one's culture.

**English as a second language (ESL).** A form of bilingual education in which standard English is taught to students with limited proficiency in English.

**Epistemology.** The branch of philosophy concerned with the investigation of the nature of knowledge.

**Equalized foundation grant.** State school finance system that provides a base amount per pupil to local school districts from a combination of state and local tax sources with the amount of state funds per pupil received by a school district being in inverse relation to the fiscal capacity per pupil of the school district.

**Equal opportunity.** A legal principle that, when applied to education, requires school districts and other agencies to develop policies and procedures to ensure that the rights of employees and students are protected and that they are given equal treatment in employment practices, access to programs, or other educational opportunities.

**Equity.** The equal treatment of persons/students in equal circumstances.

**Essentialism.** An educational theory that focuses on an essential set of learnings that prepare individuals for life by concentration on the culture and traditions of the past.

**Ethics.** The branch of philosophy concerned with the study of human conduct and what is right and wrong or good and bad.

**Ethnic group.** A subgroup of the population distinguished by having a common heritage (language, customs, history, etc.).

**Existentialism.** A philosophic belief that focuses on personal and subjective existence; the world of choice and responsibility is primary.

**Expulsion.** Exclusion of students from school for periods of time in excess of 10 days.

# F

**Fair use doctrine.** The rules that govern the reproduction and use of copyrighted materials.

**Flat grants.** A method for allocation of educational funds based on the allocation of a uniform amount per student, per teacher, per classroom, or other unit.

**Formative evaluation.** Form of evaluation designed to provide feedback while an activity is under way to improve the manner in which the activity is conducted.

**Full state funding.** A school finance system whereby all funds for the support of the public schools come from the state and from state-level taxes.

## G

**Gender equity.** In education, this term refers to the concepts of equal treatment and equal opportunity for all students, regardless of their gender.

**Globalization.** The development of multidimensional relationships and interdependent relationships among nations and cultures throughout the world.

**Grammar school.** A secondary school, originating in ancient Rome and continuing into the 19th century, which emphasized a classical education; forerunner of the high school; in current usage, an elementary school.

**Great Books.** The great works of the past, including literature, philosophy, history, and science, which represent absolute truth according to perennialist theory.

**Group instruction.** An instructional system in which teachers divide the class into groups of students (often five to eight students) and structure instruction and learning activities for this smaller number of students.

## H

**Hegemony.** A situation in which the dominant culture exercises domination over a subordinate class or group with the partial consent of the subordinate group.

**Hermeneutics.** The art or science of the interpretation of lived experience.

**Hidden curriculum.** The unexpressed perpetuation of the dominant Western culture through its rules, regulations, and rituals.

**High-stakes testing.** Testing, the results of which determine such important "stakes" as promotion or high school graduation.

**Homeschooling.** The education of children in the home; a form of private education.

**Hornbook.** A board on which a sheet of parchment was placed and covered with a thin sheath of cow's horn; used in colonial New England primary schools.

**Hostile environment harassment.** Verbal or physical conduct of a sexual nature that interferes with an individual's work performance.

**Humanism.** The dominant philosophy of the Renaissance; it emphasized the importance of human beings and promoted the literature and art of classical Rome and Greece.

**Humanistic education.** An educational program reflecting the philosophy of humanism.

## I

**Idealism.** The oldest philosophic belief, which views the world of the mind and ideas as fundamental.

**Imaginative learner.** One of four learning styles related to the perceiving and processing of information. The imaginative learner perceives information concretely and processes it reflectively.

**Inclusion.** Serving students with a variety of abilities and disabilities in the regular classroom with appropriate support services.

**Incompetence.** Lack of legal qualification, inability, or capacity to discharge the required duty. In regard to teachers, incompetence falls into four general categories: (1) inadequate teaching, (2) poor discipline, (3) physical or mental incapacity, and (4) counterproductive personality traits.

**Indirect compensation.** Payments or fringe benefits that employees receive in addition to payments in the form of money; classified as either employee benefits or employee services, such as health and life insurance, long-term disability protection, or leaves with pay.

**Individualized education program (IEP).** A program designed by a team of educators, parents, and at times the student to meet the unique needs of the child for whom it is developed.

**Inductive logic.** Reasoning from a specific fact or facts to a generalization.

**Infant school.** A type of public elementary school introduced in the United States in the 19th century to prepare children aged 4 to 7 years for elementary school.

*In loco parentis.* In the place of a parent.

**Inquiry instruction.** A problem-oriented instructional system in which students assume major responsibility for designing and structuring their learning activities and teachers serve as resource persons and facilitators.

**Insubordination.** The persistent and willful violation of a reasonable rule or direct order from a recognized authority.

**Integrated curriculum.** A curriculum design that combines separate subjects from within the same discipline, and in some instances content from two or more branches of study.

**Intelligence quotient (IQ).** A number intended to indicate an individual's level of mental development or intelligence.

**Interstate reciprocity.** A mutual agreement between states that allows teachers who are certified in one state to be eligible for certification in another.

## J

**Junior college.** An educational institution that offers courses for two years beyond high school. These courses may transfer to a four-year institution or may be complete career or vocational programs.

# L

**Language minority.** An individual whose native language is not English and who may have limited proficiency in the English language.

**Learning disability.** A disorder or delayed development in one or more of the processes of thinking, speaking, reading, writing, listening, or doing arithmetic operations.

**Least restrictive environment (LRE).** The educational setting that enables children with disabilities to have an educational experience most like that of children without disabilities.

**Lemon test.** A tripartite test used by the courts to evaluate claims under the establishment clause. Asks three questions: Does the action or policy (1) have a primarily secular purpose, (2) have the primary effect of advancing or inhibiting religion, or (3) foster an excessive entanglement between the state and religion?

**Liberty interest.** The right to a fundamental constitutional liberty (speech, press, etc.).

**Life-adjustment education.** An educational program, popular in the mid-20th century, that focused on youth who did not attend college, rejected traditional academic studies, and stressed functional objectives such as vocation and health.

**Limited open forum.** The condition said to exist when schools provide noncurriculum student groups the opportunity to meet on school premises during noninstructional time.

**Local property tax.** A tax on real property (land and buildings) levied by a local governmental unit such as a school district.

**Logic.** A method of knowing that is concerned with making inferences, reasoning, or arguing in a rational manner.

**Logical positivism (logical empiricism).** The view that no proposition can be considered valid unless it can be verified on logical or empirical grounds.

**Lyceum.** A voluntary organization sponsoring programs, demonstrations, and lectures for the education and information of its members.

# M

**Major depression.** An emotional state with persistent symptoms of sadness and hopelessness warranting referral to a mental health professional.

**Mass media.** Television, popular music, movie, music video, radio, newspaper, and magazine industries.

**Master teacher.** A teacher who is given special status, pay, and recognition but remains in the classroom as a role model for other teachers or is released from a portion of the regular classroom assignment in order to work with other teachers in a supportive, nonsupervisory role.

**Mastery learning.** An instructional system in which the desired learning and performance levels are identified and teachers work with students until they attain the desired level of performance.

**Mentoring.** Formal and informal relationships between a beginning teacher and an experienced teacher(s) that are sources of information and support for the beginning teacher.

**Metaphysics.** The branch of philosophy concerned with the nature of reality and existence.

**Monitorial school.** A school where one teacher taught a lesson to a group of older students, called monitors, who then each taught the lesson to a larger group of younger students.

**Multicultural education.** An educational strategy that provides for students whose cultural and linguistic backgrounds may prevent them from succeeding in the traditional school setting, which historically reflects the dominant Anglo-Saxon culture.

# N

**National Assessment of Educational Progress (NAEP).** A series of tests mandated by Congress and administered nationally in reading, mathematics, and science.

**National Board Certification.** National program through which a person is awarded a nationally recognized certificate that signifies successful completion of a series of activities designed to indicate excellence as a teacher. An individualized portfolio is a key component of the process. In some districts or states, these teachers receive a stipend upon successful completion of the program.

**Negligence.** A failure to do (or not to do) what a reasonable and prudent person would do under the same or similar circumstances, the result of which is injury to another.

**Neo-Thomism** The philosophy of Thomas Aquinas, which serves as the foundation for Catholic education and holds that man is a rational being who possesses both a spiritual nature and a physical nature; that truth can be arrived at through the deductive process; and that when reason fails, man must rely on faith.

**Nondirective instruction.** Student-dominated mode of instruction that incorporates the concepts of problem-based learning in which students and/or the teacher identify problems related to current experiences or problems experienced by students and proceed to solve the problems. The teacher serves as a resource person for students throughout the process.

**Nongraded school.** A school in which grade divisions are eliminated for a sequence of two or more years.

**Normal school.** Institutions established in the 1800s for the purpose of training teachers.

**Null curriculum.** Things that are not included in the formal curriculum because of their controversial nature, because they represent different values, or because of the lack of resources or information.

# O

**Object lesson.** An instructional activity that centers on concrete materials within the child's experience and involves discussion and oral presentation.

**Ontology.**  The branch of metaphysics that is concerned about the nature of existence and what it means for anything "to be."

**Open classroom.**  An architectural design for elementary schools popular during the 1960s that consisted of large, open instructional spaces not divided into traditional walled classrooms.

**Operant conditioning.**  A type of behaviorism in which any response to any stimulus can be conditioned by immediate reinforcement or reward.

# P

*Paideia.*  The general body of knowledge that all educated individuals should possess.

**Parochial school.**  A private elementary or secondary school supported or affiliated with a church or religious organization.

**Perennialism.**  An educational theory that focuses on the past, namely the universal truths and such absolutes as reason and faith. Perennialists believe the purpose of the school is to cultivate the rational intellect and search for the truth.

**Performance-based pay.**  Compensation given to an employee or group of employees based on the attainment of certain prescribed standards or outcomes (e.g., increased student achievement or lower dropout rates).

**Phenomenology.**  The study of the consciousness and experiencing of phenomena in philosophy.

**Philosophic analysis.**  The process of systematic questioning of assumptions, values, theories, procedures, and methods designed to help formulate and clarify beliefs about teaching and learning.

**Philosophy of education.**  The theory of philosophic thought that defines our views about the learner, the teacher, and the school.

**Physical abuse.**  The use of physical force, whether intentional or unintentional, against a child.

**Plenary.**  Absolute, as in the power of the state legislature to enact any legislation controlling the schools that is not contrary to the federal Constitution or the state constitution.

**Policies.**  Guidelines or principles for action adopted by a local school board to provide direction for administrative rules and regulations used in administering a school district.

**Postmodernism.**  A philosophy, ideology, movement, and process that incorporates the philosophies of pragmatism, existentialism, social reconstructionism, and critical pedagogy.

**Pragmatism (Experimentalism).**  A philosophy that focuses on the things that work; the world of experience is central.

**Praxis.**  Series of national content and pedagogical tests used to determine whether a prospective or intern teacher demonstrates the level of knowledge expected of new teachers.

**Premack principle.**  States that because organisms freely choose to engage in certain behaviors rather than others, providing access to the preferred activities will serve as a reinforcement for engaging in nonpreferred activities.

**Problem-based learning.**  A student-centered, student-directed model of instruction in which the teacher serves primarily as tutor and facilitator of learning.

**Procedural due process.**  The process by which individuals are provided fair and equitable procedures in a matter affecting their welfare (procedural due process) and are protected from unfair deprivation of their property.

**Profession.**  An occupation involving relatively long and specialized preparation on the level of higher education and governed by its own code of ethics.

**Professional development.**  Activities designed to build the personal strengths and creative talents of individuals, and thus create human resources necessary for organizational productivity.

**Progressivism.**  A theory of education that is concerned with "learning by doing" and purports that children learn best when pursuing their own interests and satisfying their own needs.

**Project method.**  An instructional methodology that attempts to make education as "life-like" as possible through the use of educative activities that are consistent with the child's own goals.

**Property right.**  The right to specific real or personal property, tangible and intangible; e.g., the right to continued employment or the use of one's name.

**Proprietary school.**  A school operated by an individual, group, or corporation for profit to serve the educational needs of a particular clientele.

**Protective factors.**  Personal attributes, family factors, and community factors that guard against maladaptive behavior.

**Proximate cause.**  The primary act or mission that produces an injury and without which the injury would not have occurred. A standard used to determine a teacher's liability in the cause of an injury.

# Q

*Quid pro quo* **harassment.**  Making a benefit of employment conditional upon the receipt of sexual favors.

# R

**Rate bill.**  A tuition fee, based on the number of children, paid by the parents during the mid-1800s.

**Realism.**  A philosophy in which the world of nature and physical matter is superior to the world of ideas. Matter exists whether the mind perceives it or not.

**Resiliency.**  Having developed the necessary coping mechanisms despite overwhelming hardships and obstacles.

**Restructuring.**  A buzzword of the 1990s, connoting a number of prescriptions for education: parental choice, year-round schools, longer school days and years, recast modes of governance, alternative funding patterns, and all-out commitments to technology.

**Reverse discrimination.**  Discrimination or bias against members of one class in an attempt to correct past discrimination against members of another class.

# S

**School board.**   As created by the state, the governing body for a local school district, with members generally selected by popular vote.

**Scientific method.**   The systematic reporting and analysis of what is observed and retesting of hypotheses formulated from the observations.

**Secondary school.**   A program of study that follows elementary school, such as junior high school, middle school, or high school.

**Self-renewal.**   Personal program of professional development designed to help a person improve teaching competencies by updating specified skills and their knowledge base.

**Sense realism.**   The belief that learning must come through the senses.

**Seven liberal arts.**   The curriculum that includes the trivium (grammar, rhetoric, and logic) and the quadrivium (arithmetic, geometry, music, and astronomy).

**Sexual abuse.**   Contact or interaction between a child and an adult when the child is being used for the sexual stimulation of the perpetrator or another person.

**Sexually transmitted disease (STDs).**   Infections such as gonorrhea or chlamydia that are transmitted through sexual activity.

**Single salary schedule.**   A salary schedule for teachers that provides equivalent salaries for equivalent preparation and experience.

**Site-based management (SBM).**   Delegation by a school board of certain decision-making responsibilities about educational programs and school operations to individual schools. Usually provides that teachers, parents, and the principal serve as the decision-making group.

**Social class.**   A social stratum in which the members share similar characteristics, such as income, occupation, status, and education.

**Social mobility.**   The movement upward or downward among social classes.

**Social reconstructionism.**   An educational theory that advocates change, improvement, and the reforming of the school and society.

**Socialization.**   The process by which persons are conditioned to the customs or patterns of a particular culture.

**Society.**   A group of persons who share a common culture, government, institutions, land, or set of social relationships.

**Socioeconomic status.**   The social and economic standing of an individual or group.

**Socratic method.**   A dialectical teaching method employed by Socrates using a questioning process based on the student's experiences and analyzing the consequences of responses, leading the student to a better understanding of the problem.

**Spiral curriculum.**   Curriculum in which a subject matter is presented over a number of grades with increasing complexity and abstraction.

*Stare decisis.*   Let the decision stand; a legal rule that states that once a court has laid down a principle of law as applicable to a certain set of facts, it will apply it to all future cases in which the facts are substantially the same, and other courts of equal or lesser rank will similarly apply the principle.

**State board of education.**   A state agency charged with adopting regulations and monitoring local school districts to ensure implementation of the constitutional and statutory mandates related to the operation of the state system of schools.

**State department of education.**   The operating arm for the administration of state education activities and functions.

**Statutory law.**   The body of law consisting of the written enactments of a legislative body.

**Student-centered curriculum.**   Learning activities that are centered on the interests and needs of the students and that are designed to motivate and interest the student in the learning processes.

**Subject-centered curriculum.**   Curriculum designed with the acquisition of certain knowledge as the primary goal. The learning process usually involves rote memorization, and learning is measured using objective test scores.

**Suicide gesture.**   A behavior that suggests a willingness to commit suicide.

**Summative evaluation (summative assessment).**   Evaluation or assessment conducted at the end of an activity or time period designed to assess overall performance or the extent to which the goals of the activity have been met.

**Sunday schools.**   Educational programs of the later 1700s and early 1800s offering the rudiments of reading and writing on Sunday to children who worked during the week.

**Superintendent of schools.**   The chief executive officer of a local school district whose educational program and related responsibilities include planning, staffing, coordinating, budgeting, administering, evaluating, and reporting. This person informs and works with the school board.

**Suspension.**   Exclusion of students from school for a period of 10 days or less.

# T

*Tabula rasa.*   Literally, blank slate; as applied to the concept of the human mind, it says that children come into the world with their minds a blank slate.

**Tax benefits.**   Tax deductions and tax credits designed to benefit patrons and nonpublic schools.

**Teacher institute.**   A teacher training activity begun in the 19th century, lasting from a few days to several weeks, where teachers met to be instructed in new techniques, informed of modern materials, and inspired by noted educators.

**Teacher-leader.**   Teacher who assumes a leadership role in the school on specific activities or on a continuing basis but does not serve in a formal capacity.

**Tenure.**   The status conferred on teachers who have served a specific period that guarantees them continuation of employment, subject to the requirements of good behavior and financial necessity.

**Theory of education.** Systematic thinking or generalization about schooling.

**Tort.** A civil wrong that leads to injury to another and for which a court will provide a remedy in the form of an action for damages.

**Transgender.** An individual who appears as, desires to be considered as, or has undergone surgery to become a member of the opposite sex.

# V

**Vernacular schools.** Elementary schools originating in Germany in the 16th century that offered instruction in the mother tongue or vernacular, as well as a basic curriculum of reading, writing, mathematics, and religion.

**Voucher.** A grant or payment made to a parent or child to be used to pay the cost of the child's education in a private or public school.

# References

*Adler v. Duval County,* 206 F.3d 1070 (11th Cir. 2000), *cert. denied,* 122 S. Ct. 664 (2001).

Adler, M. (1982). *The Paideia proposal: An educational manifesto.* New York: Macmillan.

Adler, M. (1984). *The Paideia program: An educational syllabus.* New York: Macmillan.

*Agostini v. Felton,* 521 U.S. 203 (1997).

Alexander, K., & Alexander, M. D. (2009*). American public school law* (7th ed). Belmont, CA: West/Thompson Learning.

Allegretto, S. A., Corcoran, S. P., & Mishel, L. (2008). *The teaching penalty: Teachers losing ground.* Washington, DC: Economic Policy Institute.

Alt, M. N., & Henke, R. R. (2007). *To teach or not to teach? Teaching experience and preparation among 1992–93 Bachelor's Degree recipients 10 years after college* (NCES 2007-163). U.S. Department of Education. Washington, DC: National Center for Education Statistics.

*Ambach v. Norwick,* 441 U.S. 68 (1979).

American Academy of Child and Adolescent Psychiatry. (2008). *Facts for families: Teen suicide.* Retrieved May 11, 2011, from http://www.aacap.org.

American Association for Employment in Education (AAEE). (2009). *Educator supply and demand in the United States: 2009 Executive summary.* Columbus, OH: Author.

American Association of School Administrators (AASA). (1952). *The American superintendency,* Thirteenth Yearbook. Washington, DC: AASA.

American Association of University Women (AAUW). (1998). *Gender gaps: Where schools still fail our children.* Washington, DC: AAUW Educational Foundation.

American Educational Research Association (AERA). (1999). *Standards for educational and psychological testing.* Washington, DC: Author.

American Federation of Teachers (AFT). (2000). *Building a profession: Strengthening teacher preparation and induction.* Washington, DC: Author.

American Psychiatric Association. (2000). *Diagnostic and statistical manual of mental disorders* (4th ed.). Washington, DC: Author.

American Psychological Association. (2005). *Warning signs of youth violence.* Retrieved April 28, 2005, from http://helping.apa.org/featurededtopics/feature.php.id=38.

Angus, D. L., & Mirel, J. (2001). *Professionalism and the public good: A brief history of teacher certification.* Washington, DC: Thomas B. Fordham Foundation.

Arends, R. I., & Kilcher, A. (2010). *Teaching for student learning.* New York: Routledge.

*Arizona Christian School Tuition Organization v. Winn,* 563 U. S. (2011).

Aronowitz, S. A., & Giroux, H. A. (1985). *Education under siege: The conservative, liberal and radical debate over schooling.* South Hadley, MA: Gergin & Garvey.

Arum, R., & Preiss, D. (2009). Law and disorder in the classroom. *Education Next, 9*(4), 68–76.

Association of Texas Professional Educators (ATPE). (2010). *Gender equity.* Retrieved May 20, 2011, from http://www.atpe.org.resources/student&parentissues/gender.asp.

Aud, S., Fox, M. A., & KewalRamani, A. (2010). *Status and trends in the education of racial and ethnic groups* (NCES 2010-015). Washington, DC: U.S. Department of Education, National Center for Education Statistics.

Avicenna. (1997). In *The New Encyclopedia Britannica* (Vol. 1, pp. 739–740). Chicago: Encyclopedia Britannica.

Baber, A. (2008). *State notes: State testing and assessment requirements for initial and continuing general education teachers.* Denver, CO: Education Commission of the States. Retrieved June 10, 2008, from http://www.ecs.org/clearinghouse/77/13/7713.pdf.

Bagley, W. C. (1938). An essentialist platform for the advancement of American education. *Educational Administration and Supervision, 24,* 241–256.

Ballentine, J. H., & Spade, J. Z. (Eds.). (2004). *Schools and society: A sociological approach* (2nd ed.). Belmont, CA: Thomson Learning.

Banks, J. A. (2008). *An introduction to multicultural education* (4th ed.). Boston: Allyn & Bacon.

Barnhardt, R., & Kawagley, A. O. (2005). Indigenous knowledge systems and Alaska Native ways of knowing. *Anthropology and Education Quarterly, 36,* 8–23.

*Barr v. Lafon,* 538 F.3d 554 (6th Cir. 2008). *cert. denied,* 78 U.S.L.W. 3170 (2009).

Barton, P. E. (2004). Why does the gap persist? *Educational Leadership, 62*(3), 8–13.

Beaulieu, D. L. (2000). Comprehensive reform and American Indian education. *Journal of American Indian Education, 39*(2), 29–58.

Beck, A. G. (1964). *Greek education 450–350 B.C.* London: Methuen.

Benard, B. (2004). *Resiliency: What we have learned.* San Francisco: West Ed.

Bennett, C. I. (2011). *Comprehensive multicultural education: Theory and practice* (4th ed). Boston: Allyn & Bacon.

Bennett, W. J. (1987). *James Madison High School: A curriculum for American students.* Washington, DC: U.S. Department of Education.

Bennett, W. J. (1988). *James Madison Elementary School: A curriculum for American students.* Washington, DC: U.S. Department of Education.

Bennett, W. J. (1993). *The book of virtues: A treasury of great moral stories.* New York: Simon & Schuster.

Berliner, David C. (2009). *Poverty and Potential: Out-of-School Factors and School Success.* Boulder and Tempe: Education and the Public Interest Center & Education Policy Research Unit. Retrieved March 12, 2011, from http://epicpolicy.org/publication/poverty-and-potential.

*Bethel School District No. 403 v. Fraser,* 106 S. Ct. 3159 (1986).

Biesta, G. J. (2001). Preparing for the incalculable: Deconstruction, justice, and the question of education. In G. J. Biesta & D. Egea-Kuehne (Eds.), *Derrida & education* (pp. 32–54). London: Routledge.

Biglan, A., Brennan, P., Foster, S., & Holder, H. (2004). *Helping adolescents at risk: Prevention of multiple problem behaviors.* New York: Guilford Press.

Binder, F. M. (1974). *The age of the common school, 1830–1865.* New York: Wiley & Sons.

Binderman, A. (1976). *Three early champions of education: Benjamin Franklin, Benjamin Rush, and Noah Webster.* Bloomington, IN: The Phi Delta Kappa Foundation.

Black, S. (2000). Evaluation for growth. *American School Board Journal, 187*(4), 58–61.

Blake, N., & Masschalien, J. (2003). Critical theory and critical pedagogy. In N. Blake, P. Smeyers, R. Smith, & P. Standish (Eds.), *The Blackwell guide to the philosophy of education* (pp. 38–56). Malden, MA: Blackwell Publishing.

Bloom, A. (1987). *The closing of the American mind.* New York: Simon & Schuster.

*Board of Education of Independent School District No. 92 of Pottawatomie County v. Earls,* 122 S. Ct. 2559 (2002).

*Board of Education of Westside Community Schools v. Mergens,* 496 U.S. 226 (1990).

*Board of Education v. Rowley,* 458 U.S. 175 (1982).

*Board of Regents v. Roth,* 408 U.S. 564 (1972).

Bonner, T. N. (1963). *Our recent past: American civilization in the twentieth century.* Upper Saddle River, NJ: Prentice Hall.

Borich, G. D. (2011). *Effective teaching methods: Research-based practice* (7th ed). Upper Saddle River, NJ: Pearson.

Boyer, E. (1983). *High school: Report on secondary education in America.* New York: Harper & Row.

Brendtro, L. K., Brokenleg, M., & Van Bockern, M. (2002). *Reclaiming youth at risk: Our hope for the future.* Bloomington, IN: National Educational Service.

*Bridgman v. New Trier High School District,* 128 F.3d 1146 (7th Cir. 1997).

Brosio, R. S. (2000). *Philosophical scaffolding for the construction of critical democratic education.* New York: Peter Lang.

*Brown v. Board of Education of Topeka,* 347 U.S. 483 (1954).

*Brown v. Gilmore,* 258 F.3d 265 (4th Cir. 2001), *cert. denied,* 122 S. Ct. 465 (2001).

*Brown v. Woodland Joint Unified School District,* 27 F.3d 1373 (9th Cir. 1994).

Bruner, J. (1960). *The process of education.* Cambridge, MA: Harvard.

Bruner, J. (1966). *Towards a theory of instruction.* Cambridge, MA: Harvard University Press.

Bureau of Labor Statistics. (2011). *Usual weekly earnings of wage and salary workers first quarter 2011.* Retrieved May 7, 2011, from http://www.bls.gov/cps.

*Burlington Industries v. Ellerth,* 118 S. Ct. 2257 (1998).

Butler, J. D. (1966). *Idealism in education.* New York: Harper & Row.

Butts, R. F. (1978). *Public education in the United States.* New York: Holt, Rinehart and Winston.

*C. F. S. v. Mahan,* 934 S.W. 2d 615 (Mo. Ct. App. 1996) CA: Thomson Learning.

Cain, M. (2001). Ten qualities of the renewed teacher. *Phi Delta Kappan, 82*(9), 703–705.

Callahan, C. M., & McIntire, J. A. (1994). *Identifying outstanding talent in American Indian and Alaska Native Students.* Washington, DC: U.S. Department of Education, Office of Educational Research and Improvement.

Campbell, D. E. (2010). *Choosing democracy: A practical guide to multicultural education* (4th ed.). Upper Saddle River, NJ: Merrill/Pearson.

*Carpio v. Tucson High School District No. 1 of Pima County,* 517 P.2d 1288 (Ariz. Ct. App. 1974).

Castle, E. B. (1967). *Ancient education and today.* Baltimore: Penguin.

Center for Education Reform. (2007). *Charter schools.* Washington, DC: Author.

Center for Education Reform. (2011). *All about charter schools.* Retrieved March 2, 2011, from http://www.edreform.com/printer_FVersion.efm.

Centers for Disease Control and Prevention. (2008). *Making a difference at your school.* Retrieved May 10, 2011, from http://www.cdc.gov/healthyyouth/keystrategies/index.html.

Centers for Disease Control and Prevention. (2010). *Injury prevention and control: Violence prevention.*

Centers for Disease Control and Prevention. (2010). *Youth risk behavior surveillance-United States, 2009. Morbidity and Mortality Weekly Report, 59*(SS-05). Washington, DC: Author.

Centers for Disease Control and Prevention (CDC). (2010). *Youth risk behavior surveillance-United States, 2009. Surveillance Summaries* (June 4, 2010) MMWR. 2010; 59: (No. SS-5).

Centers for Disease Control and Prevention. (2011). *Childhood overweight and obesity.* Retrieved May 10, 2011, from http://www.cdc.gov/obesity/childhood/index.html.

Centers for Disease Control and Prevention. (2011a). *Lesbian, gay, bisexual and transgender health-youth.* Retrieved May 15, 2011, from http://www.cdc.gov/lgbthealth/youth.htm.

Centers for Disease Control and Prevention. (2011b). *Vital signs: Teen pregnancy—United States, 1991–2009.* Retrieved April 15, 2011, from http://www.cdc.gov/mmwr/preview/mmwrhtml/mm6013a5,htm?s_cid=mm6013a5_w.

*Chalifoux v. New Caney Indep. Sch. Dist.,* 976 F. Supp. 659 (S. D. Tex. 1999).

*Chalk v. U.S. District Court Cent. Dist. of California,* 840 F.2d 701 (9th Cir. 1988).

Chamberlin, J. (2008). Brief teen intervention can stave off lifelong alcohol abuse. *Monitor on Psychology, 39*(4), 13.

Chapman, C., Laird, J., & KewalRamani, A. (2010). *Trends in dropout and completion rates in the United States: 1972–2008.* (NCES2011-012). National Center for Education Statistics, Institute for Education Sciences, United States Department of Education. Retrieved April 20, 2011, from http://nces.ed.gov/pubsearch.

*Cheema v. Thompson,* 67 F.3d 883 (9th Cir. 1995).

Chiang, L. (2000, October). *Teaching Asian American students: Classroom implications.* Paper presented at the annual meeting of the Midwestern Educational Research Association, Chicago, IL.

*Child Evangelism Fellowship of Maryland v. Montgomery County Public Schools,* 370 F.3d 589 (4th Cir. 2004).

Child Help. (2010). *National child abuse statistics.* Retrieved February 14, 2011, from http://www.childhelp.org/pages/statistics.

Child Trends. (2011). *Family structures.* Retrieved May 5, 2011, from http://www.childtrendsdatabank.org/?g=node/231.

*Civil Rights Division of the Arizona Department of Law v. Amphitheater Unified School District No. 10,* 680 P.2d 517 (Ariz. 1983).

*Cleveland Board of Education v. Laudermill,* 470 U.S. 532 (1985).

*Cleveland Board of Education v. Le Fleur,* 414 U.S. 632 (1974).

Clinton Foundation. (2011). *Facts about childhood obesity.* Retrieved May 1, 2011, from http://www.clintonfoundation.org/what-we-d-/alliance-for-a-healthier-generation.why-childhood-obesity.htm.

*Clonlara, Inc. v. State Board of Education,* 501 N.W.2d 88 (Mich. 1993).

Coalition of Essential Schools. (2011). *The CES Common principles.* Retrieved February 19, 2011, from http://www.essentialschools.org/items/4.

*Cochran v. Louisiana State Board of Education,* 281 U.S. 370 (1930).

Cohen, S. S. (1974). *A history of colonial education, 1607–1776.* New York: Wiley & Sons.

College Board. (2010). Next step: the SAT. Retrieved March 4, 2011, from http://www.collegboard.com/.

Collins, G. J. (1969). Constitutional and legal basis for state action. In L. S. Fuller & J. B. Pearson (Eds.), *Education in the states: Nationwide development since 1900*. Washington, DC: National Education Association.

Columbine Review Commission (2001). *The Columbine Review Commission Report to Governor Bill Owens*. Denver, CO: Author.

Committee for Economic Development. (2009). *Teacher compensation and teacher quality*. Washington, DC: Author.

Common Core State Standards Initiative. (2010). *National Governors' Association and education chiefs launch common state academic standards*. Retrieved March 1, 2011, from http://www.corestandards.org.

Conant, J. B. (1959). *The American high school today*. New York: McGraw-Hill.

Connell, W. F. (1980). *A history of education in the twentieth century*. New York: Teachers College Press, Columbia University.

*Connick v. Myers*, 461 U.S. 138 (1983).

Constantine, J., Player, D. Silva, T., Hallgren, K., Grider, M., & Deke, J. (2009). *An evaluation of teachers trained through different routes to certification*. Washington, DC: National Center for Education Evaluation and Regional Assistance, Institute of Education Science, U.S. Department of Education.

Cordier, M. H. (1988). Prairie schoolwomen, mid-1850s to 1920s, in Iowa, Kansas, and Nebraska. *Great Plains Quarterly*. Lincoln, NE: Center for Great Plains Studies, University of Nebraska.

Counts, G. S. (1932). *Dare the schools build a new social order?* Carbondale, IL: Southern Illinois Press.

Counts, G. S. (1933). *A call to the teachers of America*. New York: John Day.

Covington, R. (2007). Recovering Arabic science. *Saudi Aramco World, 58*(3), 2–4.

*Crager v. Board of Education of Knott County*, 313 F. Supp. 2d 690 (E.D. Ky 2004).

Cremin, L. A. (1962). *The transformation of the school*. New York: Knopf.

Cremin, L. A. (1970). *American education: The colonial experience, 1607–1783*. New York: Harper & Row.

Cremin, L. A. (1982). *American education: The national experience, 1783–1876*. New York: Harper & Row.

Cremin, L. A. (1988). *American education: The metropolitan experience, 1876–1980*. New York: Harper & Row.

Cromwell, S. (2006). Site-based management: Boom or boondoggle? *Education Week*. Retrieved February 4, 2008, from http://edworld.com.

Crosson-Tower, C. (2003). *The role of educators in preventing and responding to child abuse and neglect*. Retrieved May 15, 2011, from http://www.childwelfare.gov/pubs/user-materials/education/education.pdf

Cubberley, E. P. (1934). *Readings in public education*. Cambridge, MA: Riverside.

Curry, T., Jiobu, R., & Schwirian, K. (2005). *Sociology for the twenty-first century*. Upper Saddle River, NJ: Pearson.

Cushner, K., McClelland, A., & Safford, P. (2012). *Human diversity in education—An intercultural approach* (7th ed). Boston: McGraw-Hill.

Darling-Hammond, L. & Richardson, N. (2009). Teacher learning: What matters? *Educational Leadership, 66*(5), 46–51.

Darling-Hammond, L. (2007). *Reauthorization of NCLB: Key issues*. Presented at the Second Annual National Superintendent's Forum. Oct. 5–6, 2007. Palo Alto, CA.

Das, S. (2011). *What is karma?* Retrieved January 11, 2011, from http://hinduism.about.com/od/basics/a/dharma.htm

Davies, C. (April 7, 2010). *What is the importance of teacher professional development?* Retrieved February 14, 2011, from http://resume www.resume-for-teachers.com/blog/profdev/what-is-the-importance-of-teacher-professional-development.html

*Davis v. Monroe*, 119 S. Ct. 1661 (1999).

DeJong, D. H. (1993). *Promises of the past: A history of Indian education in the United States*. Golden, CO: North American Press.

*DeNoyer v. Livonia Public Schools*, 799 F. Supp. 744 (E.D. Mich. 1992).

Derrida, J. (1976). *Of grammatology*. (G. C. Spivak, Trans.) Baltimore: The Johns Hopkins University Press.

*DesRoches ex rel. DesRoches v. Caprio*, 974 F. Supp. 542 (E.D. Va. 1997).

Dewey, J. (1916). *Democracy and education: An introduction to the philosophy of education*. New York: Macmillan.

Dewey, J. (1938). *Experience and education*. New York: Macmillan.

Dewey, J. (1956). *The child and the curriculum and the school and society*. Chicago: University of Chicago Press.

Dewey, J. (1963). *Experience and education*. New York: Collier.

Diaz, C. F., Pelletier, C. M., & Provenzo, Jr., E. F. (2006). *Touch the future, teach*. Boston: Allyn & Bacon.

*Doe v. Duncanville Independent School District*, 70 F.3d 402 (5th Cir. 1995).

*Doe v. Gossage*, U.S. Dist. LEXIS 34613 W.D. Ky. (2006).

Doll, B., Song, S., & Siemers, E. (2004). Classroom ecologies that support or discourage bullying. In D. L. Espelage & S. M. Swearer (Eds.), *Bullying in American schools: A socio-ecological perspective on prevention and intervention* (pp. 161–183). Mahwah, NJ: Lawrence Erlbaum.

*Downing v. West Haven Board of Education*, 161 F. Supp. 2d 19 (D. Conn 2001).

Duncan, G. J., & Brooks-Gunn, J. (2001). Poverty, welfare reform, and children's achievement. In B. J. Biddle (Ed.), *Social class, poverty, and education* (pp. 49–65). New York: Routlege Falmer.

Dunn, S. G. (2005). *Philosophical foundations of education: Connecting philosophy to theory and practice*. Upper Saddle River, NJ: Merrill/Pearson.

EdSource. (2011). *Standards-based education*. Retrieved March 6, 2011, from http://www.edsource.org/iss_sta.html

Education Commission of the States. (2005). *Alternative certification*. Denver, CO: Author.

Education Policies Commission. (1942). *A war policy for American schools*. Washington, DC: National Education Association.

*Edwards v. Aguillard*, 107 S. Ct. 2573 (1987).

*Eisel v. Board of Education of Montgomery County*, 597 A.2d 447 (Md. 1991).

Eisner, E. (Ed.). (1985). *Learning and teaching the ways of knowing: The eighty-fourth yearbook of the National Society for the Study of Education*. Chicago: The University of Chicago Press.

Eliot, L. (2010). The myth of pink. *Educational Leadership, 68* (3), 32–36.

Ellis, A. K., Mackey, J. S., & Glenn, A. D. (1988). *The school curriculum*. Boston: Allyn & Bacon.

Emmer, E. T. (1987). Classroom management. In M. J. Dunkin (Ed.), *The international encyclopedia of teaching and teacher education* (pp. 437–446). New York: Pergamon.

*Engel v. Vitale*, 370 U.S. 421 (1962).

*Epperson v. Arkansas*, 393 U.S. 97 (1968).

Epstein, J. A., & Spirito, A. (2009). Risk factors for suicidality among a nationally representative sample of high school students. *Suicide and Life Threatening Behavior, 39*, 241–251.

*Erskine v. Board of Education*, 207 F. Supp. 2d 407 (D. Md. 2002).

*Everson v. Board of Education*, 330 U.S. 1 (1947).

Faltis, C. J., & Coulter, C. A. (2008). *Teaching English learners and immigrant students in secondary schools*. Upper Saddle River, NJ: Merrill/Pearson.

*Faragher v. Boca Raton*, No. 97-282 S. Ct. (1998).

Feinberg, W., & Soltis, J. F. (2004). *School and society*. New York: Teachers College, Columbia University.

*Ficus v. Board of School Trustees of Central School District of Green County*, 509 N.E. 2d 1137 (Ind. App.1 Dist. 1987).

*Fleischfresser v. Directors of School District 200,* 15 F.3d 680 (7th Cir. 1994).

*Florey v. Sioux Falls School District 49-5,* 619 F.2d 1311 (8th Cir. 1980), *cert. denied,* 449 U.S. 987 (1980).

Ford, P. L. (Ed.). (1962). *The New England primer.* New York: Columbia University Teachers College.

*Franklin v. Gwinnett,* 503 U.S. 60 (1992).

Franklin, B. (1947). *Proposals relating to the education of youth in Pennsylvania.* Retrieved January 24, 2011, from http://www.archives.upenn.edu/puaimdocs/1749proposals.html.

*Frazier v Winn,* 525 F.3d 1279 (11th Cir. 2008), *cert. denied,* 78 U.S.C.W. 3170 (2009).

*Freiler v. Tangipahoa Parish Board of Education,* 185 F.3d 337 (5th Cir. 1999).

Freire, P. (1973). *Pedagogy of the oppressed.* New York: Seabury.

Friend, M. (2011). *Special education: Contemporary perspectives for school professionals* (3rd ed.). Boston: Allyn & Bacon.

Gandara, P. (2010). Overcoming triple segregation. *Educational Leadership, 68*(3), 60–64.

Gardner, D. (2007). Confronting the achievement gap. *Phi Delta Kappan, 88,* 542–546.

*Garland Independent School District v. Texas State Teachers Association,* 479 U.S. 801 (1986).

Garner, B. A. (Ed.) (2009). *Black's law dictionary* (9th ed.). St. Paul, MN: West.

Garrison, J., & Neiman, A. (2003). Pragmatism and education. In N. Blake, P. Smeyers, R. Smith & P. Standish (Eds.) *The Blackwell guide to the philosophy of education* (pp. 21–37). Malden, MA: Blackwell.

Garrison, J., (1994). Realism, pragmatism, and educational research. *Educational Researcher, 23,* 5–14.

Gay, Lesbian, and Straight Education Network (GLSEN) (2008). *The principal's perspective: School safety, bullying, and harassment.* Washington, DC: GLSEN.

*Gebster v. Lago Vista Independent School District,* 118 S. Ct. 1989 (1998).

Gentile, D. A., & Gentile, J. R. (2005). *Violent video games as exemplary teachers.* Paper presented at the Biennial Meeting of the Society for Research on Child Development. April 9, 2005, Atlanta, GA.

Gilbert, W. S. (2000). Bridging the gap between high school and college. *Journal of American Indian Education, 39,* 36–58.

*Glover v. Williamsburg Local Sch. Dist. Bd. of Educ.,* 20 F. Supp. 1160 (S.D. Ohio 1998).

Goertz, M. E. (2001). Redefining government roles in an era of standards-based reform. *Phi Delta Kappan, 83,* 62–66.

Gollnick, D. M., & Chinn, P. C. (2009). *Multicultural education in a pluralistic society* (8th ed) Upper Saddle River, NJ: Merrill/Pearson.

*Good News Club v. Milford Central School,* 121 S. Ct. 2093 (2001).

Goodlad, J. (2004). Fulfilling the public purpose of schooling. *School Administrator, 61*(5), 14–18.

*Goss v. Lopez,* 419 U.S. 565 (1975).

Graham, P. A. (1974). *Community & class in American education.* New York: Wiley & Sons.

Gray, H. (2010). *New life for education malpractice: Decades of policy revisited.* Paper presented at Childlaw and Education Institute Forum, Spring, 2010. Chicago, IL: Loyola University.

Gray, R., & Peterson, J. M. (1974). *Economic development of the United States.* Homewood, IL: Irwin.

Greenberg, M., Haskins, R., & Fremstad, S. (2004). *Federal policy for immigrant children: Room for common ground?* Retrieved May 19, 2011, from http://www.brookings.edu/articles/2004/summer_demographics_ethnicity.htm

Greene, M. (2001). *Variations on a blue guitar: The Lincoln Center Institute on Aesthetic Education.* New York: Teachers College Press, Columbia University.

Greene, M. (2008). Maxine Greene: The importance of personal reflection. Retrieved January 15, 2011, from http://www.edupodia.com.html

Grossman, P., & Loeb, S. (2010). Learning from multiple routes. *Educational Leadership, 67*(8), 22–27.

*Grutter v. Bollinger,* 539 U.S. 306 (2003).

Gurian, M., & Stevens, K. (2004). With boys and girls in mind. *Educational Leadership, 62*(3), 21–26.

Gutek, G. L. (1988). *Education and schooling in America.* Upper Saddle River, NJ: Prentice Hall.

Gutek, G. L. (1991). *Education in the United States: An historical perspective.* Upper Saddle River, NJ: Prentice Hall.

Gutek, G. L. (2004). *Philosophical and ideological voices in education.* New York: Allyn & Bacon.

Gutek, G. L. (2006). George Counts and the origins of social reconstructionism. In K. L. Riley (Ed.), *Social reconstructionism: People, politics, perspectives* (pp. 1–26). Greenwich, CT: Information Age Publishers.

Gutek, G. L. (2011). *Historical and philosophical foundations of education* (5th ed.). Upper Saddle River, NJ: Pearson.

Hale, L. (2002). *Native American education: A reference handbook.* Santa Barbara, CA: ABC-CLIO, Inc.

Hare, N., & Swift, D. W. (1976). Black education. In D. W. Swift (Ed.), *American education: A sociological view.* Boston: Houghton Mifflin.

*Hazelwood School District v. Kuhlmeier,* 108 S. Ct. 562 (1988).

Headwater News. (2005, November 28). *Study explores achievement gap between Native American, white students.* Retrieved May 5, 2011, from http://www.newwest.ret/index.php/main/article/4496/htm.

*Hearn v. Muskogee Public School District,* 2004 WL 80465249 (E.D. Okla.).

Heffernan, H. (1968). The school curriculum in American education. In *Education in the states: Nationwide development.* Washington, DC: Council of Chief State School Officials.

Henderson, J. G. (2001). *Reflective teaching: Professional artistry through inquiry.* Upper Saddle River, NJ: Merrill/Pearson.

Herbst, J. (1996). *The once and future school: Three hundred and fifty years of American secondary education.* New York: Routledge.

Hess, F. M., & Meeks, O. (2010). *Governance in the accountability era.* Washington, DC: American Enterprise Institute.

Hiduje, S., & Patchin, J. W. (2010). *Cyberbullying: Identification, prevention, and response.* Retrieved May 16, 2011, from http://www.cyberbullying.us.cyberbullingresearchcenter.htm.

Hightower, A. M. (January 7, 2010). State of the states: Holding all states to high standards. *Education Week/Quality Counts 2010.* Retrieved February 1, 2011, from http://www.edweek.org/ew/articles/2010/01/12/17stateofstates.h29.html/intc=ml.

Hirsch, E. D., Jr. (1987). *Cultural literacy: What every American needs to know.* Boston: Houghton Mifflin.

Hlebowitsh, P. (2005). *Designing the school curriculum.* Boston: Allyn & Bacon.

*Hoffman v. Board of Education of the City of New York,* 400 N.E. 2d 317 (N.Y. 1979).

Hoffman, S. D. (2006). *By the numbers: The public cost of teen childbearing.* Washington, DC: National Campaign to Prevent Teen Pregnancy.

Hogan, P., & Smith, R. (2003). The activity of philosophy and the practice of education. In N. Blake, P. Smeyers, R. Smith, & P. Standish (Eds.), *The Blackwell guide to the philosophy of education.* Malden, MA: Blackwell Publishers.

Holt, J. (1981). *Teach your own.* New York: Delacorte.

Holt, M. (2001). Performance pay for teachers—The standards movement's last stand? *Phi Delta Kappan, 83,* 312–317.

Honawar, V., & Olson, L. (Jan. 10, 2008). Advancing pay for performance. *Education Week/Quality Counts 2008.* Retrieved March 12, 2008, from http://www.edweek.org/ew/articles/2008/01/10/18pay.h27.html.

*Honig v. Doe,* 484 U.S. 305 (1988).

*Hopwood v. Texas,* 518 U.S. 1033 (1996).

Horan, K. (2010). New study shows racially segregated schools not equal. *District Administrator, 46*(7). Retrieved February 15, 2011, from http://www.districtadministrator.com/view-articlepf.aspx?articleid=2476.

Horn, R. A., Jr. (2002). *Understanding educational reform: A reference handbook.* Santa Barbara, CA: ABC-CLIO.

Horn, R. A., Jr. (2004). Empowerment of teachers and students. In J. L. Kincheloe & D. Weil (Eds.), *Critical thinking and learning, an encyclopedia for parents and teachers* (pp. 211–216). Westport, CT: Greenwood Press.

*Hortonville Joint School District No. 1 v. Hortonville Education Association,* 225 N.W. 2d 658 (Wis. 1975), *rev'd* on other grounds and remanded, 426 U.S. 482 (1976), *aff'd,* 274 N.W. 2d 697 (Wis. 1979).

Human Rights Watch. (2005). *Hatred in the hallways.* Retrieved August 9, 2005, from http://www.hrw.org/reports/usight/final-04.htm.

Hupfeld, K. (2007). *Resiliency skills and dropout prevention.* Retrieved April 26, 2011, from http://www.scholarcentric.com/key_facts_students_dropouts_resilience_skills.html.

Hussar, W. J., & Bailey, T. M. (2011). *Projection of education statistics to 2019* (38th ed.). Washington, DC: U.S. Department of Education, National Center for Education Statistics.

Hutchins, R. M. (1936). *The higher learning in America.* New Haven, CT: Yale University Press.

Illich, I. (1974). *Deschooling society.* New York: Harper & Row.

*Illinois ex rel. McCollum v. Board of Education,* 333 U.S. 203 (1948).

Imber, M., & van Geel, T. (2010). *Education Law* (4th ed.). New York: Routledge.

*In Re Thomas,* 926 S.W. 2d 163 (Mo. App. 1996).

*Indiana ex rel. Anderson v. Brand,* 303 U.S. 95 (1938).

Ingersoll, R. M. (2008). The status of teaching as a profession. In J. H. Ballantine & J. Z. Spade (Eds.), *Schools and society: A sociological approach to education* (3rd ed. pp. 106–118). Belmont, CA: Wadsworth/Thomson Learning.

Ingersoll, R., & Merrill, L. (2010). Who's teaching our children. *Educational Leadership, 67*(8), 14–20.

*Ingraham v. Wright,* 430 U.S. 651 (1977).

Intercultural Development Research Association South Central Collaborative for Equity. (2011). *Six goals of education equity.* Retrieved May 20, 2011, from http://www.idra.org/South_Central_Collaborative_for_Equity/Six_Goals_of_Education_Equity/.

Jacobsen, D. (2003). *Philosophy in classroom teaching: Bridging the gap.* Upper Saddle River, NJ: Merrill/Pearson.

*Jeglin v. San Jacinto Unified School District,* 827 F. Supp. 1459 (C.D. Cal. 1993).

Joyce, B., & Weil, M. (2009). *Models of teaching* (8th ed.). Boston: Allyn & Bacon/Pearson.

Kaestle, C. F. (1983). *Pillars of the republic: Common schools and American society, 1780–1860.* New York: Hill and Wang.

Kandel, L. L. (1948). *The impact of the war upon American education.* Chapel Hill: University of North Carolina Press.

Kaplan, G. (1990). Pushing and shoving in videoland U.S.A.: TV's version of education (and what to do about it). *Phi Delta Kappan, 71,* K11–K12.

Katz, L. G., & Chard, S. C. (2000). *Engaging children's minds: The project approach* (2nd ed.). Stamford, CT: Ablex.

Keefe, J., & Jenkins, J. (2002). Personalized instruction. *Phi Delta Kappan, 83*(6), 440–448.

Kellough, R. (2011). *Resource guide for teaching* (6th ed.). Upper Saddle River, NJ: Merrill/Pearson.

Kellough, R., & Kellough, N. (2011). *Secondary school teaching: A guide to methods and resources* (4th ed.). Upper Saddle River, NJ: Merrill/Pearson.

*Kelly v. Huntington Union Free School District,* 675 F. Supp. 2d 283 (E.D.N.Y. 2009).

Kerr, C. (1963). *The uses of the university.* Cambridge, MA: Harvard University Press.

KewalRamani, A., Gilbertson, L., Fox, M. A., & Provasnik, S. (2007). *Status and trends in the education of racial and ethnic minorities* (NCES 2007-039). Washington, DC: U.S. Department of Education, National Center for Education Statistics.

*Keyes v. School District No. 1 of Denver, Colorado,* 413 U.S. 189 (1973).

*Keyishian v. Board of Regents,* 385 U.S. 589 (1967).

Kidwell, C. S., & Swift, D. W. (1976). Indian education. In D. W. Swift (Ed.), *American education: A sociological view.* Boston: Houghton Mifflin.

Kincheloe, J. L., Slattery, P., & Steinberg, S. R. (2000). *Contextualizing teaching: Introduction to education and educational foundations.* New York: Longman.

King, K., Gurian, M., & Stevens, K. (2010). Gender-friendly schools. *Educational Leadership, 68*(3), 38–42.

Kirkland, E. C. (1969). *A history of American economic life* (4th ed.). New York: Appleton-Century-Crofts.

Kishiyama, M. M., Boyce, W. T., Jimenez, A. M. Peng, L. M., & Knight, R. T. (2009). Socioeconomic disparities affect prefrontal function in children. *Journal of Cognitive Neuroscience, 21,* 1106–1115.

*Kitzmiller v. Dover Area School District,* 400 F. Supp. 2d 707 (M.D. Pa. 2005).

Kliebard, H. M. (1995). *The struggle for the American curriculum, 1893–1958* (2nd ed.). New York: Routledge.

Knapp, L. G., Kelly-Reid, J. E., & Ginder, S. A. (2010). *Postsecondary institutions and price of attendance in the United States: Fall 2009, degrees and other awards conferred: 2008–09 and 12 month enrollment: 2008–09.* (NCES2010-161). United States Department of Education, National Center for Education. Retrieved April 12, 2011, from http://nces.ed.gov/pubsearch.

Kneller, G. F. (1971). *Introduction to the philosophy of education.* New York: Wiley & Sons.

Knight, E. W. (1952). *Fifty years of American education.* New York: The Ronald Press.

*Knox County Educ. Assn. v. Knox County Board of Educ.,* 158 F.3d (6th Cir. 1998), *cert. denied,* 120 S. Ct. 46 (1999).

Kohl, H. R. (1976). *On teaching.* New York: Schocken.

Kosciw, J. G., Greytalk, E. A., Diaz, E. M., & Bartkiewicz, M. J. (2010). *The 2009 national school climate survey: The experiences of lesbian, gay, bisexual and transgender youth in our nation's schools.* New York: Gay, Lesbian and Straight Education Network.

Kozol, J. (1972). *Free schools.* Boston: Houghton Mifflin.

Kozol, J. (1991). *Savage inequalities.* New York: Crown.

Kysilka, M. L., & Brown, S. (2006). In search of curriculum theory: The reconstrucionists. In K. L. Riley (Ed.), *Social Reconstructionism: People, Politics, Perspectives* (pp. 189–210). Greenwich, CT.: Information Age Publishers.

Labaree, D. F. (2000). Resisting educational standards. *Phi Delta Kappan, 82,* 28–33.

Ladd, G. W. (2007). Social learning in the peer context. In O. N. Saracho and B. Spodek (Eds.), *Contemporary perspectives on socialization and social development in early childhood education* (pp. 133–164). Charlotte, NC: Information Age Publishing.

*Lamb's Chapel v. Center Moriches School District,* 959 F. 2d 381 (2d Cir. 1992), *rev'd,* 113 S. Ct. 2141 (1993).

*Lau v. Nichols,* 414 U.S. 563 (1974).

*Lee v. Weisman,* 505 U.S. 577 (1992).

*Lehto v. Board of Education of Caesar Rodney School District No. 175,* 962 A.2d 222 (Del. 2008).

*Lemon v. Kurtzman,* 93 S. Ct. 1463 (1971).

Lenski, S. D., Ehlers-Zavala, F., Daniel, M. C., & Sun-Irminger, X. (2006). Assessing English-language learners in mainstream classrooms. *The Reading Teacher, 60*(1), 24–34.

Lerner, M. (1962). *Education and radical humanism.* Columbus, OH: Ohio State University Press.

Madsen, D. L. (1974). *Early national education: 1776–1830.* New York: Wiley & Sons.

Magee, J. B. (1971). *Philosophical analysis in education.* New York: Harper & Row.

Manna, P. (2010, Fall). The three Rs of Obama's Race to the Top Program: Reform, reward, and resistance. *America's Quarterly,* 112–117.

Maritain, J. (1941). *Scholasticism and politics.* New York: Macmillan.

Maritain, J. (1943). *Education at the crossroads.* New Haven, CT: Yale University Press.

Markow, D., & Cooper, M. (2008). *The Met Life survey of the American teacher: Past, Present and future.* Washington, DC: Harris Interactive.

Markow, D., & Martin, S. (2005). *The Met Life Survey of the American teacher: Transitions and the role of supportive relationships.* Washington, DC: Harris Interactive Inc.

Markow, D., & Pieters, S. (2009). *The Met Life survey of the American teacher: Collaborating for student success.* Washington, DC: Harris Interactive.

Markow, D., Moessner, C., & Horowitz, H. (2006). *The Met Life survey of the American teacher: Expectations and Experiences.* Washington, DC: Harris Interactive.

Marsh, C., & Willis, G. (2003). *Curriculum: Alternative approaches, ongoing issues* (3rd ed.). Upper Saddle River, NJ: Merrill/Pearson.

Martusewicz, R. A. (2001). *Seeking passage: Post-structuralism, pedagogy, ethics.* New York: Teachers College Press.

Masten, A. S. (1997). Resilience in children at risk. *Carei research/prevention newsletter.* Retrieved April 22, 2011, from http://www.cehd.umn.edu/carei/reports/rpractices/spring97/resilience.htm/.

Mastropieri, M. A., & Scruggs, T. E. (2007). *The inclusive classroom: Strategies for effective instruction.* Upper Saddle River, NJ: Merrill/Pearson.

Mayer, F. (1973). *A history of educational thought.* Columbus, OH: Merrill.

*McCollum v. Board of Education of School District No. 71,* 333 U.S. 203 (1948).

McKinsey & Company. (2009). *The economic impact of the achievement gap in America's public schools.* Retrieved May 10, 2011, from http://www.McKinsey.com/app/media/images/page_images/offices/socialsector/PDF/achievement_gap_report.pdf.

McLaren, P. (2003). *Life in schools: An introduction to critical pedagogy in the foundations of education.* Boston: Allyn & Bacon/Pearson.

McLaren, P., & Torres, C. A. (1998). Voicing from the margins: The politics and passion of pluralism in the work of Maxine Greene. In W. Ayers and J. L. Miller (Eds.), *A light in dark times: Maxine Greene and the unfinished conversation* (pp. 190–203). New York: Teachers College Press.

McLoughlin, J. A., & Lewis, R. B. (2008). *Assessing students with special needs* (7th ed.). Upper Saddle River, NJ: Merrill/Pearson.

McManis, J. T. (1916). *Ella Flagg Young and a half century of the Chicago public schools.* Chicago: McClurg.

McNeill, M. (July 26, 2010). Civil rights groups call for new federal education agenda. *Education Week Online.* Retrieved July 20, 2011, from http://blogs.edweek.org.edweek/campaign-k-12/2010/07civil_rights_groups_call_for_new_federal_education_agenda.html.

McNergney, R. F., & McNergney, J. M. (2008). *Foundations of education: The challenge of professional practice.* Boston: Allyn & Bacon/Pearson.

*Melzer v. New York City Bd. of Educ.,* 336 F.3d 185 (2d Cir. 2003).

*Mendez et al. v. Westminister School District of Orange County,* 64 F. Supp. 544 (S.D. Cal. 1946), *aff'd* 161 F.2d 774 (1947).

*Menora v. Illinois High School Association,* 683 F.2d 1030 (7th Cir. 1982), *cert. denied,* 459 U.S. 1156 (1983).

Metcalf, K. K., & Legan, N. A. (2002). Educational vouchers: A primer. *Clearinghouse, 76*(1), 25–26.

Meyer, A. E. (1972). *An educational history of the Western world.* New York: McGraw-Hill.

Miller, P. C., & Endo, H. (2004). Understanding and meeting the needs of ESL students. *Phi Delta Kappan, 85,* 786–791.

*Mills v. Board of Education of the District of Columbia,* 348 F. Supp. 866 (D.D.C. 1972).

Min, P. G. (2003). Social science research on Asian Americans. In J. A. Banks & C. M. Banks (Eds.), *Handbook of research on multicultural education* (pp. 332–348). New York: Macmillan.

*Mitchell v. Helms,* 120 S. Ct. 2530 (2000).

Mobley, P. R., & Holcomb, S. (2010). *A report on the status of women in education: Achieving gender equity for women and girls.* Washington, DC: National Education Association.

Molnar, A., Boriger, F., Wilkinson, G., Fogarty, J., & Geary, S. (2010). *Schools and the machinery of modern marketing: The thirteenth annual report on schoolhouse commercialism trends: 2009–2010.* Boulder, CO: National Education Policy Center.

Monger, R., & Yankay, J. (2011). *U.S. legal permanent residents: 2010.* Washington, DC: U.S. Department of Homeland Security, Office of Immigration Statistics.

Monroe, P. (1939). *Source book of the history of education for the Greek and Roman period.* New York: Macmillan.

Morgan, S. (2010). *10 things charter schools don't tell you.* Retrieved March 20, 2011, from http://www.smartmoney.com/spending/rip-offs/10-things-charter-schools-don't-tell-you.

Morris, V. C., & Pai, Y. (1976). *Philosophy in the American school.* Boston: Houghton Mifflin.

Morrow, R. D. (1991). The challenges of Southeast-Asian parental involvement. *Principal, 70,* 20–22.

*Morse v. Frederick,* 121 S. Ct.2618 (2007).

Mosley, R. (2011). Jewish education in ancient times. Retrieved January 24, 2011, from http://www.restorationfoundation.org/volume-3/32-6.htm.

*Mount Healthy City School District v. Doyle,* 429 U.S. 274 (1977).

*Mueller v. Allen,* 103 S. Ct. 3062 (1983).

Murphy, M. M. (2006). *The history and philosophy of education: Voices of educational pioneers.* Upper Saddle River, NJ: Pearson.

Nabozny, B. (2007). Making it personal. *NEA Today, 25*(7), 24–27.

National Alliance for Public Charter Schools. (2009). *Charter school achievement: What we know.* Retrieved February 20, 2011, from http://www.publiccharters.org.

National Association of Secondary School Principals. (1921). *Fifth yearbook of the National Association of Secondary School Principals.* Washington, DC: Author.

National Association for Single Sex Public Education (NASSPE). (2011). *Single-sex schools/schools with single-sex classrooms: What's the difference.* Retrieved May 15, 2011, from http://www.singlesexschools.org/schools-schools.htm.

National Association of State Boards of Education. (2011). *2011 state education governance models.* Retrieved March 16, 2011, from http://nasbe.org/index.php=com_content&view=article&id=1121:2011state-education-governance-modes&cited=1034:about&Itemid=1001#csso-method.

National Board for Professional Teaching Standards (NBPTS). (2005). *About NBPTS.* Retrieved April 7, 2005, from http://www.nbpts./aboutus/newscenter.2005.

National Board for Professional Teaching Standards (NBPTS). (2011). *National Board for Professional Teaching Standards.* Retrieved February 14, 2011, from http://www.nbpts.org.

National Center for Alternative Certification. (2011). *Alternative teacher certification: A state by state analysis.* Retrieved January 15, 2011, from http://www.teacg_now.org/intro.cfm.

National Clearinghouse for Alcohol and Drug Information. (2006). *Youth orientation prevention initiatives.* Retrieved March 10, 2006, from http://www.health.org/ndcs98/iv-html.

National Clearinghouse for English Language Acquisition. (2011). *The growing number of limited English proficient students 1998/1999-2008/09.* Retrieved May 5, 2011, from http://www.ncela.gew.edu/uploads/9/growingLEP_0809.pdf.

National Commission on Excellence in Education. (1983). *A nation at risk: The imperative for educational reform.* Washington, DC: U.S. Government Printing Office.

National Commission on Teaching and America's Future. (2010). *Who will teach? Experience matters.* Washington, DC: Author.

National Council for the Accreditation of Teacher Education (NCATE). (2011). *Glossary.* Retrieved January 31, 2011, from http://www.ncate.org/standards/NCATEUnitStandards/NCATEGlossary/tabid/477/default.aspx.acf.hhs.gov/programs/ch/stats_research/index.html.

National Council of Teachers of English (NCTE). (2008). *English language learners: A policy Research Brief.* Retrieved January 21, 2011, from http://www.ncte.org/library/NCTEFiles/Resources/PolicyResearch/ELLResearchBrief.pdf

National Education Association. (2005). *NEAFT partnership.* Washington, DC: Author.

National Education Association. (2010). *Rankings and estimates of the states 2010 and estimates of school statistics 2011.* Washington, DC: Author.

National Policies Commission. (1941). *The Civilian Conservation Corps, the National Youth Administration, and the public schools.* Washington, DC: National Education Association.

National Youth Violence Prevention Resource Center. (n.d.). *Elements of effective school violence prevention plans.* Retrieved January 27, 2008, from http://www.safeyouth.org/scripts/faq/schoolplan.asp.

Native American Studies. Retrieved May 5, 2011, from www.facebook.com/topic.php?uid=311580209268&topic=14847.

Neild, R. C., & Balfanz, R. (2006). *Unfulfilled promise: The dimensions and characteristics of Philadelphia's dropout crisis, 2000–2005.* Philadelphia, PA: Project U Turn.

Neill, A. S. (1960). *Summerhill: A radical approach to child rearing.* New York: Hart.

*New Jersey v. T.L.O.*, 105 S. Ct. 733 (1985).

*New Oxford American Dictionary.* (2005). New York: Oxford University Press.

New Teacher Project. (December, 2010). Resetting Race to the Top: Why the future of the competition depends on improving the scoring process. Retrieved May 11, 2011, from http://ntp.org/assets/documents/Resetting_R2T_Dec6F.pdf

Newcomer, M. (1959). *A century of higher education for women.* New York: Harper & Brothers.

*Newdow v. Rio Linda Union School District,* 597 F.3d 1007 (9th Cir. 2010).

*Newdow v. U.S. Congress,* 292 F.3d 597 (9th Cir. 2002).

Newman, J. W. (1998). *America's teachers.* New York: Longman.

*Newport Independent School District v. Commonwealth of Kentucky,* S.W. 3d. 216 (Ky. App. 2009).

Newport, F. (January 28, 2007). *State of the states: Importance of religion.* Retrieved May 10, 2011, from http://www.gallup.com/poll/114022/state-states-importance-religion.

Ngo, B., & Lee, S. J. (2007). Complicating the image of minority success: A review of southeast Asian American education. *Review of Educational Research, 77,* 415–453.

Nichols, S. L., & Berliner, D. C. (2005). *The inevitable corruption of indicators and educators through high-stakes testing.* East Lansing, MI: Great Lakes Center for Education Research & Practice.

Nichols, S. M. C., Bicard, S. C., Bicard, D. F., & Casey, L. B. (2008). A field at risk: The teacher shortage in special education. *Phi Delta Kappan, 89,* 587–600.

NIDA for Teens. (2010). *Drug abuse.* Retrieved April 23, 2011, from http://www.teens.drugabuse.gov/facts/facts.php.

Nitko, A. J., & Brookhart, S. M. (2011). *Educational assessment of students* (6th ed.). Upper Saddle River, NJ: Merrill/Pearson.

Noddings, N. (1997). *Philosophy of education.* Boulder, CO: Westview Press.

*Null v. Board of Education of the County of Jackson,* 815 F.Supp. 937 (S.D. W. Va. 1993).

*O'Conner v. Ortega,* 480 U.S. 709 (1987).

Oakes, J., & Lipton, M. (2004). Forward. In J. J. Romo, P. Bradfield, & R. Serrano (Eds.), *Reclaiming democracy: A multicultural educator's journey toward transformative teaching (pp. vii–ix),* Upper Saddle River, NJ: Merrill/Pearson.

Odden, A. (2000). Paying teachers for performance. *School Business Affairs, 66*(6), 28–31.

Ogden, C., & Carroll, M. (2010). *Prevalence of obesity among children and adolescents: United States, trends 1963–1965 through 2001–2008.*

Oringanje, C., Meremikwu, M. M., Eko, H., Esu, E., Meremikwu, A., & Ehiri, J. E. (October 7, 2009). Interventions for preventing unintended pregnancies among adolescents (Review). *Cochrane Database of Systematic Review.* Retrieved February 11, 2011, from http://www.ncbi.nlm.nih.gov/pubmed/19821341.

Ormond, J. E. (2010). *Gender differences: Research findings.* Retrieved January 26, 2011, from http://www.education.com/print/research-findings-regarding-gender/.

Ozmon, H. A. (2012). *Philosophical foundations of education.* Upper Saddle River, NJ: Merrill/Pearson.

*Palmer v. Wanahachie Independent School District,* 579 F.3d 502 (5th Cir. 2009).

Palmer, L. B. (2007). The potential of alternative charter school authorizers. *Phi Delta Kappan, 89,* 304–309.

Pang, V. O. (2005). *Multicultural education: A caring-centered reflective approach.* New York: McGraw-Hill.

*Parents Involved in Community Schools v. Seattle School District No. 1,* 551 U.S. 701 (2007).

Partelli, J. P. (1987). Analytic philosophy of education: Development and Misconceptions. *Journal of Educational Thought, 21*(1), 20–24.

Pavlov, I. (1927). *Conditional reflexes: An investigation of the physiological activity of the cerebral cortex* (G. V. Anrep, Trans.). London: Oxford University Press.

*Pennsylvania Association of Retarded Citizens v. Pennsylvania,* 343 F. Supp. 179 (E.D. Pa.1972).

Peoples-health.com. (2011). *Facts about childhood obesity.* Retrieved May 23, 2011, from http://www.peoples-health.com/childhood_obesity_facts.htm.

Perkinson, H. J. (1977). *The imperfect panacea: American faith in education, 1965–1976* (2nd ed.). New York: Random House.

*Perry v. Sindermann,* 408 U.S. 593 (1972).

*Peter W. v. San Francisco Unified School District,* 131 Cal. Rptr. 854 (Cal. App. 1976).

Peter, K., & Hern, L. (2005). *Gender differences in participation and completion of undergraduate education and how they have changed over time.* Retrieved April 5, 2005, from http://nces.ed.gov/das/epubs/2005169/gender_2asp

Piaget, J. (1951). *The child's conception of the world.* New York: The Humanities Press.

Piaget, J. (1970). *Genetic epistemology.* New York: W. W. Norton.

*Pickering v. Board of Education,* 391 U.S. 563 (1968).

*Pierce v. Society of Sisters,* 268 U.S. 510 (1925).

Pifer, A. (1973). *The higher education of blacks in the United States.* New York: Carnegie.

Planeaux, C. (1999). *Christopher's Plato: The academy.* Retrieved August 1, 2005, from http://php.iupui.edu/~cplaneau/Plato%20and%20His%20World.Plato%20Academy%Introduction.html.

Plato. (1958). *The Republic.* (F. Carnford, Trans.). New York: Oxford University Press. (Original work 360 B.C.)

Plato. (360 B.C.). *Laws,* VII, p. 805.

*Plessy v. Ferguson,* 163 U.S. 537, 16 S. Ct. 1138 (1896).

*Plyler v. Doe,* 457 U.S. 202 (1982).

Poland, S. (2011b). Resilience and academic success: What schools can do to help create resilient students. *District administrator, 47*(1). Retrieved May 14, 2011, from http://www.districtadministrator.com/viewarticlepf.aspx?articleid=2668.

Popham, W. J. (2011). *Classroom assessment: What teachers need to know* (6th ed.). Boston: Allyn & Bacon/Pearson.

Power, E. J. (1982). *Philosophy of education: Studies in philosophies, schooling and educational policies.* Upper Saddle River, NJ: Prentice Hall.

*Prince v. Jacoby,* 303 F.3d 1074 (9th Cir. 2002).

*Progressive Education.* (1924). 1, 2.

Provasnik, S., & Dorfman, S. (2005). *Mobility in the teacher workforce.* (NCES 2005-114). U.S. Department of Education, National Center for Education Statistics. Washington, DC: U.S. Government Printing Office.

Pulliam, J. D., & Van Patten, J. (2007). *History of education in America* (6th ed.). Upper Saddle River, NJ: Merrill/Pearson.

*Pyle v. South Hadley School Community,* 861 F. Supp. 157 (D. Mass. 1994), *vacated,* 55 F.3d 20 (1st Cir. 1996).

Quintero, E. (2007). Critical pedagogy and young children's worlds. In P. McLaren & J. L. Kincheloe (Eds.), *Critical pedagogy: Where are we now?* (pp. 201–207). New York: Peter Lang.

Ravitch, D. (1983). *The troubled crusade—American education, 1945–1980.* New York: Basic Books.

Ravitch, D. (2000). *Left back: A century of failed school reforms.* New York: Simon & Schuster.

Ravitch, D. (2004). *The language police: How pressure groups restrict what schools learn.* New York: Vintage Books.

Ravitch, D. (2010). *Obama's Race to the Top will not improve education.* Retrieved February 26, 2011, from http://www.huffingtonpost.com/diane-ravitch/obama's-race-to-the-top-will-not-improve-education_666598.html

Ravitch, D. (Sep/Oct, 2011). American schools in crisis. *Saturday Evening Post.* 48-51.

Ravitch, D., & Finn, C. E. (1987). *What do our 17 year olds know? A report on the first national assessment of history and literature.* New York: Harper & Row.

Ready, D. D., & Silander, M. R. (2009). *School racial composition and young children's cognitive development.* Paper presented at the Looking to the Future: Legal and Policy Options for Integrated Education in the South and Nation Conference, April, 2009. Chapel Hill, NC: University of North Carolina.

Rebell, M. A. (2008). Equal opportunity and the courts. *Phi Delta Kappan, 89,* 432–439.

*Regents of the University of California v. Alan Bakke,* 438 U.S. 265 (1978).

*Reitmeyer v. Unemployment Compensation Board of Review,* 602 A.2d 505 (Pa. Commw. Ct. 1992).

Rhodes, S. E. (2010). *Considering sex differences for effective education.* Retrieved January 26, 2011, from http://www.education.com/print/ref-consideringsex/ingesexschools.org/schools-schools.htm.

Rickover, H. G. (1963). *Education and freedom.* New York: New American Library.

Rideout, V., Foehr, O. G., & Roberts, D. F. (2010). *Generation M2: Media in the lives of 8–18 year olds.* Washington, DC: Kaiser Family Foundation.

Rippa, S. A. (1997). *Education in a free society: An American history* (8th ed.). New York: Longman.

*Roberts v. City of Boston,* 59 Mass. (5 Cush.) 198 (1850).

Roberts, S., Zhang, J., & Truman, J. (2010). *Indicators of school crime and safety: 2010* (NCES 2011-0021/NCJ230812). National Center for Education Statistics, U. S. Department of Education, and Bureau of Justice Statistics. Office of Justice Programs, U.S. Department of Justice. Washington, DC.

Rose, S. J. (2007). *Social stratification in the United States.* New York: New Press.

Rosenberg, M. S., Westling, D. L., & McLeskey, J. (2011). *Special education for today's teachers: An introduction* (2nd ed.). Upper Saddle River, NJ: Merrill/Pearson.

Rothstein, R. (2004). A wider lens on black-white achievement gap. *Phi Delta Kappan, 86,* 105–110.

Sadker, D. (2001). Gender equity: Still knocking at the classroom door. *Equity & Excellence in Education, 33*(1), 80–83.

Sadovnik, A. R. (2004). Theories in the sociology of education. In J. H. Ballantine & J. Z. Spade (Eds.), *Schools and society: A sociological approach to education* (pp. 7–26). Belmont, CA: Thomson Learning.

*Safford Unified School District v. Redding,* 129 S. Ct. 2633 (2009).

Salend, S. J. (2011). *Creating inclusive classrooms: Effective and reflective practices* (7th ed.). Upper Saddle River, NJ: Merrill/Pearson.

Samuels, C. A. (Dec. 12, 2007). Minorities in special education studies by U.S. panel. *Education Week,* p. 15.

*San Antonio Independent School District v. Rodriguez,* 411 U.S. 1 (1973).

*Santa Fe Independent School District v. Doe,* 120 S. Ct. 2266 (2000).

Sartre, J. P. (1956). *Being and nothingness.* (H. Barnes, Trans.). New York: Philosophical Library.

Savage, T. A., & Harley, D. A. (2009). A place at the blackboard: LGBTQ. *Multicultural Education, 16*(4), 2–9.

Scheffler, I. (1960). *The language of education.* Springfield, IL: Thomas.

Scherer, M. (2005). Reclaiming testing. *Educational Leadership, 63*(3), 9.

Schimmel, D., Stellman, L.R., & Fischer, L. (2011). *Teachers and the law* (8th ed.). New York: Longman.

Schmid, C. (2001). Educational achievement, language-minority students, and the new second generation. *Sociology of Education, 74* (Extra Issue), 71–87.

*School Board of Nassau County v. Arline,* 107 S. Ct. 1129 (1987).

*School District of Abington Township v. Schempp,* 374 U.S. 203 (1963).

*Scott v. Savers Property and Casualty Insurance Co.,* No. 01-2953 (Wis. June 19, 2000).

Scott, D. (2006). Six curriculum discussions: Contestation and edification. In A. Moore (Ed.), *Schooling, society and curriculum* (pp. 31–42). New York: Routledge.

*Serrano v. Priest,* 487 P.2d 1241 (Cal. 1971).

*Settle v. Dickson County School Board,* 53 F.3d 152 (6th Cir. 1995).

Shafritz, J. M., Koeppe, R. P., & Soper, E. E. (1988). *The facts on file dictionary of education.* New York: Facts on File.

*Sherman v. Koch,* 623 F.3d 501 (7th Cir. 2009).

Shouler, K. (2008). *The everything guide to understanding philosophy: The basic concepts of the greatest thinkers of all time.* Avon, MA: Adams Media.

Silberman, C. (1970). *Crisis in the classroom.* New York: Random House.

*Skinner v. Railroad Labor Executive Association,* 489 U.S. 602 (1989).

Sleeter, C. E., & Grant, C. A. (2007). *Making choices for multicultural education: Five approaches to race, class, and gender* (5th ed.) Hoboken, NJ: Wiley.

Snyder, T. D., & Dillow, S. A. (2011). *Digest of Education Statistics 2010.* National Center for Education Statistics, Institute for Education Sciences. Washington, DC: United States Department of Education.

Sociology Central. (2011). *Agents of socialization.* Retrieved May 1, 2011, from http://www.sociologycentral.com/text/soci/agentssocialization.pdf.

Sommers, C. H. (2000). *The war against boys: How misguided feminism is harming our young men.* New York: Simon & Schuster.

Sowell, E. (2005). *Curriculum: An integrative introduction* (3rd ed.). Upper Saddle River, NJ: Merrill/Pearson.

Sowell, T. (1984). *Civil rights: Rhetoric or reality.* New York: William Morrow.

Spade, J. Z. (2004). *Gender and education in the United States,* in J. H. Ballentine & J. Z. Spade (Eds.), *Schools and society, A sociological approach* (2nd ed.). Belmont, CA: Thomson Learning.

Sparks, D. (2004). *Principals as leaders of learning results.* Oxford, OH: National Staff Development Council.

Sperry, D. J., Daniel, P. T. K., Huefner, D. S., & Gee, E. G. (1998). *Education law and the public schools: A compendium* (2nd ed.). Norwood, MA: Christopher-Gordon.

Spinelli, C. G. (2012). *Classroom assessment for students in special and general education* (3rd ed.). Upper Saddle River, NJ: Merrill/Pearson.

Spring, J. (1976). *The sorting machine: National educational policy since 1945.* New York: McKay.

Spring, J. (2008). *American education* (13th ed.). New York: McGraw-Hill.

Spring, J. (2011). *The American school: From the Puritans to No Child Left Behind* (8th ed.). New York: McGraw-Hill.

St. Charles, J., & Constantino, M. (2000). *Reading and the Native American learner: Research report.* Olympia, WA: Office of the State Superintendent of Public Instruction, Office of Indian Education.

*Stain v. Cedar Rapids Community Sch. Dist.,* 626 N.W. 2d 115 (Iowa 2001).

Stephens, J. E., & Harris, J. J., III. (2000). Teacher shortage: Implications for educators of color. *School Business Affairs, 66*(6), 44–47, 53.

*Stephenson v. Davenport Community School District,* 110 F.3d 1303 (8th Cir. 1997).

Sternberg, R. J., Grigorenko, E. L., & Bridglall, B. L. (2007). Intelligence as a socialized phenomenon. In E. W. Gordon & B. L. Bridglall (Eds.), *Affirmative development: Cultivating academic ability* (pp. 49–72). New York: Rowman & Littlefield.

*Stone v. Graham,* 449 U.S. 39 (1980).

Stopbullying.gov. (n.d.) *Know the risk factors before bullying begins.* Retrieved April 29, 2011, from http://www.stopbullying.gov/topics/risk_factors/index.html.

Strasburger, V. C. (2009). Media and children: What needs to happen now? *JAMA, 301,* 2265– 2266.

*Stratechak v. Board of Education of South Orange Maplewood School District,* 587 F.3d 547 (3rd Cir. 2010).

*Stroman v. Colleton County School District,* 981 F. 2d 152 (4th Cir. 1992).

*Stuart et al. v. School District No. 1 of the Village of Kalamazoo,* 30 Michigan 69 (1874).

*Sullivan v. River Valley Sch. Dist.,* 20 F. Supp. 2d 1120 (W.D. Mich. 1998).

*Swann v. Charlotte-Mecklenburg Board of Education,* 403 U.S. 1 (1971).

Swanson, C. B. (January 10, 2008). Teacher salaries: Looking at comparable jobs. *Education Week/Quality Counts 2008.* Retrieved March, 12, 2008, from http://www.edweek.org/ew/articles/2008/01/10/18salaries.h27.html.

Szasz, M. C. (1999). *Education and the American Indian.* Albuquerque, NM: University of New Mexico Press.

Tanner, D., & Tanner, L. (2007). *Curriculum development* (4th ed.). Upper Saddle River, NJ: Pearson.

TAP. (2010). *Multiple career paths.* Retrieved February 17, 2011, from http://talentedteachers.org/action/action.taf?page=mcp.

*Tape v. Hurley,* 66 Cal. 473 (1885).

*Taxman v. Board of Education of Township of Piscataway,* 91 F.3d 1547 (3d Cir. 1996).

Taylor, C. S., & Nolen, S. B. (2008). *Classroom assessment: Supporting teaching and learning in real classrooms.* Upper Saddle River, NJ: Pearson.

TeenSuicide.us. (2005). *Teen suicide warning signs.* Retrieved April 25, 2011, from http://www.teensuicide.us/articles2.html.

Thomas, S. T., Cambron-McCabe, N., & McCarthy, M. M. (2009). *Public School Law* (6th ed.). Boston: Allyn & Bacon.

*Thompson v. Carthage School District,* 87 F.3d 979 (8th Cir. 1996).

*Tinker v. Des Moines Independent Community School District,* 393 U.S. 503 (1969).

Tollett, K. S. (1983). *The right to education: Reaganism, Reaganomics, or human capital?* (p. 47). Washington, DC: Institute for the Study of Educational Policy, Howard University.

Totah, K. A. (1926). *The contribution of the Arabs to education.* New York: Bureau of Publications, Teachers College, Columbia University.

*Trustees of Dartmouth College v. Woodward,* 17 U.S. (4 Wheat) 518 (1819).

U.S. Census Bureau. (2011a). *American Fact Finder.* Retrieved May 1, 2011, from http://factfinder.census.gov/acs/.

U.S. Census Bureau. (2011b). *America's families and living arrangements: 2010.* Retrieved May 16, 2011, from http://www.census.gov/population/socdemo/hh-fam/cps2010.htm.

U.S. Census Bureau. (1975). *Historical statistics of the United States, colonial times to 1970.* Washington, DC: U.S. Government Printing Office, Series H 316–326.

U.S. Census Bureau. (2010a). *Facts for features, Hispanic heritage month: Sept. 15–Oct. 15.* Retrieved May 2, 2011, from http://www.census.gov/Press-Release/www/releases/archives/facts_for_features_special_editions.

U.S. Census Bureau. (2010b). *Facts for features, Black history month: February 2011.* Retrieved May 2, 2011, from http://www.census.gov/Press-Release/www/releases/archives/facts_for_features_special_editions.

U.S. Census Bureau. (2010c). *Facts for features, American Indian and Alaska Native heritage month: November 2010.* Retrieved April 21, 2011, from http://www.census.gov/Press-Release/www/releases/archives/facts_for_features_special_editions.

U.S. Census Bureau. (2011c). *Facts for features, Asian/Pacific American Heritage Month.* Retrieved April 16, 2008, from http://www.census.gov/Press-Release/www/releases/archives/facts_for_features_special_editions.

U.S. Commission on Civil Rights. (2003). *A quiet crisis: Federal funding and unmet needs in Indian country.* Washington, DC: Author.

U.S. Department of Education. (2011). *Bringing flexibility & focus to education law: Supporting state and local progress.* Retrieved July 18, 2011 from http://www.ed.gov/sites/default/files/supporting-state-local-progress.pdf

U.S. Department of Education, National Center for Education Statistics. (1994). *Condition of education 1994.* Washington, DC: U.S. Government Printing Office.

U.S. Department of Education, National Center for Education Statistics. (1997). *Job satisfaction among America's teachers: Effects of workplace conditions, background characteristics, and teacher compensation.* Washington, DC: Author.

U.S. Department of Education, National Center for Education Statistics. (2005). *The condition of education 2005.* Washington, DC: U.S. Government Printing Office.

U.S. Department of Education, National Center for Education Statistics. (2008). *Digest of education statistics 2007.* Washington, DC: U.S. Government Printing Office.

U.S. Department of Health and Human Services, Administration for Children, Youth, and Families. (2010). *Child maltreatment: 2009.* Retrieved April 12, 2011, from http://www.childwelfare.gov.

U.S. Department of Labor, Bureau of Labor Statistics. (2010). *Occupational outlook handbook.* Retrieved February 13, 2008, from http://www.bls.gov.

U.S. Secret Service. (2001). *The prevention of targeted violence in schools.* Washington, DC: Author.

Ulich, R. (Ed.). (1971). Three thousand years of educational wisdom (2nd ed.). Cambridge, MA: Harvard University Press.

United States Department of Health and Human Services. Administration for Children and Families, Administration on Children, Youth and Families, Children's Bureau. (2010). *Child maltreatment 2009.* Retrieved May 15, 2011, from http://www.acf.hhs.gov/programs/ch/stats_research/index.html.

*United States v. Board of Educ. for the School Dist. of Philadelphia,* 911 F.2d 882 (3rd Cir. 1990).

*United States v. Place,* 462 U.S. 696 (1983).

*United States v. South Carolina,* 445 F. Supp. 1094 (1977), *affirmed,* 434 U.S. 1026 (1978).

Unlimited Justice. (2011). *Paddle now pay later.* Retrieved February 25, 2011, from http://www.unlimitedjustice.co,/facts/.

Valente, W. D., & Valente, C. M. (2005). *Law in the schools* (6th ed.). Upper Saddle River, NJ: Pearson.

Ventura, S. J., & Hamilton, B. E. (2011). *Teenage birth rate resumes decline: NCHS Data Brief.* Retrieved April 27, 2011, from http://www.cdc.gov/nchs/data/databriefs/db58.htm.

*Vernonia School District v. Acton,* 115 S. Ct. 2386 (1995).

Viadero, D. (Jan. 10, 2008). Working conditions trump pay. *Education Week/Quality Counts 2008.* Retrieved March 12, 2008, from http://www.edweek/org/ew/articles/2008/01/10/18conditions.h27.html.

Villegas, A. M., & Irvine, J. J. (2010). Diversifying the teaching force: An examination of major  arguments. *Urban Review, 42,* 175–192.

Villegas, M., & Lucas, T. (2007). The culturally responsive teacher. *Educational Leadership, 9,* 28–33.

Von Drehle, D. (2007). The boys are all right. *Time, 170*(6), 38–42, 44–47.

*Vukadinovich v. Bd. of Sch. Tr. of North Newton Sch. Corp School,* 47 Fed. App. 417 2000, WL 31159318 (7th Cir. 2002).

Waid, K. B., & McNergney, R. F. (2003). Teacher. In J. W. Guthrie (Ed.), *Encyclopedia of education* (2nd ed., pp. 2435–2439). New York: Macmillan Reference.

Walker, T. (2004). Something is wrong here. *Teaching tolerance, 26,* 40–43.

*Wallace v. Jaffree,* 105 S. Ct. 2479 (1985).

Wallace, J. M., Forman, T. A., Celdwell, C. H., & Willis, D. S. (2003). Religion and U.S. secondary school students: Current patterns, recent trends, and sociodemographic correlates. *Youth & Society, 35,* 98–105.

*Walz v. Egg Harbor Township Bd. of Educ.,* 342 F.3d 271 (3rd Cir. 2003).

*Ware v. Valley Stream High School District,* 545 N.Y.S. 2d 316 (N.Y. App. Div.), *appeal denied,* 545 N.Y.S. 2d 539 (N.Y. 1989).

*Washegesic v. Bloomington Public Schools,* 33 F.3d 679 (6th Cir. 1994), *cert. denied,* 115 S. Ct. 1822 (1995).

*Washington v. Davis,* 426 U.S. 229 (1976).

*Waters v. Churchill,* 511 U.S. 661 (1994).

Watkins, W. H. (2006). Social Reconstructionism in education. In K. L. Riley (Ed.). *Social Reconstructionism: People, Politics, Perspectives* (pp. 211–234). Greenwich, CT.: Information Age Publishers.

Webb, L. D., & McCarthy, M. M. (1998). Ella Flagg Young: Pioneer of democratic school administration. *Educational Administration Quarterly, 34,* 224–242.

Webb, L. D., McCarthy, M. M., & Thomas, S. (1988). *Financing elementary and secondary education.* Columbus, OH: Merrill.

*Weigarten v. Board of Education of City School District of the City of New York,* 680 F. Supp. 2d 592 (S.D.N.Y. 2010).

Weinberg, M. (1997). Asian-American education: Historical backgrounds and current realities. Mahwah, NJ: Erlbaum.

Weinberg, M. (2009). LGBT inclusive language. *English Journal. 98*(4), 50–51.

*West Virginia State Board of Education v. Barnette,* 319 U.S. 624 (1943).

West, E. (1972). *The Black American and education.* Upper Saddle River, NJ: Merrill/Prentice Hall.

Westheimer, J., & Kahne, J. (1993). Building school communities: An experience-based model. *Phi Delta Kappan, 75*(4), 324–328.

White, J., & White, P. (2001). An analytic perspective on education and children's rights. In F. Heyting, D. Lenzen, & White, J. (Eds). *Methods in philosophy of education* (pp. 13–29). London: Routledge.

Wiles, J., & Bondi, J. (2011). *Curriculum development* (8th ed.). Upper Saddle River, NJ: Merrill/Pearson.

Wilkins, A. S. (1914). *Roman education.* Cambridge, England: Cambridge University Press.

Wingo, G. M. (1974). *Philosophies of education: An introduction.* Lexington, MA: Heath.

Wink, J. (2011). *Critical pedagogy: Notes from the real works* (4th ed.) Boston: Allyn & Bacon.

Winn, C., & Gingell, J. (2008). *Philosophy of education: The key concepts.* Florence, KY: Routledge.

Winn, C., & Jacks, M. (1967). *Aristotle.* London: Methuen.

Wittgenstein, L. (1953). *Philosophical investigations.* New York: MacMillan.

Wittrock, M. C. (1987). Models of heuristic teaching. In M. J. Dunkin (Ed.), *The international encyclopedia of teaching and teacher education* (pp. 68–76). New York: Pergamon.

*Wood v. Strickland,* 420 U.S. 308 (1975).

Woodward, W. H. (1906). *Studies in education during the age of the Renaissance, 1400–1600.* Cambridge, England: Cambridge University Press.

Wraga, W. G. (2000). *The comprehensive high school in the United States: A historical perspective.* Paper presented at the annual meeting of the American Educational Research Association, April 2000, New Orleans.

Wright, V. R., Chau, M., & Aratani, Y. (2011). *Who are America's poor? The official story.* New York:  National Center for Children in Poverty, Columbia University.

*Wygant v. Jackson Board of Education,* 106 S. Ct. 1842 (1986).

Yoo, B. (2010). *Unraveling the model minority myth of Asian American students.* Retrieved  January 16, 2011, from http://www.education.com/print/unraveling-minority-myth-asian-students.

Youth Suicide Prevention Program. (2010). *Statistics about youth suicide.* Retrieved May 16,  2011, from http://www.yspp.org/about_suicide/statistics.htm.

*Zameonik v. Indian Prairie School District No. 204,* 710 F. Supp. 2d 711 (N.D. Ill. 2010).

Zarrillo, J. (2012). *Teaching elementary social studies: Principles and practices* (4th ed.). Upper Saddle River, NJ: Allyn & Bacon/Pearson.

Zehr, M. A. (October 28, 2007). Reading seen as lag to ELL focus. *Education Week.* Retrieved January, 29, 2008, from www.edweek.org.

*Zelman v. Simmons-Harris,* 122 S. Ct. 2460 (2002).

Zimmerman, F. J., Glew, G. M., Christakis, D. A., & Katon, W. (2005). Early cognitive stimulation, emotional support, and television watching as predictors of subsequent bullying among grade school children. *Archives of Pediatric & Adolescent Medicine, 159,* 384–388.

Zirpoli, T. J. (2005). *Behavior management: Applications for teachers* (4th ed.). Upper Saddle River, NJ: Merrill/Pearson.

*Zobrest v. Catalina Foothills School District,* 113 S. Ct. 2462 (1993).

*Zorach v. Clauson,* 343 U.S. 306 (1952).

# Author INDEX

# Subject INDEX